Volume 1: To 1815

Women and Gender in the Western Past

Katherine L. French
State University of New York–New Paltz

Allyson M. Poska
University of Mary Washington

Houghton Mifflin Company   Boston   New York

Publisher: Patricia Coryell
Senior Sponsoring Editor: Nancy Blaine
Senior Development Editor: Jennifer Sutherland
Editorial Assistant: Tawny Pruitt
Senior Project Editor: Jane Lee
Editorial Assistant: Kristen Truncellito/Carrie Parker
Senior Art and Design Coordinator: Jill Haber
Senior Photo Editor: Jennifer Meyer Dare
Composition Buyer: Chuck Dutton
Associate Strategic Buyer: Brian Pieragostini
Senior Marketing Manager: Katherine Bates
Marketing Assistant: Lauren Bussard
Cover Design Manager: Anne S. Katzeff

Cover image: *Two Women in a Chariot,* fresco from Palace of Tiryns, thirteenth century B.C., Mycenaean. Credit: © National Archaeological Museum, Athens/Dagli Orti/The Art Archive.

Printed in the U.S.A.

Library of Congress Control Number: 2006926540

ISBN 13: 978-0-618-24624-3
ISBN 10: 0-618-24624-X

1 2 3 4 5 6 7 8 9-QUF-10   09   08   07   06

Text credits: pp. 24–25: From, "The Egyptian Economy and Non-Royal Women: Their Status in Public Life," presented by William A. Ward, Department of Egyptology, Brown University (NEH Lecture, Brown University, 21 June, 1995). p. 65: Diane J. Rayor, trans., *Sappho's Lyre: Archaic Lyric and Women Poets of Ancient Greece.* Copyright © 1991 by The Regents of the University of California. Reprinted by permission of the University of California Press via Copyright Clearance Center. pp. 100–101: Soranus' *Gynecology,* pp. 34–39, translated with introduction by Owsei Temkin, M.D. With the assistance of Nicholson J. Eastman, M.D., Ludwig Edelstein, PH.D., and Alan F. Guttmacher, M.D. Copyright © 1956 The Johns Hopkins University Press. Reprinted with permission of The Johns Hopkins University Press. pp. 130–131: Schaff, Philip, ed., Freemantle, M.A., The Hon. W. H., trans., *Letter CVII to Laeta* (Grand Rapids, MI: Christian Classics Ethereal Library). pp. 166–167: *Equitan, Marie de France,* translated Judith P. Shoaf © 1992. Reprinted by permission of Judith P. Shoaf. p. 171: James A. Brundage, *Law, Sex, and Christian Society in Medieval Europe.* Copyright © 1987 by the University of Chicago. Reprinted with permission of the publisher, the University of Chicago Press. pp. 198–199: Frances Beer, *Julian of Norwich: Revelations. The Motherhood of God* (Cambridge: D.S. Brewer, 1998). Reprinted by permission of Boydell & Brewer, Inc. pp. 242–243: Sarah Fyge Egerton, compiled and edited by the Beck Center at Emory University, *The Female Advocate: or, an Answer to A Late Satyr against The Pride, Lust and Inconstancy, &c. of Woman Written by a Lady in Vindication of Her Sex* (London: Printed by H. C. for John Taylor 1686). Reprinted by permission of the Beck Center at Emory University. p. 231: *The Witch Hunt in Early Modern Europe,* 2d ed., Brian Levack, Pearson Education Limited. Copyright © 1995 by Pearson Education Ltd. Reprinted by permission of Pearson Education Limited. pp. 282–283: Copyright © Marie Madeleine Jodin, 1741–1790, Felicia Godon and P. N. Furbank, 2001, Ashgate Publishing Ltd. Reprinted by permission of Ashgate Publishing Ltd.

Contents

Maps

Special Features

Preface

Women's history has transformed our understanding of the past and the historical profession itself. Only three decades ago, the field was in its infancy. Scholars who asked questions about the role of women in the past faced the bafflement of their colleagues and struggled to teach and research women's history with little institutional support. Although these conditions persist on many campuses, the field has flourished. Women's historians have produced scholarly studies of the highest quality, and the dynamism of the field is evident in the many conferences, book series, and journals dedicated to the subject. Women's history courses have become a regular part of many college and university curricula, and high school teachers increasingly integrate the historical experiences of women into their classes.

Despite these successes, teaching women's history continues to be a challenge, because many students see women's history as marginal to their education. In recent years, we have worked to bridge the gap between what our students perceive as "important" and women's history by blurring the line between women's history and more traditional fields of historical inquiry. We have integrated women's history into our Western Civilization courses and brought more of the narrative of traditional history into our women's history classes. We have shown our students that women's history is not a secondary topic to be relegated to elective courses, but an indispensable part of the study of history. However, in the process, we found that the available textbooks on European women's history did not serve our needs. Some were collections of essays that did not provide the larger historical framework; others

were survey textbooks organized in ways that made them difficult to teach.

In response, we decided to write a textbook that would integrate the critical themes of women's history into the historical narrative. *Women and Gender in the Western Past* brings students the most up-to-date scholarship on women, from the earliest days of human experience to the present. We examine the experiences of women of all classes, religions, and ethnicities and provide the most extensive coverage of women in Western political, social, economic, intellectual, religious, and cultural history available.

We recognize that students come to this course with varying levels of historical knowledge and preparation. Written at an introductory level, *Women and Gender in the Western Past* provides enough historical context to make it accessible to students from a wide variety of majors and educational backgrounds.

Women and Gender in the Western Past focuses on five major themes:

1. *The relationship between historical events and ideas and women's lives.* Our text shows women as vibrant creators of and participants in the events, ideas, and movements that shaped the past. We reject the notion that women were mostly passive victims without influence on their own lives or the world around them.

2. *The history of the family and sexuality.* For much of history, women were defined by their marital and family status. But ideas of women's place in the family and societal norms about sexuality have evolved over time, influenced by developments in religion, law, and technology. We

emphasize the scholarship that has shown that the family and sexuality are not natural categories that transcend historical forces but shifting realities that have a history of their own.

3. *The social construction of gender.* Like the family and sexuality, gender has a history. Every society constructs its own gender norms based on religious beliefs, cultural stereotypes, and other societal forces. We include extensive discussions of the evolution of gender ideologies as they apply to both women and men, as well as to relations between the sexes. Although our discussions of masculinity are limited by space constraints and the relative newness of masculinity studies, we understand that men and masculinity are integral to gender studies.

4. *The differences between cultural ideals and the lives of women.* Over the centuries, Western society has formulated and reformulated its expectations for how women should behave. We explore changes in gender expectations and how and why some women willingly acquiesced to them while others rejected them.

5. *Women's perceptions of themselves and their roles.* One of the most important contributions of women's history has been the discovery and rediscovery of writings and other works by women. Women's perspectives on their own lives and the issues facing their societies further illuminate how women understood and interacted with social expectations. Women's voices provide an important corrective to the male-dominated historical narrative and challenge assumptions about the development of Western society.

Women and Gender in the Western Past consistently addresses these five major themes as it integrates women's history into the familiar narrative of Western Civilization, making women's history easier for faculty to teach and for students to learn.

FEATURES

We have included a number of features to supplement the narrative and engage students. We encourage students to personalize historical experience by examining the lives of individual women. Each chapter includes a biography feature called "Women's Lives." We have selected women of different classes, nationalities, religions, and occupations, showing how each was shaped by and responded to historical forces and constraints. For instance, in Chapter 4, students meet Perpetua, who was imprisoned for practicing Christianity in the Roman Empire. In Chapter 11, we show how author Olive Schreiner challenged both sexism and racism in colonial South Africa.

Each chapter also includes "Sources from the Past"—short excerpts from primary sources written mostly by women. Students will learn how these writers viewed women and how women used writing to communicate their feelings and concerns. The excerpts reflect the diversity of sources that scholars use to investigate women's history. For example, the selection of Egyptian legal texts found in Chapter 1 reveals the protections and rights of Egyptian women. In Chapter 8, Marie-Madeleine Jodin's proposal on women's rights to the National Assembly may be the first signed, female-authored, feminist work of the French Revolution.

Each chapter also includes a Chronology to highlight key developments in the chapter and integrate women's history into the traditional historical narrative. Students can see at a glance the relationship between women's experiences and the major historical events of the period.

We have tried to make this text visually appealing to both faculty and students. A generous selection of maps provides geographic context for the events discussed in each chapter. The illustrations include images from a wide array of media and, whenever possible, women's representations of themselves and each other. Images of material culture created by women demonstrate women's creativity, resourcefulness, and priorities. For example, in Chapter 14, the Changi Quilt, made by women in a Japanese prisoner of war camp during World War II reveals how under the most horrific circumstances, women found ways to use traditional skills to preserve their identity and communicate with others.

We were determined to credit the work of scholars who have transformed our understanding of women's place in the past and to give students access to the sources on which our book is based. As a result, in addition to a short list of Suggested Readings at the end of each chapter, we provide extensive footnotes to the primary and secondary sources that we used to write this book. We hope that *Women and Gender in the Western Past* will inspire students and make it easier for them to pursue topics in women's history that they find particularly intriguing.

CHALLENGES

Writing this textbook forced us to deal with some of the most controversial issues in the historical profession. Our decision to refer to *the West* will be problematic for some scholars. We wholeheartedly agree that the term *Western Civilization* is problematic because it implies a particular notion of Western progress and privileges the history of white Europeans. However, we decided to work within that framework in order to make the text useful as a core or supplemental text in Western Civilization courses and to meet our goal of viewing the familiar narrative of Western Civilization through the lens of gender. We believe that women's history fundamentally challenges any teleological notion of Western progress, and we have consciously addressed the issue of ethnocentrism by being racially, ethnically, and religiously inclusive.

Chronology has also been problematic for women's historians. The traditional Western Civilization narrative was focused on powerful and influential men and events that historians believed were central to the creation of the modern Western world. However, the trajectory of women's history does not necessarily follow the traditional divisions of history. Although we generally work within that framework, some events that loom large in Western Civilization texts, such as the Peloponnesian wars, play a minimal role in *Women and Gender in the Western Past* because of the limited influence of or impact on women. In addition, based on the research in those fields, we have reconceptualized the traditional periodizations of the Middle Ages and Renaissance to reflect the transformations that most affected women. Chapter 5, "Women in the Early and High Middle Ages," covers the 400–1200 period, when most women followed the distinct rhythms of rural life, while Chapter 6, "Women and Urban Life: The Late Middle Ages," covers the 1200–1500 period, when women increasingly

participated in life and work in European towns and cities. In Chapter 6, we examine the Renaissance as an intellectual and artistic movement rather than as a time period.

Every historian must confront the problem of sources. For the ancient period, there is little written by women and, in some cases, very little written by men about women. Instead, we turned to literature, art, and archaeology to supplement the written record. Even during the modern period, there are topics that remain largely unstudied, such as the role of women in the Thirty Years War. Women's history is an evolving field, and our text reflects the limits of our current knowledge.

Space constraints also limited our ability to provide significant discussions of historiography; however, the relationship between historiography and the creation of the historical narrative was always in the forefront of our work. We have tried whenever possible to convey a sense of historical debate, as we believe that it is important for students to recognize that history is created and that the process of creation is dynamic.

Women's history is the product of many social and intellectual changes. Although previous generations of historians did not ignore women entirely, until the middle of the twentieth century, both male and female historians demonstrated little interest in the lives of women other than rulers and women directly associated with major political changes. Then, during the 1930s, the *Annalistes* and their successors in the burgeoning field of social history reconceptualized historical time to focus on the *longue durée*. They introduced the use of quantitative analysis, anthropology, sociology, and geography, in order to explore the lives of people who left no written records. These changes would prove critical for the study of women, because many of the basic structures of women's lives change very slowly and in response to factors unrelated to political events.

Women's history as a subfield of the historical discipline emerged in the 1960s and early 1970s, when the widespread application of these innovations in the historical profession came together with the social and political movements of that era. Galvanized by the second wave of feminism, many female scholars began to investigate the role of women in history. They understood the potential of historical study to gain not only a more comprehensive understanding of the past but also to contextualize their own place in society.

Women's history would challenge some of the most fundamental historical concepts. In her groundbreaking essay "Did Women Have a Renaissance?" (1977), Joan Kelly forced scholars to reconsider the meaning of the term *Renaissance*, as she asserted a decline in women's status at the height of that period. Kelly demonstrated how the traditional historical narrative and notions of progress systematically excluded women and that the inclusion of women challenged some of the dearest assumptions about Western progress. A decade later, Joan Scott, in "Gender as a Useful Category for Historical Analysis" (1988), argued that gender is central to power relations and a primary aspect of social organization. Therefore, understanding gender is critical even to the study of subjects that traditionally excluded women, such as politics.

These are just a few of the ideas that have shaped the field of women's history. For a more extensive discussion, we recommend Merry E. Wiesner-Hanks, "Gender" in *Writing Early Modern History,* edited by Garthine Walker (London: Hodder Education, 2005): 95–113. Wiesner-Hanks provides an excellent overview of the field of women's history in general and early modern women's history in particular. We also recommend the remarkable three-volume collection, *Women's History in Global Perspective,* edited by Bonnie G. Smith (Urbana: University of Illinois Press, 2005). Written with the teacher in mind, these essays provide clear, accessible introductions to the historiography in many fields of women's history.

Finally, we have taken an explicitly feminist approach to *Women and Gender in the Western Past.* We believe that patriarchy is systemic in Western culture and has been the central force curtailing the movement and rights of women. However, we do not view patriarchy as stagnant. We explore how technology, politics, religion, economics, and a variety of social forces have interacted with patriarchal norms to influence women's lives.

Gerda Lerner once said, "Women's history is the primary tool for women's emancipation." We hope that this textbook can be one small part of that project.

WEBSITE

The *Online Study Center* has been developed as a companion website for *Women and Gender in the Western Past.* Created by Marybeth Carlson, University of Dayton; Holly Hurlburt, Southern Illinois University; and Annette F. Timm, University of Calgary, it includes chapter outlines, web exercises, and pre-class quizzes to help students master the material.

ACKNOWLEDGEMENTS

We are grateful for the care with which the many reviewers read the chapters of this text. Whenever possible, we integrated their suggestions, and their insightful comments and corrections made the manuscript stronger.

Marybeth Carlson, University of Dayton

Laurel Carrington, St. Olaf College

Craige Champion, Syracuse University

Ann Chirhart, Indiana State University

Susan Conner, Florida Southern College

Michelle Den Beste, California State University, Fresno

Susan Freeman, Minnesota State University, Mankato

Jennifer Heuer, Middlebury College

Holly Hurlburt, Southern Illinois University

Erika Kuhlman, Idaho State University

Lynn MacKay, Brandon University

Amy Thompson McCandless, College of Charleston

John McClymer, Assumption College

Elizabeth Green Musselman, Southwestern University

Kenneth Orosz, University of Maine

Brian Pavlac, King's College

Tammy Proctor, Wittenberg University

Judith Sebesta, University of South Dakota

Phyllis Soybel, College of Lake County

Emily Tai, Queensborough Community College

Annette Timm, University of Calgary

Deborah Valenze, Barnard College

Marta Vicente, University of Kansas

Leigh Whaley, Acadia University

This project has been an intellectual and emotional challenge that we could not have completed without the support of many people. At the University of Mary Washington, Allyson Poska would like to thank Jeff McClurken, Claudine Ferrell, Porter Blakemore, Carole Garmon, Leonard Koos, Liane Houghtalin, Lisa Patton, Mary Rigsby, and Steve Hanna, all of whom patiently answered questions, lent books, read sections of the text, and helped in a myriad of other ways. Lorene Nickel's spinning lesson helped her to better understand that critical aspect of women's work. Jack Bales, Beth Perkins, Carla Bailey and the rest of the staff at Mary Washington's library dedicated extra time and energy to fulfilling seemingly endless, and often quite unusual, requests.

At SUNY New Paltz, Katherine French would like to acknowledge the assistance of Lee Bernstein, Stella Dean, Kathleen Dowley, Andrew Evans, Barbara Hollingshead, Susan Lewis, and John Vander Lippe.

The staff at the Sojourner Truth Library was generous with their time, expertise, and support. We would also like to thank Sandy Bardsley, Stephen Bensch, Eric Carlson, Angela Creager, Emma Dench, Ellen Eisenberg, Robin Fleming, Christine Kraus, Amy Leonard, Nancy McLoughlin, Bella Millett, Lydia Murdoch, Hal Parker, Kevin Perry, Wim Phillips, Mary Louise Roberts, John Shinners, Thomas Sizgorich, Wendy Urban-Mead, and Merry Wiesner-Hanks. Each of these scholars willingly gave of their time and knowledge. We hope that we have not forgotten anyone, but if we have, please know that we valued your assistance just as much. Christopher Kilmartin went beyond the call of duty as he proofread and commented on every chapter. However, his contributions were more than technical. His knowledge of men's studies and masculinity was critical to our conceptualization of the project.

The staff at Houghton Mifflin—Jean Woy, Nancy Blaine, Jennifer Sutherland, Tawny Pruitt, and Jane Lee, as well as freelance art editor George McLean, Maria Sas at New Graphic Design, copyeditor Laurie McGee, proofreader Ruth Jagolinzer, and photo researcher Linda Sykes— guided us through what was a very challenging process. We are grateful for their dedication to this project.

Of course, our students offered challenging questions and often heard the first formulations of our ideas. Their interest in women's history was the spark for this project.

Katherine L. French
Allyson M. Poska

About the Authors

Katherine L. French is Associate Professor of History at the State University of New York–New Paltz, where she teaches medieval and women's history. She received her Ph.D. from the University of Minnesota in 1993. She is the author of several articles on women and medieval popular religion. She is also the author of *The People of the Parish: Community Life in a Late Medieval English Diocese* (2001) and *Good Women of the Parish: Gender and Religion in Late Medieval England* (forthcoming).

Allyson M. Poska is Professor of History at the University of Mary Washington in Fredericksburg, Virginia, where she teaches European and Latin American history. She received her Ph.D. from the University of Minnesota in 1992. In addition to numerous articles, she is the author of *Regulating the People: The Catholic Reformation in Seventeenth-Century Spain* (1998) and *Women and Authority in Early Modern Spain: The Peasants of Galicia* (2005).

The Ancient Mediterranean, to 600 B.C.E.

Willendorf Venus (CA. 24,000 B.C.E.). *The Willendorf Venus, discovered in Austria in 1908, is the most famous of the so-called Venus figurines. The meaning and use of this tiny figure (only 4 3/8 inches tall) has puzzled scholars for decades. (Naturhistorisches Museum, Vienna, Austria/Erich Lessing/Art Resource, NY.)*

To take advantage of the most extensive historical record and to better understand the history of women in the West, this chapter ranges far beyond the boundaries of Europe, the focus of the rest of the text. By reaching back into human history and into the Near East and North Africa, we can see more clearly how Western gender norms evolved. In the prehistoric past and the earliest recorded civilizations, women were crucial to both human survival and the development of complex societies. However, ancient cultures had different expectations of women and offered them varying degrees of social and legal freedom.

WOMEN IN PREHISTORY, TO 3,000 B.C.E.

Without a doubt, gender distinctions between women and men are much older than the historical record. Of course, socially constructed *gender* is different from biologically determined *sex*. The sex of a person, male or female, is determined by his or her genetic makeup and generally revealed by his or her body. Biologically, women differ most from men in their ability to bear and nurse children. The gender of a person, his or her masculinity or femininity, is a set of behaviors that are culturally defined as appropriate for a person of that sex. Each society constructs its own set of gender norms based on a wide array of forces, including religious beliefs and cultural stereotypes. Even the earliest humans may have formed some basic ideas about the expected behaviors of women and men.

We must speculate on the role of gender in prehistory based on evidence that is sparse, difficult to interpret, and often very controversial. Scholars rely on several disciplines to formulate a coherent picture of prehistoric gender norms, including archaeology, paleontology, and anthropology. Based on this multidisciplinary research, feminist scholars have provided new interpretations of archaeological data that make women central actors in the social and technological developments of our prehistoric past.

1

Chapter 1 ❖ Chronology

600,000 B.P.–10,000 B.C.E.	Paleolithic period
40,000–10,000 B.C.E.	Upper Paleolithic period
25,000 B.C.E.	Habitation of Dolni Vestonice
	Venus figurines
	Cave paintings
8000 B.C.E.	Neolithic Revolution
6500 B.C.E.	Invention of pottery
3100 B.C.E.	Sumerians arrive in Mesopotamia
	Earliest evidence of writing
3000 B.C.E.	The unification of Egypt
2450	Ku-Bau rules city of Kish—first recorded female ruler
2350 B.C.E.	Akkadian conquest of Mesopotamia
	Enheduana appointed high priestess
ca. 2181 B.C.E.	Nitiqret rules in Egypt
2050 B.C.E.	Middle Kingdom Egypt
1900 B.C.E.	Babylonian conquest of Mesopotamia
ca. 1777 B.C.E.	Sobekneferu rules in Egypt
1750 B.C.E.	Code of Hammurabi (Mesopotamia)
1550 B.C.E.	New Kingdom Egypt
1500 B.C.E.	Israelite tribes begin worship of Yahweh
1470 B.C.E.	Hapshepsut rules in Egypt
1380 B.C.E.	Reestablishment of workers' community of Deir el Medina
ca. 1340	Queen Nefertiti, wife of Akhenaten of Egypt
1000 B.C.E.	Rule of David, king of the Israelites

Prehistoric Lives

Recent excavations in northeastern Africa indicate that the oldest human ancestors may have lived more than six million years ago. As they evolved into modern *homo sapiens*, their numbers grew and they slowly spread across Eurasia and Africa in small groups. We know almost nothing about most of the first six million years of human existence. Our earliest knowledge of prehistoric life comes from the Paleolithic period or Old Stone Age (600,000 B.P.–10,000 B.C.E.), and more specifically the Upper Paleolithic period (approximately 40,000–10,000 B.C.E.) with the appearance of anatomically modern humans.

Paleolithic people's lives focused on the search for food and shelter. To ensure a steady food supply, small nomadic family groups or clans followed herds of animals on their migrations. They generally sought protection in caves and rock formations, but they also built some simple structures to protect themselves from the weather.

2

They lived out in the open if the climate was moderate and food was readily available. At one of the oldest excavated human sites, Dolni Vestonice in the Czech Republic, archaeologists have unearthed evidence of an early home with a small terrace and a low wall surrounding a hearth. Posts held up some type of roof. In their search for food, the inhabitants probably remained at sites such as this for only a few days before moving on. Although their lives may seem foreign to us, Paleolithic peoples survived remarkably well. Indeed, their nomadic lifestyles contributed to their success. As they moved from place to place, they were less susceptible to contagious diseases and less exposed to unhygienic refuse than their descendants who lived in permanent settlements.[1]

Early humans were vulnerable to the unpredictable forces of nature. In order to have some sense of control over their lives, they may have practiced *animism*, the worship of spirits associated with natural phenomena, such as the earth, the rain, and the sun. They provided these spirits with offerings, usually food and prayers, hoping that in return, the spirits would respond with improvements in their daily lives, such as better weather or larger food supplies. This early religious activity expanded over the centuries. By the Upper Paleolithic period, burial sites filled with grave goods, such as tools, clothing, and jewelry, indicate that prehistoric people had also become concerned with an afterlife.

Gender and Early Work

Modern society takes the image of prehistoric man as hunter and woman as gatherer for granted. Men gained authority and prestige from the dangers of hunting, and the gendered hierarchy in food collection reflected a broader social hierarchy in which men dominated women. However, recent research presents a much more complicated view of the role of gender in prehistoric food collection. Many scholars assert that this gendering of food collection may have been accurate but that a higher proportion of prehistoric people's diets came from plant foods than meat. They argue that women were the primary collectors of plants, and thus their contributions to survival and their status were greater than many scholars had previously considered. Other scholars argue that in addition to collecting plants, women contributed to food collection through hunting. In some modern hunter-gatherer societies, women catch small game, hunt with men, or even hunt alone. In others, women provide protein for their families by collecting shellfish. Thus, scholars believe that in prehistory, gendered divisions of labor were not very rigid. Prehistoric people depended on both men and women's ability to obtain food. Indeed, among hunter-gatherers, any refusal to undertake the food-collecting responsibilities of the other sex could easily lead to starvation if a member of the clan were unable to complete his or her work.

During the Paleolithic period, humans learned to produce and use stone tools. In addition to stone flints and arrows for hunting, they relied on stone blades to manufacture a variety of objects from bone, ivory, and wood. No doubt they also fashioned objects from softer materials including leather, but like wooden pieces, those materials have not survived the centuries. With stone tools, prehistoric peoples could hunt more effectively and extract more meat from each kill.

Recently, feminist archaeologists have challenged the traditional claim that men produced Paleolithic stone tools. They assert that earlier scholars attributed toolmaking to men because in modern, Western society, men have traditionally made tools. Moreover, they associated stone flints with supposedly masculine tasks, including hunting, butchering, and warfare. However, the tools themselves provide no indication about who manufactured them, and early peoples used stone tools for a wide variety of tasks, including grinding seeds and cutting roots—work often associated with women. It seems highly unlikely that prehistoric women would wait for men to produce or sharpen their stone tools; instead, women most likely manufactured and honed their own tools as necessary.[2]

Paleolithic peoples also created cave art and art objects. Caves in France, Germany, and northern Spain, including the most famous caves at Lascaux (France) and Altamira (Spain), are decorated with naturalistic depictions of animals and humans. People returned to these caves regularly over more than ten thousand years, adding new figures and painting over old ones. Prehistoric humans may have drawn these figures as a part of religious activity or purely for decoration. Or they may have had other meanings that we do not yet understand. These are the earliest images of women in existence. One cave painting in eastern Spain depicts a figure, often interpreted as a woman, gathering wild honey from a tree. A cave in northern Spain is decorated with a number of female figures. In addition to the cave art, archaeologists have unearthed a wealth of small animal and human figurines that may have been used for religious purposes or for trade in addition to their artistic value. Scholars are particularly intrigued by the so-called Venus figurines, which date from approximately twenty-five thousand years ago and have been found in diverse parts of Europe, including the Balkans, France, Moravia, and the Ukraine. Carved in ivory, wood, and stone, many of these statues have strong female characteristics, including exaggerated hips, breasts, buttocks, and thighs and clearly outlined pubic triangles; one has a detailed vulva. Some appear pregnant. Here again, although most scholars have assumed that men created these figures, there is no reason to exclude women from the production of early art. We have no evidence to link the figurines' creation with either gender.

The only clear exception to this otherwise flexible division of labor was and is childbirth. Women in nearly all times and places faced the dual responsibilities of reproduction (childbearing) and production (labor), known to contemporary scholars as the double burden. The notion of the double burden does not imply that men never engaged in domestic work or childcare, but only that women bore the primary responsibility for such tasks. Women's reproductive role may have influenced the nature of some women's work. Historian Judith Brown has hypothesized that in order to accommodate breastfeeding and childcare, Paleolithic women undertook tasks that did not require constant attention, were easily interrupted, did not place the child in potential danger, and did not require the woman to move far from the settlement.[3] Thus, spinning, weaving, and sewing became the first productive activities that women attempted outside of food collection and caring for children. Women (and possibly men) wound plant fibers into cordage as early as twenty thousand years ago. The "skirts" on some of the Venus figurines provide evidence for early weaving

of plant materials, and impressions of these cloths in clay reveal that the plants were woven into intricate patterns.

During the Paleolithic period, technological change was quite slow; however, by approximately 8000 B.C.E., people learned to domesticate plants and animals, a transformation known as the Neolithic or Agricultural Revolution. By 7000 B.C.E., farming societies had become established in the Near East, and they expanded across Europe beginning in the southeast and moving across the continent to the northwest over the next three thousand years.

Some scholars have hypothesized that women may have been essential to the domestication of plants and animals because women remained at home more than men. Because of their childcare responsibilities, women would have been better able to observe plant growth and replicate the process. Moreover, agriculture requires a more sedentary population to tend the fields and harvest the produce, and women may have been in the best position to undertake those tasks. Moreover, anthropologists have found that in modern agrarian societies women are responsible for almost all agricultural production that relies on basic hoes or digging sticks for planting (instead of plows).[4]

The development and expansion of agriculture brought significant changes to the gender division of labor. In addition to collecting and hunting food, Neolithic peoples had to clear and prepare land for farming. Presumably, both men and women undertook most tasks without regard to gender. However, evidence indicates that as societies became more reliant on agriculture, men did proportionally more farm work and less hunting and fishing. A Neolithic female skeleton in Sweden was buried with a fishhook, suggesting that she participated in fishing.[5]

The development of agriculture allowed Neolithic peoples to produce extra food, yet until the invention of pottery around 6500 B.C.E., they had only woven baskets to store the surplus. Pottery was a major technological advance, as it allowed for more effective food storage and transportation. Scholars speculate that, as was true with other technologies, both men and women were both involved in the various stages of pottery production, from obtaining the clay and forming pots to decorating and firing them. Presumably, one person did not perform all of those tasks, and different groups of people allocated the tasks differently according to their own conceptions of the gendered division of labor.[6]

Agriculture and the domestication of animals also led to a more consistent diet, which in turn led to increases in fertility, overall health, and life span. Excluding those who died in childhood, the average Neolithic man lived to be around thirty-five years old and the average Neolithic woman closer to thirty years old. Evidence indicates men may have lived longer because they ate more meat, while women ate diets that were higher in carbohydrates and therefore less nutritious. In addition, many women died from complications from childbirth.

Neolithic peoples were less nomadic than their predecessors, opting instead for the sedentary or semisedentary lifestyle that planting and harvesting demanded. This settled lifestyle changed women's lives in a number of ways. First, Neolithic peoples constructed permanent houses. These homes allowed them to settle near water, fertile soil, and other resources, rather than in caves and other naturally formed structures in less convenient locations. Prehistoric peoples collected and stored their material possessions in their permanent homes, and groups of people formed small villages. In these villages, prehistoric people cooperated in larger projects, such as clearing land, cultivating, harvesting, herding, and butchering. With other people around, women could look to nonkin neighbors for help with household chores. Through permanent settlement, the Neolithic Revolution radically transformed many basic structures of prehistoric society.

Matriarchy and Patriarchy

Beyond educated speculation about the gendered division of labor, we know almost nothing about prehistoric gender hierarchies. Some scholars have asserted that matriarchies, societies ruled by women, existed in the prehistoric past. Some supporters of this theory believe that these cultures were egalitarian, peaceful societies or that prehistoric peoples worshipped a powerful Mother Earth goddess. Still others contend that although women did not necessarily rule, they were held in particularly high esteem and that these cultures were eventually overthrown by patriarchal, male-dominated cultures.

Those who claim that matriarchy existed in prehistory rely on three primary arguments. First, the archaeological record does not positively indicate prehistoric gender hierarchies. Without evidence to the contrary, they assert that we should not discount the possibility that egalitarian or even matriarchal systems existed. Second, many early cultures had myths that explained their origins from first mothers followed by the overthrow of that female dominance by a patriarchal society. The idea that so many early peoples would explain their origins in the same way without some connection to ancestral realities seems highly unlikely. Third, supporters of a matriarchal past focus on the Venus figurines. While some scholars have suggested that prehistoric people used these female figures for fertility magic, others have followed the lead of scholar Erich Neumann (1905–1960), who hypothesized that they represented worship of the Great Mother, an all-powerful mother goddess who was the dominant force in religion before the conception of a supreme male deity.[7] Archaeologist Marija Gimbutas (1921–1994) and others have asserted that the pervasiveness of these figures indicates the dominance of goddess worship in prehistoric Europe.[8] These scholars argue that a society with a dominant female deity would have held human females in higher esteem than a society that worshipped a dominant male deity or deities.

However, the majority of scholars dispute the possibility of matriarchal prehistoric societies. They argue that because there is no evidence for the existence of matriarchy in the modern world, there is no reason to believe that it existed among prehistoric peoples. They also present alternative interpretations of early goddess myths and traditions that focus on the creation of patriarchal dominance rather than the overthrow of female authority. Many scholars doubt the existence of a European-wide goddess religion. They argue that a religion involving deities rather than spirits was far more complex than most scholars believe existed during that period. In response to the assertions about the Venus figurines, they contend that no evidence exists to suggest who made them or their purpose. They may have been ritual or fertility objects, but they may also have been toys or used for magical purposes. Their uses and meanings may have changed over thousands of years. Moreover, while many of the figurines are female, an equal number of figurines appear to be sexless, and some are clearly male. Finally, based on evidence from later societies, scholars assert that even if some societies worshipped a dominant female goddess, there is no correlation between goddess worship and the status of women in those civilizations.

If indeed there was no clear gender hierarchy among prehistoric peoples, then how did *patriarchy* come to dominate Western society? According to historian Gerda Lerner, patriarchy is "the manifestation and institutionalization of male dominance over women and children in the family and the extension of male dominance over women in society in general."[9] In patriarchal societies, men have access to greater levels of political, economic, and social authority than women.

In her classic work, *The Creation of Patriarchy* (1986), Lerner argues that patriarchy evolved toward the end of the Neolithic period with the exchange of women and the control of female sexuality. In an agricultural society, land ownership becomes critical and as Neolithic people came to value land more, they used women to form alliances that would protect their property from warfare and to produce children to work in the fields. In this way, women became a resource to be exchanged by men through marriage and slavery. Men's control of women and women's sexuality created the patriarchal family. As we will see in more detail below, male domination expanded beyond the family with the formation of early civilizations. The authority that the leaders of these civilizations exerted over their subjects was modeled on the control that men had over their families. By approximately 3000 B.C.E., these early civilizations began to appear in the Near East and North Africa and developed in ways that would have a profound impact on European culture and its gender norms.

Feminist scholars have significantly revised women's roles in prehistoric societies. Although traditional interpretations placed men at the center of most early technological developments, women had access to the same knowledge and skills as men, and in many cases were in a better position to initiate those innovations. Certainly, women's labor was central to the success of prehistoric societies. However, transformations at the end of the Neolithic period led to the establishment of patriarchy and male dominance in the earliest civilizations.

ANCIENT MESOPOTAMIA, 3100 B.C.E.–1500 B.C.E.

Ancient Mesopotamia was home to the oldest Western civilization. The dynamic culture of the region was the product of a series of migrations to and conquests of the fertile plains between the Tigris and the Euphrates rivers (now Iraq). (See Map 1.1.) Sumerians, although not the first settlers of the region, appear in the area by about 3100 B.C.E. Although their origins remain unknown, once they settled in southern Mesopotamia, they developed a highly organized society. Not long after their arrival, around 2900 B.C.E., Akkadian-speaking Semites migrated from Arabia, and in 2350 B.C.E. their king, Sargon, conquered the Sumerian kingdoms. Under Akkadian rule, Mesopotamian society combined elements of both cultures but retained individual aspects of each. In approximately 1900 B.C.E., the Babylonians conquered the region and ruled for another three hundred years.

Our knowledge of ancient Mesopotamia, and in particular, women's lives, comes from both archaeological evidence and the earliest written texts in the Western world. Scholars debate the origins of writing. Some believe that it was a new technology that appeared in response to Mesopotamia's complex economy and record-keeping needs. Others understand the development of writing as a slow evolution from clay tokens to numerical tablets to writing by approximately 3100 B.C.E. The earliest texts are pictograms, pictures that represented words or ideas. Later, Mesopotamians used wedge-shaped signs, known as *cuneiform*, to represent sounds and abstract ideas. The oldest writing recorded economic and administrative activities, but people

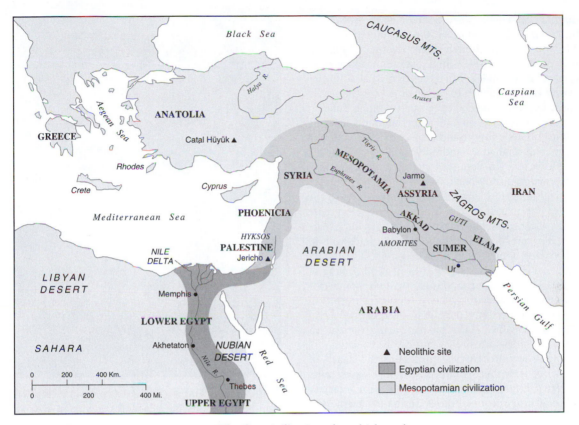

***Map 1.1* THE ANCIENT NEAR EAST.** The first civilizations for which we have extensive evidence of gender norms emerged in Mesopotamia and Egypt.

quickly came to use it for literature and personal correspondence. Certainly, most women, and indeed most men, did not learn to write. However, ancient Mesopotamia's bounty of economic, political, administrative, and legal documentation, personal correspondence, and its rich body of literature reveal much about women's roles in ancient society.

Gender and Mesopotamian Politics

Before 3000 B.C.E., the economy and culture of Mesopotamia was predominantly pastoral and agricultural, but by approximately 2000 B.C.E., many Mesopotamians had moved into walled cities. Some scholars have suggested that these early cities arose near temples, where Mesopotamians met to pray and trade. These urban centers became quite large. The city of Uruk had a population of around ten thousand, and, at its height, the city of Nippur was home to as many as forty thousand inhabitants.

Cities were the center of Mesopotamian political life. Each political entity or *city-state* consisted of one or a few urban communities and the nearby agricultural lands under its control. Although constantly at war, Mesopotamian city-states were economically interdependent and shared a common culture and history. Each city-state was governed by a king, whom people believed had been chosen by the gods. Kingship began as a temporary office during warfare and other crises, but it became permanent soon after 2600 B.C.E., as city-states constantly feuded and vied for authority. During this period, the relative power of these city-states waxed and waned with no single city-state achieving long-term dominance. Finally, the conquest of the region by Sargon the Akkadian in 2350 B.C.E. united much of Mesopotamia. Although Mesopotamian kingship was almost exclusively male, some evidence indicates that around 2450 B.C.E., Ku-Bau, a former tavern keeper, reigned for some time over the city of Kish, becoming the first recorded woman ruler in history. According to the Sumerian king list, she "consolidated the foundation of Kish, became 'king' and reigned a hundred years."[10]

However, Ku-Bau was the exception. Otherwise, women only participated in the governance of the kingdom through their relationships to the king. For example, the king's mother and wife often exerted considerable authority over palace life. The most vivid evidence of women's role in the palace comes from a later period. The letters between Zimri-Lim (r. 1775–1760 B.C.E.), king of Mari, and his queen, Shiptu, provide some evidence of the activities of royal wives. Shiptu was the daughter of one of the period's most powerful kings. She came to the palace during the fourth year of Zimri-Lim's reign but did not participate in many royal activities until after the death of the queen mother, Adad-dûri, a few years later. Shiptu's letters indicate that she took on a variety of governing responsibilities during her husband's absences, especially managing the royal palace. Zimri-Lim sent her instructions and kept her informed about certain political matters. He even relied on Shiptu to help control an outbreak of disease while he was away. When her husband was at home, she seems to have devoted herself to organizing the worship of various deities and managing the workforce of the palace.[11]

From these same letters, we also know something of the fates of Zimri-Lim's ten daughters, whom he married off to neighboring kings. Rulers commonly used women to cement political alliances, and some kings practiced *polygyny*, marrying more than one wife. Over the course of three years, Zimri-Lim married two of his daughters to Hâya-Sûmû, the king of Ilânsurâ. For his daughter Shîmatum, he provided an extensive *dowry*, a payment to the groom's family at the time of the marriage, which included jewelry, luxurious clothing, furniture, and ten female servants. When he arranged for the marriage of his daughter Kirûm to Hâya-Sûmû, he also appointed her mayor of Hâya-Sûmû's city-

WARKA HEAD URUK (CA. 3100 B.C.E.). This life-size, mask-like marble head of a Sumerian woman may have originally been part of a larger statue with inlaid eyes, eyebrows, and hair. Sumerian women are the earliest women for whom we have written records. (*Bildarchiv Preussischer Kulturbesitz/Art Resource, NY.*)

state. As a woman, Kirûm's political position was seemingly unique. Her letters to her father include political advice and admonishments when he failed to heed her counsel. However, the relationship between Kirûm and Hâya-Sûmû was fraught with conflict and the sisters quarreled continuously. Humiliated and unhappy, Kirûm pled with her father to bring her home saying, "If my lord does not write to me and does not bring me home, I shall surely die; I can no longer go on living."[12] Although Zimri-Lim maintained his alliance through Shîmatum, Kirûm's marriage was eventually dissolved and she returned to Mari. Presumably, she lost her political position as well.

Although, typically, mortal women did not rule, the goddess Inanna was critical to the acquisition of monarchical power (see **Women's Lives: Inanna, Near Eastern Goddess**). The kings of the city-state of Ur legitimized their rule through a sacred marriage with the goddess. Although scholars disagree on the details of the ceremony, the king may have had sexual relations with a queen or high priestess who represented the goddess. Sumerian hymns explicitly describe the king touching Inanna's "pure vulva" and "bed[ding] down with her." Through this act, the king received his authority directly from a deity and secured a personal tie to the heavens for both himself and for his subjects. Mesopotamian kings extolled their relationship with the goddess on their seals, describing themselves as "the beloved spouse of Inanna."[13]

With few exceptions, women could not participate directly in Mesopotamian political life. Men governed communities, and male officials supervised the city subdivisions. Male politicians used women to form alliances and may have consulted with and even relied on the advice of their wives and mothers, but unfortunately, such behind-the-scenes political activity left few marks in the historical record.

Mesopotamian Society

Mesopotamian society was class based. Class divisions distinguished wealthy, powerful women from the rest of the population and free women from unfree women. Urban society included the nobility, mostly relatives of the ruling family, free commoners, and slaves. The nobility controlled much of the wealth and exercised all of the power in Mesopotamian society. The majority of the population, free commoners, owned property and worked to support themselves in a variety of urban trades.

Slaves worked for the state, the temples, and private citizens. Most slaves were women and children taken as prisoners during the constant warfare, as the victors usually killed defeated men. Mesopotamians did not kill the women because they valued them for their ability to bear children. After Zimri-Lim defeated enemy leaders, he sent home female captives. These women, presumably members of the defeated man's

entourage, were the spoils of war. In a letter to Shiptu, Zimri-Lim determined their roles at the palace:

> To Shiptu say, thus [says] your lord. I have just sent you some female weavers. In among them are [some] ugbabātum priestesses. Pick out the ugbabātum priestesses and assign [the rest of them] to the house of female weavers. . . . Give instructions about their rations so that their appearance does not worsen.[14]

Other women became slaves when male relatives sold them to pay off debts. Men could even sell their mothers. However, the social hierarchy was remarkably fluid, and social status, even slavery, was not permanent. Slaves could be freed and free commoners might be enslaved. Even lowborn women could move into the world of the royal court. For instance, Kubatum was originally a wet nurse who breastfed other people's children. She must have borne children for the king, because later inscriptions show that she ultimately became the chief wife of King Shu-Sîn (ca. 2030 B.C.E.).[15]

Marriage was critical to the formation of the household, the basic unit of Mesopotamian society. Typically, parents arranged marriages while the future couple was still young, although Sumerian love songs indicate that girls could sometimes choose their own spouses. The families formulated a contract, often oral rather than written, that described the exchange of gifts, including a dowry. Families then celebrated the completion of the contract with a feast. To ensure the paternity of the children, the bride was expected to be a virgin. In fact, Mesopotamian law prescribed the death penalty for men who raped engaged women. Once the prospective bride reached puberty, she left her family to live in her husband's paternal home where she ideally lived until death.

Heads of household were nearly always men, who passed that title down to their eldest sons. As the head of the family, the father wielded complete authority over his wife and children. However, gender norms within marriage may have varied according to the family's ethnicity. In Akkadian-speaking areas, women were confined to the family house, while in Sumerian-speaking areas they were not. The Akkadian word for marriage meant "to

Women's Lives

Inanna, Near Eastern Goddess

Inanna was one of the oldest and most widely venerated goddesses of the ancient Near East. Although some scholars speculate that prehistoric peoples may have worshipped her, the first evidence of devotion to her appears around 3000 B.C.E., when an inscription over a storehouse names her as the protective spirit of the Mesopotamian city of Uruk's central storehouse.[1] Inanna's temple in Uruk was called Eanna, "the house of heaven." It is the oldest preserved temple in the city. In addition to religious worship, it was also the center of economic and intellectual activity.

Inanna means Queen of Heaven and indeed, she came from a distinguished heavenly family. She was the daughter of the moon god, Nanna, and his consort, Ningal. She was the Goddess of the Morning and Evening Star and was associated with the planet Venus. She ruled aspects of the heavens, the earth, and the underworld.

As far back as the fourth millennium B.C.E., Inanna was the protector of the city-state of Uruk and the source of Sumerian kingship. The king of Uruk was the consort of Inanna, with whom he was tied in a ceremony of sacred marriage. We know little about this ceremony; however, in one text, the king acquires the authority of kingship by making love to Inanna.

When on the bed he shall have caressed me,
Then shall I caress my lord, a sweet fate I shall
*   decree for him.*
I shall caress Shulgi, the faithful shepherd, a
*   sweet fate I shall decree for him.*
I shall caress his loin,
The shepherdship of all the lands I shall decree
*   as his fate.*[2]

According to a different Sumerian myth, at the time of creation, the huluppu tree was planted next to the Euphrates. The tree was swept away by the South Wind and the river, but Inanna rescued it. Although she cared for the tree for ten years, it became infected by pests. Unable to save the tree, she called upon Gilgamesh, the Sumerian god-king and epic hero. He carved a throne and a bed for Inanna from the trunk of the tree. In return, she fashioned the emblems of kingship for him from its crown and roots.[3]

Inanna appears in many forms in Mesopotamian literature. She was the goddess of warfare and fertility. Archaeologists have found a splendid crown of lapis lazuli beads decorated with tiny golden fruit trees, plants, and animals dating from 2500 B.C.E., which may have been made expressly for the goddess.[4] In the *Epic of Gilgamesh*, Inanna is a powerful, often vengeful goddess. Attracted by the beauty of the god-king Gilgamesh, she asks him to be her lover. She even offers him gifts, including a chariot of lapis

take possession of one's wife," from the same verb for "capture" or "seizure" of any goods or territory or people.[16] The sense of possession was confirmed by an economic transaction, as the husband-to-be's family paid his in-laws a *bride price* for their daughter.

The legal norms surrounding divorce reveal much about the expectations of marriage. According to one of the oldest law codes in the West, the Babylonian Code of Hammurabi (ca. 1750 B.C.E.), a woman was expected to be fertile and faithful. A man could not mistreat his wife or

neglect his children. If a man wanted to divorce a wife who had borne him children, he had to return her dowry and provide her with enough property and goods to raise their children. If the couple was childless, he had only to return her bride price and her dowry and declare himself divorced. If a woman wanted to leave her husband, she had to present evidence of his neglect or mistreatment to the authorities. If the authorities found him to be at fault, she could leave with her dowry. However, if they found that she had "ruined her house" through adultery, the Code sentenced her to be

lazuli. Despite her wooing, Gilgamesh rebuffs her, cruelly listing how she had destroyed her previous lovers. When Inanna learns of Gilgamesh's rejection, she goes to her father and asks him to send the Bull of Heaven to kill Gilgamesh. When the Bull snorted, a huge abyss opened and hundreds of men from Uruk fell to their deaths. However, Gilgamesh slays the Bull, further enraging Inanna.

Inanna was also the guardian of *me,* the divine principles that spread arts, crafts, and civilization. In the tale *The Descent of Inanna,* Inanna wants to see the underworld where her sister, Ereshkigal, is the queen. When Inanna arrives, she is stripped of all her finery, physical representations of *me.* When the sisters finally meet, Ereshkigal orders Inanna's death. Eventually Ereshkigal is calmed and has Inanna brought back to life and released. Inanna regains her fine clothing, jewelry, and *me.*

The regular conquests of the region spread devotion to Inanna across the Near East. After the Sumerians, the Akkadians adopted her worship and named her Ishtar. Enheduanna (ca. 2250 B.C.E.), the daughter of Sargon, the conqueror of Mesopotamia, was the high priestess of the moon god but was particularly devoted to Inanna. Her hymns to Inanna are among the earliest known writings and the first known compositions by a woman. Inanna's immense and wide-ranging power drew worshippers to her temples for thousands of years.

[1] Joan Goodnick Westenholz, "Goddesses of the Ancient Near East 3000–1000 BC," in *Ancient Goddesses: The Myths and the Evidence,* ed. Lucy Goodison and Christine Morris (London: British Museum Press, 1998), 73.
[2] Beverly Moon, "Inanna: The Star who Became Queen," in *Goddesses Who Rule,* ed. Elisabeth Benard and Beverly Moon (Oxford: Oxford University Press, 2000), 73.
[3] Diane Wolkstein and Samuel Noah Kramer, *Inanna Queen of Heaven and Earth: Her Stories and Hymns from Sumer* (New York: Harper and Row, 1983), 75.
[4] Wolkstein and Kramer, 146.

Sources: Diane Wolkstein and Samuel Noah Kramer, *Inanna Queen of Heaven and Earth: Her Stories and Hymns from Sumer* (New York: Harper and Row, 1983); Beverly Moon, "Inanna: The Star who Became Queen," in *Goddesses Who Rule,* ed. Elisabeth Benard and Beverly Moon, 69–81 (Oxford: Oxford University Press, 2000). Joan Goodnick Westenholz, "Goddesses of the Ancient Near East 3000–1000 BC," in *Ancient Goddesses: The Myths and the Evidence*, ed. Lucy Goodison and Christine Morris, 63–82 (London: British Museum Press, 1998).

drowned. A woman's legal rights depended on her sexual reputation and her ability to bear children.

Mesopotamians spoke frankly about sex and love. Many poems, songs, and plaques describe sexual intercourse. They often compared female genitals to sweet foods, as in this love song from 2100 B.C.E.:

> *The beer of my [. . .], Il-Ummiya, the tap-stress / is sweet / And her vulva / is sweet like her beer / and her beer is sweet! / And her vulva is sweet like her chatter / and her beer is sweet! / Her bittersweet beer / and her beer are sweet!*[17]

However, their relationships also had a sentimental side. Another love song reveals the deep feelings of a woman who suspected that her lover was interested in another woman:

> *I shall remain faithful to you, / May Ishtar-the-Sovereign be my witness: / My love will prevail, / And that evil tongue [her rival!] will be confounded. / Henceforth I shall cling to you / And I shall reward your love with mine!*[18]

Although sexual taboos were uncommon in earlier Mesopotamian societies, the Babylonians who conquered the region around 1900 B.C.E. considered women unclean for six days each month during menstruation. They referred to menstruation as "hit by the weapon."[19] We do not know whether the Babylonians were the first to develop this idea of female pollution; however, we should not underestimate its significance, as it defined women as physically inferior to men. Babylonians believed that pollution had to be contained, and as a result, they had to control women's movements and regulate their sexuality. They punished a woman's sexual transgressions more harshly than a man's. For instance, a husband's adultery was punishable only if it harmed someone other than his wife. However, a wife caught with a lover other than her husband could be drowned unless pardoned by her husband.[20]

Bearing children, particularly sons, was a woman's primary responsibility in Mesopotamian society. Sons were critical for both the continuation of the family line and the inheritance of familial property. The Code of Hammurabi even prescribed penalties for harming pregnant women. It decreed that a man who hit a free pregnant woman so that she miscarried paid her ten shekels for her loss. If she died, the assailant's daughter was executed in retribution. However, the penalties also reveal the strength of the Mesopotamian class structure. If a man struck a pregnant slave, he was to pay only two shekels and if she died, he had to provide financial compensation to her owner.

Although Mesopotamian society discouraged polygyny, a man could take a second wife or make a slave into his concubine to ensure the birth of an heir. However, he could not divorce his wife or throw her out of the house, nor was the second wife considered the equal of the first wife. Any sons of the second relationship inherited from the man's estate, and any daughters received dowries. If a man whose wife had already borne him children took a slave as his concubine, those sons only inherited if the man acknowledged them as his own.

As a widow, a woman exerted greater control over her own future and that of her family. If her children were still minors, she became the head of the family and administered the estate. According to the Code of Hammurabi, the widow could remarry and choose her own spouse, but if she had young children, officials had to verify that her first husband was dead. After receiving approval, she and her new husband became the managers of her first husband's property. The Code then admonished the widow to "keep the house in order, bring up the children, and not sell the household utensils." To protect the deceased man's legacy, a widow could not inherit from her husband's estate if she had adult sons nor could she continue her husband's business if she remarried.

Women and the Urban Workforce

Urbanization transformed the region's economy. As cities grew, a larger proportion of the Mesopotamian population worked in occupations other than agriculture. Merchants, artisans, those involved in religious and ritual activities, and members of the political elite did not grow their own food. To feed the growing number of city dwellers, powerful members of society used their authority to demand *tribute* from people below them in the socioeconomic hierarchy or from conquered peoples. Tribute was taxation in the form of goods or labor. Thus, most Mesopotamian households worked to fulfill demands for tribute as well as to provide for their own subsistence.

The wife of a ruler played a critical role in the economy of her husband's dominions. Rulers, their wives, and possibly even their children each had their own, separate households, and these royal households were centers of the local economy. The household of the wife, the *é-mí*, was largely devoted to agricultural production. As the primary administrator of these estates, she controlled a variety of activities, including sowing, harvesting, storage, canal maintenance, and equipment supplies.[21] The wife's household also often owned cattle and other livestock, employed fishermen, and manufactured textiles. In addition to managing their enormous households, wives of rulers had other economic responsibilities. Shulgi-simti, the wife of Shulgi (r. 2094–2047 B.C.E.) was in charge of the collection of animals and their distribution to the temples of Nippur and other cities and among palace workers. The wife of the ruler also handed out food rations. The head of the é-mí remained in power even after her husband died, as long as government passed peacefully to her son. When a city expanded beyond its boundaries, the kings appointed governors to rule the additional lands, and the wives of these governors, *dam-ensí*, played important roles in the local economy. In the city of Umma Ninmelam, the wife of Ur-Lisi supervised transactions involving gold, leather, wool, cloth, grain, and flour. Her commercial activities indicate that women had the legal right to enter into contracts.

Indeed, according to legal documents dating from as early as 2550 B.C.E., Mesopotamian women had extensive legal rights that differed little from those of men. They could own and dispose of property as they wished. The records of one married couple reveals that the husband, Ur-Shara, specialized in caring for the livestock, while his wife, Ama-e, owned large areas of land and seems to have been responsible for the couple's agricultural activities.[22] Women could participate fully in commerce, even buying and selling houses.

Among other legal rights, a woman could adopt another person (Mesopotamian adoption was not limited to children) to ensure the existence of an heir and to provide for her in her old age. An unmarried woman could adopt a girl with the right to either marry her off or have her work as a prostitute. Women could lend and borrow money and act as guarantors of other people. They could institute legal proceedings without the approval of their husbands and furnish legal testimony.

Women's economic roles evolved as the populations of Mesopotamian cities increased. As more people moved into the cities, there were fewer rural producers from whom to extract tribute. Gradually, Mesopotamians moved from a tribute-based economy to a manufacturing economy in which wealthier households hired employees to produce what they could no longer demand in tribute. Women formed a substantial proportion of the workforce of this new economy.

Textiles were among the most important goods that Mesopotamians produced. In addition to clothing, they used cloth for gift giving, ritual offerings to gods and goddesses, and trade with other peoples. Although initially women wove in their homes for personal use and tribute payment, by 2000 B.C.E., an almost exclusively female workforce produced most textiles in temple and palace workshops. Many of these weaving workshops were quite large. One enterprise employed more than four thousand adult (mostly women) and eighteen hundred child weavers.[23] Generally, these women worked in groups of twenty, sometimes under a male, but more often under a female supervisor. Unlike their predecessors who spun and wove at home, women in Mesopotamia's textile enterprises left home to work every day and may have taken their younger children with them.[24] While at first the fact Mesopotamian women worked outside of the home seems quite modern, these workshops actually indicate a decline in women's economic status. These women workers did not own the cloth that they produced nor did they control the amount or type of textiles that they made. Moreover, their workloads increased as supervisors forced women workers to increase production to meet higher tribute quotas in addition to continuing their domestic responsibilities.[25]

The new urban economy offered a remarkable variety of occupational opportunities for women. Women did hard labor on towboats and acted as oil pressers. Women sang and danced professionally in both religious and secular settings. Other women, known as *sabitu*, were responsible for brewing and selling beer, and still others were tavern keepers. Women may have worked in many other occupations, but many Sumerian names were used by both genders, making it almost impossible for historians to know the gender of the person mentioned in some of the texts. Despite the extent of their participation in the workforce, women were nearly always paid less than men. For instance, women usually received a monthly ration of barley of between thirty and forty liters for their work with a maximum of fifty to sixty liters per month, while men's wages usually started at sixty liters per month.[26]

Finally, the many opportunities for urban women should not obscure the fact that most people in ancient Mesopotamia carried on their traditional ways, herding goats and sheep across the plains. On farms, women worked in the wheat and barley fields, carrying and removing grain and milling flour. They helped grow the flax that other women used to make linen. While we do not know the gender division of labor among

Mesopotamian farmers, as farming technology improved with the development of plows and carts that relied on animal power, men gradually took on most of those responsibilities, while women devoted much of their energies to domestic duties such as cooking, cleaning, spinning, and caring for children.

Gender and the Gods

Religiously, Mesopotamians viewed nature, human activities, and divine action as intimately connected. Like their prehistoric predecessors, early Mesopotamians were animists, but eventually, people ascribed human characteristics to these natural forces, creating *anthropomorphic* gods and goddesses. Scholars have identified more than two thousand Mesopotamian gods and goddesses, each with his or her own powers. Some deities were more powerful than others. Their names and special associations changed over the centuries, but the power of the gods over Mesopotamian life remained constant.

The relationship between female deities and mortal women is complex. On the one hand, female deities had power over critical aspects of human life, especially fertility, and were the subject of great veneration by both men and women. However, there is little evidence that the worship of a female deity empowered female worshippers or raised their status in society. In fact, there is no evidence of any relationship between the sex of a deity and its powers or devotees. For example, the goddess Nidaba was associated with writing, despite the fact that nearly all scribes were men.[27] Nor were the genders of deities completely stable. Some deities were male in one city and female in another. Moreover, the Sumerian language has only a non-gendered word for deities, and the lack of gender-specific names and pronouns in Sumerian further complicates assigning a gender to most of the gods.

Although Sumerian creation stories changed over the centuries, goddesses played central roles in the formation of the Mesopotamian world. The earliest myth describes the world's creation from both a male (Heaven—An) and a female (Earth—Ki). Later texts, which some scholars believe actually reveal earlier traditions, name the goddess Nammu as the sole creator of all the gods and goddesses.

Mesopotamians associated most goddesses with traditionally female spheres of activity. In particular, goddesses had power over fertility-related activities, including insemination and gestation. They watched over and protected mothers during childbirth. People also connected them with food production. For instance, wine and beer fell under the jurisdictions of the goddesses Geshtinanna and Ninkasi, respectively. Goddesses also fulfilled traditionally feminine roles as the mothers, wives, and daughters of male deities.

Each city had its own patron god or goddess to whom the inhabitants dedicated a temple. For instance, Inanna (in Sumerian, Ishtar in Akkadian) was one of the best-known and most powerful goddesses and the patron of the powerful city of Uruk. (See **Women's Lives: Inanna, Near Eastern Goddess.**) Once they placed a statue of that deity in the temple, people believed that the god or goddess was present. People treated them like the most privileged of humans, clothing and feeding them every day. City deities had spouses and children, each of whom had to be attended to as well. The gods' relationships replicated human interactions. Gods and goddesses experienced the full range of human emotions. They argued, loved, hated, and became jealous. Violent outbursts by gods caused earthquakes, floods, and other natural disasters. The *Epic of Gilgamesh* (ca. 2100 B.C.E.) tells of the flooding of the world by angry gods. By carefully looking after their needs, Mesopotamians hoped to lessen the unpredictable consequences of the gods' emotions.

Each temple had an entourage of priests and priestesses. However, men appointed women to official positions in the temple hierarchy and supervised their activity. The only exception was the creation of the *entu*, the high priestess, by the Akkadian king Sargon. The entu priestess took orders from no mortal. Sargon appointed his daughter, Enheduanna, as high priestess of the moon god Nanna and his consort Ningal of Ur as a way of consolidating power over his newly conquered territories. From her exalted position, Enheduanna became an accomplished poet, the author of at least two great cycles of hymns and a collection of Babylonian hymns dedicated to her father's patron goddess, Ishtar. Enheduanna wrote in Sumerian, even as her father made Akkadian the official administrative language, a sign of her role in fusing Sumerian and Akkadian cultures. In her position as high priestess, she remained celibate all her life, symbolically married to the god. Thirteen royal priestess followed Enheduanna in the position of entu over the next five hundred years.

In addition to priestesses, royal women engaged in many forms of worship. They offered prayers for the king and his armies. They worshipped the main gods of the area through sacrifices, and women acted as professional prophetesses attached to particular gods or temples.[28]

By approximately 1800 B.C.E., cloisters of female priestesses served Mesopotamian deities. These women, known as *naditu*, lived in cloisters called *gagû*. Some scholars believe that the cloisters of women formed because high-ranking women could not find suitable spouses. Others connect them with an increase in private wealth during this period that required families to develop an institution to house women who would not have children and ensure that female heirs did not dilute male inheritance. Their situation varied from one temple to the next. The naditu of Shamash were prohibited from having sexual relations all their lives. In Babylon, the naditu of Marduk might marry, but they were forbidden to bear children. To fulfill their roles as wives, they had to provide or permit their husbands to have concubines in order to have children. With royal patronage, the gagû of Sippar was the most prestigious of all cloisters. Women came from all over the region to live there. The princesses of the royal houses of Babylon and Mari and even the sister of Hammurabi became naditu in Sippar. Their association with the gagû of Sippar brought prestige to their families and cemented relations between their families and the gods. Girls in their midteens were brought there by their fathers or guardians and remained there until their deaths. Inside the cloister, one hundred to two hundred naditu and cloister officials lived in private residences, which they either owned or rented. Slaves helped with household tasks and worked as scribes. As these women had no offspring and the institution had no means to provide for them, naditu often adopted slaves, either male or female, or younger naditu, to care

for them when they grew old. The slave would be freed when the naditu died.

Each naditu provided for herself, a situation that required considerable wealth. These women brought slaves, jewelry, and prized furniture and utensils to the cloister. Despite their enclosure, they did not lose their rights to family property upon entering. The Code of Hammurabi clearly states that a naditu could manage her own share of the family estate. If she received no portion of the estate when she entered the gagû, she shared equally in the inheritance with her brothers at her father's death. Sometimes three or four generations of women in the paternal line became naditu, as the cloister offered a good alternative to marriage. Their wealth also contributed to the local economy, as they bought and sold land and goods from local inhabitants. They were important sources for loans. Although we have extensive evidence of their economic transactions, we know little about the religious duties of the naditu except that they participated in religious offerings twice each day and marched in some religious processions.[29]

In addition to their myriad of gods and goddesses, Mesopotamians believed that evil or demonic forces could affect their lives and that witches and sorcerers could access those forces and direct them at unfortunate people in the form of illness or ghosts of the dead who haunted the living. Women, especially foreign women, were considered the most skilled at witchcraft. To protect themselves, people participated in antiwitchcraft rituals in which they had mock trials of witches in which they burned an effigy. These trials would rid both the mortal world and the underworld of witches and sorcerers. Individual witches may have been tried for their crimes and punished by drowning. However, the Code of Hammurabi attempted to control the social turmoil that witchcraft could provoke by decreeing that putting forth a false witchcraft accusation was a crime punishable by death.

Mesopotamian women faced some serious constraints. They could not participate in the political life of their burgeoning civilization, and society rigidly controlled their sexuality. In this class-based society, powerful women exploited the labor of the rest of the population. However, with extensive legal rights, women engaged in

PERIODS OF EGYPTIAN HISTORY

Period	Date	Significant Events
Archaic	3100–2660 B.C.	Unification of Egypt
Old Kingdom	2715–2180 B.C.	Construction of the pyramids
First Intermediate	2180–2080 B.C.	Political chaos
Middle Kingdom	2080–1640 B.C.	Recovery and political stability
Second Intermediate	1640–1570 B.C.	Hyksos "invasion"
New Kingdom	1570–1075 B.C.	City of Deir el Medina

commerce and acquired property and were critical participants in the dynamic economies of Mesopotamian cities.

ANCIENT EGYPT, 3000 B.C.E.– 1000 B.C.E.

During more or less the same period, a powerful civilization developed in Egypt in North Africa. Around 3100 B.C.E., Menes, the leader of Upper Egypt, conquered Lower Egypt, unifying the two kingdoms under a strong central government that ruled the peaceful and prosperous kingdom for more than one thousand years. Scholars refer to this period in Egyptian history as the *Old Kingdom* (2715–2180 B.C.E.). Toward the end of the Old Kingdom, royal authority weakened and the unified government fell into chaos. After one hundred years of political and economic difficulties, peace was finally restored around 2080 B.C.E. This period of prosperity and tranquility is known as the *Middle Kingdom* (ca. 2080–1640 B.C.E.). Political stability allowed the rulers to devote Egyptian wealth and labor to extensive irrigation and other public works projects. Traders expanded southward into Nubia and eastward into Mesopotamia. However, these contacts brought both wealth and trouble to the Middle Kingdom. A revolt by the Nubians and a general weakening of royal power allowed the Hyskos, foreign invaders from the east, to come to power in the north. The Egyptian defeat of the Hyskos and the reunification of the kingdoms initiated the

New Kingdom (1570–1075 B.C.E.). (See **Periods of Egyptian History**.) With the exception of two brief interludes, over nearly two thousand years, Egypt remained remarkably stable, and Egyptian women benefited from that stability. Both noble and common women experienced considerable freedom and equality, although they did not have full access to religious or political authority.

Gods and Goddesses

Egypt was a deeply religious society, and the Egyptians' deep-seated spirituality helped maintain social stability. As with all early peoples, Egyptians believed that natural phenomena expressed the will of the gods. Thus, to understand and more effectively control the world around them, they formed close relationships with a large pantheon of gods, including Osiris, the god of the underworld, Amun-Re, the king of the gods, and Ptah, the creator god. In addition to appeasing the gods, Egyptians also believed that their survival depended on their ability to maintain the divine order of the world, called *ma'at*, which the gods had ordained at creation. Without constant care, they feared that the gods would leave Egypt in a state of chaos. For instance, when a series of crop failures around 2350 B.C.E. provoked a series of economic and political crises, the Egyptians believed that ma'at had been disturbed.

Egyptians worshipped both male and female deities but did not associate them with stereotypically gendered spheres. Unlike the earth goddess to whom most Mediterranean peoples attributed fertility, the Egyptian god of the earth, Geb, was male, and most of the important fertility deities were male. Uniquely, the sky deity, Nut, was female. As the goddess of the sky, Nut was the mother of many of Egypt's important deities, including Osiris, Isis, Seth, and the mother of the stars. As the mother of the sun god, to whom she gave birth daily, she provided one of the necessary components of life and regulated the passage of time.

Egyptians often depicted goddesses with animal features. Many had cowlike features, connecting cows' milk-giving ability with the goddesses' capacity to give life, nurture, and feed. Egyptians also identified snakes with women, reproduction, and the home. Thus, the cobra goddess Renenutet became an important domestic deity. To protect themselves and their children from the dangers of childbirth, pregnant women often prayed to the goddess Taweret, who was represented as a hippo with a lion's feet, a crocodile back, and human breasts. Bes, a male dwarf deity, also protected women in childbirth. Bes had both human and animal features, was quite ugly, and was usually depicted with oversized genitalia. Bes amulets were popular for more than two thousand years, and during later periods, some lower-class women decorated their bodies with Bes tattoos to guard against sexually transmitted diseases or the dangers of childbirth.[30]

In addition to dealing with issues such as fertility, goddesses held authority over realms that were largely forbidden to mortal women, such as politics. When Upper Egyptians celebrated the unification of the Egyptian kingdoms, they placed the cow goddess, Bat, at the top of a commemorative shield, indicating that the fertility goddess aided the birth of both humans and states.[31] The second of the king's five titles was "He of the Two Ladies," referring to Nekhbet, the vulture goddess, and Wadjet, the cobra goddess, both of whom protected the king. The connection between the Two Ladies and politics extended beyond the person of the king. They represented the unification of northern and southern Egypt and of the divine and earthly worlds.

Egyptians also associated Isis, one of the oldest goddesses and the great mother goddess of Egypt, with politics. Widely venerated, she was the sister-wife of Osiris (the god of the underworld) and the mother of Horus, who was both a god and

considered the first king of Egypt. In one image, Isis suckles the king Thutmose III.[32] However, over the centuries, her connection with the monarchy declined in favor of her role as universal mother and the Queen of Heaven.

Hathor was probably the most powerful goddess. She was the chief goddess and divine mother of the king of Egypt.[33] Often depicted with cowlike features, her powers ranged widely. She was the nurturer of humankind and was associated with drunkenness, love, sex, joy, music, and poetry. She played an important role as a funerary goddess, helping the dead make the transition from this world to the next. Her cult was very popular among women, as is evident from the many mirrors and other personal objects owned by women that displayed her image.[34] In addition, women offered her votives when petitioning for help with fertility issues. At her shrines, archaeologists have discovered models of breasts, female genitalia, and votive cloths that name women and portray family scenes.[35]

Hathor, like other Egyptian gods and goddesses, lived both in heaven and on earth, where priests tended to their needs, cared for their cultic statues, and performed an extensive array of religious rituals and offerings. Although most priests were men, Hathor's priesthood was predominantly female until the end of the Old Kingdom. These priestesses, many of whom were members of the nobility, had considerable authority. They served the goddess and administered the revenues generated by sacred land (mainly foodstuffs and linens) and supervised workers belonging to the temple.

While priestesses were full-time clerics, laywomen with the rank of *wabet* (pure one) served the temple for one-month intervals spaced throughout the year and received the same payment for their services as men in this position. Women also served as *meret* priestesses, part of the temples' troops of sacred musicians. The "superior of the musical troop" was usually the wife of a high-ranking official.

Although the Old Kingdom witnessed a vibrant expansion of the worship of Hathor and the extension of the priesthood of Hathor to commonborn women from across Egypt, the increasing attraction of men to the cult of Hathor led to a decline in the number of female clergy. By the late

Middle Kingdom, there is no longer evidence of female commoners acting as priestesses. Occasionally, women also officiated in the cults of Neith (early creator goddess), Thoth (the god of wisdom), Khons (the moon god), and a number of other less powerful goddesses.

In addition to temple worship, Egyptians gave offerings and prayers at local shrines and community chapels. Families also engaged in religious rituals at home. Each house may have had its own shrine where the family worshipped domestic deities. A workman's house in the city of Amarna contains a depiction of a woman and a girl before the goddess Taweret, along with two small pottery beds and two female figurines. This shrine may have been connected with fertility and childbirth.[36] Egyptians also venerated their deceased relatives at household shrines.

Egyptians believed that death was not the end of life, but rather the beginning of the next stage of life, and women were actively involved in that transition. Women commonly participated in funerary rituals and could serve as funerary priests who made offerings and performed rituals for the deceased. The deceased's family often paid women as professional mourners. In elaborate funeral ceremonies, the mourning women threw dust onto their heads, ripped their clothing, wailed, and scratched their cheeks. They also impersonated the goddesses Isis and Nephthys at both ends of the funeral bier, performed funerary dances, and gave offerings.[37] Because they believed in the afterlife, wealthy Egyptians constructed elaborate tombs for both men and women and carefully mummified the bodies. They buried the bodies with a variety of goods. Women's graves often included mirrors, jewelry, and pottery. Men were generally buried with more funerary goods than women, which may indicate that Egyptians viewed men as more important than women or that women could not or did not spend as much on their burials.

Pharonic Authority and the Role of Queens

The Egyptian king, the pharaoh, was an absolute monarch, the source of all laws and moral righteousness. As the supreme ruler and priest, he was the main link between gods and mortals. In return for properly serving the gods through the construction of new temples and the maintenance of rituals, he ensured the peace and prosperity of his kingdom. He ruled in accordance with ma'at. Egyptians also believed that the gods had divinely created pharonic authority at the beginning of time. The pharaoh was the physical embodiment of the god Horus and the son of the sun god Re. Over the course of more than three thousand years, Egyptian kingship was an almost exclusively male institution. We have records of only four female rulers.

In nearly all the cases, women came to power during dynastic crises. We know little about the first recorded female pharaoh, Nitiqret, other than that she came to the throne during a troubled time (r. ca. 2181 B.C.E.). Sobekneferu (r. ca. 1777 B.C.E.) became pharaoh under similarly unclear circumstances and ruled for barely four years. Her full title reveals the difficulties of a woman occupying a traditionally male position. Fragments of statues refer to her as "the Female Horus, Meryetre, the King of Upper and Lower Egypt, Sobekneferu, the Daughter of Re, Sobekneferu." She employed the idea of a female embodiment of the god Horus in order to list herself among the other pharaohs.[38] Tausret (r. ca. 1188 B.C.E.) ruled as regent for her stepson, Merenptah-Siptah, but when he died, she took the title of pharaoh and governed briefly on her own. The Nineteenth Dynasty ended with her reign.

Hatshepsut (r. ca. 1470 B.C.E.) was the only female pharaoh to enjoy a long, prosperous reign. She was the daughter of the warrior king Thutmose I and the wife of her half brother, Thutmose II. At Thutmose II's death, she became regent for the son of her husband's concubine (her stepson/nephew). An active and ambitious regent, within seven years, she seized power and declared herself ruler and senior coregent with the young prince Thutmose III. She bolstered the economy through trading expeditions to foreign lands and instituted an ambitious building program. Among many elaborate projects, Hatshepsut built the terraced temple at Deir el Bahri, one of the greatest monuments from antiquity dedicated to a woman. Inscriptions in the private area of the temple warned the privileged few who entered that "those who shall do her homage shall live, he who shall speak evil in

HATSHEPSUT'S TEMPLE AT DEIR EL BAHRI (CA. 1470 B.C.E.). Located in Valley of the Queens, this temple housed the funerary cults of Hatshepsut, her father, and probably her father's mother. It was decorated throughout with painted reliefs, many of which depict Hatshepsut's military campaigns. This magnificent temple is a testament to the female pharoah's remarkable power. *(Courtesy of the Semitic Museum, Harvard University #SM 1907.64.470.)*

blasphemy of her Majesty shall die."[39] Despite her success, Egyptians had a difficult time describing and representing a female ruler. She appears on her monuments dressed as a man, sometimes with a false beard. Her scribes sometimes used masculine and other times feminine pronouns when referring to her. We do not know how she died, but long after her death, Thutmose III obliterated her name and image from many monuments and smashed her statues. Historian Gay Robins asserts that this destruction may have been necessary because a "female ruler violated the fundamentally masculine nature of kingship." To maintain ma'at, her successor had to erase Hatshepsut from the official record.[40]

Some queens successfully ruled as regents for their minor sons. Ahhotep II was the mother of

King Ahmose, the founder of the Eighteenth Dynasty (ca. 1550 B.C.E.). Although we know little about her role, her son dedicated a large stone slab, a *stela*, at Karnak in which he praised her as "one who cares for Egypt. She has looked after her [Egypt's] soldiers; she has guarded her; she has brought back her fugitives, and collected together her deserters; she has pacified Upper Egypt, and expelled her rebels."[41] Although officially his queen regent, she may have ruled alone for many years.[42] Archaeologists discovered a necklace of three golden flies in her tomb. This necklace was a military decoration granted only for bravery in battle, suggesting that Queen Ahhotep II may have personally led troops into battle.

During the New Kingdom, queens gained new authority. Thutmose IV (ca. 1400 B.C.E.) emphasized the divinity of the women of his family. He gave his mother the title "god's wife of Amun," directly associating her with the goddess Mut as well as Isis and Hathor.[43] Queen consorts like Tiy (ca. 1370 B.C.E.), the wife of Amenhotep III, exercised significant power through their influence with the pharaoh. Although of common birth, Tiy was Amenhotep's principal wife and was frequently depicted next to her husband. A unique tomb painting in which she is represented as a sphinx trampling two female enemies (one Nubian, one Asiatic) attests to her political skills. Queen Tiy was the first to wear the vulture headdress, blurring the lines between goddess and queen and was deified in her own temple at Sedeinga (now in the Sudan).[44] As a goddess, she was the "solar eye of Ra" who would help to restore ma'at to the world.[45]

Her daughter-in-law, Nefertiti (ca. 1340 B.C.E.), also seems to have played a prominent role at court. When Nefertiti's husband, Amenhotep IV, created a new monotheistic state cult to the sun god Aten and changed his name to Akhenaten, Nefertiti helped spread the new religion. Her figure appears frequently at the temples of Karnak dedicated to Aten, and in one building, she is depicted performing rituals that previously had been reserved for the king. She may have acted as coregent with her husband, and there is the strong possibility that briefly she ruled alone after Akhenaten's death, hiding behind a male persona.[46]

Pharaohs had many wives but chose one as the principal queen. She was usually the wife and sister or half sister of the pharaoh. Many scholars believe that pharaohs married their sisters in order to set themselves apart from their subjects and in imitation of the gods, who often married their siblings in Egyptian mythology. As the wife of a semidivine ruler and a member of the royal family, the queen had considerable public authority and was granted numerous titles and privileges. A number of pharaohs also married their daughters. As these intrafamilial relationships did not generally produce healthy children, the pharaohs took other wives, who also bore them heirs. Many wives came as gifts from foreign rulers to help solidify political alliances. Ramses II (ca. 1250 B.C.E.) was married to his sister Henutmira, three of his daughters, two Hittite princesses, a Syrian princess, and a Babylonian princess. In addition, the pharaoh's harem included numerous concubines of both noble and common birth. Ramses supposedly fathered seventy-nine sons and fifty-nine daughters with the women of his harem.[47]

The presence of so many possible successors often led to palace intrigue, as royal wives and concubines plotted to advance the careers of their sons. Late in the New Kingdom, a royal concubine named Tiy (not the queen mentioned above) plotted with her son, other palace women, and a small group of officials both inside and outside the palace, including a commander of the army and an overseer of priests. The conspirators may have hoped to assassinate Ramses III (ca. 1180 B.C.E.) and put Tiy's son on the throne. However, the plot failed and royal authorities forced the prince to commit suicide. Although some of the other conspirators were executed, we do not know the fates of the women involved.

After their deaths, the most powerful and favored royal women were buried in elaborate pyramid tombs. Pyramids equipped the dead for the afterlife and connected the heavens with the earth. During the Old and Middle Kingdoms, royal women were often buried in small pyramids near the pharaoh's pyramid. Senworsret I (1956–1911 B.C.E.) had an enormous pyramid complex constructed for himself and his family. In addition to the main pyramid, royal women, including his principal queen, Neferu, and one of his daughters, were buried in nine smaller pyramids.[48] The New Kingdom saw the construction of the great pyramids in the Valley of the Kings and the eighty tombs of the Valley of the Queens. The most spectacular of these monuments is the pyramid of Queen Nefertari (1290–1224 B.C.E.), the wife of Ramses II. This elaborately decorated tomb was covered in wall paintings and rivals the greatest of the pharaohs' tombs for its beauty.

Although most Egyptian women did not have access to political power, a few women reigned as pharaoh, and many more influenced Egyptian politics as the wives and mothers of Egyptian rulers. These women benefited from the fact that Egyptians believed that the pharaoh was part god and that they or their children had royal blood. Their connection to divinity gave them significant power and authority despite their gender.

Gender in Egyptian Society

Egyptian society was very hierarchical. At the top of the social structure, the royal family and the nobility controlled the extensive Egyptian bureaucracy and the priesthood. A vast commoner population not only supported themselves but also supplied food and other services for the elites. At the bottom of society, serfs, unfree people tied to the land, worked the lands owned by the monarchy, the temples, and sometimes individuals. Slavery was unknown during the Old Kingdom and only became important after the large-scale conquests of the New Kingdom.

Marriage was an important institution at all levels of society. Even slaves married, and Egyptians permitted marriages between slaves and free persons. However, it was an economic transaction, not a religious ritual. There was no ceremony. Families or individuals came to an agreement, exchanged goods, and the couple began to live together. Although the evidence is sparse, there seems to have been little social pressure to marry a person of equal social status. Egyptians regularly married foreigners. One advice book suggests that twenty was the right age for a man to marry and that wives were generally younger than their husbands.[49] Unlike many other early civilizations, there is no evidence that brides were expected to be virgins.

Egyptians often expressed love and affection for their spouses in tomb reliefs and conveyed tender emotions in letters between husbands and wives. Egyptian love poetry, like the excerpt below, speaks of passion and yearning between lovers:

> *I love you through the daytimes, / in the dark, / Through all the long divisions of the night, / those hours / I, spendthrift, waste away alone, / and lie, and turn, awake 'til whitened dawn. /*
>
> *And with the shape of you I people night, / And thoughts of hot desire grow live within me. / What magic was it in that voice of yours / to bring such singing vigor to my flesh, / To limbs which now lie listless on my bed without you?*[50]

As marriage had no religious significance, both men and women could end marriages for any reason, and divorce was fairly common. When the couple separated, the wife was entitled to the value of her dowry and the husband had to continue to support his children. Adulterous men rarely met with punishment, but women guilty of adultery might be forced out of their homes.

Egyptians expected women to bear children and considered childlessness shameful. Without children, a couple had no one to care for them in their old age and no one to maintain their funerary cult. Although fertility and creation were generally associated with the male, Egyptian interest in female fertility is evident in surviving gynecological manuscripts. The Kahun Papyrus (ca. 1800 B.C.E.) contains extensive discussions of fertility and childbirth. The first two pages contain gynecological prescriptions and instructions, and the third page includes seventeen prescriptions for the assessment of sterility and pregnancy. The most important medical text discovered thus far is the Ebers Papyrus (ca. 1500 B.C.E.). This work provides information on how to deal with a prolapsed uterus (a condition indicated in a number of mummies), breast milk, contraception, and sexually transmitted diseases. Because of the dangers of pregnancy and childbirth, women relied on magical charms, incantations, and prayers to help them survive the ordeal. Egyptians also developed the first known pregnancy test. To determine if a woman was pregnant, they moistened sprouts of grain or vegetables with the woman's urine. If the sprouts grew strong, the woman was pregnant (possibly due to high hormone levels in the urine).[51] Scholars have discovered many images of women breastfeeding. While it is difficult to assess the size of the average Egyptian family, late Middle Kingdom documents mention families with between two and six children while artisans at the workers' community of Deir el Medina often had eight to ten surviving children.[52]

Egyptian women were citizens just like men and shared equal legal rights. Moreover, they did not give up those rights at marriage. Women were fully independent legal beings. They never required a guardian to buy or sell property, adopt children, sue in the courts, or free slaves. We even know of one woman who sued her father over some of her possessions.[53] In some ways, Egyptian inheritance favored women over men. For instance, typically women received their inheritance in the form of a dowry, while men had to wait for their parents to die to receive their inheritance. As a result, young wives were often wealthier than their husbands for the first few years of marriage. Once married, a wife shared her husband's property and inherited one-third of his estate upon his death. Their children received the rest of the family property. Daughters inherited equally with sons unless one child could prove that the funeral expense of the parent was borne by him or her alone. If there were no children, a husband could adopt his wife and make her his sole heir (see **Sources from the Past: Egyptian Legal Texts**).

The Egyptian workplace was strictly divided according to gender. In wealthy households, male domestic servants waited on men, and women attended to women. During the Old Kingdom, female managers supervised female workers. Women held titles such as "overseers of cloth" and "overseers of ornaments" and worked as stewards in charge of storehouses.[54] However, by the Middle Kingdom, fewer women held positions of authority. Moreover, the Egyptian bureaucracy was exclusively male, presumably because schools existed for boys. There is no evidence of formal female education, but a few women may have worked as scribes. Although some elite women and wives of artisans may have known how to read and write, scholars have found no texts written by women until the New Kingdom.

As in Mesopotamia, textiles were central to the Egyptian economy, and women did most of the weaving. Flax was raised on noble and temple estates where large crews of women then made it into linen. Interestingly, while women dominated much of the production process, laundering the cloth seems to have been an exclusively male profession. Moreover, when the Hyksos introduced the more efficient vertical loom, only men used the new technology.[55]

Women also supplemented family incomes by selling in local markets. The professional and overseas merchants were mostly men; however, the wives of farmers and artisans found a ready market for their surplus food and cloth. A New Kingdom tomb depicts women selling food, drink, and other products from stalls set up on a riverbank.[56]

Female singers, musicians, and dancers appeared frequently at banquets and other festivities.

During the Old Kingdom, women are depicted playing harps and percussion while men played a much wider range of instruments, including oboes and flutes. Over time, the gendering of musical instruments changed. By the New Kingdom, women are shown playing the full range of instruments except for the trumpet.[57] Unlike other gender-segregated professions, men and women often played together in orchestras, although by the New Kingdom, wealthy Egyptians seem to have favored all-female orchestras over mixed groups or all-male orchestras.

Rural women's lives were quite different, although we have little textual evidence about them. No doubt, women kept busy preparing food and caring for the children. They farmed and spun and wove linen for consumption at home. Their lives changed little over the centuries.

Daily Life at Deir el Medina

The pyramids are the most visible and famous reminders of the power of Egyptian pharaohs; however, recent excavations at Deir el Medina, home to pyramid workers and their families, have provided fascinating insight into the lives of ordinary Egyptians. Civil servants, sculptors, and artisans who excavated, constructed, and decorated the royal tombs in the Valley of the Kings all lived in Deir el Medina, located in a secluded desert valley. The village was first inhabited as early as 1500 B.C.E., but it was abandoned under Akhenaton, who had his tomb prepared at Tell Amarna. The community was reestablished around 1380 B.C.E. and thrived for another three hundred years.

Deir el Medina was a small town. At its height, the workforce was as large as 120, but it averaged between fifty and sixty men plus their families and support staff. It was probably never much larger than two hundred inhabitants. The craftsmen worked in groups, each taking on only a small part of the overall project. The workers were reasonably well paid in rations, but to supplement their income, many artisans moonlighted, making and selling furniture and other goods in their spare time. There seems to have been ample time for such activities, as they worked only eight-hour days and had one day off every ten days. Families often worked at Deir el Medina for several generations.

Sons followed fathers into their crafts, and daughters married the sons of other craftsmen.[58]

Deir el Medina was a walled city. Each of the seventy homes had an entrance room that often contained a niche for a domestic shrine. Beyond was a larger central room with a raised platform for sitting during the day and sleeping at night. The back rooms were bedrooms and storage rooms. A courtyard served as the kitchen, and staircases led to second floors or roofs. We actually know who lived in many of these homes, as archaeologists have recovered the fragments of a register that names the owner, his wife, and any children in each house. Through other documentation, we know personal details about some of the families. For instance, the chief workman, Neferhotep, and his wife were childless so they adopted a slave as their heir. The son later dedicated a stela to Neferhotep and named his children after his adoptive parents.[59]

Because of the wealth of documentation, Deir el Medina provides a fascinating opportunity to see Egyptian women in action. Their husbands trudged off to work on the pyramids and spent many nights at the work sites. Women were responsible for getting food to their husbands, who were often a two-hour hike away from the village. Of course, women also prepared meals and cared for children, tasks that kept them busy since, as noted above, these artisan families tended to be quite large. In addition, villagers often purchased land, livestock, and slaves. With their husbands absent most of the week, women presumably managed these small estates. One of the village's scribes wrote tenderly about his dead wife's labor, noting that it was she who had tended to the couple's fields and cattle and regularly carried heavy loads.[60] Some of these women were literate, as indicated by the discovery of laundry lists and dressmaking advice.[61]

Unlike other Egyptians, the women of Deir el Medina relied heavily on goods and services the government provided. For instance, the government hired a time-shared servant girl who went from house to house to help grind the grain, and it provided a laundry service for women who lived far from the river. The government also issued clothes to the male workers. In some circumstances, that dependence led to abuse. At one point, the foreman Paneb forced himself on five women in the village, the wives and unmarried daughters of the workmen. For a long time, government administrators protected him against these and other charges, including murder, before he was finally brought to justice.[62]

Letters found at the site reveal intimate moments and the day-to-day problems of villagers. One document notes that a woman left the village for a month, probably to visit family or friends. In another, a man complains that his daughter has not sent him the cakes that he wanted.[63] The mother of a man named Padikhonsu acquired a house, which he inherited at her death. When Padikhonsu died, his wife mortgaged the house and all her property. When she failed to meet her debts, the house became the property of her creditor who later sold it to another woman named Taynetjeruy.[64]

Although their lives centered on work, there was time for recreation as well. Married couples attended drinking parties together in the courtyards of family tombs, and workers got days off to celebrate the festivals of certain deities. They also went on short pleasure trips to ancient religious sites and kept pets. Deir el Medina was a vibrant community of hardworking men, women, and children.

The wealth of archaeological evidence reveals much about the lives of Egyptian women. Although few women had access to political influence, they played meaningful roles in Egyptian religion. Moreover, as a result of Egypt's social and political stability over nearly two thousand years, women had a remarkable degree of legal freedom and a variety of social and economic opportunities.

ANCIENT ISRAELITES: BIBLICAL REASONING AND TRIBAL REALITIES, 1500 B.C.E.–600 B.C.E.

The small Semitic tribes of the ancient Israelites played a central role in the development of Western civilization. We know little about their origins. Some scholars believe that they were seminomadic tribes that migrated from Mesopotamia

Egyptian Legal Texts

Because few women could write in the ancient world, scholars must rely on other types of documents to learn about women's lives. Ancient legal texts have been particularly useful in this regard. These Egyptian legal records reveal gender expectations as expressed through law codes as well as the information about relationships that would otherwise be hidden from history.

Document I

MARRIAGE AGREEMENT BETWEEN A BRIDEGROOM AND HIS FATHER-IN-LAW

In this text, a young man agrees to face a serious penalty should he ever divorce his wife.

Ost. Bodleian Library 253

Year 23, Month 1 of the Planting Season, day 5. This day, Telmontu declared to the Chief Workman Khonsu and the Scribe Amon-nakht, son of Ipui:[1] "Cause Nakhemmut to swear an Oath of the Lord to the effect that he will not depart from my daughter."

The Oath of the Lord which he swore: "As Amon lives, as the Ruler lives, if I should turn away to leave the daughter of Telmontu at any time,[2] I will receive a hundred blows and be deprived of all profits that I have made with her.[3]

The Chief Workman Khonsu, the Scribe Amon-nakht, Neferhor, Khaemnun.[4]

Document II

THE WILL OF AMONKHAU IN FAVOR OF HIS SECOND WIFE[5]

This document is an excellent example of Egyptian inheritance practices and the ability of women to inherit from their husbands.

Pap. Turin 2021

I stand today before the Vizier and the members of the Tribunal to announce to my children the testament that I make today in favor of the Citeness Ineksenedjem, the woman who is now in my house.[6] For Pharaoh has said: "Each one should do as he wishes with his property."[7]

I bequeath to the Citizeness Ineksenedjem, the woman who is in my house, all that I have acquired with her, namely, two male servants and two female servants, total 4, and their children. (This is) my two-thirds share in addition to her one-third share.[8]

---

[1] This is not a formal hearing before a tribunal, but a private one made to responsible officials. It is in the same vein as Pap. Deir el-Medineh 27 concerning adultery, apparently settled by the families involved. In both cases, the Oath of the Lord does not seem to have the same force as if sworn in a regular tribunal.

[2] This is one example of the legal language used in this text. The Egyptian is literally "in morning after morning," meaning at any time in the future. Babylonian legal texts use a similar phrase—"day and night"—with the same sense.

[3] The prospective bridegroom here renounces all claim to any community property he and his wife may gain during the coming marriage should he leave his wife. In case of a divorce, the wife is thus better off than under normal circumstances where community property is divided. This is

a unique case in the known legal literature, but may represent a common practice.

[4] As with all legal or quasi-legal documents, a list of witnesses to the transaction is usually appended. Here, the two officials who heard the oath have added two more ordinary citizens as witnesses. Kept in the family archives of the wife's family, the document assures that the husband cannot renege on his promise at a later date.

[5] Only a few fragments of the first page and a half of this document are preserved. The text begins where translation is possible

[6] That is, his second wife.

[7] This is one of several pronouncements of kings concerning inheritance used in the courts to help render judgments. In this case, the king as the final authority in law has stated that everyone can turn over their property to whomever they wish. Since such royal statements are recorded in legal texts, it is evident they amounted to the law of the land.

[8] This is the usual division of community property. Amonkhau is here prevented from giving his children anything from his two-thirds of the community property gained during his second marriage.

And I bequeath the nine servants which fell to me in my two-thirds share with the Citizeness Tathari to my children, as well as the house of my maternal grandfather now in their possession.[9]

They (the children) shall not be deprived of anything that I acquired with their mother. I would (also) have given to them from what I acquired with the Citizeness Ineksenedjem, but Pharaoh has said: "Give the dowry of each woman to her."[10] The Vizier said to the Priest and Overseer of Workmen Ahautinefer and the Priest Nebnefer, the children of Amonkhau who stood before him, they being the elder brothers of his children: "What do you say about the testament that the Divine-Father[11] Amonkhau your father has stated? Is what he says true concerning these nine servants whom he says he gave to you from his two-thirds share that he divided with your mother, and (also) the house of the maternal grandfather?"[12] They said with one voice: "Our father is right, they are indeed in our possession."

The Vizier said: "What do you think about this testament that your father is making for the Citizeness Ineksenedjem, this (second) wife of his?" They said: "We have heard what our father is doing. As for what he is doing, who can argue with him? It is his own property. Let him dispose of it as he wishes.

The Vizier said: "Even if it was not his wife, but a Canaanite or Nubian woman who he loved and to whom he gave his property, and who might annul what he has done?" (And they said:)

"Let be given these four servants that he acquired with the Citiziness Ineksenedjem, that which he acquired with her of which he said: 'I give to her my two-thirds share in addition to her one-third share, and no son or daughter shall argue about this testament that I am making for her today.' "[13]

The Vizier said: "Let be done exactly as that which the Divine-Father Amonkhau has said, this Divine-Father who stands before me." The Vizier gave instructions to Ptahemheb, Priest and Scribe of Accounts of the Tribunal of the Temple of Ramses III, saying: "Let there be recorded the decisions that I have made on a papyrus roll in the temple of Ramses III; the same shall be done for the Great Council of Thebes."[14]

(Done) in the presence of many witnesses. The list thereof: (a list of 18 witnesses to this hearing follows.)

---

[9] Amonkhau's children by his first wife, Tathari, inherit Amonkhau's share of the community property gained during the first marriage, that is, to the children's mother. They have already been given the grandfather's house.

[10] The Egyptian word used here is unique and "dowry" is the closest equivalent. Again, this is a royal pronouncement that had the force of the law of the land. A woman's inheritance was at least her dowry plus one-third of the community property gained during the marriage; this also applied in case of divorce. In the present case, the law seems to be that community property acquired during the second marriage should be inherited by the second wife and not by the first wife or her children.

[11] "Divine-Father," a literal translation of a priestly title of the middle ranks of a priesthood.

[12] That is, the two oldest sons of the first marriage are asked to swear that they have inherited the nine servants and the grandfather's house.

[13] An important provision that prevents the children of the first marriage from contesting the will in the future. The sons agree to this provision.

[14] Two official copies of Amonkhau's testament along with the Vizier's judgments are to be deposited in the archives of a temple and the city tribunal of Thebes.

All texts from http://www.stoa.org/diotima/anthology/wardtexts.shtml. Translated by William Ward.

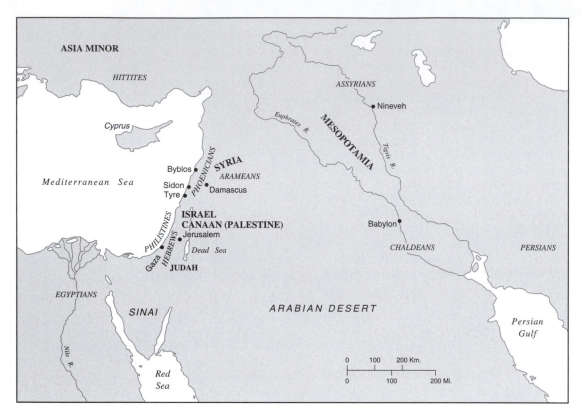

Map 1.2 ANCIENT ISRAEL. The ancient Israelites adopted monotheism, while the other peoples in the region remained polytheists.

to the eastern coast of the Mediterranean sometime before 1500 B.C.E., while others assert that they were indigenous to the area and rose to prominence around 1200 B.C.E. (see Map 1.2). Whatever the case, unlike the other peoples of the region, they gradually adopted *monotheism*, the worship of one god. Their legacy was ancient Judaism, the oldest of the major Western religions.

The study of the ancient Israelites, particularly Israelite women, is complicated by the fact that the Hebrew Bible is the sole piece of written evidence about their lives. Historians, archaeologists, and other scholars disagree over the relationship between the Hebrew Bible and Israelite history. Feminist scholars find it difficult to use the Bible for understanding women's lives because it was composed as a sacred text, not as

a historical narrative. In addition, the Hebrew Bible was compiled over many centuries, so it does not represent Israelite life in any particular period. Moreover, most of the historical books are the product of life at the royal court in Jerusalem and its bureaucrats, while the majority of Israelites lived in small, isolated rural villages. Finally, for the most part, the Hebrew Bible relates Israelite gender expectations, not the actual experience and practice of gender in daily life. Nevertheless, without other written sources, most scholars continue to rely on the Hebrew Bible, gleaning information about Israelite women's lives wherever possible. This research, combined with recent archaeological work, indicates that with the transition from polytheism to monotheism, Israelite women's activity and authority were largely confined to the home.

The Transition to Monotheism and Women's Spirituality

Although the Israelites were not the first people to experiment with monotheism, their experience was the longest lasting and most influential. The Israelites did not adopt monotheism overnight. Instead, in the period after 1500 B.C.E., Israelites gradually stopped worshipping a pantheon of male and female deities in favor of one male-gendered deity whom they called Yahweh.

Although we know little about the nature of ancient Israel's pre-Yahwistic beliefs, the Hebrew Bible makes regular references to the worship of other gods. We know that the many other peoples living in ancient Israel, including Ammonites, Edomites, and Moabites, worshipped similar pantheons of anthropomorphic gods and goddesses. Generally, male priesthoods controlled the cults of these gods, and the tribe's relationships to those gods were based on ritual sacrifice. Early worship of Yahweh had much in common with traditional religion in the area. Yahweh had anthropomorphic qualities, and Israelites made regular sacrifices to him.

However, in many other ways, Israelite monotheism worship was quite different from the polytheism of their neighbors. Yahweh was omnipotent and omnipresent. His will was unyielding and untempered by the desires of other deities. Israelites believed that Yahweh forbade the use of images. Worshippers prayed to him directly, hoping to evoke his aid and mercy. To challenge or defy his authority could result in death.

As the creator of everything, Yahweh was the source of all fertility. He created the earth alone. While women in many other cultures looked to goddesses for aid in conception and childbirth, Israelite women depended on Yahweh. In *Genesis,* Yahweh gave Sarah a son and opened the wombs of both Rachel and Leah. In *1 Samuel,* Hannah prayed to Yahweh to provide her with a son.

From the outset, all of Yahweh's critical contacts were with men. Israelites believed that he formulated his relationship with the Israelites through the covenant, offering Abraham land and fertility for his descendants in return for worship. Although both men and women were supposed to worship only him, the association of the covenant with Abraham legitimized male authority in the cult. Israelites reinforced the connection between Israelite males and Yahweh with the demand that membership in the Jewish community be marked by circumcision. In particular, this ritual marginalized women as their membership in the community could only come through their relationships to men. They could not undergo ritual circumcision nor was there any parallel ritual for women.[65] Finally, the hereditary priesthood, members of the tribe of Levi, who made ritual offerings and sacrifices to Yahweh, was also limited to men. The male priesthood presumably evolved from taboos that declared women ritually impure during menstruation and childbirth. That ritual impurity made it difficult (although not impossible) for them to act as intermediaries between the Israelite people and their male god.

Although there is extensive evidence of women praying, women's official religious activity was limited to making priestly vestments and other textiles for religious uses, preparing food for ritual purposes, and cleaning vessels and sanctuaries. Women also sang and danced as a part of certain religious festivities. However, even the most privileged Israelite women played only unofficial roles in the worship of Yahweh. Unlike their counterparts in other Near Eastern civilizations, neither queens nor female members of the Israelite elite acted as important figures in the expansion of the worship of Yahweh.[66]

Women's primary religious experience took place in the home. At household sites across ancient Israel, scholars have unearthed a diverse collection of religious artifacts, including female and animal figurines, libation vessels, and incense burners. Many homes had their own shrines, which may have been tended to and used predominantly by women. Archaeologists have found that these shrines often included small terracotta female figures. These naked statues may have been votive objects used as a part of fertility prayers. In addition, women may have employed amulets made from cowrie shells and other materials to ward off evil. Israelite women also continued to practice witchcraft and necromancy, as when Saul visits a woman to speak with the dead Samuel (*1 Samuel* 28:3–25).[67] Some domestic rituals, including female puberty rites, childbirth rituals, and harvest dances may have been exclusively female activities.[68]

Surrounded by people who worshipped many gods and influenced by their polytheistic past, some members of the Israelite community continued to pray to local deities and prophesy, while others worshipped only Yahweh. The Hebrew Bible regularly condemns the Israelites for failing to rid themselves of the idols from their polytheistic past and maintain the exclusive worship of Yahweh. Many of those gods were household deities, and women may have been slow to remove the shrines to which they were particularly devoted. For instance, in *1 Samuel* 19:13 Michal hid a household image when men searched her home for her husband, David.[69]

Moreover, Israelite women continued to practice prophesy. Huldah warned King Josiah (640–609 B.C.E.) of his fate if he did not end the worship of other gods (*2 Kings* 22:14–20). Deborah, the most important female prophet, delivered a message from Yahweh to Barak, commanding him to prepare troops for battle. She agreed to accompany him to the battle, but foretold that the coming victory would be credited to a woman (*Judges* 4–5). Many Israelites continued to believe that Yahweh communicated directly with women both as individuals and as representatives of the Israelite community.[70]

Some of the most provocative scholarship on gender and Israelite religion asserts that some Israelites may have continued to pray to the Queen of Heaven as late as the sixth century B.C.E. Associated with fertility, in the book of Jeremiah, women baked cakes and burned incense for her. Their husbands were complicit in their devotion to her:

> Then all the men who knew that their wives had offered incense to other gods, and all the women who stood by, a great assembly, all the people who dwelt in Pathros in the land of Egypt, answered Jeremiah:
>
> "As for the word which you have spoken to us in the name of the LORD, we will not listen to you. But we will do everything that we have vowed, burn incense to the queen of heaven and pour out libations to her, as we did, both we and our fathers, our kings and our princes, in the cities of Judah and in the streets of Jerusalem; for then we had plenty

> of food, and prospered, and saw no evil. But since we left off burning incense to the queen of heaven and pouring out libations to her, we have lacked everything and have been consumed by the sword and by famine." And the women said, "When we burned incense to the queen of heaven and poured out libations to her, was it without our husbands' approval that we made cakes for her bearing her image and poured out libations to her?" (Jeremiah 44:15–19)

Scholars disagree on the identity of the Queen of Heaven. Some assert that she was the Semitic goddesses Ishtar and Astarte, while others suggest that the Queen of Heaven was not one deity but a goddess who combined characteristics of a number of Semitic goddesses. Moreover, the Queen of Heaven may not have been the only remnant of premonotheistic devotions. A number of inscriptions indicate that well into the eighth century B.C.E., Israelites worshipped Asherah as the consort of Yahweh. Cult statues of Asherah were found in the Temple in Jerusalem, and Israelite women wove vestments for her (*2 Kings* 23:6–7).[71] The continued worship of female deities demonstrates both the persistence of polytheistic beliefs and women's desire for a female connection to the heavens.

The relationship between the Israelites' worship of Yahweh and the creation of the Israelite monarchy had important implications for women. Before approximately 1000 B.C.E., the Israelites were tribal peoples, ruled by leaders known as judges. However, over time, the Israelites came to desire a king. The formation of a centralized monarchy may have been related to their need for territorial expansion and better responses to attacks by neighboring tribes like the Philistines. According to the Hebrew Bible, Yahweh chose Saul (ca. 1000 B.C.E.) as the first Israelite king, establishing an explicit connection between monotheistic worship and the new monarchy and between monarchy and masculinity. Indeed, only one queen ever ruled in ancient Israel, and only in extraordinary circumstances:

> Now when Athali'ah the mother of Ahazi'ah saw that her son was dead, she arose and destroyed all the royal family. But Jehosh'eba, the daughter of King Joram, sister of Ahazi'ah, took Jo'ash the son of Ahazi'ah,

and stole him away from among the king's sons who were about to be slain, and she put him and his nurse in a bedchamber. Thus she hid him from Athali'ah, so that he was not slain; and he remained with her six years, hid in the house of the LORD, while Athali'ah reigned over the land. (2 Kings 11:1–3)

Athali'ah's reign was illegitimate, as the legitimate heir, the child Jo'ash, was hidden away. Once Jehosh'eba revealed the child, the Israelites slew Athali'ah in a violent uprising.

Queen consorts, like the wives of Solomon or Ahab's queen, Jezebel, had no recognized authority. Biblical passages typically demonize these queens. Jezebel and Ma'acah, the mother of Asa, were accused of bringing the foreign cult of Asherah into Israel; however, as already discussed, extensive evidence indicates that this cult already existed in the region. However, queen mothers may have had considerable influence, as when Bathsheba worked to bring her son Solomon (r. 961–922) to the throne.[72]

These male monarchs were more adept at unifying and leading the tribal militias and more effective at distributing resources in times of crisis than earlier tribal leaders. Saul's successors, especially David (r. ca. 1000–961 B.C.E.), increased the power of the Israelite monarchy through military expansion and the creation of an exclusively male bureaucracy. Moreover, they consolidated male authority in both religion and politics, excluding women from most sources of public power.

Gender Expectations Among the Israelites

Israelites lived tribally, and the household was the focus of all social and economic activity. Men completely controlled Israelite households, *bet ab*, literally "house of the father." Although on three occasions the Hebrew Bible mentions the *bet em*, the house of the mother, scholar Carol Meyers believes that this designation may be a remnant of an earlier tradition superseded by the patriarchal family.[73]

The entire paternal line, including uncles, brothers, sons, and grandsons and their wives, often lived in the compound. Israelite life was so concentrated in the home that there is no evidence of public buildings until the consolidation of the monarchy and the growth of urban centers around 1150 B.C.E. An Israelite traced his or her lineage through the patrilineal clan. The father was the ultimate authority over his immediate kin as well as any relatives or servants. When the head of the family died, patriarchal authority passed to the eldest son.

As a member of the clan, a woman's primary responsibility was to marry and bear children. As a result, she was always an outsider, spending her childhood preparing to leave her own family and her adulthood in her husband's family. Fathers arranged the marriages of their children and although later biblical texts forbade marriages between certain kin, early Israelites clearly married within families. The bridegroom paid the bride's father, the *mōhar* (bride price). Depending on the wealth of the family, the mōhar may have included land, household goods, and even slaves. The payment of the mōhar formalized the relationship, although the marriage might not take place immediately. Weddings were often long, elaborate affairs in which families feasted, sang, and danced for a week or more.

Children were critical to Israelite culture. Women were encouraged to bear as many children as possible, and biblical passages extol the virtues of marital sex and a large family. To ensure the creation of a family, men could even exempt themselves from military service during their first year of marriage (*Deuteronomy* 24:5). Israelites favored sons over daughters, as they would perpetuate the clan and were important sources of labor. The Israelites' constant warfare also put pressure on women's fertility. Scholars estimate that Israelite women bore an average of four children.[74] If a woman was infertile, her husband could choose another woman to bear children for him. Sarah encouraged Abraham to have sexual relations with Hagar so that she might bear him a son (*Genesis* 16:1–3) and Elkanah took P'ninah as his second wife because his first wife Hannah was infertile (*1 Samuel* 1:1-5).

In contrast, women were limited to sex within marriage. To ensure their virginity, women married while still in their teens, whereas men waited until their twenties or even later. The penalties for women who engaged in nonmarital sex were harsh. According to *Deuteronomy* 22:21–22, brides who had lost their virginity prior to their weddings were to be stoned to death by local elders, as were adulterous women. Demands for female monogamy were so strong that a girl who had been raped was supposed to marry her attacker. However, authorities also made efforts to protect the unfair blemish of a woman's reputation. If a husband falsely put forward the claim that his new bride was not a virgin, authorities were to whip him and fine him one hundred shekels of silver to be given to her father. Nonetheless, the marriage would not be terminated.

Israelites demanded female chastity in order to guarantee paternity and maintain the paternal line. Although in modern Judaism, membership in the community is passed through the female line, many scholars believe that tradition only dates to second century C.E. No mention is made of the transmission of lineage through the female in the Hebrew Bible. In fact, the text regularly stresses lineage through the father. For example, in Genesis, the description of the descendants of Adam and Eve goes from father to son, "To Enoch was born Irad; and Irad was the father of Me-hu'ja-el, and Me-hu'ja-el the father of Me-thu'sha-el, and Me-thu'sha-el the father of Lamech" (*Genesis* 4:18). Women are completely absent from the genealogy. Slightly later, in *Genesis* 4:26, a child was born without mention of a women, "To Seth also a son was born, and he called his name Enosh." Men could even marry non-Israelite women without compromising their children's membership in the tribe.

The Hebrew Bible reveals a strong concern with bodily pollution. Not only was a woman polluted during menstruation, but the pollution contaminated anything that she touched. As a result, laws mandated that menstruating women separate themselves from the family for seven days. Any physical contact with the woman or anything she touched was strictly prohibited. Pollution also accompanied childbirth. A woman was considered impure for thirty-three days after the birth of a son and for twice that long after the birth of a daughter. After her period ended or the required time had passed after childbirth, a woman took a ritual bath, which restored her purity and allowed her to sleep with her husband and prepare food for the family.

The emphasis on pollution expressed in Jewish dietary laws also shaped women's lives. Foods had to meet certain criteria and be prepared in specific ways in order to be consumed. Among other restrictions, Israelites only ate animals with cloven hooves and that chewed their cud that had been slaughtered in a specified way so as to remove any trace of blood. In addition, Israelites did not eat meat products and dairy products at the same meal. Much of the responsibility for maintaining these and other food rituals fell to women.

According to the Hebrew Bible, a woman was completely dependent on her father or husband for legal rights and protection. Her word had no legal standing; husbands and fathers had the right to annul any vow their wives or daughters made. Only the vows of widows and divorced women were as equally binding as those of adult males. Inheritance laws were equally restrictive, allowing only Israelite women without brothers to inherit from their fathers. In one biblical tale, after Zeloph'ehad died without sons, his daughters asked Moses and other leaders not to exclude them from their familial inheritance. "And the LORD said to Moses, "The daughters of Zeloph'ehad are right; you shall give them possession of an inheritance among their father's brethren and cause the inheritance of their father to pass to them. If a man dies, and has no son, then you shall cause his inheritance to pass to his daughter" (*Numbers* 27:1–8). However, these female heirs had to marry within the tribe so that the inheritance remained within the lineage:

> This is what the LORD commands concerning the daughters of Zeloph'ehad, "Let them marry whom they think best; only, they shall marry within the family of the tribe of their father. The inheritance of the people of Israel shall not be transferred from one tribe to another; for every one of the people of Israel shall cleave to the inheritance of the tribe of his fathers. And every daughter who possesses an inheritance in any tribe of the people of Israel shall be wife to one of the family of the tribe of her father, so that every one of the people of Israel may possess the inheritance of his fathers." (Numbers 36:6–9)

Wives had no right to their communal property. When a man died, his property passed to his sons. If he had no sons, his property went to the next male relative. A widow had to rely on her sons to support her. If she had no sons, she would have to return to her family of origin.[75]

Only men could initiate divorce; Jewish women's right to divorce is a much later phenomenon. However, a divorced woman could remarry. Israelite society understood that women without male protection, widows, orphans, and divorced women, were very vulnerable and needed special protections. Biblical passages such as *Deuteronomy* 14:29 required communities to provide for them when necessary.

Often, when a man died without children, his widow went to cohabitate with his brother. Through this custom, known as *levirate* marriage, the family continued to provide for the widow. However, it was also quite beneficial to the man's family. Levirate marriage ensured that the widow did not marry an outsider and jeopardize the inheritance. The first son born to this new relationship was considered the child of the dead husband.[76]

The Ten Commandments required children to honor both fathers and mothers, under penalty of death. Although this commandment reveals a strong commitment to both parents, scholars dispute its meaning to women's authority in the family. Some scholars assert that the demand that children give mothers respect equal to that of fathers gave women some authority and status in the home. However, other scholars argue that such language only strengthened the patriarchal family by giving women some small amount of status in exchange for their cooperation and sexual subordination.[77]

TERRACOTTA FIGURE OF FEMALE DRUM MUSICIAN. Biblical texts and terracotta figurines like this one indicate that Ancient Israelite women performed music. These performances brought together women of different families and offered Israelite women the opportunity for artistic expression. *(Courtesy of the Semitic Museum, Harvard University, #SM 1907.64.470.)*

Israelite Women and Work

We know little about Israelite women's work. Certainly most of their work took place in the home, and that work must have afforded them some status and authority in their families. To be successful, agricultural households require the intense labor of both men and women. Women worked in the fields and herded livestock. Biblical passages frequently refer to daughters drawing well water, spinning thread, weaving textiles, and grinding grain into flour. In addition, they devoted considerable time to food preparation and caring for children. Women were expected to teach their young children. The family relied on all of these tasks for its survival.

Biblical texts indicate that women engaged in a variety of occupations outside of the home. Despite laws to the contrary, some women worked as prostitutes. In *Joshua* 2–6, the harlot Rahab aided Israelite spies against the king of Jericho, and the dispute that Solomon famously resolved by threatening to divide a child in two was between two prostitutes (*1 Kings* 3:16–27).

Midwives aided women during childbirth. In *Exodus 1*, Israelite midwives defied the Egyptian pharaoh's command that they kill the sons of the Israelites. Women served as wet nurses for the children of wealthy women, and *1 Samuel* indicates that some women may have worked as "perfumers and cooks and bakers." In their most visible public roles, female musicians performed in a variety of contexts. This work may have emerged out of women's traditional role as public mourners and singers at funerals. Archaeologists have found terracotta figurines depicting female musicians playing flutes, lyres, and, most often, hand-drums, and biblical text mentions women's public musical performance:

> *Then Miriam the prophet, Aaron's sister, took a hand-drum in her hand; and all the women went out after her with hand-drums and dancing.* (Exodus 15:20–21)

Public performance offered Israelite women an important outlet for public expression and their main opportunity to work with women outside of their own families.[78]

For the most part, the transition from polytheistic to monotheistic worship negatively affected Israelite women. The Israelites were bound to Yahweh, the all-powerful male god, through men. The critical components of that relationship, the covenant and circumcision, marginalized women, and Israelite law excluded them from most public religious rituals. Based on the belief that their sexuality should be tightly controlled to ensure paternity, Israelite women's lives were highly circumscribed, and their opportunities for activities outside of the domestic realm were few.

CONCLUSION

This overview of prehistoric peoples and early civilizations reveals how gender expectations varied from one place to the next and changed over time. Prehistoric peoples had to be flexible in terms of their gender expectations in order to survive. Ancient Mesopotamia, Egypt, and Israel were all powerful civilizations whose legacies include the creation of the earliest political and economic systems, the development of writing, and monotheism. These innovations altered women's lives, sometimes for the better, sometimes for the worse. For the most part, women had little access to political authority; however, in ancient Mesopotamia and Egypt, women had extensive legal rights and were critical to the state-run economies. Sexual norms varied considerably from one civilization to another. Mesopotamians and Israelites emphasized virginity, while ancient Egyptians placed no particular value on premarital chastity. As these civilizations came into contact with Mediterranean and southern European cultures, their ideas about women, gender, and sexuality would be important influences on the creation of Western gender norms.

NOTES

1. Margaret Ehrenberg, *Women in Prehistory* (Norman: University of Oklahoma Press, 1989), 40, 59.

2. Joan M. Gero, "Genderlithics: Women's Roles in Stone Tool Production," in *Engendering Archaeology: Women and Prehistory*, ed. Joan M. Gero and Margaret W. Conkey (London: Blackwell, 1991), 163–171.

3. Judith K. Brown, "A Note on the Division of Labor by Sex," *American Anthropologist* 72:5 (Oct. 1970): 1073–1078.

4. Ehrenberg, 81.

5. Ehrenberg, 55.

6. Rita P. Wright, "Women's Labor and Pottery Production in Prehistory," in Gero and Conkey, *Engendering Archaeology*, 194–223.

7. Erich Neumann, *The Great Mother: An Analysis of the Archetype* (Princeton: Princeton University Press, 1974).

8. Marija Gimbutas, *The Goddesses and Gods of Old Europe, 6500–3500 BC: Myths and Cult Images* (Berkeley: University of California Press, 1982).

9. Gerda Lerner, *The Creation of Patriarchy* (New York: Oxford University Press, 1986), 239.

10. J. A. Black, G. Cunningham, E. Fluckiger-Hawker, E. Robson, and G. Zólyomi, "The Sumerian Kings List: Translation," The Electronic Text Corpus of Sumerian Literature (http:// www-etcsl.orient.ox.ac.uk/), Oxford 1998.

11. Betrand Lafont, "The Women of the Palace at Mari," in *Everyday Life in Ancient Mesopotamia*, ed. Jean

Bottéro (Baltimore: The Johns Hopkins University Press, 2001), 130, 139.

12. Lafont, 133.

13. Jerrold S. Cooper, "Sacred Marriage and Popular Cult in Early Mesopotamia," in *Official Cult and Popular Religion in the Ancient Near East. Papers of the First Colloquium on the Ancient Near East*, ed. Eiko Matsushima (Heidelbertg: Universitätsverlag C. Winter, 1993), 85, 83.

14. Bernard Frank Batto, *Studies on the Women at Mari* (Baltimore: The Johns Hopkins University Press, 1974), 27.

15. Marc Van De Mieroop, "Women in the Economy of Sumer," in *Women's Earliest Records from Ancient Egypt and Western Asia,* ed. Barbara S. Lesko (Atlanta: Scholars Press, 1989), 62.

16. Jean Bottéro, "Women's Rights" in *Everyday Life in Ancient Mesopotamia,* ed. Jean Bottéro (Baltimore: The Johns Hopkins University Press, 1992), 114.

17. Quoted in Zainab Bahrani, *Women of Babylon: Gender and Representation in Mesopotamia* (London: Routledge, 2001), 45.

18. Quoted in Bottéro, "Love and Sex in Babylon," in *Everyday Life*, 104.

19. M. Stol, "Private Life in Ancient Mesopotamia," in *Civilizations of the Ancient Near East,* ed. Jack M. Sasson (New York: Scribner, 1995), 490.

20. Bottéro, "Women's Rights," 116.

21. Susan Pollock, *Ancient Mesopotamia: The Eden That Never Was* (Cambridge: Cambridge University Press, 1999), 120.

22. Van De Mieroop, 56, 57–58, 62.

23. Pollock, 123.

24. Van De Mieroop, 65.

25. Pollock, 115–116, 148.

26. Rita P. Wright, "Technology, Gender, and Class: Worlds of Difference in Ur III Mesopotamia," in *Gender and Archaeology,* ed. Rita P. Wright (Philadelphia: University of Pennsylvania Press, 1996), 96–97.

27. Pollock, 192.

28. Batto, 123.

29. Rivkah Harris, "Independent Women in Ancient Mesopotamia?" in Lesko, *Women's Earliest Records,* 152–153.

30. Joyce Tyldesley, *Daughters of Isis: Women of Ancient Egypt* (London: Penguin, 1995), 160.

31. Barbara Lesko, *The Great Goddesses of Egypt* (Norman: University of Oklahoma Press, 1999), 17.

32. Lesko, *The Great Goddesses*, 170.

33. Lesko, *The Great Goddesses*, 82.

34. Tyldesley, 253.

35. Lynn Meskell, *Private Life in New Kingdom Egypt* (Princeton: Princeton University Press, 2002), 111.

36. Zahi Hawass, *Silent Images: Women in Pharonic Egypt* (New York: Harry N. Abrams, 2000), 166.

37. Gay Robins, *Women in Ancient Egypt* (Cambridge: Harvard University Press, 1993), 164.

38. Hawass, 32.

39. Betsy M. Bryan "The Eighteenth Dynasty before the Amarna Period," in *The Oxford History of Ancient Egypt*, ed. Ian Shaw (Oxford: Oxford University Press, 2000), 242.

40. Gay Robins, "Women in Ancient Egypt," in *Women's Roles in Ancient Civilizations: A Reference Guide,* ed. Bella Vivante (Westport, CT: Greenwood Press, 1999), 176.

41. Robins, *Women in Ancient Egypt*, 43.

42. Bryan, 228.

43. Bryan, 259.

44. Tyldesley, 201, 197.

45. Bryan, 267.

46. Jacobus Van Dijk, "The Amarna Period and the Later New Kingdom," in *The Oxford History of Ancient Egypt*, 276, 281.

47. Tyldesley, 185.

48. Tyldesley, 197.

49. Tyldesley, 51.

50. "I love you through the daytimes," in *Ancient Egyptian Literature: An Anthology*, trans. John L. Foster (Austin: University of Texas Press, 2001), 19.

51. Tyldesley, 69–70.

52. Barbara Lesko, "Rank, Roles, and Rights," in *Pharaoh's Workers: The Villagers of Deir el Medina,* ed. Leonard H. Lesko (Ithaca: Cornell University Press, 1994), 36.

53. Robins, *Women in Ancient Egypt*, 128.

54. Hawass, 135.

55. Tyldesley, 132.

56. Hawass, 136.

57. Emily Teeter, "Female Musicians in Pharaonic Egypt," in *Rediscovering the Muses: Women's Musical Traditions*, ed. Kimberly Marshall (Boston: Northeastern University Press, 1993), 79–80.

58. Lesko, "Ranks, Roles, and Rights," 22.

59. Robins, *Women in Ancient Egypt*, 77.

60. Lesko, "Rank, Roles, and Rights," 26.

61. Tyldesley, 119–120.

62. Lesko, "Rank, Roles, and Rights," 36, 24.

63. Andrea G. McDowell, "Contact with the Outside World," in *Pharaoh's Workers*, 53.

64. Hawass, 129.

65. Lerner, *The Creation of Patriarchy*, 189–191.

66. Phyllis A. Bird, *Missing Persons and Mistaken Identities: Women and Gender in Ancient Israel* (Minneapolis: Fortress Press, 1997), 98.

67. Philip J. King and Lawrence E. Stager, *Life in Biblical Israel* (Louisville: Westminster John Knox Press, 2001), 277, 381.

68. Carol Meyers, *Discovering Eve: Ancient Israelite Women in Context* (Oxford: Oxford University Press, 1988), 161.

69. Meyers, *Discovering Eve*, 159.

70. Bird, 44.

71. Bird, 92.

72. Susan Ackerman, "The Queen Mother and the Cult in Ancient Israel," in *Women in the Hebrew Bible: A Reader*, ed. Alice Bach (New York: Routledge, 1999), 179.

73. Meyers, *Discovering Eve*, 179–180.

74. King and Stager, 41.

75. Bird, 27.

76. King and Stager, 56.

77. For one perspective, see Meyers, *Discovering Eve*, 157; for another, see Lerner, 113.

78. Carol Meyers, "The Drum-Dance-Song Ensemble: Women's Performance in Biblical Israel," in *Rediscovering the Muses*, 66–67.

Suggested Readings

General

Barber, Elizabeth Wayland. *Women's Work: The First 20,000 Years Women, Cloth, and Society in Early Times*. New York: Norton, 1994. Barber provides a nice interdisciplinary overview of women and work in prehistory, focusing on the development of textiles.

Prehistoric Women

Ehrenberg, Margaret. *Women in Prehistory*. Norman: University of Oklahoma Press, 1989. This book offers a good examination of feminist archaeological and anthropological research.

Gero, Joan M. and Margaret W. Conkey. *Engendering Archaeology: Women and Prehistory* London: Blackwell, 1991. The articles in this collection reconsider traditional ideas about women and prehistory from a feminist perspective.

Lerner, Gerda. *The Creation of Patriarchy*. Oxford: Oxford University Press, 1986. Lerner has written the classic overview of the development of patriarchy, using a remarkable array of source materials.

Mesopotamian Women

Pollock, Susan. *Ancient Mesopotamia: The Eden That Never Was*. Cambridge: Cambridge University Press, 1999.

Egyptian Women

Lesko, Leonard, ed. *Pharoah's Workers: The Villagers of Deir el Medina*. Ithaca: Cornell University Press, 1994. This collection paints a vivid picture of daily life in the workers' village.

Robins, Gay. *Women in Ancient Egypt*. Cambridge: Harvard University Press, 1993. This clearly written work synthesizes the research on Egyptian women.

Israelite Women

King, Philip J. and Lawrence E. Stager. *Life in Biblical Israel*. Louisville: Westminster John Knox Press, 2001. This beautifully illustrated description of daily life in ancient Israel uses both biblical references and the most recent archaeological evidence.

Meyers, Carol. *Discovering Eve: Ancient Israelite Women in Context*. New York: Oxford University Press, 1988. Meyers examines the roles of Israelite women before the creation of the monarchy.

Chapter 2

Ancient Greece, 3100–150 B.C.E.

Woman Selling Perfume to Slave Girl (CA. 460 B.C.E.). Although the Greeks promoted ideas of female seclusion, non-elite women had to work to support their families. It must have been common to see women in the marketplace, engaging in commercial activities similar to the transaction that we see in this image. (Bernisches Museum.)

The ancient Aegean civilizations from which Greek culture emerged have left only minimal evidence about the role of women in their societies. However, it seems clear that over the centuries, Greek, and particularly Athenian, society became increasingly more rigidly defined by masculine ideals. Greek culture valued male dominance over both non-Greeks and women in warfare, politics, and even intimate relations, and it idealized the segregation of women. Nevertheless, Greek women still found meaningful ways to participate in social, economic, and religious life.

AEGEAN CONNECTIONS

By approximately 3300 B.C.E., Western peoples began to replace stone tools with metal implements. During this period, known as the Bronze Age, people, goods, and ideas moved freely among the powerful civilizations of the Near East and Europe. As a result, complex civilizations began to develop in and around the Mediterranean, the earliest of which were the Minoan civilization of Crete and the Mycenaean civilization of mainland Greece (see Map 2.1). Historians have often described these two cultures as having very different ideas about gender, but recent research reveals more similarities than differences.

Minoan Civilization, 3100–1000 B.C.E.

The Minoans, the most successful early Bronze Age civilization in the Mediterranean, lived on the island of Crete. Scholars are uncertain of the origins of the Minoans, as they were neither Greek nor Indo-European people. Some historians hypothesize that they may have been Semitic peoples from either the southern or the eastern Mediterranean, but the issue remains unresolved. By 2000 B.C.E., the Minoans had created an urban civilization marked by a dynamic economy and fine art and architecture. Minoans used a system of writing known as Linear A. Unfortunately, Linear A remains undeciphered nearly four thousand years later.

The Minoan cities of Knossos, Mallia, Phaistos, and Ayia Triadha were each home to remarkable

Chapter 2 ❖ Chronology

3100–1450 B.C.E.	Minoan civilization
1700–1375 B.C.E.	Heyday of the palace at Knossos
2000–1100 B.C.E.	Mycenaean civilization
1100–800 B.C.E.	Greek Dark Ages
700 B.C.E.	Hesiod's *Theogony* and Homer's *Iliad*
612 B.C.E.	Sappho composes her poetry
508 B.C.E.	Cleisthenes reforms Athenian government and institutes democracy
490–479 B.C.E.	Persian wars from which Athens emerges triumphant
479–404 B.C.E.	Classical Athens
451 B.C.E.	Pericles restricts citizenship to children of citizens
431–404 B.C.E.	Peloponnesian Wars
Fifth century B.C.E.	Poets Praxilla and Telesilla flourish
428–355 B.C.E.	Plato
384–322 B.C.E.	Aristotle
336 B.C.E.	Alexander the Great comes to power

palace complexes. In the early twentieth century, archaeologists assumed that kings and queens lived in these remarkable edifices, some of which were five or six stories high. They relied on the myth of King Minos of Crete to support their contention that a monarchy controlled the island. Sir Arthur Evans (1851–1941) even labeled some of the rooms of the palace at Knossos "the Queen's Megaron," based on his idea that the palace's wall paintings, or frescos, portrayed "feminine subjects." However, no other evidence exists to indicate that there was a king, let alone a queen; that women lived in those rooms; or even that those rooms were bedrooms. Nevertheless, it took a very large and well-managed labor force to construct and maintain these palaces, indicating some centralization of authority and some ability to persuade or coerce inhabitants to work collectively.

The island's economy revolved around the palaces, each of which housed artisanal workshops that produced goods, including textiles, for distribution at home and trade with foreigners. In addition to flax, the spinners and weavers of Minoan Crete used wool from the sheep that they herded to make beautiful, brightly dyed cloth that was valued as far away as Egypt. As in earlier civilizations, women were presumably the primary textile producers, making them central to the island's economy and tying them to Crete's larger trade networks across the eastern Mediterranean.

Our understanding of Minoan religion is sparse. We do not know the names of Minoan deities, although frescos and other artworks portray a large number of both gods and goddesses. Scholars have also found no evidence of buildings used exclusively as temples; however, palaces may have been centers of religious activity, and archaeologists have excavated numerous nature sanctuaries located on the tops of mountains, in caves, and in the countryside, where worshippers prayed and made offerings. Frescos portray both male and female priests leading religious activities. Priests were involved in

Map 2.1 **AEGEAN GREECE.** The Minoans and Mycenaeans were the most important Bronze Age civilizations in the Mediterranean.

sacrifices, while priestesses poured libations, led processions, took offerings to sanctuaries, and performed dances. Minoans also practiced an elaborate cult of the dead, burying the deceased in communal graves with a variety of ritual implements that included cups and jugs for ritual offerings to the gods.

The elaborate frescos that decorated palace walls provide scholars with the most extensive evidence about gender in Minoan culture. The male figures are sparsely clad, usually only in a loincloth, and the female figures are mostly covered with only their forearms and breasts exposed.

Women appear more often than men in the paintings and are active participants in the events portrayed.[1] In one painting, elaborately dressed women sit in the front row seemingly watching some type of entertainment. Behind them sit mixed groups of men and women. In one of the most intriguing frescos, two women and a man are leaping over a bull. Some scholars believe that the fact that there are many women in the paintings indicates that women had particularly high status in Minoan society. However, others disagree, noting that it is difficult to know whether the images represent mythological events or daily life.[2] Classicist

Barbara Olsen noted that women appear more frequently participating in outdoor and social activities, thereby emphasizing their public rather than domestic roles.[3] We do not understand all of the gender expectations conveyed in the paintings. For instance, males in the frescos were painted with reddish-brown skin, and women were painted with white skin. Earlier scholars argued that these colors reflected men's outdoor activities and women's association with the indoors. However, recently scholars have begun to question that interpretation, as women appear outdoors in the frescos. The skin coloration may also be related to a broader Mediterranean aesthetic. Egyptians also often painted men with dark skin and women with light skin.

The frescos at Akrotiri (Santorini) portray women at various stages of the life cycle. They indicate that Minoan women wore different hairstyles to indicate their place in society. Young girls had shaved scalps, with only a lock of hair at the forehead and in the back; adolescent girls were allowed to grow their hair, so that by the end of puberty they had full heads of hair. Women may have cut their forelocks as they moved into adulthood. Mature women wore their hair long, often tied in elaborate cloths.[4]

Archaeologists have also unearthed numerous figurines of bare-breasted women. These curious pieces, made of terracotta or faience, a glasslike substance, are dressed in corseted jackets with full-length skirts. The hair of each figurine is tied back in a bow, and each has one or more snakes entwined in her arms. Similar representations occur in frescos and on other objects, such as sarcophagi. In some depictions, a female figure is being worshiped by others, mainly women. Some scholars have argued that these figures represented a great mother or fertility goddess. Others believe that the woman with the snake may have been a real woman with magical or ritual powers, like a queen or priestess.[5]

Although Minoan art and architecture provide some insight into urban life and gender among the elites, the majority of Cretans were rural dwellers. Their lives, no doubt, differed significantly from the luxurious world portrayed in the frescos. Women processed wool and then spun it with clay spindle whorls. Archaeologists have discovered

Minoan Faience Figure (ca. 1600 b.c.e.). We know very little about gender norms in Minoan civilization. Excavated at Knossos, Crete, this female figure, and others like it, may have represented a goddess or a priestess. *(Archaeological Museum, Heraklion, Crete/ Erich Lessing/Art Resource, NY.)*

loom weights, which may indicate some rural cloth production. Rural inhabitants tended flocks of sheep and goats. Like their rural counterparts in the Near East, theirs was a chiefly agricultural society for which we are only now finding evidence.

Around 1450 b.c.e., Crete was beset by a series of catastrophes. Almost all of the palaces were devastated by fire and Minoan culture was almost completely destroyed. Although some scholars believe that invaders from the mainland devastated the culture, others assert that an immense earthquake or volcanic eruption may have precipitated its decline. Whatever the case, Minoan civilization was already being eclipsed by another vibrant civilization from mainland Greece, the Mycenaeans.

Mycenaean Civilization, 1650–1100 B.C.E.

The European mainland emerged as the center of the late Bronze Age Mycenaean culture, which most scholars view as the formative civilization from which classical Greek gods, myths, and customs emerged. The Mycenaeans became an imperial power, conquering the Minoans around 1400 B.C.E. and spreading their empire east into portions of Asia Minor. Mycenaeans were literate peoples, whose writing, known as Linear B, was an early form of Greek.

At its height, from 1400 to 1250 B.C.E., Mycenaean civilization was composed of at least fifteen autonomous principalities, each centered on an easily defended citadel or palace. Some scholars have speculated that they were ruled by princes, possibly the area's largest landowners. We know nothing about the rulers of each principality; however, it is clear that the head of each kingdom played an important role in religious affairs. Mycenaean palaces acted as storage and distribution centers for goods produced on lands controlled by the palace and those collected through taxation. One room of the palace of Nestor at Pylos had thousands of clay drinking cups stored in stacks. Other rooms held enormous urns full of wine, olive oil, and grains. After the collection and storage of these goods, palace officials then reallocated them across the kingdom.[6]

Mycenaean palaces were also the focus of a highly centralized and specialized craft production. Men and women often worked in single-sex workgroups and were paid the same rations of wheat, barley, figs, or olives. The fact that men and women received the same compensation may reflect the greater importance of women in the Mycenaean labor force than in Near Eastern societies like Mesopotamia. Professions were highly specialized and divided according to gender. Linear B tablets list large numbers of occupations and workers, but many of the professions seem to have been followed exclusively by women, as no male equivalent ever appears. Most of the more than thirty female-only occupations listed involved textiles and clothing production. Some of the textile workers may have been captives or refugees.[7] Recently discovered evidence indicates that, in addition to palace workgroups, a piecework system was also in place in which a woman completed one stage of production in her home and then sent it to another woman to complete the next stage.[8]

Mycenaean religion is generally understood as the basis of Classical Greek religion. Linear B tablets include the names of approximately thirty gods and goddesses, many of whom became important Greek deities, like Zeus, Hera, and Poseidon. The anthropomorphic deities of Mycenae owned property, even slaves. People worshipped these deities in small cult rooms in palaces and country shrines. Offerings included jewelry, pottery, small vessels for perfume, and human and animal figurines. People may have placed figurines in sacred areas as stand-ins for worshippers. Other archaeological evidence indicates that ritual feasting and processions were important to Mycenaean rituals.[9]

Priestesses were the most prestigious of Mycenaean religious women. Each was probably devoted to one cult. Four priestesses served at Pylos and at least three at Knossos. Priestesses served the popular Cretan cult of the Winds, and the priestess Erita led the cult of Pa-ki-ja-na, which was associated with the goddess Potnia, the chief female deity at Pylos. Erita was also a wealthy landowner. She had her own assistants who were also prosperous landowners, one of whom owned nearly as much as the priestess herself. Erita's involvement in a land dispute with local officials indicates that priestly women were legally independent and could take legal action without the assistance of a man.[10]

In addition to priestesses, some women served as Keybearers, important cult officials who, among other duties, controlled the sacred treasure at the cult site. For instance, we know that the Keybearers at Pylos donated temple bronze for military purposes before the fall of that city to invaders. Karpatia, a Keybearer at the sanctuary at Pylos, appears frequently in the written records and owned land. Other women held positions that were closely associated with the local priestesses. For instance, a board of wealthy women, known as the *ki-ri-te-wi-ja*, appears on tablets at Knossos and Pylos. Female attendants or servants, *do-e-ra*, served a priestess, while others directly served the deity. Do-e-ra sometimes held land and their names appear on tablets, characteristics usually confined to persons in religious positions and/or high status. The duties of the do-e-ra seem to have involved sacred metals such as gold and bronze, primary metal used in Mycenaean society. They often had fathers and husbands who were bronze smiths.[11]

Some early researchers asserted that Mycenaean society was much more militarily oriented than its Minoan predecessor and thus more masculine. Certainly, as most of its palaces were built for defense, they were smaller and less ornate. Moreover, Mycenaean frescos often depict men in battle, scenes that rarely occur in Minoan art, and Mycenaean artisans produced highly skilled weaponry and body armor, which are found frequently in tombs. However, warfare was not unknown in Minoan society, and the artistic creations of the Minoans were not necessarily an indication of their civilization's feminine nature. Most scholars now reject such characterizations as too simplistic.

For reasons that still puzzle scholars, by 1300 B.C.E., Mycenae came under attack. We do not know if the source of the aggression was interstate rivalry or an external threat, but attackers destroyed nearly all of the major centers and palaces. Some believe that Homer's epic of the Trojan War, *The Illiad* (ca. 750 B.C.E.), might have its roots in the end of Mycenaean civilization. Archaeological evidence indicates a steady wave of destruction and abandonment of sites starting around 1200 B.C.E., and by 1100 B.C.E., Mycenaean civilization had vanished completely and writing had ceased. It would take another three hundred years for Greek society to emerge from the trauma.

EARLY GREEK CIVILIZATION, 750–500 B.C.E.

For three hundred years after the collapse of the Mycenaean civilization, the region stagnated politically, culturally, and economically. Then,

around 750 B.C.E., major cultural transformations began, first in Ionia and the islands near the coast of Asia Minor, then on the Greek mainland. Writing reemerged based on the Phoenician alphabet, and iron gradually replaced bronze as the primary metal for tools and other objects. The period also witnessed a revival of the trade in wine, olive oil, and other goods around the Mediterranean. This era of vibrant rebirth is known as the Archaic period and lasted until the fifth century B.C.E.[12]

The impact of these developments on women is difficult to assess. Because of the scarcity of sources, it is often difficult to distinguish the lives of Archaic women from those of their successors in the Classical period. However, the oldest Greek myths provide some insight into the basis for later gender expectations as they presented idealized visions of male and female behavior. Moreover, Archaic political structures may have created a situation in which women were more important to family dynamics than they would be in later centuries.

Homer, Hesiod, and the Greek Pantheon

Although the reappearance of writing provides historians with textual evidence about Archaic Greece, those sources are not without problems for the study of women and gender. On the one hand, the narratives were based in oral traditions passed from one generation to the next, and women were probably active participants in the creation and transmission of these oral traditions. On the other hand, the earliest written versions of the Greek myths are the eighth-century epic poems by Hesiod and Homer. As written texts, they became static reflections of the interests of the authors' gender and class. Thus, they describe the gender expectations of well-to-do, educated men, and the relationship between those expectations and those of the Greek population in general remains unclear. Despite their limitations, feminist scholars use these epics because they portray a wide variety of female characters, from goddesses to queens to monsters, who provide some interesting insights into Archaic Greek religion and Greek gender norms.

The Greek poet Hesiod was a farmer from Boeotia who lived around 700 B.C.E. His work, the *Theogony,* which was based on much older material, became the standard Greek version of divine evolution, and it portrays women in very negative terms. The poem depicts the progression from early female-dominated generations to the superior and masculine reign of Zeus. According to the myth, the earth goddess Gaia appeared in the wake of Chaos. Gaia, without intercourse with a male, produced Uranus, god of the sky. Gaia then had sex with her son and produced a race of monstrous children. Uranus did not want the children, so he hid them deep inside Gaia. Gaia, along with her son by Uranus, Cronus, then plotted the overthrow of Uranus. With a sickle created by Gaia, Cronus castrated his father the next time he came to have sex with Gaia. Cronus then had sex with his sister, who gave birth to the six major Greek deities. One of Cronus's children, Zeus, overthrew his own father and established patriarchal rule on Mount Olympus. In contrast to those of his predecessors, Zeus's new regime was marked by moral order and culture. He denied power to females and even took away their monopoly over reproduction by giving birth to Athena through his head and Dionysus from his thigh. Zeus replaced the chaotic and disorderly (female) world with a new enlightened government controlled by men.[13]

Hesiod went even further in his negative portrayals of women by attributing all of humankind's woes to the first woman, Pandora. According to Hesiod, men were created separately from women. The craftsman god molded the first woman under instructions from Zeus. "From her comes all the race of womankind, The deadly female race and tribe of wives, Who live with mortal men and bring them harm" (*Theogony,* 590–592). In another of Hesiod's compositions, *Works and Days,* Pandora, opened the jar filled with all the pains and evils of the world, scattering them among the earth's inhabitants. Her rash act introduced humanity to an array of problems including hard labor and disease.

The female characters in Homer's works are more diverse. Homer's *Iliad* is the story of a war between the Greeks and Troy, prompted by the abduction of Helen, the most beautiful woman in the world, by the Trojans. The few women who appear in *The Iliad* perform very traditional roles. Although Helen's abduction is central to the epic's

narrative, she is treated more like property than a person. Andromache is the loyal wife of Hector, the great defender of Troy. She pleads for her husband not to go to war, but he reminds her that her authority is limited to the home. "Please go home and tend to your own tasks, / the distaff and the loom, and keep the women / working hard as well" (*The Iliad,* Book VI, 304–305). Women play more critical roles in *The Odyssey,* the tale of Odysseus's wanderings after the Trojan War. More than once on his travels, Odysseus encountered female-dominated environments, like the island of the enchantress Circe. Women, including Circe and Athena, aid the hero during his journey. Homer describes Queen Arete as "a woman of great intelligence, who is regarded as a god by all her people," and who "dissolves quarrels even among men." (*The Odyssey,* 7 lines 73–74). But, not all the depictions are positive. Queen Clytemnestra commits adultery and murders her husband. Although Penelope remains ever faithful to her wandering husband, Odysseus, she is unable to maintain control over his dominions in Ithaca.

Homer and Hesiod populated Mount Olympus with six powerful goddesses: Athena, Artemis, Hestia, Aphrodite, Hera, and Demeter. The fact that female divinities were both powerful and numerous is important, but their relationship to mortal women was complex. Greek goddesses differed from their human counterparts in many ways. In addition to their immortality, Greek goddesses often had personalities deemed inappropriate for women, and they engaged in activities unavailable to mortal women. For instance, the goddess Athena displayed both masculine and feminine characteristics. At times, she was female in appearance and was associated with female handicrafts like spinning and weaving. Other times, she was associated with masculine qualities like wisdom and was often portrayed wearing military armor. When necessary, she disguised herself as a man to help her favorites.[14] Goddesses were actively involved in the world outside of the domestic sphere, while, as we will see, ideally their mortal counterparts were confined to the home.[15]

Virginity also differentiated goddesses from Greek women. All the male Olympians were sexually active, but of the six females, Athena, Artemis, and Hestia were dedicated virgins and

Hera, Zeus's sister and consort, was able to renew her virginity every year by bathing in a sacred spring. Ancient Greeks viewed virginity as potent and sacred, and these goddesses maintained their power through their virginity. In contrast, women were supposed to remain virgins only until they submitted to male authority through marriage and reproduction. Greek myths rarely glorify motherhood in the divine world. Only the goddess Demeter is a good mother; other goddesses kill and even consume their offspring.

In addition to goddesses, Greek mythology includes stories about the Amazons, a mythological race of warrior women who lived without men, wore masculine clothing, and took part in male activities like hunting and fighting. They reproduced by visiting a mountainous border area each year for two months for random sexual encounters with local men. In terms of their relationship to real women, Amazons were everything that Greek women were not supposed to be. They were publicly active and self-governing. They refused to marry and were either asexual or sexually promiscuous. In contrast with the dominant values of Greek culture, Amazons valued baby girls more than boys. Some versions of the myth even have them cutting off one breast in order to be better archers. In contrast, Greek women were to be passive and chaste.

As widespread as the story was, there is no clear evidence for the existence of an Amazon community. Recent archaeological excavations in Kazakhstan have revealed women buried with weapons, and their bodies indicate that they were killed in battle. While these women were unlikely to have been the Amazons of Greek myth, as they date from approximately 600 B.C.E. and lived much farther east, they may have influenced the development of the legend.[16]

The Greeks never admired the Amazons. The Greeks always defeated the Amazons because of their feminine weaknesses, and the notion of warrior women may have been merely a familiar trope used to feminize Greek enemies. Of course, we do not know how Greek women received the myth of the Amazons. Although traditional interpretations considered a culture dominated by women as barbarous, it is certainly possible that some women found these tales of female independence provocative or even inspiring.

The Polis and the Oikos

Scholars believe that after the fall of Mycenae, Greeks colonized much of the Aegean and parts of Asia Minor. Initially, tribal monarchies governed hundreds of small territories. Gradually the *polis,* or city-state, emerged from these monarchies as the primary unit of Greek society. The polis was a self-governing community of the citizens and noncitizens of a city and its surrounding countryside. The city was the center of commerce, worship, and political decision making. Most poleis were small—about the size of an American county—with populations in the low thousands. The economy of the polis was agrarian, with each relying on its own hinterland to feed the urban population. Some, like Corinth and Athens, also had some residents who worked in trade or manufacture. While no particular form of government was associated with the early polis, during the Archaic period political power generally rested in the hands of a traditional landholding aristocracy. There was considerable rivalry among the city-states. Although each polis had its own political and cultural identity, we have the most documentation about Athens and Sparta, city-states that would dominate during the Classical period.

Within the polis, the basic unit in Greek society was the *oikos,* which referred to both the family and the household. The head of the household was always a man. Women spent their entire lives under the legal control of a male guardian, or *kyrios*: a father, a husband, a son, or some other male kin. Even marriage solidified a relationship between the guardian and the groom, not between the man and the woman. During the Archaic period, brides were often passed from one man to another in exchange for *hedna*, gifts from the groom's father. In fact, the Greek word for woman, *gynē*, was also the word for wife. Through this exchange, women played important, although secondary roles, in Archaic politics through their value in cementing alliances and providing wealth.

We know little about women's daily lives. In his *Works and Days*, Hesiod describes a clear gendered division of labor. Men worked outdoors while women work indoors. Homer's *Odyssey* indicates that women may have spent free hours weaving. A gold distaff and a silver box on wheels were among the luxurious gifts given to Helen. She then used the box to hold her expensive purple wool (*The Odyssey*, Book 4). The god Mercury finds the nymph Calypso "busy at her loom, shooting her golden shuttle through the warp and singing beautifully" (*The Odyssey*, Book 5). Archaic-era images show girls using spindles and distaffs.[17]

Outside of the home, religion provided women with regular opportunities for public activity. Women's most public role came as they laid out bodies for burial and loudly lamented the loss of the dead during the funeral procession. The families of the deceased sometimes hired professional women mourners to participate in the funerals of wealthy citizens. The mourning rituals were often dramatic; women tore their hair, scarred their cheeks, ripped their clothing, and beat their breasts. Women also expressed their religious devotion by making dedications to deities, generally female divinities, especially Athena and Artemis, while men made dedications to both male and female deities. Most of the women who made these dedications were probably members of the aristocracy and quite wealthy. Some of the most famous dedications from this period were the life-size marble statues of young maidens called *korai*. The statues, dressed in elaborate clothing and jewelry, may have been the likenesses of the dedicators. Some were also funerary markers for wealthy women. Less wealthy women dedicated mirrors, clothing, cakes, spindles, and bobbins. Through these personal gifts, Greek women reinforced connections to the goddesses upon whom they relied for aid and comfort.[18]

Sappho

Certainly, the most renowned woman of the Archaic period was the poet Sappho, although she remains shrouded in mystery. We know almost nothing about her private life. She seems to have been born around 612 B.C.E. to an aristocratic family and lived on the island of Lesbos. Although some texts state that she was married and had a daughter, many scholars believe that these were fictions asserted by later authors. She composed nine books of poetry, but only one complete poem and a number of fragments survive. Her love poetry is full of passion and sex, and her works

KORE FIGURE (ARCHAIC PERIOD). These life-size free standing stone figures of young deceased women were originally brightly painted. They were used as grave markers, and were usually dedicated to a goddess. (*Acropolis Museum, Athens, Greece/ Nimatallah/Art Resource, NY.*)

speak of the pain and suffering that she felt when marriage took her female companions from her.

Sappho's sexuality has been the subject of much debate. Female homosexuality was not unknown in ancient Greece; vases depict women engaging in sexual acts. However, the association of the island of Lesbos with female homosexuality appears long after Sappho's time. In ancient Greece, the women of Lesbos were famous for their uninhibited and creative heterosexual sex.[19] Scholars have described Sappho as heterosexual, bisexual, and a lesbian, depending on their readings of her works and their understanding of Archaic sexuality and poetic conventions. Based on the idea that Archaic poetry was written to be performed in public, some argue that she wrote using a male voice. Thus, their erotic content does not necessarily represent Sappho's own sexual desire, but imitates expressions of male heterosexual desire. Others focus on the fact that her poems were to be sung by female choirs. Therefore, they were not necessarily expressions of individual emotion. Those who believe that she was married hypothesize that she was bisexual. Most feminist scholars assert that these poignant verses could only be produced by a woman who had experienced such desire for women and that her works differ significantly from male-authored poetry. However, without more detailed knowledge about her personal life, we can only speculate about the relationship between Sappho's sexuality and her poetry.

Whatever the case, Sappho clearly did not live outside or in opposition to traditional Greek culture. She also composed wedding songs that pointed to the importance of marriage in Greek society. She was famous in her own time and intellectuals knew and discussed her works for generations. Greeks admired her beautiful and complex works without regard to her sexuality.

Although our understanding of women's lives in Archaic Greece is limited by a lack of sources, the early works of Greek literature provide some indications about how gender shaped their world. Moreover, in these texts, we see the origins of many gender norms would become fundamental to later Greek society.

Classical Athens and Sparta, 500–404 B.C.E.

Athens came to political prominence from among the Greek poleis with its defeat of the powerful Persian Empire in 480 B.C.E. During this period of

Lesbian Scene (ca. 510 b.c.e.). Although we know much more about male homosexuality in ancient Greece, female homosexuality was not unknown. In this scene from inside a wine cup, a naked woman holds a perfume jar while being fondled by another woman. *(Tarquinia Museum.)*

cultural and political domination, Athenian men idealized the segregation of men and women in nearly all aspects of life. However, as often as not, the ideal went unrealized, as Athenian women regularly participated in the civic life of the polis. In sharp contrast, Sparta's militaristic society valued women's ability to manage independently both in public and in private. As we will see, Athenian women and Spartan women may have engaged in similar activities, but each city-state's culture perceived their roles very differently.

Athenian Women at Home

Ideally, Athenians believed that women should be completely segregated from public life. A woman should not be found standing in a doorway or at a window, as such exposure compromised her reputation. Women were not supposed to be discussed by men, let alone seen by them. Orators avoided naming living respectable women in order not to mar their reputations. In his famous Funeral

Oration, the Athenian statesman Pericles (ca. 495 –429 B.C.E.) told Athenian widows that "Great will be your glory in not falling short of your natural character; and greatest will be hers who is least talked of among the men, whether for good or for bad" (Thucydides, *History of the Peloponnesian War*, Book 2). On most occasions when citizen women appeared in public, they probably wrapped a mantle or veil around their heads to protect their modesty.

Indeed, from conception, a woman's life was precarious. Female fetuses were believed to be weaker than male fetuses and take longer to develop. Children were the property of their kyrios, usually their fathers. He had the right to decide whether to rear them in his oikos or commit infanticide. Greeks viewed infanticide as a practical means to control family size; however, it is unclear how often a kyrios took advantage of his right to expose a newborn. It is likely, although not certain, that girls were exposed more often than boys. A female child was an economic liability, since she cost the family a dowry but did not carry on the family name. Unwanted children were left exposed to the elements, although some may have survived and were collected by other women, including prostitutes.

Greeks held elaborate ceremonies for the naming of newborn males, on the fifth or seventh day after the birth. Although some girls may have been named at this point (with fewer festivities), they were given names that indicated their inferior status, including the feminized forms of male names, names embodying male military ideals, or abstract virtues. Only their families could speak their birth names. If it was necessary to mention a girl in public, the speaker referred to her by the possessive of her father's name. Once married, a wife was identified by her husband's name.[20]

Greek literature describes the division of elite homes by gender. Women lived in the women's quarters of the house, the *gynaikonitis*, while men inhabited the *andron*, the men's quarters. According to Xenophon's (430–357 B.C.E.) *Oeconomicus*, "I also showed her the women's apartments, divided from the men's apartments by a bolted door, so that nothing can be taken from inside which should not be, and the inhabitants cannot have children without us knowing" (9.2–5). However, recent archaeological research indicates that Greek households were not so clearly demarcated. Archaeologists have found domestic utensils in most parts of Greek homes, indicating that household chores took place there. Based on that evidence and the floor plans of excavated sites, it appears that women had access to most areas of the house. However, some homes had specific areas that could be used for entertaining guests without any unsupervised contact between women and men from outside the household.[21]

Young Athenian girls participated in a coming-of-age ceremony known as the *Arkteia*. During this festival, celebrated at the temple of Artemis at Brauron and other shrines, girls "played the bear," as a part of their transition to adulthood. According to a Greek legend, a bear scratched a young girl. Her brothers then shot the bear, offending Artemis. In retribution, the goddesses demanded that young girls serve her by "playing the bear" before marrying. Vases found at the site depict girls of various ages dancing and racing. These festivities "tamed" uncontrolled female sexuality and prepared them for motherhood.[22] Indeed, Artemis was the object of much devotion for girls when it came time to marry. Girls dedicated their toys and a lock of their hair to the goddess. The cutting of the hair was a critical moment in a girl's transition to adulthood.[23]

Athenian women had no true rights to property. By the fifth century, the hedna had been replaced by a dowry made up of the daughter's share of the inheritance from her father. Women's dowries were usually in the form of money or valuables, not land (which was passed exclusively to sons). However, the dowry never belonged to her. If the couple divorced, the husband had to return the dowry to his ex-wife's guardian. Thus, dowry allowed the woman's family to retain some control over the husband and the marriage. Dowry also ensured a decent standard of living for the woman, as inheritance by a woman was rare. In the event that there were no sons to inherit and to perpetuate his oikos, a daughter could be named the *epikleros*. The epikleros was not an heiress. She could not inherit the property herself, and the only way that a man could access the inheritance was by marrying her. A man might adopt a son to marry his epikleros, but if no adoption were made, she and the property passed to the next available male kin: her paternal uncle, his eldest son, or some other male relative. Even then, neither the woman nor her husband ever held complete control over the property. Her husband merely held it in trust until any sons born from that relationship came of age.[24] Despite the fact that women had little or no say in their choice of spouse and could not control either their inheritance or their dowries, exchanges of women and property through marriage created complex political and social networks among citizen families that made women valuable members of the oikos.

Wedding processions generally took place by torchlight and brought the bride from the father's house to the husband's home in a small chariot. The bride's mother led the procession to the door of the groom's home, where his mother waited in the doorway. The transition to marriage must have been a traumatic experience. A woman did not choose her own spouse; her kyrios did that for her. The terms of the marriage and the contract were negotiated between the girl's father and the prospective groom. She then left the comfort of her own oikos for a new household about which she probably knew very little. Depending on her husband's age and his status in the family, she might live under the same roof with her in-laws.

Although Greek women's primary role was to bring children into the world, they did have access to some contraception. Medical treatises described vaginal suppositories made from wool alone or treated with spermicides such as cedar gum, vinegar, or olive oil. Amulets and prayers may have been less effective, but women relied upon them nevertheless. Greek women also had access to a variety of abortifacients. Medical writers of the period describe women who aborted after ingesting toxic potions, violently jumping up and down, and inserting objects into their uteruses.

In the ancient world, giving birth could be quite dangerous. A small percentage of women died during or just after giving birth as did many of their newborn children. As a result, pregnant women often visited temples to invoke the gods' help during childbirth. In particular, women sought the aid of Artemis, Demeter, and Eileithyia, the goddess of childbirth. Pregnant women brought offerings, usually pieces of clothing, to the temple of Artemis at Brauron. Many high-status women came from far away to plead with the goddess for a safe delivery or to thank her for successful childbirth.[25]

BABY ON STOOL WITH MOTHER, ATHENS (CA. 460 B.C.E.). Although Greek women's primary function was to bear and raise children, this image is one of the few depicting a mother interacting with her child. The child's seat may have also functioned as a potty chair. *(Musée Royaux d'Art et d'Histoire, Brussels.)*

When the moment arrived, most women relied on female relatives and midwives rather than doctors to help them through the delivery. A woman may have been embarrassed to allow men to have such intimate access to her body, and her husband may have been generally unwilling to allow another man to see his wife in such an immodest position.

As is true in many cultures, once a woman passed childbearing age, she had more freedom. Widows often appear in the speeches of orators as actively involved in the business of the oikos. They could walk through the streets and speak with men. They were afforded these privileges because Greek society viewed them as having lost their value as childbearers. However, older women were not completely free of male influence. Their sons usually became their kyrios and managed their affairs.

Just as older women were allowed to emerge from the oikos, the ideal of confined women did not seem to have affected women of the lower classes. Their work was too necessary for the survival of their families. Although they must have been a significant proportion of the Athenian population, there are few surviving descriptions of their lives. Murals show men fishing, which required them to leave home for long periods, and Athens's extended wars mobilized large numbers of men throughout the Classical period. Their absence must have given their wives some measure of independence. We also know that lower-class male and female citizens, *metics,* resident foreigners and slaves often worked alongside one another in craft shops. Some lower-class women engaged in the retail trades, selling foodstuffs, garlands, and perfumes, and were famous for their vulgar shouting in the market. Others were tavern keepers, wool workers, and wet nurses. However, women never participated in the most profitable trades, such as importing luxury goods.

Although Athenians believed in an ideal of female seclusion, the reality was much more complicated. From birth, women lived under the guardianship of a man. Women could not inherit property and their sole function was to bear children. However, as we will see, women regularly appeared in public for both religious and other civic activities.

Athenian Women in Public

Athenian women's marginalization from public life increased with the creation of democratic government. Political turmoil began in the seventh century B.C.E., when aristocrats ruled harshly over the rest of the population. Social tensions increased as the rich got richer and the poor became increasingly poorer. Hoping to avoid civil war, Athenian elites chose Solon (ca. 594 B.C.E.) to resolve the impending crisis. Solon introduced a series of reforms that relieved the lower classes of their debts, increased political participation by nonelites, and restructured the economy. Unfortunately, his reforms failed to alleviate class tensions, and in 546 B.C.E. a tyrant, Pisistratus, took power. After another period of civil unrest, both aristocrats and commoners supported the rule of Cleisthenes (ca. 508 B.C.E.), a prominent aristocrat. Cleisthenes took Solon's notions of expanded political participation and created direct democracy in Athens. His reforms divided the city into ten political units, thereby successfully dismantling the city's traditional political alliances. He enfranchised all adult citizen males over the age of twenty-one. Citizen males met regularly in a voting assembly, the *ekklesia,* in which each citizen had one vote and could speak in public debate. Although the expansion of political rights created the most extensive democracy in the ancient world, it completely excluded women.

Athenian democracy was at its height during the time of Pericles. Elected to the governing council, he championed democracy, working to ensure that even poor citizens could participate in the political process; however, his most important reform was his citizenship law of 451–450 B.C.E. The law restricted citizenship to the children of two Athenian citizens, permanently excluding Athens's large population of metics from political participation. While on the one hand this law made citizenship equally dependent on one's maternal and paternal lineage, it also limited women's political roles. Citizen women's sole political act was to bear sons who would become the next generation of Athenian citizens and daughters who would be their wives. During the Golden Age of Athenian democracy, female citizenship existed merely to determine the citizenship of women's children (see **Women's Lives: Aspasia**).

Women also had only limited access to the legal system. Citizen women received legal protection, but they never appeared in court. In some circumstances, they could give testimony privately before family members, but they always had to be represented in litigation by their male guardian. Metics had access to Athenian courts, but metic women, like their citizen counterparts, did not represent themselves. In one case, when the metic woman Zobia was accused of failing to pay her tax, her citizen sponsor represented her in court.[26] As might be expected, slave women had no legal rights. They could be bought, sold, and beaten by their masters without interference from authorities.

Beyond politics and law, women were better integrated into Greek society than the Athenian ideal would suggest. Most important, women actively participated in many of Athens's religious festivals. During the *Panathenaea,* the commemoration of the goddess Athena's birthday, men, women, children slaves, and non-Greeks celebrated together. Women of all classes participated in the religious processions that filled city streets.

Of course, class distinctions did not disappear. Girls from noble families preceded those from the ordinary citizen class in the processions that criss-crossed the city. Even among men, older men marched separately from men of military age. Girls also performed specific ritual functions, like weaving the *peplos* robe for Athena, washing the cult statue, grinding the grain for ritual cakes to offer to Athena or Demeter, or carrying special ritual olive branches as they processed to the temple of Apollo Delphinios. One privilege reserved to Athenian girls was being named a basket-carrier, *kanephoros*, in religious processions. However, there were limitations. Girls and women could not participate in some particular blood sacrifices, but they could participate in many of the ritual activities leading up to the sacrifice itself and could receive sacrificial meat. Moreover, participation in most of these rituals was limited to a few girls of aristocratic birth. Nevertheless, the activity gave girls in general some degree of ritual prominence in the city.[27]

Citizen women figured prominently in the *Thesmophoria*, the celebrations to honor Demeter and Kore, the goddesses who protected the city's grain crops. The festival in Athens was three days long. On the first day, women left their homes and encamped on the Pnyx, the site of the ekklesia, imitating life before agriculture. On the second, they fasted in imitation of Demeter, who fasted as she searched for her lost daughter, Persephone, and on the third, they feasted and celebrated in honor of birth. All public business at the Agora, Athens's central gathering and commercial place, was suspended for the festival. In addition, women participated in other festivals surrounding the harvest cycle, including Haloa (a woman's festival in honor of Demeter and Dionysus, the god of wine) and Skira (a threshing festival). It is interesting that women participated in these fertility-related festivals, even though men were primarily responsible for agricultural work in ancient Greece. In addition, scholars suspect that despite the desire for female seclusion, women of all classes must have participated in festivals as spectators. Women's participation in religious activity took them so far outside the Greek ideal that some Greek thinkers even suggested that religion was a dangerous influence that could lead women into adultery.

Some women also participated in the worship of Dionysus. As a part of their worship, these women fell into madness or mania, and they were known as *maenads*. Gathering in the mountains each winter, they danced ecstatically, whirling in circles and beating drums. They let their hair fall loose, contravening basic Greek notions of propriety. They may have even gotten drunk. Men were not allowed to attend.

A few women dedicated themselves to the service of a particular cult. Priestesses often led the cults of female divinities. In cults with both male and female priests, women were not subordinated to men, but held authority separate from them. In one famous case, the priestess of Demeter even sued a priest for performing sacrifices that should have been exclusively hers. Priestesses were common, and their age, status, and duties differed according to their cult. Some priesthoods were hereditary while others were purchased. Some priestly offices were lifelong while others were not. The priest and priestess of Artemis Hymnia in Mantineia had to remain virgins their entire lives, while married priestesses served in cults of married deities like Hera. Unlike other Athenian women, a priestess could act on her own behalf, signing documents, administering cult affairs, and suing in court. The pay of a priestess varied according to the wealth of her cult. Rich cults such as the Eleusinian Mysteries paid their priestess of Demeter fees from each initiate and one hundred drachmas annually. The priestess of Athena Nike received less than fifty drachmas and a portion of the sacrifices.[28]

Priestesses tended to the personal needs of the devotees and the ritual needs of the polis. At Kyrene, the priestess of the cult of Artemis performed rites for new brides, and at Athens, the priestess of Athena visited the homes of newly-weds. The Greek polis relied on priestesses for its survival and prosperity. In Athens, it was the priestess of Athena Polias who prayed on behalf of the polis to its patron deity. No priest had a comparable role in the city's relationship with the divine. Certainly, women's most prominent public religious role came as priestesses at Greece's most prestigious center of prophecy, the oracle at Delphi. The priestess, the *Pythia*, was chosen by lot from among the Delphian women. She was the mouthpiece of Apollo on issues as disparate as

Aspasia

We know very little about individual Greek women. Greek men were not only uninterested in the lives of women but believed that it was inappropriate to talk about them in public. As Greek women were generally illiterate, they could not leave written descriptions of their own lives. As a result, Aspasia is one of the only Greek women for whom we have enough information to compose a brief biography. She was well known during her lifetime and was mentioned in a number of contemporary texts. In addition, the Roman historian Plutarch (45–120 C.E.) discusses her in his *Life of Pericles,* written around 75 C.E. Aspasia has been the subject of much scholarly debate, but it is clear that she was an intellectually and politically influential woman in a world that rarely credited women with such talents.

Aspasia was born in the Greek city of Miletos on the coast of Asia Minor. She probably came to Athens around 451 B.C.E. Although later writers call her a *porne,* a common prostitute, and many modern scholars refer to her as a *hetaira* or courtesan, there is no contemporary evi-dence to suggest that she participated in the sex trade.

At some point after her arrival in Athens, Aspasia met the great politician Pericles. Pericles had been married and had two sons, but he had divorced his wife. As a metic, a free non-Athenian woman, Aspasia's options for a relationship with Pericles were limited. The earliest literary mention of her from approximately 440 B.C.E. describes her as a concubine. Although it was not yet illegal for Athenians to marry non-Athenians, as Pericles had legitimate sons by his wife, there was no benefit in formalizing their relationship. According to Pericles's own citizenship law (451/450 B.C.E.), any children whom their liaison produced would not be citizens.

During her lifetime, Aspasia was renowned for her intellect. As Pericles's companion, she participated in many discussions with the members of Socrates's (469–399 B.C.E.) circle. Plutarch says that Socrates visited her often and that sometimes her male philosopher friends would bring their wives to listen to her. She is the only historical woman who "speaks" in Plato's works. In his *Menexenus,* a dialogue between Socrates

war, famine, and the fate of children Once a month, Apollo's priestess gave oracles, prophecies, to all who came to the god for advice. The inquirers, both men and women, had to make their questions known to the attendant male priests in advance. Most of the prophecies that survive relate elite politics or philosophical questions, but ordinary people could also ask the oracle questions about issues such as a couple's childlessness.

Few women achieved fame in this very masculine world. We know of only four female poets from the period, none of whom came from Athens. Myrtis of Anthedon (fl. sixth century B.C.E.) is the earliest known woman writer of the Classical period. No remnants of her work exist, but she is remembered as the mentor of Corinna (fl. sixth century B.C.E.), who was known for defeating the male poet Pindar (ca. 522–ca. 443 B.C.E.) in a poetic contest. One short fragment, three one-word quotations, and many brief references to her poems in the works of other authors are all that remain of the works of Telesilla of Argos (fifth century B.C.E.). Although her poems were mainly for women, she was well known to Greek chroniclers and grammarians. Praxilla of Sicyon (fifth century B.C.E.) wrote poetry of several different genres and was famous for writing songs that were a favorite part of drinking party music in fifth-century Athens. These women's renown

and Menexenus, the men discuss a hypothetical speech honoring the Athenian war dead. Socrates asserts that he could compose an excellent speech on short notice because he has an excellent teacher of rhetoric—Aspasia. Socrates then gives a funeral oration that he attributes to her. Antisthenes (fl. ca. 445 B.C.E. and 360 B.C.E.) and Aechines, both pupils of Socrates, wrote dialogues entitled *Aspasia*. Xenophon (430–356 B.C.E.) mentions her on a number of occasions as an expert on male-female relations. Although scholars debate her treatment in these works, she was clearly important enough to provoke discussion among the great thinkers of her time.

Plutarch says that Pericles loved her for her "knowledge and skill in politics." He, like many others, considered her to have been influential in Pericles's decision to go to war against Samos, a move that would have aided her home city of Miletos.

Aspasia's high profile left her open to criminal accusations of impiety and of procuring free women. The accusations may have been politically motivated. Two of Pericles's other associates, including the philosopher Anaxagoras, were also accused of crimes at about the same time. The charge of impiety may have involved unconventional views of divinity, linked to her association with Anaxagoras. The accusation that she was a procuress were probably spurious and an attack on Pericles. She was acquitted after a passionate defense by Pericles.

After an epidemic in Athens in 430 B.C.E. killed both of Pericles's sons by his wife, he was forced to ask for an exemption for his illegitimate son by Aspasia from the citizenship law, which he himself had enacted. The people of Athens agreed to his request.

Pericles died in 429 B.C.E., and sometime later Aspasia moved in with and may have married a man named Lysicles. She is said to have borne him a son, but she would have already reached middle age by that point. Her participation in Athenian intellectual life seems to have ended, and like many other Greek women, we do not know when or where she died.

Sources: Matthew Dillon, *Girls and Women in Classical Greek Religion* (London: Routledge, 2002), pp. 186–189; and Madeleine M. Henry, *Prisoner of History: Aspasia of Miletus and her Biographical Tradition* (New York: Oxford University Press, 1995).

during their lifetimes did not translate into the type of broad-based cultural influence of the Greek philosophers or even of male poets. Women's voices in Classical Greece were heard but rarely listened to.

Spartan Women

Spartan gender expectations varied considerably from Athenian ideals. According to legend, in the early seventh century B.C.E., the Sparta lawgiver Lycurgus bestowed a set of laws called the *Rhetra* that made Sparta into a militaristic society ruled by two kings. Organized around war and around the state rather than the family, Spartan society trained men from an early age to focus their relationships on other men, leaving women unsupervised and in control of considerable property.

Housed in military barracks from the age of seven, all male citizens were full-time professional warriors. They lived, ate, and trained with other Spartan males for most of their lives. Even after Spartan men married in their early twenties, they continued to live in barracks with other warriors until they reached thirty. After that, they could set up their own households, but they still ate every night in a common mess with their male companions. Their primary intellectual, emotional, and even sexual relationships were with other men. This masculine culture had unexpected gender implications. Since boys grew up without their fathers, the authority of the individual father declined in importance. Spartan boys addressed all older men as father, and these fathers had the right to discipline them as if they were their own sons.[29]

This arrangement must have enhanced the role of the Spartan mother, as Spartan society channeled male energies into military life rather than their families. Generally, the father did not live in his home for the first ten years of the marriage. So, for the first few years of a boy's life, he might have little or no contact with his father. By the time the father returned, the boy might have moved out into the barracks. Raised in a female-dominated household, Spartan girls must have formulated strong relationships with their mothers. Moreover, unlike Athenian women, their lives did not center on domestic work. The prevalence of servants and slaves in upper-class Spartan households meant that mothers were not bound solely to domestic duties. In fact, weaving and other sedentary activities were seen as unfit for a free woman.[30]

While physical conditioning was critical to a boy's military education, the Spartan state also prescribed public education for girls that included a significant physical component. At the festival of the *Heraia*, dedicated to the goddess Hera, unmarried girls competed in foot races. The competition, held every five years, may have been a prenuptial initiation rite.[31] Girls also participated in wrestling, throwing the discus and javelin, and chariot races. Depictions and descriptions of these athletic competitions reveal that Spartans also had very different sensibilities about the female body than their Athenian neighbors did. Girls may have been nude or seminude during the contests, just like the boys. Such intense physical conditioning for unmarried girls, *parthenoi*, was meant to enable them to bear vigorous sons. After marriage, women stopped their physical training.

While Athenian girls married at puberty, Spartan girls supposedly married later, around age eighteen. They probably had no say in the choice of a spouse. Scholars continue to debate the meaning of Spartan marriage customs. There are allusions to marriage by capture, but scholars believe that that was probably part of a marriage ritual rather than actual kidnapping. On the night before the wedding, a bridal attendant cut the bride's hair short, dressed her in male clothing, and laid her on a mattress in the dark. The bridegroom ate his meal in the barrack's dining hall, then slipped secretly into the bride's room and took her to their marriage bed. The couple had sex and he returned to the barracks. The masculinization of the bride through her dress and haircut has been difficult for historians to explain. Traditionally, unmarried women wore their hair long, while married women cut it short. The male dress may have been part of a cross-dressing ritual intended to confuse evil spirits or may have been part of temporary role reversal prior to marriage. It may also have eased the transition from homosexual to heterosexual relationships.[32]

After marriage, sexual intercourse between husbands and wives was supposed to be infrequent in order to be more potent. Some evidence suggests that Spartans shared wives on occasion. As a Spartan woman's primary task was to give birth to Spartan warriors, older or infertile husbands may have allowed others to have sex with their wives in order to procreate. It is also quite possible that Spartan women engaged in extramarital affairs. Outside of Sparta, they were famous for their promiscuity and independence. The fact that warfare left married women alone for long periods made it easy for them to have such liaisons. Moreover, the legitimacy of Spartan children was not a serious concern, as individual paternity was not as important to the state as the bearing of children itself.[33]

Spartan women performed more or less the same activities as Athenian women, managing their households and raising their children. However, Greeks considered Athenian wives to be dependent and submissive while Spartan women were viewed as independent, powerful, and integral to the Spartan state. In part, Spartan women's perceived power was due to their ability to own property through both inheritance and dowry. With men away at war for long periods, Spartan society relied on women's ability to manage family estates and had eased inheritance laws to allow them to possess considerable wealth. In fact, some later Greek thinkers, including Aristotle, believed that the accumulation of Spartan wealth by women was partially responsible for the decline of Sparta in fourth century B.C.E.[34]

Although they had no official political authority, royal mothers and wives of kings were influential in the outcomes of Sparta's third-century revolutions. In Plutarch's first-century descriptions, King Agis IV (ca. 244–241) and his successors initiated the Spartan revolutions in order to put an end to unequal distribution of wealth and political power in the polis. The consolidation of political power into the hands of a few citizens and the fact that through their successful conquests, non-Spartans and *helots*—Spartan serfs or unfree agricultural workers—outnumbered citizens by more than seventy to one eroded Spartan dominance. According to Plutarch, by the third century B.C.E., only one hundred of the seven hundred remaining old Spartan families owned land, and most were heavily in debt.[35] These rulers attempted to alleviate income inequality through a series of reforms. As aristocratic Spartan women owned considerable quantities of land, they played critical roles in both sides of the revolution. Some royal women willingly turned over their wealth to the communities as a part of the reform efforts. Other women refused to give up their lives of luxury and influence and thus played a decisive role in the failure of the reforms.

Like their Athenian counterparts, Spartan women were active in the religious life of the state. Women feasted and drank along with men. At one festival, they ate cakes shaped like breasts.[36] They sang and danced, sometimes in the presence of men. Foot races were associated with the worship of Dionysus. Priestesses called *poloi* "fillies" supervised unmarried girls who raced in the god's honor.[37] One of the most remarkable spectacles in Spartan life came with the death of either of the two kings. Women traversed the city of Sparta, beating on cauldrons, bringing out a man and a woman from each household to mourn.[38]

Classical Athens may have idealized female seclusion, but women's segregation was far from complete. Greek religious events brought women of all ages and classes into public on a regular basis, and lower-class women probably felt few constraints on their lives. Moreover, other poleis, such as Sparta, rejected the Athenian emphasis on seclusion. Sparta's militaristic society relied intensely on women's ability to run the household in the absence of men.

SEX AND SEXUALITY IN CLASSICAL GREECE

Greek ideas about sex and sexuality are key to understanding gender norms in Classical society. Greek male sexuality was not confined to marriage. In fact, Greeks viewed marital sexuality almost exclusively as a means to produce citizens and heirs. Greek men were encouraged to find emotional and sexual satisfaction in relationships with other men and a variety of female prostitutes. All these relationships, sexual or not, were based on dominance of older, powerful men over younger, powerless men and women. The ideas of dominance and male superiority became central to the formulation of Greek philosophy on biology, reproduction, sex, and gender.

Greek Masculinity and Homosexuality

Women's status in Greek society was, in large part, determined by the fact that Greeks placed a high value on masculine virtues. Men had three avenues to prove their masculinity. First, a man's success as the head of his oikos determined his character. Although Greeks valued a man's public persona over his private self, his ability to control the lives of his wife, children, and servants, and to perpetuate a successful household was critical to his masculinity. Second, masculinity was proven on the battlefield. As Greeks extolled the masculine virtues of honor, strength, and excellence, *arête,* war became central to the formation of male identity, and the battlefield acted as an arena for gaining fame and glory. This warrior culture exhorted men to fight on behalf of their polis. Athenian men remained liable for military service from the age of eighteen until they reached sixty. By the seventh century B.C.E., Greek warrior culture was manifested most strongly in the *hoplite* armies. Originally, most armies were composed of male citizens who could afford to arm themselves. This arrangement reserved military service, and thus the opportunity to demonstrate one's strength and courage, for the elites; however, by the seventh century, iron and bronze weapons and shields of wood and leather had become affordable to most craftsmen and small farmers. This extension of military participation to nonelites not only provided them with regular opportunities to display their masculine prowess, but it also showed results on the battlefield as phalanxes of armed infantrymen proved to be undefeatable. This military culture also created the *gymnasium,* the third place where men displayed their masculinity. The gymnasium provided an intense physical training program intended to condition young men for warfare. They were to employ the skills honed through individual athletics in defense of the polis.

A culture that valued masculinity over femininity and dominance over submission created the setting for intense male-male relationships. Greek homosexual relationships reflected these values as they were not typically between equals, but pederastic relationships between an older (in his twenties) man of high status, *erastes*, and a younger (often prepubescent) partner, *erômenoi*. Not everyone participated in these relationships. Indeed, many nonelite men may not have approved of male-male sex. For those who did participate, these relationships were tightly constrained by Greece's rigid social hierarchy. Citizen males could only pursue younger citizen males. Free noncitizens could only have relations with servants and foreign boys. Greek culture emphasized the dominant masculinity of the active partner over the submissive, feminine role of the passive partner. The passive partner was supposed to acquiesce only reluctantly to the seduction by the active partner. Dominance was also evident in other relationships. Noncitizens (resident aliens and slaves) were subordinated because they could not engage in any public activity (politics or warfare) in which they could prove their social worth (masculinity). Women were relegated to even lower status, as they were believed to be physically weak, submissive, deceptive, naive, and irrational.

Citizens saw their homosexual relationships as part of the mentorship and training of young men in the pursuit of Greek virtues. These relationships were also about companionship and sexual pleasure. Greek pottery vividly depicts men having sexual relations with other men. However, even physical pleasure was constrained by the social hierarchy. Sexual pleasure was the goal of the active, never the passive partner.

Homosexual relationships were not substitutes for heterosexual sex. Eventually, the active partner would reach marriageable age, around thirty, and forgo his sexual relationships with men. The passive partner would then become an active, dominant partner in another relationship. Even when these relationships continued after marriage, wives may not have distinguished between homosexual affairs and heterosexual affairs. There is, in fact, no indication that Greeks differentiated between the two, as the distinction between active and passive roles was more important than the gender of a man's sexual partner. Young men and women were always the passive recipients of sexual activity due to their lack of political and social status.

Prostitution

Outside of marriage, three different types of women served the heterosexual needs of Athens's men: courtesans, prostitutes, and concubines. Courtesans called *hetairai*, "companions to men," were generally metics. As they were beautiful, educated, and artistic, men preferred them to their uneducated, unworldly wives. Hetairai accompanied men to symposia and other male gatherings from which wives were generally excluded. Such companionship came with a hefty price tag. Courtesans often commanded fees one hundred times that of an ordinary prostitute. As a result, hetairai may have controlled significant amounts of money.[39] In fact, Greeks often gossiped about their lavish lifestyles. In one of the most outrageous stories, Rhodopis, an Egyptian courtesan freed by Sappho's brother supposedly supplied the funds to build a pyramid.[40] Although scholars disagree on whether or not she was a hetaira, Aspasia's extramarital relationship with Pericles brought her fame and power (see **Women's Lives: Aspasia**). For other courtesans, life was more precarious. Athenian men were known to fight over hetairai, and some women may have faced threats from male suitors.

Whether well paid or not, hetairai did not have the legal protection of wives. The Greek orator Apollodoros (fourth century B.C.E.) wrote of a courtesan, Neaira, who was bought by two young men from Corinth from a brothel owner for their sexual pleasure. Neaira was already an adult and a relatively expensive hetaira by that point. She served as their sexual slave for around a year until both men decided to marry. They sold Neaira her freedom on the condition that she never practice her trade in Corinth again. Having no money of her own, she approached her former clients, who gave her the necessary funds. After obtaining her freedom, she went to Megara where she had a difficult time supporting herself. There, she met another man who took her back to Athens, but one of her former clients who had helped pay for her freedom went to her home and tried to drag her off. He claimed that Neaira was his slave, and that she had run away from him. Although that dispute was eventually resolved, she was later involved in another legal case. Her lover and Apollodoros had an ongoing feud. As a part of that feud, Apollodoros eventually prosecuted Neaira for breaking the law. Not only was the marriage of an Athenian citizen and a noncitizen illegal, but he charged Neaira with masquerading as a citizen, which was also prohibited under Athenian law. Although seemingly freer than other Athenian women, hetairai were also very constrained by Athenian society.

The cities of Classical Greece were also home to large populations of ordinary prostitutes, *pornai*, both male and female. Prostitution flourished partly because of the emphasis on female chastity for citizen women and the late age of marriage for men. Most prostitutes were foreign slaves who worked from brothels run by either a man or a woman who paid taxes on the profits to the polis. Prostitutes dressed in highly sexualized fashions. Some may have even worn sandals with studs affixed to the bottoms that spelled out provocative messages in the street as they walked.[41] In addition to sex, some women offered musical performances and played harps, flutes, and lyres as a part of their entertainment. The government tightly regulated prostitution. All prostitutes in Athens had to be registered and pay a special tax and the price of their entertainments was set by law. A prostitute, whether slave or free, could be granted freedom by her owner or arrange to buy it by contracting a loan from a benefit club sometimes made up of past clients. She would repay the loan with her earnings collected as a free prostitute. Some then purchased slave girls and collected abandoned female newborns to train in the pro-

fession and to ensure an income in their old age. We know that a brothel keeper and former slave purchased Neaira as a child.

Some wealthy Greek men also kept concubines with whom they had informal, but more or less permanent relationships. Most of these women were slaves or metics, but a surprising number were free-born Athenians. Presumably, they were forced into concubinage by poverty. Concubines came under their partners' guardianships and received some legal protections. A man who raped or seduced a concubine was punished as if he had committed the crime against another man's wife. However, concubines suffered an important loss of status after the Periclean citizenship law decreed that the children whom they bore to citizen men could no longer be considered citizens.

The only evidence that we have that married women opposed their husbands' relationships with hetairai, prostitutes, and concubines are accounts that admonish men against bringing prostitutes home and spending lavish amounts of money on them. In general, however, Greeks made no distinction between heterosexual and homosexual relationships; thus prostitutes probably bothered a woman no more or less than her husband's male lovers. Indeed, these women actually served an important purpose for unmarried men who desired heterosexual contact, as Athenian society forbade them from engaging in sexual contact with unmarried citizen women.

Sex, Gender, and Greek Philosophy

As many Greek philosophers attempted to understand what the world was made of and how it functioned, they began to examine the differences between men and women. Although Anaximander (ca. 540 B.C.E.) determined that men and women had come about at the same time and under the same circumstances, unlike the secondary creation of women described in Greek myths, most Greek thinkers found rationales for sexual inequality in the natural world.

Democritus (460–370 B.C.E.) was the first of many Greek philosophers to describe the male not only as different from, but as superior to, the female. Indeed, the theory of male superiority dominates what we know as the Hippocratic corpus. This body of work has been attributed to

Hippocrates, but actually consists of sixty to seventy medical treatises written by anonymous doctors from around the Greek world in the fifth and fourth centuries B.C.E. They united sex difference and humor theory to formulate theories of medical science that would dominate Western thought for more than one thousand years. Humor theory asserted that the body was composed of four humors: blood, yellow bile, black bile, and phlegm. Those humors could be hot, cold, dry, or moist. The Hippocratic corpus associated hot and dry with the male and cold and moist with the female. Male embryos were stronger than female embryos and developed more quickly. The texts also assert that men and women could contribute gendered seeds to conception, and that the combination of seeds determined personal characteristics. If both partners contributed male seeds, they would generate highly intelligent male children.

> If the secretion of both parents be female, the offspring proves female and fair, both to the highest degree. But if the woman's secretion be female and the man's male, and the female gain the mastery, the girls are bolder than the preceding but nevertheless they too are modest. But if the man's secretion be female and the woman's male, and the female gain the mastery, growth takes place after the same fashion but the girls prove more daring than the preceding, and are named "mannish." (Hippocrates, Vol. IV, Regimen I, 269–271)

A balance of the humors was the key to health, and to maintain that balance, a healthy adult woman had to be constantly pregnant, lactating, or menstruating. Women whose bodies were not involved in these activities were subject to a variety of physical and mental disorders. For instance, the womb, when not filled with child or semen, would migrate to various parts of the body causing "hysterical" symptoms. (The Greek word for womb is *hystera*.) In Greek medical thought, the womb was an almost independent organism. Unused, the womb might attach itself to a moister organ of the body, such as the liver, the heart, or the brain. If it did not return to its proper place spontaneously, a doctor could manipulate it back into place using odiferous substances at either end

of a woman to entice it back. The womb was not the only site of dangerous imbalances for women. Greeks believed that an overabundance of blood collected in the breasts caused a woman to go mad. Virgins were supposedly prone to suicide because their menstrual flow was partially blocked; they had to be married off so that their hymens could be pierced during intercourse.

In addition to biological differences between the sexes, Xenophon's (430–357 B.C.E.) *Oeconomicus* (*Household Management*) asserted that separate spheres, public for men, private for women, were divinely ordained. In the dialogue, one speaker, Isomachus, explains Xenophon's view:

> "Since both indoor and outdoor matters require work and supervision," I said, "I believe that the god arranged that the work and supervision indoors are a woman's task, and the outdoors are the man's. For the god made a man's body and soul better able to endure the cold and heat of travel and military service, so that he assigned to him the outdoor work. But the god endowed the woman with a body less able to endure these hardships and so," Ischomachus told me he said, "I believe that he assigned the indoor work to her."

He goes on to present the dangers of transgressing those gender boundaries.

> "Now, my dear," I said, "since we both understand what has been assigned to us by the god, each of us must try to accomplish the work appropriate to us. This is what the law intends," Ischomachus told me he said, "when it yokes man and wife. Since the god made them partners in their children, so the law makes them partners in their household. And that the law shows that the arrangement that the god made each more competent in certain respects. For it is better for a woman to remain indoors than to go outside, and it is more disgraceful for a man to remain inside than to take care of the work outside. If anyone does something contrary to the nature the god gave him, it is quite possible that his disorderliness will not escape the notice of the

*gods and that he will pay the penalty for
ignoring his proper work or doing a woman's
work" (7.29–7.31).*[42]

Thus, undertaking the work of the opposite sex
was a violation of divine law.

Both Plato (428–355 B.C.E.) and Aristotle
(384–322 B.C.E.) agreed that the male was the true
and superior form of humanity. Plato connected
women to a lack of control and to the world of
sensations rather than that of intellect. However,
in his *Republic*, Plato complicated his view by
arguing that biological differences between men
and women did not automatically constrain
women's ability to participate in the governance
of the state. Indeed, women who developed the
masculine traits of relying on intellect and self-
control might be more suited to belong to the ruling class than many men. He also advocated
similar education for boys and girls; however, he
did not think that women's capacities as rulers
would be the same as men's, as women were, in all
areas, less gifted than men.

Aristotle made the most long-lasting contribution to Western civilization's conceptualization of
male and female. Based on humeral theory,
according to Aristotle, the key difference between
men and women was the amount of heat in their
bodies. Heat served to concoct matter. The more
heat an animal is able to generate, the more developed it will be. As women generate less heat than
men, women are less perfect. Indeed, women's relative lack of heat accounts for a wide variety of
"defects"—women were smaller than men, less
muscular, thinner, and more knock-kneed. To
Aristotle, the original form of the human was
male and women were "mutilated male[s]"
formed from embryos that did not properly
develop. The physical defects of women affected
their intellectual abilities. Like their bodies,
women's minds were, at best, imperfectly developed. Aristotle then asserted that physical differences led to differences in male and female
natures, describing women as:

*more compassionate than man, more easily
moved to tears, at the same time is more
jealous, more querulous, more apt to scold
and to strike. She is, furthermore, more prone
to despondency, and less hopeful than man,*

*more void of shame, more false of speech,
more deceptive, and of more retentive
memory. She is also more wakeful, more
shrinking, more difficult to rouse to action,
and requires a smaller quantity of nutriment.*
(History of Animals, 608b 9–13)

Because of a woman's biological inferiority, it was
necessary for men to rule her. Like an animal or a
slave, a woman required the supervision of a man,
because she could not control her passions. A
woman could only be virtuous through her obedience to a virtuous man.

Greek intellectuals affirmed Greek assumptions
about the roles of men and women in society.
They looked to the natural and spiritual worlds
for evidence of male superiority. Those ideas
would last long after Greece faded from political
and cultural dominance, forming the "scientific"
basis of Western gender expectations for centuries
to come.

Gender and Gender-Bending in Greek Drama

Classical Greek drama vividly depicted the tensions about sex and gender that pervaded
Athenian society. Many performances took place
during the annual spring festival in honor of
Dionysus, god of wine, that included processions,
feasting, and plays. The event was a spectacular
display of civic unity. In addition to Athenian citizens, foreigners, metics, and representatives of
allied states and other poleis were present for the
festivities. Before the plays began, generals poured
ritual libations, tribute from across the Athenian
empire was displayed onstage, the orphans of the
war dead who had come of age were invested with
hoplite armor, benefactors of the city were honored, and the names of emancipated slaves were
proclaimed. Scholars continue to debate whether
women were allowed to attend. The evidence is
contradictory. On the one hand, it is unlikely that
women were the only group excluded from the
festival, which was open to all Greeks. Most certainly, lower-class women sold food and other
products outside of the performances, and prostitutes must have taken the opportunity to sell
their wares. On the other hand, since the theatrical

presentations were about Athenian military, civic unity, and identity—traditionally masculine ideals—women probably did not have any official place in the spectacles, even in the audience. Even onstage, women were absent. Although female characters figure prominently in most Greek plays, they were all portrayed by male actors.[43]

Many of the plays show the dangers of women who assert their power over others. For example, the strong-willed Queen Clytemnestra in Aeschylus's (525–456 B.C.E.) *Oresteia* trilogy conspires against her husband, Agamemnon, who is fighting in the Trojan War. After persuading him to return to her, she kills him and Cassandra, his lover who has accompanied him from Troy. In this way, Clytemnestra achieves uncontested rule with her lover, Aegisthus, at her side. Subverting Greek gender roles, she undertakes masculine activities, governing alone during Agamemnon's absence, committing first adultery, and then murder. The tragedies that result leave a clear message: rule by a woman is unnatural.

Similarly, in Sophocles's (496–406 B.C.E.) *Antigone*, Antigone leaves the seclusion of the palace to bury her brother, Polyneices, whom King Creon has denied a proper burial. By doing so, Antigone challenges Creon's authority as both her king and her guardian. In contrast, her sister, Ismene, reiterates Greek expectations that women submit to male authority. When faced with the decision to contravene Creon's decree, she meekly asserts, "Remember, we are women / we're not born to contend with men" (*Antigone*, 52). Even Antigone regrets that by submitting to divine law, she will not fulfill her socially determined role as a mother. When Creon discovers that it is Antigone who has defied his decree, her insubordination is worse because she is a woman. Outraged, he shouts, "Now I swear that she is a man and I am not, if she is to prevail in this and go unpunished" (*Antigone*, 484–485). However, although Creon sentences her to be walled into a cave, she subverts his authority one last time by hanging herself. Antigone pays for her transgressions of Athenian gender norms with her life.

Conflicts between men and women in Greek theater often expressed the tensions between the public and the private, the polis and the oikos, in Greek life.[44] The women of Aristophanes' (c. 448–380 B.C.E.) comedy *Lysistrata* attempt to

end the ongoing wars among the poleis. As they discuss their plans, one of the women questions their ability to move from the private to the public, "But how should women perform so wise and glorious an achievement, we women who dwell in the retirement of the household, clad in diaphanous garments of yellow silk and long flowing gowns, decked out with flowers and shod with dainty little slippers?" (*Lysistrata*, 42–45), The women then band together, take over the city treasury, leave their domestic tasks undone, and refuse to have sex with their husbands unless peace is made between the warring factions.

The *Lysistrata* and other works by Aristophanes present problematic views of women. His comedies were meant to be funny and irreverent. He was not advocating the power of women, and his audience would have thought that women taking authority was ridiculous. While drama often reflected tensions in Greek society, the Greek stage did not reflect reality. On the stage, men played women and mortals played gods. In that world, female characters frequently acted and spoke in ways that were unavailable to them in reality.

The transvestism of the Greek stage further complicates our understanding of gender in Greek drama. Some scholars have downplayed the importance of cross-dressing on the Greek stage, arguing that for a Greek audience, a man playing a woman was no different from a man playing the role of a god. However, for many scholars, it is critical to both the narrative and the play's reception that the male actors portrayed female characters. Women never represent themselves or speak for themselves. A drama's full impact required the double transgression of gender norms: a woman crossing the boundaries of expected behavior and a male actor feminized. Froma Zeitlin has argued that Classical Greek theater was designed to educate its male citizens. Thus, dramatists carefully constructed women as the other so that both the players and the audience might explore female experiences as a means to come to a more complete understanding of their male identities. In Aristophanes' comedy *Ecclesiazuse*, the male actors perform the role of female characters who infiltrate the male-only assembly dressed in their husbands' clothing. The conflicts, irrationalities, and struggles that female characters faced were intended to educate men about themselves, not to confront issues faced by Greek women; transvestism only heightened the experience.[45]

While we cannot know how Greek audiences responded to the complicated interactions of sex and gender onstage, Classical Athens was a very masculine society. Its political innovations excluded women, and its culture idealized the seclusion of women. Greek philosophy reinforced the notion that such male dominance was based in nature. However, despite the rhetoric of seclusion and exclusion, there were limits on masculine authority. Masculine domination could not extend into women's religious activity, as women too required access to the gods. A myriad of devotions and cults provided expressive outlets for women of all ages and classes. Even as Athenian men entered the theater for entertainment, they passed groups of lower-class women who crowded the streets of Athens. Men in Classical Greece could not ignore the women who lived among them.

EAST MEETS WEST: GENDER AND THE HELLENISTIC WORLD, 450–150 B.C.E.

The political and cultural supremacy that Athens gained from its defeat of the Persians was short-lived. In 431 B.C.E., Sparta challenged Athenian dominance on the peninsula. For nearly thirty years, the two poleis clashed in the Peloponnesian Wars, and the extended conflict brought dramatic changes for the citizen women of Athens. Pericles urged married women to bear more children, and the pressure to bear sons increased as men were killed in battle. At the same time, the high death tolls in the wars must have decreased the pool of potential husbands for unmarried women. During and immediately after the wars, with their husbands away or dead, many citizen women were compelled to work outside the home in order to provide for their families. Sources indicate that citizen women undertook work as wet nurses, wool workers, and fruit pickers—tasks that were usually confined to slaves.[46]

The Peloponnesian Wars weakened the Greek city-states both demographically and financially and left the peninsula without a dominant power. However, Philip II (r. 359–336 B.C.E.), the king of Macedon and a participant in those wars, was strategically placed to fill the power vacuum. Macedon, to the north of Greece, was populated by Greek-speaking peoples, but had remained tribally based and had not adopted the polis structure. Once he consolidated his authority over the northern tribes, Philip turned his troops against his southern neighbors. In 338 B.C.E., Philip and his armies slaughtered the coalition led by Athens and Thebes at the Battle of Charonea, paving the way for him to take control of all the Greek city-states except Sparta. Philip's consolidation of authority did not rely exclusively on the success of his armies. Philip used marriage as a mechanism of conquest and alliance, taking at least six wives, most of whom were not native Macedonians. Each wife solidified his dominance over yet another Greek city-state.

Unlike Athenian women who could not participate in politics, the women at the Macedonian court were powerful forces both at home and on the battlefield because of their wealth, their influence with the king, and their ability to produce heirs. Philip's first wife was probably Audata, an Illyrian princess who took the name Eurydice when she married him. She bore him a daughter, Cynane (ca. 357–322 B.C.E.), who campaigned with her father in his conquest of Illyria and killed an Illyrian princess during combat. Cynane remained powerful when her half brother, Alexander, came to power. She was able to negotiate a strategic marriage for her daughter and died during battle as the head of a mercenary force that she had engaged with her own monies. Because of their assertiveness, women were often blamed for the jealousies and intrigues that constantly befell the Macedonian court. Philip's murder in 336 B.C.E. was attributed to Olympias, another of Philip's wives and the mother of Philip's son, Alexander. After Olympias succeeded in placing Alexander on the throne, she presided over his court and competed for power with Alexander's viceroy.[47]

Philip's untimely death brought twenty-year-old Alexander (r. 336–323 B.C.E.) to the throne. Alexander was well prepared to rule. He had been taught the arts of war and was trained in philosophy by Aristotle. He quickly consolidated his authority in Greece and began a series of successful campaigns against his enemy to the east, the Persian Empire. After defeating the Persian king Darius III, he turned his attentions to Phoenicia, destroying the great seafaring power. In 332 B.C.E., he swept into Egypt nearly unopposed. There he was crowned pharaoh and founded the city of Alexandria. Alexander then returned to deal with his enemies the Persians. Crossing the Tigris and Euphrates rivers, he soundly defeated them at Gaugamela in 331 B.C.E. In an attempt to conquer the known world, Alexander pressed eastward to India, but his troops mutinied and he returned home. Alexander died in 323 B.C.E. in Babylon at only thirty-two years of age. After Alexander's death, his wife, Roxane, and his son were murdered. His generals then divided his empire into a number of smaller kingdoms: the Seleucid king-

dom in Persia, the Ptolemaic kingdom in Egypt, the Antigonid kingdom in Macedonia, and a series of smaller states in Greece and Asia Minor (see Map 2.2). Despite the breakup of his empire, Alexander's legacy remained in the spread of Greek culture, language, and thought, *Hellenism,* to Asia Minor and the Near East. This interaction between Greek and non-Greek cultures profoundly altered gender norms around the Mediterranean world.

Royal Women

As we have seen, the women at the Macedonian court were not passive wives living in the shadows of their ruling husbands. Long before Alexander, Macedonian queens, unlike women in most Greek city-states, could control their own property. Their

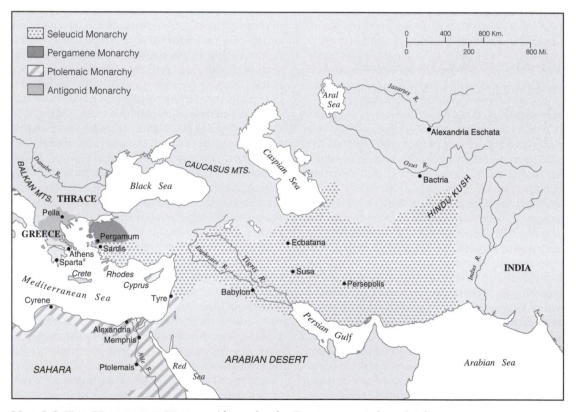

Map 2.2 **The Hellenistic World.** Alexander the Great conquered much of the Mediterranean world. After his death in 323 B.C.E., his empire dissolved, but Greek culture continued to influence the monarchies that succeeded him.

access to wealth increased their authority in other arenas, such as religious offerings, charitable activities, and dowries for poor girls. Alexander's conquests and the subsequent interactions between Greeks and non-Greek peoples dramatically increased the visibility and authority of many royal women around the Mediterranean. However, much of our understanding of those women has been filtered through Greek sensibilities, cultural prejudices, and narrative traditions.

As a result, stories of Persian queens told by Greeks tend to emphasize their outlandish behavior, especially their cruel and violent actions. One of the most infamous tales is that of Queen Parysatis (r. 424–405 B.C.E.), who played dice with her son, the king, with the life of a eunuch at stake. The queen won and the eunuch was flayed alive. According to Maria Brosius, these sensational tales were products of both the centuries-old antagonism between Greeks and Persians and the contrast in behavioral expectations for Greek and Persian women. Earlier Greek writers, such as Herodotus (fifth century B.C.E.), expressed surprise that Persian queens appeared in public and that Persian noblewomen attended feasts and other celebrations. The Greeks pointed to the presence of women in public as a sign of the effeminacy of the Persian court.[48]

Some of the most prominent queens ruled in Hellenistic Egypt. They ruled alone, controlling large amounts of wealth and spending it on public works and large armies. Hellenistic culture flourished as writers sought their patronage. Not only did these women command great wealth and authority, but their influence extended beyond this life into the next. They were worshipped through dynastic cults introduced by Greeks to Egypt, through native Egyptian cults as successors of pharaohs, and as various incarnations of both Greek and Egyptian deities.

The reign of Arsinoë II (316–271 B.C.E.) demonstrates the power that Egyptian queens acquired. Although she was the daughter of Ptolemy I, Arsinoë II came to prominence through her marriages to powerful men. She was married to her first husband, Lysimachus, the much older king of Thrace, at the age of sixteen. She bore him three sons but was accused of complicity in their oldest son's death. Lysimachus promised that she would eventually rule Thrace, and when he died,

she used her wealth and power to engage mercenaries to protect her authority. She then married her half brother, Ptolemy Ceraunus, the king of Macedon, who killed two of her sons. Finally, she fled to Egypt where she married her full brother, Ptolemy II, the pharaoh, who was eight years younger. Arsinoë's marriage to Ptolemy initiated a series of brother-sister marriages among the Ptolemies. Incestuous marriages eliminated foreign influences at court and made pharaohs more like gods than mortals (see Chapter 1). Moreover, Egyptians worshipped both Arsinoë and Ptolemy as divine. Later, a cult developed to Arsinoë alone, as coins show her wearing a diadem, evidence of her deification. She ruled alongside her brother/husband for five years until her death in 271 B.C.E. Her political career has been the subject of historical debate. Some scholars believe that she was quite powerful and responsible for expansion of Egyptian sea power, while others argue that she was not so politically astute and that her brother/husband was the primary decision maker.[49]

The queens of the eastern Seleucid kingdom were active in promoting their husbands' agendas and solidifying support for the new dynasty. Queen Apame, the wife of Seleucus I (r. 305–281 B.C.E.) helped carry out her husband's foreign policy, strengthening the relationship with the city of Miletus. Her role was important enough that the Milesians made certain to thank her. In 299 B.C.E., Demodamas of Miletus decreed that Queen Apame be honored, for her "goodwill and support of the Milesians campaigning with King Seleucus, and . . . she has been especially zealous about the building of the temple at Didyma." Similarly, Laodice I, the wife of Antiochus II (r. 261–246 B.C.E.), provided the city of Iasos with corn for their destitute population in return for their continued support of her husband.[50]

Royal women were also intimately involved in the intrigues that accompanied royal marriages. When Antiochus II made peace with the Egyptians, the pharaoh made a marriage alliance between his daughter Berenice and the Seleucid monarch. She came with such an enormous dowry that she was known as the "Dowrybringer." The new wife meant that Antiochus was expected to divorce Laodice, his current wife, and disinherit her four children by him. When Berenice arrived, he gave Laodice and her sons some estates, and she retired with them to the city of Ephesus. At some point, Antiochus grew tired of Berenice, returned to Laodice, and named their son, Seleucus, as his heir. Upon Antiochus's death (some sources say that Laodice poisoned him), Laodice became queen and coregent with her son. Laodice had the last word in that power struggle. To ensure the succession of Seleucus, she had the other claimant to the throne, Berenice's son, and Berenice killed.[51]

Although much of what we know about Hellenistic queens has been filtered through Greek gender expectations, these women asserted their political and religious authority for both themselves and on behalf of their husbands and sons. As royal women, they were able to transcend gender expectations and use the resources available to them to consolidate their power.

Nonroyal Women

In the wake of Alexander's victories, Greeks settled newly conquered areas like Egypt and founded new cities across the empire. Women were critical to the spread of Hellenism as Alexander used marriage to assimilate conquered peoples into the Greek Empire. He encouraged his Greek and Macedonian troops to intermarry with conquered peoples and saw to it that one hundred of his generals married highborn Persian women. He set an example by marrying the daughter of the Persian emperor, Darius, and later Roxane, the daughter of a central Asian king.

Through marriage, Greek soldiers spread Greek language and culture around the Mediterranean, although not always to the benefit of women. For instance, the practice of female infanticide continued among Greek soldiers. Unlike farmers who relied on daughters as an additional source of labor and as an opportunity to create an advantageous marriage alliance, the thousands of Hellenistic soldiers had little reason to raise daughters. Soldiers usually married into other soldier families so there was no advantage to be gained through marriage alliance, and the cost of feeding an extra child outweighed any benefit from her labor. Evidence indicates that one-child families were common and that soldier families seldom reared more than one daughter.[52]

Relationships between local peoples and their Greek overlords varied across the Hellenistic world. In general, the economic and legal position of women improved, especially among the Greek elites outside of Greece. Although they were still prohibited from participating in most political activities, a few very wealthy elite women were awarded public honors in recognition of their personal generosity. One inscription records the existence of a female magistrate in Histria during the second century B.C.E. A century later, Phile of Priene (Asia Minor) used her great wealth to construct a reservoir and an aqueduct, prompting local officials to give her a magistracy. She held the title, "first among the women" of Priene, indicating that she may have been the first woman to hold that office. Men holding the same position were expected to perform sacrifices and hold feasts for male residents of the city. As a woman, it is unlikely that Phile undertook the same tasks.[53]

Hellenization was often superficial, and native peoples often resented attempts to impose Greek language and culture. Tensions between Greeks and non-Greeks sometimes led to violence. The most famous of these revolts was the Maccabean revolt of Jews in second-century B.C.E. Jerusalem. In this instance, the relationship between the Jews of Jerusalem and their Greek overlords was complicated. On the one hand, evidence suggests that the impulse to Hellenize came from some members of the Jewish community during the last half of the second century B.C.E. On the other hand, Seleucid leaders like Antiochos IV Epiphanes (r. 175–164) made clear attempts to force their Jewish subjects to accept Greek ways. According to *1 Maccabees,* Antiochos banned Jewish religious and social practices and introduced statues of Greek gods into the Temple in Jerusalem, actions that provoked rebellion by some of his Jewish subjects. During the suppression of the revolt, the Seleucid rulers held women responsible for the maintenance of Jewish traditions in defiance of government decrees. Women who had their sons circumcised were put to death, and their dead infants were hung from their mothers' necks (*1 Maccabees* 1:60–61).

In contrast, the interactions between Greeks and non-Greeks in the Ptolemaic kingdom in Egypt affected women differently depending on their ethnicity. Egyptian and Jewish women continued to live according to their traditional cultures and conduct legal and economic transactions without the intervention of a male guardian, whereas Greek women were still bound by Greek constraints on independent public activity. However, there are many indications that Greek women in Egypt adopted local notions about female participation in the economy. Women often appear in Greek documents leasing land. Women with Greek names generally dealt in private land, while women with Egyptian names were more likely to deal with sacred lands that were owned by temples but could be leased or purchased by secular individuals.[54]

Other evidence indicates that Greek women adopted Egyptian norms. Some women in the Greek cities of Egypt bore the designation *aste,* citizen. Although that status entailed no particular political rights, it affected the status of their children. In Alexandria, which was home to large numbers of foreigners, citizenship was limited to the children of citizens. These restrictive laws actually protected native-born women, giving them an advantage in the marriage market since only their children could become citizens. Among the Greek population, these laws encouraged the rearing of daughters, as there was no incentive to abandon female children. Not only was infanticide not traditional among Egyptians, but the Greek ruling class in Egypt had no trouble attracting bridegrooms for their daughters, since the supply of Greek brides was so limited.[55]

The interactions between Greeks and non-Greeks also transformed religious beliefs, as Greeks connected their pantheon with the gods of other Mediterranean peoples, especially the Egyptians. For instance, Greeks identified Aphrodite with Isis, whom the Egyptians worshipped as a compassionate mother goddess. Isis was believed to show a personal interest in her devotees, making her extremely popular among women with whom she shared her experience as a wife and mother. She was the goddess of married life, the protector of childbirth and infants, and the inventor of spinning and weaving. Not surprisingly, women held a number of official positions in her cult and were responsible for large numbers of dedications to her, although in many cases female priests were daughters of high-ranking men. Their priestly offices may have been related to their fathers' positions.[56]

Women and Hellenistic Culture

Although the majority of men and women remained illiterate, there seems to have been a slight increase in female literacy during the Hellenistic period. At Teos, boys and girls were taught together for the first three grades. At Pergamon, girls were awarded prizes for poetry, reading, and penmanship.[57] Similarly, in Egypt more women signed their names to contracts than in earlier periods.

At the same time, we see the emergence of some renowned female poets. Erinna of Telos (late fourth century B.C.E.) wrote her famous poem, "The Distaff," by the age of nineteen and was praised by ancient critics. Anyte of Tegea (fl. ca. 300 B.C.E.) was one of the first Hellenistic poets to write bucolic poetry, while Nossis (early third century B.C.E.) of Lokri (Italy) wrote lyrics and epigrams for and about women (see **Sources from the Past: The Epigrams of Nossis of Lokri**). The cosmopolitan connections of the Hellenistic world brought women's works to public attention as they traveled to festivals to recite their poetry. The men of Lamia awarded one female poet, Aristodama of Smyrna (ca. 217 B.C.E.), public honors.

The Hellenistic world also gave rise to a number of women artists, but we know little about them. Most of them were daughters of male artists. Helena, the daughter of the artist Timon of Egypt, lived at the end of the fourth century B.C.E. and painted a famous scene of battle of Issus. According to Pliny the Elder, Laia or Lala (first century B.C.E.) of Cyzicus (in Asia Minor) painted portraits of women, and "her artistic skill was such that the prices she obtained far outstripped the most celebrated portraitists of the day" (Pliny, *Natural History,* 35:147).

Some new trends in Greek philosophy opened up possibilities for women. The Cynics, founded by Antithenes (445–365 B.C.E.), encouraged men and women to live simply. They argued that the rejection of material things was the key to freedom and encouraged their followers to withdraw from public life and its hypocrisies. Their philosophy, while difficult to adhere to, was open to both men and women. Hipparchia from Thrace (third century B.C.E.) learned Cynic philosophy from her husband, Crates, and she became a well-known philosopher in her own right. According to Diogenes Laertius

The Epigrams of Nossis of Lokri

The poet Nossis came from Lokri in southern Italy. She wrote both love poems and epigrams, but her love poetry has all been lost. All the known female poets of the early Hellenistic period wrote epigrams. The word epigram *means "inscription" and the earliest epigrams were probably inscriptions on tombstones; however, over time, it developed into a popular literary genre. Female poets like Nossis made important contributions to epigrammatic literature by publishing them under their own names and addressing them to issues specific to women.*

1. Nothing is sweeter than love, all other riches second: even honey I've spat from my mouth. This Nossis says: Whomever Kypris[1] hasn't kissed knows nothing of her flowers, what sort of roses.

2. Stranger, if you sail to the land of lovely dances, Mitylene,[2] to catch fire from the blossom of Sappho's graces, say that a friend to her and the Muses, the Lokrian land bore me. And knowing my name is Nossis, go on!

3. Shields[3] Bruttians threw from their doomed shoulders—struck by the hands of the Lokrians quick in battle? lie in the gods' shrines, praising their bravery, not longing for the cowards' forearms they left.

4. O Honored Hera, who often descending from heaven view your incense-scented Lakinian shrine, take the linen robe that Kleocha's daughter Theuphilis[4] wove for you with her noble child Nossis.

---

[1] Kypris is another name for Aphrodite. Roses are a symbol of both the Muses's poetic gift and of Aphrodite's sexuality.

[2] Mitylene was Sappho's native city.

[3] Soldiers from Lokri dedicated to the gods shields captured from Bruttian men, from southwest Italy.

[4] Kleocha was Theuphilis's mother. It is interesting that Nossis refers to her maternal line rather her paternity as was the more formal form of address.

(third century B.C.E.), she donned men's clothes and sparred with male philosophers. Cynicism encouraged its adherents to flout convention, and Hipparchia took advantage of that philosophy to defy gender expectations.

Similarly, Epicurus (341–270 B.C.E.) admitted women to his school. Epicureanism emphasized the pursuit of pleasure through knowledge, friendship, and living a virtuous and temperate life, a pursuit that men and women could undertake equally. His followers may have included both men and women who lived together in community, probably chastely. However, neither philosophy attracted many prominent adherents or had significant impact on official attitudes toward women.

The Cynics' pursuit of virtue through simple living inspired Stoicism, the most popular Hellenistic philosophy. Stoicism stressed happiness through the pursuit of virtue, the unity of men and the universe, and a community of brothers. Zeno (335–263 B.C.E.), the founder of the Stoic school, identified pleasure with excellence, *arête*. Men and women achieved excellence by living according to the masculine notion of reason. However, Stoicism did not advocate equality among the sexes. Zeno even encouraged the sharing of wives, as a part of the utopian community of men that he envisioned.

The decline of Athens brought new opportunities to women. Unlike their Athenian counterparts,

5. When we go to the temple, let's see Aphrodite's status, skillfully worked with gold. Polyarchis erected it, having reaped so much gain from her body's own splendor.[5]

6. It seems that Aphrodite took with joy this hairband, an offering from Samytha—it's skillfully worked and smells sweetly of nectar, with which the goddess too anoints fair Adonis.

7. Kallo dedicated her portrait in the house of golden Aphrodite, the picture painted true to life. How gentle her stance, see how her grace blossoms! Greet her with joy, for she has a blameless life.

8. This portrait captures Thaumareta's form—it renders well the spirit of youth of the gentle-eyed woman. The house watchpup, looking at you, might wag her tail, thinking she sees the mistress of the house.

9. Melinna herself is re-created: notice the face is gentle; she seems to gaze serenely at us. How truly the daughter resembles her mother in all—how fine when children are like their parents.

10. Even from a distance, this picture is known by its form and majesty to be of Sabaithis. Look closer—I think you can see her wit[6] and serenity. May you fare well, blessed woman.

11. When you've laughed out loud and said a friendly word to me, pass by. I am Rhinthon of Syracuse, a little nightingale of the Muses, but from tragic burlesques[7] I picked my own ivy crown.

12. O Artemis of Delos and lovely Ortygia, lay down your pure archery in the laps of the Graces; washing your skin clean in Inopos, enter the house to deliver Alketis from difficult labor.[8]

---

[6] Here wit means wisdom or understanding.
[7] Rhinthon wrote thirty-eight burlesques of tragedy.
[8] Some scholars do not attribute this epigram to Nossis.

From Diane Raynor, *Sappho's Lyre: Archaic Lyric and Women Poets of Ancient Greece* (Berkeley: University of California Press, 1991), 133–136 and notes 192–193.

---

[5] Polyarchis was a prostitute.

women were key political actors at the court of Philip of Macedon. With the conquests of Alexander, royal women often exerted authority as a part of powerful dynasties, and ordinary women were important to the expansion of Greek culture. The interactions between Greeks and non-Greeks brought new ideas and new opportunities to women around the Mediterranean.

CONCLUSION

Greek gender expectations evolved from the dynamic Bronze Age cultures of the Aegean Sea. During the Archaic period, women were valued for their utility in creating marriage alliances, but the creation of democracy in Athens marginalized women from political life. Athenian society's emphasis on intimacy between men over male-female relationships and its idealization of female segregation further disempowered women. At the same time, women's religious activities gave them public visibility that confounded any desire to isolate them from civic life. In the wake of Alexander's conquests, local traditions tempered the harshness of Greek gender expectations and Hellenistic women were actively engaged in politics, economics, and culture. However, Classical Greek gender expectations would remain important in Western society due to the influence of thinkers such as Aristotle and Plato.

NOTES

1. Mary Ann Eaverly, "Color and Gender in Ancient Painting: A Pan-Mediterranean Approach," in *From the Ground Up: Beyond Gender Theory in Archaeology*, ed. Nancy L. Wicker and Bettina Arnold (Oxford: Archeopress, 1999), 5–6.

2. Margaret Ehrenberg, *Women in Prehistory* (Norman: University of Oklahoma Press, 1989), 110–112.

3. Barbara A. Olsen, "Women, Children, and the Family in the Late Aegean Bronze Age: Differences in Minoan and Mycenaean Constructions of Gender," *World Archaeology* 29:3 (1988): 390.

4. Ellen N. Davis, "Youth and Age in the Thera Frescos," *American Journal of Archaeology* 90 (1986): 399–401.

5. Ehrenberg, *Women in Prehistory,* 116.

6. Charles Gates, *Ancient Cities: The Archaeology of Urban Life in the Ancient Near East and Egypt, Greece, and Rome* (London: Routledge, 2003), 138–139.

7. Jon-Christian Billigmeier and Judy A. Turner, "The Socio-Economic Roles of Women in Mycenaean Greece: A Brief Survey from Evidence of the Linear B Tablets," in *Reflections of Women in Antiquity*, ed. Helene P. Foley (New York: Gordon and Breach Science, 1981), 3–6.

8. E. J. W. Barber, *Prehistoric Textiles: The Development of Cloth in the Neolithic and Bronze Ages* (Princeton: Princeton University Press, 1991), 284–285.

9. Cynthia W. Shemerdine, "Review of Aegean Prehistory VI: The Palatial Bronze Age of the Southern and Central Greek Mainland," *American Journal of Archaeology* 101 (1997): 577–579.

10. Billigmeier and Turner, 6–7.

11. Billigmeier and Turner, 8–9.

12. Art historians often divide the nearly seven hundred years between 1100 and 480 B.C.E. into smaller periods of time variously known as the Dark Ages, the geometric period, the orientalizing period, and the archaic period.

13. Sue Blundell, *Women in Ancient Greece* (Cambridge: Harvard University Press, 1995), 20–21.

14. Sarah B. Pomeroy, *Goddesses, Whores, Wives, and Slaves: Women in Classical Antiquity* (New York: Schocken Books, 1995), 4–5.

15. Blundell, 25.

16. Jeannine Davis Kimball, "Warrior Women of the Eurasian Steppes," *Archaeology* 50:1 (January–February 1997): 44.

17. Barber, *Prehistoric Textiles,* 54, 70.

18. Matthew Dillon, *Girls and Women in Classical Greek Religion* (London: Routledge, 2002), 12–14.

19. Pomeroy, *Goddesses, Whores, Wives,* 53–54.

20. Nancy Demand, *Birth, Death, and Motherhood in Classical Greece* (Baltimore: The Johns Hopkins University Press, 1994), 8–9.

21. Lisa C. Nevett, *House and Society in the Ancient Greek World* (Cambridge: Cambridge University Press, 1999), 155, 124–125.

22. Demand, 107–113.

23. Dillon, 215.

24. Roger Just, *Women in Athenian Law and Life* (London: Routledge, 1989), 95–98.

25. Demand, 89–90.

26. Marilyn A. Katz, "Women, Children, and Men," *The Cambridge Illustrated History of Ancient Greece*, ed. Paul Cartledge (Cambridge: Cambridge University Press, 1998), 110.

27. Dillon, 37–38.

28. Dillon, 91, 75, 85.

29. Blundell, 151.

30. Blundell, 151.

31. Nancy Serwint, "The Female Athletic Competition at the Heraia and Prenuptial Initiation Rites," *American Journal of Archaeology* 97:3 (1993): 418.

32. Sarah B. Pomeroy, *Spartan Women* (New York: Oxford University Press, 2002), 42–43.

33. Pomeroy, *Spartan Women,* 38.

34. Pomeroy, *Spartan Women,* 80–82.

35. Pomeroy, *Spartan Women,* 86.

36. Dillon, 43–44, n. 234.

37. Pomeroy, *Spartan Women,* 118.

38. Dillon, 270.

39. Katz, 119.

40. Pomeroy, *Goddesses, Whores, Wives,* 91.

41. Debra Hamel, *Trying Neaira: The True Story of a Courtesan's Scandalous Life in Ancient Greece* (New Haven, CT: Yale University Press, 2003), 5.

42. Translated in Mary R. Lefkowitz and Maureen B. Fant, *Women's Life in Greece and Rome: A Source Book in Translation* (Baltimore: The Johns Hopkins University Press, 1992), 199–200.

43. Katz, 121–122.

44. Froma Zeitlin, *Playing the Other: Gender and Society in Classical Greek Literature* (Chicago: University of Chicago Press, 1996), 354.

45. Zeitlin, 345.

46. Blundell, 138.

47. Sarah B. Pomeroy, *Women in Hellenistic Egypt: From Alexander to Cleopatra* (New York: Schocken Books, 1984), 6.

48. Maria Brosius, *Women in Ancient Persia, 559–331 BC* (Oxford: Clarendon Press, 1996), 96, 109–115.

49. Pomeroy, *Women in Hellenistic Egypt*, 17–18.

50. Susan Sherwin-White and Amelie Kuhrt, *From Samarkhand to Sardis. A New Approach to the Seleucid Empire* (Berkeley: University of California Press, 1993), 26, 127.

51. Pomeroy, *Women in Hellenistic Egypt*, 14.

52. Sarah B. Pomeroy, "Infanticide in Hellenistic Greece," in *Images of Women in Antiquity*, ed. Averil Cameron and Amélie Kuhrt (Detroit: Wayne State University Press, 1983), 215–216.

53. Riet van Bremen, *The Limits of Participation: Women and Civic Life in the Greek East in the Hellenistic and Roman Periods* (Amsterdam: J. C. Bieben, 1996), 31–32.

54. Pomeroy, *Women in Hellenistic Egypt*, 152.

55. Pomeroy, *Women in Hellenistic Egypt*, 46–47, 123.

56. Pomeroy, *Women in Hellenistic Egypt*, 57.

57. Susan G. Cole, "Could Greek Women Read and Write?" in *Reflections on Women in Antiquity*, 231.

SUGGESTED READINGS

Blundell, Sue. *Women in Ancient Greece*. Cambridge: Harvard University Press, 1995. An accessible overview of the lives of Greek women through the Classical period.

Demand, Nancy. *Birth, Death, and Motherhood in Classical Greece*. Baltimore: The Johns Hopkins University Press, 1994. An excellent discussion of the complicated cultural expectations of women through the life cycle.

Dillon, Matthew. *Girls and Women in Classical Greek Religion*. London: Routledge, 2002.

Hamel, Debra. *Trying Neaira. The True Story of a Courtesan's Scandalous Life in Ancient Greece*. New Haven: Yale University Press, 2003. A well-researched and entertaining look at the life of a hetaira and one of Greece's most scandalous trials.

Pomeroy, Sarah B. *Spartan Women*. Oxford: Oxford University Press, 2002. Rather than contrast Spartan women with Athenian women, this work explores them in the context of their own culture.

———. *Goddesses, Whores, Wives, and Slaves: Women in Classical Antiquity*. 2nd ed. New York: Schocken Books, 1995.

Women in Ancient Rome, 800 B.C.E.–200 C.E.

Altar of Augustan Peace, dedicated 4 July 13 B.C.E. Augustus and his family are portrayed in traditional Roman clothing to emphasize the Imperial family's connection with the past and to Republican virtues. Augustus's wife, Livia, wore the married woman's stola to portray her as the mother of the country. (Museum of the Ara Pacis, Rome, Italy/Scala/Art Resource, NY.)

While Greece dominated the eastern Mediterranean, Rome transformed itself from a tiny city-state to the ruler of the Mediterranean world. Over the course of nearly one thousand years, Roman gender norms changed as the empire grew and evolved. Following the ideals of Greece, early Romans tried to restrict women's involvement in public life. During the Republic, Roman women became more independent as military service took men away from home for long periods and left women to care for families. However, daily independence was tightly constrained by Roman law that placed women under the authority of men. Then, as the Republic crumbled, women emerged as powerful negotiators of their own interests. Finally, women took advantage of Imperial Rome's vibrant society. In Rome's attempt to reconcile the difference between gender ideals and realities, women came to symbolize Rome's successes and failures.

AN AGE OF LEGENDS: WOMEN AND THE FOUNDING OF ROME AND THE EARLY REPUBLIC, 800–300 B.C.E.

Roman history can be traced back to the eighth century B.C.E., when a variety of Iron Age peoples inhabited the Italian peninsula. They farmed, fished, and mined the region's rich deposits of iron, copper, and tin. Two of the most powerful and influential of these peoples were the Greeks, who had colonized the south, and the Etruscans, who had formed city-states in the northwest. Etruscan women seem to have had relatively high status and public visibility. Ultimately, both societies were conquered by a small group of people who settled around what would become the city of Rome. Uncomfortable with Etruscan gender norms, Romans condemned women's political activity in their founding legends. Then, with the establishment of the Republic, Rome formally excluded women from the political process; however, women still found ways to participate, largely through their influence with men.

Chapter 3 ❖ Chronology

753 B.C.E.	Romulus's legendary founding of Rome
509 B.C.E.	Legendary suicide of Lucretia
509 B.C.E.	Republic is declared
450 B.C.E.	Twelve Tables established
216 B.C.E.	Battle of Cannae
215 B.C.E.	*Lex Oppia* established
186 B.C.E.	Wives permitted to choose their own guardians at the deaths of their husbands
100 B.C.E.	Fannia of Minturnae successfully sues ex-husband for her dowry
44 B.C.E.	Assassination of Julius Caesar
43 B.C.E.	Hortensia protests before the Senate the taxation of Rome's fourteen hundred richest women
First century B.C.E.	Sulpicia writes her poems
9 C.E.	*Lex Poppae* established
14 C.E.	Death of Caesar Augustus
47 C.E.	Boudicca's revolt
79 C.E.	Vesuvius destroys Pompeii
Early second century C.E.	Soranus writes his *Gynecology*
197 C.E.	Septimus Severus permits soldiers to marry

The Archaeological Past

Scholars do not know the origins of the Etruscans, although they were not Indo-European peoples. Originally herding peoples, Etruscan tribes gradually coalesced into a sophisticated confederation of city-states. Our earliest evidence of Etruscan life dates from about 700 B.C.E., with the appearance of pottery with Etruscan inscriptions. By 650 B.C.E., they occupied Rome and had become the dominant political force in the area. By the fifth century, the ruling military-aristocratic elite had given way to an urban elite who expanded the cities, building public squares and communal sanctuaries, large public buildings, and elaborate private homes. Etruscan cities were home to artisans who produced sophisticated metalwork, pottery, and sculpture, and merchants who traded goods from around the Aegean Sea.

Many scholars believe that Etruscan women had relatively high status and public visibility, but the evidence is sparse. Although the Etruscans gradually adopted an alphabetic script and developed a literary tradition and written bureaucracy, only a few inscriptions on pottery and metal have survived. However, among the most common archaeological artifacts are large numbers of women's mirrors, decorated with mythological scenes and inscriptions that identified the owner or commemorated a god or goddess. The inscriptions on these mirrors sug-

SARCOPHAGUS OF AN ETRUSCAN MARRIED COUPLE FROM BANDITACCIA NECROPOLIS, CERVETERI. CA. 530–520 B.C.E. Unlike their Greek contemporaries, Etruscans often depicted husbands and wives socializing together, possibly implying that Etruscan women had high status in their society. *(Louvre, Paris, France/Erich Lessing/Art Resource, NY.)*

gest that some Etruscan women could read, and they show that free Etruscan women, as opposed to slaves, had their own names, not female forms of their father's names as would become common in the later Roman Republic. Their independent identification indicates a legal and social status that distinguished them from their Greek counterparts.[1] In fact, Greeks were amazed at Etruscan women's freedom. The Greek historian Theopompus (fourth century), coming from a society that idealized the seclusion of women, was astounded to find women making toasts at banquets and mingling with friends and relatives. Moreover, unlike the Greeks, Etruscan couples are frequently portrayed in artworks as socializing together and showing affection; sarcophagi and tomb paintings show couples embracing and men and women dining and watching sporting events together.

Tombs indicate that some elite women acquired an impressive amount of wealth. The richest tomb excavated at the *Castel di Decima*, outside of Rome, is that of an Etruscan woman. It was filled with more than ninety bronze and ceramic items, as well as Etruscan glaze ware. The body was adorned from head to toe with gold, silver, and amber jewelry.[2]

Like women in many other ancient societies, Etruscan women worked in textile production. Archaeologists have recovered from women's tombs large quantities of spindle whorls, distaffs, and loom weights, which women used to produce a remarkable array of different styles of clothing. Paintings show that Etruscan clothing was more complicated than simple rectangles draped over the body and that men and women dressed differently. During the sixth and fifth centuries, men typically wore a belted tunic and women wore both short and long dresses. Some clothing had set-in sleeves and decorative trim.[3]

Ethnically and culturally different, the Romans did not initially grant women the same visibility as Etruscan women had. Early Roman history, which is shrouded in myth, depicts Etruscan women as exotic and foreign. Roman legends express a profound unease about Etruscan women's political influence, often contrasting their influence and visibility with a Roman ideal that women belonged at home.

Roman Legends and the Creation of Feminine Ideals

Women played prominent roles in the legends of Rome's founding, and the female protagonists served as powerful models for later generations of Roman women. Modern historians must use these tales with caution because they were written down centuries after Rome's founding. Livy (59 B.C.E.–17 C.E.) recorded these legends in his *History of Rome* when Rome itself was changing from a Republic to an Empire. Thus these legends also record Livy's anxiety about women's political behavior in his own time. However, most scholars believe that the legends' basic narratives originated in oral tradition and contain insights into the priorities and ideologies of pre and early Republican Rome.

According to legend, Romulus, one of a pair of twins abandoned at birth and raised by a she-wolf, founded Rome. The legend's antiquity is clear from other sources, including a bronze statue of a she-wolf that dates from the sixth century. According to Livy, in 753 B.C.E. Romulus set himself up as king of Rome. The city soon became a haven for "a promiscuous crowd of freemen and slaves" (*History*, 1.8) but had few women to ensure the city's future. When Romulus's overtures to other city-states for alliances and intermarriage were rebuffed, he plotted an event that became known as the "Rape of the Sabine Women." Romulus invited the Sabines to a public celebration, and Roman youths abducted the Sabine women while their families watched the spectacle. Pleased to have women with whom to expand his population, Romulus granted a request by his wife, Hersilia, to make the women citizens of Rome. War between the Romans and

the Sabines ensued, but the Sabine women, now the mothers of Roman children, stood between their Roman husbands and their Sabine fathers. The Sabines sued for peace rather than kill their daughters and sisters. Romulus named the city wards after these founding mothers in honor of their loyalty.

Although there is little evidence of the historicity of the Sabine legend, it expresses two prominent themes in Roman history. First, it emphasizes Rome's willingness to integrate non-Romans into their society in stark contrast to Greek practice. If the legend provides any insight into this process, it shows that like other conquering peoples, Romans extended their influence through sexual conquest, making women mediators between their natal and marital families. Second, the legend stresses the role of law in legitimizing Roman actions. In glossing over the horrific details of the rape, Livy emphasized that the Roman men married their captives, granting them citizenship, property, and legal rights. Thus, their children were legitimate. This legend makes the connection between legitimate birth and marriage an early principle of Roman law: women's reproductive capabilities transmitted both legitimacy and citizenship.[4]

A second set of legends concerns the evolution of Roman government from a monarchy to a republic. Livy claims that an Etruscan dynasty that ruled Rome started with Tanaquil, an elite woman who married a Greek from Corinth named Lucomo. After hostility to their intermarriage prompted the couple to move to Rome, Lucomo assumed the name Lucius Tarquinius Priscus (Tarquin) and found great favor at the king's court. When the king died, Tanaquil engineered her husband's election to the throne and established an Etruscan dynasty in Rome. When political rivals murdered Tarquin, Tanaquil kept his death a secret until she could arrange the succession of her son-in-law Servius Tullius.

Stories of Etruscan women's political influence continued in successive generations. Livy's portrayal of Tanaquil's granddaughter, Tullia, draws on characterizations found in Greek tragedy and introduces the stereotype of an evil and unnaturally ambitious woman. According to Livy, Servius Tullius had two daughters, the younger of whom, Tullia, was politically ambitious. She conspired with her equally ambitious brother-in-law, Lucius Tarquinius, and after the double murder of her husband and her sister, Tullia married her brother-in-law. Hoping to emulate her grandmother's king-making, she convinced Tarquinius to kill her father. She then hailed her husband king before the Senate, but the Senate denounced her for interjecting herself into political matters. Tarquinius sent her home while he waited for the Senate to confirm his rule. Her dismissal reaffirmed that politics was an exclusively male activity. On her way home, Tullia ran over her father's body with her chariot. Tullia's act was not only dishonorable, it was shocking and further emphasized Tullia's unnatural nature and, by association, the unnaturalness of women in politics.[5]

As Romans grew increasingly unhappy with their monarchy, the legend of the "Rape of Lucretia" and the founding of the Roman Republic vividly depict their dissatisfaction and provides detailed descriptions of female gender expectations. According to the legend, between military campaigns, the Etruscan king, Tarquinius Superbus, and his men contrived a contest to see who had the most virtuous wife. Upon returning to their homes, all the men except for his general and cousin Tarquinius Collatinus found their wives drinking and dining with friends. Collatinus's wife, Lucretia, was at home, working her wool. Her virtue and modesty aroused the king's son, Sextus Tarquin, and he returned to seduce her. When she rebuffed him, he threatened to kill her and place her body with that of a slave, thereby implicating her in a scandalous relationship. After giving in to Tarquin, Lucretia denounced him to her husband and father. She then killed herself rather than live with the shame of the rape. Vowing revenge, Lucretia's family paraded her body through the streets, goading the Roman populace into action. The crowd took up arms and overthrew the king. In 509 B.C.E., the Republic was declared.

The legend of Lucretia reveals the priorities of the early Republic. Lucretia's fate served not only as a sign of royal corruption, but also as a symbol of the connection between male political action and female honor. Using the image of Lucretia dutifully working wool, ancient Roman historians and politicians emphasized their self-sufficient past and simple culture. Moreover, Lucretia became the epitome of Roman womanhood, modest, industrious, and willing to sacrifice herself for her family's honor. She remained at home tending to her domestic duties, unlike Etruscan women who spent their time socializing and drinking.

We do not fully understand the relationship between Roman legends and the Roman past; however, these three legends expressed critical notions about female behavior. Romans were clearly uncomfortable with Etruscan women's visibility. Roman legends emphasized women's contributions as cultural integrators and as bearers of new citizens, but their political aspirations and sexual selves had to be kept carefully in check.

Patricians and Plebeians: Women and the Struggle of the Orders

In the fifth century, Rome was essentially an agrarian society divided into two groups: patricians and plebeians. Some scholars speculate that patrician status grew out of archaic priestly functions, which gave them certain religious obligations and privileges. Their prestige and wealth gave them rights, including exclusive access to most public offices. The plebeians evolved out of the much larger group of families who did not have these privileges. Their origins are unclear, but they were associated with military and agricultural work. Livy believed that conflict between these two groups over access to government office marked the first two centuries of the Republic's history.

Dissatisfaction with despotic monarchs led the Romans to build a government designed to prevent one man or one family from acquiring exclusive power. Although the government continued to evolve, its basic structure throughout the Republic called for two magistrates, known as *consuls*, to rule in place of a king. The consuls had extensive administrative, judicial, religious, and military authority. To prevent them from gaining too much power, they could only serve for one year and could not serve more than one term. The consulship was the pinnacle of a man's political career. It came after long service, first in the military, and then in a series of ever more responsible government offices. The Senate, initially a group of one hundred men, advised the consuls. Government service earned no salary, but officials had responsibility for maintaining public works and feeding the poor. They paid for these expenses out of their own pockets as a sign of their power, largess, and commitment to the state. Under this system, only the wealthiest, whether patrician or plebeian, could afford public office. However, by the end of the fifth century B.C.E., patricians had a virtual monopoly on government offices, controlled the priesthoods, and levied harsh taxes on plebeians.

From the outset, rich and educated plebeians resented their exclusion from government. Plebeian leaders mobilized the growing numbers of poor by promising them better representation in the government, land reform, freedom from enslavement for debt, and a written law code that guaranteed their rights. Their agitation led to protracted conflicts throughout the fifth and fourth centuries B.C.E. Later Roman historians termed these conflicts the Struggle of the Orders.

The Struggle of the Orders resulted in a series of reforms that gradually reopened government service to plebeians. In 494 B.C.E., one reform created the office of *tribune*, to ensure that the government passed no laws detrimental to the plebeians. This arrangement gave the tribunes a tremendous amount of power because they could block legislation in the Senate. The *Lex Ovinia* passed between 339 and 318 B.C.E. made both plebeians and patricians eligible for the Senate, excluding only those guilty of serious misconduct. The plebeians were partially successful in their fight largely because they constituted the majority of the military. When they refused to defend Rome, the patricians had to accede to some of their demands.

Despite these reforms, Roman women had no official role in government; however, as they moved freely in public, they presumably encountered information about politics in their daily activities. Although women could not vote or hold office, elections to all governmental positions started with a series of local assemblies that all Romans could attend, including women. Moreover, Roman women were in a position to influence their husbands' votes.

According to Livy's history, the plebeians owed their victory in the Struggle of the Orders to women's ability to influence their husbands. M. Fabius Ambustus (consul 360 B.C.E.), a patrician,

had married his older daughter, Fabia Major, to a patrician and his younger daughter, Fabia Minor, to a plebeian. Fabia Minor was visiting her sister's house when a knock at the door startled her. Her sister laughed at her because she was so unused to a busy household, and Fabia Minor went home upset at her unequal marriage and overall lack of status. When her father learned of her distress, he and her husband agitated for political reforms that would bring plebeians into the government. Livy credits Ambustus with the rule that one of the two consuls be a patrician and the other a plebeian. Although probably fictitious, Fabia Minor's actions highlights the influence a Roman woman could have over the men in her family.

Romans were proud of their history, but they were also troubled by it. Livy's histories highlight the difficulties in creating a new government. His descriptions of Sabine women who went out in public, Tanaquil as kingmaker, Tullia as regicide, and Fabia Minor as instigator of political change, point to the violence and cultural misunderstandings that arose from integrating different peoples into Rome. Women's behavior, political influence, and public visibility produced anxiety because Greeks, Etruscans, and Romans all had different attitudes toward them. Romans attempted to reconcile these conflicts by placing these problematic women squarely in the realm of legend.

WOMEN, WAR, AND REPUBLICAN EXPANSION, 300–70 B.C.E.

The Roman historian Polybius (ca. 200–ca. 118 B.C.E.) celebrated the ease with which Rome transformed itself from a small city-state to the dominant power in the Mediterranean. Indeed, the Roman Republic spent much of its energy and resources on conquering neighboring kingdoms. First it conquered Italy and then turned to North Africa, Greece, and the Iberian Peninsula. Warfare left many women unsupervised for long periods of time, and the conquest of new territory altered Rome's economy in ways that dramatically affected women's daily lives.

Republican Wars of Expansion

The fear of invasion, the need for increased food supply, and a desire for greater wealth inspired Rome's policy of expansion and conquest. Warfare was so pervasive that many Romans saw it as a national characteristic, and Polybius intimated that peace led to effeminacy in Roman men. Rome's conquests started in the 490s with a victory over the Latins south of Rome and the piecemeal conquest of the Etruscans to the north. Roman aggression came with its share of setbacks. Around 390 B.C.E., the Gauls sacked Rome; however, Rome survived the invasion and ultimately conquered the entire Italian peninsula south of the Po River. Once the Italian peninsula was under its control, Rome turned its attention to the rest of the Mediterranean. A series of three wars against the North African city of Carthage, called the Punic Wars, and wars against Macedonia and Greece gave Rome control of the entire Mediterranean (see Map 3.1).

Until the start of the First Punic War in 264 B.C.E., warfare was a seasonal duty. Roman men left home in the summer to fight and returned to their families and farms in the autumn. However, Roman warfare changed when troops started fighting outside Italy. The wars in Sicily, Africa, and Greece increased mortality and kept those who survived away from home for years. During these absences, soldiers' wives supervised family farms alone and tried to stave off creditors. Long troop mobilizations contributed to the decline in small independent farms. If we are to believe contemporary accounts, many a farmer came home from the wars to discover his family sold into slavery for defaulting on debts and his farm taken over by a wealthy landowner. For instance, in 256 B.C.E., the consul M. Atilius Regulus's military successes in Africa earned him an unprecedented second term in the field. However, he declined this offer because back home, his hired hands were victimizing his wife and children and stealing his equipment and livestock. His family was starving and the farm was in danger of foreclosure. Although in the end, the Senate provided for Regulus's wife and children, most families were not so fortunate. The Senate saw unsupervised wives as a problem and by the end of the Republic, it resolved the issue by prohibiting soldiers from marrying.[6]

Warfare changed women's public behavior. In the Second Punic War (218–201 B.C.E.), the Carthaginian general Hannibal (247–182 B.C.E.) led an army with elephants from Carthaginian territory in Iberia across the Alps. Once on Roman soil, he inflicted the Republic's worst military loss at the Battle of Cannae in 216, killing more than seventy thousand Romans. Without knowing who had survived and who had been killed, Roman women began their traditional mourning. Their grieving was so loud that one senator proposed removing them from the streets, in violation of tradition. With the publication of the casualty list, their mourning became even more passionate, hindering their performance of household and civic religious duties. Women in mourning could not participate in the annual rites to Ceres, goddess of grain and the food supply, and because nearly all women were in mourning, the Senate contemplated canceling her rites. Unwilling to risk offending the goddess and jeopardizing the food supply, the Senate issued unprecedented rules that limited the mourning period to thirty days so that the women could perform their rites. Later, when Hannibal sent Roman prisoners to beg the Senate to pay their ransom, women pleaded with the senators for their men's lives. The Senate refused and the women escorted the prisoners to the city gates. Livy commented on how extraordinary it was that women engaged in public dispute with men. The war had begun to disrupt daily life and erode the constraints on women's behavior.[7]

The Senate took action to curtail such brazen behavior. Motivated by both the need for gold to pay for military action and a sense that women's public behavior was morally dangerous, in 215 B.C.E., the Senate passed sumptuary legislation called the *Lex Oppia*. These laws limited the amount of gold that women could own, the clothing that they could wear in public, and their ability to ride in a horse-drawn vehicle. It passed similar limits on men's wealth and dress in 210 B.C.E. Roman military fortunes began to change, and Roman general Publius Scipio Africanus (236–ca. 184 B.C.E.) ultimately defeated Hannibal in 202. The next year, Rome invaded Carthage, forcing it to pay huge indemnities, to sink its fleet, and to turn over its holdings in Iberia. With the end of the Second Punic War, Romans tried to return to life as normal, and two tribunes

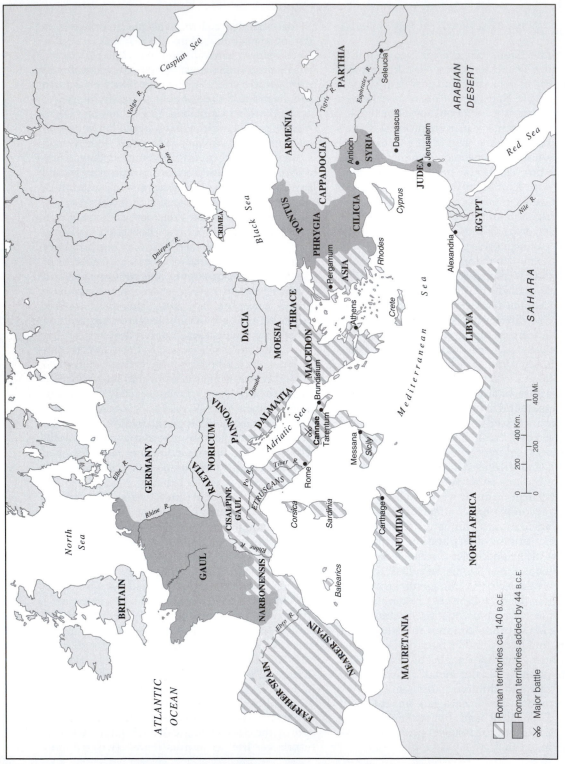

Map 3.1 Roman Conquests During the Republic. Roman military expansion took soldiers away from home for long periods of time, leaving their wives and daughters in charge of family farms and property.

Roman territories ca. 140 B.C.E.
Roman territories added by 44 B.C.E.
Major battle

proposed the repeal of the *Lex Oppia*. When conservative senators opposed this legislation, women listened to the debates and tried to convince the senators to support the repeal. The Roman orator Cato the Elder (234–149 B.C.E.) was in favor of keeping the law. He believed that women's finery and property threatened their traditional place in the home and turned their attention away from their families. In contrast, L. Valerius (fl. 195 B.C.E.) supported the repeal of the law, arguing that it would restore a key element of women's culture and identity. According to L. Valerius, finery revealed a woman's status and respectability and should be restored now that the war was over and the Senate had lifted other wartime measures. Threatened with a veto of the repeal, women from the city and the surrounding countryside blockaded the offending politicians' houses until they withdrew their opposition. The women were successful and the Senate repealed the *Lex Oppia*.

Women and Conquest

The Iberian Peninsula was one of the first places outside Italy to experience Roman conquest. Long a part of the Greek and the Phoenician trading networks, Iberia boasted a diverse Iron Age population who lived in hilltop forts and were ruled by local oligarchies. The conquest of Iberia was difficult, especially in the north. At Numantia, in 134 B.C.E., the Roman general Scipio Aemilianus (ca. 177–129 B.C.E.) put his soldiers on daily forced marches to acclimate them to the difficult climate. He reportedly expelled two thousand women from the camp in an effort to discipline his troops. Roman historians claim that these women were prostitutes and undoubtedly many were, but some were wives and mothers of the soldiers who helped make military life more bearable by doing the laundry, cooking meals, and providing comfort and companionship. Many women preferred to follow their husbands and sons rather than face hardship alone.

When the Romans finally brought the peninsula under their control, many of the Roman soldiers decided to settle there. In 171 B.C.E., the Senate took the exceptional step of granting citizenship to four thousand offspring of local women and soldiers and then settled them in a Roman colony on the Iberian Peninsula. However,

Roman settlement did not erase variations in regional customs. Archaeological evidence shows that Iberian women wore a variety of hair and clothing styles. Some followed the Greek practice of wearing veils, while other women shaved or plucked the front halves of their heads. Some women served as priestesses in local cults. As Roman influence spread, statues of women wearing Roman clothing and hairstyles began to appear. Whether because of local traditions or the influence of Rome, women in Iberia owned property and had some influence in local urban affairs. For example, a woman built the public baths at Tagli and created an endowment to maintain them in perpetuity.[8]

The conquest of Greece had a more profound impact on Roman culture than its settlement of Iberia. Rome started its wars with Greece in 200 B.C.E. and by 146, it had sacked the city of Corinth. After the conquest, Romans actively sought out Greek art and emulated Greek styles of painting, sculpture, architecture, and drama. Greek had long been the international language, and so Roman parents made sure that their sons and daughters learned Greek. Greek nurses and nannies were especially popular with the wealthy because they could teach Greek to the children when they were first learning to talk. The earliest Roman literature survives from just after the First Punic War and it self-consciously imitated Greek literary forms. The Roman playwright Plautus (ca. 254–184 B.C.E.) adapted Greek comedies for Roman audiences. Educated Greek slaves worked as teachers, writers, and artists. Some of Rome's greatest historians, such as Polybius and Quintus Fabius Pictor (fl. 190 B.C.E.), either came from Greece or wrote in Greek rather than Latin. Rome remained the capital, but Greece became the economic and cultural center of the new empire.

Although the Romans were attracted to most of Greek culture, they believed that the Greeks were self-indulgent and overly fond of luxury, behavior that conflicted with Roman values of restraint and austerity. However, male homosexuality was not a part of this anxiety. Latin writers quickly appropriated Greek terms for male and female homosexual activity, but paid little attention to female homosexual acts. Homosexual sex was acceptable as long as it was between a free adult male and a boy or a slave and the free man was the "active" partner. However, sex between two free men or a free man playing the "passive" role was unacceptable. The Romans also condemned *pederasty*, in the sense of a romantic and sexual relationship between a male citizen and a freeborn youth, as wrong. For the Romans, sex implied domination and authority. Free men could dominate women, slaves, and children, but freemen and free boys were not to be treated that way. So, while the Romans might imitate Greek culture, they remained distrustful of what they viewed as Eastern decadence.[9]

The Roman Economy and the Expansion of Slavery

Roman conquest transformed the economy through the creation of large agricultural estates and the expansion of slavery. This process began as the Senate made the newly conquered lands available only to wealthy elites. Instead of producing food to meet a family's needs, the owners of these large estates called *latifundia* used gangs of slaves to produce crops that would earn huge profits. The rise of latifundia displaced many rural inhabitants who then flocked to the cities in search of work and food. During the fourth century, the urban population doubled, and archaeological excavation indicates an increase in new construction. While Roman officials built new homes for their families, the burgeoning urban poor lived in squalid tenements rented by the room.

Urban residents could not grow enough food to feed themselves, nor did they produce enough goods to satisfy consumer needs. Rome became reliant on imports, paying for its food and luxury items with wealth earned from taxes, booty, and leases on state-owned forests, fisheries, mines, and saltworks in North Africa and Iberia. The Senate imported grain from Africa to feed the military and the urban poor, while the agricultural areas produced cash crops such as wine, olives, fresh fruit and vegetables, and meat for those urban residents who could afford them.

To meet the demands of the growing cities, landowners relied on slave labor. By the end of the Republic, some 30 percent of the total population was enslaved. Romans captured men in battle and women and children during assaults on cities. One

Roman historian reported that when the Romans captured Carthage in 146 B.C.E., they took thirty thousand men and twenty-five thousand women as slaves.

Cato the Elder's manual on estate management, *De Agricultura* (ca. 160 B.C.E.), the oldest surviving piece of Roman literature, provides glimpses of rural slave life. Male and female slaves did not live together and were unable to form permanent families; however, Cato believed that regular sex kept his male slaves from rebelling, so he charged admission to the female slave quarters. His wife, Licinia, nursed the children born of these casual unions.

Slaves could not marry, and female slaves were denied the virtues of modesty and chastity that were valued in free Roman women. Roman men expected their slaves to be sexually available to them, and the promiscuous slave girl was a common character in Roman literature. Many slave women bore children, and some slave owners specifically bought female slaves to produce children for future sale. Owners believed that children born to slaves were less rebellious because they had no memories of a free life and no distant families to inspire escape. However, Rome's continued military expansion meant that captured slaves made up the majority of the slave population.

By the second century, large numbers of slaves also worked in cities in manufacturing, in brothels, or as domestics in the houses of the elite. Both male and female slaves cared for children, dressed hair, bathed their masters and mistresses, and cooked, cleaned, and sewed. Romans often used Greek slaves for tasks requiring literacy, such as writing messages, keeping accounts, and teaching children. Literacy was not limited to men. According to an undated epitaph, one female slave, Virgilia Eupitrosyn, worked as a copier of manuscripts.[10] The number of slaves who made up the retinue of a nobleman or noblewoman became a status symbol, and many domestic slaves did little else but accompany their masters or mistresses in public. Slaves of both sexes provided sexual favors to their male masters; however, it was against the law for a free woman to have sexual relations with a slave, and the crime brought shame and severe penalties if discovered.

Epitaphs on graves indicate that there were large numbers of freed slaves in the population.

One such inscription declares: "To Juno. [The tomb] of Dorcas, hairdresser of Julia Augusta [the Empress Livia], born a slave on Capri [in the imperial house]. Lycastus, polling clerk, her fellow freedman, [put this up] for his dearest wife and for himself."[11] Like the hairdresser Dorcas, most freed slaves were urban artisanal or former domestic slaves, and they continued to work at their crafts after manumission. For instance, the wealthy widow Sassia freed her doctor and provided him with a storefront from which to practice medicine. Slaves could also purchase their freedom with their earnings from tips and side businesses. In fact, the crafty, enterprising slave was a stock character in Roman comedy. Freed slave women were midwives, bakers, wool workers, seamstresses, and nurses. Once free, they could marry and produce free children.[12]

However, most slaves never experienced freedom. They worked chained together in agricultural or mining gangs. Slave owners treated them brutally, all the while complaining that slaves ran away, were lazy, and vandalized property. Sometimes slave discontent resulted in rebellion. Three revolts grew so large that they required extensive military interventions.

Sicily and southern Italy were the center of most violent slave revolts, and female slaves participated in the uprisings. During the first slave war (139 or 135–132 B.C.E.), the leader Eunus allowed the housemaids of a particularly brutal mistress to torture and execute her. After his initial success, Eunus set himself up as a king and took as his queen a female slave who had participated in the rebellion. Roman chronicles state that the wife of the free gladiator, Spartacus, took part in the third slave war (73–71 B.C.E.). She came from Thrace and was a prophetess in the cult of Dionysus. As a gladiator's wife, she shared his difficult life, and when he started the rebellion, she followed him. What happened to her remains a mystery.[13] Presumably, many more women risked their lives in these uprisings.

Military expansion changed Rome from within. With men away at war, women undertook new responsibilities. When the Senate passed legislation constraining their activity, they stepped into politics, challenging Rome's wartime policies. They were also a critical part of Roman settlement. As Rome came to rely on imports and slave labor, women were both the owners and the workers in the new economy.

SOCIETY DURING THE ROMAN REPUBLIC, 300–20 B.C.E.

Although Roman expansion had created new opportunities for women, Roman legal norms seriously restricted their ability to act independently. Women lived their entire lives under the guardianship of men. They could not decide their own futures and had few rights to property. Roman religion helped to enforce social status. As Rome's religious beliefs evolved, the state used these beliefs to emphasize its power and the importance of women's place within the home.

The Roman Family

As the Struggle of the Orders yielded a place in Roman government to plebeians, a Roman law code ended the patricians' monopoly of the law. Promulgated by the Senate around 450 B.C.E. it created the principle of equality before the law for all free men. The Twelve Tables were so important that Roman schoolboys memorized them as part of their lessons. Ironically, given their importance, no complete copy survives; only one-third of them are known, and those are only quoted in other works.

The Twelve Tables limited the family's autonomy by taking revenge out of its jurisdiction. Thus, only fifty years after Lucretia's family had allegedly avenged her rape, their actions became illegal. However, the Twelve Tables still left an enormous amount of power in the hands of the male head of the family, the *paterfamilias*. These laws declared women's need for constant legal and moral supervision by men, preferably their fathers or husbands.

The Roman family consisted of biological kin, slaves, freed slaves, and clients, all of whom fell under the guardianship of the paterfamilias, the oldest, most powerful male member of the family. His power was immense and his guardianship included responsibility for the family's livelihood and maintaining the integrity of family property. The paterfamilias had the right to sell his children into slavery or even punish them with death, although by the end of the Republic, they rarely exercised this right.

The paterfamilias maintained his authority throughout his life. Even an adult man was not legally independent and had no fortune of his own until his father's death; whatever he earned or inherited belonged to his father. No Roman subject to the authority of the paterfamilias could conduct business in his own name or possess any goods. He could not even choose his occupation. The paterfamilias might provide him with an allowance and some independence, but doing so was purely a personal choice; it had no legal basis. Similarly, the paterfamilias might choose to grant a son his freedom through emancipation, but he was not expected to do so.

Just how many people fell under the paterfamilias's control depended on his wealth. A peasant family probably consisted of a husband, wife, and children. Other close family members might help with farm labor, cooking, and childcare. In addition to family members, artisans, merchants, and low-level government officials might have owned a few household slaves. Elite families would have had hundreds of household slaves and gangs of slaves working on the latifundia.

Roman law required the paterfamilias to raise all healthy male babies, but only the first healthy female baby. Although women would have had many pregnancies, high infant mortality probably meant that neither wealthy nor poor women had many surviving children. Historians disagree over how frequently parents chose to abandon or expose their children rather than raise them. However, low population growth and the matter-of-fact reporting of exposure suggest that it was common. Moreover, unbalanced sex ratios imply that families raised more sons than daughters.[14] Although poor families may have exposed their children because they could not afford to feed them, elite Roman families had different motivations. They wanted to ensure a decent fortune for their other children. Physically weak or deformed children were automatically abandoned, while slave traders collected healthy ones to sell. Indeed families seem to have expected this and left chil-

dren in locations where they were likely to be found. Roman comedies frequently included stories about abandoned children finding their parents. Men without children could also adopt an heir to carry on the family lineage.

Evidence about urban working classes and the peasantry does not appear until the middle of the first century C.E. However, nostalgic literary descriptions and archaeological and documentary evidence hint at Roman peasant life. Roman freeholders and their families generally farmed small plots for personal consumption. Crops varied with the region, with grain more common on the plains and grapes and olives in the hills. In the more rugged territory of Etruria to the north of Rome, small farmsteads continued to survive up into the second century C.E., with the inhabitants living off a combination of livestock raising and cereal and vegetable crops.[15]

Later Roman writers expected male and female farmers to follow prescribed gender roles. Columella (ca. 10–70 C.E.), in his work *De Re Rustica*, explains that

> since man's food and clothing had to be prepared for him, not in the open air and in woods and forests, as for the wild animals, but at home and beneath a roof, it became necessary that one of the two sexes should lead an outdoor life in the open air, in order that by his toil and industry he might procure provisions which might be stored indoors. . . . God, therefore, assigned to man the endurance of heat and cold and the journeys and toils of peace and war that is of agriculture and military service, while he had handed over the woman, since he had made her unsuited to all these functions, the care of domestic affairs. (12. preface, 2–6)

However, economic necessity made it unlikely that many peasant women led the idealized lives Roman moralists described. In reality, they probably undertook a wide variety of tasks in addition to "domestic affairs" to make up for their husbands' absences and lack of slave labor.[16]

Roman expansion created a new professional class composed of men, whose origins were in the equestrian branch of the military, and their families. Their relative wealth placed them above the infantry. Typically, this class worked as artisans, merchants, tax collectors, or government contractors, occupations that Rome needed but that senators could not perform by law. Because this class's wealth did not come from the land, the elites looked down upon them. Plautus's comedies mocked their wives for their social pretensions and aping of elite manners and clothing.[17]

We know much more about the lives and concerns of the Roman elite. Roman parents took significant steps to care for their children. Wealthy families usually hired wet nurses for infants and employed nannies and tutors for the day-to-day supervision of children. Children developed terms of affection for the adults who raised them; *mama* and *tata* were the Latin equivalents of "mommy" and "daddy" and may have referred either to their biological parents or to the men and women who cared for them. Parents and guardians also provided Roman children with toys. Archaeologists have recovered rag dolls, toy carts with horses, balls and bats, and dog tags for family pets. Artwork also depicts Roman children at play.[18]

Roman children received an education appropriate to their class and sex. Slave tutors taught elite boys and girls at home. By the late Republic, many parents sent their children to public schools, although girls probably left school by their early teens in order to get married. Some girls may have continued to study with tutors at home until their weddings. Elite parents wanted both boys and girls to be literate in Greek, as well as knowledgeable about literature, rhetoric, geometry, and philosophy.[19] Children of the artisanal class received practical educations. Sons and male and female slave children served apprenticeships, so that they could work in skilled jobs such as weaving and pottery. For slave owners, it was a means of recovering the costs of raising the slave. Girls from artisanal families apparently did not work as apprentices, but probably learned domestic skills from their mothers or female guardians.[20] We have no evidence of the education of peasant children, but they too probably learned the skills necessary for their adult lives at home.

Women and Marriage

The power of the paterfamilias is clearly evident in Roman marriage, a private institution available only to free citizens. Roman society expected all citizen women to marry, and the sole purpose of marriage was to produce legitimate citizen children. Although love and companionship were desirable, they were considered irrelevant when arranging a marriage. Of course, we know the most about patrician marriages. The paterfamilias arranged marriages for his children with his social and economic aspirations in mind, but he was legally bound to obtain his daughter's consent for both her engagement and marriage. Because girls were raised to be submissive and passive, most probably granted their permission quite readily.

Roman girls married their first husbands in their early teens. Boys waited a few years after they had officially entered adulthood, as signified by putting on the plain white toga associated with adult men. This ceremony did not occur at a fixed age; the father decided when his son was mature enough to assume adult responsibilities. As a result, grooms were older than their brides. Roman politician and philosopher Cicero (106–43 B.C.E.) married off his daughter, Tullia (76–45 B.C.E.), while she was in her teens to a man in his late thirties. He died when he was just over forty. Tullia married two more times, divorcing her second husband and dying in childbirth when she was thirty-one. The difference in age between husbands and wives meant that many women could expect to be widowed young. However, the age gap might not be as large in a woman's second or third marriages, and she might ignore her father's choice. Tullia and her mother disregarded Cicero's wishes when arranging Tullia's final marriage.

The Romans recognized two kinds of marriages: one placed the woman under the control of her husband's family and the other kept her in the control of her natal family. In a marriage *cum manu*, all of the woman's property, dowry, or inheritance, passed to her husband. In effect, she became an adopted daughter of her husband's paterfamilias, with no independent property or legal rights. However, if the woman stayed in her father's house for three nights a year, she would remain under her father's guardianship. In this form of marriage, called a free marriage, or *sine manu*, a woman's dowry and property remained in her father's control, and her husband could not permanently gain from this liaison.[21]

MURAL OF BRIDE FROM POMPEII, VILLA OF THE MYSTERIES (60–40 B.C.E.). Roman society expected Roman citizen women to marry and produce children. They married quite young and their husbands were much older. (*Museo Archeologico Nazionale, Naples, Italy/Erich Lessing/Art Resource.*)

It is difficult to know which form of marriage benefited women more. A woman who married cum manu lived under the direct control of her guardian, but became independent with the death of her husband. In contrast, a woman who married sine manu spent her day-to-day life beyond her guardian's watch, but she could not be independent until the last direct male descendant died.[22] Suzanne Dixon has remarked that marriage divided women's loyalties: "Politically, married women of the elite promoted the interests of their brothers and sons rather than those of their husbands. Economically, they favored their children. Emotionally, they showed great affection and loyalty towards their husbands."[23]

The negotiation of the dowry was a critical aspect of Roman marriage. Under Roman law, women could inherit equally with their brothers; however, females generally inherited less than their male siblings. Usually, they received their portion of the inheritance in the form of a dowry. Strictly speaking, a woman had no ownership of her dowry. Her husband was supposed to use it to help maintain her, but he could sell it without her permission. Conflicts over dowries frequently ended up in the courts. In 100 B.C.E., Fannia of

Minturnae sued her husband for not returning her dowry when he divorced her for adultery. Fannia argued that her husband knew her character and only married her so that he could divorce her and get her property. Fannia was notable because she conducted her case herself and won.[24] The playwright Plautus used the figure of the timid husband fearful of his well-dowered wife to address Roman anxieties about dowries.

If the class differences were too great between the man and the woman, in particular if the woman were a freed slave, the couple might live together and she would be his concubine. Monogamous relationships such as these recognized the woman's lack of status, not her lack of honor or virtue. However, children from these relationships were illegitimate, could not inherit, and legally speaking, were outside of the man's guardianship.

In the earliest Roman marriage laws, it was impossible for a woman to obtain a divorce, but a husband could divorce his wife without grounds if he were willing to forgo her property. If he divorced her for using poisons, drinking, substituting children, or committing adultery he acquired all her wealth. Traditionally, these laws were ascribed to Romulus at the founding of Rome. Remarriage after either divorce or widowhood was a possibility, although the Romans held up the ideal of the *univira*, a woman married to only one man. Univirae gained a special place in Roman society, including the right to perform some religious rituals. We do not know how common this status was. Poor women with no property probably found it difficult to remarry, and wealthy widows probably found it difficult to stay single.[25]

In the third century B.C.E., social reforms modified Roman marriage practices, ending women's extreme disadvantage in both marriage and divorce. Some changes were a consequence of the Struggle of the Orders; others were the result of men's long military enlistment. The net effect was that cum manu marriages declined.

The first reforms ended discrimination against patrician women married to plebeian men. Many assumed that plebeian men married patrician women to gain unearned prestige and as a result, Romans limited the ability of such women to participate in some religious activities, in particular

the cult of *Pudicitia Patricia* (Patrician Virtue). Founded by a Roman official in 331 B.C.E., the cult maintained that only the most modest and virtuous patrician women who had been married only once could pray at the shrine; women who were married to plebeians were expressly excluded.[26]

In 307 B.C.E., the Senate expelled one of its members for divorcing his wife without cause, signaling a change in attitudes toward divorce. Wealthy men who could afford to lose their wives' property could no longer simply repudiate them without consequences. The man who initiated this change was Lucius Volumnius Flamma, a plebeian married to a patrician woman named Verginia. Verginia was also motivated to change marriage laws. In 296 B.C.E., she established a shrine in her home dedicated to *Pudicitia Plebeia*, Plebeian Virtue, in retaliation for her exclusion from the cult of Pudicitia Patricia. She urged plebeian women to do likewise and exceed patrician women in their modesty and chastity. The cult did not survive, but Verginia's actions were unprecedented as a form of women's public action.[27]

Rome's continued military success brought further changes to Roman marriage practices. Male absence and military casualties made it impractical to restrict the role of wives and mothers in family decisions. After the Punic Wars, sine manu marriages became available to every woman. By 186 B.C.E., a husband could grant his wife the right to choose her own guardian at his death. Additional reforms also made divorce easier and more equitable. A wife could divorce her husband and remove herself from his guardianship, freeing her from any male guardianship. By the end of the Republic, couples did not have to establish grounds for divorce; they simply had to work out a settlement. In terms of dowry, for all practical purposes, a husband no longer owned his wife's dowry, but only had custody of it for the duration of their marriage. Since law is essentially conservative, it is likely that these legal changes reflected earlier changes in practice.[28]

These marriage reforms came at a time when Roman class structure was becoming more rigid. Marriages were increasingly between men and women of the same class. As sine manu marriages made it possible for women's families to hold on to their property, marriage became a less successful means for men's advancement. There is other evidence that social mobility slowed in the late Republican period. The rule that one consul was to come from the plebeian class initially brought new families into government, but by the end of the Punic Wars, the plebeian and patrician families that had provided consuls had melded into an exclusive class or de facto nobility. Rich plebeians from outside this clique of twenty or so families found it increasingly difficult to be elected to government positions. As marriage reforms gave women more independence, they also made it harder for families to improve their social status.

Women and Roman Religion

Although Roman religion brought women into public and gave them public roles, it ultimately justified and maintained their secondary social status. Religion played a major role in Roman society, although religious practices varied widely reflecting both indigenous Roman beliefs and imported ones. Romans, who gave gods gifts in the form of rituals and sacrifices and expected favors in return, paid a great deal of attention to signs and omens and tried to discern the gods' desires through augury, fortunetelling, and astrology. Religion served the Roman state, and Romans believed that disasters, such as the loss of the Battle of Cannae, were signs of divine disfavor. Regaining favor required sacrificial offerings and moral behavior. Many Roman cults such as the cult of Pudicitia Patricia linked women's behavior to the health of the state. Maintaining divine favor and maintaining women's submission to men amounted to the same thing.[29]

Greek influence made Roman religion more sophisticated. Deities increasingly assumed the attributes and purviews of Greek gods and goddesses. Romans also adopted Greek legends, which Ovid (41 B.C.E.–17 C.E.) recounted in his works the *Metamorphoses* and *Fasti*. For the most part, Roman gods and goddesses have exact counterparts in the Greek pantheon. For example, Hera was the Greek goddess of marriage, fertility, and childbirth, and the consort of the king of heaven; for the Romans, she was Juno. The Greek goddess of harvest and grain was Demeter, and for the Romans, she was Ceres.

Women's religious practices were usually private and directed at maintaining female virtue.

Women tended household shrines with these hopes in mind. Other religious rituals focused on specific stages in the life cycle or social status. When a young girl married, she dedicated her childhood toga to the goddess Virgo as a sign that she was now under the goddess's protection and put on the *stola*, the dress of respectable married women. Upon marriage, she made a sacrifice to Praenesta, a cult in honor of Juno, the patron goddess of mothers and childbirth. There were also cults for widows, slave women, and lower-class women, each of which articulated ideals for Roman life and female behavior.

Maintaining temples was part of the elite's responsibilities, but it also allowed wealthy women to act on their own or their family's pious concerns. To facilitate these obligations, many cities had women's associations, such as the cults of Pudicitia Plebeia and Pudicitia Patricia. Some of these groups were burial societies dedicated to tending graves, providing tombs for poorer members, and honoring the dead. Some had charitable duties, and others may simply have been social groups. When lightning struck the temple of Juno Regina in Rome in 207 B.C.E., women's organizations raised money for its repair.

The most important cult and the heart of Roman religion was the cult of Vesta, the goddess of the hearth. This cult directed women's fertility to the protection of the state by requiring its priestesses to remain virgins. Six Vestal Virgins, all chosen from patrician families before they reached puberty, oversaw the cult's public rituals and kept the sacred flame lit. Vestals served for thirty-five years. As lifelong virgins, the Vestals were unusual in Roman society and they enjoyed special privileges unavailable to other Roman women. Vestals could make wills even if their fathers were still alive; they could appear in court and administer their own affairs without a tutor or guardian; and they sat in places of honor at banquets and public events.

The Vestals' behavior reflected on Rome's fortunes. The Romans deemed unusual behaviors, natural disasters, monstrous births, or odd weather to be prodigious and attributed them to either the extinction of Vesta's sacred flame or the loss of a Vestal's virginity. The Senate blamed the loss at Cannae on two Vestals losing their virginity. An unchaste Vestal had to be buried alive with only a day's worth of food and a lamp, unless she killed herself first. Her grave was hidden to prevent future commemorations. After the second century, the execution of Vestals became rare. The virgins' chastity was essential for redirecting their regenerative powers toward the health of the state. Scholars argue that these women reinforced traditional gender roles by acting quite differently from most other women. By inverting the traditional gender order, the cult called attention to how women ought to behave.[30]

As early as the second century B.C.E., the cult of the Egyptian goddess Isis (see Chapter 1) specifically attracted Roman women. Romans portrayed her as a mourner, a loving mother, and a wife and prayed to her during marriage, childbirth, and death—moments that particularly marked a woman's life. In Athens and Rome, a high percentage of cultic inscriptions were from women. Cultic involvement encouraged women to go to the temples to pray alone. Rituals to Isis involved more public emotion and elaborate displays than other Roman cults. This cult also attracted both men and women of the lower classes. The combination of lower-class support and exuberant displays opened up the cult to accusations of immorality and lasciviousness. In 43 B.C.E., Octavian banned the cult as a political threat, although subsequent rulers restored it, hoping to gain favor with the masses.[31]

Another popular cult that involved women was that of *Mater Matuta* (the Good Mother), imported from Asia Minor. It involved univirae, women who had only been married to one man. Male priests, called *galli*, who had castrated themselves as a sign of their devotion to the goddess, led the rituals. Univirae practiced ecstatic rituals that included beating and expelling a slave woman from the temple precinct. Both the galli's effeminate behavior and the univirae's expulsion of the slave called attention to proper gender and social roles by enacting inappropriate behavior. In this way, the cult affirmed women's accepted gender roles.[32]

Although the Roman Republic initially gave women no public authority and few legal rights, women saw their status increase following military expansion. Other changes resulted from continued tensions between the plebeians and patricians. By the late Republic, women had lost their extreme disadvantage in marriage and divorce and could control

significant resources. Religion helped Romans cope with these changes by ascribing religious meaning to women's continued subordination.

WOMEN AND POLITICS AT THE END OF THE REPUBLIC AND THE BEGINNING OF THE EMPIRE, 70 B.C.E.–14 C.E.

By the late Republic, Rome was a wealthy and powerful state. However, this wealth was unequally distributed, and the Senate had stopped setting up colonies and now leased or sold newly conquered territory to the wealthy. The rise of private contractors meant that the Senate abdicated much governmental responsibility for this land. The growing urban population resented their lack of access to land and declining political influence. Although their unhappiness inspired attempts at economic reform, these reforms failed to redistribute either wealth or political power, and by the first century B.C.E., the Republic was in its last days. This period of crisis brought women into public life, as they used their influence with powerful men to influence political life. However, with the creation of the Empire, Augustus rejected this new Roman woman as emblematic of all that had gone wrong with Rome.

Women and the End of the Republic

Disparities of wealth led to class tension and even violence in the late Republic. Urban populations, particularly in Rome, continued to swell with unemployed men and women from rural areas. By the first century B.C.E., Rome's population was nearly five hundred thousand, with more than half relying on the dole, public handouts of food. Through such handouts, the elite hoped to expand their patronage networks and garner popular support for their own political aspirations.

The Gracchi brothers, Tiberius (ca. 163–132 B.C.E.) and Gaius (ca. 157–121 B.C.E.), led the most famous attempts to prevent the coming social crisis. They were the sons of Cornelia (ca. 197–ca. 117 B.C.E.), the patrician daughter of Scipio, who had defeated Hannibal, and Tiberius Sempronius

Gracchus (d. 153 B.C.E.), an illustrious plebeian politician. Powerful orators and skilled politicians, the brothers served as tribunes and used their office to try to institute reforms based on principles of popular sovereignty. One of their goals was to redistribute illegally occupied public lands to the poor and landless. Most senators saw this as an attack on their own status and wealth and ultimately assassinated Tiberius in 132 B.C.E. and then Gaius in 121 B.C.E. The murder of the Gracchi and their followers precipitated further political violence and instability.

Cornelia, mother of the Gracchi, was as notable as her sons. Her behavior and honor generated much admiration and emulation. She was well educated and erudite. While her husband was alive, she hosted literary salons, where the greatest thinkers of the time came to exchange ideas. She refused to remarry after her husband's death, assuming the honored status of univira. As a widow, she raised and educated her twelve children, only three of whom reached maturity. Honored for her modesty, she reportedly told a heavily bejeweled matron that she needed no adornment; her sons were her jewels. After Tiberius's murder, she retired to her country estate outside of Naples. She continued entertaining and regaled her guests with stories of her father and her sons. According to Cicero, she never showed her grief, but spoke about her sons as if they were men of early Rome. The historian Cornelius Nepos (late first century B.C.E.) claimed to have preserved one of her letters to her younger son, Gaius. In this letter, Cornelia shows herself to be fully engaged in the political concerns of the day, willing to support the programs of her oldest son, Tiberius, but thinking that Gaius was too radical and too susceptible to the crowd's praise. Her letter demonstrates that her politics were firmly those of a patrician, despite the fact that she had married a plebeian. Although she lacked official political power, Cornelia exercised great influence, on Rome's future.[33]

The political assassinations of the Gracchi heralded even greater political strife, with the rise of client armies who were more loyal to their generals than the Senate. Gaius Marius (ca. 157–86 B.C.E.) used his military strength to intimidate the Senate into granting him favors and political office. As consul, Marius did away with property requirements for military service, opening the military to landless men, who enlisted hoping that booty and plunder would end their poverty and propel them into respectability. Lucius Cornelius Sulla (ca. 138–78 B.C.E.) was even more devastating. After great military success outside the Empire, he conquered Rome in 82 B.C.E. Fearful of Sulla's army, which had killed more than three hundred thousand men, women, and children, the Senate declared him dictator. Sulla consolidated his power through *proscription*, declaring his enemies as enemies of the state, confiscating their property, and sentencing them to exile or death. There were great rewards for catching an enemy of the state, so ambitious and unscrupulous persons turned in innocent men, creating widespread fear and sending many people into hiding.

Sulla's retirement opened the way for other military rulers. Three such men, Gnaeus Pompey (106–48 B.C.E.), Julius Caesar (100–44 B.C.E.), and Marcus Licinius Crassus (ca. 115–53 B.C.E.), each with their own client army, formed an alliance hoping to rule Rome together. However, personal ambition and mutual distrust made the triumvirate unstable. Caesar tried to strengthen it by marrying his daughter Julia to Pompey, but after Julia died in childbirth, Caesar and Pompey's relationship disintegrated. In 49 B.C.E., after his successful conquest of Gaul, Caesar returned to Rome and was elected consul without opposition. He then defeated Pompey, forcing him to retreat to Egypt. At the time, Egypt was a client state of Rome, and Egyptian rulers tried to curry favor with Rome in order to prevent outright conquest. A Greek dynasty had ruled Egypt since 332 B.C.E. When Caesar followed Pompey to Egypt, Ptolemy XIII and his sister Cleopatra VII (69–30 B.C.E.) were fighting each other for the right to rule the kingdom alone.

Cleopatra was a central and complex figure in the Roman civil wars. Because of her relationships with many Roman leaders, Roman historians often wrote negatively about her. Her enemies saw her as exotic, corrupt, beautiful, and immoral. Sarah Pomeroy argues that although she was quite unlike Roman women, she was not unusual in Ptolemaic Egypt. Like other Ptolemaic queens, she married and eliminated two of her brothers in succession in order to rule alone. She also rode horses, hunted, and fought, a list of accomplishments that further distinguished her from Roman women.[34]

Caesar met Cleopatra in 48 B.C.E. She had been aiding Pompey, believing him the stronger man and a necessary ally. Her alliance with Pompey outraged her subjects, who forced her to flee Alexandria. Caesar summoned Cleopatra and her brother to settle their differences. While Ptolemy arrived with an army, Cleopatra smuggled herself into Caesar's room in a rolled-up carpet, getting to him first and securing his favor before her brother. Plutarch, in his *Lives*, described this critical moment in their relationship, "Caesar was first captivated by this proof of Cleopatra's bold wit, and afterwards so over come by the charm of her society that he made a reconciliation between her and her brother on the condition that she should rule as his colleague in the kingdom."[35] Caesar and Cleopatra became lovers (Caesar was already married). Ptolemy and Pompey died in the ensuing violence between Egyptian and Roman forces. Cleopatra bore Caesar a son in 47 B.C.E. and went to Rome the next year to celebrate Caesar's victories. Romans despised her as a symbol of the decadent East and a threat to the Republic.

When Caesar returned to Rome, he had the Senate declare him dictator for life. This assertion of power angered his enemies, and a conspiracy formed to eliminate him. Some conspirators were motivated by jealousy, others by Republican sentiments. On March 15, 44 B.C.E. Julius Caesar was assassinated. Cleopatra fled Italy for Egypt.

The death of Caesar left a void in the government. Although many wanted to return to the Republic, too many ambitious men stood in the way. Two men in particular, Mark Antony (ca. 83–30 B.C.E.), who was Julius Caesar's fellow consul, and Octavian (63 B.C.E.–14 C.E.), Julius Caesar's adopted heir, competed for control. By the time Octavian triumphed, the Republic could not be revived.

The New Woman

The long years of civil war, political instability, and fear changed Roman culture in ways that profoundly affected women. In the fifty or so years before 1 C.E., Roman women acted with unprecedented assertiveness and with greater attention to their own needs and feelings. Some scholars argue

these "new women" were a counterpoint to the new politicians who demonstrated little respect for old ways.[36]

Sulla's proscriptions fundamentally altered relations between the paterfamilias and his charges, effectively giving wives, mothers, and slaves life and death power over their husbands, sons, and masters. Proscriptions forced them to choose between loyalty to the state or the paterfamilias, making elite Roman homes places of betrayal and suspicion. One woman threatened to turn her husband in if he fled without her, and in another instance, a former female slave, upset by the end of their sexual relationship, turned in her former master. In both cases, they used proscription to advance their interests over the interests of the paterfamilias.[37]

During the crisis of the civil war, women found new opportunities to assert their political interests. In 43 B.C.E., in order to raise money and weaken their rivals, Octavian and Mark Antony levied a tax on the personal wealth of Rome's fourteen hundred richest women. These women rebelled against the tax. At first, they employed traditional methods of influence. A group of women appealed directly to Antony's mother and wife and to Octavian's sister. When Mark Antony's wife, Fulvia (d. 40 B.C.E.), rebuffed them, they took their case to the forum where Hortensia, the daughter of the famous orator Hortensius (114–50 B.C.E.), pled:

> *As befitted women of our rank addressing a petition to you, we had recourse to the ladies of your households; but having been treated as did not befit us, at the hands of Fulvia, we have been driven by her to the forum. You have already deprived us of our fathers, our sons, our husbands, and our brothers whom you accused of having wronged you; if you take away our property also, you reduce us to a condition unbecoming our birth, our manners, our sex. If we have done you wrong, as you say our husbands have, proscribe us as you do them. But if we women have not voted any of you public enemies have not torn down your houses, destroyed your army or led another one against you; if we have not hindered you in obtaining offices and honours,—why do we*

> *share the penalty when we did not share the guilt? (Appian,* Roman History, *IV.5.32)*

Hortensia's speech emphasized women's lack of political power and the impact of the civil war on them. Her words were so persuasive that the Senate reduced the number of taxed women to four hundred. Both Fulvia's rebuff and Hortensia's protest reflect women's emerging political influence.[38]

The new woman is also evident in the Roman literature of this period. In his histories, Livy juxtaposed assertive women alongside traditional ones and explored the nature of women's influence. His portraits were not always positive, but taken together they show women rejecting the ideal of a sheltered and demure life. Often women claimed the same sexual license as young men, seeking out lovers and dispensing with them when they tired of their company. The poems of Valerius Catullus (ca. 85–ca. 54 B.C.E.) trace the rise and fall of his relationship with Lesbia, a married woman, who ultimately cast him off in favor of another man. Unlike the sexually adventurous Lesbia, the poet was committed to love and willing to explore his feelings about love. His mistress's behavior might be scandalous, but it gave him the opportunity to express his emotions. In many ways, it was a kind of sexual role reversal.[39]

Sulpicia (first century B.C.E.), one of the few known female writers whose works survive, expressed similarly daring emotions in her elegiac love poetry. We do not know Sulpicia's age or marital status or when she wrote these poems. She portrays herself in her works as a young, unmarried woman of education and elite status. She engages in the same vivid descriptions of her physical and emotional involvement in love affairs as Catullus. Sulpicia provides an extraordinary and innovative representation of a woman's emotions.

> *Whatever day, Cerinthus [her lover], gave you to me, this day will have to be blessed by me and always celebrated among the holidays. When you were born the Fates sang of a new form of love's slavery for women, and gave you proud reams of power. But I am set on fire more than all other women. This thrills me, Cerinthus, that I am ablaze, there is a shared fire in you that has spread from me. . . . Birthday spirit, stay, gladly*

> *receive offering of incense and look favorably upon my vows, if only when he thinks of me, he is heated with passion . . . and may you not be unfair, Venus; either let each of us submit equally in bondage to love's slavery or remove my own bonds.*[40]

Compared with the women who came before her, such as Cornelia, Sulpicia expressed surprising sensuality and emotional intensity.[41]

Scholars have speculated about whether these new ideas were widespread or merely a passing literary fashion. The fact that writers such as Cicero repeatedly commented on the sexual exploits of elite women suggests that Roman women were experiencing an unprecedented degree of sexual freedom and self-expression. Scholars have also asserted that Greek literary influences coupled with political and social instability created a climate that permitted women to openly seek sexual satisfaction and gratification.[42]

Mark Antony's Women: Octavia, Fulvia, and Cleopatra

After the assassination of Julius Caesar, Octavian and Mark Antony vied for control of Rome. Although Octavian defeated Antony at the Battle of Modena in 43 B.C.E., Julius Caesar's assassins opposed Octavian, hoping to restore the Republic, which forced Octavian to join with Antony to defeat the Republicans. In 42 B.C.E., Octavian and Antony triumphed and Antony toured the eastern provinces to collect tribute and demonstrate his power. Women were not only victims and pawns in these violent politics; they were also key players, negotiating between factions, arguing politics, and in one case even raising an army. Still, Roman men tended to understand women's contributions solely in terms of images and symbols that reflected Rome's overall moral health and well-being.

Mark Antony was married three times, and his political career was closely connected to the women in his life. His first wife, Fulvia, was quite wealthy. She had been married twice before and took an active role in politics. Her first public appearance was in 52 B.C.E. as a witness at the trial of her first husband's murderer. It was a political murder and Fulvia's eloquent expression of pain and grief outdid Cicero's defense of the accused. Fulvia appeared in public several more times on Antony's behalf during his struggle against Octavian. When the Senate tried to declare him a public enemy, Fulvia visited the senators hoping to convince them to support Antony. The morning of the vote, she appeared in mourning clothes, as was the custom of female relatives of criminals. Usually this display was designed to garner support for the condemned criminal. Fulvia had a subtler goal; she directly challenged the constitutionality of the Senate's vote because it would not allow Antony to defend himself. When Antony left Italy shortly after, Fulvia appeared before Antony's soldiers with her children urging them to remain loyal to him until he returned. As war between Antony and Octavian became certain, she raised military reinforcements for him. She led the assault herself, wearing a sword, haranguing the solders, and holding strategy sessions. She then joined Antony in the Gulf of Corinth, where she died. Because she was on the losing side, Tacitus (55–117 C.E.) and Cicero portray her as grasping, lustful, and manipulative.[43]

Antony's second wife, Octavia (d. 11 B.C.E.), was the sister of his rival Octavian and quite different from Fulvia. Octavia's marriage to Antony was an attempt to unite the two men, similar to Pompey's marriage to Julius Caesar's daughter, Julia. Historians portray Octavia as a traditional, loyal wife who put the state's needs ahead of her own concerns. Octavia married Antony in 39 B.C.E., bore him several children, and raised not only her own children, but his children by Fulvia as well. In 37 B.C.E., Antony married Cleopatra in an Egyptian ceremony that allowed for polygamy. In an effort to win back his support, Octavia sent him military supplies for his Armenian campaign in 35 B.C.E; however, he continued to ignore her. Octavian ordered her to divorce Antony because of his poor treatment, but she refused. Ultimately, Antony repudiated her for Cleopatra in 32 B.C.E.

Antony's third wife was Cleopatra of Egypt. After Julius Caesar's assassination, Cleopatra returned to Egypt and refused to take sides with either Octavian or Antony. Antony met Cleopatra in 41 B.C.E., while touring the eastern provinces. He wanted tribute and an explanation for why she had supported the Republicans. Cleopatra needed an alliance with the new Roman strong man. According to Plutarch, Cleopatra made their meeting an elaborately staged event. Cleopatra sailed to meet Antony in a barge with a gilded stern, purple sails, and rowers who kept time to music. She dressed herself like Venus and her maids like sea nymphs. Antony was captivated. However, the Roman sources are no kinder about Cleopatra's relationship with Antony than they were about her relationship with Julius Caesar. They claim that she seduced Antony, who agreed to rule with her rather than conquer Egypt. When Antony succumbed to Cleopatra, Roman historians saw him as emasculated by a voracious woman. Men were supposed to dominate women, not the other way around.

Antony stayed in Egypt and waged a series of military campaigns against various Eastern kingdoms. Cleopatra financed them and he was successful enough that his union with Cleopatra and his own military strength threatened Octavian back in Rome. In 32 B.C.E., when Antony repudiated Octavia, he made his will in favor of his Egyptian children by Cleopatra, and he requested an Egyptian burial. Romans considered this a betrayal and turned against him. Octavian declared war on Cleopatra, conquering Egypt two years later. Antony and Cleopatra chose suicide rather than face capture and public humiliation.

The different roles that Antony's wives played in Roman politics illustrate the tensions surrounding women's political activity. Fulvia exhibited the independence of the "new woman," while Octavia fulfilled traditional expectations for wives but was ultimately humiliated. Cleopatra's needs as the ruler of Egypt put her in the position of having to challenge Roman domination. The differences in cultural traditions between Rome and Egypt made her a target of vicious gossip and Roman condemnation.

The Imperial Family and the New Morality

With the defeat of Mark Antony, Octavian ruled Rome alone. Although he had no intention of restoring the Republic, he was savvy enough to use its images, titles, and institutions, such as the Senate, to foster a sense of continuity with the past even as he forged an imperial government. Octavian took the name of Caesar Augustus and cobbled together a list of offices and titles. Although he created the title *princeps,* or "first citizen," rather than emperor, he substantially decreased the Senate's power. The women in his life, particularly his wife, Livia (58 B.C.E.–29 C.E.), and his daughter, Julia (ca. 39 B.C.E.–14 C.E.), had to live according to his ideas about morality and Roman society. Augustus tried to restore the traditional behavior of the Republic by promoting marriage and female chastity. To accomplish this, he gave new legal rights to wives and mothers.[44]

Augustus's reform program was both conservative and innovative. Much of it was enshrined in new laws, first issued in 18 B.C.E. and then reissued as the *Lex Papia Poppaea* in 9 C.E. These laws applied to both free and freedwomen. They released free women who produced three living children from their tutors or guardians. A freedwoman with four children could be free of guardianship and able to make a will, thus removing her from a freed slave's legal and financial obligations to a former master. To further encourage marriage, the laws made it difficult for men and women who remained unmarried or childless to inherit property. Adultery had been a family issue, as the law defined adultery as sex with a married woman or a woman who "belonged" to a man, such as a daughter. The new laws made adultery a criminal charge that anyone, even someone outside the family, could bring before the courts; however, a married woman who had been raped could no longer be charged with adultery. Sex with female slaves, prostitutes, and barmaids remained beyond the laws' concern. Augustus did not design these legal changes, sometimes referred to as the emancipation of women, to create equality between men and women; rather, he wished to restore moral attitudes that he believed Rome had lost during the civil wars.[45]

Virgil's (70–19 B.C.E.) great Roman epic, *The Aeneid,* described marriage as a service to the state. In this poem, the hero, Aeneas, was unable to keep a wife until he fulfilled his destiny of founding Rome. When he met Dido, the widowed queen of Carthage, she fell madly in love with him, despite her oath of loyalty and chastity to her deceased husband. She made him her co-ruler of Carthage, much as Cleopatra had done with Mark Antony. Yet, unlike Antony, Aeneas did not succumb to that exotic "foreign" life. He left Dido, telling her that his duty was to the future of Rome, not to the marriage bed. In her grief, Dido killed herself. For the Roman audience, the message was that marriage was not a private matter between a man and a woman; it was a service to the state.[46] Yet at the same time, Virgil and other writers of the period, such as Livy, understood women's behavior as having political consequence. Their repetition of the legends of the rape of the Sabines and of Lucretia were in part a search for the meaning behind women's behavior and an attempt to make sense of the contradictions between ideals of women's behavior and women's actual behavior.

Augustus presented his own family as a model for his new morality. Artists depicted the imperial family, complete with children, as the guarantor of peace, fecundity, and prosperity. The Augustan Peace Altar in Rome showed the imperial family dressed in traditional Roman clothing: Augustus wore a toga and Livia wore a stola, a dress worn over a tunic, rather than the Greek styles currently popular in the first century. Women did not wear the stola until marriage. The stola symbolized the modesty and fertility expected of a married woman. Augustus felt that Roman women had abandoned these traditions in favor of personal pleasure. Placing traditional clothes on the figure of Livia represented her as the *mater patriae,* the mother of the country, whose fertility and honor served the state. Beyond these images, Livia created the role of the princeps wife. She dedicated temples, interceded on behalf of people in trouble, and received local and foreign dignitaries. She had the right to use a special ceremonial vehicle, the *carpentum,* to move about Rome, usually reserved for Vestal Virgins and evocative of elite women of the past. She was responsible for the hostage children of princes, sent as insurance of their father's good behavior toward Rome. Caring for them elaborated on her role as mater patriae. Her public persona drew simultaneously from traditional ideas of women as keepers of the house and from male political duties and privileges.[47]

Livia's honors gave her considerable political power, which she used to promote her own agenda. Palace gossip accused her of manipulating Augustus and resorting to poison to remove enemies. She hoped to convince Augustus to make

Tiberius (r. 14–37 C.E.), her son by her first marriage, his heir. Tacitus even suggests that she murdered Augustus. Whether she did or not, Tiberius succeeded to the throne in 14 C.E. At Augustus's death, his reported last words were "Livia remember our marriage and farewell."[48] When she died in 29, she was celebrated for her chastity and modesty and was deified.

Augustus expected his daughter, Julia, to uphold imperial ideas of morality at the cost of her own happiness. Roman writers continually gossiped about Julia. Although she dutifully married three times to suit her father's political needs and bore five living children, she reportedly took many lovers, especially while pregnant so as to hide her actions. One writer claimed she also worked as a prostitute. Angered by her sexual promiscuity, Augustus publicly denounced her and exiled her to a barren island. In the public mind, she was the first *meretrix Augusta*, the imperial whore, in many ways a counterpart to the image of Cleopatra. We can also see her as a victim of a changing political climate and as paying the penalty for embracing the attitudes of the Roman new woman.[49]

The dramatic political upheavals that ended the Republic expanded women's public roles. Although moralists might have wished that women remained at home, women, especially elite ones, pleaded before courts, engaged in politics, and followed their emotional desires. Augustus's moral reforms claimed to return Rome to the old ways in an effort to lessen the impact of his own radical break with Rome's past. Subsequent emperors and empresses continued to use Augustus's image of the imperial family as moral standard for the Empire, which further idealized women's behavior and widened the gap between expectations and practice (see **Women's Lives: Messalina, Roman Empress**).

WOMEN IN IMPERIAL ROME, 14 C.E.–200 C.E.

Imperial Rome was more diverse and mobile than Republican Rome. Wives could accompany their husbands to colonial posts, and by the third century, the emperor permitted soldiers to marry. Women also increasingly moved out of the countryside and into cities in search of work. As a result, women spread Roman culture around the Empire and encountered new ideas about how they should behave, making it difficult for them to conform to traditional Roman gender expectations. Further changes came in the third century, as Roman writers began to reconsider some traditional assumptions about women and women's bodies.

Women and Territorial Expansion

By the first century C.E., Rome's territorial holdings and colonies spread across the Mediterranean from Spain and North Africa and up into what are now France and Switzerland (see Map 3.2). However, Romanization was a piecemeal process that affected various classes and groups differently. Roman rule communicated expectations about women's status and behavior to people in the conquered areas, and Roman women brought Roman lifestyles and expectations with them when they accompanied their husbands to the colonies.

In 21 C.E., the Senate allowed commanders to bring their wives to their military postings, and by 24, the Senate granted the same right to provincial governors. Although the law had prohibited soldiers from marrying since probably the time of Augustus, they frequently formed permanent unions with women.[50] Some of these families followed their soldiers from post to post despite their lack of legal status. Finally, in 197, Emperor Septimus Severus (r. 193–211) permitted soldiers to marry, making Roman women more common in the colonies and creating many couples of mixed ethnicity. For example, Vibia Pacata, who was probably born in Africa, married Flavious Vereundus, a soldier born in Pannonia (modern-day Hungary). Both died in Northern Britain.[51]

The presence of families in the colonies meant the introduction of Roman domestic culture and behavior. Women brought clothing, jewelry, and household items with them. Roman administrators built Roman-style houses and engaged in Roman activities such as going to the theater and the public baths. A rare letter from a Roman woman living in northern England illuminates

Messalina, Roman Empress

Messalina was one of the most notorious empresses of the early Roman Empire. Through her relationship with her husband she quickly acquired power and influence that she used for her own gain, not the benefit of the state. Descriptions of her also show that Romans despised her and linked her behavior to the moral health of Rome. Roman writers attributed her behavior to the bad influence of Eastern decadence that was corrupting Roman life and power.

Messalina was the great-niece of Augustus. She grew up in the court of the emperor Caligula (r. 37–41), a cruel and sexually promiscuous emperor at best and a psychopath at worst. Messalina reportedly lost her virginity to him at an early age. Life in Caligula's court taught Messalina a great deal about political intrigue, self-promotion, and sexual promiscuity. When Messalina was around fifteen years old, Caligula married her to his uncle Claudius (10 B.C.E.–54 C.E.), a man of about fifty. Claudius had a birth defect, which gave him a wobbling head, spindly legs, and a speech impediment. Messalina resented marrying such an old and unattractive man; nevertheless, she dutifully bore him a daughter and a son.

In 41, Caligula's guards murdered him and proclaimed Claudius emperor, making Messalina the empress. Claudius refused to give her the title of Augusta, a slight that always upset her. However, Claudius did grant her the right to ride in the carpentum, sit in the front seat at gladiatorial games, and hold independent audiences. Messalina used these privileges to gain great wealth and promote her favorites and lovers. One of her supporters, the consul L. Vitellius was so taken with her that he asked for one of her shoes. He carried it with him at all times, frequently taking it out to fondle and kiss. Claudius was unable to deny her anything and reportedly sentenced people to death at her insistence.

Roman historians make much of Messalina's sexual exploits, seeing them as evidence of Eastern corruption imported by Caligula. They reported that she took many lovers and liked to work as a prostitute under the name of Lycisca. Her sexual appetites were supposedly so great that when she held a contest to see which woman could tire out the most men, she won. She made women commit adultery while their

aspects of Roman colonial life. In this letter, Claudia Severa invites her friend Lepidina to her birthday party.

> *Claudia Severa to her Lepidina greetings. On 11 September, sister, for the day of the celebration of my birthday, I give you a warm invitation to make sure that you come to us, to make the day more enjoyable for me by your arrival, if you are present (?). Give my greetings to your Cerialis. My Aelius and my little son send him their greetings. I shall expect you, sister. Farewell, sister, my dearest soul, as I hope to prosper, and hail. To Sulpicia Lepidina, wife of Cerialis, from Severa.*[52]

The language that Claudia uses in her letter shows her to be educated and likely familiar with the kind of elegiac poetry that Sulpicia wrote. Back in Rome, a birthday party would have been a family occasion supervised by women. By calling Lepidina "sister" and by inviting her to a birthday party, Claudia forged intimate and familial-like ties with Lepidina, perhaps trying to re-create the family she had left behind for this remote outpost.[53]

Rome's colonies were very diverse. Britain, Germany, and Gaul were home to Iron Age peoples who lived in clans or tribes, while Egypt was a sophisticated and literate society with a high level of technological development. No matter how far from home, the Romans built towns and fur-

husbands watched, and if anyone complained, she had them arrested on charges of adultery, still a crime under Augustus's laws. Claudius remained unaware of her behavior because, says Cassius Dio, she kept him plied with female slaves and bribed or punished those who could inform on her.

Rome's population held Messalina in contempt for abandoning traditional Roman values of conservatism, morality, and decency, the values that Livia had publicly promoted. Moreover, Claudius's reputation suffered because many felt that Messalina took advantage of him.

In 48 C.E., during one of Claudius's absences from Rome, Messalina arranged a bigamous marriage with Caius Silius, "the handsomest man in Rome" (Tacitus, *Annals,* XI.12). At Messalina's insistence, Silius divorced his wife and agreed to marry her. Messalina turned her marriage ceremony into a Bacchanalian orgy, another sign of her decadence and irreverence. Messalina's enemies, led by a freedman named Narcissus, informed Claudius of her betrayal. When Messalina's supporters could not rally Claudius to their side, Silius and other supporters were convicted of treason and adultery and were executed or allowed to commit suicide.

Claudius asked to hear Messalina's defense personally, but fearing that he would forgive her out of love, Narcissus reinterpreted the message as a command to execute her. When told of her death, Claudius asked no questions and allowed the Senate to remove her name from all public and private places. In compensation, Narcissus received honors that made him eligible for the Senate.

Messalina's story exemplifies what Roman historians saw as the problem of women's influence in politics. The imperial family was supposed to serve as a model of good behavior for the Roman people. An emperor who could not control his household was likely to lose control of his empire. This was, in fact, what happened. Claudius's fourth wife, also his niece, murdered him to make room for her own son by a previous marriage. He became the Emperor Nero.

Sandra Joshel, "Female Desire and the Discourse of Empires: Tacitus's Messalina," in *Roman Sexualities,* ed. Judith P. Hallett and Marilyn B. Skinner (Princeton: Princeton University Press, 1998), 221–254; Suetonius, "Claudius," in *The Twelve Caesars;* and Tacitus, *Annals.*

---

nished them with Roman amenities. They constructed baths with elaborate mosaics and plumbing to pipe in the water from the natural hot springs in the city of Bath in Britain and an amphitheater in Caerwent, Gwent (Wales).[54] Nevertheless, life in Roman Britain was difficult. Excavations of cemeteries, such as Poundbury, Dorset, show that inhabitants suffered from parasitic infections, lead poisoning, and untreated broken bones. Poundbury is also notable for the high mortality of young adults. Archaeologists assume that the women died in childbirth, but they have no explanation for the large number of dead young men.[55]

Life in Egypt appears to have been easier, and it is certainly better documented than Britain. As in much of the premodern world, 50 percent of all children died before the age of five, and only 1 percent could expect to live to age eighty. Disease was only one factor; malnutrition, accidents, and disease also shortened men's and women's lives. Women experienced the additional dangers of childbirth. Women who survived to the age of fifteen had an average life expectancy of forty-eight years, while men could expect to live to fifty-five years old.[56]

Roman rule in Egypt changed the lives of women there. The Romans reformed Egyptian marital practices, bringing them into line with their own. Surviving marriage contracts suggest that nearly a quarter of Ptolemaic Egyptian marriages were within families and many were between

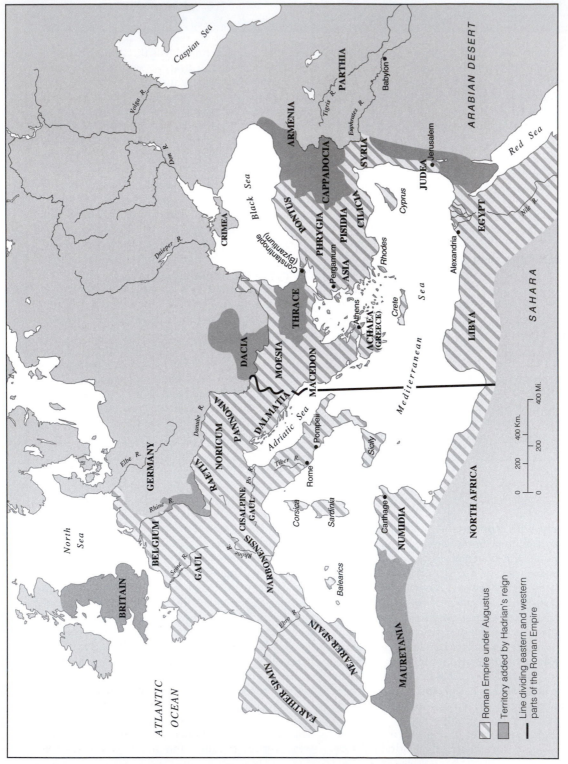

Map 3.2 **Roman Conquests Under the Empire.** Imperial expansion raised the standard of living for women and allowed them to move more easily around the Empire.

FIRST-CENTURY TOMBSTONE OF UMMA WHO LIVED IN NORICUM (MODERN AUSTRIA). Umma's tombstone shows a blending of Germanic and Roman customs. The tombstone is Roman in style, but her hat is Germanic. *(Niederoesterreichisches Landesmuseum, St. Poelten, Austria/Erich Lessing/Art Resource, NY.)*

siblings. This arrangement allowed families to maintain control of family land and alleviated the need for dowries for their daughters. The Romans outlawed such marriages, and endogamous and incestuous marriages significantly declined. Dowries also became more common as a result.[57]

Regular revolts against Roman rule made life in the provinces violent and uncertain. Many a Roman general made his fame by suppressing a provincial rebellion. Women were often caught in the middle of these revolts, but in two instances, British women played leading roles. In 47, Boudicca, queen of the Iceni, a tribe in eastern England, led a violent revolt against the Romans. Her husband, Prasutagus, was a client king of Rome. We have two different accounts of this

revolt. According to Tacitus, when Prasutagus died in 47, he left his kingdom to his two daughters and the Roman emperor, Nero (r. 54–68 C.E.). Roman soldiers then turned on Boudicca, flogged her, and raped her daughters. Boudicca then led an army of Iceni who sacked Roman London, massacring the Roman inhabitants. Cassius Dio's account makes no mention of the rape, but claims the rebellion was over money that Rome had confiscated from the Iceni.

Cartimandua's revolt against the British shows how Roman intervention affected tribal politics. Cartimandua was leader of the Brigantes in northern England, another client kingdom of Rome. She helped Rome secure its northern border, even turning over tribal members who challenged Rome's authority. In 57, she and her husband had a falling-out, and some of the Brigantes supported her husband. The Romans helped put down the revolt. In 69, she divorced her husband and married his armor bearer. Her troops deserted her and followed her husband. Tacitus calls Cartimandua's behavior scandalous, but the Romans rescued her again. This time, they put her former husband in charge of the Brigantes. Unable to keep her people in order, the Romans no longer found Cartimandua useful.

It is difficult to separate out the truth from Roman propaganda and moralizing. Romans such as Tacitus were uncomfortable with women as political leaders. It was also standard practice for Rome to work through sympathetic local tribes. In both conflicts, we see the toll that Roman domination took on local populations. They faced violent soldiers, new taxes and financial obligations, and insensitivity to their local customs.[58]

Women's Work and Urban Life

During the Empire's first century, Roman-style urbanization spread throughout the Empire, the economy expanded, and the quality of life for much of the population improved. Although the Romans glorified rural simplicity as the source of Roman virtue, they flocked to live in cities. Urban life was one of great contrasts in wealth and experiences. Wealthy women had elaborate palaces and slaves, whereas lower-class urban women worked at manufacturing and in the service economy, in addition to their domestic obligations.

Although women are not well represented in many occupations, few seem to have been completely closed to them.

The ruins of the city of Pompeii provide a unique view of urban women's lives. Pompeii was a port city in the Campania region of Italy at the mouth of the Sarnus River. It had been in Rome's political orbit since the fourth century, but culturally it looked to Greece. During the civil wars, Sulla settled at least two thousand of his veterans and their families in the city, which brought more Roman culture to the city, including a new amphitheater, and the shift to Latin instead of the local language. When Mount Vesuvius suddenly erupted in 79 C.E., it destroyed the city, preserving its ruins in ash and lava. Although most people escaped, the eruption caught some individuals in the midst of mundane activities and preserved the tools, artifacts, and settings of daily life.

Scholars estimate that approximately sixty-five hundred people lived in Pompeii, but we do not know what percentage of Pompeii's women were slaves, freed, or free women. Most women in Pompeii worked in service occupations such as midwifery, hairdressing, food selling, and clothing and jewelry retail. Poor women took up seasonal work in vineyards outside the city or harvested grain. Other part-time work included employment as a professional mourner at funerals. Whether in the countryside or the city, women's work was understood as a moral statement about her, her husband, and her family. Even when a woman worked in her family's business, society praised her as a mother and as a pious housekeeper, who worked with wool, cared for the children, and prepared the food.

Patronage ties between former slaves and their masters made it difficult for rural women migrating into the city to find work. At the same time, patronage networks were one of the ways that the poor and working classes interacted with the elite. For example, the well-to-do Pompeian woman

MIDWIFE'S SIGN FROM A TOMB IN THE ISOLA SACRA NECROPOLIS (MID-SECOND CENTURY C.E.). This terra cotta relief might have advertised the services of a midwife whose salary would have supported her and her family. *(Museo Ostiense, Ostia, Italy/Erich Lessing/Art Resource, NY.)*

Eumachia served as a priestess to one of Pompeii's temples of Venus and donated a building to the fullers (cloth workers). The fullers in turn honored her with a statue and commemorated her gift in an inscription over the door to their building.[59]

Many poor women ended up as prostitutes. Roman cities tended to have many brothels, generally staffed by slaves, but also by freed slaves and other free men and women unable to support themselves by other means. Some brothels were luxurious, but most were dank and cramped, with little light or ventilation. The graffiti in Pompeii provides ample and vivid evidence of a thriving sex trade. Clients recorded on walls and benches their impressions of the women who served them. Some women were especially noted for their willingness to perform particular sexual acts; others were known for their beauty or physical abnormalities. Two graffiti celebrate the prostitute Novellia Primigenia of Nuceria. "In Nuceria, near Porta Romana, in the district of Venus, ask for Novellia Primigenia" and "Health to Primigenia of Nuceria. For just one hour I'd like to be the stone of this ring, to give to you to moisten it with your mouth, the kisses I have impressed on it."[60] Roman men's desire for prostitutes made the sex trade an easy option for women moving into the city.[61]

To distract the poor from their difficult lives, the wealthy provided regular distributions of free food, and entertainment in the form of gladiator shows. Gladiators fought each other or wild animals to the death. These bloody and violent shows grew more popular during the Empire, and donors of Pompeii's new amphitheater intended it to hold such shows. The rich hosted these shows to celebrate a daughter's marriage, a son's coming of age, or a successful military campaign. Successful games increased a host's reputation and signaled civic commitment and generosity. The majority of gladiators were men, but female gladiators began to appear in the late Republic and became common enough to provoke the satirist Juvenal (first century C.E.) into mocking them. "Look at the noises she makes when she drives home the blows her trainer showed her, at the weight of her helmet, how solidly she sits on her haunches (like the binding around a thick tree) . . ." (*Satires* 6. 111). Their exact role in the arena is unclear, but in one instance at least, women fought with swords.

Later laws forbade women from fighting in single combat, suggesting that at one point they had. Life as a female gladiator and performer apparently became so popular that in 19 C.E. the emperor Tiberius passed a law prohibiting elite women from becoming entertainers.[62]

Elite Women and Urban Life

The urban elite lived in lavish houses and engaged in the pleasures and diversions of city life, such as theater performances, shopping, politics, public baths, and a myriad of religious and social obligations. The poet Sulpicia celebrated the greater attractions of urban life in one of her poems. "My birthday approaches, and I will have to spend it in sorrow in the nasty country and without Cerinthus (her lover). What is nicer than the city? Or is a farmhouse a fit place for a girl- or a freezing river around Arezzo?"[63] However, for elite women, enjoying the distractions of the city meant going out in public, an act that could harm their reputations. Elite women who followed traditional morality faced hours of inactivity and tedium, a difficult option when faced with urban amusements.

The elite adorned their lavish houses with elaborate murals, decorative courtyards, and large gardens. In the elite houses of Pompeii, the images that greeted visitors depicted scenes from Roman history and mythology. Some of the scenes were explicitly erotic or violent. For example, at the House of Menandro one of the rooms off the atrium contains a mural of scenes from the Trojan War, specifically the rape of Cassandra and the return of Helen to Menelaus so that he could rape her. These graphic scenes were popular with the emperor Nero, who was known for his dissolute and ruthless nature. These scenes allowed the artist to depict naked women and male domination, images that promoted the male house owner's role as a powerful man who kept his house in order and kept up with politics and current artistic styles. Such scenes also allowed the viewer to participate in the domination of women, and depending on the sex and status of the viewer, gain a sense of superiority or submission from the image.[64]

The elites hosted musical performances, literary salons, political debates, and large banquets in their houses. In the preface to his work *Illustrious Lives* (first century B.C.E.), Cornelius Nepos, a contemporary and friend of Cicero, wrote, "No Roman thinks it shameful to take his wife to a dinner party. As mistress of the household the wife occupies the place of honor and, as hostess, presides of its social life."[65] Indeed, the banquet was a chance for the host to display wealth and largess. The host served the best wines and food, and he or she expected the guests to lecture on a subject, play an instrument, or recite literature. Banquets lasted long into the night, with wine flowing freely long after the food was gone.

The senatorial class did not work. Laws specifically prevented them from engaging in trade, or working with their hands. Instead, they lived off the proceeds of their agricultural lands. Elites held those who worked with their hands in contempt, even as moralists condemned the leisurely and luxurious lifestyle of the senatorial class. Pliny the Younger's (61–113 C.E.) letters about why the widow Ummidia had been a risky guardian for her grandson underscore his disgust at such lifestyles:

> *She kept a troupe of pantomime actors and used to indulge them more freely than was suitable in a lady of rank. . . . When she was passing her grandson into my keeping for training, she told me herself that, as a woman of leisure, she was in the habit of relaxing with gambling games and that it was her practice to watch her own pantomime performers. (Letters 7.24)*

Elite women were decorations that adorned the family, and their behavior brought it either honor or shame.

Although some women supervised household slaves and oversaw their children's education, a wealthy household had slaves to perform these tasks, and many Roman matrons lived a life of enforced idleness and boredom. Elite women did not even nurse their own infants; instead, their husbands contracted wet nurses to live with the family. Men complained of tensions between new wives with few duties and slaves responsible for running the household. Women were not expected to leave the house unaccompanied, and their movements were supervised not only by older family members but also by a retinue of slaves.

Because elite women controlled money and property, many found ways to promote their interests and indulge their tastes. Ummidia did more than gamble and amuse herself with acrobats. She built an amphitheater in her hometown of Casinum, refurbished the one given by her father, and donated a temple. Through these gifts, Ummidia shaped a public reputation. She honored her father, promoted her family's religious concerns, and established her reputation as a civic patron. Women property owners created their own patronage networks and used their wealth to promote their families' prestige.[66]

Property ownership required women's oversight, even if they hired on-site supervisors. Cicero's wife, Terentia, owned two blocks of tenements in Rome. She also owned some forests near Tusculum and a farm that she nearly sold to offset the family's financial problems when Cicero was sent into political exile during the civil wars. She seemed to have conducted most of her financial dealings without Cicero's interference, and when their thirty-year marriage came to an end, Cicero accused her of embezzlement. Although the charges may have been the result of bitterness over their marriage, his accusations underscore Terentia's financial independence.

Women and Roman Philosophy

With conquest came access to new ideas. The Romans were particularly interested in Greek philosophy and avidly copied Greek manuscripts. Most Roman philosophy derived from Aristotle and did not advance beyond his understanding of women's moral and physical inferiority. However, when Roman philosophers addressed how individuals could serve the state or the relationship between morality and the state, they occasionally considered women and their role in society. In the second century, medical knowledge began to diverge from Aristotle and offered new insights into women's moral capacities and physiology.

Augustus's new morality owed much to Stoicism, the Greek philosophy that most influenced Roman society. As we saw in Chapter 2, Stoicism advocated happiness through the pursuit of virtue. In striving for this goal, men were to practice moderation in all things, especially eating, sleeping, and sex. Heightened emotions and sexual pleasure should be curbed for the pursuit of more important matters. Stoics believed that the mind should master the body. The emperor Marcus Aurelius (r. 161–180), following Stoic ideas, waited until he was an adult before losing his virginity, as a sign of his control over his body. This behavior differed from that of most elite men who learned that sex was power and that active, even predatory sex with women, slaves, boys, and prostitutes displayed their masculinity. Attitudes toward women in Roman Stoicism derived largely from Aristotle. Marcus Aurelius used the term "womanish" in a derogatory way, associating women with weakness and a lack of control over passions.[67]

Stoic philosopher Musonious Rufus (ca. 30–101) offered a very different vision of women. He believed that both husbands and wives were critical to the creation of a perfect marriage. In his treatise on "What Is the Chief End of Marriage?" he states, "For without sympathy of mind and character between husband and wife, what marriage can be good, what partnership advantageous?"[68] He also considered marriage as the foundation of society, and one in which both men and women played central roles. "That the home or the city does not depend upon women alone or upon men alone, but upon their union with each other is evident. One could find no other association more necessary nor more pleasant than that of men and women. For what man is so devoted to his friend as a loving wife is to her husband?"[69] Musonious was unusual in asserting women's emotional and moral importance to the union. Women were more than simply property— husbands and wives owned everything in common, even each other's bodies. He believed that this concept of marriage was the cornerstone of Roman society, the city, and in fact, the human race.[70]

To achieve the ideals of a virtuous life, Musonious advocated that women be educated. According to his treatise entitled, "Should Women Study Philosophy?" women had the same capabilities for reason, wisdom, and virtue as men, but these qualities revealed themselves differently in women's actions and lives. Musonious explained how a woman's life could display the classical virtues of justice, courage, and self-control:

> *Let us examine in detail the qualities which are suitable for a woman who would lead a good life, for it will appear that each one of them would accrue to her most readily from the study of philosophy. In the first place, a woman must be a good housekeeper; that is a careful accountant of all that pertains to the welfare of her house and capable of directing the household slaves. It is my contention that these are the very qualities which would be present particularly in the woman who studies philosophy, since obviously each of them is a part of life, and philosophy is nothing other than knowledge about life.*[71]

Musonious went on to explain that household management requires women to exercise self-control, avoid recklessness, and be a sympathetic helpmate to her husband. The cultivation of all these qualities required the study of philosophy.

Although the Stoics did not move much beyond Greek thought, by the second century C.E., two medical writers challenged some of Aristotle's ideas about male and female physiology. Their observations about women would influence the evolution of Western medicine for centuries to come.

Soranus (98?–138?), a medical practitioner from Ephesus, wrote twenty books on medicine and anatomy that were innovative for their emphasis and reliance on empirical observation (see **Sources from the Past: Soranus's Gynecology**). One of his major contributions to women's health was the connection he posited between a mother's habits and the formation of the fetus. He specifically saw alcohol consumption as harming the fetus. To encourage moderation in medical treatments, he made the distinction between an abortifacient and a contraceptive, advocating the latter as healthier for the woman. Soranus also respected women's knowledge of their bodies, explaining that menstruation flow varied and women would know what was appropriate for them. Soranus also offered advice on child-rearing and nursing. He believed that mothers should nurse their own children because it was healthier and would foster a closer bond between mother and child. When this was not possible, he urged mothers to consider carefully the wet nurse's character because she

Soranus's *Gynecology*

In this selection from Soranus's Gynecology, we can see how he combines Aristotle's theories of the four humors with observations he himself has made based on his own medical practice. Soranus also argues from analogy, likening conception to planting a seed in the earth, and arguing that women prepare themselves carefully like the farmer carefully prepares the soil for planting.

x. What Is the Best Time for Fruitful Intercourse?

36.   Just as every season is not propitious for sowing extraneous seed upon the land for the purpose of bringing forth fruit, so in humans too not every time is suitable for conception of the seed discharged during intercourse. Now so that the desired end may be attained through the well-timed practice of intercourse, it will be useful to state the proper time. The best time for fruitful intercourse is when menstruation is ending and abating, when urge and appetite for coitus are present, when the body is neither in want nor too congested and heavy from drunkenness and indigestion, and after the body has been rubbed down and a little food been eaten and when a pleasant state exists in every respect. "When menstruation is ending and abating," for the time before menstruation is not suitable, the uterus already being overburdened and in an unresponsive state because of the ingress of material and incapable of carrying on two motions contrary to each other, one for the excretion of material, the other for receiving. Just as the stomach when overburdened with some kind of material and turned by nausea is disposed to vomit what oppresses it and is averse to receiving food, so according to the same principle, the uterus, being congested at the time of menstruation, is well adapted for the evacuation of the blood which has flowed into it, but is unfitted for the reception and retention of the seed. And the time when menstruation starts is to be dismissed because of the general tension, as we have said; likewise the time when menstruation is increasing and at its height because the seed becomes very moist and gushes forth together with the great quantity of excreted blood. Just as a wound does not unite if accompanied by a hemorrhage, and even if united temporarily opens again when the hemorrhage sets in, neither can the seed unite with and grow into the fundus of the uterus when it is repelled by the bloody substance excreted therefrom. Consequently, the only suitable time is at the waning of the menses, for the uterus has been lightened and warmth and moisture are imparted in right measure. For again, it is not possible for the seed to adhere unless the uterus has first been roughened and scraped [as it were] in its fundus. Now just as in sick people food taken during a remission and before the paroxysm [is retained], but is ejected by vomiting if taken during the paroxysm itself, in the same manner the seed too is safely retained if offered when the menses are abating. But if some women have conceived at another time, especially when menstruating a short while, one must not pay attention to the outcome in a few, but must point out the proper time as derived from scientific considerations.

37.   We added "when the urge and appetite for intercourse are present." Just as without appetite it is impossible for the seed to be discharged by the male, in the same manner, without appetite it cannot be conceived by the female. And as food swallowed without appetite and with some aversion is not well received and fails in its subsequent digestion, neither can the seed be taken up or, if grasped, be carried through pregnancy, unless urge and appetite for intercourse have been present. For even if some women who were forced to have intercourse have conceived, one may say with reference to them that in any event the emotion of sexual appetite existed in them too, but was obscured by mental resolve. Similarly in women who mourn, appetite for food often exists but is obscured by grief from their misfortune. Indeed,

later they are compelled to eat by reason of exceeding hunger, putting aside their resolve.

38.   The time, therefore, is suitable which corresponds with the sexual desire, provided that the body is neither overloaded nor in want; for it is not enough to feel the urge towards intercourse unless the condition of the body is suitable too. We often crave food while the things already eaten are in a poorly digested and corrupted state, and if, at this time we partake of something, complying with the force of the appetite, we make this corrupt too. Similarly the proper time does not depend solely upon the craving for intercourse if in addition we do not consider the rest of the circumstances; for in the more lecherous women the urge towards intercourse exists at any time. In fact, the body must be neither in want nor weak, for it stands to reason that together with the whole the parts too are weak. Thus if the uterus is too weak, it will be so, in all likelihood, regarding its functions too, and conception is a function of the uterus. Thus intercourse shall be practiced neither when the body is in want, nor, on the other hand, when it is heavy as it is in indigestion and drunkenness. First because the body in a natural state performs its proper functions but it is not in a natural state at the time of drunkenness and indigestion. and just as no other natural functions can be effected in such a state, neither can conception. Second, because the seed when attached must be nourished, and takes food from the substance containing blood and pheuma which his brought to it. But in drunkenness and indigestion all vapor is spoilt and thus the pneuma too is rendered turbid. Therefore danger arises lest by reason of the bad material contributed the seed to change for the worse. Furthermore, [the] satiety due to heavy drinking hinders [the] attachment of the seed to the uterus. Just as in drunken people the wine, but vigorously rising up makes the wounds difficult to unite, it stands to reason that the attachment of the seed is disturbed by the same cause.

39.   What is one to say concerning the fact that various states of the soul also produce certain changes in the mould of the fetus. For instance, some women, seeing monkeys during intercourse, have borne children resembling monkeys. The tyrant of the Cyprians who was misshapen, compelled his wife to look at beautiful statues during intercourse and became the father of well-shaped children; and horse-breeders, during covering, place noble horses in front of the mares. Thus, in order that the offspring may not be rendered misshapen, women must be sober during coitus because in drunkenness the soul becomes the victim of strange phantasies; this furthermore, because the offspring bears some resemblance to the mother as well, not only in body but in soul. Therefore, it is good that the offspring be made to resemble the soul when it is stable and not deranged by drunkenness. Indeed, it is utterly absurd that the farmer takes care not to throw seed upon very moist and flooded land, and that on the other hand mankind assumes nature to achieve a good result in generation when seed is deposited in bodies which are very moist and inundated [by] satiety.

40.   Together with these points it has already been stated that the best time is after a rubdown had been given and a little food been eaten. The food will give the inner turbulence an impetus towards coitus, the urge for intercourse not being diverted by appetite for food; while the rubdown will make it possible to lay hold of the injected seed more readily. For just as the rubdown naturally aids the distribution of food, it helps also in the reception and retention of the seed, yesterday's superfluities, as one may say, being unloaded, and the body thoroughly cleansed and in a sound state for its natural processes. Consequently, as the farmer sows only after having first cleansed the soil and removed any foreign material, in the same manner we too advise that insemination for the production of man should follow after the body has first been given a rubdown.

Source: *Soranus's Gynecology,* trans. Owsei Temkin (Baltimore: The Johns Hopkins University Press, 1956), 34–39.

would affect the child's development. Soranus had extensive experience with treating women, and thus his observations and personal experiences tempered his understanding of Aristotle. He challenged many of Aristotle's ideas about women's bodies, questioning the notion that a woman's womb could wander, and he was unusual for his discussion of menopause. In fact, Soranus studied the health of women with multiple pregnancies and lifelong virgins and concluded that the virgins were healthier. Although he did not advocate virginity, his belief that sex could be harmful flew in the face of contemporary ideas about women's bodies needing sex, menstruation, and childbirth to release pent-up humors.

The other influential medical writer was Galen (ca. 130–ca. 200), a physician and natural philosopher from Pergamum who also based his medical observations on experience. Before moving to the court of Marcus Aurelius in Rome, he attended to gladiators. He was not only well versed in Greek medical writing but also a keen observer and diagnostician. He combined a thorough knowledge of ancient medical texts with dissections and observations of the human body. Like Aristotle, Galen thought that women's bodies were imperfect male bodies and he accepted the belief that women's bodies were cold and men's bodies were hot. Women's coolness led to their imperfection. An imbalance in temperature led to sickness, and healing required restoring the proper balance of temperature in the male or female body. Without heat, her reproductive organs could not escape outside like a man's and thus she was imperfect. However, he disagreed with Aristotle on women's role in conception. He believed that a woman released a seed when she had an orgasm. Thus, women's pleasure in sex was important for producing children. Galen did not think that women's seed was as important as the man's seed for procreations. Nonetheless, his notion of the existence of a female seed was a radical departure from

other medical writers who had relegated women to the role of vessels for fetal development only. Although both Soranus and Galen were influenced by Aristotle, their hands-on experience as physicians permitted them to move beyond Aristotle in ways that would influence women's health care for centuries.

Rome was a vibrant, cosmopolitan empire in which women moved about more freely than they had in earlier times, bringing Roman gender norms and culture to the edges of the known world. Especially in the Empire's cities, working-class women worked in most occupations while elite women enjoyed the luxuries of urban life that Rome's military success brought to its citizens. In this setting, Roman thinkers began to reconsider many Greek ideas about women and their bodies.

CONCLUSION

Greek models of family and gender influenced Roman ideas about women, but they had to be continually modified or reasserted in the face of Roman expansion. Early Romans rejected the high status of Etruscan women in favor of a more submissive, domesticated Roman woman. During the Republic, class conflict and military expansion led to increased opportunities for women, but Roman law restricted their ability to act independently. Nevertheless, moralists continued to believe that women's behavior reflected the health of the Roman state, and they lamented the fact that few women could meet the high standard set by the mythical Lucretia. Because of these moral concerns for women's behavior, marriage and household concerns gradually evolved from private to state issues. As we will see in the next chapter, during the coming centuries, the rise of Christianity would be the critical force in transforming Roman gender expectations.

NOTES

1. Sybille Haynes, *Etruscan Civilization: A Cultural History*, (Los Angeles: J. Paul Getty Museum, 2000), 1, 133; Larissa Bonfante, "Etruscan Couples and their Aristocratic Society," *Reflections of Women in Antiquity*, ed. Helene P. Foley (New York: Gordon and Breach Science Publishers, 1981), 333.

2. T. J. Cornell, *The Beginnings of Rome: Italy and Rome from the Bronze Age to the Punic Wars (c. 1000–264 B.C.)* (London: Routledge, 1995), 82.

3. Haynes, 10, 131–133, 255.

4. Jo-Marie Claassen, "The Familiar Other: The Pivotal Role of Women' in Livy's Narrative of Political Development in Early Rome," *Acta Classica* 41 (1998): 83.

5. Claassen, 87.

6. John Patterson, "Military Organization and Social Change in the Later Roman Republic," in *War and Society*, ed. John Rich and Graham Shipley (London: Routledge, 1993), 98–99.

7. Richard A. Bauman, *Women and Politics in Ancient Rome* (London: Routledge, 1992), 24–25.

8. Leonard A. Curchin, *Roman Spain: Conquest and Assimilation* (London: Routledge, 1991), 4, 82.

9. Craig Williams, *Roman Homosexuality: Ideologies of Masculinity in Classical Antiquity* (New York: Oxford University Press, 1999), 72; Holt Parker, "The Teratogenic Grid," in *Roman Sexualities*, ed. Judith Hallett and Marilyn B. Skinner (Princeton: Princeton University Press, 1997), 47–48.

10. Kim Haines-Eitzen, "'Girls Trained in Beautiful Writing': Female Scribes in Roman and Antiquity and Early Christianity," *Journal of Early Christian Studies* 6 (1998): 632.

11. Mary R. Lefkowitz and Maureen B. Fant, ed., *Women's Life in Greece and Rome: A Source Book in Translation*, 2nd ed. (Baltimore: The Johns Hopkins University Press, 1992), 222.

12. Suzanne Dixon, *Reading Roman Women* (London: Duckworth, 2001), 101.

13. Keith Bradley, *Slavery and Rebellion in the Roman World 140–70 B.C.* (Bloomington: Indiana University Press, 1989), 59, 92–93.

14. Gillian Clark, "Roman Women," in *Women in Antiquity*, ed. Ian McAuslan and Peter Walcot (Oxford: Oxford University Press, 1996), 38.

15. Walter Scheidel, "The Most Silent Women of Greece and Rome: Rural Labour and Women's Life in the Ancient World," part I, *Greece and Rome*, 2nd series, 42 (1995), 210–217.

16. John K. Evans, *War, Women, and Children in Ancient Rome* (London: Routledge, 1991), 113–117.

17. H. Hill, *The Roman Middle Class in the Republican Period*, reprint. (Westport, CT: Greenwood Press, 1974), 30–31.

18. Keith Bradley, ed., "*Tatae* and *Mammae* in the Roman Family," in *Discovering the Roman Family: Studies in Roman Social History* (Oxford: Oxford University Press, 1991), 76; Suzanne Dixon, *The Roman Family* (Baltimore, MD: The Johns Hopkins University Press, 1992), 180–181.

19. Emily A. Hemelrijk, *Matrona Docta: Educated Women in the Roman Elite from Cornelia to Julia Domna* (London: Routledge, 1999), 18–25.

20. Bradley, "Child Labor in the Roman World," in *Discovering the Roman Family*, 108–110.

21. Jane F. Gardner, *Women in Roman Law and Society* (Bloomington: Indiana University Press, 1991), 71.

22. Gardner, 67.

23. Dixon, *The Roman Family*, 77.

24. Bauman, 49–50.

25. Augusto Fraschetti, "Introduction" in *Roman Women*, ed. Augusto Fraschetti (Chicago: University of Chicago Press, 1993), 7–8.

26. Bauman, 15–16.

27. Sarah B. Pomeroy, *Goddess, Whores, Wives, and Slaves: Women in Classical Antiquity*, 2nd ed. (New York: Schocken Books, 1995), 208.

28. Bauman, 18–19; Dixon, *The Roman Family*, 81–91; Gardner, 103–105.

29. Ross Shepard Kraemer, *Her Share of the Blessings: Women's Religions Among Pagans, Jews, and Christians in the Greco-Roman World* (New York: Oxford University Press, 1992), 55.

30. Mary Beard, "The Sexual Status of Vestal Virgins," *Journal of Roman Studies* 70 (1980): 17–18; Holt N. Parker, "Why Were the Vestals Virgins? or Chastity of Women and the Safety of the Roman State," *American Journal of Philology* 125 (2004): 563–602.

31. Sharon Kelly Heyob, *The Cult of Isis Among Women in the Graeco-Roman World* (Leiden: Brill, 1975).

32. John Ferguson, *The Religions of the Roman Empire* (Ithaca, NY: Cornell University Press, 1970), 27–28.

33. Corrado Petrocelli, "Cornelia the Matron," in *Roman Women*, 49–50; Hemelrijk, 64–67.

34. Sarah Pomeroy, *Women in Hellenistic Egypt: From Alexander to Cleopatra* (New York: Schocken Books, 1984), 24–25.

35. Plutarch, "Caesar," in *Lives of Noble Grecians and Romans*, trans. John Dryden (New York: Modern Library, 1932), 883.

36. Elaine Fantham, Helene Peet Foley, Natalie Boymel Kampen, Sarah B. Pomeroy and H. Alan Shapiro, *Women in the Classical World* (New York: Oxford University Press, 1994), 280–281.

37. Ronald Cluett, "Roman Women and Triumviral Politics, 43–37 BC," *Echos du Monde Classique/Classical Views* n.s. 42 (1998): 71–78.

38. Cluett, 82–88.

39. Fantham et al., 282–288.

40. Quoted in Judith Hallett, "Women in the Ancient Roman World," in *Women's Roles in Ancient Civilizations: A Reference Guide*, ed. Bella Vivante (Westport, CT: Greenwood Press, 1999), 279.

41. Hallett, "Women in the Ancient Roman World," 277–283.

42. Fantham et al., 220–221.

43. Bauman, 85–86; Catherine Virouvet, "Fulvia the Woman of Passion," in Fraschetti, *Roman Women*, 100–117.

44. Nicholas Purcell, "Livia and the Womanhood of Rome," in *Proceedings of Cambridge Philological Society* n.s. 212:32 (1986): 78–79.

45. Gardner, 77–78, 194–197.

46. Fantham et al., 279–280.

47. Judith Sebesta, "Women's Costume and Feminine Civic Morality in Augustan Rome," *Gender and History 9* (1997): 529–541; Purcell, 88–94.

48. Quoted in Purcell, 94.

49. Fantham et al., 291–292.

50. Sara Elise Phang, "The Families of Roman Soldiers," *Journal of Family History* 27 (October 2002): 353, 359.

51. Lindsay Allason-Jones, *Women in Roman Britain* (London: The British Museum Publications, 1989), 58.

52. Vindolanda Tablets, online at http://vindolanda.csad.ox.ac.uk/ (Tablet 291).

53. Hallett, "Women in the Ancient Roman World," 285–287.

54. Allason-Jones, 79.

55. D. E. Farwell and T. L. Molleson, *Excavations at Poundbury, 1966–1988.* Vol. 2. *The Cemeteries* (Dorchester: Dorset Natural History and Archaeological Society, 1993), 207–212.

56. Jane Rowlandson, ed., *Women and Society in Greek and Roman Egypt: A Sourcebook* (Cambridge: Cambridge University Press, 1998), 84.

57. Rowlandson, 84–85.

58. Jane Crawford, "Cartimandua, Boudicca, and Rebellion: British Queens and Roman Colonial Views," in *Women and the Colonial Gaze*, ed. Tamara L. Hunt and Micheline R. Lessard (New York: New York University Press, 2002), 25–28.

59. Dixon, *Reading Roman Women*, 107.

60. Quoted in Lefkowitz and Fant, 213.

61. Fantham et al. 338; Gardner, 132–134.

62. Lefkowitz and Fant, 213; Paul Zanker, *Pompeii: Public and Private Life*, trans. Deborah Lucas Schneider (Cambridge, MA: Harvard University Press, 1998), 70–71.

63. Lefkowitz and Fant, 131.

64. Ann Olga Koloski-Ostrow, "Violent Stages in Two Pompeian Houses: Imperial Taste, Aristocratic Response, and Messages of Male Control," in *Naked Truths: Women, Sexuality, and Gender in Classical Art and Archaeology*, ed. Ann Olga Koloski-Ostrow and Claire L. Lyons (London: Routledge, 1997), 243–265.

65. Quoted in Dixon, *Reading Roman Women*, 101.

66. Dixon, *Reading Roman Women*, 96–97, 109–110.

67. Prudence Allen, *The Concept of Woman: The Aristotelian Revolution 750 BC–1250 AD* (Montreal: Eden Press, 1985), 164–165, 185–186.

68. Cora E. Lutz, *Musonius Rufus: The Roman Socrates* (New Haven, CT: Yale University Press, 1947), 91.

69. Lutz, 93–95.

70. Allen, 173–180.

71. Lutz, 41.

Suggested Readings

Bauman, Richard A. *Woman and Politics in Ancient Rome*. New York: Routledge, 1992.

Dixon, Suzanne. *The Roman Family*. Baltimore: Johns Hopkins University Press, 1992. Follows the changes to the Roman family both culturally and legally and how these changes shaped the lives of members.

Gardner, Jane E. *Women in Roman Law and Society*. London: Croom Helm, 1986.

Haynes, Sybille. *Etruscan Civilization: A Cultural History*, Los Angeles, CA: J. Paul Getty Museum, 2000. Beautifully illustrated history of Etruscans with the latest scholarship.

Hemelrijk, Emily A. *Matrona Docta: Educated Women in the Roman Elite from Cornelia to Julia Domna*. London: Routledge Press, 1999. Discusses the content of women's education and its use in promoting motherhood and womanly virtue.

Heyob, Sharon Kelly. *The Cult of Isis Among Women in the Graeco-Roman World*. Leiden: Brill, 1975. Scholarly treatment of the cult of Isis and the changes in the participation of women.

Gender and the Evolution of Early Christianity, 60 B.C.E.–600 C.E.

Lime Stone Roundel of Thekla with Wild Beasts and Angels (Fifth Century, Egypt).
Thekla exemplified the new social experiences that Christianity brought to women. She
rejected marriage, faced persecution in the arena, and lived in the desert as a hermit. (The
Nelson-Atkins Museum of Art, Kansas City, Missouri. Purchase: Nelson Trust, 48-10.)

Many peoples conquered by the Romans resisted their rule and faced persecution as a result. In particular, tensions between Jews in Palestine and their Roman overlords reached the breaking point in the first century C.E., as Jewish leaders and preachers challenged Roman domination. One of those preachers, Jesus (d. ca. 30 C.E.), attracted a large following of both men and women. Gradually, the followers of Jesus founded a new religion, Christianity, which redefined women's value to society by encouraging celibacy and virginity rather than fertility and marriage. Early followers of Jesus lived in relatively egalitarian communities, and their leaders asserted the radical notion that men and women were equal before God. However, as the church emerged as an institution, Christian leaders reaffirmed women's inferiority on earth. Thus, although women found spiritual fulfillment in Christianity, they constantly struggled to assert their place in Christian society.

WOMEN AND JUDAISM IN THE FIRST CENTURY, 60–100 C.E.

The Jewish population was relatively small, only about 4 percent of the population of the Roman Empire.[1] However, even among the many religions of the Roman Empire, Jews stood out from the rest of Roman society. Their monotheism prevented them from worshipping Roman deities and unlike other inhabitants of the Empire, they followed dietary restrictions, observed the Saturday Sabbath, and circumcised male babies. After the conquest of the largely Jewish kingdom of Judea (now Israel) in 63 B.C.E., Rome ruled the region through puppet kings who were often despised by the Jewish population. For the most part, Romans were tolerant of Jews, allowing them to practice their religion and govern themselves without interference as long as they paid their taxes. Nevertheless, the inhabitants of Judea resented Roman rule and the taxes that they paid to support it. Periodic persecutions by Roman overloads only flamed that resentment. A Jewish rebellion in 66 C.E. unleashed the full force of Roman repression, and four years later, the Romans destroyed the Temple in Jerusalem. In response to the loss of

Chapter 4 ❖ Chronology

ca. 30 c.e.	Crucifixion of Jesus
ca. 35	Paul's conversion
48	Council of Jerusalem
ca. 50	Paul writes his earliest surviving letter, *1 Thessalonians*
ca. 65	Martyrdom of Peter and Paul
70	Destruction of Jewish Temple in Jerusalem
ca. 80	*Gospel of Mark* written
Second century	Deutero-Pauline letter *1 Timothy* written
End of second century	Formation of the Talmud
Third century	*Didascalia* written
313	Edict of Toleration
324	Council of Nicea
391	Christianity made the state religion of Roman Empire
414	Christian mob murders Hypatia for being a pagan
430	Death of Augustine
ca. 533	Justinian finishes *Corporus iuris civilis*

the center of Jewish worship, the community developed new practices that affirmed women's domestic roles and limited their public participation in religious activity.

Gender and Diversity Among the Jews in the Roman Empire

Rome ruled Judea through the puppet king Herod (37 B.C.E.–4 B.C.E.). As a client king, Herod worked with Rome and benefited from its patronage and protection. One of his great achievements was the rebuilding of the Temple in Jerusalem, the center of Jewish worship, after its destruction in the sixth century B.C.E. by the Babylonians. However, much of the Jewish population resented his inconsistent policies and repression of those who opposed him. He created conflict not only between Romans and Jews, but also among Jews themselves over how to deal with their coreligionists who had achieved

political and economic success by collaborating with the Romans.

Late antique Judaism was divided into many sects. These sects disagreed over how Jews should work with Herod and assimilate into Roman life. The Sadducees, mainly the landed aristocracy and members of the priestly class, emphasized worship at the Temple in Jerusalem and accepted some assimilation and collaboration with Roman authorities in order to keep the Temple secure. In contrast, the Pharisees rejected any assimilation or compromise with Roman culture, and instead advocated complete separation from non-Jewish society. The Pharisees emphasized Jewish dietary and purity laws and other forms of private observance, as well as the importance of synagogue worship.

In addition to these two prominent sects, communities of Jewish ascetics sprang up in the surrounding desert in the first century. They shunned commercial activity and contact with Romans.

Some of these groups, such as the Essenes, produced writings that predicted the end of the world. They may have excluded women, although the evidence is contradictory. Another group, the Therapeutae, was a community of highly educated men and women living and praying together but observing strict celibacy. The Jewish philosopher Philo of Alexandria (ca. 20 B.C.E.–ca. 50 C.E.) says that the women in this group were old and lifelong virgins or widows from well-to-do families. When men and women worshipped, they sat in separate rooms so that they would not see one another but could hear one another. Membership in the Therapeutae required members to cut themselves off from their families and dedicate themselves to the contemplative life. Philo believed that philosophers should aspire to a mystical union with God. To do this, they had to purge themselves of physical concerns. Philo believed that the Therepeutrides had achieved this status by remaining childless or reaching menopause. By rejecting their feminine bodies, women past childbearing age could converse with God.[2]

Wealth and status further differentiated Jews. Women of the landed elite had slaves and servants to help them with their household chores, while among the artisanal classes in Judea, women worked in a variety of occupations from the traditional textile-producing trades and midwifery to baking, glass making, and wine producing. One group of first-century Jewish women joined together to organize an egg-hatching business.[3] Tenant farmers and their families had the most difficult time. During Herod's reign, drought, earthquakes, and locusts repeatedly destroyed crops and caused famine. Like farmers everywhere, they bore the brunt of Roman taxes and had few resources to rely on when crisis struck.[4]

While many Jews strictly maintained their religious and cultural practices, others gradually assimilated into Roman culture. Most Jews outside of Judea spoke Greek as their primary language and within Judea, most also spoke Hebrew and Aramaic. Jews living in Rome also spoke Latin. In general, there were few differences between Jewish and Roman households.[5] Like their Roman counterparts, Jewish women worked with their husbands, raised children, and tended households. Archaeological excavation of houses in Jewish and non-Jewish neighborhoods shows many similarities. Kitchens were typically located in the same part of the house, and both groups of women used the same kinds of pots, storage vessels, and looms. Although some Jewish homes had special baths (*mikvot*), so that women could observe menstrual purity laws, and some had *menorahs*, ritual candelabras, many others did not. Roman governors did not require that Jews live in particular neighborhoods, yet Jews tended to live near one another, making it easier for housewives to buy kosher food, for families to practice communal rituals, and for parents to find Jewish spouses for their children.[6]

Jews worshipped differently in Jerusalem than they did in the rest of the Roman Empire. In Jerusalem, the Temple was the center of all religious activity. The priestly class controlled the Temple. It was the only place they could make the sacred sacrifices required by the Hebrew Bible. The Temple was divided into progressively more restrictive sections. Jewish law considered menstruating women and women who had recently given birth impure and Temple priests prohibited them from entering even the outer reaches of the Temple where non-Jews could assemble. Near the exterior was the Court of the Women. Women could enter the Temple there, and men and women worshipped together during certain festivals. All women were excluded from the interior of the Temple, and only priests could enter the area where the sacrificial altar stood. The inner sanctum, the Holy of Holies, could only be accessed by the high priest under certain circumstances.

Outside of Jerusalem, the synagogue was the center of Jewish social, religious, and commercial life. Scholars differ on whether men and women worshipped together in synagogues. However, archaeological excavation indicates tremendous architectural variation, and not all synagogues had separate galleries for women. Whatever the case, Judaism stressed the importance of female attendance at religious services, and women played active roles in their synagogues, although those roles varied according to the local culture.[7] Inscriptions show that women served in leadership positions in some synagogues. For example, a second-century inscription from Asia Minor states "Rufina, a Jewess, head of the synagogue, built this tomb for her freed slaves and the slaves raised in her house. No one else had the right to bury anyone (here)."[8] In Crete in the fourth or fifth centuries, a woman named Sophia held a similar position. Bernadette Brooten asserts that these positions were not merely honorific but allowed certain women to exercise some authority. Moreover, female participation in synagogue leadership may have been more common in synagogues with large numbers of recent converts from Greco-Roman religions in which women sometimes held positions of authority. Although much of this material dates from the second century or later, Brooten argues that there is no reason to believe that women's leadership in the synagogue was a new trend. The range of titles associated with women suggests that some women had access to money, education, and influence. Many inscriptions attest to women's substantial donations to their local synagogues. In certain circumstances, women also seem to have represented their communities in interactions with other Jewish communities, non-Jews, and Roman authorities.[9]

Roman violence against Jewish inhabitants increased during the first century, but scholars disagree about whether this was a conscious change of policy or a response to local tensions. For example, in 38 C.E., a Greek mob sacked the Jewish quarter in Alexandria. They looted shops, raped women, burned houses, and erected statues of the emperor in the synagogues. The Roman Emperor Caligula (r. 37–41 C.E.) intended to take similar action against other Jewish communities, but he was murdered before he could do so.[10] In 66 C.E., conflicts between the Jews and the Greeks in the city of Caesarea provoked a Jewish revolt in the region. For four years, the Jews fought to end Roman domination. According to the historian Flavius Josephus (37–ca. 101), a Jewish historian with Roman sympathies, Jewish rebels at the rock fortress of Masada chose to die by their own hands rather than be killed by the Romans. One of the seven survivors supposedly told Josephus that the rebel leader voiced his concern about the women and children saying, "Let our wives die before they are abused, and our children before they have tasted of slavery, and after we have slain them, let us bestow that glorious benefit upon one another mutually" (*The War of the Jews*, VII: 8:6). In 70 C.E., after the Romans defeated the rebels, authorities abolished both the office of

WALL PAINTING OF THE RESCUE OF MOSES FROM THE DURA SYNAGOGUE IN SYRIA (NOW RECONSTRUCTED IN THE MUSEUM OF DAMASCUS, ca. 250). The contemporary clothing worn by the women in this picture shows the continued vibrancy of Judaism after the fall of the Temple. *(Art Resource, NY.)*

high priest and the Jewish legal council known as the *Sanhedrin* to prevent a resurgence of Jewish resistance. They also destroyed the Temple and prohibited further worship. The soldiers looted it of its sacred objects and brought them back to Rome as booty. The Romans forced all Jews to donate the tax that they had paid to the Temple to the temple of Jupiter in Rome, but Jews remained exempt from emperor worship.

The first century after the destruction of the Temple was a period of turmoil for the Jewish community. The Pharisees, who had refused to work with the Romans, became the dominant force in Judaism. Many Jews moved out of Judea, adding to the Diaspora, or dispersion of the Jews, as they migrated to communities around the eastern Mediterranean. For the next two centuries, Jews sought out new ways to structure their lives and identities without the Temple. The composition of the Talmud was one solution. The ultimate transformation of the followers of Jesus into the new religion of Christianity proved to be another.

Women and the Talmud

As Jewish communities expanded around the eastern Mediterranean, Jewish leaders worried that Jewish identity and religion would be subsumed by Roman culture. At the end of the second century, a group of Pharisees still living in northern Judea produced a collection of Jewish law known as the *Mishnah*. This work and the other legal commentaries that make up the Talmud dictated how Jewish law would organize everyday life in the post-Temple world and would define Jewish women's activities for many centuries. These texts reflect both traditional concerns and new anxieties about Jewish life without the Temple.

In the *Mishnah,* the earliest of these classical rabbinic texts, women fall into two categories, dependent and autonomous, based on who controlled their reproductive ability. Men controlled the fertility of dependent women: minor daughters, wives, and levirate widows, widows under the control of their deceased husband's brother. For example, a Jewish father collected monetary compensation from a man who raped or seduced his minor daughter, because the violation decreased her value in the marriage market. Autonomous women, adult daughters, divorcées, and widows controlled their

own reproduction.[11] As Judith Wegner explains "The *mishnaic* system thus inextricably, links a woman's social identity to ownership of her sexuality."[12]

Jewish law severely limited women's participation in religious life. It clearly articulates women's responsibilities for lighting the candles at the onset of the Sabbath, making dough offerings when making bread, and observing the rituals surrounding menstruation, pregnancy, and childbirth. In addition, women played a primary role in the supervision of dietary laws, participated in mourning, and prepared the bodies of the dead. Like men, the Talmud required women to observe the Sabbath and the festivals of the Jewish calendar such as Sukkoth, Passover, Rosh Hashanah, and Yom Kippur. However, it was the Talmud's exemption of women from a variety of other religious obligations that accentuated the gender hierarchy within Judaism. The Talmud exempted women from studying Torah, from daily prayers, and from a variety of holy day observances. By virtue of their sex, men could observe all the commandments and thus serve the Jewish God Yahweh fully. Women could only fulfill some of the commandments. Although some scholars have viewed these exemptions as practical accommodations to women's domestic activities, feminist scholars have emphasized that in the long run, those exclusions negatively affected women's status.

While establishing the parameters of female religious participation, the Talmud offers interesting evidence about women's lives. For instance, the Talmud discusses whether the wife of a scholar could lend her cooking pots to or grind grain with the wife of a man who was not careful in his observances of religious rituals. This example indicates a diverse adherence to the dietary and menstrual purity laws among Diaspora Jews and hints that Jewish women may have focused more on cooperation and companionship than on maintaining ritual purity.[13]

Rabbinic law also codified Jewish marital practices. Like Romans, Jewish families sought marriages for their children that forged political and economic alliances and reinforced existing social connections. As in the rest of the Mediterranean, Jewish women married young, and the production of children, especially sons, was critically important. From time to time, Jews also practiced polygyny;

however, the expense of more than one wife limited this practice to wealthier households. Jewish law allowed men to seek a divorce, although rabbis differed over the justifications for divorce. One rabbi said it was permissible if a man found his wife's cooking unsatisfactory; others taught that it was permissible only if the wife was unchaste.[14] Although bad cooking might seem frivolous, cooking was an important part of maintaining ritual purity, and thus, the failure to observe dietary rituals compromised the entire household. In contrast, women could not initiate divorce.

As a legal commentary, the Talmud does not provide much information about how Jewish women actually lived or even if they followed the laws. To understand the realities of daily life, we must turn to the often incomplete inscriptions and fragmentary papyri that survive from Roman Egypt. One woman, Babatha, who was born about 100 C.E. and probably died in the Jewish revolt of 135, left a personal archive that fills in some gaps in our knowledge of Jewish women. While Babatha was not literate, she nonetheless engaged in lawsuits to protect her property, inherited land from her father, and apparently arranged her own second marriage after her first husband died. When she married a man named Judah around 125 C.E., he already had another wife. Polygyny among Jews was dying out and Babatha's marriage is the only known Jewish polygynous marriage in this period. The records also show that Babatha lent her husband money for his daughter's dowry, but upon his death, Babatha had to sue the girl's mother, Judah's first wife, for repayment. Babatha's private archive attests to the wide range of activities in which Jewish women participated and demonstrates that the Talmud and other rabbinic sources do not reveal the full extent of women's activities and concerns.[15]

Talmudic law helped to resolve part of the religious crisis brought on by the destruction of the Temple. Not all Jews followed this path; others followed leaders who preached that the end of the Temple was a sign of the end of the world and that Jews needed to abandon Jewish laws and practices for new laws and new ways of life until that end came. For those who believed that the end of the world was near, traditional family life and gender roles held little appeal.

FEMALE FOLLOWERS OF JESUS, 50–150 C.E.

Rome's domination of the Jews shaped the foundations of Christianity. Many wandering Jewish preachers, a common sight in Jerusalem, called for an end to Roman rule and predicted the end of the world. Jesus of Nazareth belongs to this tradition of charismatic preaching. Because we have virtually no information about the historical Jesus outside of the religious texts generated by the movement, it is difficult for scholars to reconstruct his life. Scholars generally agree that he was a Jew raised in Nazareth in Galilee. His preaching and healing mission attracted many male and female followers. The Romans believed that Jesus's message posed a political threat and they arrested and executed him as a criminal around 30 C.E. Scholars do not agree on either his social status or that of his followers. Some describe him as a peasant who avoided cities, while others understand him as primarily influenced by the cosmopolitan Jewish city of Sepphoris, only three miles away from the village of Nazareth.

Jesus's followers produced three main historical sources: the letters of Paul, the canonical Gospels, and the so-called Gnostic Gospels, non-canonical, or not officially recognized texts. These records are the written accounts of earlier oral traditions and writings. As followers of Jesus grappled with their relationship to Judaism and to the rest of Roman society, these texts offered competing visions of women's roles in the new religion.

Women According to Paul

Paul was central to the formation of early Christian views of women. The letters of Paul constitute the earliest documentary evidence about the followers of Jesus, and Paul's own activities are chronicled in the later source the book of *Acts*. Paul was a Jew and a Roman citizen, raised in the Asia Minor city of Tarsus. He was educated as a Pharisee, yet because he had grown up in a Greek city, he was also familiar with Greco-Roman society. Sometime between 30 and 35 C.E., Paul had a conversion experience and dedicated his life to spreading the message of Jesus. The success of Christianity owes much to Paul's work. Initially, he worked within the Jewish communities in Asia Minor, but he understood Jesus's message as also applying to non-Jews, or Gentiles, as well. According to *Acts,* at the Council of Jerusalem in 48 C.E., Paul's decision to evangelize to Gentiles led to serious disagreement with other disciples, particularly Peter (d. ca. 65 C.E.), over the meaning of Jesus's life and death for Jews and Gentiles. Paul's acceptance of non-Jewish followers was a pivotal decision in the formation of the new religion. He traveled around the Aegean coast asserting that Jesus was the new law and the fulfillment of Jewish Scripture. Paul's teachings would eventually lead his followers to split permanently from Judaism. When Paul's travels took him to Rome, the Roman authorities arrested and executed him sometime between 60 and 65 C.E. (see Map 4.1).

Paul wrote letters to maintain contact with his new followers. In his letters, Paul encouraged believers, answered questions, and corrected erroneous beliefs and practices. He wrote his earliest

surviving letter, *1 Thessalonians,* between 50 and 52 C.E. Of the original thirteen letters traditionally ascribed to him, scholars agree that he wrote seven of them. Scholars refer to the letters that Paul did not write, *1* and *2 Timothy, Titus, Ephesians,* and *Hebrews,* as the deutero-Pauline letters. (Scholars are split over whether Paul wrote *Colossians* and *2 Thessalonians.*) The deutero-Pauline letters contain elements of Paul's ideas, but Paul's followers wrote them in the century following his death as a way to spread his teachings.

Paul was celibate and he wished his followers to be so too, because he believed that marriage distracted a person from God. However, he asserted that for those unable to give up sex, marriage was better than promiscuity. This rejection of sexuality grew in part from Paul's familiarity with Greek philosophy. Greek philosophers asserted that the mind and body or the spirit and flesh made conflicting demands on a person and that a philosophical life was incompatible

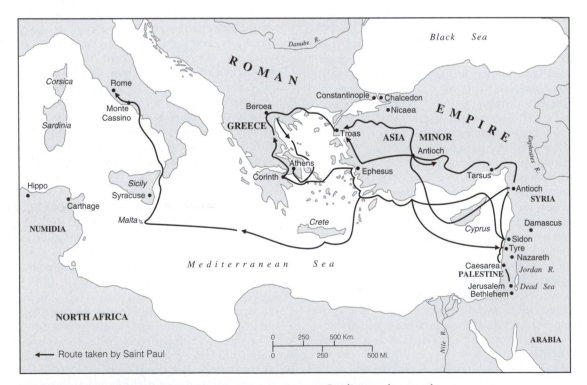

Map 4.1 THE JOURNEYS OF PAUL, CA. 46–CA. 64 C.E. Paul's travels spread Christianity to the major cities of the Roman Empire.

with marriage and sex. Paul's advocacy of celibacy freed women from the control of fathers, husbands, or children, as they were no longer defined by their reproductive abilities. In fact, the women named in Paul's letters are not typically listed in conjunction with male relatives or a household. Thus, they might have been single, widowed, or divorced, or their independence might be evidence of the community's different priorities. If, as Paul's followers preached, the end of the world was at hand, then women drawn to the movement would have had little interest in family, property, marriage, or childbearing.[16]

The household served as the earliest unit of worship for followers of Jesus. Missionaries worked through family and household relationships, as they provided some privacy and safety from the harassment of Roman soldiers and nonbelievers. Paul's letters often address householders, both male and female. When Paul commented in *1 Corinthians* that "Chloe's people" had informed him of quarreling about doctrine, scholars believe he is referring to members of Chloe's household (*1 Corinthians* 3:11). The centrality of the household formed the basis of later Christianity's assumption that men were to be religious leaders and that they should exert their strong authority over its members, much like the Roman paterfamilias (see Chapter 3).[17]

One-fifth of the individuals named in the letters were women, and Paul indicates that they played important roles in early Christianity. They allowed followers to meet in their houses, funded missionary activities, and served as group leaders. For example, Phoebe, whom Paul greets at the end of his letter to the Romans, was a leader and benefactor of another Pauline community, and Paul notes that Prisca and her husband risked their lives for him. Paul describes these women variously as "sister," "coworker," and "deacon," and in the case of Junia he calls her an "apostle" (*Romans* 16:7).[18] For centuries, scholars identified Junia as a man because they did not believe women could be apostles, despite the fact that all other known individuals with this name were women.[19]

Paul's letters provide some indications of women's social status in his communities. According to Wayne Meeks, who has done extensive analysis of Paul's followers, most of these women were not Jewish, but instead came from the Greco-Roman urban middle classes.[20] Many were small-scale artisans and foreign-born merchants, such as the traders Euodia and Syntyche, who were members of the community in Philippi and who worked together as missionaries. Converted female slaves and slave owners also appear in the texts.

The communities that followed Paul were very different from one another. The community at Philippi appears to have been well organized, and women held prominent leadership roles. Some scholars have suggested that this community accepted women's authority because they were already prominent in local pagan cults to the goddesses Diana and Isis. An important feature of women's worship in the community at Corinth was prophecy and ecstatic prayer. Corinthian women spoke in tongues, performed miracles, and conducted initiation rituals such as baptism. Some members of the community in Corinth believed that they had attained perfection, a state that separated the body and the spirit by denying bodily needs through fasting, celibacy, and even sleep deprivation. They believed that disciplining the body enhanced the spirit. These ascetic female followers rejected the Greco-Roman association of women with fertility, childbirth, and sexuality.[21]

These different communities fiercely debated the proper roles and behavior of women and Paul's letters reveal the contradictions in early practices. For example in *1 Corinthians* 11:2–16, Paul explained how men and women were to pray and prophesy. He says "any man who prays or prophesies with this head covered dishonors his head, but any woman who prays or prophesies with her head unveiled dishonors her head—it is the same as if her head were shaven" (*1 Corinthians* 4–6). Later in the same letter, he admonished women to be silent in church and rely on their husbands to teach them, "As in all the churches of the saints, the women should keep silence in the church. For they are not permitted to speak, but should be subordinate, as ever the laws says. If there is anything they desire to know, let them ask their husbands at home. For it is shameful for a woman to speak in church" (*1 Corinthians* 14:33b–36). The first selection assumes that women participated in public prayer, while the second prohibits them from such activity. Many scholars believe that this second instruction is a later addition to the letter. Early manuscript versions of the letter move these verses around, suggesting that copiers found them contradictory and confusing. Despite the contradictions, later church leaders used both verses to keep women out of church leadership positions and to affirm women's physical impurity.

Feminist scholar Ross Kraemer argues that Paul's mandate that women cover their heads while in church identified men as men and women as women when they were in a state of religious ecstasy. Religious prophecy had a long tradition in the area around Corinth. Perhaps when men and women entered into religious trances, they behaved in the same way and the blurring of gender identities disturbed Paul. In such circumstances, head coverings would differentiate between men and women. As we saw in Chapter 3, in many Roman cults such as the cult of Vesta or the *Mater Matuta*, women behaved or appeared like men. Moreover, respectable Greco-Roman women covered their heads when they went outside, and in Jewish law, unbound hair indicated an adulteress. Paul may have felt it necessary to distinguish his community from pagans and clearly identify the women in this church as respectable.[22]

The new roles women assumed in early Christianity strongly challenged traditional Jewish and Greco-Roman practices. The noncanonical work the *Acts of Paul and Thekla* reveals some of the issues and tensions facing women who chose roles other than those of wife and mother. Written during the second century, the *Acts* tell the story of Thekla, an elite Roman girl about to marry. Upon hearing Paul preach, she left her family, converted to Christianity, and began to preach and teach alongside him. Roman officials arrested and imprisoned her once for refusing to marry her fiancé and another time for rejecting the sexual advances of the Roman official. She only escaped death in the Roman arena when the animals refused to hurt her and the women in the audience intervened. Finally Thekla moved to the desert, where she lived as a hermit dressed as a man. Although Thekla's life is probably fictitious, her story explores Paul's emphasis on the renunciation of fleshly desires and its implications for women.

The Pauline letters offer various interpretations of the proper role for women. Some letters recognized women as community leaders while others portrayed women as subservient to men. Some of the letters seem to assert that women should become ascetics, practice prophecy, and reject social conventions. As Jesus's followers debated the role of women in their communities, leaders sought to legitimize their ideas and practices through references to Paul. Ultimately Christian leaders used the differences and contradictions found in Paul's letters to choose roles for women that reflected their own concerns and beliefs and not necessarily the practices of early Christianity.

Women and the Gospels

The four canonical Gospels, *Matthew, Mark, John,* and *Luke,* retell the story of Jesus's life and teachings from perspectives that reflect disagreement about the events surrounding the crucifixion and the nature of Jesus, specifically his humanity and divinity, the physicality of the resurrection, and the meaning of his preaching. These differences also show the followers of Jesus moving beyond Judaic theology and tradition and formulating their own theologies and gender expectations. The four Gospels are only a fraction of the writings dedicated to exploring the nature of Jesus. During the third century, theologians declared some of these scriptures canonical and others heretical. However, this distinction reflects the concerns and theological battles of the third century rather than those of the early followers of Jesus. In the early second century, when the theology of the Christian church was still developing, the differences between orthodoxy and heresy were not yet clear and gender norms were still in flux.

We know nothing about the authors of the Gospels except that they composed them after Jesus's lifetime. New Testament scholars refer to three of the Gospels, *Matthew, Mark,* and *Luke,* as the synoptic Gospels because they share some basic information. Of these three, *Mark* is probably the earliest, composed by someone living in either Galilee or Syria around 80 C.E. The author was clearly influenced by the destruction of the Temple in 70 C.E. The authors of *Matthew* and *Luke* include material from *Mark*. The author wrote *Matthew* at the end of the first century probably in Syria because he (or she) relies on interpretations and legal and pious observances common to that region and time. The last synoptic Gospel, *Luke,* was composed between 90 and 145 C.E. Biblical scholars believe that the same author wrote *Luke* and the *Acts of the Apostles* and they often treat them as one book. It is the first book to use the word *Christian* and is the most narrative of the four Gospels. The community that produced *Luke-Acts* appears to have been very well organized and heavily influenced by Greco-Roman social norms. The *Gospel of John* draws on an independent tradition for Jesus's life and mission. Some believe it was the last Gospel written down, others argue it is roughly contemporary with *Mark.* The author of *John* used little material from the other Gospels and came from a community that had recently separated from a Jewish synagogue. It focuses on prophecy rather than communal offices, titles, and hierarchies. The differences among the Gospels reflect both changes in early Christianity in the century and a half after Jesus's death and regional variations.[23]

The four Gospels tell the story of the birth, mission, and death of Jesus of Nazareth. According to the Gospels, Jesus, the son of a Jewish woman, was born in Bethlehem and learned both carpentry and Jewish law. At about the age of thirty, he went to the desert alone, where he had a spiritual awakening. When he returned, he took up the preaching begun by his cousin, a hermit known to Christians as John the Baptist. Jesus gathered followers, called disciples, from among the fishermen of Galilee, healed the sick, and taught that a better world was coming and that repentance and forgiveness would gain one entry into this world. Jesus preached his message to Jews in an atmosphere of political tension, and his mission attracted attention and controversy. The Romans understood his message as political and arrested and executed him by crucifixion, a method they reserved for revolutionaries, pirates, and slaves. After three days, his followers, led by Peter, claimed that he rose again from the dead, visited them, and then ascended bodily into heaven. After his death, Jesus's followers took the story of his missionary and healing work and his resurrection around the Roman Empire.

Like the Pauline letters, the canonical Gospels name several women among Jesus's followers. Their presence has created much debate about Jesus's vision of gender roles. Who were these women and how were they empowered by Jesus's message? As with the Pauline letters, it is difficult to discern a single answer to these questions because there is so much variation within the Gospels.

The Gospel narratives describe Jesus talking to women in both public and private. In Greco-Roman and Jewish culture, these interactions imply that he took women seriously and considered them a part of his mission. Additionally, women witness the resurrection in all Gospel accounts, although the letters of Paul place only men at the scene. Only a few of the named women in the Gospels were Jewish. Most Jewish women would have been married with children and social pressure on women to conform to traditional gender norms would have hindered their participation in the movement.[24] In fact, most of the Jewish women named in the Gospels were ill, single, lower-class women, prostitutes, or widowed women without children—all women who lived on the margins of late antique society.

The Gospels imply that Jesus advocated celibacy for his followers. Jesus stated that those who became eunuchs, castrated men, for the Kingdom of Heaven were blessed (*Matthew* 19:27). He argued that lust in the heart was as sinful as committing adultery (*Matthew* 5:27), and that after the Second Coming there would be no marriage (*Matthew* 22:30; *Mark* 12:25; *Luke* 20:35–36). Taken together these teachings suggest that Jesus was far from committed to traditional Greco-Roman or Jewish family life.

Much scholarly research on women in the Gospels has focused on Mary of Magdala, or Mary Magdalene, a Jewish women healed by Jesus of demonic possession and who then became a follower. She found Jesus's tomb empty after the crucifixion and was the first person to meet Jesus after his resurrection. Later authors claimed that Mary Magdalene was a prostitute before she converted and followed Jesus; after his resurrection, she lived in the desert as a hermit. These stories come from a conflation of Mary Magdalene with the unnamed women in the Gospels, such as the prostitute who washed Jesus's feet with her hair (*Luke* 7:36–50). Later theologians also identified the other Marys mentioned in the Gospels, such as Mary, the sister of Martha who offered Jesus hospitality while he preached in their house (*Luke* 10:38–42), and Mary the sister of Lazarus, whom Jesus was said to have raised from the dead (*John* 11:1–55) as Mary Magdalene. Despite these historical mistakes, feminist scholars have come to understand Mary Magdalene as a female disciple, an apostle, and a witness to Jesus's resurrection.[25] Her presence in the Gospels demonstrates that women were members of Jesus' inner circle and were central to his mission.

Luke-Acts reveals some of the tensions between early Christianity's radical ideas about gender and the broader Greco-Roman social norms. In contrast to the women in earlier texts, the women in *Luke-Acts* appear to be well-to-do, somewhat educated, and generally under the control or guidance of men. For example, although a female prophet anoints Jesus in the other three Gospels, there is no female prophet in *Luke-Acts*. The only woman to anoint Jesus in this Gospel is an unnamed sinful and repentant woman who does so with her hair. Women do not prophesy in *Luke-Acts,* but instead emphasize Jesus's role as a prophet. What is more, when the author mentions women, he usually mentions them in conjunction with a man, not as individuals or in pairs as we see in Paul's letters. Scholars have interpreted these variations as the author's concern for respectability and an attempt to counter Roman accusations that Christians were superstitious, foolish, and dishonorable. In an effort to show that this was not the case, the author of *Luke-Acts* describes gender expectations similar to those of the Greco-Roman world.[26]

Women and Gnosticism

The canonical Bible does not include all the writing that the followers of Jesus produced. Irenaeus (fl. 180 C.E.), the bishop of Lyon and author of the five-volume work *The Destruction and Overthrow of Falsely So-Called Knowledge*, destroyed many texts that he believed were heretical. The scarcity of these writings makes it difficult for scholars to reconstruct the ideas and experiences of those deemed heretics. Detractors often argued that heretical sects advocated free love and sexual promiscuity in contravention of Paul's teachings about women and sex. However, recent discoveries of lost texts indicate that their beliefs were much

more complicated than their enemies understood. Within these communities, women played prominent and nontraditional roles.

In 1945, a young boy, digging in an Egyptian cave near the village of Nag Hammadi, found a ceramic pot filled with papyrus scrolls. His discovery has made it possible to reconstruct some of these other Christian beliefs. These thirteen scrolls contain fifty-two texts written in Coptic, a form of Egyptian written in Greek script. Among the texts are poems, hymns, letters, magical instructions, and secret Gospels, such as the *Gospel of Thomas* and the *Gospel of Philip*. A related Gospel, the *Gospel of Mary Magdalene,* found elsewhere, is also part of this tradition. The people who followed these writings had very different ideas about the nature of Jesus and the structure of early Christianity than those who adhered to the canonical Gospels.

These texts are usually referred to as Gnostic texts. Gnosticism is a general term that includes a range of beliefs connected by the idea that a believer found the divine through intense introspection. Gnostic writings gave Jesus an important role in leading this search for spiritual understanding and enlightenment. In those works, he appears as a teacher and spiritual guide, not a savior. In contrast, orthodox Christian writers focused on Jesus's role as a savior and redeemer of sins. Although orthodox believers insisted on an unconquerable divide between the creator and humanity, some Gnostics believed that self-knowledge was the knowledge of God and that the self and God were the same. Canonical writings emphasized that Jesus was unique and distinct from the rest of humanity as was evident in his physical death and resurrection. Among some Gnostics, however, Jesus did not suffer death and resurrection; his crucifixion did not touch or change his spiritual dimension, which they believed was eternal. Still other Gnostic writers believed that Jesus did not experience a physical resurrection and that the resurrection could only be known through visions.[27]

The spiritual and otherworldly focus of Gnostic theology called for a separation of the physical world, which was corrupt and inferior, from the spiritual world. Sin was not behavior, as it was in orthodoxy, but a mixing of the physical and spiritual realms. Each realm was gendered; the spiritual realm was masculine and the physical realm was feminine. Moreover, the God of the Gnostic writers had both feminine and masculine aspects, whereas orthodox writers gendered their image of God as masculine, as the title "God the father" implies. Some Gnostic writers understood the dual nature of the godhead as two gods: one of light, spirit, and understanding, the other of darkness, physicality, and ignorance. This type of dualist belief appeared in a variety of religions around the Mediterranean throughout the Roman, late antique, and medieval periods.[28]

Women have higher status in the Gnostic Gospels than in the orthodox Gospels. The Gnostic texts depict Mary Magdalene as Jesus's favorite disciple, whose strong faith in Jesus and prophetic visions contrast with the doubt and disbelief of the male disciples. The *Gospel of Philip* even describes the relationship between Mary and Jesus in erotic terms. The author explains that Jesus "loved her more than all the disciples and used to kiss her often on the mouth" (*Gospel of Philip,* 63:34–64). She receives the fullest and most positive treatment in The *Gospel of Mary,* which is purported to be her own account of the secret teachings that she received from Jesus. In this text, Mary Magdalene is the ideal leader who remained steadfast in her faith while the male disciples wept with fear and ignorance. At Jesus's departure, Peter asks her to recount the teachings of the Savior that she had received but that the other disciples had not. With this request, we see the acknowledgment of Mary Magdalene's status and special relationship with Jesus, because she alone understands and communicates Jesus's message of salvation. Mary acknowledges having received special instructions in a vision, which she recounts to the other disciples in the form of a dialogue between herself and the Lord. Peter initially challenges her teachings, but the Gospel ends with an affirmation of the truth of her vision and her authority to teach it to the male disciples:

> Then Mary wept and said to Peter, "My brother Peter, what do you think? Do you think that I thought this up myself in my heart, or that I am lying about the Savior?" Levi (another disciple) answered and said to Peter, "Peter, you have always been hot-tempered. Now I see you contending against

the woman like the adversaries. But if the Savior made her worthy, who are you indeed to reject her? Surely the Savior knows her very well. That is why he loved her more than us." (Gospel of Mary, 18)

Followers of the Gnostic texts saw themselves as special Christians whose knowledge of the secret teachings of Jesus augmented the four Gospels. According to *Mark* 4:11–12, Jesus said to his disciples "To you has been given the secret of the kingdom of God, but for those outside everything is in parables; so that they may indeed see but not perceive, and may indeed hear but not understand; lest they should turn again, and be forgiven." Gnostics believed that these texts were those secret teachings and that people who had access to them had special status.

Many groups adhered to Gnosticism, including the Montanists, a charismatic movement that believed in the imminent end of the world. Although this idea had been popular in the first century, most Christians abandoned it during the second century. The founder of the sect, Montanus, taught that all sex was evil and that followers would only achieve salvation and spiritual knowledge with complete celibacy. He also taught that the Holy Spirit directly inspired prophecy. Two women, Maximilla and Priscilla, were in Montanus's immediate circle. The community believed that these women had received direct revelations from the Holy Spirit. Priscilla's vision was of Jesus descending from heaven in the form of a woman to announce the end of the world. According to his critics, Montanus also allowed women to baptize converts, preach, and celebrate the Eucharist. For their part, the Montanists justified this decision with Paul's assertion that "in Christ there is neither male nor female" (*Galatians* 3:28). Another Gnostic leader, Marcus, encouraged women to view themselves as prophets. He is supposed to have said when he initiated women into the group, "Behold Grace has come to you; open your mouth and prophesy."[29] The Gnostic followers of Carpocrates (second century) in Alexandria had a woman teacher named Marcellina who traveled to Rome to represent her community before orthodox authorities. Her sect claimed to have received secret teaching from biblical women, including Mary, Salome, and Martha.

Some scholars believe that women had considerable authority in Gnostic communities, because the Gnostics understood the divine as having female attributes or characteristics, and because many women were members of this movement. Scholar Elaine Pagels argues that because there was a female component to the godhead, women had more authority in the movement than in other Christian sects. Others have speculated that Gnosticism's origins in Egypt, where women had greater roles and visibility, influenced the gender norms of the sect. Still other scholars assert that the women leaders and priests in the Gnostic sects were wealthy elites who would have had status and visibility anyway, so their prominence reflects the importance of wealth, not gender, in the sect. Elisabeth Schüssler Fiorenza argues that although Gnosticism attributed some femaleness to the godhead, salvation in Gnostic thought required the annihilation and destruction of this female aspect. Thus, she does not see a positive relationship between Gnosticism's female imagery and Gnostic practice.[30]

The canonical Bible and the noncanonical works reveal the diversity of beliefs that existed in early Christianity. As new communities of followers sprang up around the eastern Mediterranean, they interpreted preachers' messages through their own local traditions and experiences. Some tried to merge these new ideas with what they already believed, while others completely rejected traditional beliefs in favor of new ones. The role of women in this emerging religion was often a major point of contention.

The initial success of Jesus's mission reflected the anguished moments that followed the destruction of the Temple. As followers of Jesus attempted to redefine their relationship to the rest of society, many thought it was the end of history. In anticipation of that moment, they constructed a society in which women played new and exciting roles. The feminine perspective of some of the Gnostic texts suggests that women might even have interpreted theology. Both orthodox and Gnostic writings indicate that women were central to the development of Christianity.

LIVING AND THINKING AS A CHRISTIAN, 100–400

Initially, Romans could not distinguish between Jews and Christians. As far as the Romans knew, both groups refused to participate in the cult of emperor worship, a critical part of Roman life. However, the followers of Jesus actively proselytized, bringing them to the attention of Roman authorities. Under the Emperor Diocletian (r. 284–305), the cult of the emperor became the state religion and the government identified Christians as traitors and executed them. Despite these dangers, Christianity spread and its internal organization began to reflect Greco-Roman social and gender concerns. Women found themselves redefined by their marital status and denied the ability to preach and prophesy as they had in the decades after Jesus's death. At the same time, their sex did not protect them from the horrors of Roman persecution. When Christianity became legal in the fourth century, church members faced new challenges of incorporating their beliefs into Roman law and practice.

Christian Women Confront the Roman Empire

Roman rulers believed that Christians were superstitious and foolish because they were followers of a man condemned for treason and magic. Moreover, Romans believed that Christians were atheists since they referred to the Roman gods who protected the Empire as devils and demons. The Roman historian Tacitus (ca. 56–ca. 117) observed one of the first persecutions of Christians by the Emperor Nero (r. 54–68). Nero blamed the Christians for a massive fire in Rome and had them arrested and killed by wild animals and gladiators in the arena. Although Tacitus seems to have understood that they were being used as scapegoats, he nonetheless held them in contempt. One pagan critic writing in the second century referred to Christianity as a religion of women, children, and slaves—individuals who had few rights and little or no political power in the Roman world.

Until Christianity became legal in the fourth century, persecutions waxed and waned according to government interest. The Emperor Domitian (r. 81–96), who wanted to be worshiped as a god, harshly persecuted both the followers of Jesus and the Jews. In contrast, Emperor Antoninus Pius (r. 138–161) engaged in little persecution and even permitted Jews to circumcise their male children. The Emperor Marcus Aurelius (r. 161–80) saw Christians as exhibitionists with a morbid interest in death, but he generally left them alone. Diocletian's efficient military government was the most effective in capturing and persecuting Christians. Not surprisingly, surviving Christian texts are highly critical of his reign.

During the persecutions, many early Christians embraced martyrdom as a chance to share in Christ's human sufferings. Martyrdom bound Christians together and impressed outside observers with Christians' commitment to and compassion for each other. Tertullian (ca. 160–ca. 217), an educated second-century writer, said that he converted to Christianity after witnessing the heroic deaths of Christians in the arena. The second generation of Christian leaders drew inspiration from the apostles' martyrdom and accused the Gnostics, who had little interest in Jesus's death, of avoiding martyrdom and ridiculing those who sought it. In pursuing martyrdom, early Christian women defied Roman and Christian gender expectations. By sacrificing themselves for their faith, they horrified Romans by relinquishing their role as mothers (see **Women's Lives: Perpetua, Christian Martyr**). Christian writers emphasized how female martyrs overcame the weakness of their sex and made strong "manly" affirmations of faith.

One of the earliest female Christian martyrs was Blandina, a slave girl living in Lyons in Roman Gaul. The Romans were particularly hard on the Christian community in Lyon. Local magistrates forbade Christians from even appearing in public and when they did, they faced brutal harassment. We do not know what led to Blandina's arrest along with her Christian master and many others in 177. However, Roman officials tortured her: "her entire body was mangled and broken," according to the fourth-century account by Eusebius (ca. 263–339). Nevertheless, Blandina maintained her faith, exclaiming "I am a Christian, and there is nothing vile done by us." In the amphitheater, Blandina and others underwent a series of violent contests. First, the authorities scourged her, and then they placed her in a hot iron chair that roasted her skin. When the Christians remained steadfast, Blandina was hung upside down from a stake to be devoured by wild animals. The animals miraculously refused. Finally, her tormentors enclosed her in a net and threw her before a bull to be gored. They left her decimated body to wild dogs and then burned her remains. Eusebius describes Blandina as "small and weak and despised," yet "the heathen themselves confessed that never among them had a woman endured so many and such terrible tortures" (*Ecclesiastical Hist.* V: 1:17–57).

There is no doubt about the power of martyrdom in early Christian society, even if later authors, such as Eusebius, fictionalized some of the drama of the contests and exaggerated the martrys' steadfastness. To perpetuate their memory, devoted followers composed biographies of the saints, known as *hagiographies*, which Christians widely read and recounted. Many lives of saints used masculine and military vocabulary, likening martyrs to soldiers of Christ. Male martyrs expressed their masculinity in their willingness to confront death, their self-restraint, and their chastity. Female martyrs behaved like men when they overcame their feminine weaknesses and exhibited similar restraint and steadfastness. As a result, Christians never understood martyrdom as feminine, and often described female martyrs as manly.

The bodies and graves of martyrs became the focus of Christian devotion. Christians gathered regularly at the gravesites of martyrs and other dead Christians to pray, celebrate, and even reenact the Last Supper. Believers tended their graves and prayed to them, not as gods, but as models of Christian behavior and as powerful intercessors with God and Christ. The veneration of martyrs further distinguished Christians from pagans, because pagans considered dead bodies unclean. Some church leaders complained about the enthusiasm that many had for the bodies of martyrs. Yet, leaders also recognized that the graves of martyrs were a source of power and influence. The communities near martyrs' graves counted themselves as especially blessed, and Christian leaders worked hard to preserve and promote local saints' cults. This reverence for the bodies of martyrs

Perpetua, Christian Martyr

The Roman government persecuted pious women and men, creating martyrs who served as witnesses to the power of Christianity. One of the most vivid accounts of martyrdom comes from the diary of Vibia Perpetua, a young Roman woman living in Carthage (North Africa). She came from an elite family with citizen status and she was well educated and well loved by her family. Her diary tells about the Christian community in Carthage, her theology, and the horrors of death in the Roman arena. Through her experiences, we can see the relationship between her gender and her religious experience.

In 203, while still nursing her infant son, Perpetua and a young pregnant slave named Felicity were arrested along with the other members of their Christian community. At her trial, both her father and the magistrate pleaded with her to make the required sacrifice to the emperor, which would end her imprisonment. Both played on her loyalty to her family and her obligations as a daughter and mother. The magistrate said, "Have pity on your father's grey head; have pity on your infant son. Offer the sacrifice for the welfare of the emperors." When Perpetua refused and confessed to being a Christian, she terminated her familial ties. After her confession, Roman soldiers beat her in front of her family and took her to die in the arena with the rest of her group. She left her son with her parents. After her milk dried up, she wrote, "As God willed, the baby had no further desire for the breast, nor did I suffer any inflammation; and so I was relieved of any anxiety for my child and any discomfort in my breasts." Because Roman law did not permit the execution of pregnant women, Felicity feared she would not be martyred. However, she gave birth early and joined the others in the arena.

While in prison Perpetua had four dreams that comforted her and her companions and foretold their futures. In her visions, Perpetua worked out many of the issues of her identity as a daughter and mother and her relationship to the community of Christians. Her first vision focused on the love of her new Christian family, and her second and third visions focused on a dead brother who attained salvation through her prayers. Her final vision foretold her martyrdom in the arena. In this dream, Perpetua saw that when her clothes were ripped off, she had no breasts, in her words, "suddenly I was a man." She had been transformed from female to male, from believer to martyr.

Perpetua's complicated visions indicate that she was familiar with a variety of Roman and Christian writings. The Gnostic work the *Apocalypse of St. Peter* informs her images of the heaven that she and her companions would reach after martyrdom. Her understanding of hell came from *Revelations*. Ultimately, it was Perpetua's belief in the physical suffering of Jesus and her willingness to accept martyrdom that made her writings orthodox, yet the Gnostic influences indicate that later distinctions between heretical and orthodox ideas were not yet clear.

Someone else completed Perpetua's diary, as it gives a moving and vivid account of her experience with the gladiators and animals. In the end, she had to steady the hand of the young gladiator assigned to kill her so that he could plunge the knife into her breast. The narrator explains that she was the last to die, and because of the gladiator's inexperience, it was a more painful death than it might have been otherwise.

The *Passion of Saint Perpetua* is one of the few surviving early Christian writings by a woman. It reveals the difficulties Christian women faced living under Roman rule. By submitting to martyrdom, Perpetua challenged Roman authority and Roman gender expectations. In defense of her faith, she sacrificed her family, her child, and eventually herself.

Sources: The text of Perpetua's visions is available at: www.fordham.edu/halsall/source/perpetua.html; and see Joyce Salisbury, *Perpetua's Passion: The Death and Memory of a Young Roman Woman* (New York: Routledge, 1997).

became known as the cult of the saints, and it was an important part of late antique and medieval Christianity.[31]

The Role of Women in the Early Church

Roman persecutions of Christians compelled Christian leaders to define clearly both the structure and theology of the Christian church, so that it could survive persecution. By emphasizing common structures, practices, and beliefs, church leaders hoped to strengthen Christian communities. During this period, church leaders approved the canonical Bible and rejected the Gnostic texts. Those same leaders also agreed on permanent offices and church hierarchies, which reasserted traditional Greco-Roman gender norms.

During the second century, church leaders began curtailing women's leadership opportunities. Initially Clement, the bishop of Rome (ca. 100 C.E.), emphasized the distinction between the laity and the clergy, but he considered social distinctions within the laity less important. The clerical hierarchy consisted of bishops, priests, and deacons, a structure that later writers declared mirrored that of heaven. Leaders legitimized the new hierarchy by arguing that believers could only know God with the help of priests and the church, a position that challenged the personal understanding of God advocated by Gnostics. It also gave a few, chosen men great influence and power over the rest of Christian believers. Church authorities required that bishops, priests, and male deacons undergo ordination and prohibited women from undergoing the ritual.

Widows are the only women who appear in positions of responsibility in the second-century church. The deutero-Pauline letter *1 Timothy,* and later writings, such as the third-century *Didascalia Apostolorum,* a general statement on church organization and the conduct and responsibilities of the laity, include many descriptions of the necessary qualities that widows should possess in order to play a prominent role in the church. The authors of *1 Timothy* and the *Didascalia* both distinguished between the "good" widow, who was silent, pious, and obedient, and the "bad" widow, who talked too much, gossiped, gave into sensual

CATACOMB PAINTING OF A WOMAN, MID-FOURTH CENTURY. Early Christian communities depended on the patronage and support of women to survive when Christianity was illegal. *(Scala/Art Resource, NY.)*

desires, spread false teachings, and even cursed. These descriptions suggest that widows had great influence in Christian communities. Moreover, prohibitions in the *Didascalia* against widows prophesying, teaching, baptizing, and converting pagans indicate that women regularly participated in these activities. The authors of *1 Timothy* and the *Didascalia* found such public activity incompatible with second- and third-century Christian gender expectations.[32]

According to the *Didascalia,* good widows could serve as deacons. Some time between 111 and 113, the pagan governor of the Roman province of Pontus-Bythinia, in northern Asia Minor arrested two female slaves who called themselves deacons. In general, deacons assisted the bishop's work with the laity and the church needed female deacons to work among women converts. After a bishop, priest, or male deacon baptized a woman, a female deacon anointed the new female member with oil. The implication is that anointing included some physical contact with women that was inappropriate for men. Female deacons also instructed female converts and visited sick women, especially those who lived in the homes of pagans.

The authors of the deutero-Pauline letters (*1-2 Timothy, Titus, Ephesians,* and *Hebrews*) struggled to understand the role of marriage and celibacy in their communities. The women who received their letters heard messages in line with traditional Greco-Roman beliefs that women should marry, a message quite different from Paul's teachings. Although Paul clearly thought celibacy was the best option, the author of *1 Timothy* instructed young widows to remarry and produce children: "So I would have younger widows marry, bear children, and rule their households, and give the enemy no occasion to revile us" (5:14). Scholars have speculated that these changes developed out of a need for Christians to appear respectable to Roman authorities. Young widows in Christian communities caused scandal or suspicion unless they remarried, and as a result, the writer of *1 Timothy* felt it necessary to prescribe more traditional behavior for them.[33]

As part of the second-century debate over the role of marriage in Christian social organization, Christian thinkers reconceptualized the figure of Mary, the mother of Jesus. Although Mary played a limited role in the canonical Gospels, she appeared extensively in a text called the *Protoevangelium of James* (ca. 120–150), which portrayed her as a perpetual virgin for the first time. According to that biographical material on Mary, the midwife who helped at Jesus's birth did not believe that Mary was a virgin, so she felt to see if the hymen was still in place. It was, and the midwife's hand withered with her doubt, only to be restored by the infant Jesus. This emphasis on Mary's perpetual virginity required a new interpretation of the brothers and sisters of Jesus who appeared in the Gospels. Later writers argued that those siblings were not blood relatives, but instead metaphorical relations. The acceptance of Mary's perpetual virginity meant that, some Christian

writers, like Tertullian, unfavorably compared ordinary women who did not remain virgins to Mary. Tertullian referred to women as the devil's gateway, coined the phrase "original sin," and blamed women for causing the fall of man in the Garden of Eden. Through Mary's example, some Christian thinkers presented celibacy as the ultimate sign of devotion to God. The new image of Mary put women in a difficult position, because unlike her, they could not both remain virgins and be mothers.

The Legalization of Christianity

Emperor Constantine (r. 312–337) passed the Edict of Toleration in 313, making Christianity legal and giving Christians the right to practice their religion without interference. We do not know Constantine's personal beliefs. Although he ultimately attributed his successes to the Christian god, historians remain uncertain about his beliefs immediately after he conquered Rome. His triumphal arch credited an unnamed deity with his victory. However, he was a savvy politician and was well aware of Christianity's increasing popularity.

No doubt, Constantine's mother, Helena (ca. 250–ca. 330), greatly influenced her son's familiarity with and interest in Christianity. If she was not a Christian, she was certainly intrigued by Christian beliefs. Once Christianity became legal, Helena embraced a life of Christian piety. She donated large sums of money to the church and built several churches and monasteries. Helena also undertook a pilgrimage to the Holy Land, where she endowed and lavishly decorated numerous churches, including one near the Grotto of the Nativity in Bethlehem and another on the Mount of the Ascension near Jerusalem. This pilgrimage produced the famous legend that she brought back a piece of the cross that the Romans had used to crucify Jesus. Her patronage of the church and her travels to holy sites created a new model of behavior for Christian royal women to imitate.

Although Constantine seems to have cared little for the particulars of Christian theology, he attempted to eliminate Christians who disagreed with the bishops under his patronage. Gnostics were his first target, but he also attacked the followers of an Egyptian priest named Arius (ca. 250–336) as heretics. Arius argued that Christ was not of the same substance as God because he came to earth as the son of God. In 324, Constantine called a church council at the city of Nicaea where he urged the bishops to decide whether Arian Christianity was orthodox. At the council, the bishops formulated the Nicene Creed, which declared the Trinity—the Father, the Son, and the Holy Spirit—indivisible. Christ and God were of the same substance. The council excommunicated Arius, thereby excluding him from all sacramental activity until he recanted and asked for forgiveness. The council also set Easter as the first Sunday after the first full moon that followed the spring equinox. Before that, Christians had celebrated it on a variety of Sundays around Passover.

Despite the council's best efforts, Arianism remained vibrant. Both Arians and orthodox missionaries worked to spread their versions of Christianity. The Arians were especially active among the Germanic tribes east of the Danube. Arianism even divided Christian families. The sixth-century chronicler Gregory of Tours (ca. 538–ca. 594) told the story of a woman who hosted a dinner party for her Catholic priest and her husband's Arian advisor. A competition ensued. As servants brought each dish from the kitchen, the Arian blessed it, making it impossible for the Catholic priest to eat, as he refused to consume food blessed by heretics. Finally, the Arian choked on an omelet of olives and grapes and died, signaling the triumph of the priest and orthodox Christianity.

Constantine's protection of Christianity did not turn Rome into a Christian empire overnight, nor did later Christian emperors automatically legislate in accordance with Christian morality. However, Christianity quickly began to influence Roman law in areas such as marriage legislation. As early as 320, Constantine abolished Augustus's laws against celibacy (see Chapter 3). Constantine also made divorce much more difficult for both men and women to obtain, because marriage was created by God and analogous to the relationship between Jesus and the church. A woman could only divorce her husband if he had committed murder, sorcery, or had desecrated a tomb. If a woman filed for divorce and could not prove these grounds, she was declared "presumptuous," and she forfeited all her property down to her last

hairpin and was exiled to an island. A man found it similarly difficult to divorce his wife but did not suffer the same punishments for an unsuccessful attempt. He had to give back his wife's dowry, and he was not supposed to remarry, but if he did, his first wife could confiscate the second wife's dowry. Christian suspicion about remarriage also appeared in the legislation concerning widows as guardians. Widowed mothers and grandmothers could become guardians of their children and grandchildren only as long as they did not remarry.[34]

Christianity also influenced ideas about child abandonment. As we saw in the previous chapter, child exposure was the way Romans disposed of unwanted children. During the first century, pagan Roman officials became concerned about underpopulation and began to oppose the exposure of children, while early Christian writers openly denounced the practice. Constantine did not make exposure illegal, but he did make it possible to sell children rather than simply abandon them. Moreover, people who raised abandoned children could decide the legal status of the child and that status could not be changed even if the birth father later found and attempted to claim the child. In 322, Roman government officials in North Africa passed an edict giving aid to indigent families so that they would raise their children rather than sell them or expose them. Finally, in 374, Emperor Valentinian I (364–375) outlawed child exposure, although the law was difficult to enforce.[35]

In 391, Emperor Theodosius (r. 379–395) made Christianity the state religion of the Roman Empire, and soon after Christians began to express the same intolerance for pagans that they had experienced under the Romans. One of the most infamous Christian persecutions of pagans was the murder of Hypatia (d. 412), the daughter of a famous Egyptian philosopher. She was well educated and became the head of the Neo-Platonist school in Alexandria around 400. An eloquent, charismatic teacher, she attracted large numbers of students. She also compiled and edited ancient mathematical treatises. Some Christians opposed this kind of scholarly work as pagan and antithetical to Christian spiritual goals. In 412, Cyril became head of the Christian church in Alexandria. His rival, the pagan prefect Orestes, was a close friend of Hypatia. As Christians lashed out against pagans in the city, a Christian mob, which felt threatened by her scientific approach to knowledge and her association with Orestes, murdered Hypatia.

As Christianity spread, many Roman emperors persecuted its followers for not worshipping them; however, Christians turned martyrdom into the ultimate manifestation of holiness. They praised female martyrs' ability to overcome feminine weakness and found spiritual strength in the cult of the saints. By the second century, the ongoing interactions between Christians and Romans changed Christian practice. Church leaders limited women's participation in the church in order to comply with Greco-Roman expectations for women's behavior. When Christianity became legal, its emphasis on celibacy changed Greco-Roman society profoundly, giving it a new set of values and expectations for women.

LIVING LIKE A MAN: THE CHRISTIAN ASCETIC IDEAL, 300–450

Christianity's emphasis on celibacy offered women opportunities largely unavailable in the pagan world and altered official attitudes toward women and gender. In particular, many women expressed their spirituality through monasticism and asceticism. Practitioners of monasticism and asceticism believed that personal and physical desires were sinful and hindered the pursuit of salvation. They rejected sex and most material and personal comforts in order to focus on their relationships with God. Women who gave up sex, motherhood, and the physical comforts of home challenged traditional gender expectations, as many considered their behavior "manly."

The Lure of Monasticism

Christian monasticism arose in and around the Egyptian desert. Tradition holds that the first Christian monk was Anthony (251–356), an Egyptian peasant moved by a Christian preacher who encouraged his listeners to renounce material possessions. Anthony took this message to heart, sold his inheritance, and went to live in the desert. With his asceticism, Anthony hoped to reclaim the purity of Adam before the Fall. His example and teachings attracted many followers, and by 305, a community of men and women assembled periodically to receive Anthony's instruction, although they did not live together permanently. Anthony urged those who wished for Christian fulfillment to reject the sinful temptations of urban life, especially sex and women.

According to the *Life of Anthony* written around 350, before undertaking the monastic life, he sent his orphaned sister to live with a community of consecrated virgins. Thus, we know that even before Anthony decided to become a monk, there were already dedicated communities of Christian women.[36] The community that took in Anthony's sister was probably in Alexandria. We do not know much about these urban communities, or whether they were exclusively composed of women. However, Christians quickly came to associate urban monasticism with women and desert monasticism with men, despite the presence of women.[37]

Monastics who preferred to live alone in the desert became known as hermits or anchorites. Christian authorities discouraged women from living in the desert because it placed them in physical danger, and many male thinkers believed that women posed a sexual threat to male hermits. Increasingly, monastic writers presented women as a temptation to men. One desert hermit warned that even if an elderly nun patted the foot of a sick and elderly bishop, both would instantly fall in to fornication.[38] Despite such sentiments, many women sought the solitude of the desert. The "desert mothers" performed elaborate feats of asceticism, living in caves, eating roots, fasting extensively, and praying continuously. Through self-denial, they subordinated the body to the spirit and brought themselves closer to God. Hagiographers reported that some hermits went without food, sleep, or bathing for years at a time. By disciplining their flesh, women made their bodies like men's. Indeed, limited food and other deprivations may have stopped women's menstrual cycles. The sayings of some desert fathers and mothers reveal that although they struggled to deny their sex, women's desert experiences were still gendered. One female hermit, Amma Syncletia (second century) stated, "Just as sturdy clothes, trodden and turned in washing, are made clean and white, so a strong soul gains in strength by voluntary poverty. But those souls, which have weaker reasoning power, experience the opposite. Even if they are only slightly pressed down, they are destroyed, like clothes which are torn: they cannot stand the washing given by virtue."[39] Even in the Egyptian desert, female hermits relied on the domestic imagery of clothing and laundry to describe their religious experience.

The life of a hermit could be a form of penance for former prostitutes. Many such legends exist, although the story of Mary Magdalene is probably the most popular. According to the tale, after eschewing her life as a whore, Mary went to live in the desert as a hermit. In stark contrast to her luxurious life as a prostitute, she became like a wild woman, covered with hair and living on little food. Her long hair, which had symbolized her life as a prostitute, then symbolized her repentance and hermitic life. Stories such as these are mostly apocryphal, but they provided a model for others to admire if not emulate. Mary Magdalene gave up not only her riches and comfortable life but also her beauty.

True communal or *cenobite* monasticism developed in southern Egypt. Pachomius (ca. 292–346) wrote the first rule for his monastery outside of the Egyptian city of Thebes in 326. It required strict discipline and rigorous prayer and emphasized two critical notions—discipline and the need for total obedience to a rule and the community's leader, the abbot. Both concerns became central themes in subsequent monastic rules. Discipline included virginity or chastity, physical labor, and routine prayer. Infractions not only jeopardized the individual's soul, but also the souls of the entire community. Abbots punished uncooperative members with beatings and expulsion.

People from all classes joined monasteries. Sometimes entire families joined. The hagiographies of early Christian monastic saints claimed that many monks and nuns came from humble roots, as did Anthony and his sister, and had little education. The White Monastery in southern Egypt boasted eighteen hundred women and twenty-two hundred men during the tenure of its third abbot, Shenoute (ca. 348–ca. 464).[40] Monastic discipline provided members with the assurance of salvation, but the poor peasants of Egypt also relied on the daily food, certain shelter, continued employment, and regular contact with family members who had already joined the community.

Although solitary and communal monasticism hoped to erase social and gender distinctions, both influenced daily life in monastic communities. Women performed all types of work in exclusively female communities; however, in mixed-sex communities, women performed traditional women's work. In the larger, more permanent monasteries such as the White Monastery, men and women lived in separate sections, and women made cloth and clothing, which supplied the monastery and the nearby village. Cloth making was easy to combine with prayer and a life of personal deprivation. As monasteries also provided charity for the poor, female monks probably helped to deliver babies and tended to the medical needs of laywomen. The men wove baskets and farmed.

Shenoute's letters to his female monks show how difficult it was for members of monastic communities to abandon their family ties. Female monks continued to replicate family life by caring for particular individuals, and in some cases even hoarding food to help weaker individuals overcome strict fasting regulations. Shenoute's letters also hinted that close personal relationships developed in monastic houses. He condemned younger female monks who "run after their companions in a fleshly desire."[41] Monastic rules repeatedly tried to redirect attention away from other monks and toward God.

Ideally monastic life allowed adherents to give up their gender identities. Yet in reality, this process was more complicated. Thekla, who lived as a hermit and dressed as a man, was a model for this goal, but male monastics rarely ignored the fact that these ascetics were women. Asceticism was the denial of the body, and the body was associated with femininity. Although female monastics might perform extreme feats of denial and asceticism like their male counterparts, the men who recorded their lives described their accomplishments as manly because of the great efforts they expended to deny their female needs and weaknesses. However, male ascetics who denied their body could not be described as feminine, because the spirit was associated with masculinity. Denying physical needs was by definition a masculine behavior.

The Evolution of Christian Theology and Gender Ideologies

With the legalization of Christianity, theologians focused on how to live openly as a Christian and how to create a Christian society. They looked to both Greco-Roman philosophical and medical ideas and monastic ascetic experiences to formulate Christian beliefs about women, sex, and gender. For instance, Soranus's idea that virgins were healthier helped justify Christians' belief that virginity was the perfect state (see Chapter 3). Many monastic leaders, such as Anthony believed that virginity was the condition of Adam and Eve in the Garden of Eden before the Fall. Christian theologians learned from Aristotle that women were imperfectly formed men, that women were prone to emotion and irrationality and intellectually and physically weak, and that heterosexual sex was between an active person (the man) and a passive person (the woman). Based on these ideas and experiences, theologians struggled to reconcile Christian theology with Greco-Roman society.

Two of the most important theologians of the fourth century were Augustine (354–430) and Jerome (ca. 340–420). Both were teachers at Roman schools when they underwent their conversions to Christianity, yet their careers and attitudes toward women and sex were very different. Jerome lived much of his life in Italy. He translated the Hebrew Bible and the New Testament from their original languages of Hebrew, Aramaic, and Greek into Latin. Known as the *Vulgate*, because it was in the vulgar or vernacular language of the time, it was the standard translation of the Bible for centuries. Jerome also served as advisor and confidant to a wide range of followers, many of whom were ascetic women. In his correspondence to his followers, of which approximately 120 letters still survive, Jerome tried to conceptualize Christianity as a religion for everyone, not just a few enthusiasts. Augustine came from North Africa and converted to Christianity after a long

spiritual and intellectual struggle. Unlike Jerome, he became part of the church hierarchy and from his position as a pastoral leader, he wrote extensively about the meaning of Christianity for ordinary Christians. Augustine and Jerome are known as church fathers because their writings are so central to the development of the Christian theology.

Augustine's autobiography, the *Confessions,* reveals how his own experiences with sex were critical in his development of Christian ideas about gender, virginity, and marriage. Born in North Africa to a pagan father and a Christian mother, Augustine received both a Christian and a classical education in Carthage. Before his baptism, he spent his time in Roman schools, attending parties, and having sex. His pious mother Monica attempted to calm his wild lifestyle urging him "not to commit fornication; but especially never to defile another man's wife." Augustine responded that this "seemed to me womanish advices, which I should blush to obey" (*Confessions*, 2.3.7). Ignoring his mother's advice, he lived with a concubine who bore him a son. Around 373, he joined the Manicheans, a religious sect that saw the world as ruled by opposing forces of Light (God) and Dark (the Devil). Eventually, Augustine went to Rome to teach rhetoric and continue his education. He ended up in Milan, where his mother joined him. Under her influence and that of the great preacher Ambrose (ca. 340–397), Augustine began to explore Christianity seriously. He sent his concubine of fifteen years away, accepted Christianity, and embraced a life of celibacy. His mother's faith guided him in his spiritual quest. At her death, he described her as a woman "in female garb with masculine faith" (*Confessions*, 9.4.8). His wisdom and oratory skills propelled him into the church leadership. He was ordained and returned to North Africa to become bishop of Hippo.

Jerome and Augustine disagreed over the role of virginity. Jerome believed that women's bodies were inherently sinful and polluted and that women needed to work harder to achieve salvation than men. His models were the ascetic women he counseled. He had close relationships with these women, relied on them for advice, and was well aware of their spirituality and religious devotion. Yet, he still believed that women were inferior to men and were more susceptible to sin and temptation. He advised men to leave women alone because marriage and sex were stains on the soul that were difficult to remove.

Augustine's experiences with women and sex and the particular problems he faced leading the North African Church gave him a more pragmatic view on women, marriage, and sex than Jerome. During the Roman persecutions, North African Christians particularly suffered, and many denied their faith to escape torture and death. Once Christianity was legal, surviving Christians resented those who had collaborated with the Romans. As a result, Augustine led a bitterly divided church.

Augustine believed that reconciliation of the North African Church required finding a social role for both virginity and marriage. Augustine argued that Christians should limit sex to marriage. Marriage was a sacramental binding of two people that could not be dissolved, even in cases of infidelity or infertility. Moreover, North African priests were usually married, unlike those advised by Jerome in Rome. Augustine knew that imposing celibacy on his priests would make recruitment difficult. Augustine also placed a higher value on martyrdom than virginity. Many of the North African female martyrs he admired, such as Crispina of Theveste and Perpetua, were mothers. Unlike Jerome, Augustine believed that sex was a part of God's plan for Adam and Eve even in Eden. Augustine's view of Eden had much the same gender hierarchy as the fourth-century Greco-Roman world. Women were to be subservient to their husbands. However, although Augustine understood the importance of marriage and sex to society, he still had a low opinion of sex and the power of sexual attraction. He viewed sex as a terrible distraction that overcame reason. When men became enamored with women and women's bodies, they became detached from God.[42]

Finally, by arguing that women were not failed or inferior versions of men, Augustine differed from the dominant Aristotelian view. Augustine also argued for the importance of free will for both men and women. As free will was a gift from God, both women and men could seek a virtuous life through the correct use of their free will. In a society that granted little freedom to women, this

ASCENSION OF JESUS INTO HEAVEN, WHILE MARY PRAYS, RABBULA GOSPELS (CA. 589). Although only appearing briefly in the Christian Bible, the Virgin Mary took on a much larger role in Christianity as the religion spread. *(Biblioteca Mediceo Laurneziana, Florence/Art Resource.)*

idea had tremendous significance. For instance, it explained a woman's preference for a Christian life of celibacy over marriage or a daughter's wish to live as a pagan when her father wanted her to be a Christian.

Domestic Asceticism and the Cult of Virginity

The legalization of Christianity attracted new followers; however, many of them lacked the fervor and commitment of those who had suffered through the persecutions. Many new converts joined the church for political or economic reasons rather than spiritual ones. The Roman state offered tax breaks to bishops, making the office attractive to ambitious rather than spiritually devout men. Pious and opportunistic Christians lived side by side. For the sincere, who could no longer prove their religious devotion through martyrdom, asceticism offered a rigorous Christian lifestyle. In particular, Roman women embraced asceticism, which they could practice in their homes. Scholar Kate Cooper has argued that asceticism allowed women some opportunity to choose their own fates by rejecting traditional Roman emphases on family status and marriage alliances. When a woman became an ascetic, she was introduced to new social networks of people who admired her Christian behavior. For Roman women accustomed to self-effacement and self-sacrifice, asceticism enhanced their identities and gave them and their families privileged status.[43]

Much of what we know about women's domestic asceticism comes from the letters of Jerome to his female followers. He advised this large circle on a variety of topics, including how to raise children in an ascetic household (see **Sources from the Past:** "Letter of Jerome to Laeta"). At the beginning of Jerome's career, he believed that these women should leave home and cut themselves off from their families, because he feared that they would distract the young ascetics with worldly concerns. Jerome gradually changed his opinion, realizing that living alone was dangerous for women and that their connections to kin could convert others to the ascetic lifestyle. Marcella (d. ca. 382), one of his early followers, strongly influenced his early opinions on female asceticism. Marcella became an ascetic but continued to live with her mother, who pressured her to marry an elderly wealthy suitor. She refused, but Jerome noted how difficult it was for Marcella to ignore her family. Marcella was also highly educated and helped Jerome with his biblical interpretation and theological writings. When Jerome had to leave Rome after losing a political dispute, she took over for him and addressed several religious controversies. She always carefully attributed her ideas to the Bible or to Jerome so as not to disobey the biblical ban on women teaching.[44]

Jerome's relationship with Paula (ca. 347–404) also influenced his ideas on women. A wealthy mother of five, she became an ascetic after her husband's death, limiting her consumption of food and drink, sleeping as little as possible, and devoting herself to charity. She became close to Jerome, and after going on a pilgrimage to the Holy Land with her daughter Eustochium, she settled in Bethlehem. With Jerome's guidance, she and Eustochium founded a double monastery (separately housing men and women); Paula learned both Greek and Hebrew and became Jerome's closest confidante as well as his caretaker.

The women in Jerome's circle were elite women of prominent families. Their austere lifestyles and wealth gave them a great deal of freedom. Like men, these women traveled, conversed with church leaders, and studied theology. They retreated to country estates to practice their asceticism and engage in physical labor. In the Roman world, poverty was a serious social problem and many of these well-off women gave away huge fortunes. They founded religious houses with their own money and donated their dowries when they refused to marry. When necessary, they relied on their status to get them out of trouble.[45]

Melania the Elder (d. 410) was the daughter and granddaughter of consuls. She married young and had one son. At about the age of twenty, her husband died and she took up asceticism. In the 370s, she left Rome to travel to the East, meeting with bishops and other ascetics. When Egyptian authorities arrested her for vagrancy and consorting with dubious characters, she informed them of her family connections and they allowed her to continue her work. She founded a convent and monastery with her own substantial fortune and eventually supervised fifty virgins, although we know little about them or their community. When word reached her that her son was trying to prevent her granddaughter, Melania the Younger (d. 439), from taking up the ascetic lifestyle, the grandmother returned to Rome to oversee her granddaughter's education and conversion. Ultimately convinced of her granddaughter's commitment to asceticism, Melania the Elder returned to Egypt and her studies.

Melania the Younger followed her grandmother's ascetic model. Like a traditional Roman woman, she married young, but she spent much of her marriage trying to convince her husband to allow her to become an ascetic. He only relented after she bore him two children, eventually taking up the ascetic life himself. Melania the Younger then left Rome for the East. While in Constantinople, she mingled with the royal court and argued theology. Her *Life* claims that she saved several women from doctrinal error and brought them back to the orthodox, or correct, form of Christian belief. She also converted her worldly uncle to Christianity on his deathbed. She founded a convent in Jerusalem, but unlike her grandmother, refused to become abbess. She nevertheless maintained a strong presence in the community.

Early Christian writers emphasized that these women acted and looked different from traditional Roman women. In addition to protecting their virginity in the face of family pressure to marry, they did not dress like other women of their class. Jewelry, hairstyle, and dress were all markers of status and family honor in the Roman world. Well-off female ascetics gave up silk, a sign of wealth, for the shapeless garments of cotton or linen generally worn by the poor. Some wore white as a sign of purity and because it showed dirt and blood, while others wore black as a sign of repentance and sinfulness. Still others believed that natural colors were best because they did not require either bleaching or dyeing, signs of wealth and vanity. They also preferred uncomfortable clothing, especially shirts made of goat hair that rubbed the skin raw and reminded the wearer of the suffering of Jesus.[46] Hairstyles also conveyed messages about female sanctity. Some women kept their heads covered as a sign of humility; others wore their hair down and unkempt in opposition to the elaborate hairstyles of pagan women and to show their lack of vanity. Ascetic women often imitated Mary Magdalene's long, coatlike hair. Jerome tells the story of Eustochium, Paula's daughter, whose hair became matted and dirty. Her aunt, who tried to fix it, became fatally ill as divine punishment, and Eustochium maintained her unkempt appearance.[47]

Although female ascetics acted and dressed in ways that denied their femininity and their feminine weakness, Christian authorities found it unacceptable for women to cut their hair and dress in men's clothing. The legendary Thekla had dressed as a man when she left home to follow Paul, but she was the exception. Overcoming feminine weakness was permissible, but denying one's sex denied God's creation. After the fifth century, church councils insisted that women wear female clothing and cross-dressing women could not enter churches.

Asceticism and virginity as Christian values posed challenges to Roman men. As we saw in the last chapter, men demonstrated their masculinity through sex and military activity. In response, Christian leaders often used Stoic ideas of moderation and restraint to assure Roman men that adopting Christianity would not feminize them. Initially Christian leaders used military vocabulary to describe martyrdom so that men could embrace the image of "soldier of Christ." Martin (d. 397), who served unwillingly in the Roman military, finally renounced his life as a soldier to become a Christian ascetic. When his commanding officer accused him of cowardice, he agreed to "go unscathed through the enemy's columns" without arms or armor.[48] While spurning military combat, Martin still asserted his masculinity through bravery. Noblemen, who at this point did not serve in the military, also used military images to describe their battle against sin.[49] As a result, elite men, such as Melania the Younger's husband, Pinian, could retire to their country estates and live as ascetics without compromising their masculinity.

The legalization of Christianity brought changes to both Christianity and Greco-Roman society; one of the most profound was the shift from an emphasis on marriage and motherhood to virginity and celibacy as women's highest spiritual calling. As women looked to maintain their virginity in the service of God, they practiced new lifestyles that took them away from their families and taught them new behaviors. Their efforts to deny their physical natures drew admiration from male church leaders who applauded their triumph over female physicality and weakness.

WOMEN AND THE RISE OF BYZANTIUM, 330–800

With the Roman emperor's support for Christianity, Christianity dominated Roman society and Roman institutions. In the eastern half of the Empire, Roman institutions, Greek culture, and Christianity flourished in what became known as the Byzantine Empire. At its height in the seventh century, Byzantine territory included

Letter of Jerome to Laeta

In this letter, Jerome answers Laeta's questions about how to raise and educate her baby daughter, whom Laeta has consecrated as a virgin. His educational program encourages some aspects of Roman culture and rejects others for baby Paula. He is especially concerned that Paula learn to read so that she can read Scripture.

4.   Thus must a soul be educated which is to be a temple of God. It must learn to hear nothing and to say nothing but what belongs to the fear of God. It must have no understanding of unclean words, and no knowledge of the world's songs. Its tongue must be steeped while still tender in the sweetness of the psalms. Boys with their wanton thoughts must be kept from Paula: even her maids and female attendants must be separated from worldly associates. For if they have learned some mischief they may teach more. Get for her a set of letters made of boxwood or of ivory and called each by its proper name. Let her play with these, so that even her play may teach her something. And not only make her grasp the right order of the letters and see that she forms their names into a rhyme, but constantly disarrange their order and put the last letters in the middle and the middle ones at the beginning that she may know them all by sight as well as by sound. Moreover, so soon as she begins to use the style upon the wax, and her hand is still faltering, either guide her soft fingers by laying your hand upon hers, or else have simple copies cut upon a tablet; so that her efforts confined within these limits may keep to the lines traced out for her and not stray outside of these. Offer prizes for good spelling and draw her onwards with little gifts such as children of her age delight in. And let her have companions in her lessons to excite emulation in her, that she may be stimulated when she sees them praised. You must not scold her if she is slow to learn but must employ praise to excite her mind, so that she may be glad when she excels others and sorry when she is excelled by them.

Above all you must take care not to make her lessons distasteful to her lest a dislike for them conceived in childhood may continue into her maturer years. The very words which she tries bit by bit to put together and to pronounce ought not to be chance ones, but names specially fixed upon and heaped together for the purpose, those for example of the prophets or the apostles or the list of patriarchs from Adam downwards as it is given by Matthew and Luke. In this way while her tongue will be well-trained, her memory will be likewise developed. Again, you must choose for her a master of approved years, life, and learning. A man of culture will not, I think, blush to do for a kinswoman or a highborn virgin what Aristotle did for Philip's son when, descending to the level of an usher, he consented to teach him his letters.[1] Things must not be despised as of small account in the absence of which great results cannot be achieved. The very rudiments and first beginnings of knowledge sound differently in the mouth of an educated man and of an uneducated [one]. Accordingly you must see that the child is not led away by the silly coaxing of women to form a habit of shortening long words or of decking herself with gold and purple. Of these habits one will spoil her conversation and the other her character. She must not therefore learn as a child what afterwards she will have to unlearn. The eloquence of the Gracchi is said to have been largely due to the way in which from their earliest years their mother spoke to them.[2] Hortensius became an orator while still on his father's lap.[3] Early impressions are hard to eradicate from the mind. When once wool has been dyed purple who can restore it to its previous whiteness? An unused jar long retains the taste and smell of that with which it is first filled.[4] Grecian history tells us that the imperious Alexander who was lord of the whole world could not rid himself of the tricks of manner and gait which in his childhood he had caught from his governor Leonides.[5] We are always ready to imitate what is evil; and faults are quickly copied where virtues appear in attainable. Paula's nurse must not be intemperate, or loose, or given to gossip. Her bearer must be respectable, and her foster-father of grave demeanour. When she sees her grandfather, she must leap upon his breast, put her arms round his neck, and, whether he likes it or not, sing Alleluia in his ears. She may be fondled by her grandmother, may smile at her father to shew that she recognizes him, and may so endear herself to everyone, as to make the whole family rejoice in the possession of such a rosebud. She should be told at once whom she has for her other grandmother and whom for her aunt; and she ought also to learn in what army it is that she is enrolled as a recruit, and what Captain it is under whose banner she is called to serve. Let her long to be with the absent ones and encourage her to make playful threats of leaving you for them.

9.   And let it be her task daily to bring to you the flowers which she has culled from Scripture. Let her learn by heart so many verses in the Greek, but let her be instructed in the Latin also. For, if the tender lips are not from the first shaped to this, the tongue is spoiled by a foreign accent and its native speech debased by alien elements. You must yourself be her mistress, a model on which she may form her childish conduct. Never either in you nor in her father let her see what she cannot imitate without sin. Remember both of you that you are the parents of a consecrated virgin, and that your example will teach her more than your precepts. Flowers are quick to fade and a baleful wind soon withers the violet, the lily, and the crocus. Let her never appear in public unless accompanied by you. Let her never visit a church or a martyr's shrine unless with her mother. Let no young man greet her with smiles; no dandy with curled hair pay compliments to her. If our little virgin goes to keep solemn eves and all-night vigils, let her not stir a hair's breadth from her mother's side. She must not single out one of her maids to make her a special favourite or a confidante. What she says to one all ought to know. Let her choose for a companion not a handsome well-dressed girl, able to warble a song with liquid notes but one pale and serious, sombrely attired and with the hue of melancholy. Let her take as her model some aged virgin of approved faith, character, and chastity, apt to instruct her by word and by example. She ought to rise at night to recite prayers and psalms; to sing hymns in the morning; at the third, sixth, and ninth hours to take her place in the line to do battle for Christ; and, lastly, to kindle her lamp and to offer her evening sacrifice. In these occupations let her pass the day, and when night comes let it find her still engaged in them. Let reading follow prayer with her, and prayer again succeed to reading. Time will seem short when employed on tasks so many and so varied.

------

[1] Quintilian, *Institutio Oratoria*, I. 1. Aristotle taught Alexander the Great, see Chapter 2

[2] Quint. *Institiutio Oratoria*, I.1; Cornelia was very educated and purportedly educated her sons, see Chapter 3.

[3] The contemporary and rival of Cicero.

[4] Horace, *Epistles*, I. ii 69.

[5] Quint. *Institutio Oratoria*, I. 1.

Source: Christian Classics Ethereal Library, Calvin College; http://www.ccel.org/ccel/schaff/npnf206.v.CVII.html#fnb _v.CVII-p57.2.

Asia Minor, the Middle East, Greece, and the Balkans (see Map 4.2). The center of the Byzantine Empire was the capital of Constantinople. Constantine's legalization of Christianity had alienated many of the old pagan families who dominated Rome, so he built a glorious new capital city for his empire on top of the decaying Greek city of Byzantium, located on the Bosporus. Constantine named the city, which was financed in part by the plundered gold and silver of the old pagan temples, for himself and dedicated it on May 11, 330. The new capital also placed the emperor close to the main battlefronts of the lower Danube and the Euphrates. It was a hub for goods traded between the East and West and was far richer than Rome. Rome continued to have great symbolic value because of its history and

because it had the relics of Saints Peter and Paul, but culturally it was no longer the center of the Empire or the source of its wealth. Increasingly, the Western Empire suffered economic decline and political chaos, while the East enjoyed wealth and political stability. Gender norms in the Byzantine Empire differed significantly from those in Rome. Byzantine women had to negotiate not only Christian ideas about the value of their virginity, but also the traditional Greek ideal of female seclusion.

Gender in the Byzantine Palace

Byzantine women, like their Roman counterparts, played no official role in government and politics but relied instead on their family relationships to influence the court. However, the fact that many

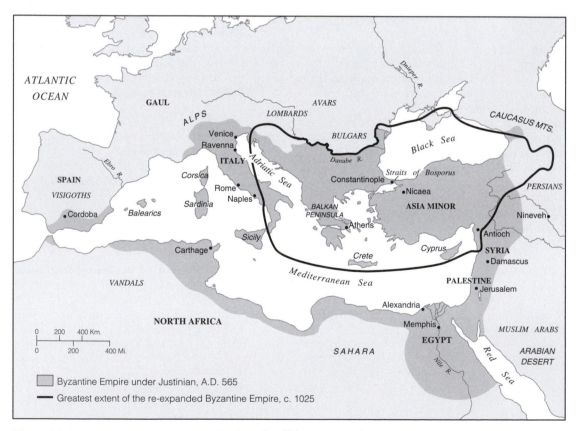

Map 4.2 THE BYZANTINE EMPIRE. During the fifth century, the Byzantine Empire emerged from the Eastern Roman Empire, combining Eastern and Western cultures to create a new and vibrant society.

Byzantine government functions were under the control of eunuchs indicates that Byzantine culture understood gender very differently than the Romans. Eunuchs were men who had been castrated, usually at birth but sometimes after puberty, to enhance their value as slaves. Eunuchs had been common as household slaves in the East and prized for their loyalty and their inability to impregnate women. Males castrated at birth do not go through puberty, thus their bodies share many of the characteristics of women—soft skin, no facial hair, high voices, and later in life, even swollen breasts. Males castrated after puberty look like other men but cannot father children. Katherine Ringrose argues that a Byzantine eunuch's disassociation from family and reproduction, the primary component of masculine and feminine gender in the Greco-Roman world, made them neither masculine nor feminine. In fact, Byzantines understood a eunuch's negative traits—weakness, emotionality, deceitfulness, and irrationality—in feminine terms and saw their positive traits—loyalty, rationality, and vigor—as masculine. The presence of large numbers of eunuchs gave Byzantium three genders: masculine, feminine, and eunuch.[50]

Attitudes toward eunuchs changed over the course of Byzantine history. Like many other Eastern imports, Romans did not particularly trust eunuchs; they found their sexual ambiguity troubling. Christian leaders, believing that one must leave the body as God had made it, also found eunuchs problematic. Although some eunuchs were celibate, the church was suspicious of their commitment, believing that they did not have to wrestle with and conquer their sexual desires like whole men. Other eunuchs worked in the sex trade and the church believed that because they were infertile they only had sex for pleasure, making them debauched. However, by the eighth century, a positive view of eunuchs emerged and the church allowed eunuchs to serve in positions of authority. Ignatios the Younger, a eunuch, was patriarch, or head of the church, in Constantinople in the ninth century.

Eunuch slaves dominated the imperial bureaucracy of Byzantium. Eunuchs often served as mediators, filling roles and performing tasks inappropriate for physically whole men or women. Court eunuchs managed money, tutored children, supervised the feeding and dressing of their masters and mistresses, and organized court ceremonies. Eunuchs also worked in the households of Byzantine empresses. Within the women's quarters, eunuchs oversaw their ceremonial life and served as go-betweens for the various segments of the imperial household. Some eunuchs became very powerful, wealthy, and influential, as many empresses came to depend on them as confidants and advisors.[51]

The only women involved in Byzantine politics were members of the royal family. Although not legally barred from the throne, a female ruler was highly unusual, and the women who ruled had difficulty maintaining power and the confidence of their advisors. Instead, the empress's power derived from her ability to influence the emperor as his wife or as the mother of the heir. Thus, lacking a male heir to the throne, an empress or princess conveyed imperial power to her husband rather than rule herself. Several men became emperor in this way. Emperor Leo I (d. 474) died leaving only a daughter, Ariadne. She first married Zeno (r. 474–491), and then when he died without a male heir, she married Anastasios I (r. 491–518), who succeeded to the throne.

Theodora (ca. 497–548), the wife of Justinian (r. 527–565), is the best-known Byzantine empress. However, most of our information about Theodora comes from a scandalous and malicious account of her life, *The Secret Histories*, written by Prokopios (d. 562), a Byzantine administrator. Although Prokopios wrote several respectful histories of Justinian's reign, *The Secret Histories* is full of animosity. Theodora was a close advisor to her husband and exercised considerable authority at court. Prokopios disapproved of her influence and accused Justinian of becoming effeminate because of his dependence on her. Prokopios wrote that Theodora was the daughter of a bear trainer and worked as an actress and prostitute before she met and married Justinian. We do not know how accurate Prokopios's accusations are because he drew heavily from classical literary traditions, making his work more a piece of rhetoric and polemic than a historical narrative.[52]

Theodora's role in public life is difficult to untangle. Less vindictive sources, and even Prokopios himself, tells us that Theodora engaged in many charitable acts. Theodora helped unmarried girls at court find husbands, and she founded a convent for repentant prostitutes. It is tempting to see great empathy for women in these acts of imperial charity. Yet, compared with other empresses' charitable works, they do not appear unusual. Constantine's mother, Helena, founded several churches in the Holy Land, and the Empress Eudokia (d. 460) was a patron of scholars and schools. Theodora also established several monasteries for men, demonstrating that she did not limit her charity to women. We should also remember that her ability to step outside of traditional feminine activities was constrained by the fact that her power came largely from her ability to influence Justinian, not from any independent authority. She was interested in court politics and helped to design the court rituals that accentuated imperial authority, but her activities took place almost exclusively within the palace. Her influence on the outside world was predominantly through her husband the emperor, not through her generosity.[53]

Theodora's niece, Sophia (ca. 530–ca. 601), exercised more direct power as empress than Theodora. Her marriage to Justin II (r. 565–578) was the result of Theodora's patronage. When Justinian died without an heir and successor, Sophia helped secure the throne for her husband. Sophia apparently took charge of the treasury, establishing Justin's fiscal policy and helping oversee his building program for the city. Within a few years, Justin's mental health declined, and by 572, Sophia ruled alone. During this period, Sophia's name appears on royal decrees and coins. Although most empresses, with the exception of Theodora, appeared only on special coins minted for specific occasions, Sophia appeared on coins used in regular business. As Justin's conditioned worsened, Sophia had to pick a successor. She chose a nobleman named Tiberios (r. 578–582). Court gossips claimed that she wanted to marry him and continue ruling through him, but Tiberios was already married. Sophia refused to move out of the palace and let Tiberios's wife assume her duties as empress. Sophia hung on to power as long as she could and disappears from the records without information on her fate. She left the Byzantine Empire with the legacy of a strong empress, who wielded more power than her notorious aunt.[54]

Women in Byzantine Society: Elites and Peasants

After Constantine's death, the Roman Empire had split in two and Emperor Justinian was determined to reunite the two halves of the empire under his rule. After he successfully conquered most of the Mediterranean basin, Justinian sponsored a series of legal reforms that would both integrate Christian theology into Roman law and

EARLY BYZANTINE IVORY PANEL, POSSIBLY OF EMPRESS SOPHIA. Although Byzantine empresses could not rule directly, Sophia took direct control of the treasury, established fiscal policy, and aided in civic building programs. When her husband's health declined, she ruled alone, until forced to pick a successor. *(Bargello, Florence, Italy/ Art Resource, NY.)*

improve the government of his expanded empire. Although his military conquests did not last beyond his lifetime, his legal reforms provided the basis of European law for the next millennium. His compilation of statutes, opinions, and interpretations, known collectively as the *Corpus iuris civilis* (ca. 533), rationalized Roman law by eliminating redundancies and inconsistencies. In the process, these legal reforms codified a new set of Christian gender norms.

The *Corpus* reveals a legal system struggling to reconcile its pagan legal heritage with its Christian identity, and the results had serious implications for women. Justinian rejected the Christian belief that marriages were indissoluble, yet he made divorce more difficult to obtain. Moreover, he tried to ensure that men and women would be treated equally by abolishing the Roman tradition of consensual divorce and forcing both men and women to plead a legally recognized cause in order to terminate the marriage. Justinian also elevated the status of concubines, making them nearly equal to wives and allowing their children to inherit. A married man convicted of adultery lost all rights to his wife's dowry and she could sue for divorce. However, the husband of an adulterous wife could beat his wife and put her in a convent.[55]

The combination of Greek ideas about secluding women and the Christian emphasis on virginity meant that a well-bred Byzantine woman was expected never to leave home without a chaperone. Later Byzantine women also veiled themselves so that men outside of their families would not see their faces. The only proper outside activities for women were attending funerals, going to church, or visiting shrines. Although men and women apparently ate together with other family members, when a male guest came to the house, women kept to their quarters, eating and conversing only with other women. Seclusion did not prevent women from expressing their tastes or their personalities inside their homes. Wealthy women could spend a great deal of money on personal adornment and could acquire luxury items from around the known world. Byzantine elites particularly favored elaborately dyed or embroidered silk. Women also wore expensive jewelry made by the skilled gold and silversmiths of Constantinople. Byzantine women's use of makeup provoked the

criticism of clergymen, who argued that it was a sign of vanity and a source of deception—it made them look more beautiful than they were.[56]

Upper-class families taught their daughters to read, write, count, and sing, although they did not receive the same level of education as their brothers. Byzantine society considered education helpful in preparing women for marriage. Some of the education was practical, such as knowledge of herbs and medicine. In the first half of the ninth century, three women had enough education to compose poetry and religious hymns. Kassia, Theodosia, and Thekla used their skills to defend the use of icons, or images of the saints, in worship.[57]

Like other Mediterranean cultures, Byzantine women married young, generally by the age of twelve or thirteen. They left their parents' homes and moved in with their husbands' families or set up new households with their husbands, who were usually ten to fifteen years older. As in Roman culture, parents arranged marriages with an eye to economic concerns and family status. The wedding ceremony could be elaborate. Preparations started with a ritual bath for the bride, followed by a procession to the church, where a priest blessed the couple's union. After the ceremony, the couple and their guests went to the groom's house for the reception. In wealthy families, these celebrations could last for days. However, the couple only stayed through the wedding feast and then went to their bedroom, specially decorated for the occasion, where they consummated their marriage.[58]

Both church and state law attempted to discourage second or third marriages by women. As a result, widows headed as many as 20 percent of households in some rural communities. The state allowed them to control their own property and resources, and for some women, widowhood brought greater independence. For most, however, it probably brought poverty as well.[59]

Women were the key mourners in funerals. First, they prepared the body, sprinkling it with fragrant oils and spices and wrapping it in a shroud. During the processions, they wailed, tore their clothes and hair, and even lacerated their cheeks with their fingernails. The wealthy might even hire mourners to add to the spectacle. Many clergymen disapproved of these traditions. They argued that such emotion was unseemly and that women exposed too much of their bodies. In response, the church tried to reform Byzantine funerals, turning them into solemn and dignified occasions with trained choirs of monks and nuns singing religious hymns, thereby removing women from yet another public sphere.[60]

For lower-class women, social norms were not as restrictive. Whether urban or rural, lower-class Byzantine women tended to the kitchen garden, went to the well for water, and prepared the family's food and clothing. Wealthy women also depended on their maids and slaves to go to the marketplace for household provisions. There is little information on the work of rural women. Ivory carvings show women working in vineyards and helping with the harvest of grain, but a medieval Byzantine text states that women harvested only in emergencies, such as during war, when the men were away fighting. There are also references to women working as shepherdesses, but this was also considered scandalous, so we do not know how common it was. Families often depended on the income women generated, making it difficult to keep women completely confined.[61]

In Byzantine cities, women worked in a variety of capacities. They were artisans, retailers, midwives, bathhouse attendants, and moneylenders. Some women worked for wages in workshops, but there were also female owners of shops and workshops. Moreover, Byzantine law granted property rights to all Byzantine women, not just members of the upper class. Women could inherit and choose beneficiaries, and sons and daughters inherited equally. Women also owned the goods and property of their dowries, although in reality their husbands usually administered them, thereby limiting women's real economic independence.[62]

As in classical Roman culture, women provided most of the health care to other women. They served as midwives, nurses, wet nurses, and occult healers who combined folk medicine and charms with Christian prayer. In Constantinople, there were seven maternity wards with as many as forty beds each. Establishing hospitals for pregnant women was an important act of charity. Poor women could give birth, spend a week recovering, and receive a third of a gold coin at their departure. In the female ward of the hospital of the Pantokrator monastery in Constantinople, there was a female physician on staff. We know little about her. Whatever her train-

ing, she received half the salary of her male colleagues and less food.[63] Court cases also mention that lawyers called upon midwives and female doctors to testify to the virginity of a bride or a woman's state of pregnancy. One woman, Metrodora (fl. some time between the first and sixth centuries), wrote at least two original medical treatises that do not depend on Soranus and Galen (see Chapter 3). Her surviving work shows that she was engaged in several medical debates of the time, including one on the classification of various kinds of vaginal discharges. She also advanced some original theories about these discharges, linking them to parasites found in the rectum. Some of her remedies are unique to her and are not part of the late antique medical tradition. The fragment of her work that survives shows that she was more than a theorist; she practiced medicine as well.[64]

Women and the Byzantine Church

Over the centuries, Byzantine Christianity came to differ from western or Latin Christianity. After Constantine, Eastern emperors routinely participated in theological debates. Eastern priests could marry; there was an elaborate Greek, not Latin, liturgy; and the Virgin Mary was a more important focus of devotion than in the West. The Eastern liturgy also made extensive use of icons, painted pictures of the saints, the Virgin Mary, and Jesus. Worshippers used icons to feel closer to God and the saints.

Icons were an important aspect of female piety because they could be located in private homes. However, because icons became associated with idolatry, they became a source of controversy, and in 726, Emperor Leo III (ca. 680–741) banned them. Banning icons was also an attempt to curb monastic power. Monasteries produced most of the icons, giving them both a spiritual and an economic influence that rivaled the emperor. During this period, nuns and secular women suffered martyrdom for trying to defend or hide their icons. One woman, Theodosia, led a group of women from Constantinople to resist Leo's attempts to burn the image of Christ removed from the Chalke Gate. Theodosia and her companions were executed.[65] In 741, Leo III's widow, the Empress Irene (769–802), became regent for their son and restored icon worship. Empress

Theodora (830–ca. 867) ended another wave of iconoclasm in 843.

Although monastic lifestyles varied considerably, both male and female houses looked to Basil (330–379) as the founder of Byzantine monasticism. His rule expected religious foundations to be not in the desert, but in the city, where monks and nuns could serve as models for society and provide charity and prayers. Monasteries also provided what limited medical care was available. Increasingly, they acted as social welfare providers when the state could no longer afford to do so. Unlike the Roman dole (see Chapter 3), when Byzantine elites dispensed food as charity, they usually relied on monks or nuns as intermediaries, instead of the state. As a consequence, monasteries gained tremendous influence among the urban poor. Monks also acted as clergy for many local churches, which increased their influence.[66]

There were fewer convents than monasteries, and monks and nuns lived rather differently despite the similarities in their rules. Monks often moved from monastery to monastery, living in several over the course of their lives. In contrast, authorities expected nuns, like secular women, to remain in place. Nuns devoted their daily lives to praying, singing, and maintaining the monastery. They wove and embroidered beautiful liturgical vestments and wall hangings that adorned their churches and the chapels of their patrons. Women entered convents for a variety of reasons. Some were drawn to this life for religious reasons, but others used the monastic life to escape brutal marriages or poverty. Parents also placed mentally ill or disfigured daughters in convents, knowing that it would be difficult to find husbands for them. Having gained control of their money, many widows endowed convents to which they retired.[67]

Women also contributed to the vibrancy of Byzantine culture by founding and decorating churches, monasteries, and convents. One Byzantine princess, Anicia Juliana (late fifth century), used her wealth to commission lavish manuscripts. She also provided elaborate liturgical vessels for several churches in Constantinople. Women's association with cloth production also meant that less well off women donated cloth, embroideries, and wall hangings to adorn local churches. Wealthy women donated expensive silks, while lower-class women offered wool or linen. The Empress Sophia commissioned the funeral pall for Justinian's funeral. It had embroidered scenes from Justinian's reign and was decorated with gold and precious jewels.[68]

By merging Roman, Christian, and Greek institutions and concerns, the Byzantine Empire forged a new culture, familiar to Romans yet different in emphasis and worldview. Women's rights and status drew from Christianity and Roman law, but culturally, the prevalence of eunuchs made the meaning of femininity different and the understanding of gender decidedly unlike Rome. As the western half of the Roman Empire faced political instability and declining wealth, Byzantium grew, spreading Eastern Christianity and its gender norms into Russia and the Slavic lands.

CONCLUSION

The development of Christianity from a sect of Judaism to a separate religion had a profound impact on women in the Western world. Instead of being valued for their childbearing capacities, Christianity urged them to remain virgins and serve God. The gender expectations that emerged in communities of Jesus's followers often clashed with Roman expectations. Early followers of Jesus believed the end of the world was at hand and espoused radical notions of egalitarianism among the classes and between the sexes. However, early Christian writers were deeply influenced by Greco-Roman ideas about women and gender and gradually restricted women's official roles. Nevertheless, women found spiritual comfort in asceticism and monasticism. Women benefited from Christianity's assertion that women and men were spiritually equal, but they did not achieve social or legal equality in the Christianized Roman Empire.

NOTES

1. Erich S. Gruen, *Diaspora: Jews Amidst Greeks and Romans* (Cambridge, MA: Harvard University Press, 2002), 15.

2. Ross Shepard Kraemer, *Her Share of the Blessings: Women's Religion Among Pagans, Jews, and Christians in the Greco-Roman World* (Oxford: Oxford University Press, 1992), 114–115.

3. Miriam B. Peskowitz, *Fantasies: Rabbis, Gender, and History* (Berkeley: University of California Press, 1997), 64.

4. D. A. Fiensy, *The Social History of Palestine in the Heriodian Period* (Lewiston, NY: Edwin Mellen Press, 1991), 99–103.

5. Gruen, 29.

6. Santiago Guijarro, "The Family in First-Century Galilee," in *Constructing Early Christian Families: Family as Social Reality and Metaphor*, ed. Halvor Moxnes (London: Routledge, 1977), 49–55.

7. Léonie J. Archer, "The Role of Jewish Woman in the Religion, Ritual and Cult of Graeco-Roman Palestine," in *Images of Women in Antiquity*, ed. Averil Cameron and Amélie Kuhrt (Detroit, MI: Wayne State Press, 1985), 281.

8. Quoted in Bernadette J. Brooten, *Women Leaders in the Ancient Synagogue: Inscription Evidence and Background Issues* (Chico, CA: Scholars Press, 1989), 5.

9. Brooten, *Women Leaders*, 11, 139–151.

10. Gruen, 55.

11. Judith Romney Wegner, "The Image and Status of Women in Classical Rabbinic Judaism," in *Jewish Women in Historical Perspective*, 2nd ed., ed. Judith Baskin (Detroit, MI: Wayne State University Press, 1998), 76.

12. Wegner, 77.

13. Kraemer, *Her Share of the Blessings*, 99.

14. Peskowitz, 140–141.

15. Ross Shepard Kraemer, "Women's Judaism(s) at the Beginning of Christianity," in *Women and Christian Origins*, ed. Ross Shepard Kraemer and Mary Rose D'Angelo (Oxford: Oxford University Press, 1999), 55–56.

16. Elizabeth A. Castelli, "Paul on Women and Gender," in *Women and Christian Origins*, 225.

17. Wayne Meeks, *The First Urban Christians* (New Haven, CT: Yale University Press, 1983), 75–77.

18. Margaret Y. McDonald, "Reading Real Women Through the Undisputed Letters of Paul," in *Women and Christian Origins*, 202–211.

19. Bernadette Brooten, "Junia . . . Outstanding Among the Apostles," in *Women Priests: A Catholic Commentary on the Vatican Declaration*, ed. Leonard J. Swidler and Arlene Swidler (New York: Paulist Press, 1977), 141–144.

20. Meeks, 53.

21. Kraemer, *Her Share of the Blessings*, 148; MacDonald, "Rereading Paul: Early Interpreters of Paul on Women and Gender," in *Women and Christian Origins*, 239–240.

22. Kraemer, *Her Share of the Blessings,* 149–150.

23. Mary Rose D'Angelo, "(Re)Presentations of Women in the Gospels of John and Mark," in *Women and Christian Origins,* 130–131.

24. Ross Shepard Kraemer, "Jewish Women and Christian Origins," in *Women and Christian Origins,* 46.

25. Mary Rose D'Angelo, "Reconstructing 'Real' Women from Gospel Literature: the Case of Mary Magdalene," in *Women and Christian Origins,* 105–128.

26. D'Angelo, "(Re)Presentations of Women: in the Gospels: John and Mark," in *Women and Christian Origins,* 180–190.

27. Elaine Pagels, *The Gnostic Gospels* (New York: Random House, 1979), 11–12.

28. Pagels, 49–52.

29. Quoted in Elizabeth Clark, "Devil's Gateway and Bride of Christ: Women in the Early Christian World," *Ascetic Piety and Women's Faith: Essays on Late Ancient Christianity* (Lewiston, NY: Edwin Mellen Press, 1986), 35.

30. Pagels, 59–60; Elisabeth Schüssler Fiorenza, *In Memory of Her: A Feminist Theological Reconstruction of Christian Origins* (New York: Crossroads Press, 1983), 274.

31. Peter Brown, *Cult of the Saints: The Rise and Function of Latin Christianity* (Chicago: University of Chicago Press, 1981).

32. Francine Cardman, "Woman, Ministry, and Church Order in Early Christianity," in *Women and Christian Origins*, 302–314.

33. Cardman, 312–314.

34. James Brundage, *Law, Sex, and Christian Society in Medieval Europe* (Chicago: University of Chicago Press, 1987), 94–96.

35. W. V. Harris, "Child Exposure in the Roman Empire," *Journal of Roman Studies* 84 (1994): 19–22.

36. Jo Ann McNamara, "Muffled Voices," in *Distant Echoes*, ed. John Nichols and Lillian Thomas Shank (Kalamazoo, MI: Cistercian Publications, 1984), 13–14.

37. Jo Ann McNamara, *Sisters in Arms: Catholic Nuns Through Two Millennia* (Cambridge, MA: Harvard University Press, 1996), 62.

38. Peter Brown, *The Body in Society: Men, Women, and Sexual Renunciation in Early Christianity* (New York: Columbia University Press, 1988), 242.

39. Gillian Clark, *Woman in Late Antiquity: Pagan and Christian Lifestyles* (Oxford: Oxford University Press, 1993), 102.

40. Rebecca Krawiec, *Shenoute and the Women of the White Monastery* (Oxford: Oxford University Press, 2002), 3.

41. Kraewic, 37.

42. Brown, *Body and Society*, 396–408.

43. Kate Cooper, *Idealized Womanhood in Late Antiquity* (Cambridge, MA: Harvard University Press, 1996), 74–83.

44. Elizabeth Clark, "Ascetic Renunciation and Female Advancement: A Paradox of Late Antique Christianity," in *Ascetic Piety and Women's Faith*, 182–183.

45. Clark, "Ascetic Renunciation," 188.

46. Clark, *Woman in Late Antiquity*, 111–118.

47. Clark, *Woman in Late Antiquity*, 115.

48. Sulpicius Severus, "The Life of St. Martin," trans, F. R. Hoare, in *Soldiers of Christ: Saints and Saints Lives From Late Antiquity and the Early Middle Ages*, ed. Thomas F. X. Noble and Thomas Head (University Park: Pennsylvania State University Press, 1995), 8.

49. Mathew Kueflier, *The Manly Eunuch: Masculinity, Gender Ambiguity, and Christian Ideology in Late Antiquity* (Chicago: University of Chicago Press, 2001), 118.

50. Kathryn Ringrose, *The Perfect Servant: Eunuchs and the Social Construction of Gender in Byzantium* (Chicago: University of Chicago Press, 2003), 5, 40.

51. Ringrose, 82, 165.

52. Averil Cameron, *Prokopios and the Sixth Century* (Berkeley: University of California Press, 1985), 69–70.

53. Cameron, 74–75; Anne McClanan, *Representations of Early Byzantine Empresses: Image and Empire* (New York: Palgrave-Macmillan, 2002), 98–106.

54. Lynda Garland, *Byzantine Empresses: Women and Power in Byzantium, 527–1204* (London: Routledge, 1999), 40–57.

55. Brundage, 114–119.

56. Alice-Mary Talbot, "Women," in *The Byzantines*, ed. Guglielmo Cavallo (Chicago: University of Chicago Press, 1997), 120, 127, 132.

57. Talbot, "Women," 120; Alexander P. Kazhdan and Alice-Mary Talbot, "Women and Iconoclasm," *Byzantinische Zeitschrift* 84/85 (1991/1992): 400.

58. Talbot, "Women," 122.

59. Talbot, "Women," 129.

60. Talbot, "Women," 134.

61. Talbot, "Women," 130–131.

62. Talbot, "Women," 130–131.

63. Alice-Mary Talbot, "Byzantine Women, Saints, and Social Welfare," in *Through the Eye of a Needle: Judeo-Christian Roots of Social Welfare*, ed. Emily A. Hanawalt and Carter Lindberg (Kirksville, MO: Truman State University Press, 1994), 116.

64. Holt N. Parker, "Women Doctors in Greece, Rome, and the Byzantine Empire," in *Women Healers and Physicians: Climbing a Long Hill*, ed. Lilian R. Furst (Louisville: University of Kentucky Press, 1997), 138–140.

65. Kazhdan and Talbot, "Women and Iconoclasm," 392.

66. Alice-Mary Talbot, "A Comparison of the Monastic Experience of Byzantine Men and Women," *Greek Orthodox Theological Review* 30 (1985): 1–18.

67. Talbot, "A Comparison of the Monastic Experience," 1–18.

68. Garland, 42.

SUGGESTED READINGS

Brooten, Bernadette J. *Love Between Women.* Chicago: University of Chicago Press, 1996. Detailed and scholarly study of Christian attitudes toward love between women.

Brown, Peter. *The Body and Society: Men, Women, and Sexual Renunciation in Early Christianity.* New York: Columbia University Press, 1988. Classic work on changing ideas about sexual renunciation and monastic life in early Christianity.

Clark, Elizabeth A. *Ascetic Piety and Women's Faith: Essays on Late Ancient Christianity.* Lewiston, NY: Mellen Press, 1986.

Connor, Carolyn. *Women of Byzantium.* New Haven, CT: Yale University Press, 2004.

Cooper, Kate. *The Virgin and the Bride: Idealized Womanhood in Late Antiquity.* Cambridge, MA: Harvard University Press, 1996. Innovative work that addresses the underlying attraction of domestic piety for Roman women.

Ilan, Tal. *Jewish Women in Greco-Roman Palestine.* Peabody, MA: Hendrickson Publishers, 1995.

Kraemer, Ross Shepard and Mary Rose D'Angelo, eds. *Women and Christian Origins.* New York: Oxford, 1999. Collection of essays that offer feminist interpretations of first-century Judaism and early Christian texts.

Krawiec, Rebecca. *Shenoute and the Women of the White Monastery*. Oxford: Oxford University Press, 2002. Close study of the letters of Shenoute and what they reveal about Egyptian women's monastic life.

Schüssler Fiorenza, Elizabeth. *In Memory of Her: A Feminist Theological Reconstruction of Christian Origins*. New York: Crossroads, 1983.

Women in the Early and High Middle Ages, 400–1200

Woman Milking a Cow (ca. 1225–1250). Most people in medieval Europe were peasants. *Men and women often performed different tasks to keep their families fed and the taxes paid. (Bodleian Library, Oxford.)*

*I*n the fourth century, the Roman Empire
showed signs of decline. Incompetent emperors, internal unrest, and economic stagnation
all contributed to the deterioration of political, economic, and social institutions in western Europe.
As Rome gave way to Germanic successor states, a
process of cultural integration started that would
continue throughout the Middle Ages. This cultural
integration would create a highly stratified society
run by a military elite, which left women vulnerable
to violence, but also offered them avenues of power
and influence. Efforts to control this violence
through religious conversion and social pressure
drew on Roman and Christian traditions that
defined women as weak and in need of supervision.
Nevertheless, women created dynamic court and
religious cultures in the face of political and social
turmoil and oppression.

GENDER IN GERMANIC SOCIETY

The Germanic peoples living on Rome's borders
gradually moved into Roman territory in the face
of Roman decay (see Map 5.1). By the sixth century, Germanic tribes established successor kingdoms from England to Dalmatia. As they spread
across Europe, they assimilated Roman ideas about
law and property that profoundly altered the status
of Germanic women, and German conversions to
Christianity furthered the process of assimilation.
The creation of Germanic successor kingdoms was
chaotic and often violent, allowing some women to
ignore new gender expectations and act on their
own ambitions, while others sought protection and
support from the church.

Gender Among the Germanic Tribes

The Germans were not one people, but many
tribes living east of the Danube and Rhine rivers.
Contact between the Romans and Germans came
in the first century B.C.E., when the Romans
pushed north. Germans fought in the Roman
army and traded for Roman goods, and Roman
soldiers probably engaged in sexual relationships
with German women. By the first century C.E.,
Germans and Romans had interacted along the
Roman frontier for more than two centuries.

Chapter 5 ❖ Chronology

410	Visigoths sack Rome and capture Galla Placidia
ca. 490	Burgundian King Gundobad issues first Germanic law code
507	Clovis converts to Christianity
512–534	Caesarius of Arles writes the first monastic rule for women
ca. 595	Muhammad marries Khadija
664	Hild oversees the Council of Whitby
711	Muslims invade Iberia
800	Charlemagne crowned emperor
841	Vikings raid London and Paris
1055	First Cluniac convent founded at Marsigny
1065	Investiture Controversy begins
1148	Anna Komnena completes her *Alexiad*
1179	Hildegard von Bingen dies
Twelfth century	Trota writes her *Practical Medicine According to Trota*
Late twelfth century	Marie de France writes her lais

Much of what we know about Germanic gender norms comes from Cornelius Tacitus, a Roman senator (ca. 56–115) who wrote about them in his work Germania. Warfare shaped gender expectations among first-century Germans. Men's relationships were linked to loyalty and success in battle, and the death of a chief brought shame to the entire fighting company. Women were also integral to Germanic warfare. During the battles, women cheered on their husbands, fed the combatants, and cared for the wounded. According to Tacitus,

> *It stands on record that armies already wavering and on the point of collapse have been rallied by the women pleading heroically with their men, thrusting forward their bared bosoms, and making them realize the imminent prospect of enslavement—a fate which the Germans fear more desperately for their women than for themselves* (Germania, 8).

German women's presence in battle reflected their household and familial loyalties.

Although Tacitus was not always reliable, later sources and archaeology confirm many of his statements about German gender norms. Germans divided work according to gender, and men and women made equally important contributions to the household. According to Tacitus, German men trusted their wives with maintaining the household and the family's possessions, while men fought and hunted. Both men and women farmed, but families depended on women to produce pottery and textiles and to brew ale. In addition to their military activities, men tended livestock and produced weapons. Tacitus also claims that Germanic women nursed, raised, and educated their own children. Cemetery excavations show that women's graves rarely contained weapons and often included spindle whorls and loom weights.

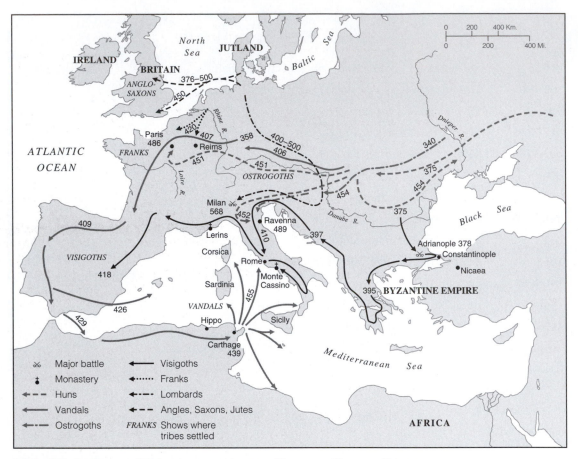

Map 5.1 GERMANIC MIGRATIONS INTO THE WESTERN ROMAN EMPIRE, CA. 300–500. Germanic tribes migrating into western Europe imposed new ideas about women's place in society.

Tacitus stated that the Germans were monogamous, and that husbands and wives were as loyal to each other as warriors were to their leaders. Indeed, later sources indicate that only wealthy Germans practiced polygyny. Scholars also believe that Germans recognized three kinds of marriages. In a free marriage, a woman contracted a marriage on her own. A man could also force a woman to marry him by abducting her. Marriage by purchase required the exchange of goods or money. According to Tacitus, the husband brought his wife livestock, horses, and weapons as marriage gifts, while she presented him with weapons. He claimed that the exchange of weapons reaffirmed their partnership in this warrior society:

the woman must not think that she is excluded from aspirations to many virtues or exempt from the hazards of warfare. That is why she is reminded in the very ceremonies which bless her marriage at the outset, that she enters her husband's home to be a partner of his toils and perils, that both in peace and in war she is to share his suffering and adventures (Germania, 18).

Germans believed that women had great spiritual powers. According to Tacitus, "They believe that there resides in women an element of holiness and a gift of prophecy; and so they do not scorn to ask advice or disregard their replies" (*Germania*, 8).

Not even the Romans doubted German women's abilities to predict the future. For example, in the midst of a political crisis, Roman Emperor Domitian (r. 81–96) consulted with a German diviner named Ganna.

Archaeological excavations imply that German men Romanized more quickly than women. Women tended to wear traditional German-style tunics, whereas men adopted Roman-style clothing.[1] Women's graves at Rohrbach in western Germany included traditional German grave goods, while men's graves more often followed Roman practices and did not include any grave goods. Archaeologist Peter Wells suggests that German women held on to native culture and identity longer than men as their form of resistance to Rome.[2] German men's involvement with the Roman military may have influenced their earlier Romanization.

During the fifth century, the Huns, nomadic peoples from central Asia moved eastward, conquering and enslaving the Germans and disrupting German-Roman relations. Germans who escaped the Huns migrated south and westward, challenging the Germanic peoples who lived closer to the Roman border. In 376, Roman Emperor Valens (r. 364–378) allowed one group of Germans, the Visigoths, to move into the Roman Empire, where the two cultures quickly came into conflict. In 410, the Visigoths sacked Rome and captured a Roman princess, Galla Placidia (ca. 390–423).

Galla Placidia's life reveals the blending of German and Roman culture that was already under way. After four years of captivity. Galla Placidia wed Athaulf, the Visigothic king (r. 410–416). Their wedding ceremony was a surprising combination of Roman and Germanic cultures. The Gothic groom wore Roman robes, but he gave his Roman bride German-style gifts of war loot. A puppet emperor, whom Athaulf had both appointed and then deposed, entertained the royal couple with Roman songs. Athaulf died within a year, and Galla returned to Rome to marry the western Roman emperor.

Throughout the fifth and sixth centuries, Germanic tribes would slowly migrate into Roman territory. Motivated by fear of the Huns and the lure of Roman riches, and facilitated by political and military instability, Germanic peoples ultimately conquered most of western Europe. The new dominant Germanic society combined aspects of both Roman and Germanic cultures.

Germanic Legal Codes and the Restructuring of Society

Once settled into the former Roman Empire, German leaders transformed themselves from tribal warlords into kings. Imitating Roman ideas of law and order, they promulgated law codes as a means of expanding their authority and codifying some traditional Germanic practices. The Burgundian king, Gundobad (r. 474–516) issued the earliest German law code at the end of the fifth century. Germanic law codes replaced familial control with royal authority, a process that emphasized social and gender hierarchies.

The codes established monetary values, or *wergelds*, for all members of society, which created a clear social hierarchy based on sex, age, and status. Kings and great warriors had the highest wergelds. A woman's wergeld depended on her social status and childbearing ability. According to the Salian Frankish law code, pregnant women had a wergeld of seven hundred shillings, but a woman beyond childbearing had a wergeld of only two hundred shillings, the same as an ordinary man.[3] Slaves had no wergeld. When a crime was committed against a person, the perpetrator paid the appropriate wergeld to the victim or his or her family as well as a fine to the king. After the payment, the victim's family could no longer exact retribution. However, failure to pay the wergeld put the perpetrator outside the king's protection and at the violent mercy of the wronged party.

Contact with Roman practices changed German women's status. The earliest German law codes, such as the fifth-century version of the Salic Code, followed German practices and would not allow women to inherit property. Revisions in the sixth and seventh century, which reflect greater Roman influence, relaxed these prohibitions and gave Frankish women rights commensurate with Roman women. They could inherit, but while married, their husbands controlled their property. Like Roman women, they were also legal minors. The Visigothic Code, promulgated in Iberia in the seventh century, reflected greater Romanization. It required that sisters inherit equally with their brothers, and widows had the right to goods acquired during the marriage. It also allowed women to use the court system to protect their property rights. Like Roman widows, German widows acquired legal and economic rights that had been unavailable to them while they were married. At her husband's death, a widow gained control of what she brought to the marriage and what her husband had paid as part of the marriage settlement. Historian Suzanne Wemple has argued that giving a widow the power to inherit weakened her and her husband's natal families by preventing them from breaking up her household. Still, limitations on married women's property ownership reflect the ambiguous position of women and a fear that they might give away family land to husbands and children outside the maternal line.[4]

In an effort to control kinship and limit the power of families, the law codes changed marriage practices, giving wives greater access to property. They eliminated a woman's right to contract a free marriage but continued to recognize marriage by capture, distinguishing between capture with and without the woman's consent. The Germanic tradition of the groom paying a bride price to his betrothed's family evolved into a groom's gift to the bride, and many codes also standardized the provision of dowries. In addition, after the wedding night, the groom paid an additional sum, the *morgengabe*, morning gift, to compensate the bride for the loss of her virginity. In the event of divorce, abandonment, or repudiation, the wife kept the wedding gift and the morgengabe. These practices helped limit the amount of power a woman's natal family had over her property and made divorce costly to the husband.

Regulating marriage also meant defining disruptive sexual behavior. The codes imposed fines on men who abducted women and women who consented to be carried off by men other than their fiancés. They also punished adulterers of both sexes. Other laws protected woman, compensating them when they were victims of physical crimes such as rape and incidents of public harassment or dishonor. The Burgundian Code fined perpetrators for insulting a women or cutting her hair. Loose or cut hair implied that a women lacked virtue; thus, cutting a woman's hair challenged the honor of her male family members charged with protecting her and her reputation.

Law codes further restricted women's ability to participate in war. Only free men could legally carry and use weapons. Slaves and women could not. This change removed Germanic women from warfare, making it a masculine pursuit as it had been in Roman society. This change also made women vulnerable to attack and in need of male protection.

Germanic Queens

Through military and diplomatic perseverance, strength of personality, and strategic marriages, kings consolidated their rule. Their queens played critical roles in this process. Queens helped run the court, controlled access to the king, dispensed charity and favors, and rewarded supporters. Many nobles expected kings to wed other Germanic princesses in order to unite tribes. The Frankish king, Sigibert (r. 561–575), wed Brunhild (ca. 550–613), a Visigothic princess, to help legitimate his reign and expand his alliances. Indeed, Anglo-Saxon poetry often refers to queens as "peace-weavers." However, Germanic kings still practiced polygyny and divorce, so a queen had to work hard to maintain her position. A wife's best hope was to produce a son who would protect her if her husband died or divorced her. Kings also married slaves whom they found desirable, or kept them as concubines. If those women bore children, they often fought to have their sons inherit rather than the legal wife's children. Although law codes attempted to control the problem, feuding between former wives and concubines occurred frequently. Kings had no incentive to consider long-term marriage strategies when choosing a wife because of the availability of divorce and polygyny.

The experiences of three Germanic queens, Amalasuntha (d. 535), Fredegund (d. 597), and Radegund (518–87), reveal the different ways that royal women functioned in early medieval society. Their experiences also show that law codes described an ideal for female behavior that was not always reflected in practice.

Amalasuntha was the daughter of Theodoric (r. 493–526), the Ostrogothic king in Italy. Amala-suntha learned Latin and Greek, in addition to her native Germanic language. She married a Visigoth to whom she bore a son and daughter. After Theodoric's death, she ruled as regent for her son, Atharlaric, and ensured that he received a Roman education. If her husband was still alive, he was irrelevant. As regent, Amalasuntha went to war with the Franks and Burgundians, promoted and rewarded supporters with money and titles, and exchanged letters with the Byzantine rulers, Justinian and Theodora. While regent she issued laws in her son's name, one of which tried to outlaw concubinage by turning concubines into slaves of the wronged wife. During her reign, the Ostrogoth's Arianism in defiance of both the papacy and the Byzantine Empire also became an issue. Theodoric had persecuted Orthodox Christians at the end of his reign, but Amalasun-tha was more moderate. In 534, Atharlaric died, and Amalasuntha quickly remarried, this time choosing an Ostrogothic cousin, Theodahad. She ruled with her husband until 535 when he imprisoned and then killed her. Her death prompted Justinian's invasion of Italy (see Chapter 4). Amalasuntha's status as her father's heir was not enough to give her power; she needed to be associated with a man, either her son or a husband. She could only rule alone as a regent for her son, not as the daughter of a king.

The chronicles describe Fredegund (d. 597), the third wife of Frankish King Chilperic I of Soisson (r. 560–584), as a ruthless and ambitious woman. She was a slave who attracted Chilperic's attention. He murdered his wife, rather than give back her dowry, in order to make Fredegund his queen, initiating a forty-year feud between Fredegund and the murdered wife's sister, Brunhild. Chronicles also accused Fredegund of murdering Chilperic when he suspected her of adultery. Whatever the case, Chilperic's death left her a widow with a four-month-old son, Clothar (r. 584–629). Fredegund established herself as regent to secure her son's inheritance, but her brother-in-law challenged Clothar's legitimacy and Fredegund's right to the regency. In response, she assembled three bishops and three hundred nobles who swore to Chilperic's paternity. Fredegund even defended herself on the battlefield. According to the chronicles, she took control of the military and led her troops to victory against her opponents while carrying the baby Clothar in her arms. One chronicler described how she disguised her men as trees and launched a surprise attack, noting that "she returned home with much booty and many spoils."[5] With a military victory and a full treasury, Fredegund then

ruled as regent. According to one chronicler, she continued to oversee the assassinations of rivals, ordering the poisoning of a bishop who supported her brother-in-law, and then offering him her personal physician to cover her tracks. When she died in 597, she was buried in great splendor at the basilica of Saint Vincent in Paris. Fredegund's experience demonstrates that even when chosen by the king, a queen was vulnerable. Her claim to power was as mother of a prince, not as a queen.

Because of their status as property holders and their relationships to royal families, women often suffered brutally during the constant warfare between Germanic kingdoms. Survival required not only luck, but also the ability to garner support in a hostile environment. Radegund, a princess from the Germanic kingdom of Thuringia, was raised in the household of an uncle who had murdered her father. Her uncle later broke a treaty with the Franks, provoking war between the Thuringians and the Franks. In revenge, the Franks murdered most of the Thuringian ruling family. The Frankish king, Fredegund's son, Clothar, captured Radegund and, after gambling with his brothers, won her as his wife. She was quite young, somewhere between six and twelve years old. Clothar then left her to be raised at one of his country homes until she reached puberty. Clothar, a pagan with a number of wives, then married Radegund. Her royal blood made her a status symbol. After about ten years, she fled the Frankish court hoping to dedicate herself to Christian piety. Later, Clothar killed her brother, her only surviving family member. She recorded the horror of these events in a powerful poem entitled "The Thuringian War," which Radegund either composed herself or in collaboration with her friend and priest Venantius Fortunatus (530–609):

> *Brother, I salute you, and stand accused of this impiety: You only died because of me and I gave you no sepulcre. / Twice am I captive who only left my country once, / Having endured again the enemy while my brother lay fallen. / Then, father and mother, uncle and kindred, / This grief recalls them whom I should mourn in the tomb.*[6]

Radegund's support of the church gave her powerful allies outside of the court, and ulti-

PORTRAIT OF BAUDONIVIA WRITING THE *LIFE OF ST. RADEGUND* (LATE ELEVENTH CENTURY). Baudonivia's *Life* reflects the close relationships nuns had with each other as well as the education available to them.

mately Clothar acceded to her wishes. He established a convent at Poitiers where Radegund became abbess and dedicated her wealth to supporting the church. Both Fortunatus and Baudonivia, a nun in her convent, wrote biographies of her. From Fortunatus, we learn of Radegund's political life, her public acts of charity, her devotion to Christianity, and the humiliation and pain of royal politics. From Baudonivia, we learn of her convent life, her personal acts of humility, and her relationships with the other nuns in her convent. Her close contact with the church provides evidence of the patronage networks available to women outside of the military culture of the court.

Women and the Expansion of Christianity

Although a few of the early Germanic kingdoms were nominally Christian, women were critical to the large-scale conversion of Germans and the Christianization of German culture. Christianity was a source of Roman influence. Most clergy were from Roman families and as they spread Christianity to Germans, they spread Roman culture as well. As queens, women used their influence over their husbands on behalf of their faith. As nuns and patrons of convents, they exerted powerful influence over church policy and Christian culture.

Germanic kings rarely converted to Christianity because of their great piety, but rather because it was politically expedient. As a result, church officials found Germanic queens to be important allies in their missionary efforts. Clovis (r. 481–511), the Frankish king, decided to accept Christianity at the insistence of his wife, Clotild (d. 545). Unlike the Visigoths and the Ostrogoths who were Arian Christians, Clotild was a Roman Christian, and Clovis's decision to convert to the Roman church gave him important alliances with Byzantium and the papacy. Similarly, the Anglo-Saxon king of Kent, Ethelbert (r. 860–866), was a pagan, but his wife, Bertha, a Frankish princess, was a Christian. Bertha convinced her husband to allow Christian missionaries to enter his kingdom and, eventually, he too converted. Both Clotild and Bertha eventually earned sainthood for their evangelical work, while their husbands used the new religion and its ties to Rome to enhance their own status.

Monasticism helped spread Christianity and provided women with an important alternative to marriage. Pious noble and royal widows used their considerable wealth to establish monastic houses in newly Christianized regions, and women flocked to these new foundations. A son or daughter in a monastery forged an alliance with God, much like marriages created alliances between kingdoms or families. Between 600 and 649, in what is modern-day France and Belgium, one-quarter of all new monastic houses were for women, a number that rose to one-third during the last half of the seventh century. A century later, in England, 40 percent of new monastic foundations were for women.[7] These houses generally attracted women from the same families and served as mechanisms for female networking and patronage. Daughters often followed their widowed mothers as abbesses, and celibate sisters often joined similarly inclined aunts. The Anglo-Saxon queen, Aethelthrith, founded a convent in Ely. Her sister Seaxburh succeeded her as abbess. Seaxburh was then succeeded by her daughter, and later by her granddaughter. For some, monasticism filled a spiritual longing; for others it was an appealing alternative to arranged marriages, the dangers of childbirth, or the shame of infertility. However, not all women preferred the convent. A few tried to flee after male relatives placed them in convents against their will. The consequences could be brutal. At one point during her tenure as abbess, Radegund imprisoned and starved a rebellious nun until she reformed.

These early monastic houses were autonomous, and organized daily life and the litany of prayers and services around any number of monastic rules. Many monastic institutions, such as Luxeuil in the Frankish kingdom, were double houses where monks and nuns lived in separate quarters under the rule of an abbess. They owed their inspiration to Irish monasticism, which emphasized the spiritual equality of men and women. The Irish monk Columban (d. 640) had established a number of monasteries in the Frankish kingdom in the late sixth century. Set in remote and isolated locations, men and women living in double houses entered into spiritual partnerships, supporting the community through work and prayer. The rule for Luxeuil limited contact between men and women by having them work in groups and sleep in single-sex dormitories. Double houses could be quite large; the one at Laon founded in 641 had three hundred nuns.[8]

Other houses were single sex, like the one Caesarius (ca. 470–542) founded in the city of Arles for his sister Caesaria sometime between 512 and 534. The rule that he composed for this house prescribed a strict regimen. The nuns were to have no servants, and no one under the age of six or seven could become a nun. All women following his rule had to leave the outside world forever and renounce all worldly goods. According to Caesarius, "Nuns who have possessions cannot achieve perfection."[9] The rule assumed that nuns would spend most of the day in prayer, but that manual labor such as spinning, carding, weaving, and embroidery would

help support the convent. Caesarius also expected the nuns to learn to read Scripture. This requirement helped expand the use of Latin beyond the Roman clergy. The nuns may have even established a school for new members who could not yet read. Caesarius's rule became quite popular and was adopted by many houses, including Radegund's convent in Poitiers.

Nuns' familial connections often influenced both political and ecclesiastical policy. Hild (614–680), the powerful abbess of the double house at Whitby in the north of England, had strong connections to power. She was the great-niece of one king and the aunt of another, and her connections aided the careers of the men in her monastery. Whitby became known as the nursery of bishops; five Anglo-Saxon bishops began their religious careers there. Hild's influence was so great that when officials of the church in Rome wanted to meet with their counterparts from the Celtic Church to eliminate differences in organization, liturgy, and the ecclesiastical calendar, they met at her abbey for the Council of Whitby in 664.

Convents helped spread Christianity in newly converted parts of Europe. An Anglo-Saxon nun named Leoba (d. 779) helped Boniface (680–754), an Anglo-Saxon monk, establish the Christian church in Germany. Boniface spent most of his professional life among pagan Germans, using monasteries and convents to spread Christianity. As a staunch supporter, Leoba at first only corresponded with Boniface, sending him encouragement, books, and liturgical items to help with his mission. Later, Boniface asked her to join him in Germany, where he put her in charge of the first convent in Germany at Bischofsheim.

Convents also had responsibilities and influence beyond their spiritual mission. They educated the children of the nobility and royalty, created luxurious liturgical vestments and altar clothes, copied manuscripts, fed the poor, and cared for the sick. In times of crisis, people turned to powerful abbesses for guidance. For instance, Leoba organized the local citizenry to put out a major fire, and the citizens of Poitiers went to Radegund for help during an epidemic. These determined women were critical to the long-term success of the church.

Beginning in the fourth century, Germanic peoples overtook the fading Roman Empire. Germanic gender norms, tied closely to their warrior culture, demanded the active participation of women. However, as German leaders established new kingdoms, legal codes influenced by Roman law redefined women's place in society, taking them off the battlefield and making them conduits of property and political power. These kingdoms were fraught with internal conflict, allowing some German queens to wield considerable authority, which they used to further their own interests. While some women promoted family concerns, others dedicated themselves to the spread of Christianity.

CAROLINGIAN TRANSFORMATIONS

The most successful Germanic kingdom developed in the eighth century under the leadership of Charlemagne (r. 768–814) and his heirs. Charlemagne reunited the Franks and through conquest gradually extended his empire beyond modern-day France to much of Germany and northern Italy (see Map 5.2). In 800, the pope crowned him Holy Roman Emperor. The rise of his dynasty, known as the Carolingians, was no mere shift in political authority from one family to the next, but rather the beginning of what many historians consider the first medieval European monarchy. To control such an extensive kingdom, Charlemagne imitated Roman institutions and implemented intellectual, religious, and social reforms that altered the lives of women across Europe.

Restraining Female Piety

Charlemagne consciously styled himself a Christian monarch in imitation of the Roman emperors in Constantinople. He built his capital at Aachen as a new Byzantium and intervened in religious debates, as had many Byzantine emperors. In fact, he wanted to be more than just the king of the Franks; he wanted to be anointed Holy Roman Emperor. However, a woman stood in his way. The Byzantine queen, Irene (752–803), officially held the title of "Emperor" after she deposed her son. Charlemagne based his claim to the title on the fact that a woman could not, in medieval men's minds, be either an emperor or an effective ruler. According to the *Lorsch Annals,*

Because the title of emperor was at this time lacking among the Greeks and they had among them the rulership of a woman, it seemed to the pope, the holy fathers and the rest of the Christian people that they ought to give Charles himself the title of emperor.[10]

The pope, among others, was persuaded by this logic and gave Charlemagne his emperorship.

Charlemagne justified his claims to being emperor because of his interest in church reform, especially monastic reform. The centerpiece of his religious reforms was the promotion of the Rule of Saint Benedict (ca. 480–553) for all monasteries. This rule was more moderate in its pursuit of asceticism than most rules, but it discouraged monks and nuns from leaving their monasteries. Enclosure meant that nuns could no longer go on pilgrimage or have contact with people outside the convent walls. Male church officials were also increasingly distrustful of double houses, and some well-publicized scandals about seduced nuns fueled their skepticism. Gradually, they shut down double houses or converted them into single-sex institutions. Often Charlemagne placed them under royal patronage so that he could gain access to their resources. He also discouraged the founding of new houses for women, except in newly conquered lands. These reforms systematized Carolingian monastic life and curtailed religious opportunities for women.

Charlemagne's reforms de-emphasized nuns' roles in their own convents. A new emphasis on the celebration of the mass shifted the devotional activity away from prayers and psalms and forced nuns to rely on priests to administer this sacrament. A succession of church councils prohibited abbesses from hearing confession, preaching, singing the Gospel, leaving their convents to consult with others, and avowing novices—the process of inducting new members into the convent. Male priests took over all of these duties. Strict enclosure also made nuns dependent on monks and priests to check on their property, supervise repairs, collect rents, or buy and sell goods in the market. As a result, many convents fell into financial ruin, which limited their educational opportunities and the quality of convent libraries. Female houses also declined in status, number, and quality. Saints' lives reveal the ideals

Map 5.2 THE CAROLINGIAN WORLD, 768–814. Charlemagne united much of western Europe into a rural, Christian empire.

that these reforms sought for female religious. Carolingian hagiographies of female saints emphasize the qualities of enclosed and submissive nuns, focused on praying for their families outside and caring for their sisters inside.

The regular repetition of edicts requiring nuns to stay within convent walls and to stop preaching and teaching suggests that women did not easily acquiesce to the new rules. The case against a woman named Theoda heard at the Council of Mainz in 847 demonstrates one woman's resistance. The council condemned Theoda for preaching the end of the world. In fear, many people stopped attending their own churches and instead followed her and gave her money. She was arrested and publicly flogged. The records state, "Whereupon with shame she gave up the ministry of preaching that she had irrationally seized upon and presumed to claim for herself against the custom of the church and perplexed, she put an end to her soothsaying."[11] She was not the only woman to express her piety in public. In fact, women like Hild and Leoba had also preached and acquired followers. However, the Carolingian Church was strong enough to effectively limit the movement and activities of female religious, isolating them from the centers of ecclesiastical power and authority and weakening them vis-à-vis their male counterparts.

Carolingian Marriage Reform

As a part of their religious reforms, Charlemagne and his son Louis the Pious (r. 814–840) vigorously pursued marriage reform. Although the church had been unable to influence the marriages of their predecessors, Charlemagne and his son emphasized Christian ideas about the sanctity and permanence of marriage. To some extent, Charlemagne's motivations were political. His family were usurpers and they needed episcopal support for their dynasty. However, as a self-styled Christian ruler, strongly influenced by Saint Augustine, Charlemagne also felt ideologically moved to reform his kingdom.

Charlemagne specifically attacked Germanic laws on divorce. As a young man, he had had several temporary relationships and had divorced two wives. However, Charlemagne ceased to repudiate his wives and only remarried after the deaths of each of his five wives. He did not remarry after the death of his last wife, Liutgard, in 800, but he did have a succession of four concubines, all of whom bore him children. Although Charlemagne reformed divorce laws, he was also concerned with preserving his power and so forbade his daughters from marrying. Yet he let them conduct their own sexual relationships, much like Germanic free marriage. This strategy prevented any potential husbands from threatening his power.

Louis the Pious's marriage reforms went further than his father's. He curtailed the rights of concubines, rejecting the legitimacy of their children and their ability to inherit. Louis even found his own sisters' sexual activity unacceptable and sent them to convents. His new laws further clarified the rules regarding marriage. A legitimate marriage required parental consent, a property settlement, and a bride gift. Some ecclesiastical authorities also required consummation of the marriage, while others demanded a clerical blessing. These legal changes applied to peasants and nobles alike, but they were more strictly enforced among the upper classes, whose marriages had political and territorial significance.

Louis's marital problems with his second wife, Judith, illustrate how far marriage reform had come. Judith was much disliked at court for her promotion of the career of her own son at the expense of her stepsons. One faction at court levied accusations of infidelity, sorcery, and debauchery against her; however, Louis did not dissolve the marriage. Powerful nobles could no longer demand that a king repudiate his wife.

Enforcement of marriage and divorce laws varied over the next 150 years. Divorce became difficult to obtain and incest taboos expanded. The conjugal family became the dominant social and economic unit. Marital permanence changed marriage strategies. Motivated by long-term political and territorial concerns, noble families no longer permitted their sons to marry lower-class women who caught their eye, because they could no longer repudiate them when they ceased to be attractive or when they needed to marry for political reasons. As a result, wives gained status within the family, because they were no longer disposable.

Women and the Carolingian Renaissance

Charlemagne believed that the success of his Christian empire depended on a literate clergy and secular leaders. This policy would help transform his nobles into something more than violent, half-Christian warlords. One of Charlemagne's great contributions was the creation of an educated elite through a palace school. He attracted the great scholars of the period to his palace at Aachen, where they trained aristocratic children. The extension of schooling even included some elementary schools that may have provided basic literacy skills to children of both free parents and peasants. They learned Latin and presumably the vernacular language of the region.

Charlemagne ensured that his daughters received good educations, and other women at court followed suit. His sisters, daughters, and at least one wife were all literate. At one point, his sister and daughter begged the great scholar Alcuin (ca. 740–ca. 804) to write them a commentary on the *Gospel of John*.[12] Intellectuals at his court advocated for women's education as a means of spreading Christianity and Roman culture more broadly, consciously imposing the education that Jerome had laid out for Paula in his letters to Laeta. (See **Sources from the Past** in Chapter 4.) Most of the few privileged girls who could take advantage of this emphasis on education were taught in convents by nuns. In a touching reminder that these students were just children, one ninth-century work includes a schoolgirl's plea to her teacher, "Mistress Felhin, give me leave to keep vigil this night with mistress Adalu, and I affirm and swear with both hands that I shall not cease either reading or singing on behalf of our Lord the whole night through. Farewell, and do as I ask."[13]

One of the few known female authors of the period is Dhuoda (ca. 785–ca. 843), the wife of Bernard, Count of Septimania, a major figure in the Carolingian court. She composed her *Liber Manualis*, an advice book for her son, between 841 and 843. While Bernard remained at court with a concubine, Dhuoda maintained the family holdings and raised two sons. After Bernard backed the losing heir in a Carolingian succession dispute, he offered their eldest son, William, as a pledge for his loyalty and took the infant to be raised by another woman. To cope with her grief and loneliness, Dhuoda composed the *Liber*, asking that William convey it to his younger brother when he was older. In it, she expressed her hope that William might be safe and find favor with both God and the king. Her work reveals a thorough knowledge of the Bible, as well as texts by Ovid, Augustine, and many lives of the saints.[14] She extolled learning, "There are no riches where stupidity reigns, and nothing is wanting, nothing an obstacle, in matters where gentle speech prevails. Whoever tries to be numbered among the wise can be welcome to both God and man and pleasing in every way to his earthly lord."[15]

Dhuoda was not alone in her ability to create original works. Hugeburc (fl. 778–786) an Anglo-Saxon nun living in Germany, tells the story of the travels of her brothers in her *Hodoeporicon*. Despite reforms that shut down or impoverished convents, Carolingian nuns across Europe cultivated their intellectual skills. Convents exchanged books with each other, and many abbesses maintained active correspondence with leading thinkers and theologians. At least some convents had *scriptoria* in which female scribes copied manuscripts for use by nuns. It is likely that they also composed original material, in particular, some of the many saints' lives written during this period. Traditionally, scholars assumed that works by anonymous authors were written by men; however, new understandings of the quality of women's intellectual life during the Carolingian Renaissance cast doubt on that long-held hypothesis.[16]

The Second Agricultural Revolution

As part of his drive to consolidate his empire, Charlemagne pursued economic reforms and agricultural improvements. The second agricultural revolution brought positive changes to peasant's lives. Among many reforms, Charlemagne employed new agricultural technology, such as the horse collar and heavy plow, on his estates. He also introduced new planting cycles with the three-field system, which divided the arable land into three parts: the first planted with wheat or rye in the fall; the second planted with legumes such as peas, lentils, broad beans, and chick peas, or other spring crops such as barley or oats; and the third field was left fallow. Each year, the fields rotated. This system had numerous advantages. It put more land under cultivation and grew more food. Legumes revitalized soil depleted of nitrogen from growing wheat. It also increased the variety of food grown, which helped protect against catastrophic crop failure and improved the nutrition of the population. Legumes in particular added needed iron to women's diets, which was lost through menstruation and childbirth. Because women were healthier, they had fewer miscarriages and nursed stronger babies. The three-field system also distributed the work of plowing and planting more evenly across the year, making work easier for peasant families. Taken together, the agricultural revolution improved female fertility and longevity and improved peasants' lives over all. Charlemagne did not invent these agricultural improvements. He adopted practices from around his empire and imposed them on his own lands.

Charlemagne's empire unified much of Europe. In his attempt to imitate the Roman emperors of

Byzantium, he undertook extensive cultural reform. He pushed monastic institutions to accept the Benedictine Rule and diminished nuns' control over their own spiritual lives. He also strengthened the laws surrounding marriage. Among some of his most important achievements, the emperor brought the continent's most important scholars to his palace at Aachen and encouraged women to participate in the cultural renaissance. Finally, Charlemagne pursued new agricultural techniques that made life better for even the poorest peasant. For the most part, women benefited from the unity and innovation of Charlemagne's empire.

WOMEN ON THE FRONTLINES: THE SECOND WAVE OF INVASIONS

The political unity and religious reform the Carolingians created ended with the death of Louis the Pious in 840. Following Germanic practice, he divided his empire among his surviving sons. Competition among them brought renewed political instability to Europe. This political turmoil and economic growth across the continent attracted a new wave of invasions. The Vikings came from the north, the Magyars came from the east, and the Muslims came from the south, each bringing with them their own gender expectations (see Map 5.3). Although women were often victims of horrific violence, they were also key participants in the settlement and integration of these new peoples into European society.

Women and the Viking Invasions

The Viking invasions of the ninth century again transformed European society. The invading Danes, Swedes, and Norwegians shared similar polytheistic religions, languages, and social structures, but they were not unified politically. Much of what we know of Viking culture during this period comes from outside observations, archaeology, and oral traditions recorded centuries later in stories called *sagas*. Composed by monks in the thirteenth century after the Vikings had converted to Christianity, the sagas describe Viking conquests, settlements, and family relations. They reveal a society that placed greater emphasis on personal prowess than on biological differences

between men and women. Consequently, women might acquire significant power, while old men might not.[17] The sagas include stories of women engaging in feuds, choosing husbands, and leaving their families and setting out on their own. Although most women tended farms, raised children, and sewed, some went on raiding expeditions and engaged in trade.

Population growth and changes in inheritance practices drove ambitious Vikings to the seas to seek their fortunes. Land became scarce and fathers increasingly left their property to the eldest son instead of dividing it among all the heirs. The Vikings first established permanent bases in Dublin and along the coast from which they attacked England. One saga mentions a redheaded woman who led raids on Munster in the tenth century. In 841, simultaneous raids on England and France took the Vikings all the way to London and Paris. By the early 850s, groups of Vikings wintered in France and England, taking advantage of the warmer climate. The Vikings also colonized Iceland and Greenland. Unnr, the daughter of a chieftain, settled in the Hebrides (Scotland) as an agent of King Harald Fairhair (d. ca. 932). When her husband was killed, she built a boat and took her family to Iceland where she married off her many granddaughters and became a major landholder by 900.[18]

Around the year 1000, the Vikings, led by Erik the Red, landed on the coast of modern-day Newfoundland. There, archaeologists have discovered spindle whorls indicating that women lived in this colony.[19] *The Vinland Saga* specifically mentions that Freydis, the daughter of Erik the Red, accompanied him on the voyage. The Vikings encountered native Inuit peoples, whom they called "skraelings." This contact was usually violent, and the *Vinland Saga* describes Freydis fighting the skraelings while pregnant. Ultimately, the Vikings were too few in number and the natives too numerous. The Vikings left the New World and returned to their colonies in Iceland and Greenland.

When the Vikings landed on European shores, they terrorized and destroyed monasteries and convents and sold conquered peoples into slavery. The *Annals of Ulster* note that in 821, the Irish city "Etar [Howth] was plundered by the heathens, [and] they carried off a great number of women into captivity."[20] Monasteries and convents were

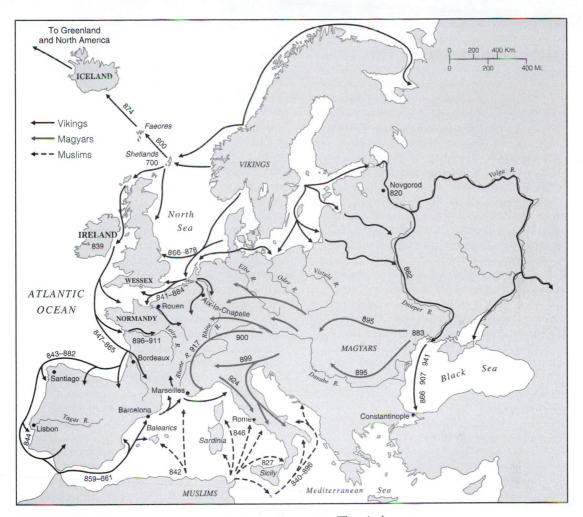

Map 5.3 The Great Invasions of the Ninth Century. The ninth-century invasions made life more dangerous for women, but in the political chaos that followed, some women gained considerable political power.

favorite targets because they were largely unguarded and filled with rich liturgical furnishings, jewel-encrusted book bindings, and unarmed monks and nuns. Monastic chronicles are filled with grisly stories of Viking attacks on convents, where the invaders raped and killed the nuns. In 870, the Danes burned all the nuns at the English convent of Barking, and one year later, they attacked the convent at Ely. By 1066 only ten monastic houses for women remained in England.[21]

Hoping to end the violence, Frankish and Anglo-Saxon kings negotiated with the Vikings and used their daughters to cement alliances with the invaders. Charles the Simple (r. 893–929), the king of the Franks, married his daughter Gisela to a Viking leader, Rollo (r. 911–31). In exchange, Rollo received the county of Normandy, converted to Christianity, and defended the Frankish coastline from further Viking attacks. In England, the Viking raids unified the Anglo-Saxons under the leadership of Alfred (r. 871–99), the king of Wessex (see **Women's Lives:** Aethelflaed, Lady of the Mercians). He repulsed Viking invasions in all but the eastern half of England. He then negotiated

Aethelflaed, Lady of the Mercians

It is difficult to piece together the lives of women from the early Middle Ages, because most sources deal with issues of war and land, not with the events of daily life or personal growth. However, the life of Aethelflaed, daughter of King Alfred the Great, is reasonably well documented because of her importance as a ruler. Her reign demonstrates that expedience could overcome gender ideology and that political crises offered some women greater opportunities. During the Viking raids on Britain, Aethelflaed's military prowess and intelligence made her a successful queen.

As a result of the Viking attacks, most of Britain's Anglo-Saxon kingdoms united under the rule of King Alfred (871–99). Sometime around 887, Alfred married Aethelflaed to his ally Aethelred (d. 911), king of the semi-independent kingdom of Mercia. When Aethelred became incapacitated in 910, Aethelflaed ruled on her own, becoming one of the most powerful people in Britain.

The ten charters that Aethelflaed witnessed reveal that she worked with her husband, cooperated with her father, and after her father's death, collaborated with her brother Edward the Elder (r. 899–924). Because contemporaries did not quite know how to classify her, charters variously refer to her as "Lady of the Mercians," queen, or provide no title. Aethelflaed's charters show that she excelled at royal management, ably balancing the needs of her secular and religious communities.

The Vikings' onslaught required successful rulers to be powerful warriors. Aethelflaed's military actions suggests that she had modified her father's ideology of kingship to suit her own concerns. Alfred believed kings should protect and expand their territories. However, Aethelflaed's military actions were purely defensive.[1] Between 910 and 918, she organized and built ten fortresses. This extraordinary accomplishment suggests a great deal of support from her nobles. The contemporary *Anglo-Saxon Chronicle* implies that she personally participated in these projects.

Aethelflaed also led successful military ventures against the Vikings. She recaptured their strongholds of Derby and Leicester and compelled the people of York, a Viking city in the north of England, to swear loyalty to her. She then orchestrated an alliance of northern kings against the Vikings, further evidence of her political foresight.

The Vikings were not her only military concern. Mercia shared a boarder with Wales, and after punitive raids on her people, Aethelflaed sent an army to Wales and brought back a Welsh queen as a hostage. She also faced competition from her brother. Although they cooperated in other ventures, when Aethelred died, Aethelflaed's brother took Oxford and London away from her. Scholars suggest that some of her fortresses were as much to protect herself from her brother as from the Vikings. Yet Aethelflaed remained on good enough terms that she helped raise Edward's son.

Aethelflaed's importance to the region was well recognized, and chronicles in Ireland and Wales note her death in 918, but not those of her brother or husband. She passed her kingdom on to her daughter Aelfwynn (born ca. 888). Aelfwynn ruled briefly, but her uncle Edward the Elder deposed her and absorbed Mercia into his holdings. Aethelflaed's legacy as a powerful Anglo-Saxon queen would not be repeated.

---

[1] Mary Dockray-Miller, *Motherhood and Mothering in Anglo-Saxon England* (New York: St. Martin's Press, 2000), 63.

Sources: Mary Dockray-Miller, *Motherhood and Mothering in Anglo-Saxon England* (New York: St. Martin's Press, 2000); and Christine Fell, *Women in Anglo-Saxon England* (London: Colonnade Books, 1984).

as the border between Anglo-Saxon territory and what became known as the "Danelaw."

As Viking settlements became more permanent in western Europe, some men married Anglo-Saxon women, while others sent for their wives and children. One French chronicle tells of a band of Vikings who settled in the abandoned town of Angers along with their wives and children.[22] The *Anglo-Saxon Chronicle* describes how, during a battle between the Anglo-Saxons and the invaders in the 890s, the Viking Haesten came down the Thames with eighty ships and was routed by English troops, who then captured "all that was therein money, women, and children and brought all to London."[23] The chronicle goes on to note that before another battle the Danes had left their wives in East Anglia.

In Viking settlements in eastern England, there are signs that even local women were more independent than their counterparts in Anglo-Saxon areas. Although we have little evidence before the eleventh century, the *Domesday Book* (1086), a survey of land compiled by the Norman conqueror William I (r. 1066–1087), lists a number of female landowners with Scandinavian names. One woman named Gunnvör owned three manors.[24]

Continual Viking attacks and weak successors left the Anglo-Saxon kingdom vulnerable, and in 1016, the Viking Cnut (r. 1016–1035) declared himself king of England. He consolidated his power by marrying the last Anglo-Saxon king's widow, Emma (d. 1052). Emma, through her connections to both English and Viking kings, was central to the evolution of the English monarchy. The daughter of the count of Rouen (France) by his Danish second wife, she was sent to England as a young woman to cement an alliance with the Anglo-Saxon king Aethelred (978–1016) against the Vikings. She quickly established her place at court and bore him three children. During their marriage, Aethelred held the Vikings at bay by paying them not to harass his territories. However, after a few years, the Vikings again stepped up their attacks, forcing Aethelred and his family to flee to Normandy. Aethelred was briefly restored to power, but died in 1016. Eighteen months after his death, Emma married his rival Cnut, becoming his second wife. Their marriage helped establish a permanent peace between the English and the Vikings. Emma's influence was both political and religious, as she con-

verted her new husband to Christianity and regularly participated in meetings with the king and his counselors.[25] She became the mother of a king, when Cnut sent their son, Harthacnut (r. 1040–1042), to rule Denmark. After Cnut's death, she promoted the succession of Harthacnut over the claims of her sons by Aethelred and Cnut's sons by his first wife. Facing increasing criticism, Emma commissioned a chronicle of the events, the *Encomium Emmae Reginae* (1041–42), which defended her involvement in the succession conflict. After Harthacnut's brief reign, his successor—his half-brother and Emma's eldest son by Aethelred—Edward the Confessor (r. 1042–1066), tired of Emma's political interference and put her into a convent in the Low Countries. When Edward died without an heir, Emma's great-nephew William of Normandy pressed his claim to the throne, conquering England and ending both Viking and Anglo-Saxon rule in 1066. Throughout this period, queens were an important conduit for political power.

Invaders in Eastern Europe

Eastern Europe was also beset by invaders who disrupted political, religious, and economic life. Hoping to trade with Damascus, Swedish Vikings traveled down the Dnieper River into Russia and into the Black Sea. They made several assaults on Constantinople and nearly conquered the city. By 852, they had founded Novgorod and went on to capture the city-state of Kiev. Intermarrying with the Slavic population, the Vikings set up a society designed to facilitate trade. Byzantium was central to that trade, bringing silk, coins, and other valuables from the east to the west and timber and furs in the other direction.

The Viking incursions into Russia set the stage for their conversion to Orthodox Christianity, as missionaries from Byzantium were active among them as early as the ninth century. In the end, Vladimir, the Viking prince of Kiev (r. 978–1015), agreed to convert to Orthodox Christianity in order to marry Anna, the sister of the Byzantine emperor Basil II (r. 976–1025). Vladimir was a pagan, although his grandmother, Olga, had been a Christian and venerated as a saint. To marry Anna and gain the prestige, money, and influence that such a union would bring, Vladimir repudi-

QUEEN FROM THE LEWIS CHESS SET (CA. TWELFTH CENTURY). By the end of the eleventh century, chess was popular among both men and women. The style of this piece, made of walrus ivory and discovered in Scotland, shows the continued influence of Scandinavia in Britain. *(The British Museum/HIP/Art Resource, NY.)*

ated his pagan wives and converted. Anna promoted Orthodox Christianity among her new people by founding churches and monasteries across Russia.

Generally, women were legally disadvantaged in medieval Russian society. A daughter had no inheritance rights unless she had no brothers. Parents or brothers arranged marriages for single women, although a law code supposedly issued by Vladimir's son, Iaroslav (d. 1054), attempted to protect unhappy daughters, noting that parents were responsible if a daughter injured herself rather than submit to an unwanted marriage or if her parents refused to allow the marriage of her choice. Once a woman married, one of Iaroslav's laws punished her if she hit her husband, but the law was silent on men who hit their wives. Russian custom allowed for divorce, but the new laws discouraged men from repudiating their wives for trivial reasons or when they were chronically ill.[26] The code also opposed any type of intermarriage. An Orthodox Christian woman was harshly fined for marrying a nonbeliever; the fine was five times higher than for a man who committed the same crime.[27]

The interaction of pagan and Christian cultures redefined women's honor. Some pagan rituals, such as abduction games during marriage rites, continued into the twelfth century. The laws did not automatically punish participants in such rituals; however, if the ritual caused the woman embarrassment, it was illegal. The wording of the law reveals much about the relationship between paganism and Christianity at this early point in Russian history, "If cheese is cut for a maiden, for the cheese the fine is a *grivna*, and three *grivny* to the maiden for her shame; and she shall be compensated whatever was lost. The metropolitan shall receive six grivny, and the prince shall punish the offender." Cheese was the pagan symbol of fertility, and to cut cheese for a maiden indicated that she was no longer a virgin. The woman, the church, and the state all received compensation for the crime of sexual dishonor.[28]

The Vikings were not the only invaders in eastern Europe. During the ninth century, the Magyars, nomadic pagans from western Asia, moved westward. They first appeared in Germany in 862 but did not constitute a serious threat until the end of the century, when they gave up their nomadic life and challenged German nobles for their lands. In 917, Magyars made it as far west as Provence and Burgundy. As they pillaged the countryside, they massacred entire villages, taking only young women and children as hostages.[29] Like the Vikings, they burned monasteries and convents and depopulated the countryside as peasants fled to safer places. Finally, the territory of the German king Otto I (r. 936–973) defeated the Magyars in 955 at the Battle of Lech, forcing them into what is now Hungary, where they settled and gradually converted to Christianity.

In 1001, King István (also known as Stephen; r. 997–1038) organized the Magyars into the Hungarian kingdom and accepted his crown from the pope, thus declaring his allegiance to the Latin Church. Like so many kings before him, István's Christian wife, Gisela, a German princess, paved the way for his conversion. Contacts between the new kingdom of Hungary and the West continued as István married his daughter Agatha to an Anglo-Saxon king. István maintained strong contacts with Byzantium, and he even founded a monastery for Greek nuns on Hungarian soil.

István also issued a series of new laws aimed at ending pagan practices among the Magyars. He prohibited the nomadic custom of forcing widows to marry against their wills and the tradition of abducting women. István imposed punishments against men who "fled their wives by leaving the country" and against the husband who, "because of the hatred he bears towards his wife," sells himself as a slave.[30]

The Magyar invasions that had begun with such violence ultimately created a powerful European monarchy. Their acceptance of Christianity changed women's status, linking them to women in the rest of Europe and cutting ties to nomadic practices.

Women Under Islam

Christian Europe's struggle against invaders from the north and the east was complicated by the formation and expansion of Islam. As had been true with Christianity, women were instrumental in the rise and spread of the new religion. According to Islamic texts, its founder, Muhammad (ca. 570–632), was born to a poor branch of a powerful tribe centered on Mecca, where he worked as a caravan leader for a wealthy widow named Khadija (ca. 555–619). When she was forty, Khadija married Muhammad, then twenty-five. After their marriage, Muhammad turned to full-time study and meditation. While meditating in a cave, Muhammad had a vision of the angel Gabriel. Khadija and Muhammad consulted one of her relatives, a Christian educated in Hebrew Scripture, who explained that Gabriel had appeared to both Moses and Mary, which placed Muhammad's vision alongside important Jewish and Christian revelations. Muhammad's revelation formed the basis of Islamic Scripture, the Qu'ran. Khadija was Muhammad's first convert.

Like Judaism and Christianity, Islam developed as a monotheistic religion, with Muhammad as its prophet. Devout Muslim men and women adhered to both moral and ceremonial obligations. Moral obligations included kindness and consideration, respect and mercy. Women must be chaste, but men had to treat their wives with kindness and restraint. Ceremonial obligations, known as the five pillars of Islam are: daily affirmation that there is no God but Allah, prayer five times a day, charity, fasting and atonement at Ramadan, and pilgrimage to Mecca at least once in a lifetime.

Before the advent of Islam, the peoples in the Middle East followed a variety of marriage and inheritance systems. Khadija's ownership of a caravan and her proposal of marriage to a younger man without the apparent approval of a male guardian demonstrate the degree of independence that some Arab women achieved. While Khadija was alive, Muhammad was monogamous. However, after her death in 619, he took multiple wives. The very different marriage experiences of Khadija and 'Aisha (614–678), his second and favorite wife, point to the changes that Islam brought to the region. Unlike the older, widowed Khadija, 'Aisha was the young daughter of one of Muhammad's major supporters. An intermediary had arranged her marriage when 'Aisha was six, and Muhammad consummated the relationship when she was nine or ten. While married to 'Aisha, Muhammad married other women. Many wives helped him forge necessary alliances with other families. Muhammad's later marriages, traditionally numbered at eleven, effectively normalized polygyny and patrilineality as orthodox Islamic practice. The Qu'ran allowed a man to have four wives, if he could maintain them equally.

Muhammad's marriages altered Muslim expectations of women in other ways. In opposition to local tradition, but in accordance with Byzantine and other Mediterranean customs, he secluded his wives, keeping them inside and out of the sight of other men. This practice distanced his family from his numerous followers who came to hear him preach or to have him settle disputes. Although he separated his wives from the rest of the world, he spoke of men's and women's spiritual equality. He often consulted with his wives, depended on their advice, and relied particularly on 'Aisha's wisdom.

Muhammad's sudden death in 632 left the new faith leaderless, and tribal conflict quickly ensued. The first two successors, called caliphs, ruled without opposition, but the election of Uthman (r. 644–656), one of Muhammad's sons-in-law and a member of the Umayyad family, incited considerable opposition. Among other complaints, opponents accused him of favoritism toward members of his own family. When Uthman was assassinated in 656, many Muslims supported Ali, another of the prophet's sons-in-law and the husband of Muhammad's only surviving daughter, Fatimah. However, 'Aisha refused to support him and led three thousand soldiers in what is known as "the battle of the camel." After Ali's murder, war erupted between Ali's sons and Uthman's family. 'Aisha gave critical support to the Umayyads. Ultimately, the Umayyads were successful, and they went on to revere 'Aisha, preserving much of her knowledge of Muhammad's life and attitudes as well as her knowledge of medicine and poetry. This split between the supporters of Ali and Uthman continues today in the divisions between Shi'a and Sunni Muslims.

Muslims debated whether the constraints that Muhammad had imposed on his wives should be the model for all women's behavior. Increasingly, Muslim women were confined to their homes, veiled when in public, and excluded from public discourse, religious or otherwise. Initial notions of religious equality between Muslim men and women gradually gave way to legal traditions that bound women to a patriarchal social structure. By the time of the Abbasid caliphate (750–1258), the successor to the Umayyad dynasty, elite men commonly had harems of hundreds of wives and concubines. Concubines were considered property, existing only to gratify male sexual desires, a concept that Arabs may have learned in Persia. Concubines had no status and few rights until they bore children, whom the father was bound by law to support. Upon his death, the concubine was granted her freedom. However, unless her children cared for her, she still had few options. Women's relegation to the status of sexual objects was not universally accepted. A grieving ninth-century father lamented at the death of his daughter, "We live in an age . . . when he who weds his daughter to the grave has found the best of bridegrooms."[31] Lower class men could not afford to keep their wives secluded, nor could they afford harems.

Islam's expansion throughout the Mediterranean basin accelerated after Muhammad's death in 632. Forging a political and religious state, Muslims conquered Persia by 651 and then swept across North Africa into Iberia.

Islamic Spain

In 711, Muslims crossed the Straits of Gibraltar and conquered the faltering Visigothic kingdom on the Iberian Peninsula. They ultimately settled in Iberia along a line marked roughly by the Duero and the Ebro rivers (excluding the county of Barcelona). For nearly three centuries, the Muslim state of Al-Andalus comprised more than two-thirds of the peninsula. Starting in 827, Muslims also began a slow conquest of Sicily and southern Italy.

The Iberian Peninsula was far more ethnically diverse than the rest of Europe. Andalusi society included Arabs, North Africans—known as Berbers—Hispano-Romans, Germans, Jews, Muslims, and Mozarabic Christians. In this complicated cultural mix, intermarriage was an important way to tie the Muslim conquerors to the local elite. Sara the Goth was the granddaughter of the next to last Visigothic king, Witiza (r. 702–710). Her high status and extensive land holdings in the region around Seville made her an attractive marriage partner and she married two Arab chiefs in succession.

Al-Andalus was a site of constant rivalry and competition. Successive groups of Muslims, each with its own ethnic identity and political and religious ideas, invaded the peninsula. In 756, Abd ar Rahman (731–788), a member of the Umayyad family that had controlled the caliphate, fled to Spain where he overthrew the governor. He made peace with the Christians in the northern kingdoms and further consolidated his power by working with Christians and Jews. From his capital at Córdoba, he created a vibrant Islamic culture largely independent of the rest of the Islamic world. Portions of poetry from Mut'a, a female slave of the ninth-century poet Ziryab, who came to al-Andalus from Baghdad, survive as evidence of women's contribution to this intellectual renaissance. At a literary gathering, she declared her passion for Amir 'Abd al-Rachman (r. 822–852) in heart-rending verse:

> *Oh, you that hide your passion! Who can*
> *   hide the day?*
> *I was owner of my heart, then love seized*
> *   me and it fled away*
> *Was it mine, alas or only borrowed? I love a*
> *   Qurashī,*
> *And abandoned shame for his sake.*[32]

Slaves like Mut'a, who were often educated for entertainment, often had more creative liberty than their free counterparts.

By the tenth century, Córdoba had a population of about one hundred thousand people, making it roughly the same size as Constantinople and several times bigger than the largest cities of western Europe. Its court rivaled that of Baghdad. Home to a dynamic array of scholars and artists, the city also boasted of one of the largest libraries of the Muslim world, with no fewer than four hundred thousand books from as far away as Persia. The Umayyad princess Wallada, the daughter of the caliph of Córdoba al-Mustakfi (r. 1025–1131), wrote poetry and maintained a literary salon. Some of her verses, which were embroidered on her clothes, proclaim both spiritual and emotional independence:

> *Worthy am I, by God, of the highest, and*
> *   Proudly I walk, with head aloft.*
> *My cheek I give to my lover and, to those*
> *   who wish them,*
> *I yield my kisses.*[33]

We also know that a woman named Labbāna worked both for the ruler himself and for the royal librarian, and that Fatima was in charge of acquisitions in the royal library. Between the eighth and eleventh centuries, 116 well-educated Andalusi women are recorded in biobibliographical dictionaries. Their expertises included grammar, jurisprudence, theology, and medicine. Islamic schools in Córdoba routinely employed female copyists. The poet Ibn Hazm credited women with teaching him the Qu'ran, poetry, and calligraphy. These examples suggest a willingness, at least on the part of the Muslim elites, to educate women.[34]

In 1108, the Umayyad dynasty came to an end, breaking Al-Andalus into several rival kingdoms.

This fragmentation made the region vulnerable to attack from both Africa and the Christian kingdoms in the north. At this point, Christian Europe had already begun an ambitious, two-pronged assault on the Islamic world.

Women and the Crusading Spirit

Christian Europe attempted to recapture its territories lost to Islam through the reconquest of Spain, the *reconquista,* and the Crusades, wars directed at retaking the Holy Land (see Map 5.4). The reconquest of Spain was a series of ongoing attempts by Christians to retake the peninsula. Urraca (r. 1109–1126), queen of León-Castile, proved to be one of the great warriors of her time. In addition to fighting her Christian rivals, in 1117, her troops reconquered the cities of Sigüenza, Atienza, and Medinaceli, consolidating Christianity's hold on northern Spain and making it a staging ground for future reconquests. During the early thirteenth century, a combined force of Castilians, Navarrese, and Aragonese soldiers had captured all the major Muslim cities, including Córdoba and Seville. Granada alone remained in Islamic hands and became the capital of the Nasrid dynasty, which would survive relatively isolated from the rest of the Islamic world until 1492.

The reconquista served as a model for the Crusades to the Holy Land, whose loss to Islam was a constant source of anxiety for medieval Christians and had isolated Byzantium from the rest of Christendom. However, until the end of the eleventh century, neither western Europe nor Byzantium had the organization or the military might to act on their concerns. Finally, an appeal from the Byzantine emperor, Alexius I Komnenus (r. 1081–1118), to halt the Muslim advance sparked a call from Pope Urban II (r. 1088–1099) in 1096 for a crusade to reconquer the Holy Land.

The call for crusade captured the imagination of western Europeans. In 1097, four armies of French knights and a fifth army of peasants left for the Holy Land. Although the pope had envisioned a crusade led by kings, instead he got uncontrolled armies of knights and peasants. The Popular Crusade wreaked havoc on its way to the Holy Land, looting villages and murdering Jews. The

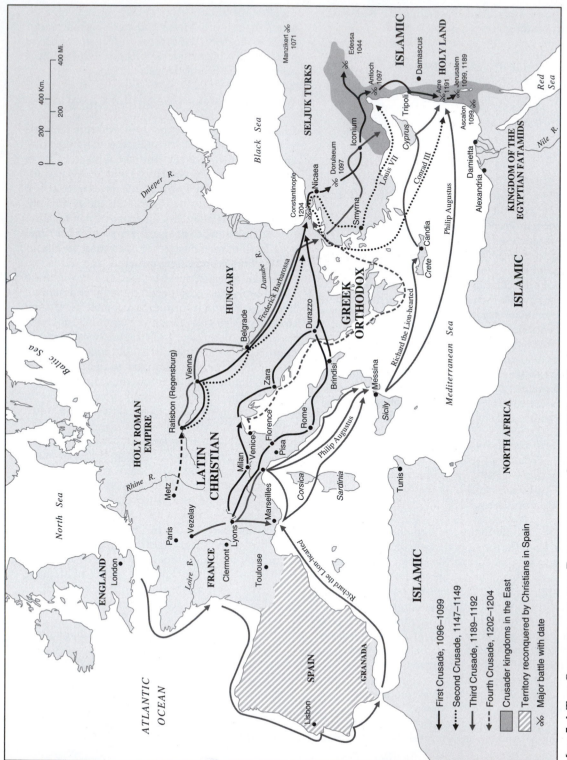

Map 5.4 **The Crusades and the Reconquest of Spain, 1095–1291.** As Christians attempted to retake land in Spain and the Middle East from Muslims, they settled women and families to promote a Christian society.

professional armies of knights behaved only slightly better. Alexius's daughter, Anna Komnena (1083–ca. 1148), described in her *Alexiad* (completed 1148), a biography of her father, how the arrival of Crusaders at the gates of Constantinople terrified the city's inhabitants. Emperor Alexius quickly sent them on their way.

When the Crusaders first arrived in the Middle East in 1097, conflict among the Muslims worked to the Crusaders' benefit. In short order, they were able to conquer the region and create four Crusader kingdoms; however, their successes did not last long. Once Muslim forces regrouped, they retook much of the European's territory, precipitating further crusades.

Amid the violence, the settlement and administration of the Crusader kingdoms offered Europeans some unique problems. The kingdoms existed in the midst of a hostile population and suffered continually from underpopulation. Crusaders had to import Christian families and brides from Syria and Armenia to resettle the countryside so that the Europeans would not be reliant on the local Muslim population for their supplies.

Although men did most of the fighting, they relied on women to support their efforts. Hundreds of European women from queens to laundresses, nurses, and prostitutes traveled to the Holy Land. Queen Eleanor of Aquitaine (1122–1204) and some of her court accompanied her husband, the French king Louis VII (r. 1137–1180), on the Second Crusade (1147–48), reportedly dressing as Amazons for the occasion. Queen Berengaria of England (ca. 1165–1230) went with her husband, King Richard of England (r. 1189–1199), on the Third Crusade (1187–1193). Most women on crusade helped make life easier for the soldiers, while queens lent prestige and gave legitimacy to the cause. In Europe, women raised money to help supply the crusading armies, donated money to settlers, and went on pilgrimages to the holy sites secured by the Crusaders.

The Crusader kingdoms encouraged Christian settlement by granting favorable terms for landholding. Initially, laws allowed women to inherit land in the absence of male heirs, but the need for continual military support left rulers less inclined to allow women to control land on their own. The Crusader governments also pressured noble widows to remarry quickly so that their land would be ruled by armed and loyal men. This policy created resentment among women and their families. Rulers even tried to reward lower-class knights for loyal service with the hand of a wealthy widow or heiress. When this happened, it was called *misalliance*, and women often went to court to prevent such marriages. Gradually families asserted their rights to negotiate marriages, effectively stratifying a society that had been more flexible than the one left behind in Europe.

Containing the political turmoil of the Crusader kingdoms required a strong ruler. When the king of Jerusalem, Baldwin II (r. 1118–1131), died, his daughter Melisende (1105–1162), her husband, Fulk V, the count of Anjou (d. 1143), and their infant son were crowned co-rulers. After Fulk died, Melisende ruled as regent for their son, Baldwin III (r. 1143–1162), and then refused to hand over power when Baldwin came of age at fifteen in 1145. She ruled for seven more years, appointing military commanders, issuing charters, and negotiating with various political factions. Melisende proved to be a capable defender of the kingdom. Not until 1152 did Baldwin III muster enough support to finally rule Jerusalem alone, and even then his mother continued to be influential in local politics.

Pagan and Muslim invaders quickly destroyed the unity and prosperity of Charlemagne's empire and introduced new gender expectations to Europe. Conversion to Christianity helped bridge the gulf between the Viking's seafaring ways and the settled life of their victims. While northern Europe grappled with those pagan invaders, southern Europe faced the rapid expansion of and conquest by Islam, whose urban and monotheistic culture was not easily reconciled to European ways. Christian Europe would not tolerate the presence of infidels on "Christian" soil, and the Crusades sought to reintroduce Christianity to Muslim lands through conquest and settlement.

MEDIEVAL SOCIAL ORGANIZATION

Repeated invasions created a military elite who lived off the labor of a dependent population. Medieval European theologians described their society as comprising three orders: those who fight, those who pray, and those who work. Of course, they were talking about men, but they also recognized that women fit into this scheme. In the twelfth century, the bishop of Limerick wrote: "I do not say that the function of women is to pray or toil, let alone fight, but they are married to those who pray, toil and fight and they serve them."[35] This vision implied more social stability than was the case. Even as the bishop wrote, men and women from these three orders were fleeing to new or revitalized cities in search of a life outside the military concerns of the countryside.

Aristocratic Women

Although they made up less than 5 percent of the population, the priorities of the nobility formed the basis of medieval gender norms. Aristocratic men displayed their power and wealth through land ownership and formed political, military, and marriage alliances to protect and enhance their territories. Lords sought men to become their vassals, offering them protection, financial rewards, access to power, and, most important, land (fiefs). In return, vassals provided counsel, military service, and financial support. As transmitters of property and bearers of children, aristocratic women helped bind this military society.

With the support of the church, noblewomen attempted to limit men's violence with the creation of a court culture. By the twelfth century, the nobility developed a court culture known as chivalry that placed warrior behavior within a Christian framework. At tournaments, men displayed their prowess as Christian knights through feats of bravery in combat. Rules that respected an opponent's valor and skill and demanded loyalty to one's lord further regulated the violence. Women's place in the chivalric world was as passive and aloof observers. Their beauty and favor inspired men's actions. In the pursuit of women, men often fell in love with the wives of other men, making unfulfilled sexual longing and adultery constant sources of emotional tension in chivalric culture.

Courtly love poetry and chivalric stories like the Arthurian romances of Chrétien de Troyes written in the late twelfth century spread chivalric values and behavior. Many of these romances explored gender roles and the implications of con-

flicted loyalty. In the Arthurian romances, one of King Arthur's knights, Lancelot, loves and has an adulterous affair with Arthur's wife, Queen Guinevere. Lancelot is torn between his love for Arthur and his love for Guinevere and endures many physical tests to prove his loyalty and worthiness to both. In Chrétien de Troyes's romance *Lancelot or the Knight of the Cart*, Lancelot suffers several humiliations. To rescue the kidnapped Guinevere, he must ride in a cart reserved for criminals on their way to execution, and later he is locked in a tower and is rescued by a woman.

Far from always being passive recipients of chivalric culture, women, such as Eleanor of Aquitaine and her daughter Marie de Champagne (1145–1198), encouraged its spread by patronizing *troubadours*, lyric poets who composed songs about courtly love and chivalry. Chrétien de Troyes wrote *The Knight of the Cart* for Marie. Some women wrote their own romances, offering a feminine perspective on this otherwise masculine-centered code of conduct. Female troubadours, like Beatriz, Countess of Dia (b. ca. 1200), extolled the equality of love through beautiful music and lyrics. In the late twelfth century, a woman called Marie de France wrote many *lais*, or chivalric poems, that present active and resourceful heroines who fought oppressive marriages and rigid social conventions. In these poems, Marie shows an acute awareness of women's vulnerability when they engage in extramarital affairs, especially with men of higher status (see **Sources from the Past:** *Equitan, a Romance of Marie de France*).

Conservation and expansion of territory and the maintenance of family bloodline not only dominated military goals, they shaped noble social organization. Noblemen did not marry until they had land. Men typically had to wait until they inherited or conquered land, so they married late if at all. Lack of inheritance forced many younger sons to seek their way in the world as landless knights. As a result, demographers estimate that in thirteenth-century France, between one-third and one-quarter of noblemen remained unmarried their entire lives.[36]

Women often married at puberty, as they were highly sought after for the land included in their dowries. The marriage of the French king, Louis VII, to Eleanor of Aquitaine in 1137 more than doubled the lands under his control. After they dissolved their marriage in 1152, on the grounds that they were too closely related, Louis lost control of Aquitaine, because it was Eleanor's land. When Eleanor remarried, Aquitaine passed into the control of her new husband, King Henry II (r. 1133–1189) of England, Louis's rival. Eleanor effectively managed much of this land herself and battled Henry over the right to choose her own heir for it.

The importance of property made women with large dowries good marriage candidates, but women did not control that property during their marriages. By the High Middle Ages, legal codes across Europe stipulated that no married women regardless of class or status could own land; any lands she brought to the marriage passed immediately to her husband. During their marriage, a husband could use the dowry as he wished as long as he did not sell dowry land without his wife's permission, mismanage it, or cause it to decline in value. While a cruel or indifferent husband could effectively cut out his wife from any influence over their estates, practically speaking, this was unwise. Noblemen spent so much time away from their lands fighting or serving their overlords that they relied on their wives to manage and defend the families' estates.

Although church doctrine prohibited divorce, the reality was more complex. At times, the church attempted to force couples to remain together despite marital problems. For instance, in the thirteenth century, ecclesiastical officials ordered Edmund, the Earl of Cornwall, to return to his wife, Margaret de Clare, and care for her with proper marital affection. She alleged that he neglected her and treated her with such cruelty that she feared for her life. However, when their attempt at reconciliation failed, the church annulled the marriage. An annulment declared that the sacrament of marriage had not been legitimately administered because of some mistake, such as when the couple was too closely related. However, annulments were rare. More often unhappy couples decided to separate permanently with or without church approval. Eleanor of Aquitaine took both routes to end her unhappy marriages. She had her first marriage to King Louis VII annulled, and separated from her second husband, King Henry II, after many years of

TOMB OF ELEANOR OF AQUITAINE (1122–1204) AT FONTREVAULT. One of the most powerful and influential queens, Eleanor controlled considerable territory, which made her highly sought after as a wife. She married two kings, and patronized music and literature to create a vibrant court culture. *(Erich Lessing/Art Resource, NY.)*

conflict over his mistresses and his attempts to control her land. They lived apart for many years, first by agreement, and then because Henry imprisoned her after she encouraged their son Richard to rebel against him.

Since noblewomen married so young, they could expect to have between four and six children, in addition to many more pregnancies that did not go full term and children who did not survive. In most circumstances, a local midwife attended the delivery, helped perhaps by the woman's ladies in waiting—her female attendants at court—or her own mother. Professional physicians only attended difficult births. Noblewomen did not usually nurse their own children but sent

Equitan, a Romance of Marie de France

This selection of the lai or romance by Marie de France illustrates the tensions between love and sexual attraction and marriage and loyalty. Although all are important to an individual's life, only marriage and loyalty have public meaning. These tensions do not affect men and women equally, and Marie shows great awareness of women's vulnerability and inequality when entering into an adulterous affair.

Equitan had a seneschal,
A good knight, worthy, loyal,
Overseer of all his estate,
His manager and magistrate.
Except for war, no task, no thing—
No emergency—could draw the king
From his hunting and his pleasure,
And enjoying the river's leisures.
The seneschal had taken a bride
Who later brought evil to the countryside.
She was terribly beautiful,
Well-bred and respectable,
With a nice body, a good figure.
She was a masterwork of Nature:
Grey eyes in a lovely face,
Lovely mouth, nose in the right place.
In the kingdom she had no peer.
Her praises reached the king's own ear.
Often he would send to greet her
Gifts he'd have his men bring her.
He desired her without seeing her.
Soon as he could, he got to meet her.
Hunting pleasure of a private sort,
He went into the country for sport.
In the manor of his seneschal,
The castle where the lady stayed,
The king took shelter at nightfall;
He needed rest, so hard he'd played.
Now he can talk to her, apart,
Reveal his worth, show her his heart.
He finds her courtly, wise, proper,
Beautiful in face and figure,

Friendly, too, lively, not cold.
Love enlists him in his household.
Love shot an arrow in his direction
And the wound it made's immense.
He hit his heart; this infection
Does not call for prudent sense.
This lady's love's assault is rude:
He becomes sad, thoughtful, subdued.
Now he puts himself on trial,
Offers no defense or denial:
That night he gets no sleep in bed,
But blames and scolds himself instead.
"Alas," he says, "what has fate tried,
Leading me into this countryside?
I saw this lady; now a dart
Of agony has struck my heart.
It makes my body shake and shiver.
I think I really have to love her.
If I love her, it's wrong, after all:
She's the wife of my seneschal.
I must keep faith with him lovingly,
As I want him to do unto me.
If by some trick he found out,
I know it would bother him a lot.
Still, wouldn't it be a pity
If just for him I went crazy?
The lady's so lovely, it'd be sad
If she didn't love, if no lover she had!
What good are all her courtly ways
If she never learns love's plays?
Under heaven, any man, if she loved
Him, would be terribly improved!
If he does hear it somewhere or other,
The seneschal shouldn't bother,
For he can't have her to himself!
Indeed, I want to share his wealth."
He said this, and he sighed so deep,
Then lay thinking, without sleep
Then spoke and said, "Now, just what
Is troubling me? I'm so worried, but
I haven't yet tried to discover
If she'll take me for her lover.
I will find out, right away!
If she feels what I feel,
My sorrow can begin to heal.
God! It's so long yet until day!
I won't get any rest this slow

Night—I lay down so long ago."
He lay awake till it was light,
Longing for dawn in this sad plight.
He got up, he left for the hunt,
But soon, weary, back he went.
He didn't feel well, he said;
He went to his room and to bed.
The seneschal is chagrined;
He doesn't know what ill wind
Blows shivers and trembling on the king.
His wife is the reason for everything.
To amuse himself and to console
Him, he has her come chat in his room.
He opens up his heart and soul,
Tells her: for her he's near his doom;
She alone can grant him cheer,
Or decide his death is near.
"My lord," the lady tells the king,
"I need to think about this thing.
This first time, you understand,
I haven't thought it out or planned.
You are a king of the highest nobility;
I am not rich—well, little me,
You shouldn't think of me this way,
As a lover or partner in love-play.
If you did what you want with me,
I am sure as sure can be
Pretty soon you'd leave me there,
And I would be the worse for wear.
If it happens that I love you,
And what you ask for I give you,
Still it's not an equal share;
As lovers, we're an uneven pair.
Since you are a king of royal might,
And my husband owes you such respect,
You may be thinking, I expect,
To collect a love-tax as your right.
Love's worthless without equality.
Better a poor man's loyalty
If sense and worth are in that man;
And his love gives greater joy than
That of a king or prince, if he
Holds in his heart no loyalty.
If any one loves up higher

Than one's wealth lets one aspire,
Then one is afraid of everything.
The rich man fears, for his part,
Someone may steal his lady's heart,
For he wants her just because he's king."
Equitan's answer cannot wait:
"Lady, please, please don't say it!
These are not courtly men or women,
No, it a bourgeois bargain,
If for wealth or feudal respect
They work so hard towards a low object.
Under heaven's no lady, wise and nice,
Courtly—and how noble a heart, hers,
Setting on love a good high price
So she's not always changing partners—
So poor, her cloak's her whole estate,
But a rich prince in a castle royal
Wouldn't suffer for her, and wait,
And love her well, and be loyal.
Fickle lovers, who think they're slick,
Always ready to play some trick,
Are themselves deceived—they lose face.
We've seen this in more than one case.
If they lose out, it's not surprising;
They earned it by their enterprising.
Dear lady, I give myself to you!
Don't think of me as your king; do
Call me your friend and servitor!
I swear to you, I tell you sure,
That I will do whatever you say.
Don't let me die for you today!
You're the lady, I'm the servant here;
Proud one, hear this beggar's prayer!"
The king talked on and on, and he
Begged her so to have mercy,
He convinced her his love was true,
So she gave him her body, too.
They pledged their troth, exchanging rings,
In faith forever—each other's kings.
They kept faith, as lovers and friends;
They died of it, and met their ends.

Trans. Judith P. Shoaf ©1992 http://web.english.ufl.
edu/exemplaria/marie/equitan.pdf

them to wet nurses. As lactation tends to suppress fertility, women who hired wet nurses became pregnant more quickly and had more children. Despite the healthier diet available to noblewomen, infant mortality rates were quite high. Some scholars estimate that among noble families 36 percent of male babies and 29 percent of female babies died before their fifth year.[37] A mother did not usually attend the baptism of her child, as custom dictated that she remain confined to the house for a month after giving birth. During this period, women friends and attendants cared for the new mother, assuming many of her responsibilities. Gradually, noblewomen returned to managing their property and households, in addition to caring for their children.

Scholars used to believe that because so many children died, medieval parents had few emotional attachments to their children and treated those who survived as little adults. Recent scholarship had demonstrated that this was far from true. Even when wet nurses cared for noble babies, their mothers still spent much time with them. Although medieval parents certainly experienced the deaths of more children than parents in the modern industrialized world, they did not mourn less deeply those who died or fail to give those who lived every advantage they could. Medieval parents did not romanticize childhood the way modern parents do, but they recognized childhood as a stage of life that required instruction and guidance.

Medieval society believed that for boys and girls to learn appropriate gender norms, fathers should rear sons to be warriors and mothers should raise daughters to be noble ladies. Nonetheless, mothers were usually their children's first teacher. Some medieval noblewomen were literate and passed this knowledge on to their children. However, boys' education focused on fighting rather than literature. As a result, noblewomen may have been more literate than men. By the age of six or seven, families sent their sons and daughters to live with other families. Sending children off to another noble household furthered their educations, strengthened connections with other powerful families, and set the stage for future marriages.

The constant warfare in medieval society took a demographic toll; between the twelfth and the fourteenth centuries, nearly half of all noblemen died violently and noblewomen outlived noblemen. Approximately 50 percent of noblewomen who reached maturity could expect to live to the age of fifty, but only about 18 percent of noblemen could expect such a long life.[38] Consequently, medieval Europe was populated by large numbers of widows.

A woman gained control of her property upon the death of her husband. She could then sell it, donate it, or live off the income. Many widows remarried, but others chose to remain single and administer their lands on their own until their children came of age. Some were so powerful that they were counted as lords in their own right. Upon the death of her husband, in the early thirteenth century, Blanche of Navarre swore loyalty to the king of France. She administered and protected her husband's lands in the county of Champagne, and in 1222, turned them over to her son in better condition than when her husband had died. Not all medieval laws were so favorable to widows. In England, widows did not automatically receive the guardianship of their children, and the king had the right to arrange the marriages of noble widows if they held royal land grants in order to prevent them from marrying rivals.

Peasant Women

Maintaining an aggressive military elite required a subservient population dedicated to growing food for them. The majority of the population in medieval Europe were peasants—dependent, unfree agricultural workers. By the end of the Carolingian period, slavery had ceased to be economically viable in the countryside, and serfdom had replaced slave labor. Serfs were tied to the land, they could not be sold away from their families, they could marry and have legitimate children, and they had legal rights in the local court. Much of what we know of the medieval peasantry comes from legal sources that the nobility created to control their peasants and advance the wealth of their estates.

Peasants generally lived in villages, but the unit that regulated their labor and extracted the surplus was called a manor, and scholars often refer to the process by which the labor of peasants was turned into food for the nobility and monastic lords as *manorialism*. Peasants spent part of the week working the lord's land, and much of the produce of their own lands went to the lord in exchange for basic rights, including living on the land, using the manor mill or oven, and brewing ale. In exchange, lords typically owed their peasants protection from invasion and customary privileges that included grazing rights on the common and the sponsorship of a few annual feasts.

Economic necessity created some flexibility in the gender roles observed by peasant men and women. Although both men and women worked the fields and tried to keep the family fed, housed, and clothed, they performed different jobs to achieve this end. Plowing was typically male work, while women worked in the kitchen gardens, looked after the livestock, and cooked and cleaned the houses. Women's labor was integral to the household. Although they might plow if their husbands could not, families also depended on women to make extra income by brewing ale, spinning wool, or caring for village children. In coastal areas, peasant women took on even more work, as men were often away fishing for long periods. They were not only responsible for farming, but they oversaw all the family's property and often negotiated their children's marriages. Peasant women's labor also provided them with regular contact outside the home, as they went to the market to sell or buy produce, strolled to the well to get water, did laundry, or dealt with itinerant peddlers.

Peasant women married between the ages of eighteen and twenty, later than aristocratic women, and their husbands tended to be close to them in age. Couples married either when they had saved enough to buy some land or when they had inherited enough to begin an independent life together. However, by the fourteenth century, as many as one-third of women never married. Single women had extensive freedom to buy and sell land, hire additional labor, and earn money at various occasional occupations including brewing, spinning, and sewing, thus marriage was not necessary for survival.

Because peasant women tended to marry later than noblewomen, they had fewer pregnancies and fewer children. Virginity was less important at marriage than the knowledge that a woman was fertile, and many peasant women were pregnant at their weddings. Childbirth was dangerous and many women and children died as a result of disease,

poor nutrition, lack of prenatal care and rest, and unsanitary conditions. Infant mortality rates may have been as high as nearly 50 percent. Children and fertility were so valued that some manorial bylaws gave pregnant women special rights and privileges. German manors gave pregnant women access to special foods, such as nuts, fish, and fruit.[39]

Because of the dangers involved in childbirth, women of all classes employed a variety of methods either to inhibit conception or to end an unwanted pregnancy, despite clerical injunctions against these practices. Beatrice de Plannisol, a minor French noblewoman who had an affair with the local priest, wore a bag with secret ingredients around her neck when they had sex to prevent conception.[40] Herbalists also recommended soaking lamb's wool with a mixture of certain caustic herbs and honey and inserting the wool into the vagina before sex. Infanticide was apparently rare, a legacy of both Christianity, which forbade it, and Germanic custom, which did not practice it.

Peasant babies faced numerous dangers. Coroners' reports from England show that toddlers had a high accident rate, falling into wells and ditches and being mauled by wild animals.[41] Those who survived rarely received any formal education. However, like their noble counterparts, peasant children learned skills appropriate to their class and gender roles. Boys followed their fathers into the fields, and girls learned housekeeping alongside their mothers. Adolescents also might work as servants for another family or the lord of the manor in order to earn money for their futures.

Old age was difficult for peasants. A lifetime of hard work left bodies sore, enfeebled, and prone to illness. Teeth and eyesight failed, and many an elderly peasant died when a misplaced candle set the house afire. Aging peasants who did not live in extended families did not necessarily rely on or expect their children to care for them. Widows often contracted with a niece or nephew to live with them in exchange for some land or other inheritance.[42]

Although peasants were ignorant of all but the most basic of religious tenets, Christianity was a powerful force in their lives. While clerics tried to use Christianity to control aristocratic violence,

Christianity taught peasants hard work and submission. To regulate men's and women's behavior, clerics relied on *penitentials*, handbooks of sins and their associated punishments that allowed the sinner to work off sins in this life. Penitentials assumed that women were lascivious and would supplement their Christian devotions with spells, incantations, and consultations with the village wise woman or man. They assigned harsh penalties, such as fasting, for violations of Christian sexual norms like homosexuality and adultery. Some penitentials offered very detailed discussion of sex, stipulating proper positions and times of day. No one was to have sex on Sundays or holy days, or for the entire forty days of Lent. The penitentials taught that sex was for procreation, and that sexual pleasure led to the sin of lust. It is unlikely that anyone but the most pious peasants closely followed these prescriptions.

Peasants learned about Christianity through their parish priest. The parish was the basic unit of public worship, moral instruction, and religious taxation. At the parish church, peasants paid taxes to support the church hierarchy, learned about Christian behavior from sermons, and received the sacraments. Some religious activities were sex segregated. During Sunday services, women sat or stood on one side of the church and men on the other. Wall paintings of biblical stories and saints' lives reinforced Christian ideology and gendered behavior. In Hungary and Byzantium, images of female saints were located at the section of the church where women stood or sat.[43] To earn the saints' favors and ensure health, healing, abundant crops, or safety on a journey, peasants visited local shrines and presented their patron saints with gifts of candles, votives, and prayers. Women prayed to Saint Margaret for safe childbirth and borrowed "relics" of girdles, necklaces, and headpieces from the saints to help with childbirth. During the twelfth century, both men and women increasingly prayed to the Virgin as their primary intercessor in heaven, and images of her filled parish churches.

Urban Women

Although western Europe was predominantly rural, in the first two centuries after the year 1000, small groups of merchants, artisans, and traders banded together to form the first new cities in Europe since the Roman Empire. They constituted a different kind of society from the militarily-oriented countryside. Merchants and traders built walled cities in former defensive outposts, Roman crossroads, and monastic centers in order to protect their markets and warehouses from attacks by knights. Old Roman cities, often the strongholds of bishops, also flourished. Commerce not war was the central activity in medieval cities, and city leaders were often the wealthiest men in town. Initially, only a trickle of hearty, independent souls flowed into the tiny, walled towns. Serfs escaping the violence and poverty of their manors helped swell the urban population. By the late twelfth century, more and more people were attracted to the freedoms of city life. The populations of Cologne, Milan, and Florence quickly exceeded fifty thousand inhabitants. Paris, Europe's largest city, boasted a population of more than two hundred thousand in 1300.[44]

With the success of the reconquista, Spanish kings in the eleventh and twelfth centuries founded towns to promote stability and bring prosperity to the reconquered territories. City founders viewed women as critical to a city's success. The kings of Castile granted settlers favorable financial terms to encourage their formation. In some towns, military men were declared nobles, in others, criminals were exonerated, and in still others, men, as heads of households, had total control over the behavior of women, giving women little recourse to courts when they had been wronged. The government encouraged all men heading for these new towns to bring women, even if they had to abduct them. Town laws exempted men with wives from some taxes or, if one married a local woman, the town might pay for the wedding. Some municipal laws also allowed women to inherit, purchase, or sell property and to designate heirs, as a woman with property was an asset for the town. For some women, the reconquista was a chance to begin a new life.[45]

Because trade and urban development required cash and wealth, cities promoted new inheritance systems and changed marriage laws in order to concentrate wealth in the hands of a few. These changes prevented women from taking property away from their natal families through their dowries and inher-

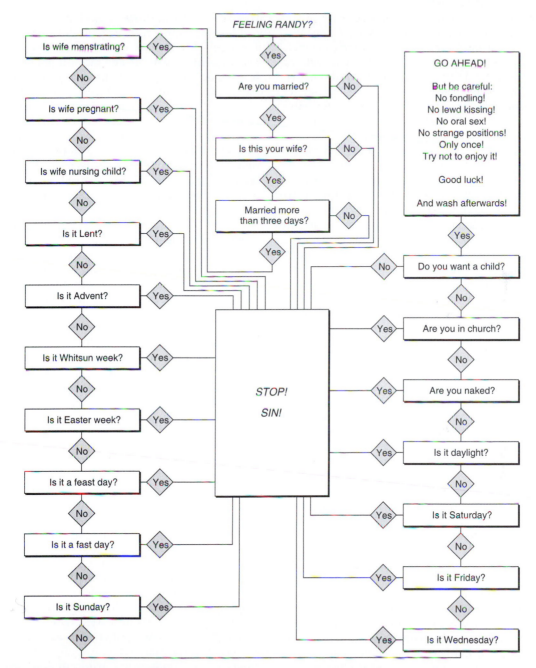

SEXUAL DECISION-MAKING PROCESS ACCORDING TO THE PENITENTIALS. In an effort to teach the peasants about Christianity and sin, the clergy composed penitentials, which prescribed specific punishments for specific sins. This chart illustrates the medieval clergys' ideas that sex was exclusively for procreation not recreation. *(James Brundage,* Law, Sex, and Christian Society in Medieval Europe *[Chicago: University of Chicago Press, 1987], 162.)*

itance. In Genoa, the city government, or commune, specifically changed traditional marriage practices. Both Roman and Germanic law required a dowry, a counter-dowry or bride price (usually about half the amount of the dowry), and a promise of portion, called the *tertium* (usually a quarter to a third of her husband's estate), at widowhood for a woman's maintenance. In 1130, Genoa made all three components negotiable. In 1143, the city further limited the size of both the bride price and the tertium. Minimizing the tertium meant that sons inherited more land or property upon the death of their fathers, and they did not have to wait until their mothers died. In Milan, the dowry came to be viewed as a loan, and husbands could be called to repay it. As a consequence, the numbers of female property holders in Italian cities declined over the course of the twelfth century.[46]

Widows were the most active women in urban commerce. Between 1155 and 1216, 24 percent of commercial contracts with the Genoese city government were with widows.[47] Those widows who had acquired substantial resources at the deaths of their husbands could loan money for long-distance trade missions and set up workshops for manufacturing of goods, usually cloth.

The great wealth of these new cities made them attractive prey for land-hungry knights. However, cities and their wealthy inhabitants wanted to run their affairs without the interference of nobles, who could inhibit urban freedom and growth through taxes or violence. Cities hired militias to defend them, but also tried appeasing local nobles through alliances. Urban patriarchs sought to marry their daughters into noble families and thus tie the nobility to the city. After the count of Ventimiglia made peace with the inhabitants of Genoa, his sons had to marry Genoese women, and his own daughter had to marry a Genoese man.[48]

As gathering spots for a diverse and an affluent population with fewer military ambitions, cities developed a culture quite different from the countryside. In the southern Italian cities, particularly in Salerno, physicians and other medical practitioners gathered to teach and practice medicine. They drew upon Islamic, Greek, and Roman texts readily available in this region. City records show a number of women working in the local medical profession. The most famous but illusive of these was Trota, who authored a twelfth-century medical text and apparently practiced medicine. Her *Practical Medicine According to Trota* attests to her range of knowledge and medical practice, but it gives no further information as to her age or social status. Until quite recently scholars also attributed *Treatments for Women,* generically called *The Trotula,* to her. Trota did not in fact write this tremendously popular medical treatise. The section titled "Women's Cosmetics" explains that some of the preparations were from Saracen women, demonstrating the integration of Arabic and local medical knowledge in Salerno.[49]

The class-based society of the Middle Ages was dominated by the military ambitions of the nobility. Aristocratic women living in a culture that promoted male violence found ways to limit its daily impact on their lives. Peasant women, who faced a daily struggle to feed their families and elude noble violence, participated in a culture designed to ensure their hard work and subservience. The rise of cities challenged this military culture, but to survive, town leaders formed alliances with the nobility through marriages. At the same time, cities offered immigrant women willing to leave the familiarity of rural life new experiences and opportunities.

WOMEN AND CHURCH REFORM

By the eleventh century, the political situation in Europe had stabilized to such a degree that church leaders again focused on reform. From the church's perspective, the chaos of invasion had again permitted women too much freedom. As new forms of monasticism introduced new ideas about spirituality and the role of women in the church and society, reformers again defined women as dangerous and weak and in need of constant supervision, rather than helpful to the pursuit of spiritual perfection. By connecting monastic vocations to the priesthood, reformers effectively separated the laity from the clergy and removed nuns from the ecclesiastical hierarchy. Nevertheless, female religious created a vibrant culture that reflected their own spiritual and emotional priorities.

Women and Monastic Reforms

The foundation of a new monastery called Cluny in the region of Burgundy in 909 by Ingelberga and her husband, William, Duke of Aquitaine, was a turning point for the medieval church. The monks of Cluny emphasized their separation from the world. Unlike most monasteries, Cluny was outside the control of the local bishop and under the direct control of the papacy. This policy freed its ambitious abbots to pursue their own initiatives free of local interference. As a result, Cluny became increasingly wealthy and powerful over the course of the tenth and the eleventh centuries. Through its own interpretation of the Benedictine Rule, Cluny created an elaborate liturgy, which removed monks from manual labor. The Cluny monks also insisted on the ordination of monks as priests. By emphasizing the connections between monasticism and the priesthood, Cluny elevated male monks above nuns because as women, nuns could not be ordained. The Cluniac notion that women were physically and morally inferior to men because they could not be priests justified a range of practices and policies designed to limit women's involvement in the church.

Although many female houses attempted to imitate the Cluniac ideal, Cluny did not establish a house for women until 1055, when Abbot Hugh (1049–1109) founded a convent at Marcigny, near Cluny. He wanted a suitable home for his mother, to protect her from her second husband who had already killed one of Hugh's brothers. He further explained that it was to be a "glorious prison" for all the wives abandoned by men who wanted to join Cluny. Three of Hugh's sisters and two nieces joined her.[50] The nuns' enclosure both protected them from temptation and prevented them from tempting male religious. The nuns of Marcigny took this enclosure seriously, coming to view themselves as "penitents immured in a living tomb."[51] When a fire threatened to destroy the convent and kill them all, the nuns refused to leave, despite the pleas of the monks. They trusted God to protect them, and the fire died down before it reached the convent. Although it housed female members of illustrious noble families, Marcigny was never as rich and beautiful as Cluny, and Cluny's lack of interest in female houses inhibited their expansion. Moreover,

Marcigny and its houses never gained the same degree of political independence as Cluny. While the monks at Cluny elected their own abbot, Hugh gave the office of abbess of Marcigny to the Virgin Mary and appointed a prioress, who had few administrative and minimal liturgical duties. Although Cluniac monks were happy to have the prayers of the Marsigny nuns and praised their piety and virtue, it was, in their eyes, a house filled with women, who were by their very nature sinful and dangerous.

Cluny's lifestyle and influence attracted criticism and prompted the creation of new monastic orders. One of the most popular and ultimately the most powerful of these post-Cluniac orders were the Cistercians, whose head monastery was located at Cîteaux in eastern France. Unlike the Cluniacs, the Cistercians, led by the dynamic mystic Bernard of Clairvaux (1090–1153), pursued a simple life that placed equal emphasis on prayer and manual labor. Bernard and the Cistercians hoped to reinvigorate the self-sufficiency of the Benedictine Rule through a life of apostolic poverty. Although Bernard was a riveting preacher and attracted many followers, he was indifferent to women who wanted to join his order. The Cistercian statutes prohibited monks from having any contact with women, whether they were servants, women who came to the churches to pray and attend services, family members, or nuns. The notion that women threatened male chastity had become firmly entrenched, and Bernard wanted little to do with those who might sully the reputation of his monks.

Nevertheless, the Cistercian Order remained popular among women who longed for its life of apostolic poverty and found Bernard's spiritual goal of a personal relationship with God appealing. Like Cluniac nuns, Cistercian nuns accepted claustration as a sign of obedience and piety. Despite women's enthusiasm for Cistercian monasticism, they were not recognized as a part of the order. As a result, their houses did not receive the same tax benefits or freedom from episcopal intervention as their male counterparts. They were excluded from the order's business, and the Cistercians regularly converted convents that they defined as beyond reform into monasteries. In Laon, Bernard called the women's community "a house of debauchery," and in 1128, he replaced the nuns with monks.[52] The Cistercian belief in the corruption of women was so strong that in 1348 the order forbade the founding of new female houses.

Despite the misogynist nature of Cluny and the Cistercians, one reforming male cleric understood the power of female spirituality and worked to cultivate it. At the beginning of the twelfth century, Robert d'Arbrissell (ca. 1045–1116), an itinerant preacher, set out to create and maintain a new style of religious life for women. In founding the Order of Fontevrault, he created a mixed community, reviving a monastic structure not seen since the eighth century. He strictly limited contact between men and women and divided the work of the community according to sex. Robert "commended the more tender and weaker sex [women] to psalm-singing and contemplation, while he applied the stronger sex [men] to the labors of the active life."[53] His preaching attracted many followers, and Robert spent the next fifteen years expanding his order. In 1115, just before he died, he ensured the continuation of the female side of the order by choosing one of his early followers, a widow named Petronilla of Chemillé (r. 1115–1149) as the abbess. He specifically chose a widow, because he feared that a woman without worldly experience might not be able to supervise the priories and oversee the order's property. Eventually, Fontevrault attracted both papal and royal support. King Henry II of England and Eleanor of Aquitaine were buried there, as was their son Richard the Lionheart, also the king of England.

The Gregorian Reforms and the New Gender Order

The Cluniac reforms set the stage for the Gregorian reforms, the first European-wide attempt at ecclesiastical change and reorganization since the Christianization of western Europe. Cluny's influence meant Cluniac monks came to staff many ecclesiastical offices. They spread Cluny's ideas about the separation of the laity and the clergy and the connection between monastic and clerical vocation.

By the ninth and tenth centuries, the papacy had lost most of its international influence and had fallen under the control of a few Roman families. Electing a pope had become a family affair, not an international one. The head of the Roman nobility, Theophylactus (d. 916), and his wife, Theodora (early tenth century), arranged the election of Pope Sergius III (r. 904–911). Sergius and their daughter Marozia (mid tenth century) had either been lovers or married, and their relationship had produced a son. After Theophylactus's death, his widow, Theodora, along with Marozia and her other daughter, Theodora II, continued to oversee family interests. This meant arranging for their own candidates to become pope. Eventually, Marozia orchestrated the election of her son by Sergius, John XI (r. 931–935), and the election of her grandson Pope John XII in 955.

Although aristocratic intervention in papal politics was not new, observers harshly criticized the influence of women on the pope. Calls for reform began with a smear campaign. One clerical chronicler famously referred to this period as a "pornacracy." He wrote that Theodora I was a "shameless strumpet who ruled Rome in the manliest fashion," and added that she made John the pope "because she feared that she wouldn't be able to satisfy her lust often enough if he were two hundred miles away."[54] Another chronicler declared the papacy so corrupt that a woman disguised as a man ruled as pope. However Pope Joan, as she is known, never existed. Chroniclers portrayed women involved in politics as debauched and "manly" and defined politics as a purely masculine activity.

In the wake of these criticisms and with the support of the Holy Roman Emperor, cardinals drawn from Cluny initiated a series of reforms designed to liberate the papacy from Roman politics, strengthen ecclesiastical organization, and improve clerical morality. The most zealous of these reformers was Pope Gregory VII (r. 1073–1085). He wanted the church to control both the appointment of clergy and the revenue associated with individual churches, as well as eliminate nepotism (the preference of relatives over qualified candidates for church office), simony (the selling of church offices), and clerical marriage. Ending nepotism and simony theoretically gave the church more control over who became clerics and what offices they filled, thereby removing the church from familial influences.

The Gregorian reforms provoked debate and resistance, but the most heated controversy involved the end of lay investiture. Traditionally the nobility appointed the clergy in their lands. This privilege assured their support, as no ruler wanted confrontation with powerful ecclesiastics. By ending this practice, Gregory hoped to liberate the church from secular politics. In ending lay investiture, Gregory asserted that the pope was the supreme ruler in Christendom, a position that challenged the authority and power of secular rulers, specifically the Holy Roman Emperor, who saw himself as divinely appointed and with legitimate influence over the church.

The Investiture Controversy, as it is called, sparked a military and ideological confrontation between the papacy and the Holy Roman Emperor Henry IV (1056–1106) in 1065. Henry had come to the throne as a child, and during his long minority, his nobles had grown powerful and independent. Henry relied on lay investiture to curb their authority. Henry wanted to appoint clergy who would be loyal to him, but Gregory refused to allow it. In the military conflict that ensued, Matilda, countess of Tuscany (1046–1115) took Gregory's side. She led her troops to defend both papal superiority and her territory from Henry's incursions. Gregory excommunicated Henry for his refusal to accept papal supremacy, denying him the sacraments and releasing his nobles from their oaths of loyalty to him. In 1077, Henry appeared at the papal palace at Canossa dressed as a barefoot penitent, begging for forgiveness. Their reconciliation was short-lived. As soon as the excommunication was lifted, Henry renewed the conflict.

Gregory's uncompromising stance on the supremacy of the papacy over temporal lords alienated many rulers who would otherwise have supported him in his fight with the Holy Roman Emperor. With Gregory's death, a compromise emerged. Secular leaders had the right to submit a list of acceptable candidates for church offices and the pope chose one and invested him with his ecclesiastical authority.

For the masses of Europeans, Gregory's enforcement of a ban on clerical marriage was truly revolutionary. The church had never been comfortable with married priests, but it had done little to stop the practice. However, Gregory and his supporters argued that women were a source of pollution and a distraction to priests administering the sacraments. Gregory also believed that clerical wives challenged their priest-husband's loyalty to the church and compromised church property, which married priests passed down to their children. By ending clerical marriage, the pope made the clergy more like monks, elevating them above the laity as a separate caste. At the same time, he asserted that marriage was the only legitimate life choice for the laity.

Although enforcement of the new clerical rules on marriage was sporadic and many village priests continued to have concubines, by the twelfth century, it was generally accepted that the ordained clergy were not supposed to marry. The end of clerical marriage had a profound effect on priests' wives, who had been integral to the parish's life and liturgy. They had special prayers, robes, and roles in the liturgy, and they had cared for the sacred space of the church. When priests gave up their wives and children, they must have seriously disrupted village life, and priests genuinely attached to their wives and families suffered personal tragedies. We do not know what happened to these women; however, the church made no provisions for them.

Historian Jo Ann McNamara has argued that the emphasis on clerical celibacy dramatically altered the gender system of medieval Europe. Whereas masculinity had always been asserted through physical strength and heterosexual practices, a celibate clergy had no such options. Thus, reformers emphasized women's sinfulness instead. In this way, women's submission was affirmed and men's superiority was maintained despite the inability to engage in heterosexual relationships.[55]

Female Monastic Culture During the High Middle Ages

Despite the church's unwillingness to involve women in monastic reform, the convent remained central to many women's pursuit of spiritual and intellectual fulfillment. For some women it was a genuinely attractive lifestyle full of the promise of salvation. Although many women's houses voluntarily enclosed themselves in imitation of Cluniac and Cistercian practices, cloistration did not always inhibit the intellectual vitality of medieval convents or the desire to create new forms of women's monasticism. During the twelfth and thirteenth centuries, convents produced numerous dynamic women thinkers and artists and flourished as centers of female culture.

A collection of letters from the convent at Admont in the diocese of Salzburg, in present-day Austria, attests to the level of learning in many convents. Far from being cut off from the world, the nuns' correspondence reveals their independent notions about monastic life and their regular interactions with family members and episcopal officials. These nuns wrote their own sermons to be given when the monk-preachers from the neighboring monastery of Admont were away. The nuns even felt free to interpret the rules for themselves. One letter explained that the nun dictated it in Latin to a nun-scribe in the middle of the night, noting that as long as she was speaking in Latin, she was not violating the rules of silence.[56]

Although they could not perform Mass or administer the sacraments, women used their intellects and creativity to broaden their participation in the liturgy. In some communities, the abbess presented the bread and wine to the altar. Nuns also decorated their churches with elaborately embroidered altar cloths. They regularly performed chants and dramatic reenactments. The link between liturgy and drama produced some of the most famous dramatists of the period. Playwright Hroswitha of Gandersheim (d. ca. 1001) flourished in the convent where she had access to an excellent library. She received much of her education from her abbess, Gerberga (b. 940), and relied on encouragement and advice from her fellow nuns. Her literacy and Latinity is evident in her use of the bawdy works of the Roman writer Terence (195–159 B.C.E.) as one of the models for her many plays. However, while Terence's humor often relied on female frailty, Hroswitha's plays celebrate the triumph of women's virtue over the weaknesses of men.

Nuns also created important works of art. The works of Herrad of Landsberg (ca. 1130–1195), the abbess of the convent of Hohenbourg, Germany, provide some evidence of their skill. She compiled the *Hortus Deliciarum,* or *Garden of Delights*, an extensively illustrated encyclopedia of knowledge intended to train the novices in her convent. The work includes 336 illustrations done by Herrad, including everything from literary and theological themes to portraits of individual nuns. She also composed a series of poems to accompany the work.

Probably the most creative and versatile artist within convent walls was Hildegard von Bingen (1098–1179). The founder and abbess of a Benedictine convent on the banks of the Rhine, she achieved fame as a mystic, theologian, composer, and author of medical texts. She corresponded with the pope and Bernard of Clairvaux over church policy and doctrine. She was apparently the only woman permitted to preach. She composed seventy-seven religious songs mainly in honor of women such as the Virgin Mary for her nuns to sing. She also composed an extraordinary morality play, *Ordo virtutum*, around 1150 for the consecration of her monastery. It broke new musical ground in the way it combined emotion, text, musical instruments, and human voice. Hildegard also experienced visions, and her explanations and discussions of them constitute important theological discussions of the nature of divinity.

Female religious life presented women with many paradoxes. Nowhere are the opportunity and constraints of the High Middle Ages more obvious than in the unique and passionate correspondence of Abelard (1079–1142) and Heloise (ca. 1100– 1164). Heloise was raised by her uncle Fulbert, a canon of the Parisian cathedral of Notre Dame. He recognized Heloise's brilliance and hired one of Paris's most renowned and controversial thinkers, Peter Abelard, from the newly founded University of Paris to be her teacher. Peter and Heloise fell in love, and she became pregnant. Despite her insistence that marriage would interfere with his work, Abelard and Heloise married secretly. Fearing that Abelard was going to repudiate Heloise, Fulbert hired thugs to castrate Abelard. Humiliated, Abelard fled to a monastery and after much pressure, he finally convinced Heloise to become a nun.

The couple had no contact for nearly a decade, but Heloise initiated a correspondence with him after she read his autobiographical *History of My Misfortunes*. Her letters reveal both her continued passion for him and her ambivalence about her monastic career. As she came to accept her role as Abelard's sister-in-Christ, their correspondence turned to monastic and spiritual issues. She issued a particularly harsh criticism of the Benedictine Rule, which she viewed as unable to accommodate women's physical and spiritual needs. Heloise's life as a nun took place in the midst of monastic reforms. Abott Suger (ca. 1181–1151) of the Royal Monastery of St. Denis wanted her convent for his monks. He accused the nuns of mismanagement and immorality and scattered them. Abelard came to Heloise's rescue by giving her some land for a new house, and with great determination, she founded a new convent, named the Paraclete, whose houses rapidly expanded under her attentive supervision and capable administration.

The religious reforms of the High Middle Ages altered the gender norms of medieval Europe by institutionalizing beliefs in women's inherent weakness and sinfulness. The Clunaic reforms devalued nuns' contributions to monastic life because they could not be ordained and the Gregorian reforms that followed further limited women's options by declaring marriage and submission to a husband to be a laywoman's duty. Nevertheless, medieval convents were sites of a flourishing women's culture marked by art, literature and great piety.

CONCLUSION

During the Middle Ages, women's opportunities expanded and contracted with the waves of chaos and political stability of repeated invasions. Perhaps counterintuitively, women realized their greatest cultural and political influence in times of loose social organization and political disruption. The reassertion of control by either kings or the church restricted women's opportunities. Peasants found it difficult to leave the land in search of better opportunities, and aristocratic women found their legal rights constrained. Political stability also allowed the church to consolidate its influence usually at the expense of women religious who had worked on the frontlines of Christianity to convert pagans and settle frontiers. One of the paradoxes of medieval history is that women's greatest influence on society came at moments when as a group they were most threatened by violence, rape, and dispossession. Political stability brought greater physical safety, but often at the expense of their mobility and agency.

NOTES

1. Peter Wells, *The Barbarian Speaks: How the Conquered Peoples Shaped Roman Europe* (Princeton: Princeton University Press, 1999), 158–159.

2. Wells, 169–170.

3. "Salic Law," in *Selected Historical Documents of the Middle Ages*, ed. Ernest F. Henderson (London: George Bell and Sons, 1896).

4. Suzanne Wemple, *Frankish Women: Marriage and the Cloister, 500 to 900* (Philadelphia: University of Pennsylvania Press, 1981), 49–50.

5. Quoted in Wemple, 28.

6. "The Thuringian War," in *Sainted Women of the Dark Ages*, ed. and trans. Jo Ann McNamara and John E. Halborg with E. Gordon Whatley (Durham, NC: Duke University Press, 1992), 69.

7. Jane Tibbetts Schulenburg, "Women's Monastic Communities, 500–1100: Patterns of Expansion and Decline," *Signs* 14:2 (1989): 268–269.

8. Wemple, 161.

9. "Caesarius' Rule for Nuns," in *Women's Lives in Medieval Europe: A Sourcebook*, ed. Emilie Amt (New York: Routledge, 1993), 222.

10. Quoted in Janet Nelson, "Women at the Court of Charlemagne: A Case of Monstrous Regiment?" in *Medieval Queenship*, ed. John Carmi Parsons (New York: St. Martin's Press, 1993), 49.

11. Quoted in Wemple, 145.

12. Rosamond McKitterick, *The Carolingians and the Written Word* (Cambridge: Cambridge University Press, 1989), 226.

13. Steven A. Stofferahn, "Changing Views of Carolingian Women's Literary Culture: The Evidence from Essen," *Early Medieval Europe* 8:1 (1999): 72.

14. Patricia Ranft, *Women in Western Intellectual Culture, 600–1500* (London: Palgrave-Macmillan, 2002), 13.

15. Dhuoda, *Handbook for William: A Carolingian Woman's Counsel for her Son*, trans. Carol Neel (Washington, DC: Catholic University of America Press, 1999), 27.

16. Rosamond McKitterick, "Women and Literacy in the Early Middle Ages," in *Books, Scribes, and Learning in the Frankish Kingdoms, 6th–9th Centuries* (Aldershot, England: Variorum, 1994), esp. 22, 26–27.

17. Carol J. Clover, "Regardless of Sex: Men, Women, and Power in Early Northern Europe," *Speculum* 68:2 (1993): 365.

18. Judith Jesch, *Women in the Viking Age* (Woodbridge, Suffolk: The Boydell Press, 1991), 82–83.

19. Jesch, 183.

20. Jesch, 107.

21. Sally Thompson, *Women Religious: The Founding of English Nunneries After the Norman Conquest* (Oxford: Oxford University Press, 1991), 2.

22. Jesch, 104.

23. *The Anglo-Saxon Chronicles*, trans, G. N. Garmonsway (London: Dent, 1953), 86.

24. Christine Fell, *Women in Anglo-Saxon England* (London: Colonnade Books, 1984), 135.

25. Simon Keynes, "Introduction to the 1998 Reprint," *Encomium Emmae Reginae*, ed. Alistair Campbell (Cambridge: Cambridge University Press, 1998), xxiv.

26. Simon Franklin and Jonathan Shepard, *The Emergence of Rus, 750–1200* (London: Longman, 1996), 296–297.

27. Eve Levin, *Sex and Society Among the Orthodox Slavs, 900–1700* (Ithaca, NY: Cornell University Press, 1989), 102.

28. Levin, 224.

29. Pál Engel, *The Realm of St. Stephen: A History of Medieval Hungary, 895–1526* (London: I. B. Tauris, 2001), 16.

30. Engel, 46.

31. Quoted in Leila Ahmed, *Women and Gender in Islam: Historical Roots of a Modern Debate* (New Haven, CT: Yale University Press, 1992), 85.

32. Quoted in María J. Viguera, "Asluhu Li'L-Māʼali. On the Social Status of Andalusī Women," in *The Legacy of Muslim Spain*, ed. Salma Khadra Jayyusi (Leiden: E. J. Brill, 1992), 710. Qurashī is a tribal or family name, probably a variant of Quraish, an old aristocratic tribe from Mecca that included Muhammad.

33. Quoted in Viguera, 709.

34. Viguera, 718.

35. Quoted in George Duby, *The Three Orders: Feudal Society Imagined* (Chicago: University of Chicago Press, 1980), 287.

36. Shulamith Shahar, *The Fourth Estate: A History of Women in the Middle Ages* (London: Methuen, 1983), 139.

37. Shahar, 139.

38. Shahar, 129.

39. Werner Rösener, *Peasants in the Middle Ages*, trans. Alexander Stützer (Urbana: University of Illinois Press, 1992), 183.

40. Emmanuel Le Roy Ladurie, *Montaillou: The Promised Land of Error* (New York: Vintage Books, 1979), 172–173.

41. Barbara A. Hanawalt, *The Ties That Bound: Peasant Families in Medieval England* (New York: Oxford University Press, 1986), 180.

42. Elaine Clark, "Some Aspect of Social Security in Medieval England," *Journal of Family History* 7 (1982): 308.

43. Sharon E. Gerstel, "Painted Sources for Female Piety in Medieval Byzantium," *Dumbarton Oaks Papers* 52 (1998): 91–92.

44. Fritz Rörig, *The Medieval Town* (Berkeley: University of California Press, 1967), 112–113; Paul M. Hohenberg and Lynn Hollen Lees, *The Making of Urban Europe, 1000–1950* (Cambridge: Harvard University Press, 1985), 10–11.

45. Heath Dillard, *Daughters of the Reconquest* (Cambridge: Cambridge University Press, 1984).

46. Patricia Skinner, *Women in Medieval Italian Society, 500–1200* (London: Longman, 2001), 167–168.

47. Skinner, 169.

48. Skinner, 162.

49. Monica Green, ed., *The Trotula* (Philadelphia: University of Pennsylvania Press, 2001), 9.

50. Bruce L. Venarde, *Women's Monasticism and Medieval Society in France and England, 890–1215* (Ithaca, NY: Cornell University Press, 1997), 48.

51. Jo Ann McNamara, *Sisters in Arms: Catholic Nuns Through Two Millennia* (Cambridge: Harvard University Press, 1998), 218.

52. McNamara, *Sisters in Arms*, 227.

53. Penny Schine Gold, "Male/Female Cooperation: The Example of Fontevrault," in *Medieval Religious Women*, vol. 1, *Distant Echoes*, ed. John A. Nichols and Lillian Thomas Shank (Kalamazoo, MI: Cistercian Publications, 1994), 152.

54. Quoted in Jo Ann McNamara, "Canossa and the Ungendering of the Public Man," in *Render Unto Caesar: The Religious Sphere in World Politics*, ed. Sabrina Petra Ramet and Donald W. Treadgold (Washington, DC: American University Press, 1995), 137.

55. Jo Ann McNamara, "The *Herrenfrage*: the Restructuring of the Gender System, 1050–1150," in *Medieval Masculinities: Regarding Men in the Middle Ages*, ed. Clare Lees (Minneapolis: University of Minnesota Press, 1994), 4–5.

56. Alison I. Beach, "Voices from a Distant Land: Fragments of a Twelfth Century Nun's Letter Collection," *Speculum* 77 (2002): 40–41.

SUGGESTED READINGS

Atkinson, Clarissa W. *The Oldest Vocation: Christian Motherhood in the Middle Ages*. Ithaca, NY: Cornell University Press, 1991. Discussion of the intellectual and social context for medieval attitudes toward motherhood.

Blamires, Alcuin. *The Case for Women in Medieval Culture*. Oxford: Oxford University Press, 1997. Study of the intellectual debate over the nature of women.

Evergates, Theodore, ed. *Aristocratic Women in Medieval France*. Philadelphia: University of Pennsylvania Press, 1999. Collection of essays examining the legal and territorial power of aristocratic women.

Hambly, Gavin, ed. *Women in the Medieval Islamic World: Power, Patronage, and Piety*. New York: St. Martin's Press, 1998. Collection of essays that challenges the stereotypes of Islamic women as passive.

Hanawalt, Barbara. *The Ties That Bound: Peasant Families in Medieval England*. New York: Oxford University Press, 1986. Study of medieval peasant families using coroners' rolls and location of death to discuss peasant gender roles.

Jochans, Jenny. *Women in Old Norse Society*. Ithaca, NY: Cornell University Press, 1995.

Johnson, Penelope D. *Equal in Monastic Profession: Religious Women in Medieval France*. Chicago: University of Chicago Press, 1991. Study of women's monastic life that argues that nuns were not any more corrupt or lax than monks.

Wemple, Suzanne Fonay. *Women in Frankish Society: Society, Marriage, and the Cloister, 500 to 900*. Philadelphia: University of Pennsylvania Press, 1985.

Women and Urban Life: The Late Middle Ages, 1200–1500

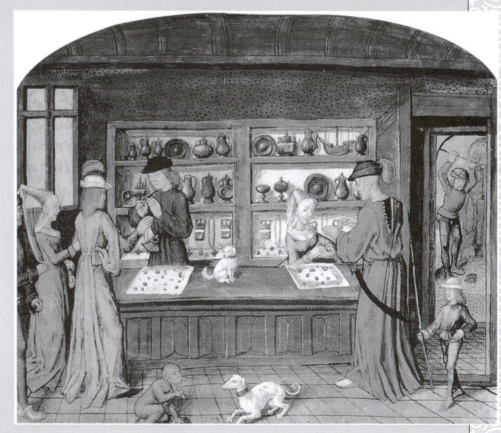

Female Shopkeeper. As cities grew, women became a critical part of urban economies. Women both produced goods and sold them in shops. In some parts of Europe, women even owned their own businesses. (Bibliothèque nationale de France.)

Around 1200, cities dramatically expanded and became a much more important part of medieval society (see Map 6.1). As they grew, cities became centers for economic development, intercultural and intellectual interaction, innovative forms of piety, and artistic activity; however, they were also bastions of masculinity. Only men could participate in city government and university study, and men dominated many sectors of the economy. Nevertheless, urban life offered women new opportunities unavailable in the countryside. Women owned businesses, led armies and religious movements, and inspired others through their holiness. They created magnificent works of art and patronized the great artists of the period. Despite increasing constraints, women made a productive space for themselves in late medieval society.

GENDERING URBAN LIFE

During the late Middle Ages, urban power and authority remained almost exclusively in the hands of men. Women could not participate in government, and their citizenship offered them only basic rights. Universities admitted only men, created a masculine culture, and propagated notions of female inferiority. Male guilds controlled most of the urban economy. However, women still found ways to take advantage of urban commerce. They learned new trades and made livings performing traditional tasks for city governments. Although city authorities tried to control women's work, most of it was so basic to daily life that it eluded regulation.

Masculinizing Civic Identity

Most medieval cities were governed by some type of city council. These councils attempted to guarantee fair justice and well-regulated marketplaces. They also carefully distinguished between citizens—people who would be allowed to take advantage of urban institutions—and noncitizens—those who would not. In return, citizens paid taxes and defended the city from attack. Citizenship was highly desirable for both the opportunities and the status that it brought.

Chapter 6 ❖ Chronology

ca. 1200	Foundation of the University of Paris
1208	Albigensian Crusade
ca. 1209	Francis of Assisi founds the first Mendicant Order
1263	Clare of Assisi founds the Order of the Poor Clares
1290	Expulsion of the Jews from England
1346	Brigitta founds the Order of the Most Holy Savior at Vadstena
1348–1351	The Black Death
1358	The Jacquerie
1381	The English Peasant Revolt
1405	Christine de Pizan writes *Book of the City of Ladies*
1417	End of the Great Schism
1431	Execution of Joan of Arc
1500	Leonardo da Vinci's portrait of Isabella d'Este

The qualifications for citizenship varied from town to town, but generally, one had to be of legitimate birth and a resident of the city for a specific length of time. In many English towns, a citizen also had to own a house within the city walls. Most cities allowed women to become citizens, but only by passive means, either by marrying citizen men or because their parents were citizens. As members of citizen households, they had access to some rights and some protections; however, women could neither vote nor hold office. Moreover, although men might provide their wives and daughters with citizenship, the reverse was not always true. Men who married female citizens did not automatically become citizens.

Because citizenship was linked to familial ties, the large numbers of adult single women and widows who moved into cities looking for work often had a difficult time becoming citizens. For instance, the city of Lille (now in France) defined citizenship as a privilege of property owners, so between 1291 and 1459 it registered no immigrant women as citizens. However, in Bruges (now in Belgium), women made up approximately 10 percent of the new citizens registered between

1331 and 1460. In some years, more than one-quarter of the new citizens were female. The city leaders of Bruges were more interested in a citizen's ability to work, and therefore granted easier access to its privileges.[1]

Whether citizens or not, urban women had some legal rights, many of which were closely tied to marital status. Single adult women could own property and transact business with few constraints. Upon marriage, a woman's legal status was known as *femme couverte*. Literally "covered" by her husband, she was legally dependent on him and had to have his permission to make business contracts. Yet, married women were not completely at the mercy of their spouses. When a husband was unwilling to give his wife access to the financial resources necessary for business, she could petition local officials for permission to act independently. Becoming a *femme sole* allowed a married woman to transact business on her own, and she alone was responsible for any debts incurred as a part of her business. Once widowed, women regained their legal independence.

Although medieval legal theory often conceptualized women as legal minors in need of male

182

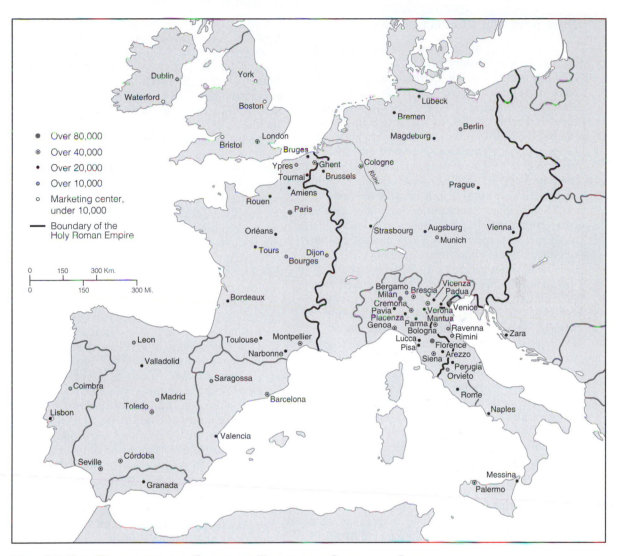

***Map 6.1* THE POPULATION OF EUROPEAN TOWNS AND CITIES, CA. LATE
THIRTEENTH CENTURY.** The expansion of urban centers during the late Middle
Ages offered women a wide range of new opportunities.

guardianship, women had rights to justice and
historians have been surprised by how often
women used medieval legal systems. Typically,
adult, unmarried women could litigate alone.
Under most circumstances, married women were
supposed to have their husbands' consent, but
there were numerous ways to circumvent that
requirement. Women also acted as witnesses in

both civil and criminal suits; however, courts
often preferred the testimony of men, and magistrates often judged the quality of a woman's testimony based on her sexual reputation. The
testimony of female witnesses or the legitimacy
of a woman's case could be discounted if the
court deemed her dishonorable or of question-
able character.

Masculinizing Intellectual Life

In cities such as Salamanca, Naples, Paris, and Oxford, the university played a critical role in defining women's place. During the early Middle Ages, elite men received their educations from monasteries or local cathedral schools. Over time, famous teachers attracted students from beyond the immediate area. As their numbers grew, students and master teachers organized into associations to better regulate their curricula and protect their interests in conflicts with church and city officials. Those associations became the first universities. Medieval universities dominated the cultural landscape. In addition to training in law, medicine, arts, and theology, they created a group of educated men who formulated and circulated new ideas about gender in medieval society.

Medieval universities excluded women from their classrooms, although a few women may have defied gender barriers to study. A small cohort of women may have studied at the University of Bologna, and the fifteenth-century scholar Christine de Pizan (see later in this chapter) noted that Novella d'Andrea (d. 1333) lectured at the university where her father was a renowned professor of law. Her sister Bettina d'Andrea, also a lawyer, taught at the University of Padua. However, these women were truly exceptions to the rule.

Without women, university culture reflected the class interests and masculinity of the student body. The teenage sons of nonaristocratic elites who made up the majority of the students wrote home regularly asking for money for fashionable clothes, new books, and entertainment. University students became known for their drinking, fighting, and carousing with townswomen. The 1355 Saint Scholastica Day riots in Oxford began when two students threw wine in a bartender's face. Several townspeople and university members died in the subsequent riots. In an attempt to control rowdy behavior, university authorities forbade students from having any contact with young women, especially prostitutes. These regulations only accentuated the university's masculine culture, as students had few positive interactions with women, particularly of their same social class.[2]

In addition to training young men, scholars at medieval universities engaged in spirited philosophical and religious discussions about the nature of women, often based on the works of Aristotle. Although Aristotle's texts had been lost to western Europe, they had been preserved in the Muslim world and translated from Greek into Arabic. During the twelfth century, the increased interaction between Christian and Muslim intellectuals in Iberia led to their translation into Latin and their reintroduction into European thought.

Medieval universities were dominated by scholastics, men who wanted to prove that Christianity was rational and who hoped to use reason to prove what they believed on faith. Although initially many scholars expressed concerns about teaching the works of a pagan, in 1255 Aristotle's texts became required reading at the University of Paris. His discussions of women's biological inferiority provided undeniable evidence for Christian scholars that men were created in the image of God and were thus closer to God than women.

Thomas Aquinas (1224–1274), a theologian and scholar at the University of Paris, was the most important scholastic thinker of the late Middle Ages. He based many of his ideas about gender on Aristotelian notions of sexual difference; however, as a Christian theologian, he complicated the Greek philosopher's ideas in order to allow for women's salvation. Aquinas believed that woman reflected the image of God less perfectly than man, that women were the passive, inferior partners in reproduction, and that they had only weak capabilities in both virtues and reasoning power. Women were only equal to men in theological virtues (faith, hope, and charity) and in the ability to receive God's grace. Aquinas's ideas became central to Christian thought, and, as we will see, his notions of female inferiority would dominate European gender norms for centuries to come.

Young men both defined and were defined by these centers of intellectual and social life. They neither experienced women as intellectual equals nor believed that women were capable of scholarly pursuits. As students returned home to become leaders in their families and communities, they carried those gender expectations far beyond the city walls.

The Guilds

Cities were also commercial centers and men controlled much of the economic activity. To regulate each craft and trade, the citizens of many European towns banded together into trade-based associations known as *guilds*. The guilds ensured quality and protected profits. They watched out for members' mutual interests, regulated markets, distributed charity, and organized social activities. Guilds reflected the gender expectations of medieval society. Many excluded women altogether, and even guilds that admitted women rarely gave them equal status with men or allowed them to influence guild policies.

A medieval worker learned a trade by studying as an apprentice with a guild-approved master. Because medieval society expected urban girls to marry young, girls began their apprenticeships around age twelve, while boys often had to be fourteen or older. As the girls usually lived in the master's household, families were careful to apprentice girls to women or to couples whom they found through family connections and trusted to protect their chastity. The length of apprenticeships varied. London city law required that apprenticeships last a minimum of seven years, but in other parts of Europe, they tended to be shorter—only four to five years. By the time most young women had completed their apprenticeships, they were ready to marry. In some cases, a woman could buy herself out of her apprentice contract if she decided to marry before the completion of its terms. However, even when a woman married before the end of her apprenticeship, her education was not wasted. She could use the knowledge and skills she had acquired to contribute to the family income.[3]

Some trades, in particular aspects of cloth production, became extensively or even exclusively associated with women. At times, women even banded together in informal groups to protect their economic interests. In 1386, female silk workers in London successfully petitioned the crown for protection against competition from male Italian silk workers.[4] However, women workers rarely formed guilds. Women's guilds existed only in Rouen, Cologne, and Paris. Medieval Rouen had five female-dominated guilds, each representing different aspects of the cloth industry. In thirteenth-century Paris, there were seven exclusively female or female-dominated guilds, all of which specialized in detailed handiwork such as weaving silk ribbons or producing purses. In these guilds, women supervised apprenticeship contracts, inspected the quality of members' work, and enforced guild ordinances. However, men held the leadership positions. For example, in the purse makers guild of Paris, male officials supervised the all-female membership, even though most of the officials had never made a purse in their lives.

Women also made livings at trades controlled by male guilds. By working alongside their husbands and fathers day after day, they learned the craft or business and shared in many of the responsibilities. With time, many women became skilled enough to take over the family trade after their husbands' deaths, and guilds generally allowed widows to continue working in the trade unless they remarried outside the guild. Women's familiarity with guild structures and policies often helped them succeed. In Montpellier (France), wealthier widows used the capital and connections that they had acquired during their marriages to become merchants in the silk trade. However, women never traded in the most profitable goods like spices nor did they participate in the large trade fairs of Champagne and northern Germany, where male merchants traded products from around the world. The fairs were not only dominated by male guilds and merchants, but also would have required extensive travel that was considered inappropriate for widows.[5]

In addition to regulating the craft, guilds served other functions in urban society. Members cared for each other during personal crises. When the wife or child of a guild member fell ill or suffered an injury, the guild provided comfort, food, and help with expenses. Members often socialized together in annual celebrations for the guild's patron saint. At a guild member's death, the surviving members mourned with the family at the wake and accompanied the funeral procession to the cemetery.

Regulating Women's Work

As city governments extended their influence over daily activities, they attempted to regulate women's work outside of guilds. They began to pay women to do traditional women's work on behalf of the city, and cities took on a variety of social services that formerly had been the responsibility of lords or depended on private initiative. However, the fact that cities needed women's skills did not lend these jobs prestige or lead to high pay. For instance, during the fifteenth century, the city of Montpellier in southern France took responsibility for caring for abandoned children, paying women to nurse children in their homes. By the 1490s, the city was paying an average of twenty-six women each year to care for municipal foundlings. The pay was very poor, about half that of a female grape harvester.[6] Moreover, in these official positions, women often had to submit to a variety of examinations and regulations. The city of Nuremberg (Germany) created an official list of midwives and a governing council of elite women charged with supervising them. City midwives had to be examined and swear oaths just like other city officers. Their salaries were also quite low, although the city often helped them collect debts and gave them free grain or firewood. City midwives gave up some freedom when they took those positions. For instance, they could not leave town without permission and they could not choose their patients.[7]

City authorities invested considerable time and effort in the regulation of prostitution. Medieval society was highly ambivalent about prostitution. Although sex outside of marriage was considered sinful, medieval society believed that without prostitution, men's natural uncontrolled lust would lead to rape, adultery, homosexuality, and sodomy. To prevent these vices, cities across Europe established licensed and even municipally owned brothels. City officials regulated nearly all aspects of prostitutes' lives, often requiring them to wear some distinguishing clothing, like striped hoods or prohibiting them from wearing certain types of ornamentation such as fur, which was reserved for respectable women. Laws barred prostitutes from living in or practicing their trade in certain parts of the city. In some places, prostitutes could not attend church, while in other cities officials closed municipal brothels on holy days and forced the prostitutes to listen to sermons. Cities often set the fees and working hours, as well as the circumstances under which a woman could leave the profession. Some towns even restricted who could visit a brothel. According to municipal ordinances, brothels were supposed to turn away men who were forbidden to engage in sexual intercourse with prostitutes, including married men, clerics, and Jews.[8]

Women provided most premodern medical care and by the late Middle Ages, government and university authorities became more interested in regulating who practiced medicine. There were many types of healers, from herbalists to surgeons and university-trained physicians. Only a few, determined women were able to study at the medical schools at the universities in Salerno, Naples, Rome, and Pavia. More frequently, women apprenticed themselves to surgeons in order to learn the trade, and authorities often recognized those skills. In the Kingdom of Naples, records from the thirteenth century list twenty-four female surgeons, half of whom were licensed to practice specifically on women.[9]

Generally, practitioners received no official training. For a small fee, they merely passed on the knowledge that they had acquired from their parents or community elders. These unlicensed healers faced frequent harassment by local authorities. As early as 1271, the medical faculty at the University of Paris insisted that all medical practitioners be examined and licensed, despite the fact that the university excluded women from medical studies. Unable to obtain the necessary licensure, a number of women, including thirty-year-old Jacqueline Felicie, were arrested for illegally practicing their trade. At her 1322 trial, witnesses testified that she examined patients' urine, prescribed tonics, and made follow-up visits. Authorities punished her with a fine and excommunication.[10] However, overall such interference from authorities had little effect. Patients—from the slightly sick to the very ill—continued to seek out female healers for relief from what ailed them.

Despite these attempts to control women's work, most women found ways to earn livings outside of government regulation. For instance, much of the activity in the marketplace evaded the watchful eyes of city officials. Women were mostly petty retailers, hawking nuts, candles, and used clothing. Sometimes, they bought and resold fruits and other foodstuffs that had gone unsold by male grocers. Women also used the skills that they learned at home to earn some extra income. They made food items for sale to urban workers, spun thread, and washed other people's clothes. Brewing, ale selling, and candlemaking were also predominantly female trades. Lower-class women did whatever they could to survive, while wealthy women invested in local businesses, made loans, and bought, sold, and leased property in local real estate markets.

As medieval cities expanded, authorities limited women's participation in civic life. Citizen women could not participate in politics, and brilliant women could not attend university. Even the most talented clothworkers made less than their male counterparts. However, urban women were not completely marginalized. Using their property rights and their business acumen, women prospered in bustling urban economies.

URBAN DIVERSITY

City streets and markets brought together women from many walks of life. Rural women moved to the city hoping to make some money and find husbands. In Mediterranean Europe, the slave trade brought women from Africa, the Middle East, and the Balkans to cities to work as domestic servants. Many cities across Europe had small Jewish communities that lived according to their own laws and traditions, as did Muslim communities in southern Spain. These cross-cultural interactions were often fraught with tension and the late Middle Ages witnessed a surge of intolerance against non-Christians.

Rural Women

The largest group of immigrants were women who moved from rural areas to nearby cities. Some moved as their husbands and fathers relocated to take advantage of new economic opportunities. For instance, in an attempt to develop its textile industry, in 1230 the city of Bologna offered loans, tax exemptions, and citizenship to artisans who would move there. More than 150 artisans and their families migrated to the city in the next year.[11] As we saw in the previous chapter, frontier cities in Spain offered similar financial incentives to convince families to settle in newly reconquered towns.

Cities were magnets for young rural women seeking employment and husbands. They offered freedom from parental supervision and the possibility of economic independence, as well as a world of new tastes, sights, and smells. Most women sought work as domestic servants. They negotiated their own contracts with employers, usually wages, food, and lodging in return for their labor. Few female servants remained in a household for long; rather, they moved from position to position hoping to improve their working conditions. Domestic service was exhausting. Servants were at their employers' beck and call twenty-four hours a day. When the servant had a good relationship with her employer, she became a part of the family; however, a position with the wrong family could be dangerous. For instance, after a servant woman named Joan responded inappropriately to her master, court records report that "the said John Lorymer took up a club and struck her on the head and elsewhere as is proper."[12] Many servants were forced into unwanted sexual relationships with masters or their sons. Given the potential for abuse, it is not surprising that most women left domestic service as soon as they could by marrying other servants or men they met in the marketplace or at church. These women tended to marry later than their peers who worked in other occupations.

Life was difficult for single women who worked outside domestic service. With few skills and far from their families, they struggled, barely making livings as laundresses and in the cloth trades. Sometimes they practiced prostitution to help make ends meet. Because their livings were so unpredictable, they relied heavily on local hospitals and other charitable institutions. Single women also tended to cluster together in certain neighborhoods, sharing lodging, relying on one another for social networks, and helping one another during illnesses and other crises.[13] Despite the challenges of living on their own, they rarely returned to the countryside.

Slaves

Not all urban immigrants came willingly. Slaves made up a small but ethnically diverse segment of many Mediterranean cities. The majority of female slaves worked as domestics, and many were as young as nine or ten. Around the Adriatic Sea, slave raids captured many girls, while families sold others into slavery to pay off family debts.

Nearly 90 percent of the slaves in thirteenth-century Ragusa (modern Dubrovnik) were captured women from rural areas. In addition to domestic work, some did heavy labor, including lifting cloth bales and processing wax.[14] On the Italian peninsula, Venetians and other traders imported Russian, Bulgarian, Armenian, and Muslim women from around the Mediterranean as slaves. The trade in both male and female slaves was particularly active on the border between the Christian and Muslim kingdoms—Christians bought Muslim girls to work in their households, while across the border, Muslims purchased Christian girls. Like their Greek and Roman predecessors, medieval Christians enslaved non-Christians and people whom they had conquered, not necessarily those whose skin color was different.

During the fifteenth century, the numbers of African slaves in Europe increased as Portuguese explorers and traders became deeply involved in the slave trade. Indeed, the trade in West Africans flourished on the docks of Lisbon. In this booming metropolis, female slaves worked as washerwomen and garbage collectors, as well as in domestic service.[15]

Seville was home to what was probably Europe's largest slave population, the majority of whom were Africans. Slavery was so common that nearly every family who could afford to owned a slave. By the end of the fourteenth century, the community of freed slaves and slaves who lived apart from their masters had grown large enough that the church established a hospital and a confraternity in the largely black parish of San Bernardo. On occasion, Seville's black population even intermarried with its poor white population, creating a small, but growing mixed-race community.[16] In addition to being relatively well integrated into Spanish society, slave women had many legal rights. For instance, in the Kingdom of Valencia, slave women could attempt to gain their freedom by filing paternity suits against their masters. In twelve cases brought before authorities between 1450 and 1500, only two were unsuccessful. Although enslaved, the plaintiffs, including some Russian and African women, knew how to use the legal system to their own advantage.[17]

Jews and Muslims in Christian Europe

Especially during the late twelfth and early thirteenth centuries, many European towns were also home to Jewish communities. Overall, the European Jewish population was small, never more than 1 percent of the population, except in Spain, and no medieval city ever had a Jewish population larger than fifteen hundred members.[18] Most Jewish communities had negotiated the right to follow their own religious laws and customs under the protection of the monarch or local ruler. Generally, they lived in separate communities, sometimes by choice but sometimes by force.

Jewish women lived under different constraints than their Christian counterparts. For instance, nearly all Jewish women married. Jewish culture emphasized a woman's role as wife and mother and there were few opportunities for single women. According to Jewish custom, parents arranged marriages between young children, around age nine, and the couple married when the girl reached puberty. Early marriages not only helped avoid the possibility of premarital sex, but they also allowed parents to contract marriages when it was financially opportune. When the wedding eventually took place, parents often provided large dowries for their daughters. Families may have hoped that these contributions to the new couple would help prevent domestic abuse and serve as an incentive for husbands to remain in difficult marriages. Jewish law increasingly protected the interests of married women. For instance, Judaism allowed divorce under a number of circumstances, but the husband had to return the dowry. Moreover, over the course of the Middle Ages, rabbis in northern Europe outlawed polygyny for Jews in Christian countries, although it continued to some degree in Muslim Spain. They also determined that no woman could be divorced against her will. These legal changes further solidified a woman's place in the marriage.[19]

Jewish women enjoyed some influence in daily affairs that their Christian counterparts did not. Jewish life was highly regulated by religious law, and the observance of religious rituals in the home fell largely to women. Mothers taught their daughters how to maintain Jewish dietary laws and Sabbath rituals, and women were expected to ensure that the family fulfilled all religious obligations. Jewish women also had significant control over their own bodies. Although married couples had to avoid intercourse around menstruation, rabbinic authorities viewed pleasurable sexual activity as critical to a healthy marriage and they allowed for the use of the cervical cap during intercourse in order to prevent pregnancy.

Like Christian widows, Jewish women experienced much more independence after the deaths of their husbands. Jewish widows could be heads of households and guardians of their children. Although a Jewish widow could not inherit from her late husband, at his death she received the dowry that had been provided for her in the marriage contract.[20] That money and/or property was hers to do with as she pleased. She could be active in business or use her wealth to advance the family through the negotiation of advantageous marriages for her children.

Outside the home, Jewish women's lives were constrained by Judaic law and custom. Women did not hold any religious or secular leadership positions, nor could they testify in legal cases. However, some evidence suggests that within the synagogue, some women may have carved out new roles during religious services. As men and women worshipped separately, some women from elite rabbinic families may have led prayers for the other women.[21]

Jewish women regularly interacted with Christians in the lively markets of medieval cities. Jews typically acted as moneylenders so that Christians could avoid the sin of usury (charging interest on a loan). In fact, to prevent Jewish merchants from competing with Christians, authorities forbade Jews from engaging in most other occupations. As a result, Jewish women often became prominent in financial transactions between the Jewish and Christian communities. Licoricia of Winchester (England) was a successful Jewish businesswoman whose transactions with the king of England included large donations for the construction of a chapel and shrine dedicated to the king's favorite saint, Edward the Confessor, at Westminster Abbey.[22] In Spain, a Jewish merchant woman named Doña Encave supplied the nobility with embroidered purses, silk, silver, and jewels.[23] Beyond commercial activities, a few Jewish women obtained royal permission to practice medicine in the Kingdom of Aragon, and

Jewish midwives helped Christian women through the pains of childbirth. Jewish wet nurses even suckled Christian infants from time to time.

In places like Spain, Italy, and southern France, where Jews and Christians walked the same streets and attended public festivities together, some Jewish women became involved with Christian men. These interfaith relationships must have been quite difficult. Those who avoided violent reactions from family and neighbors would have had a hard time earning a living or even purchasing basic goods, as neither community tolerated their presence. Interfaith couples required royal permission to live together. In a petition to King Jaume I (1213–1276), a thirteenth-century Jewish woman from Catalonia described how she and her Christian lover were "burning in their love for each other." Their previously granted permission to cohabit was about to expire and she felt like "a thief whom the lord has ordered to be hanged." Only the king could remedy her situation.[24]

To prevent socializing between members of the two communities, Christian authorities often mandated that Jews wear distinctive marks on their clothing, such as a yellow or red badge. Historian David Nirenberg has described the clothing regulations as one way to create a visible sexual boundary that neither group could transgress. Nevertheless, interfaith relationships continued and women who had sex with men from outside their communities faced harsh penalties. For instance, the Jewish authorities of Zaragoza asked the king to have the face of Oro de Par disfigured and that she be sent into exile after she was accused of having intercourse with both Muslim and Christian men. In other cases, the community sought royal permission to punish the offending men using their own systems of justice.[25]

Christian elites' reliance on Jews as moneylenders and general anxiety about the presence of non-Christians led to an increase in anti-Semitic activity in the late Middle Ages. In 1215, the Catholic Church forbade Jews to hold any public office, prohibited them from going outdoors during the last days of Holy Week, and ordered them to wear distinguishing clothing. Many Christian monarchs refused to tolerate any Jewish presence in their dominions. The English king expelled all Jews from his lands in 1290, as did the king of France in 1306. Many of these Jews moved to Poland, where in 1264 King Boleslav V (r. 1243–1279) had promised protection for Jews who would bring trade and commerce to his kingdom.

In addition to their Jewish populations, many late medieval Spanish cities also included Muslim communities. We have limited evidence about Muslim women living under Christian rule. They remained tightly under the control of their families and tended to marry their paternal cousins. These endogamous marriages not only gave the bride's relatives control over the bridegroom but also helped keep the reproductive power of the daughter and her inheritance within the lineage. Life was often hard for women who married into other families. Any children a woman bore belonged to her husband's family, so when her husband died, a widow lost custody of her children. A Muslim woman's status relied almost exclusively on her ability to maintain her chastity. Any woman who lost her chastity, whether through consensual sex or by rape, brought shame to the entire family. The dishonor that female promiscuity brought was so great that Muslim authorities often sentenced adulterous women to be executed; however, their Christian overlords generally commuted the death sentence to slavery. Although they escaped death, dishonored women became pariahs in their communities.[26]

When it came to punishing interfaith relationships, relationships that reaffirmed Christian dominance, like those between Christian men and Muslim women, received lesser penalties than those that undermined the hierarchy, like those between Muslim men and Christian women. Thus, in late medieval Valencia, Christian men caught with Muslim women faced the humiliation of being whipped naked through the streets, but a Muslim man convicted of intercourse with a Christian woman was subject to execution. Christian men discovered with Jewish women were supposed to be burnt at the stake. Because relationships between Christians and Jews upset the already tense relationship between the two communities, they received the harshest punishments.[27]

On city streets, newly arrived rural women mingled with city elites and slaves from distant places. Although Jewish and Muslim women spent most of their time in their own communities, their interactions with Christians enriched and complicated medieval society. However, the diversity that marked medieval cities did not translate into social tolerance. Interfaith relationships based on sex and money caused serious tensions that often resulted in violence.

THE BLACK DEATH

Beginning in 1348, epidemic disease disrupted the lively commercial and intellectual activity of Europe's medieval cities. The infection probably entered western Europe through Sicily and spread quickly to the mainland (see Map 6.2). Historically scholars have believed that the bubonic and other types of plague caused the epidemic; however, recently some scholars have begun to question that diagnosis. Whatever the cause, its effects were devastating. Between 1348 and 1351, the Black Death killed twenty-five million in western Europe alone—approximately one of every three people. In some places, the death toll was even higher, closer to 50 percent. Although fewer died in subsequent outbreaks, their unpredictability continued to terrify survivors. In their search for an explanation for the disaster, many contemporary thinkers blamed women. However, those gender tensions gave way to religious and class tensions as the epidemic subsided.

Caring for the Sick

Although men and women died at more or less the same rates, as the plague struck, women experienced the epidemic differently through their roles as family caregivers. With no understanding of germs, bacteria, or contagion, medieval medicine could do little for those who contracted the disease. The symptoms were horrifying—black sores filled with pus, raging fevers, and bloody coughs—and spread from one family member to another. Of course, families called upon women to wash their sores, calm their fears, and pray for their recoveries. Wives, daughters, and mothers acted as caregivers in addition to their daily tasks: feeding the family, doing the laundry, and caring for livestock. Many wives took over their husbands' businesses when they fell ill. As some families fled to the

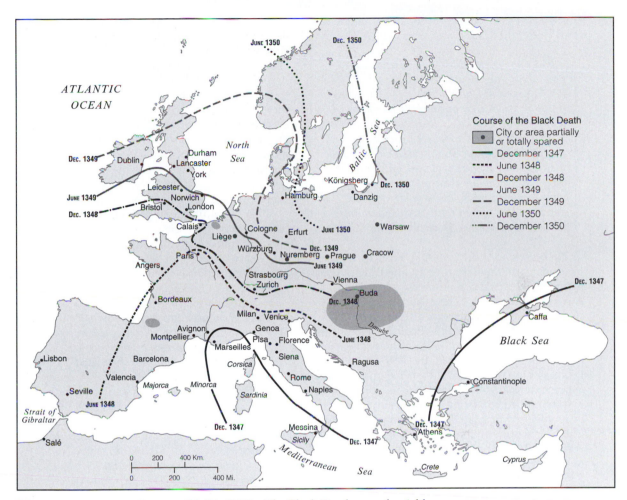

Map 6.2 THE BLACK DEATH, 1347–1350. The Black Death spread quickly across Europe, transforming European society with its high mortality rates.

countryside and others sought refuge in the city, mothers and sisters packed up belongings on short notice and set up new households in strange places. In fact, women's role as caregivers was so important to maintaining some normalcy in that time of chaos that many chroniclers saw women's failure to care for their loved ones as a sure sign of social decay.

Women joined their communities in religious processions that invoked God's mercy on the stricken population. In 1348, barefoot and wearing hairshirts, they marched through the streets of

Avignon, hoping that such dramatic displays of contrition would mitigate God's anger.[28] Thousands of similar processions took place all over Europe. Others went on pilgrimages to holy sites, appealing to saintly intercessors for assistance in ending the epidemic. An Irish chronicler noted that "everybody in fact, women as well as men, gathered in droves from all over Ireland to make the pilgrimage to Tech-Moling."[29]

Because of the staggering death toll, women could not fulfill their traditional roles in death rituals. According to Giovanni Boccaccio's *Decameron*

(1348–1351), a collection of tales composed shortly after the Black Death:

> *it had once been customary, as it is again nowadays, for the women relatives and neighbors of a dead man to assemble in his house in order to mourn in the company of the women who had been closest to him . . . but as the ferocity of the plague began to mount, this practice all but disappeared entirely and was replaced by different customs. For not only did people die without having many women about them, but a great number departed this life without anyone at all to witness their going. (Decameron, Introduction)*

No one escaped the suffering. From the poorest peasant to the highest royalty, the disease decimated families and communities. According to an Austrian chronicler, "The misery increased daily to a pitch never before recorded in the history of the world." A letter from the English king Edward III (r. 1327–1377) describes the sadness that many families must have endured. In 1348, his daughter Princess Joan died from the plague and the king expressed his anguish to the parents of her fiancé, "No fellow human being could be surprised if we were inwardly desolated by the sting of this bitter grief, for we are human too."[30] Nor was his misery over. Two more of his daughters, Mary and Margaret, would succumb in the outbreak of 1361–62.

Blaming Women

Medieval people believed that the Black Death was God's punishment for sinful behavior. After more than half the population of Scandinavia died, King Magnus II of Sweden (r. 1319–1363) declared, "God for the sins of men has struck the world with this great punishment of sudden death. By it, most of our countrymen are dead."[31] Contemporary observers often cited women's dress as a reason for God's displeasure. One English chronicler who condemned fancy hosiery, pointed toe shoes, and other "grotesque" fashions alerted his audience to expect the Lord's vengeance for such ostentatious displays. Another implied that the elaborate dress and sexual activity of women at tournaments had brought God's wrath upon the European population.[32]

In an attempt to prevent new outbreaks of disease, municipal officials passed sumptuary laws that regulated the type of clothing that each social class might wear. Although many of these laws predate the Black Death, they took on new meaning during the epidemic. One 1363 English law directly attributed "great destruction and impoverishment of the whole land" to "the outrageous and excessive apparel of many people."[33] Still, most sumptuary laws were aimed at a more insidious danger; during the social chaos of the epidemic, members of the lower classes were passing themselves off as members of the upper class.

Observers often complained that during and immediately after the epidemic, women experienced unprecedented and dangerous freedoms that led to other sinful behaviors. Some were horrified that previously modest women showed their bodies to men. Boccaccio noted that:

> *there grew up a practice almost never previously heard of, whereby when a woman fell ill, no matter how gracious or beautiful or gently bred she might be, she raised no objection to being attended by a male servant. . . . Nor did she have any scruples about showing him every part of her body as freely as she would have displayed it to a woman, provided that the nature of her infirmity required her to do so; and this explains why those women who recovered were possibly less chaste in the period that followed. (Decameron, Introduction)*

According to many texts, daughters pursued young men without parental supervision and promiscuous wives caroused while their husbands lay ill at home. The *Decameron* includes a number of stories in which women married despite the disapproval of male kin and in which women freely engaged in nonmarital sex. Although the *Decameron's* stories were fictional, contemporary chronicles echoed such concerns about female sexuality. A Scottish account of an outbreak of plague in 1361 noted that, "Widows, forgetting the love they had borne towards their first husbands, rushed into the arms of foreigners or, in many cases, of kinsmen, and shamelessly give birth to bastards conceived in adultery."[34] One English chronicler accused women of undermining the class structure by "coupl[ing] with their inferiors—

turning away from the more eminent and lowering themselves to baser men."[35] If sexual infidelity was the cause of the plague, many believed that the epidemic would only abate with the restoration of morality. Authorities in the Belgian city of Tournai mandated that men marry their concubines or end those relationships. To ensure compliance, city officials would inspect homes to remove and banish the women if necessary.[36]

The Aftermath

Historians have uncovered contradictory evidence about the impact of the plague on women who survived. In Sussex, England, postplague prosperity encouraged young people to marry younger than they had before the Black Death, with the groom in his early twenties and the bride in her late teens. Similarly, in the city of Prato (Italy), girls married quite young, around sixteen years old, in the decades after the Black Death.[37] One benefit of these early marriages was that couples had more children, slowly replacing the millions who had died in the epidemics.[38] In fact, a French chronicler commented, "Everywhere women conceived more readily than usual. None proved barren, on the contrary, there were pregnant women wherever you looked."[39] However, in other parts of Europe many young women may have delayed marriage, as they had more economic opportunities and faced a shortage of possible marriage partners.[40]

Women who survived their husbands faced tremendous social and economic insecurity. At times, the state intervened to ease the transition. In Iberia, the Castilian parliament officially reduced the traditional mourning period of one year after the death of a husband to six months, so that widows could remarry sooner. Indeed, widows seem to have remarried more often in postplague years. In London, although only 36 percent of widows remarried during the first half of the fourteenth century, 73 percent remarried between 1389 and 1458.[41]

Some of the most striking short-term consequences of the Black Death were economic. In some places, urban labor shortages encouraged the large-scale migration of women from the countryside. In York (England), the labor crisis was so severe that in 1381 city officials allowed women to work in traditionally male trades such as smithing and carpentry.[42] For the most part, however, the types of work available to women did not change, and, in fact, there is some indication that the number of occupations open to women actually declined as men sought to protect their own status in certain trades.

The shortage of workers led to increases in both men's and women's wages. In Florence, the wages of female servants more than doubled and overtook those of male servants.[43] However, most women did not experience such dramatic changes in their standard of living. Although wages rose in England, the best-paid female harvesters still received about the same wage as the worst-paid male harvesters. Thus, although many women had neither fathers nor husbands to help support them and often had children and other family members to support, their wages bought only two loaves of bread while a man's wage purchased three.[44] Moreover, women remained confined to unskilled, low-paying jobs alongside boys and old and/or disabled men, while men took the better-paying jobs left open after the epidemic.

In rural areas, male laborers and craftsmen often used their higher wages to purchase land, a move that significantly altered many women's daily lives. While men continued their trades (at the higher postplague wages), they relied almost entirely on their wives to farm the larger plots.[45] As a result, these women spent a greater portion of their lives in unpaid work on their own land than did women of the same class before the Black Death.

Women and Postplague Conflict

The Black Death increased religious and class tensions and led to a number of violent social conflicts. For many, the cause of God's anger was clear: the Jewish community. Thus, the Black Death provoked a wave of anti-Semitic pogroms, or riots, across Europe. Christians regularly accused Jews of having spread the plague by poisoning the city wells. Christian mobs attacked Jewish quarters in Avignon (1348), Zurich (1348), and Frankfurt (1349). In 1349, Emperor Charles IV pardoned the inhabitants of the town of Nuremberg in advance for any damage caused to the Jews under his protection, at which point mobs burned 562 Jewish men and women.

In Spain, the plague exacerbated preexisting religious tensions. The belief that the mere presence of Jews in a Christian kingdom polluted the rest of the community provoked irate mobs to attack the Jewish quarter of Barcelona in May 1348, ravaging property and killing twenty Jews. Even greater anti-Semitic violence would engulf the Spanish kingdoms in 1391, as Christians killed thousands of Jews and forced thousands of others to convert.

Peasants and workers were often frustrated when elites hindered their ability to take advantage of better wages. In May 1358, a revolt began in France when a member of the local bourgeoisie organized a general strike and seized control of the government of Paris after the English captured the French king John II (r. 1350–1364) and some of his nobles. Soon a peasant rebellion arose in the surrounding countryside, fed by resentment over the taxes collected to pay the ransom for the king. Rebels plundered and burned aristocratic homes, and, although he may have exaggerated the extent of the brutality, chronicler Jean Froissart (ca. 1337–1410?) vividly described the violence against noblewomen. According to Froissart, rebels broke into one castle, bound the knight to a post, and "violated his wife and daughter before his eyes. Then they killed the wife, who was pregnant, and the daughter and all the other children, and finally put the knight to death with great cruelty and burned and razed the castle" (Froissart, *Chronicles,* Book 1). The nobility quickly crushed the uprising, known as the *Jacquerie.*

In 1381, peasants and townspeople in England revolted after the English Parliament levied new taxes three times in four years and attempted to keep wages artificially low. A number of women were accused of leading the uprising. According to one account, Julia Pouchere from Essex, "came to meet with men from Canterbury and the country of Essex where they had risen in rebellion . . . [and] persuaded them . . . with the result that the above-mentioned maintainers and evil-doers tore down the above-mentioned jail and destroyed it. . . . And Julia was a party to this and encouraged it." Another woman, Johanna Ferrour, was described as "the chief perpetrator and leader of a great society of rebellious evildoers from Kent."[46]

Of course, many other women were victims of the violence that spread through the countryside.

Scholars have not extensively researched the role of women in these violent outbreaks, but it seems clear that each disturbance exacerbated the difficulties of eking out a living in the Middle Ages and put extra burdens on women. Strikes left families without regular incomes, and riots disrupted their access to food and markets, making it difficult to feed their families. Bands of pillaging rebels and the armies of frightened aristocrats wreaked havoc on family fields, destroyed businesses, and made off with livestock.

The Black Death struck men and women with equal vengeance, yet women experienced the epidemic differently. Wives, daughters, and mothers had to care for those whom premodern medicine could not cure. Despite women's hard work, medieval thinkers often blamed the epidemic on women's indiscretions. In the wake of the epidemic, survivors struggled to rebuild their lives, taking whatever work was available and hoping that they could make a new start. Most painful of all, men and women, many of whom had survived the epidemic, then suffered through the violent deaths of their loved ones during uprisings that followed.

LATE MEDIEVAL RELIGION

During the late Middle Ages, many women were attracted by renewed calls for a more intense spiritual experience. However, the church was not always comfortable with the freedom that such a life entailed. Clergy often rejected women's attempts to live in apostolic poverty and minister to the needy. In response, some special women expressed themselves through mysticism and other spiritual outlets outside of male control. However, for most people, the parish community provided them with a rich array of religious activities that connected them to one another, to the church, and to God.

Gendering Mendicant Monasticism

Many Catholics hoped to find spiritual fulfillment through a life of simplicity and poverty just as

Jesus and his followers had. The concept, known as *Imitatio Christi*, the imitation of Christ, dramatically changed medieval Christianity. Indeed, Francis of Assisi (1182–1226) transformed monasticism through his assertion that only by imitating Christ's poverty could the church return to its true, pure origins. By the end of the thirteenth century, twenty-eight thousand members of his new order, the Franciscans, or Friars Minor, abandoned traditional monastic isolation to teach and preach in European cities. Based on similar principles, Dominic de Gúzman (1170–1221) formed his order of Preaching Friars, the Dominicans, in 1216. The Franciscans and Dominicans became known as the begging or Mendicant orders, as they refused to own any property and supported themselves only through begging and preaching.

Many medieval women were attracted to the poverty of the Mendicants and their emphasis on charity. In the early days, while Francis's male followers preached to urban audiences, his female followers kept hospices near the town and supported themselves through manual labor. Their work soon attracted the attention of Clare (1194–1253). As the story goes, while still dressed in her bridal outfit, seventeen-year-old Clare renounced her family and fled her marriage to join Francis at his retreat at Saint Damiens near Assisi (Italy).

From the outset, these two passionate individuals found their spiritual goals at odds. Clare fought for a rule for female religious that would allow them to live according to Francis's imitation of Christ among laypeople. However, Francis's vision of the Franciscan Order did not include female followers living outside of male control, and despite Clare's protests, he demanded that the women accept the Benedictine Rule (see Chapter 5) and remain in a convent. Far from the life of activity and poverty that Clare sought, the rule that Francis composed for his female followers emphasized claustration and silence, and the male rule ordered the Friars to avoid them. Clare eventually obtained permission from the pope to live in apostolic poverty, but both he and Francis refused to allow her to found a female order.

After Francis's death in 1226, Clare renewed her struggle to live in abject poverty and serve the needy. However, although the pope allowed the women living at Saint Damiens to live in poverty,

he refused to allow four other women's houses in France and twenty-three houses in Italy to do so. He even forced female followers in Perugia to accept donations of books and estates against their will and forbade them to give them away. The church insisted that the imitation of Christ was for men only.

In 1253, Clare defied the papacy by composing her own rule. It set up a grille to separate nuns from visitors and restricted travel except for good and necessary purposes, but allowed for work outside the convent. Clare insisted on poverty, although those who worked outside the convent could wear shoes and did not have to strictly fast. However, the sisters continued to be bound by vows of silence, able to preach only by example.

As Clare lay dying, Pope Innocent IV (r. 1243–1254) confirmed her rule for Saint Damiens and a few other houses, but he refused to allow the women to beg. Nevertheless, letters from the pope to bishops across Europe indicate that the female followers of Francis and Clare continued to leave the convent to beg in contravention of the papal decree. Finally in 1263, Urban IV (r. 1261–1264) recognized the Clarisses, or the Poor Clares, as a separate order but did not impose Clare's rule.

The Poor Clares attracted followers from England to Poland and Bohemia. Agnes, the queen of Bohemia (1205–1282), fought the pope on Clare's behalf and eventually gained the privilege of poverty as well. The order spread quickly. By 1400, there were about four hundred Clarissen houses: two hundred fifty in Italy and most of the rest in Spain and France, with a few in England, Germany, and eastern Europe. In all, about fifteen thousand women belonged to the Poor Clares. However, they were neither fully independent of nor completely incorporated into the Franciscans.[47]

Unlike Francis, whose relationship to Clare was fraught with tension, Dominic encouraged his devoted female follower Diana d'Andalo (d. 1236) to form a companion order to his preaching Friars. Dominic's connection to Diana began in Bologna when she was only eighteen years old. She had already vowed herself to religion when she met Dominic in 1219 and suggested a female order. Along with some other young noblewomen, she took personal vows from Dominic and made plans for the foundation of a new convent, Saint Agnes of Bologna. For the next few years,

Dominic worked closely with the women, visiting and preaching to them; however, Diana's family was opposed to her pious vocation and tried to remove her by force from the convent, injuring her in the process.

Dominic eventually created a rule for the women's order and was interested enough in their welfare to have his brother supervise them. However, the relationship between the men and women changed after Dominic's death in 1221, when the Dominicans forbade the formation of new convents, afraid that they would distract energy and resources from their work and their university studies. After Diana's death in 1236, the Dominicans paired convents with monasteries so that male and female communities might share farms and other facilities. While the men fulfilled Dominic's vision through study and preaching, Dominican nuns remained inside praying, singing, sewing, and embroidering.[48]

At the end of the thirteenth century, papal politics stymied the expansion of women's orders once again. In 1298, Boniface VIII (r. 1294–1303) decreed that all religious women *everywhere* must be cloistered. Boniface believed strongly in the medieval idea that women were sexually dangerous. Based on that notion, Boniface argued that women could not hope to remain chaste and fulfill their religious vows as long as they had contact with men.

Undaunted by these obstacles, Birgitta (1303–1373), a powerful Swedish noblewoman, made the last medieval attempt to establish a reformed order for women. At the age of only thirty-one, the widowed mother of eight renounced her wealth and title in order to fulfill the miraculous visions that she had experienced since childhood. In those visions, Christ commanded her to reform the church through the creation of a new monastic order for women and dictated a detailed rule for that new order. Birgitta formed a small community of sixty strictly cloistered nuns who lived by a rule based on the Benedictine or Cistercian model. Men and women were to live as equals in a double monastery under the direct supervision of the bishop. Within the cloister, the abbess had complete authority over all the members and responsibility for their spiritual care. Despite Birgitta's claims to divine inspiration, the church prohibition on new orders hindered her efforts. However, in 1370, Pope Urban V (r. 1362–1370) finally

offered a compromise, giving her permission to found separate male and female monasteries, but not her double monastery. Birgitta agreed since he allowed her to keep other aspects of her own rule, but she continued to send Pope Urban transcripts of her revelations that included the Virgin Mary's disapproval of his failure to fulfill her divinely inspired requests. Even after Birgitta's death, the Order of the Most Holy Savior's original foundations at Vadstena, Sweden, and Syon, England, flourished. Attempts by church officials to control the abbey at Vadstena were continually thwarted by the belief among its inhabitants that its foundation had been directly revealed by Jesus.[49]

Holy Women, Saints, and Mystics

Not all women were willing to wait for the papacy to reconsider its stance on female orders. Some intensely spiritual laywomen formed their own communities in cities outside of convent walls. In northern Europe, these women were known as *Beguines*. They had no male leader and lived by no formal monastic rule. They tended to be reclusive, sharing residences, pooling property, working together, and pledging themselves to chastity and poverty. They devoted themselves to prayer and performing charitable acts in the community. In Spain and Portugal, these women were known as *beatas*. Beatas were typically poor and sometimes preached (an activity usually denied to women) or ministered to the community. Beatas and Beguines experienced poverty, heightened spirituality, and independence, but male ecclesiastics were generally suspicious of them. After papal decrees mandated full enclosure for female religious, most Beguines moved into formal monastic communities under the supervision of male clerics.

Other women pursued holiness alone, achieving sainthood for their extraordinary piety. During the late Middle Ages, the proportion of women proclaimed saints rose from less than 10 percent in the eleventh century to about 28 percent in the fifteenth century.[50] Some of these women fell squarely into early medieval spiritual traditions, such as that of the pious queen. For instance, Jadwiga (1375– 1399) was sent to Poland in 1384 at age nine to be crowned king (rex), because there was no precedent for a female ruler. She eventually married Jagiello (1348–1434),

THE REVELATIONS OF SAINT BIRGITTA OF SWEDEN (CA. 1400). During the late Middle Ages, many women engaged in mystical activity and sometimes used the religious legitimacy of those experiences to circumvent male authority. Based on her revelations, pictured here, Saint Birgitta founded the Order of the Most Holy Savior, despite opposition from the papacy. *(The Pierpont Morgan Library/Art Resource, NY.)*

the ruler of Lithuania. The countries were united in 1385 and under pressure from Jadwiga, Jagiello converted Lithuania from paganism to Catholicism. The couple ruled Poland together until Jadwiga's early death from complications from childbirth in 1399. She was renowned for her piety during her lifetime, and Poles venerated her for nearly six hundred years before the papacy officially granted her sainthood.

Other late medieval women's spiritual experiences often included mystical trances and visions. Catherine of Siena (ca. 1347–1380) was one of the most important mystics of the period. The illiterate daughter of a Sienese dyer, she demonstrated remarkable devotion from an early age. She refused to marry and decided to live by the Dominican rule. In her mystical experiences, she repeatedly endured the Passion and had a mystical marriage with Christ. Her reputation for sanctity attracted large numbers of followers. Although she never learned to read or write, she dictated at least 350 letters to important correspondents, including popes. She used the power and fame that she achieved through her mystical experiences to urge church reform, peace among Christians, and crusades against Islam.

Mystical experiences took their toll on a woman's mind and body. God communicated secrets to her and even transported her to distant, holy places. When she was closest to God, she lost all sense of her bodily self. Dozens of female saints claimed to have had the five visible wounds of Christ (stigmata). Some lost complete control of their bodies. Trances, levitations, catatonic seizures, miraculous elongation or enlargement of body parts, and ecstatic nosebleeds were rarely reported by male saints, but were quite common in the lives of late medieval female saints. Many, including Catherine of Siena, reported the inability to eat anything but the Eucharist. Such incidents of self-starvation also led to other miraculous bodily events such as the failure to menstruate or excrete. A number of thirteenth-century Netherlandish mystics experienced miraculous lactation. Lidwina of Schiedam (1380–1433) shed skin and bones that gave off a sweet odor. Ida of Louvain's body swelled as if she were pregnant with Christ.[51] Over half of late medieval female saints were renowned for their patient suffering from painful illnesses.[52] The writings of Julian of Norwich (ca. 1342–ca. 1420) are moving descriptions of the physical torments that preceded her mystical experiences (see **Sources from the Past:** Julian of Norwich, *Revelations of Divine Love*).

Some mystics' expressions of faith were highly sexualized. Angela of Foligno (1248–1309) spoke of Christ as her lover. In her raptures, she kissed him and he held her body tightly against his. The physicality of these experiences could be dangerous. Angela spoke with such passion that ecclesiastical authorities worried that her ecstasies may have been the work of the devil.

Julian of Norwich, *Revelations of Divine Love*

We know almost nothing about the life of Julian of Norwich (ca. 1342–ca. 1420) except that as a young woman she had a series of mystical experiences. She then became an anchoress, living alone in a cell attached to the parish church of Saint Julian in Norwich, where she was visited by many, including Margery Kempe. Her mystical experiences began in 1373. We do not know if she wrote down her revelations herself or dictated them to someone else. These passages reflect two important aspects of Julian's mystical experiences. The first two sections describe her physical torments and near death experience. In the third section, Julian emphasizes the maternal aspects of God.

CHAPTER II

When I was thirty and a half winters old, God sent me a physical illness in which I lay for three days and three nights. On the fourth night I took all the rites of holy church and did not think that I would live until morning. After this I lingered two days and two nights; on the third night I often thought that I was going to die, as did those who were with me. I was truly sorry at this. The thought of dying seemed hateful, not because of anything in this life that I wanted to live for, nor for anything that I feared, since I trusted in God. But I wanted to live so as to love God better, and for a longer time, that I might, by the grace of that living, have a fuller knowledge and love of God in the bliss of heaven.

Since all the time I might live seemed so slight and so brief in contrast to endless bliss, I thought, Good Lord, is there no further way my living can honor you? Yet I was answered in my reason, and by the feeling of my pains, that I should die. So I assented fully, with all my heart, to God's will.

Thus I endured until morning, by which time my body was without feeling from the midst downward. I was anxious to be set upright, with my head supported by bedclothes, to give my heart more freedom to be at one with God's will, and to allow me to think about him as long as my life should last. Those who were with me sent for my curate, the parson, to be with me when I died. He came, along with a child, and brought a cross with him; by then my eyes had set and I could not speak. The parson placed the cross before my face and said, "Daughter, I have brought you the image of your savior. Look upon it and comfort yourself with it, in reverence for him who died for you and me."

It seemed to me that I was doing well, since I was looking upwards towards heaven, where I hoped to go. Nevertheless, I agreed, if I could, to fix my eyes on the face of the crucifix, so as to postpone the time of my ending; for it seemed to me I might endure longer looking straight ahead than upwards. After this my sight began to fail. The chamber was as dark and murky as if it had been night, except for common lights that surrounded the image of the cross, though I did not understand how this could be. Everything but the cross was as ugly to me as if it had been inhabited by devils.

After this the feeling in the upper part of my body began to die. My hands fell down on either side, and out of weakness my head settled to one side. The greatest pain that I felt was shortness of breath and failing of life: I thought I was truly at the point of death.

But suddenly my pain departed and I was as well, especially in the upper part of my body, as ever I was before or after. I marveled at this change, for it seemed to me a mysterious act of God, rather than one of nature. Yet despite this feeling of ease, I did not believe that I could continue to live, nor was the respite a relief to me: since my heart had at last consented, I would rather have been delivered from this world.

CHAPTER III

At once I thought to wish for the second wound, which, by our lord's gift and grace I had formerly sought: that he would fill my body with feeling for his blessed passion. I desired his pain to become my pain through compassion, followed by a greater closeness with God. In this way it seemed that I might with grace, share his wounds, as I had before wished. Yet from God I sought neither bodily sight, nor any manner of revelation—only the compassion that it seemed to me any kind soul might feel for our lord Jesus, who for love had become a mortal man. I wanted to suffer with him, while living in my mortal body, as God would give me grace.

CHAPTER LVIII

God is never displeased with his chosen wife; of the three properties in the trinity: fatherhood, motherhood, and lordship; how our essence is in each person of the trinity, but our sensuality is in Christ alone.

God the blissful trinity everlasting being, endless without beginning, had as his eternal purpose the creation of mankind, whose fair nature was first ordained for his own son, the second person. And when he wished, with the full accord of the trinity, he made us all at once. . . . Thus in our creation God almighty is our natural father, and God all-wisdom our natural mother, who together with the love and goodness of the holy ghost are all one God, one lord. And in the knitting and the uniting he is our own true spouse, and we his beloved wife and fair maiden, with whom he is never displeased; as he says, "I love you and you love me, and our love shall never be divided.". . .

Our essential nature is the higher part, which we have in our father God almighty. In our essential creation, the second person of the trinity is our natural mother, in whom we are grounded and rooted; but in taking on our sensuality he has also become our merciful mother. Thus our mother works in diverse ways, whereby our parts are kept united. For in our mother Christ, we profit and increase: in mercy he reforms and restores us, and by the power of his passion and his death and resurrection unites us with our essence. In this merciful way our mother acts towards all children who are submissive and obedient. . . .

Thus in our father, God almighty, we have our being; and in our merciful mother, through whom our parts are united and made perfect, we have our reforming and restoration; and by the gracious rewarding and giving of the holy ghost we are fulfilled. Our essence is our father, God almighty; our essence is our mother, God all-wisdom; and our essence is our lord the holy ghost, God all-goodness. In each person of the trinity, which is one God, our essence is complete. But our sensuality is only in the second person, Christ Jesus, in whom are the father and the holy ghost; in him and by him are we mightily delivered from hell and from the wretchedness of earth, and gloriously brought up into heaven, blissfully united with our essence, magnified in splendor and nobility, all by the power of Christ and the grace and co-operation of the holy ghost.

Source: Frances Beer, *Julian of Norwich: Revelations. Motherhood of God* (Cambridge: D. S. Brewer, 1998), 27–28, 61–63.

Although most women who had mystical experiences were either nuns or Beguines, Margery Kempe (ca. 1373– 1438/9) was an English laywoman who tried to imitate the mystics. Margery was married and bore fourteen children. She began having visions of Christ soon after the birth of her first child. In her revelations, she attended the Virgin's birth, cared for the Virgin as a baby, and was present at the birth of Christ. Although she was illiterate, Margery seems to have been familiar with the important mystical writings of her time. Her autobiography, *The Book of Margery Kempe,* which she dictated to two priests, demonstrates how deeply mysticism had permeated medieval society and the role of oral transmission in spreading knowledge of mystical experiences. Margery's autobiography also indicates that not everyone shared her religious enthusiasm. Even her most pious neighbors and family members found it difficult to get along with her.

Joan of Arc's (1412–1431) mystical experiences brought her both fame and tragedy. Joan rose to prominence during the Hundred Years' War (1337–1453) between England and France, when the two nations fought over a number of issues, most importantly the succession to the French throne and the support of papal candidates during the Great Schism. After a series of English victories, young Joan of Arc came upon the scene in 1429. The illiterate daughter of a peasant farmer, Joan told the dauphin, the heir to the French throne, that she had heard the voices of Saints Margaret and Katherine and the archangel Michael since she was thirteen. Those voices told her that a victory at Orléans (then besieged by the English) would precede the dauphin's coronation. Encouraged by Joan's revelations, the dauphin provided her with the finest army in France. Clothed in armor, Joan led the troops and amazingly lifted the siege by the English. With that victory, she accompanied the dauphin to the city of Reims to be crowned Charles VII, just as her voices had instructed. With that goal accomplished, Joan tried to retake Paris from the English. However, she faced a series of defeats and was wounded in the process.

Finally, in 1430, the Burgundians captured Joan. They sold her to the English who, after three months of questioning, charged her with seventy different counts of heresy, ranging from worshipping false gods (the saints of her voices) to witchcraft to making herself into an idol by dressing as a man. Eventually, the authorities condensed the accusations into twelve main charges. Joan initially recanted, but later admitted to hearing the voices again and returning to wearing men's clothes. She was burned at the stake in May 1431. However, the complicated tale of Joan of Arc does not end there. Twenty-four years later, the French held a second trial. In this trial, the French attempted to repair Joan's reputation and transform her from a heretic to a hero.

Joan's trial reflects the period's conflicting notions about religion, mysticism, and female sexuality. Some of the initial charges against her claimed that she was a prostitute and a camp follower, although in the end authorities withdrew the charges of sexual promiscuity. Many of the accusations referred to her transvestism. Biblical law forbade wearing the clothing of the other gender, yet many female saints, including Saint Margaret, wore male clothing to avoid marriage or to enter a monastery against their parents' will. According to the authorities, Joan's did not dress like a man for religiously acceptable reasons, although she said that Saint Katherine and Saint Margaret told her to wear men's clothing in her visions. Most important, Joan's male clothing did not hide the fact that she was a cross-dressing woman, especially since she did not hide her breasts. She was something outside of nature—part man, part woman, and in the words of the accusation, she "made herself an idol for the people."

Although Joan troubled church officials, her followers revered her for her virginity. When she first arrived at the French court, the queen and her ladies physically examined her to ensure that her virginity was intact. Medieval Christians were comfortable with the idea that God might convey his will through virgins. In fact, the power of that image was strong enough that although some military leaders ridiculed her presence on the battlefield, troops willingly followed her into battle. They believed that fighting beside a holy virgin could help them achieve salvation.[53]

Scholars have hypothesized that the regular crises of the late Middle Ages created the setting for the increase in mystical activity. As society suffered through regular outbreaks of plague, economic crises, clerical abuses, and political instability, mystics provided people with a connection to heavenly power. Although few women sought the intense religious experience of saints, mystics, and holy women, their influence was greater than their numbers. They not only inspired others with their piety, they attracted the attention of popes and kings. Strengthened by their belief that they knew God's will, they used their influence with these powerful men to change the course of history.

Piety and Parish Religion at the End of the Middle Ages

Most women were neither nuns nor holy women, but we know little about their personal piety beyond descriptions of their public religious activity. Most laywomen expressed their religiosity through parish activities. For instance, individual women donated funds or goods to decorate a favorite saint's image in their parish church. When they made their wills, they revealed their religious priorities by leaving money or gifts to monasteries, convents, or saints' shrines. Even relatively poor women donated some trinket, like a candle or a kerchief, to their parish church. Burial sites also revealed women's special devotions. A woman with a special devotion to Saint Margaret might request that she be buried near the statue, painting, or relics of that saint.

Parish religious activity centered on expressions of communal piety such as Corpus Christi celebrations, attendance at Mass, and participation in lay religious groups known as confraternities or guilds in England. Mendicant orders spread these lay organizations dedicated to the devotion to one particular saint across Europe. Parishes had both mixed-sex and single-sex confraternities, usually supervised by a priest. Women participated in these groups by preparing Easter breakfasts, holiday plays, and local festivals. In some English parishes on Hocktide, the second Monday and Tuesday after Easter, the women raised money for their parish. On Hock-Monday, they went about the parish capturing the men and tying them up, releasing them only after the payment of a ransom. On Tuesday, the roles were reversed. At other times of the year, women's guilds put on

parish ales as fundraisers. These charitable and social activities were important events in parish religious life.

Women also expressed their piety through life-cycle rituals usually celebrated in the parish church. Although mothers were not typically present at the baptisms of their children, female friends and relatives were. They lovingly sewed baptismal gowns for the child and prepared feasts for the family. Women also served as godmothers, vowing to raise children according to Catholic doctrine in case the parents died. At weddings, women helped prepare the banquets and other festivities. At the end of one's life, they tended to the dying, made the burial shroud, prepared the body for burial, and laid out the food and drink for the wake. They accompanied the coffin to the parish church for the funeral and prayed for the soul's journey to the afterlife. Female family members also honored the dead by providing annual offerings of bread and other foods to the church.

In general, laywomen were devoted to saints whom they believed could affect their lives. Parish churches held many shrines and chapels dedicated to the saints, and much parish activity focused on maintaining and honoring the saints and the Virgin. Women also prayed to male saints who might help ease their physical suffering, such as Saint Roche, the plague saint, and Saint Blaise, who combated sore throats. Moreover, medieval Europeans venerated numerous local saints whose life histories were unknown to outsiders, but who were well loved by parishioners. These saints included individuals who had been martyred by invaders, such as Saint Quiteria in Spain and holy men hailed for their piety, such as Saint Drogo in France.

The boundary between official and semi-official religious activities that the church did not sanction was blurred. To gain more control over their difficult lives, women engaged in a variety of semireligious activities. Sometimes they used holy water taken from the baptismal font to heal a sick child, or herbs and amulets to ease pain in childbirth. Many women believed that jet, a popular stone for necklaces, helped alleviate menstrual problems. They did not view these activities as superstitious, but as additional means to access heavenly power.

Veneration of the saints took women out of their parishes on pilgrimages. Women sought the relics of saints for consolation or heavenly intervention. Pilgrimage might resolve crises ranging from dying relatives and heavy debts to relief from aches and pains. Most women could only visit local shrines, but some particularly pious women like Margery Kempe went on pilgrimages to the Holy Land, Rome, and Santiago de Compostela. As socially acceptable reasons for female travel, many women found great freedom in pilgrimages. In Geoffrey Chaucer's *The Canterbury Tales* (1387–1397), a collection of fictional stories recounting the adventures of a band of pilgrims journeying to Canterbury Cathedral, the Wife of Bath is on her third pilgrimage.

Despite the fact that the church increasingly constrained the activities of female monastics, women found other powerful ways to express their piety and other opportunities to act on behalf of their own salvation. Their intense devotion energized late medieval religious life from the parish to the papacy.

WOMEN ON THE FRINGES OF CHRISTIANITY

During the late Middle Ages, the Catholic Church was in crisis. Increasingly, medieval kings vied for control over the papacy's wealth and power. In 1309, the French king forced Pope Clement V (r. 1305–1314) to move the papal court to Avignon. After the papacy returned to Rome in 1377, Pope Urban VI (r. 1378–1389) attempted to reform the church; however, the cardinals declared his election invalid and chose a second pope, Clement VII. Clement moved his papal court back to Avignon while Urban ruled from Rome, creating the Great Schism. The crisis grew as another group of powerful clerics and theologians elected yet a third pope in 1409. Finally, in 1417 the Council of Constance deposed all three men and elected a new pope, Martin V (r. 1417–1431), ending the schism once and for all.

While politics plagued the papacy, the church also suffered from accusations of clerical corruption and incompetence. Clergy cohabitated with local women and passed benefices on to their sons. Few clergy received the education that their positions required. Bishops and monasteries became wealthy, politically influential landowners who dedicated little time to their religious duties.

Disgusted with the state of affairs in the Catholic Church, many Europeans found spiritual comfort in new Christian heresies that arose during the twelfth and thirteenth centuries, many of which were centered in cities. Scholars used to claim that women joined heretical sects in large numbers because traditional Catholicism could not fulfill their spiritual needs. However, recent research indicates that men dominated all but one of the movements and that women may have been underrepresented in most heretical sects. Despite their unorthodox religious ideas, most heretical groups restricted women to traditional female roles.

Waldensians

Many medieval heretical movements criticized the wealth of the Catholic Church and its abandonment of the poverty of the apostles. During the second half of the twelfth century in Lyon, France, a man named Waldes, known by some as Peter Waldo (fl. 1180), gave up his career as a well-to-do merchant for a life of apostolic poverty. He preached and distributed his money to the city's poor, quickly attracting followers. Although the church could not find fault in his charitable work or his self-inflicted poverty, it was increasingly uncomfortable with his preaching. He rejected any doctrines that he believed did not have basis in Scripture, including purgatory and excommunication. In 1184, church officials declared Waldes a heretic for preaching without a license, persecuting him and his followers. Eventually, the church forced the Waldensians to move underground and set up their own independent religious hierarchy.

Waldes never discussed his views on women. In fact, he placed his two daughters in the convent at Fontevraux (see Chapter 5) before he took his begging and preaching to the streets of Lyon, and he addressed his calls to renounce private property and preach penitence only to men. However, many women became active members of the sect and participated as equal members. They discussed religion, sought out new followers, and allowed members to stay in their homes. The Waldensians did not develop clearly defined roles for women and men and in testimonies before the Inquisitors, Waldensians rarely referred to gender, and scholars believe that it was not a critical factor in participation in the movement.[54]

While Waldes preached in France, another group of Christians zealously dedicated to poverty formed in northern Italy. The Humiliati attracted a wide variety of adherents, including clergy, unmarried laity, and married couples. They worked in the local cloth industry, refused to take oaths or undertake litigation, dressed simply, and gave away most of their belongings. Unlike the Waldensians, they did not beg, but they preached in the streets, and often got into trouble for doing so without a license. The church declared them heretics in 1184 along with the Waldensians, but in 1201, Pope Innocent III reorganized the group and licensed the Humiliati as a male monastic order. In addition, the pope created a separate order of laymen and women, known as a Second Order, and a Third Order of lay married couples. After the reorganization, women made up the majority of the Second Order Humiliati. They often lived in female-only houses, which they administered themselves.

Northern Italy was also home to one of the most enigmatic heresies of the Middle Ages, the short-lived Guglielmites. Although they never numbered more than one hundred, they were highly visible as they were closely tied to Milan's elite families. Women outnumbered men in the sect, which believed that God had both male and female aspects and that their spiritual leader, Guglielma (ca. 1210–1281), embodied the Holy Spirit. Guglielma was a Bohemian princess who came to Milan around 1260 and became famous for her piety and charitable works. She supposedly had the marks of the Crucifixion, the stigmata, on her body. Based on their belief that God had both male and female aspects, they gave women equal status in their community. They believed that Guglielma would be resurrected and then replace the church hierarchy with a pure church in which women would serve as popes and cardinals. After Guglielma's death, the group's female leader, Maifreda, conducted Mass, ordained women, and was revered as Guglielma's choice for the new female papacy. Despite their small size, the church saw them as a threat, no doubt because of the prominent role of women. After the church

burned the Guglielmites' leaders at the stake, and disinterred and burned Guglielma's bones to prevent them from becoming sacred relics, the sect came to a quick end.[55]

Cathars

Unlike the Waldensians and the Humiliati, which had their roots in local culture, Catharism may have originated in the tenth-century Bogomil Church in parts of Macedonia and Bulgaria. By the mid-twelfth century, followers had brought the sect as far west as France and northern Italy. Cathar doctrine viewed the sacraments as worthless and denied the Crucifixion and Resurrection since they believed that God could not have taken human form. In their dualistic conception of the world, the source of good created the spiritual world and the source of evil was a being who had fallen from heaven and who then created earth and all its temptations. The source of evil trapped souls in matter, preventing them from ascending to the spiritual world. Any physical indulgence indicated an allegiance to the creator of evil.

Cathars pursued a life of simplicity, purity, and chastity. They divided their communities into two groups: the perfects and the believers. The perfects led very ascetic lives. They gave up their possessions, refused to eat anything they viewed as a product of sex, such as meat, eggs, or cheese, and were celibate. The majority of Cathars were believers who supported the perfects but did not live according to such rigorous rules. Instead, they hoped that on their deathbeds they could summon a perfect to carry out an important Cathar ritual, the *consolamentum*, to make them perfects so that they would move directly into the spiritual realm.

The Cathar Church was highly organized with its own hierarchy and clerical offices. By 1200, there were eleven Cathar bishops in western Europe. In southern France, local clergy and nobility tolerated and even supported the Cathar presence. The Count of Foix, an important local noble, was a Catholic, but his wife, Philippa, headed a convent of female perfects. Two of the wives of Toulouse count Raymond VI (1156–1222) left him to dedicate themselves to Catharism. His first wife entered a Cathar nunnery, and his fourth wife's faith led her to become a celibate perfect, thus ending their marriage.[56]

Women of all social classes were active in the Cathars. The Cathar hierarchy was exclusively male, but women could receive the consolamentum and thereby become perfects, or Good Women. Once designated as perfects, women could preach and administer the consolamentum, activities that made them equal to most Cathar men. In a series of trials held between 1308 and 1313, 40 percent of those who appeared before the Inquisition were women, many of whom had provided shelter to believers and participated in religious discussions with both women and men. However, despite women's enthusiastic support, Cathars voiced considerable anxiety about women's bodies. According to Cathar beliefs, women were central in the devil's seduction of the angels away from God. Sexual intercourse was a sin, and they believed that lactating women were spiritually and physically unclean. Male perfects were not to touch women under any circumstances.[57]

At first, the church attempted to reconvert the Cathars to orthodoxy through intensive preaching by Dominican Friars. However, frustrated by the lack of success, the pope ordered the Albigensian Crusade to suppress the heresy in 1208. It was the first crusade against European heretics. Church officials sent knights to fight them and replace their bishops with orthodox Catholics. The result was the large-scale slaughter of Cathars and the eventual destruction of the sect.

Lollards and Hussites

Heresy in England took the form of Lollardy, a movement that originated at Oxford University in the 1380s inspired by John Wyclif. At first, most of Wyclif's followers were connected with the university and members of the gentry. As preachers spread his message across southern and central England, they attracted large numbers of artisans and members of the middling class. Lollardy was virulently anticlerical. Lollards not only condemned clergy for their unholy lives but also denied that ordination gave them any special powers. Some believed that clergy should not administer the seven sacraments. Sect members asserted that fasting, pilgrimages, saints, images, and holy days had no basis in Scripture and refused to participate in those activities. Lollardy also had an

CATHARS BEING EXPELLED FROM CARCASSONE (CA. 1415). Many women were attracted to heretical movements because of their promise of heightened spirituality. As members of movements such as the Cathars, they experienced persecution when the Catholic church suppressed the heresies. *(HIP/Art Resource, NY.)*

apocalyptic side that believed clerical abuses represented the presence of the antichrist in the world. The central concept in Lollardy was the formation of a new church, based on the primacy of Scripture and a congregation of the predestined. In this new church, the clergy would only preach and teach the word of God; in all other respects, they were like laypeople. Lollards emphasized the importance of vernacular works and the ability to read them in order to close the gap between clergy and laypeople.

Women usually followed other family members into Lollardy. In some communities, mothers introduced daughters to the heresy, while in others siblings introduced each other to the ideas. Women were not typically leaders in Lollardy as the movement generally prevented them from teaching and preaching. The few women with some authority were from the upper classes. For instance, Alice Rowley, a widow and member of Coventry's wealthy merchant elite, led groups of male and female Lollards. She converted men and women to her faith, taught other members, and was active in the Lollard book trade.[58]

As a professor at Oxford, Wyclif taught many students, one of whom was Jan Hus (1373–1415), a Bohemian who carried his ideas back to eastern Europe. Hus charged that clergy were too worldly and emphasized contemplation, prayer, reading Scripture, and frequent communion. He demanded changes in the way that clergy administered the Eucharist and that the clergy be deprived of their secular authority.

Despite the fact that Hus accepted the medieval view of women as inherently sinful, he urged women to be active in spiritual teaching, to see themselves as created in the image of God, and to participate in the reform of the church. Women were encouraged to share their feelings and ideas at religious meetings, and Hussite preachers admonished followers not to regard women as sex symbols. One reformer, Matthew of Janov, even believed that women, who were more inclined to modesty, chastity, and sobriety than men, were closer to the Holy Spirit than men and had the prophetic spirit.

Hussite views on sex and marriage varied greatly. Some radical groups may have granted divorce. A few reformers prohibited priests from having sex with women, while others allowed clergy to marry. The radical Chiliasts led by Martin Húska asserted that in the Hussite utopia, women would conceive without men and childbirth would occur without pain.[59]

Many women enthusiastically followed Hus and were important in the early stages of the Hussite movement. After Hus was excommunicated from the Catholic Church, Lady Anna Mochova of Usti gave Hus sanctuary in Kozí when it became too dangerous for him to stay in Prague. Queen Sophia, the second wife of King Wenceslas of Bohemia (r. 1378–1419), acted as a patron for the Hussites. Prague's communities of Beguines backed Hus's radical priests and often used violence to stop priests from performing religious services in the traditional manner. When Catholic armies attacked Hussite strongholds, Hussite women took up arms and fought alongside men. Anka of Prasetín, a gentry woman, dressed as a man and fought for the Hussites for twenty years. On July 12, 1420, Hungarian troops reported that they had captured 156 Hussite women dressed as men with their hair cut, armed with swords and stones. Still other women took to the battlefield without concealing their gender.[60]

The heyday for Hussite women seems to have been from 1416 to 1420. By the end of 1420, efforts were under way to exclude them from all but the most basic participation in religious rituals. As the movement fell into disunity, the Hussite leadership accepted traditional gender stereotypes and gradually excluded women from positions of authority and from meetings, and even blamed them for the conflict among the reformers. Hus was condemned by the Council of Constance in 1415 and burned at the stake.

Heretical movements attracted women for many different reasons. Some women joined heretical movements along with other family members. Others longed for the independence that some movements seemed to offer. Many women were attracted by the emphasis on apostolic poverty that was central to most of the heretical movements. In every case, they risked their lives in their search for a more fulfilling social and spiritual experience.

THE RENAISSANCE

In the midst of the turmoil of the late Middle Ages, some parts of Europe experienced a series of political, intellectual, and artistic changes that have become known as the Renaissance. Although the notion of a late medieval Renaissance, or "rebirth," is largely a nineteenth-century concept, many scholars continue to employ the term to describe a number of innovations during this period, particularly (but not exclusively) on the Italian peninsula. Traditionally, scholars understood the Renaissance based almost exclusively on the experiences of men. They studied Republican governments, new intellectual currents, and great art as the creations of men for other men. However, ideas about sex and gender deeply influenced the changes of the Renaissance and brought both new restrictions and new opportunities for women.

Communes

During the eleventh and twelfth centuries, the German emperor and the papacy fought regularly over the cities of northern Italy. As the conflict sputtered to stalemate, the cities formed *communes*, sworn associations of merchants and members of the lower nobility who pledged to defend the city from invasion and to protect their social and economic privileges. The largest of these communes were Venice, Florence, Genoa, and Milan. As the communes acquired additional territory, they grew into small city-states. However, communal governments were not always stable. By 1300, despots had usurped power in the communes of Milan and Ferrara, and merchant oligarchies controlled the republics of Florence and Venice. Although the republics looked democratic with their constitutions and complicated voting systems, the wealthy merchants who controlled their political systems restricted citizenship to other wealthy men, excluding the majority of the male population and all women. In fact, as women could never rule, they had fewer opportunities for power and influence than in medieval monarchies. In Florence, civic authorities barred women from even entering the government palace, the Palazzo Vecchio.[61]

In addition to excluding women from government, the ruling elites of the Italian city-states actively regulated sexuality in order to assert control and maintain public order. Florentine elites created the *Ufficio dell'Onestà* to regulate brothels and prostitution and the *Ufficiale di Notte* to prosecute sodomy. Both organizations were intended to discourage consensual homosexuality, which Florentine society largely accepted as long as it was discreet. City governments also encouraged male heterosexuality in order to repopulate the city after the epidemic of 1348.[62] Similarly, during the fifteenth century, Venetian authorities vigorously prosecuted and burned homosexuals.

The republican governments also intervened in marriages between elite families. In 1424–25 the Florentine government established the *Monte delle Doti*, a dowry fund. Authorities created the fund to encourage marriage and alleviate the fiscal crisis that Florence faced. They invited the fathers and guardians of Florentine girls to make cash deposits for a term of either seven and a half or fifteen years. At the end of the period, the deposit yielded a significant dowry. Once the girl consummated her marriage, the officials of the fund paid her dowry to her husband or his representative. If the girl died before the required period passed (even if she had married and consummated the marriage) or if she never married, the monies reverted back to the state. If she married after the predetermined period, her husband received only the predetermined sum without any additional interest. The state took advantage of the invested money as the girls grew up, and the parents were guaranteed an appropriate dowry for their daughters. Venice set up a similar fund to help slow dowry inflation and set maximums for marriage settlements. There, authorities worried that fathers deprived their sons of their rightful inheritance in order to provide elaborate dowries, thus giving their daughters too much social and familial power.

The dowry fund forced fathers to decide their daughters' destinies early. To take advantage of the Monte delle Doti, a father made his first deposit when his daughter was only six years old. Wealthy girls then entered convents and remained there until their marriages. Daughters who did not marry became nuns, taking the veil between the ages of nine and eleven and final vows after they were twelve or thirteen years old.[63]

Although they had little or no choice about whether or whom to marry, Italian women had extensive inheritance rights and could dispose of their property as they wished. One of the greatest concerns in the Italian city-states was the extensive power of well-dowered widows. Men tended to marry first at around age thirty, while their brides were generally in their midteens. As a result, women tended to be widowed at relatively young ages. They were less likely to remarry than men, no doubt because widows could make their own decisions about their futures. Since they were able to reclaim their dowries when widowed, they could use that money either to remarry or to live independently. They might also use it to influence their children's futures through dowries and other marriage gifts. In fact, the magistracy in charge of looking after the interests of fatherless children in Florence regularly approved widows' petitions for permission to administer their deceased husbands' property and to raise their children. Italian society clearly acknowledged a widow's right to undertake these legal activities without the supervision of a man.[64]

Humanism and the *Querelle des Femmes*

Although scholasticism dominated in northern Europe, many Italian intellectuals conceptualized the world differently. Instead of emphasizing canon law, humanist thinkers focused on the study of the humanities: grammar, rhetoric, poetry, history, and moral philosophy. They admired the ancient Greeks and Romans, rediscovered many ancient texts, and strove to speak and write primarily in Latin. They believed that these skills would best serve the citizens of the Italian republics.

In spite of their emphasis on learning, male humanists remained divided over the issue of educating women. Although humanists did not deny that individual women might be great thinkers or artists, they defined such women as exceptional and even unnatural. Male humanists associated creativity with masculinity—women could not be creators and those who did create were, in some essential way, not female. Moreover, since humanism trained men to participate in politics and commerce, it had little relevance for women. Indeed, humanists like Leonardo Bruni (1369–1444) believed that while training in the liberal arts might be appropriate for a noblewoman under certain circumstances (primarily to keep her mind occupied and thus protect her chastity), such skills were otherwise unbecoming for a woman. The humanist Isotta Nogarola (1418–1466) suffered miserably from that prejudice. The daughter of a noble family from Verona, her widowed mother provided both of her daughters, Isotta and Ginevra, education with the finest tutors. Adept and curious, as adolescents they were famed for their intellect and received admiring letters from several male humanists. After her sister married and quit her studies, Isotta insisted on continuing her scholarly pursuits. She corresponded extensively with some of the great male thinkers of her era; however, she was discouraged by the fact that they were willing to compare her intellectual skills only to those of other women and not to men. As a result, they viewed her as a bizarre prodigy rather than an intellectual equal. Some male scholars viciously asserted that her willingness to write for a public audience indicated her sexual promiscuity. One scholar even accused her of incest. Frustrated by her inability to participate fully in the intellectual world that she craved, in 1441, at the age of twenty-three, Isotta pledged herself to virginity and became a recluse in her home.[65]

Although most male intellectuals found little value in educating women, some determined parents worked to bring their daughters the best education available. (see **Women's Lives:** Laura Cereta, Italian Humanist). Aristocratic and elite parents hired private tutors or sent their daughters to be educated in convents. Even for the lower ranks of society, basic schooling for children of both sexes became more widely available across Europe. Some children attended elementary schools in Florence from the fourteenth century and in Venice from the beginning of the fifteenth century. Paris, London, and other major cities across Europe also had at least a few schoolmistresses to provide some education for young girls. In Brussels, a 1320 decree allowed parents to send daughters as well as sons to secondary schools, and a few German cities had schools in which girls could learn that were partially supported by city councils.[66]

Despite the increased access to schooling, female literacy rates remained much lower than men's at all levels of society. By the fifteenth century, some of the elite guilds in London required apprentices to have an education before beginning their apprenticeships, but those were exclusively male trades and families had no obligation to educate their daughters. Moreover, parents often had difficulty finding teachers for their daughters, as notions of sexual propriety prevented girls from being taught by males except in exceptional circumstances, and female schoolteachers were usually less educated than their male counterparts. However, in at least one case, a female teacher's skills led to tension. In the German city of Uberlingen in 1456, a male teacher complained to city authorities that a schoolmistress in town was so well respected that "some people in this city have decided to have their boys learn German as well and have sent them to her. She has understood that this has brought difficulties to me and my school. So I request that she be ordered to pay

Women's Lives

Laura Cereta, Italian Humanist

Although Laura Cereta was not the first female humanist to gain notoriety among late medieval European intellectuals, her life is a prime example of the challenges that a young female scholar faced. Laura was the eldest of six children from a noble family from Brescia in Italy. At around eight years old, her father, a lawyer and magistrate, sent her to be educated in a nearby convent where she learned to read and write. After two years, her father sent for her and he undertook the next stage of her education. To this point, her education was typical for a young woman of her social status. Many daughters of the Italian nobility received some education in convents supplemented by teaching by fathers or tutors.

Laura married a local merchant at age fifteen and soon after took charge of an extended household that included her father, her younger siblings, and her husband. Laura spent her days taking care of the house, but dedicated the nights to study and writing after everyone else had gone to bed. It was during this period of intense study that Laura discovered her thirst for knowledge and her aptitude for humanist ideas. She was first drawn to mathematics and then to astrology, but it was philosophy that sparked her passion. After her husband died only eighteen months into their marriage, Cereta threw herself into her studies.

Cereta was not content to learn alone. She visited nearby convents for intellectual discussions and participated in one of the many groups of scholars that flourished during the period. She also began corresponding with many of the great thinkers of her day. Cereta wrote in traditional humanist forms—letters, orations, and invectives. In 1488, she edited her letters, *Epistolae familiares*. The manuscript circulated among scholars, but it was not published until the mid-seventeenth century.

Although she had supporters among many well-regarded humanists of the period, others scorned her intellectual achievements. One male correspondent wondered whether she had copied her ideas from other books, and others asserted that her father had written her letters. Initially she did not respond to the rumors but later retorted, "What have I done [that you should] vomit forth muddy opinions from the bilgewater of envy?"[1] She was infuriated by their disrespect, "Full of their mockery of me, these men did not hesitate to dishonor me with their spittle, while I was hard-pressed by my wounds"[2]

Laura Cereta did not view her achievements as exceptional. She believed that she exemplified the intellectual capabilities of all women, and her life and works reiterate the importance of encouraging female scholars. In one of her letters, she refers to a "republic of women" who have persisted in their love of literature over the centuries and to which she pertained.

Laura Cereta could not fully participate in fifteenth-century humanism because of her sex. Both men and women distrusted and felt threatened by her abilities. However, she dedicated her life to the pursuit of academic excellence and demonstrates the powerful influence of humanist thought on women. She died suddenly of unknown causes at age thirty.

---

[1] Albert Rabil, Jr., *Laura Cereta: Quattrocento Humanist* (Binghamton, NY: Medieval and Renaissance Texts and Studies, 1981), 13.

[2] Laura Cereta, *Collected Letters of a Renaissance Feminist*, transcr., trans., and ed. Diana Robin (Chicago: University of Chicago Press, 1997), 39.

Sources: Albert Rabil, Jr., *Laura Cereta: Quattrocento Humanist* (Binghamton, NY: Medieval and Renaissance Texts and Studies, 1981); and Laura Cereta, *Collected Letters of a Renaissance Feminist*, transcribed, translated, and edited by Diana Robin (Chicago: University of Chicago Press, 1997).

me three schillings per year for every boy that she teaches, because my own income has been diminished, and that she give this to me without stalling or objections." His request was granted.[67] The message was clear; women could be good teachers, but only as long as they did not compete with men.

As a result, girls' educations reflected traditional gender expectations. They learned how to read in the vernacular, mainly religious texts, and spent the rest of their education improving their domestic skills, including sewing, embroidery, and cooking. Of course, for the late medieval peasantry, education remained almost entirely unavailable regardless of gender.

Humanists expanded the discussion over the nature and place of women in European society in an ongoing literary debate known as the *querelle des femmes*. Giovanni Boccaccio provoked considerable controversy when he attempted to depict the achievements of women in his *Concerning Famous Women* (1380). In this work, Boccaccio detailed the lives of 106 exemplary women from the Bible to his own time. However, his biographies put forward contradictory expectations for female behavior. On the one hand, Boccaccio described all the women as active and productive; on the other hand, he used the biographies to promote traditional female virtues such as chastity, silence, and obedience. Although he found women to be strong and capable, he also believed that nontraditional female behavior was extraordinary and miraculous, and therefore impossible for other women to emulate.

The debate intensified in response to seventeen thousand new verses that the poet Jean de Meun (ca. 1240–1305) had added to a famous but incomplete thirteenth-century poem, *The Romance of the Rose*. Some later readers, including the humanist author Christine de Pizan (1365–1430), were shocked by Meun's disparaging comments about women and the way he encouraged sexual promiscuity despite the fact that it would ruin women's reputations. Born in Italy, Christine was raised in France, where her father was the court astrologer to King Charles V (r. 1364–1380). She received an excellent education and while still young, she married a notary who encouraged her to continue her studies.

When he died only a few years into their marriage, the support of their three children, a niece, and her elderly mother fell to Christine. At age twenty-five, she embarked on a literary career that eventually returned her to the French court where she wrote poetry and published thirty books, including the official biography of King Charles V and the only contemporary account of Joan of Arc.

In her initial forays into the *querelle des femmes*, Christine vigorously defended women against the misogynist ideas of Meun, whose additions to the *Romance* constructed love as sexual conquest and denied female virtues. In both her correspondence and her famous work, *The Book of the City of Ladies* (1405), a response to Boccaccio's *Concerning Famous Women*, Christine asserted that all women were not sinful nor should they be blamed for falling for men's deceptions. Countering the charges of female weakness, Christine elaborated on the virtues of women throughout history, carefully noting when women proved to be superior to men. In particular, she praised women's intellect and criticized men who discounted women's knowledge:

> *Now you can recognize the massive ingratitude of the men who say such things; they are like people who live off the goods of others without knowing their source and without thanking anyone. You can also clearly see how God, who does nothing without a reason, wished to show men that he does not despise the feminine sex nor their own, because it so pleased Him to place such great understanding in women's brains that they are intelligent enough not only to learn and retain the sciences, but also to discover new sciences themselves, indeed sciences of such great utility and profit for the world that nothing has been more necessary.* (Book of the City of Ladies, *I. 37.1*)

However, Christine did not promote broader social change. Her next work, *The Treasure of the City of Ladies* (1405), reaffirmed women's subordination to men and the rigid class structure of her time. Despite the traditional nature of some of her ideas, her contribution to the *querelle des femmes* was critical. It was the first intervention by a woman and provided the foundation for an ongoing debate on the nature of women among early modern intellectuals of both genders.

Women as Patrons and Producers of Renaissance Art and Literature

The Renaissance has become best known for its remarkable flourishing of the arts. While men from Michelangelo (1475–1564) to Lorenzo de Medici (1449–1492) have become household names, scholars have learned that women played a much more extensive role in both the patronage and creation of Renaissance art than we previously understood.

Since the early Middle Ages, secular and religious authorities had encouraged women's patronage of the arts. As we saw in Chapter 5, queens and other elite women expressed their piety or pursued their spiritual goals by founding, building, and decorating convents, monasteries, churches, and chapels. They commissioned family tombs and altarpieces as well as statues and paintings of favorite saints. During the Italian Renaissance, art patronage continued to be a socially condoned outlet for women—one that promoted family interests, provided a focus for one's piety, and allowed a woman to express her particular taste or point of view.

The wealthiest of Renaissance women commissioned art to improve and expand family estates. As a woman decorated her palaces, her aesthetic decisions reflected the family's wealth, power, and influence. For instance, at her father's death in 1495, Donna Agnesina Badoer took over completion of the Badoer family chapel in Venice. The chapel was highly visible and an important sign of the Badoer family's status. His will directed her to spare no expense. She dutifully undertook the task, but in carrying out his wishes, she made a number of alterations to his original plan that reflected both her own artistic ideas as well as her family's changing needs.[68]

Most elite women became active in art patronage only after they had raised their children or were widowed. Without children, they had more time to pursue their artistic interests, and without husbands, they gained access to the financial resources necessary for commissioning works of art, as did Caterina Piccolomini, the sister of Pope Pius II (r. 1458–1464). As a widow, she had her Palazzo delle Papesse in Siena strategically built to aid her family's political ambitions.[69]

Probably the most famous female patron of the period was Isabella d'Este (1474–1539). Her parents, Ercole d'Este (1431–1505), the ruler of Ferrara, and Eleanora of Aragon (1431–1457), an active patron in her own right, gave Isabella the best humanist education available. When in 1490 she married Francesco Gonzaga (1466–1519) and became the marchesa of Mantua, she created Italy's most active artistic court and was a patron

ISABELLA D'ESTE (1499). Women were great patrons of art during the Renaissance. Isabella d'Este brought Europe's best musicians, artists, and writers to her court in Mantua. Her power and influence was immortalized in this sketch by Leonardo da Vinci. *(Louvre, Paris, France/Scala/Art Resource, NY.)*

of some of the period's most famous painters, including Leonardo da Vinci (1452–1519) and Raphael (1483–1520).

We have considerable insight into Isabella's relationships with artists through her correspondence. She was not shy about expressing her own ideas about the content of many of the paintings that she commissioned. When she contracted Perugino (ca. 1445–1523) to paint *Battle of Love and Chastity* (1503), she sent a detailed sketch to the artist. However, her strong opinions sometimes conflicted with those of the artist. She asked Giovanni Bellini (c. 1430–1516) to paint a mythological scene for her, but although he did not want to lose the commission, he had no interest in the subject matter. In response, he delayed beginning the work, hinting to Isabella that another subject might be completed faster. Isabella finally conceded saying, "If Giovanni Bellini is as reluctant to paint his history as you say, we are content to leave the subject to him, provided that he paints some history or ancient fable." Bellini continued to delay and eventually convinced Isabella to accept a Nativity scene.[70]

Isabella's patronage extended beyond painting into other art forms, especially music. She brought two of the major composers of the period, Marchetto Cara (1470–1525) and Bartolommeo Tromboncino (1470–1535), to her court, and her own musical abilities were highly regarded. At Mantua, she brought the best instructors from all over Europe to give her lessons in voice, clavichord, lute, and viola da gamba. She made Mantua famous for its vibrant musical culture.[71]

A queen's ability to commission art could transform court culture. In one of the most vivid examples of cultural exchange, Sophia (Zoe) Paleologue, the niece of the last Byzantine emperor, was sent to Moscow to marry Ivan III (r. 1462–1505) of Russia in 1472. Educated in Rome, she brought many of the ideas of the Italian Renaissance to Russia. She attracted European artists and intellectuals to her court in Moscow, and her influence is evident in her husband's decision to rely on Italian architects and masons to rebuild the Kremlin walls.[72]

Art commissioned by women patrons often related to particularly female concerns such as childbirth, children, and family. This was clearly the case with Fina Buzzacarini (d. 1378), whose husband ruled Padua during the middle of the fourteenth century. Fina used her own wealth to commission the frescos in the baptistery of Padua and appears frequently in them. Her inclusion in the scene of Birth of the Baptist reveals her concern with the well-being of her own son, who was born late in their marriage.[73]

The wives of rulers were not the only women in financial and legal positions to commission works of art. Convents too had regular sources of income, which they invested in art that beautified their spaces and heightened their spiritual experiences. Rood screens (which separated the body of the church from the chancel where the high altar was situated), altarpieces, chapel paintings, stained glass, and statuary all manifested important aspects of their religious devotion. Sometimes their commissions also asserted their independence from local authorities. For instance, the abbess of San Pier Maggiore in Florence commissioned a painting from Jacopo di Cione (d. ca. 1398) of the coronation of the Virgin for the enthronement of a new bishop in Florence in 1370. In this work, Saint Peter, the patron saint of the convent, holds a model of the church, emphasizing the convent's submission to papal authority rather than to that of the new bishop.

Although only women of wealth and power could contract with Europe's great artists, bourgeois women patronized local artists and artisans. In parishes throughout Europe, the wives of artisans and local elites commissioned decorations for their parish churches. In 1457, Andrea, the wife of Barberino the tailor, commissioned a painted curtain depicting Tobias and the archangel Raphael from the Florentine artist Neri di Bicci (1419–1491).[74] Women's guilds and confraternities helped raise money for the rebuilding of decrepit parish churches and the purchase of new ornaments and furnishings. In these ways, ordinary women also influenced Renaissance culture.

Books connected women to both the world of art and the world of literature. Late medieval women were influential in the expanding world of book buying and printing, a practice that may have been reinforced by the many medieval paintings of the Virgin Mary surrounded by books or reading prior to giving birth. These portraits became quite common and made the association between books and women respectable. Late medieval women had a special relationship to books. Since both scholastics and humanists excluded women from public study, privately owned books were important for women's spiritual and intellectual nourishment, and as mothers, women were often the primary teachers of the next generation. Here again, medieval artwork encouraged women, as paintings of Saint Anne teaching the Virgin to read became commonplace. Books also connected generations of women. Wealthy women used medieval Books of Hours (prayer books) for both devotional and educational purposes, and it may

have been traditional for mothers to commission them as wedding gifts for daughters.[75]

As few women were trained in Latin, women played important roles in the development of vernacular translations. Noblewomen like Mahaut, the Countess of Artois, (1224–1288) used their wealth and access to literate culture to become avid book collectors. Mahaut ordered numerous manuscripts and commissioned Bibles in French and a variety of devotional texts between 1300 and 1360.[76] Margaret of Beaufort (1443–1509), the mother of the English king Henry VII, was an enthusiastic advocate of the early English book industry. She encouraged William Caxton (1422–1491) to translate and print the first English book, *The History of Troyes*, in 1476. Isabella d'Este was also an active book collector.

Before the advent of printing, books were available only to noblewomen. However, the invention of the movable type printing press in the mid-fifteenth century made books more widely available and affordable to women of all classes. Women also entered the printing trades, usually working alongside their fathers or husbands.

Although women regularly practiced and excelled at painting, sculpture, embroidery, and music, a woman rarely became famous as an artist in her own right. Since most women produced their artwork in workshops, their names do not appear on their pieces. For instance, although women completed nearly all of the elaborate embroidery work of the period, we do not know their names. Other women, like Paolo Uccello's (ca. 1396–1475) daughter Antonia, learned their skills from renowned fathers and husbands but were never credited with the final product. Both contemporaries and later scholars tended to ignore the women's contributions to the family workshop.

As had been true in the early and High Middle Ages, convents offered religious women excellent opportunities to hone their artistic skills. Religious women both created artwork and repaired or repainted older pieces in order to avoid interacting with men. Although scholars have dismissed many of these art pieces as imitative, others, like the drawings by a nun of the convent of Saint

FEMALE READER (CA. 1470). Women were both the subject of literary debates as well as the readers of literary works. This image from *Boccaccio's Concerning Famous Women* shows a woman deeply engaged in reading. The woman, Proba, a Roman who converted to Christianity, is one of only three women Boccaccio praised for her writing. *(Spencer Collection, The New York Public Library, New York/Art Resource, NY.)*

Walburga in Germany, have been praised for their originality. This anonymous nun drew some remarkably unconventional images of female saints and New Testament scenes.[77] Probably the most famous female artist of the period was not only a religious, but later became a saint. Caterina dei Vigri (1413–1463) was born to a wealthy Bolognese family. After she became a nun, she became famous for her skills in music, painting, and manuscript illumination. She went on to become abbess of her convent, and after her death, a cult formed around her after miracles were attributed to her. She was canonized in 1707. Music, of course, filled the cloisters of many convents, and nuns often composed their own religious hymns. The Dutch nun Christina Hospenthal, known as Suster Bertken (1426–1514), published two books, one of which includes the lyrics for eight songs.

During the Renaissance, the Italian republics regulated sexuality and women as a means to exert government control and limit the power of competing families. Even many humanists believed that restricting women's access to knowledge was an important means of maintaining femininity. However, women with great minds and or great wealth assertively defied such attempts at control. Through the flourishing of the arts that was centered on Italy, but reverberated throughout Europe, women expressed their piety, their identities, and their skills in a world dominated by men.

CONCLUSION

Women from many cultures and backgrounds took advantage of Europe's growing cities. Although they could not participate in city government nor attend universities, they profited from the commercial life of the city. Unfortunately, the city could also be dangerous for women. Poverty, disease, and violence threatened their lives and the lives of their loved ones. Nevertheless, women challenged traditional authority through mystical and heretical religious activity and expressed themselves through art patronage and literary debates. They created exciting opportunities despite the masculine nature of late medieval society.

NOTES

1. Martha C. Howell, "Citizenship and Gender: Women's Political Status in Northern Medieval Cities," in *Women and Power in the Middle Ages*, ed. Mary Erler and Maryanne Kowaleski (Athens, GA: University of Georgia Press, 1988), 41, 46.

2. Ruth Mazo Karras, "Sharing Wine, Women, and Song: Masculine Identity Formation in Medieval European Universities," in *Becoming Male in the Middle Ages*, ed. Jeffrey Cohen and Bonnie Wheeler (New York: Garland, 1997), 187–202.

3. Barbara Hanawalt, *Growing Up in Medieval London: The Experience of Childhood in History* (New York: Oxford University Press, 1993), 142–143.

4. Maryanne Kowaleski and Judith M. Bennett, "Crafts, Gilds, and Women in the Middle Ages: Fifty Years After Marian K. Dale," in *Sisters and Workers in the Middle Ages*, ed. Judith M. Bennett, Elizabeth A. Clark, Jean F. O'Barr, and B. Anne Vilen (Chicago: University of Chicago Press, 1989), 17–19.

5. Kay Reyerson, "Women in Business in Medieval Montpellier," in *Women and Work in Preindustrial Europe*, ed. Barbara Hanawalt (Bloomington: Indiana University Press, 1986), 121–122, 133–135.

6. Leah Otis, "Municipal Wet Nurses in Fifteenth-Century Montpellier," in *Women and Work in Preindustrial Europe*, 84, 89.

7. Merry E. Wiesner, *Working Women in Renaissance Germany* (New Brunswick, NJ: Rutgers University Press, 1986), 55–60.

8. Ruth Mazo Karras, *Common Women: Prostitution and Sexuality in Medieval England* (New York: Oxford University Press, 1996), 21–22, 33.

9. Monica Green, "Women's Medical Practice and Health Care in Medieval Europe," in *Sisters and Workers*, 47.

10. David Herlihy, *Opera Muliebra: Women and Work in Medieval Europe* (Philadelphia: Temple University Press, 1990), 133.

11. Carlo M. Cipolla, *Before the Industrial Revolution: European Society and Economy, 1000–1700*, 2nd ed. (New York: Norton, 1980), 90.

12. P. J. P. Goldberg, *Women, Work, and Life Cycle in a Medieval Economy: Women in York and Yorkshire, c. 1300–1520* (Oxford: Oxford University Press, 1992), 183.

13. Sharon Farmer, "Down and Out and Female in Thirteenth-Century Paris," *American Historical Review* 103:2 (April 1998), 368–369.

14. Susan Mosher Stuard, "To Town to Serve: Urban Domestic Slavery in Medieval Ragusa" in *Women and Work in Preindustrial Europe*, 44.

15. William D. Phillips, Jr. *Slavery from Roman Times to the Early Atlantic Trade* (Minneapolis: University of Minnesota Press, 1985), 158.

16. Ruth Pike "Sevillian Society in the Sixteenth Century: Slaves and Freedmen," *Hispanic American Historical Review* 47 (August 1967), 345–346, 357.

17. Debra Blumenthal, "Slaves Molt Fortes, Senyors Invalts: Sex, Lies, and Paternity Suits in Fifteenth-Century Spain," in *Women, Texts, and Authority in the Early Modern Spanish World*, ed. Marta V. Vicente and Luis R. Corteguera (Aldershot, England: Ashgate Press, 2003), 19.

18. Kenneth R. Stow, *Alienated Minority: The Jews of Medieval Latin Europe* (Cambridge: Harvard University Press, 1992), 6.

19. Judith R. Baskin, "Jewish Women in the Middle Ages," in *Jewish Women in Historical Perspective*, 2nd ed., ed. Judith R. Baskin (Detroit: Wayne State University Press, 1998), 109–110.

20. Renée Levine Melammed, "Sephardi Women in the Medieval and Early Modern Periods," in *Jewish Women in Historical Perspective,* 146, n. 69.

21. Baskin, 117.

22. Suzanne Bartlet, "Three Jewish Businesswomen in Thirteenth-Century Winchester," *Jewish Culture and History* 3:2 (Winter 2000): 46.

23. Melammed, 134.

24. David Nirenberg, *Communities of Violence: Persecution of Minorities in the Middle Ages* (Princeton: Princeton University Press, 1996), 140.

25. Nirenberg, 133, 136–137.

26. Mark D. Meyerson, *The Muslims of Valencia in the Age of Fernando and Isabel: Between Coexistence and Crusade* (Berkeley: University of California Press, 1991), 237, 248–251.

27. Nirenberg, 140–141.

28. Rosemary Horrox, ed., *The Black Death* (Manchester: Manchester University Press, 1994), 44.

29. Horrox, 82.

30. Horrox, 60, 250.

31. Robert S. Gottfried, *The Black Death: Natural and Human Disaster in Medieval Europe* (New York: The Free Press, 1983), 57.

32. Horrox, 130–133.

33. Horrox, 340.

34. Horrox, 87.

35. Horrox, 85.

36. Horrox, 52.

37. Christiane Klapisch-Zuber, "Demographic Decline and Household Structure: The Example of Prato, Late Fourteenth to Late Fifteenth Centuries," in *Women, Family, and Ritual in Renaissance Italy* (Chicago: University of Chicago Press, 1985), 28.

38. Mavis E. Mate, *Daughters, Wives, and Widows after the Black Death: Women in Sussex, 1350–1535* (Woodbridge, England: The Boydell Press, 1998), 49.

39. Horrox, 57.

40. Goldberg, 229ff.

41. Hanawalt, *Growing Up in Medieval London*, 96.

42. David Nicholas, *The Later Medieval City, 1300–1500* (London: Longman, 1997), 72.

43. Christiane Klapisch-Zuber, "Women Servants in Florence during the Fourteenth and Fifteenth Centuries," in *Women and Work in Preindustrial Europe*, 65.

44. Sandy Bardsley, "Women's Work Reconsidered: Gender and Wage Differentiation in Late Medieval England," *Past and Present* 165 (November 1999), 11–12.

45. Mate, 51.

46. Sylvia Federico, "The Imaginary Society: Women in 1381," *Journal of British Studies* 40 (April 2001), 167–168.

47. Jo Ann McNamara, *Sisters in Arms. Catholic Nuns Through Two Millennia* (Cambridge: Harvard University Press, 1996), 306–311.

48. McNamara, 314–315.

49. McNamara, 317–320.

50. Donald Weinstein and Rudolph M. Bell, *Saints and Society: The Two Worlds of Western Christendom, 1000–1700* (Chicago: University of Chicago Press, 1982), 220.

51. Caroline Walker Bynum, *Holy Feast and Holy Fast: The Religious Significance of Food to Medieval Women* (Berkeley: University of California Press, 1987), 121–122, 124

52. Weinstein and Bell, 234.

53. Kelly DeVries, "A Woman as Leader of Men: Joan of Arc's Military Career," in *Fresh Verdicts on Joan of Arc*, ed. Bonnie Wheeler and Charles T. Wood (New York: Garland, 1996), 5.

54. Shulamith Shahar, *Women in a Medieval Heretical Sect: Agnes and Huguette the Waldensians*, trans. Yael Lotan (Woodbridge, England: The Boydell Press, 2001), 40, 100, 109–110.

55. Shahar, 27–30.

56. Malcolm Barber, *The Cathar: Dualist Heretics in Languedoc in the High Middle Ages* (London: Pearson, 2000), 52.

57. Peter Biller, "Cathars and Material Women," in *Medieval Theology and the Natural Body*, ed. Peter Biller and A. J. Minnis (York: York Medieval Press, 1997), 103.

58. Shannon McSheffrey, *Gender and Heresy: Women and Men in Lollard Communities, 1420–1530* (Philadelphia: University of Pennsylvania Press, 1995).

59. John Klassen, "Women and Religious Reform in Late Medieval Bohemia," *Renaissance and Reformation* 5:4 (1981), 207.

60. Klassen, 213–214, 216.

61. Natalie Tomas, "Alfonsina Orsini de' Medici and the 'Problem' of a Female Ruler in Early Sixteenth-Century Florence," *Renaissance Studies* 14:1 (March 2000): 74.

62. Michael Rocke, *Forbidden Friendships: Homosexuality and Male Culture in Renaissance Florence* (Oxford: Oxford University Press, 1996).

63. Christiane Klapisch-Zuber, "Childhood in Tuscany," in *Women, Family, and Ritual,* 109.

64. Stanley Chojnacki, *Women and Men in Renaissance Venice: Twelve Essays on Patrician Society* (Baltimore: The Johns Hopkins University Press, 2000), 49–50.

65. Margaret L. King, *Women of the Renaissance* (Chicago: University of Chicago Press, 1991), 195–198.

66. Erika Uitz, *The Legend of Good Women: Medieval Women in Towns and Cities* (Mt. Kisco, NY: Moyer Bell, 1990), 97.

67. King, 170.

68. Catherine E. King, *Renaissance Women Patrons: Wives and Widows in Italy, c. 1300–1500* (Manchester: Manchester University Press, 1998), 54–57.

69. A. Lawrence Jenkins, "Caterina Piccolomini and the Palazzo delle Papesse in Siena," in *Beyond Isabella: Secular Women Patrons of Art in Renaissance Italy,* ed. Sheryl E. Reiss and David G. Wilkins (Kirksville, MO: Truman State University, 2001), 83.

70. Peter Burke, *The Italian Renaissance: Culture and Society in Italy* (Princeton: Princeton University Press, 1986), 108.

71. William F. Prizer, "Una "Virtu Molto Conveniente A Madonne": Isabella D'Este as a Musician," *The Journal of Musicology* 17:10 (Winter 1999): 23.

72. Natalia Pushkareva, *Women in Russian History from the Tenth to the Twentieth Century*, trans. Eve Levin (Armonk, NY: M. E. Sharpe, 1997), 27.

73. Benjamin G. Kohl, "Fina da Carrera, née Buzzacarini: Consort, Mother, and Patron of Art in Trecento Padua," in *Beyond Isabella*, 30.

74. Rosi Prieto Gilday, "The Women Patrons of Neri di Bicci," in *Beyond Isabella*, 54.

75. Susan Groag Bell, "Medieval Women Book Owners: Arbiters of Lay Piety and Ambassadors of Culture," in *Sisters and Workers*, 150–151.

76. Bell, 143, 150.

77. Jeffrey Hamburger, *Nuns as Artist: The Visual Culture of a Medieval Convent* (Berkeley: University of California Press, 1997), 10–16.

SUGGESTED READINGS

Bennett, Judith M. Elizabeth A. Clark, Jean F. O'Barr, and B. Anne Vilen, *Sisters and Workers in the Middle Ages*. Chicago: University of Chicago Press, 1989. A fine collection of research on the wide variety of activities that women participated in during the late Middle Ages.

Bynum, Caroline Walker. *Holy Feast and Holy Fast: The Religious Significance of Food to Medieval Women*. Berkeley: University of California Press, 1987. A transformative work on the relationships between late medieval women's spirituality and their bodies.

Mate, Mavis E. *Daughters, Wives, and Widows After the Black Death: Women in Sussex, 1350–1535*. Woodbridge, England: The Boydell Press, 1998. A detailed investigation of the social, economic, and political changes that Englishwomen experienced after the tragedy of the Black Death.

Nirenberg, David. *Communities of Violence: Persecution of Minorities in the Middle Ages.*

Princeton: Princeton University Press, 1996. Although not explicitly about gender, this examination of late medieval Spain includes extensive discussions of interactions between men and women.

Reis, Sheryl and David G. Wilkins. *Beyond Isabella: Secular Women Patrons of Art in Renaissance Italy*. Kirksville, MO: Truman State University Press, 2001.

Early Modern Europe, 1500–1700

Sofonisba Anguissola, Self Portrait at an Easel (ca. 1556). Anguissola's talents as a portrait painter won her international acclaim, despite the fact that many people believed that self-portraits compromised a woman's femininity. (Muzeum Zamek w Lancucie, Lancut, Poland/Erich Lessing/Art Resource, NY.)

Between 1500 and 1700, Europeans' understanding of the world was transformed. Protestant reformers successfully challenged the Catholic Church's monopoly on Christian belief, and the Catholic Church responded with its own program of reform. Women enthusiastically entered these religious conflicts, some joining new Protestant churches and others defending Catholic orthodoxy. However, both Protestant and Catholic leaders reaffirmed traditional beliefs about women's inferiority and attempted to constrain women's religious activities, forcing women to come up with new, innovative forms of religious participation. The religious turmoil led to anxiety about the state of society, and both Catholics and Protestants persecuted witches and non-Christians. Women were frequently the victims of these pressures for cultural homogeneity. Nevertheless, from queens to artisans' wives, women struggled for power against enemies of their countries and opponents of their sex. They eagerly ventured into new creative arenas and new lands, taking advantage of the unsettled nature of early modern life.

THE PROTESTANT REFORMATIONS

Despite the many unsuccessful attempts to reform the Catholic Church during the Middle Ages, the pressure for reform did not abate. At the beginning of the sixteenth century, Martin Luther's attacks on the Catholic Church found enthusiastic support across Europe, and other Protestant reformers quickly offered their own novel interpretations of the Christian theology (see Map 7.1). Many women were attracted to Protestant ideas and even risked their lives to support their faith; however, Protestant leaders continued to defend traditional gender roles and hierarchies, rejecting women's attempts to become leaders in their religious communities.

The Lutheran Reformation

Although many others had criticized Catholic doctrines and practices, Martin Luther (1483–1546), an Augustinian monk, formulated the most successful challenge to the power of the Catholic

Chapter 7 ❖ Chronology

1492	Defeat of Muslim Kingdom of Granada and Expulsion of Jews from Spain
1519	Martin Luther posts his ninety-five theses
1525	Caritas Pirckheimer defends her convent from assault by Lutherans
1534	King Henry VIII of England breaks with the papacy
	Anabaptists establish religious state in Münster
1535	Angela Merici founds the Order of St. Ursula
1541	Calvin reforms Geneva
1545–1563	The Council of Trent meets to define Orthodox Catholicism
1553	Mary Tudor becomes the first English queen since the formation of the monarchy
1559	Elizabeth I becomes head of the Church of England
1572	Thousands of Protestants killed in Saint Bartolomew's Day Massacre
1598	Henry IV of France issues the Edict of Nantes granting limited toleration to Protestants
1609	Moriscos expelled from Spain
1685	Revocation of the Edict of Nantes

Church. Angered by the church practice of granting *indulgences* for the remission of sins in purgatory, he came to believe that the institution of the Catholic Church stood in the way of Christian salvation. In 1517, hoping to spark a debate, Luther posted ninety-five theses that questioned both church doctrine and papal authority. The theses enraged church authorities and Luther fled into the protection of Frederick, the Duke of Saxony (r. 1486–1525). Luther was later declared a heretic and excommunicated.

Challenging Catholic doctrine, Luther asserted that God granted salvation through faith alone and that no amount of good works could alter one's relationship with God. He also denied the special authority of the clergy, instead declaring that Christians belonged to a "priesthood of all believers." He believed that Scripture contained everything necessary for individual salvation, and that Christians should learn to read and interpret Scripture on their own. Luther denied the value of

the sacraments not explicitly mentioned in Scripture and decreed that the intercession of saints, pilgrimages, relics, and miracles were useless. He also rejected monasticism and clerical celibacy.

Luther's views on women were complex. He believed that women were created by God and could be saved by faith alone. Thus, women, like men, no longer had to rely on the intervention of priests for their salvation. However, unlike Catholicism, Luther did not promote female models of spiritual power. Luther's God was not influenced by the Virgin Mary or supported by the work of female saints. Instead of the Virgin Mary, Luther extolled the virtues of Martha, the sister of Lazarus, who stayed in the kitchen, prepared the food, and oversaw the household. In fact, the image of woman as wife and mother dominated Luther's life and work. Soon after leaving the monastery, he married a former nun, Katherine von Bora (1499–1550), who eventually bore him nine children. He believed that men and women fulfilled God's will through

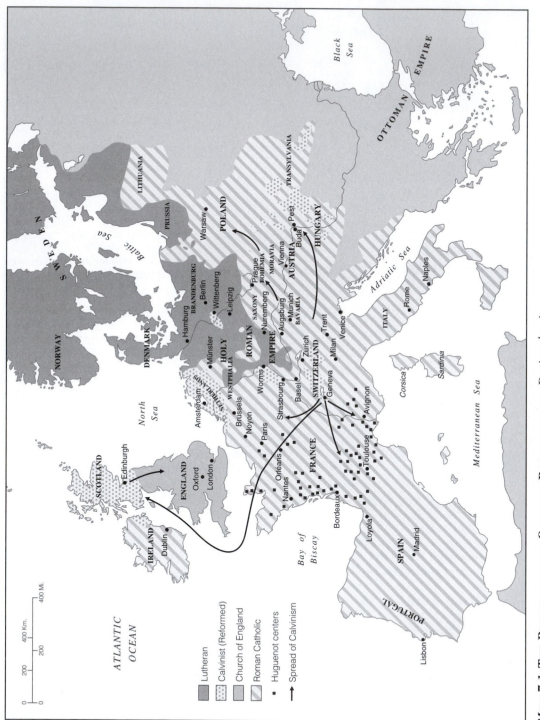

Map 7.1 **THE PROTESTANT AND CATHOLIC REFORMATIONS.** During the sixteenth century, Protestantism broke the religious monopoly of the Catholic Church in western Europe. Many women converted to the new faiths, although the majority of men and women remained Catholic.

marriage. The decision not to marry went against the natural sex drive, which he believed was greater in women than in men.

The conversions of monarchs and municipal authorities to Luther's ideas changed the lives of women in their jurisdictions. Every Protestant territory passed a marriage ordinance that stressed wifely obedience, and city officials established new courts to handle marriage and morals cases that had previously fallen under the jurisdiction of church courts. Luther's emphasis on reading Scripture led authorities to establish schools for both girls and boys. However, Luther opposed too much learning for women, saying, "There is no dress that suits a woman as badly as trying to become wise."[1] As a result, Lutheran education for girls focused on religious morality, not intellectual achievement, and often lagged far behind men's. Protestantism also affected female artisans and merchants in unanticipated ways. People bought fewer votive candles, which were often made and sold by women, and as people began to eat meat on Fridays, the demand for fish declined, cutting into the profits of female fishmongers.[2] Poor women also suffered as Luther dissolved Catholic charitable institutions.

When local authorities assumed control over convents and their property, they released nuns from their vows and usually offered them dowries so that they would marry. Women who had entered the convent unwillingly or who were attracted by Luther's message rejoiced at leaving their convents, thrilled to be freed from their vows. However, others who remained Catholic or wanted no other life resisted. Caritas Pirckheimer (1467–1532), the abbess of a Clarissen convent in Nuremberg, refused to comply with that city's demand that she release her nuns from their vows. The city pressured the nuns to leave voluntarily, but they refused. According to Pirckheimer, when family members entered the convent and tried to drag their daughters out, "The children cried out that they did not want to leave the pious, holy convent, that they were absolutely not in hell, but if they broke out of it they would descend into the abyss of hell."[3] In Strasbourg, nuns in three convents refused to leave, and the city's elite, who relied on the convents to educate their daughters until they were married, supported their resistance. In the end, the city allowed the convents to

remain open only as schools for girls. Even when the convents defied city laws by encouraging girls to become nuns, city magistrates did not close them.[4]

Beyond these pockets of resistance, many women displayed remarkable enthusiasm for the new faith; however, that enthusiasm threatened many men. City officials prohibited women from preaching and discouraged them from even gathering to discuss religion. Lutheran men silenced even their most prominent female supporters. Argula von Grumbach (1492–1563), a noblewoman from Bavaria, wrote open letters to the Duke of Bavaria and other officials protesting the treatment of Lutherans in Catholic territories, urging them to support the reformers, and arguing for open debate on religious issues in which women could participate. Her letters were printed and widely distributed, selling nearly thirty thousand copies in two years. She even met with both Martin Luther and a representative of the Holy Roman Emperor to press her case. However, Protestant men attacked her, not because they disagreed with her ideas, but because she was a woman. She received threats to wall her up, to break her fingers, and even to kill her. Her husband lost his job because of his failure to keep her under control. She eventually stopped writing but continued to support local Protestants.

Luther's reforms provoked a war between Lutheran and Catholic forces that devastated the continent for nearly forty years. Thousands died, and economic disruption and destruction was widespread. The violence only ended with the Peace of Augsburg (1555) in which the Lutheran princes and Charles V (r. 1519–1556), the Holy Roman Emperor, guaranteed a degree of religious toleration in the Empire. According to the settlement, the ruling prince would decide the religion of all the people in his territory. Subjects who disagreed with the ruler's faith would have to move elsewhere. As a result, some women followed family members or husbands into the new faith and new lands; for others, the adoption of Lutheranism by local authorities compelled them to convert.

Calvinist Discipline

Following on the heels of Martin Luther, John Calvin (1509–1564), a French humanist and legal scholar, became committed to church reform in his early twenties and converted to Protestant beliefs around 1533. In 1536, when he was only twenty-seven years old, Calvin published his major theological work, *The Institutes of the Christian Religion.* He had much in common with Luther; but, according to Calvin, God decided a person's fate before his or her birth and few would receive God's grace. Nevertheless, Calvin declared that Christians should try to please God at all times and make every effort to lead lives worthy of those few, the elect, who were predestined for salvation.

Calvin took his reformed ideas to Geneva (Switzerland) in 1536, but city officials rejected them as too radical. When new elections brought Calvin's supporters to power in 1541, he returned to establish a perfect Christian community based on strict discipline. The Consistory, a group of carefully chosen male citizens, enforced adherence to Calvin's theology. Laws forbade everything from decorative buttons to gossip, and the Consistory had jurisdiction over a wide variety of infractions, including blasphemy, divorce, marriage disputes, and the practice of Catholicism. It had the authority to excommunicate and even execute offenders, but more often it merely admonished Genevans to behave appropriately.

Like Luther, Calvin believed that both men and women were created in the image of God and had equal opportunity for both sin and salvation. But, unlike many reformers, Calvin insisted that both sexes were responsible for sin and evil, as both Adam and Eve had sinned in the Garden of Eden. However, Calvin clearly asserted the inferiority of women to men. He described women with the same misogynist stereotypes as Catholic theologians, stating, "Men are preferred to females in the human race. We know that God constituted man as the head and gave him a dignity and preeminence above that of the woman. . . . It is true that the image of God is imprinted on all; but still woman is inferior to man."[5] He promoted motherhood as women's true calling and made clear that women's inferiority began with Eve's creation. As a result, he denied women positions of authority in his church.

The Consistory adopted Calvin's views on women and particularly monitored women's lapses in faith. At first, the Consistory did not punish women more often or more harshly than men, although it regularly interrogated women about their attendance at church and their knowledge of prayers. However, after Calvin's death, the Consistory reverted to a pre-Reformation double standard, sentencing female adulterers to be whipped and/or banished while punishing men with only fines and excommunication.[6]

Reformed missionary efforts were remarkably successful. John Knox (1513–1572) spread reformed ideas across Scotland where Calvinist ministers worked alongside *kirks,* parish committees of lay male elders similar to the Consistory. The kirks punished an array of moral offenses, but they focused on extramarital sex. They fined people who had sex outside of marriage and forced them to appear in church on the "stool of penitence" for three successive Sundays. Adulterers had to face the same humiliation for twenty-six consecutive Sundays. Sometimes the kirk punished recently married couples because it was clear that the wife had become pregnant before the wedding.[7]

Calvinism attracted many converts in France, where members became known as Huguenots. Violent conflict between Huguenots and French Catholics culminated in the deaths of more than six thousand Huguenots during and after the Saint Bartholomew's Day Massacre in 1572. Calvinist narratives describe incredible violence directed at Huguenot women, including the murder of pregnant women and the desecration of female bodies. Women were the perpetrators as well as the victims of the violence. In one case, in the city of Aix-en-Provence, a group of Catholic women butchers harassed and eventually hanged a Protestant woman from a nearby tree. In reaction, Protestant women marched through the streets and rioted alongside their husbands.[8]

Huguenots suffered through years of civil war, eventually moving their families to Protestant strongholds created by the Edict of Nantes (1598). The Edict, issued by King Henry IV (r. 1589–1610), granted limited toleration of Calvinism. However, that toleration did not last long. Louis XIV (r. 1643–1715) revoked the Edict in 1685, forcing nearly a quarter of a million Huguenot women and their families to flee France for the safety of Germany, England, and North America.

Calvinism also spread to parts of the Netherlands, Germany, Poland, and Hungary, and Dutch traders took Calvinism to Indonesia where they converted native islanders from the Catholicism that the Portuguese brought. Most converts to Calvinism were members of Europe's growing middle class. By the end of the sixteenth century, it had become the largest Protestant denomination.

The Radical Reformation

Luther's belief that every Christian should read and interpret the Scriptures paved the way for many varieties of religious thought. The Anabaptists were among the most radical of the Reformation sects. The word *Anabaptist* comes from the Greek word meaning "to baptize again," and Anabaptists believed that only adults could make free choices about religious faith, baptism, and entry into the Christian community. They considered the idea of baptizing infants preposterous and wanted to rebaptize all adult believers. Anabaptists took the Gospels literally and favored a return to the kind of church that they believed had existed among the earliest Christians—a voluntary community of believers who had experienced an inner light.

Anabaptist communities developed in Switzerland, southern Germany, Moravia, the Baltics, and the Netherlands, but they never formed any overarching institutions or hierarchy. Indeed, women may have been attracted to Anabaptism because its lack of a formal hierarchy allowed some female leadership. At least in the early stages of the Anabaptist movement, numerous women chose Anabaptism over the objections of their spouses. Some divorced their unbelieving husbands and married other Anabaptists. Many women sought to convert others, and at least one fervent Anabaptist, Hilla Feicken, attempted to assassinate the Catholic bishop of Münster.[9] A number of women became Anabaptist prophets, and some Anabaptist communities even admitted women to the ministry. However, Anabaptist women did not enjoy leadership or clerical roles in the most infamous Anabaptist community, Münster, Germany.

Anabaptism's hold on Münster began with the migration of large numbers of followers from the Netherlands in the early 1530s. Led by the prophet Jan Matthys (d. 1534) and his loyal follower Jan Bockelszoon (d. 1535), the immigrants intended to make Münster into the New Jerusalem. They took over the city and created a utopian community. Anabaptist leaders outlawed private property and money, confiscated the property of Catholics, and began to stockpile food and clothing.

Once Matthys and Bockelszoon had established Anabaptism as the sole religion, it took a much less woman-friendly turn. They introduced polygyny in 1534, when the already-married Jan Bockelszoon wanted to marry Jan Matthys's widow to bolster his claim to the community's spiritual leadership. The authorities decreed that all women under a certain age must marry or face expulsion, justifying their decision through Biblical references to "be fruitful and multiply" and "to fill the earth with 144, 000." However, the male leadership also encouraged polygyny because women made up nearly 80 percent of the city's population. Although most early modern cities had a surplus of women, the demographic imbalance in Münster was especially severe after thousands of men fled during the Anabaptist takeover. They left their wives to look after family property, believing that the Anabaptists would be less likely to kill non-Anabaptist women. When the Anabaptists forced all the city's inhabitants to be rebaptized, the female majority could not flee and most probably did not convert to Anabaptism willingly. Polygynous marriages to Anabaptist men helped the city's leaders ensure that no women lived outside of male control. In fact, when some inhabitants rose up in opposition to polygny, the authorities fiercely crushed their movement, killing more than two hundred rebels. Women who opposed polygyny, including one of Jan Bockelszoon's many wives, were imprisoned or even executed.[10]

In addition, the city established a legal code that decreed the death penalty for insubordinate wives and forbade religious ecstasy and prophecy, both of which were associated with women. Münster's political-religious leadership even tried to deny Anabaptist women direct access to salvation and sanctity. They asserted that women were to their husbands as their husbands were to Christ and that they could only receive salvation through their husbands and then through Christ.

Anabaptist Münster only lasted for about a year. Catholic troops besieged the city and famine soon followed. Finally, in June 1535, a mercenary opened the city gates and, after bloody fighting, Bockelszoon and his supporters were captured, tortured, and executed.

Anabaptists in other communities often suffered persecution from both Protestants and Catholics. In Amsterdam, a small group of Anabaptists (seven men and five women) ran through the streets without clothes, proclaiming that the truth had to appear naked. They later stormed the city hall. In reaction, city authorities moved to repress the sect, executing seven Anabaptist women by drowning.[11] However, many less radical Anabaptist communities survived, and many members eventually emigrated to the Americas. These small, often isolated communities advocated pacifism, lived communally, and provided women with new forms of spiritual comfort.

Women and the Formation of the Anglican Church

In England, conflict between King Henry VIII (r. 1509–1547) and the papacy, rather than theological differences, led to religious change. Soon after Henry succeeded to the throne in 1509, he married Catherine of Aragón, the widow of his deceased elder brother, Arthur. However, she bore him only a daughter, Mary, and as a queen had not ruled England since the formation of the monarchy, Henry feared that without a male heir England would be plunged into civil war. Henry wanted his marriage to Catherine annulled so that he could marry Anne Boleyn (1507–1536), a beautiful young courtier just arrived from France. When Pope Clement VII (r. 1523–1534) denied Henry's request, Henry broke with the papacy and forced Parliament to make him the head of the English, or Anglican, Church. Anne and Henry were secretly married in 1533. Anne supported Protestant clergy and writers and discussed religious reform with members of the royal court. She may even have influenced Henry's decision to sever all ties with Rome in 1534.

Despite his break with the Catholic Church, the theology of the English Church was still essentially Catholic and Henry actively persecuted self-identified Protestants. In one of the most famous cases, Anne Askew (1521–1546), a well-educated

member of a gentry family, defied her husband and joined the reformed church. In 1545, authorities charged Anne with heresy for preaching in London. When she refused to recant, she was tortured and executed in 1546 at the age of twenty-five.

However, even women who remained faithful Catholics felt the impact of Henry's policies. In Exeter, when officials arrived to shut Saint Nicholas's Hospital as a part of Henry's dissolution of the monasteries, women appeared with pitchforks to run off the workmen dismantling the building. Many women also were angered when Henry closed England's convents. In doing so, he abolished Englishwomen's primary means to an education and removed any trace of female authority from the English church. Parliamentary legislation even limited women's access to the English Bible. Among the nobility and gentry, both men and women could read the Bible in private, but only men could read aloud to their families. Male merchants, but not their wives or daughters, could read Scripture in private. Lower-class men and women were prohibited from reading the Bible at all.[12]

Henry's marital life continued to affect England's political and religious situation. Disappointed that his relationship with Anne did not produce a male heir, Henry had her arrested, charged with adultery and treason, and beheaded. He then married another courtier, Jane Seymour, who died giving birth to Henry's only son, Edward, in 1537. Henry had three more wives before dying in 1547. His last wife, Catherine Parr, was also an enthusiastic Protestant.

Despite Henry's split with Rome, the monarchy only began to create a truly Protestant church in England during his son, Edward's, short reign (r. 1547–1553). As Edward was still a minor, England was governed by regents, first the Duke of Somerset and then the Duke of Northumberland, both Protestants. They instituted a Protestant liturgy, created the Anglican prayer book, the *Book of Common Prayer,* and forced Catholics into hiding. However, England's flirtation with Protestantism ended at Edward's death at the age of sixteen. When Mary (r. 1553–1558), Edward's half sister, succeeded him in 1553, she returned the country to Catholicism by force. She condemned almost three hundred Protestants, nearly 20 percent of whom were women, to death in heresy trials. Most of the female Protestant martyrs were married, poor, and steadfast in their advocacy of the new faith.[13] The wives of Anglican bishops and clergy also suffered. Mary required clergymen to reject their wives and be celibate.

The English Reformation ultimately succeeded during the reign of Edward's other half sister, Elizabeth I (r. 1558–1603), daughter of Anne Boleyn. In 1559, Parliament reinstated the Act of Supremacy, which made Elizabeth the Supreme Governor of the Church of England and the first female head of a Protestant church. Although she pursued and executed staunch Catholics and forbade Catholic services, she paced her reforms and the reinstitution of Protestantism so that England avoided the religious violence that plagued the continent. The Anglican liturgy was similar to the Catholic services, except that it was in English. Elizabeth even allowed her clergy to redefine the meaning of the Eucharist to suit her style of reform, taking a middle ground between Catholic and Protestant thought.

Some members of the Church of England believed that the church should undergo more intense reform than Elizabeth had allowed. They wanted the church to be purified. Their detractors often referred to them as Puritans, but they called themselves, "the godly." Puritanism was attractive to women because they were free to participate in the two critical aspects of the Puritan experience, the pursuit of a personal experience of God and the practice of godly behavior that reflected their standing as God's elect. They could also be spiritual advisors to both men and women.[14]

During the transition to Protestantism, many women continued to be active Catholics. Although *recusants*, those who refused to attend Protestant services and use the *Book of Common Prayer*, were a small percentage of the population, many were women. Recusant women continued Catholic practices at home, gave religious instruction to their children, and sent their daughters to convents on the Continent. Some recusant women harbored priests, despite the fact that such an act was punishable by death.

Women across Europe enthusiastically accepted Luther's call for Christians to read and interpret Scripture and Calvin's injunction to live a disciplined, Christian life. However, both men promoted traditional views of women. Anabaptism provided the most flexible gender expectations, but its lack of centralized authority led to both horrific abuses and widespread discrimination against its adherents. In England, religious instability challenged pious women of all beliefs. Although the new Protestant churches offered women alternative paths to salvation, men continued to control their public displays of faith.

THE CATHOLIC REFORMATION

The Catholic Church was not unaware of the problems that Luther highlighted. Indeed, attempts to reform the Catholic Church from within began long before Martin Luther. Among others, humanist theologian Desiderius Erasmus (1469–1536) criticized the clergy's ignorance, the luxurious lifestyles of the church hierarchy, ostentatious liturgies, and the superstitious beliefs of the masses. However, these critiques had little impact on Catholic institutions and clergy until 1545 when Pope Paul III (r. 1534–1549) called a church council to stop the spread of Protestantism and end abuses within the clergy. The council met on and off in the Italian city of Trent for nearly twenty years (1545–1563), dodging wars, plagues, and international politics. The decrees the Council of Trent issued clearly defined orthodoxy and presented a program of reform that came to be known as the Catholic or Counter Reformation.

Among its many decrees, the Council of Trent condemned Lutheran ideas, reasserted that both church tradition and Scripture formed the basis of church doctrine, and reiterated that both faith and good works were necessary for salvation. The decrees insisted on clerical celibacy and promoted the education and reform of the clergy at all levels by directing bishops to establish seminaries to train priests. The Council also attempted to end clerical corruption, reform the monastic orders, and strengthen the power of bishops. Finally, the Council encouraged the expansion of extended religious education for the laity and emphasized participation in the seven sacraments and the veneration of saints. As the Catholic Church attempted to clearly explain doctrine and behavioral expectations, and to ensure consistency of practice and beliefs, it expressed increased suspicions about women and worked hard to constrain female sexuality.

Laywomen and the Catholic Reformation

Laywomen were most affected by the church's regulation of the sacraments of baptism and marriage and its enforcement of prohibitions on extramarital sex. For centuries, midwives had baptized newborn babies who were in danger of dying; however, reforming bishops attempted to end that practice, urging parishioners to call the parish priest to the woman's bedside. If a priest was not available, the church preferred that a layman administer the sacrament. According to the reforms, a midwife was only supposed to administer baptism when no knowledgeable man was present. Bishops also increasingly required the examination of midwives to make certain that they understood the ritual and added no unorthodox words or ceremonies.

The church's emphasis on sexual morality led to renewed attempts to end clerical concubinage. At the time of the Reformation, many parish priests had concubines. These women often played critical roles in local religious activities, including acting as godmothers for parish children, helping administer last rites to the dying, and distributing charity to the needy. Bishops forced clergymen to remove their concubines and their children from their homes without making any provisions for their care. Both the priest and his concubine suffered. When a church official confronted a parish priest from Catalonia about his concubine, the priest replied, "that in conscience he could not do anything about it because he had lived with her for so long that to leave her now would destroy her."[15] As a result, some priests merely moved their female companions to nearby homes and continued their relationships in secret.

In a move that affected millions of Catholics, the church standardized marriage ceremonies. Prior to the Council of Trent, people relied on local customs and sexual mores when they decided to marry. Generally, families considered couples who promised marriage and had sexual intercourse married even if there were no witnesses. Although binding, these clandestine marriages often circumvented church prohibitions against marrying blood relations and frustrated family marriage strategies. According to the new decrees, a marriage was not legal until a priest had announced it three times from the pulpit of the parish church (a practice known as posting banns) and a clergyman had administered the nuptial blessing in front of witnesses. Women often benefited from the new procedures as they helped prevent bigamy and protected women from the unscrupulous behavior of men who promised marriage only to seduce them.

Church authorities hoped to end extramarital sex by shaming unmarried sexually-active women and their illegitimate children. The Council's decrees required parish priests to keep records of each child's birth that included the name and marital status of both parents. Priests and midwives were expected to pressure women to reveal the names of the fathers of their illegitimate children at the moment of the most intense labor pain. These decrees had little impact on fathers and did not take into account the circumstances of the sexual encounter, such as rape. Enforcement varied from parish to parish. In central areas and in large cities, efforts to end nonmarital sexual activity were quite successful, and in much of Europe, illegitimacy rates dropped to less than 2 percent. However, in many rural and peripheral areas of Europe, from northern Portugal to parts of Austria, illegitimacy rates remained high. The church even tried to control sex within marriage, by reiterating prohibitions against sexual activity during Advent and Lent and on a variety of holy days throughout the year.

The Catholic Reformation Church also attempted to make parish religious activity more uniform and solemn. Church officials rededicated many of the local shrines that women favored to more universally recognized venerations such as the Virgin Mary and the Holy Sacrament. As bishops made regular visits to parishes to ensure compliance with the decrees, they increasingly deemed local religious practices in which women played critical roles as "superstitious," such as the use of holy water for fertility rites. Bishops and priests carefully supervised local pilgrimages and festivals to prevent the sexual activity, drunkenness, and brawling that had become commonplace. For instance, in the bishopric of Speyer (Germany), ecclesiastical authorities were appalled to find that on Ash Wednesday, women controlled the village, chased after men, and drank heavily during the "women's carnival."[16] Despite their efforts, that festival, like many others across Europe, continued into the eighteenth century.

Church officials urged cities to close brothels and establish asylums, called Magdalene houses, to shelter repentant prostitutes. Some of these institutions were very strict. Female supervisors oversaw an exhausting regimen of work and prayer intended to prevent the women from returning to their immoral lives. In some Magdalene houses, the women learned Christian doctrine, lived by strict enclosure, and eventually professed as nuns. In Spain, in response to King Philip II's (1556–1598) request that she run a women's prison in Madrid, Madre Magdalena de San Jerónimo proposed a program of hard work, silence, and shaven heads. Madre Magdalena boasted that her regime to rehabilitate prostitutes was particularly harsh because it had been "invented by a woman against women."[17] Although these measures may have helped some women leave the streets, they did little to end prostitution.

Women and the Inquisitions

Ecclesiastical officials in southern Europe turned to the Inquisition to discipline Catholics who did not conform to the church's expectations. During the Middle Ages, the Inquisition was established by papal decree only when the authorities uncovered potential heretics and was disbanded as soon as the heresy was suppressed. However, during the early modern period, monarchs established permanent Inquisitions in the Spanish kingdoms, Portugal, and parts of Italy. The Inquisition in Castile was created in 1483 at the request of Queen Isabel (r. 1474–1504) to ensure that her kingdom's population of newly converted Jews and Muslims, known in Spain as *New Christians*, did not relapse to their old faiths. Over the next century, the Spanish monarchy established twenty-one Inquisitional tribunals across the peninsula and in Spanish territories in Europe and the Americas.

Because women made up only a minority of defendants who faced the Inquisition, for that reason alone, it must have been a particularly frightening experience. All the Inquisition officials, from its judges and jailers to its executioners, were male. In addition, the punishments often had a different impact on women than on men. For instance, for many crimes, Inquisitors sentenced the guilty person to be stripped naked to the waist and whipped as he or she rode a mule through the city streets. For men, such punishment may have been painful, but women also had to endure the humiliation of public nudity.

Old Christian women, those free of Muslim or Jewish blood, were most often accused of blasphemy for asserting that the virginity of Mary was impossible, that marriage was better than celibacy, or that it was better to be the concubine of a good man than to be married to a bad man. They were mostly illiterate and misinformed peasant women, who saw themselves as righteous Catholics and loyal believers, not heretics. Inquisitors reacted accordingly. Most of the guilty were forced to publicly recant and pay a fine.

The Spanish Inquisition rarely pursued witchcraft accusations. Prosecutions for crimes involving superstition and witchcraft accounted for only 7.9 percent of the total number of cases between 1540 and 1700.[18] However, some women were accused of both asking for and providing love magic. A woman who desired the attentions of a particular man sought out a healer who then gave her incantations and recipes for concoctions that would make the man love only her. In one incantation, the woman repeated, "I conjure you / blood from the crimson fountain—or my fountain—make [man's name] follow [woman's name] like the lamb after the sheep."[19] Other women looked to healers to help them end abuse, impotence, or adultery by their husbands. The church viewed love magic as dangerous because the incantations often used the names of saints and God blasphemously and because such magic infringed on the man's free will.

As early modern people did not really understand female homosexuality, few women were charged with having sex with other women. In one case, in the mid 1650s, community members denounced two women for their sexual activity to the Aragonese tribunal, and they were convicted, while in another case, the officials of the Inquisition in Madrid told the Saragossa tribunal not to prosecute two women since they had not used an artificial phallus.[20] In contrast, thousands of men were denounced to both the Spanish and Portuguese Inquisitions for having sex with other men. Inquisitors were more likely to convict and burn a foreigner, particularly a native of France, or a slave of sodomy than a Spaniard. Both accusers and Inquisitors associated sodomy with foreignness and religious heresy, especially Lutheranism. Sexual activity between slaves and freemen, especially black slaves, disrupted class and racial hierarchies.

The Permeable Cloister: Women Religious After Trent

Reiterating medieval papal decrees, the Council of Trent demanded that all female religious live in cloistered religious communities. Reformers pursued a two-pronged approach to enclosure: active enclosure, which completely prohibited nuns from leaving the cloister, as well as passive enclosure, which limited the access of outsiders to the convent. Bishops frequently wanted convent buildings altered to make them as impenetrable as possible. They ordered convent doors locked and garden walls constructed and instructed abbesses to guard the keys to doors and windows. If male visitors, such as confessors and doctors, had to enter the community, a trustworthy, often older nun had to accompany them. The abbess appointed a listener to monitor conversations between nuns and laypeople in the convent's visiting parlors. In Milan, officials attempted to prevent even accidental contact between nuns and the outside world by mandating that nuns could only take in washing if both the wearer and the washer were anonymous.[21]

Some communities willingly accepted enclosure and retreated from the world. However, across Europe, many convents obstinately resisted the reformers' demands. Convents refused to undertake the required alterations to their facilities and chased off clergy charged with enforcing enclosure. Frequently, they claimed that these demands ran counter to the customs and traditions of their communities and argued that their observance of monastic rules was already sufficiently rigorous.

Full enclosure also threatened the ability of convents to maintain their ties to their secular patrons and their economic interactions with local communities. As owners and administrators of nearby towns and lands, convent officers had to interact with municipal authorities on a regular basis, and many continued to do so despite the prohibitions. Because many nuns were supported by income from family property, convents continued to enter into litigation to protect their incomes. Thus, although enclosure changed the functioning of many Catholic Reformation convents, for others it never became a reality.

The Council of Trent also acted to end abuses in convents. Women had to be sixteen years old before taking final vows, and the Council reiterated previous decrees that prohibited families from forcing young women to profess. Finally, the church prohibited women from joining tertiary orders in which they took simple vows but lived outside of convents. As a result, one-third of the women in a Franciscan tertiary convent in Munich left rather than submit to full enclosure.[22]

Both the Inquisition and other church courts grew increasingly suspicious of female mystical activity. Church officials regularly accused female mystics of preaching, engaging in inappropriate relationships with confessors, and even faking their mystical ecstasies. To avoid suspicion, the Spanish abbess and reformer Teresa of Avila (1515–1582) counseled the nuns in her convent not to do anything to provoke religious raptures, such as fasting or not sleeping enough.

Despite the restrictions, many women believed in the goals of the Catholic Reformation. In her reform of the Carmelite Order, Teresa of Avila embraced the goals of the Catholic Reformation Church, emphasizing obedience and contemplation, while still meeting the spiritual needs of her nuns. She encouraged mental prayer, which many church officials feared would lead women into diabolical possession. Teresa argued that she and her nuns used their prayers as a weapon in the church's struggles. Even when her ideas led to conflicts with her opponents and investigations of heresy by the Inquisition, Teresa remained enthusiastically supportive of the reformers' goals.

A number of women attempted to fulfill the gender expectations of Catholic orthodoxy and work in the world at the same time. Angela Merici (ca. 1471–1540), founder of the Order of St. Ursula (the Ursulines) in 1535, established a community of pious laywomen who worked in orphanages and schools for abandoned girls and reformed prostitutes. Initially, the Ursulines effectively avoided enclosure, purposely dressing differently from nuns and living among those they served. However, despite their piety, Catholic Reformation clerics felt threatened by these independent, chaste women. After Merici's death, authorities gradually forced most members into the cloister.

English Catholic Mary Ward (1585–1645) encountered similar obstacles when trying to work outside the convent. Beginning in 1609, Ward established schools known as the "Institutes of the Blessed Virgin Mary" across the continent from the Netherlands to eastern Europe. Ward modeled her organization after the Jesuits, a monastic order founded in 1540 by the Spaniard Ignatius Loyola (1491–1556). He and his followers preached throughout Europe and the Spanish colonies and staffed the new seminaries designed to educate the Catholic clergy. Although Loyola did not allow women to join his order, Ward and her followers sought to emulate the Jesuits' great learning and strict Catholicism. In her schools (some of which were free and open to the poor), female lay teachers taught Latin, Greek, mathematics, religion, and the arts. However, her assertiveness and the success of the Institutes incurred the disapproval of the ecclesiastical authorities. Gossipmongers accused her of being sexually intimate with her Jesuit confessor and even of living disguised as a man in a Jesuit community. More dangerous yet, many clergy and powerful laymen believed that Ward and her followers were improperly usurping men's roles in the reassertion of Catholicism in England. In 1630, Pope Urban VIII suppressed the Institutes and Ward was denounced as a heretic for refusing to submit to enclosure.

Only Vincent de Paul's (1581–1660) Daughters of Charity successfully avoided enclosure. In 1633, he asked his friend Louise de Marillac (1591–1660) to help him train women to minister to the community. The women took private vows that each renewed annually. To prevent enclosure, De Paul never constructed any building to house the Daughters, so that nothing existed that church authorities might call a cloister. Backed by powerful, wealthy patrons, the Daughters ran hospitals, hospices, and insane asylums across northern France, and by the eighteenth century, they were France's premier nursing community.

In response to criticism from both Protestants and Catholics, the Catholic Church aggressively pursued its own reforms. Some women's lives changed substantially as ecclesiastical officials attempted to end nonmarital sexual activity, control marriage, and regulate life within the convent. However, not all women eagerly accepted the new restrictions. They challenged the church's reforms and found creative ways to fulfill their spiritual goals.

LIFE ON THE MARGINS: WITCHES, JEWS, AND MUSLIMS

The same religious enthusiasm that energized the Protestant and Catholic Reformations also produced fears about the presence of evil in Christian society. As a result of those fears, both faiths persecuted witches and non-Christians—people who were viewed as dangerous. The fight against evil and the pursuit of religious homogeneity had serious implications for women living on the margins of Christian society.

The Early Modern Witch-Hunts

Medieval and early modern Europeans believed in the constant presence of the supernatural in the world and in the ability of some people to access supernatural power. The clergy could access that power through the administration of the sacraments and through their access to certain objects, such as holy water, holy oils, and the Eucharist. Other people, including mystics, healers, and midwives (all occupations associated with women) could also call upon supernatural power through the use of magic. Good magic, like healing and divination, existed for everyone's benefit. Black magic (*maleficia*) caused harm. Although people might believe that witches existed and that some people practiced magic, no one identified himself or herself as a witch. People used "witch" as a slur against men and women whose magical abilities had become suspect.

Although local people made the initial accusations against witches, educated government and ecclesiastical officials controlled the judicial processes. Many of these men were influenced by a famous treatise on witch-hunting known as the *Malleus Malificarum* (1486), (*The Witches Hammer*), by two Dominican inquisitors, Heinrich Kramer and Jacob Sprenger. The *Malleus* emphasized the relationship between women and witchcraft and put forward the notion that some women who practiced magic had sex and made pacts with the devil. Witches supposedly danced naked with the devil, kissed his ass, and engaged in sexual relations with him.

Witchcraft trials had taken place in the Middle Ages, but witch-hunts (large-scale trials) were purely an early modern phenomenon. In addition to the general anxiety of the period, many scholars have attributed early modern witch-hunting to some key changes in the way that witchcraft was prosecuted. During the Middle Ages, the injured party accused a witch in public. If the accused confessed or if the accuser offered substantive proof, the judge would find the defendant guilty. If not, the judge would look to God to judge the accused through an ordeal, such as carrying a hot iron or placing a hand in boiling water. By the early modern period, most courts had adopted inquisitorial systems in which local authorities might also bring accusations. The judges and judicial systems then undertook investigations that included interrogations and witness depositions. Trials were no longer contests of right and wrong before God, but rather official procedures in which judges decided results based on the rules of law. The use of torture also changed witch trials. Although the Mediterranean Inquisitions required that any confession made under torture had to be repeated without torture, other judicial systems did not have that safeguard. Torture often elicited the names of supposed accomplices in addition to confessions, thus creating a witch-hunt from a single accusation. In England, the system was different, as torture was prohibited in witchcraft cases and juries of laymen decided the guilt or innocence of the accused.

WITCH GIVING RITUAL KISS TO THE DEVIL (1626). During the early modern period, elite ideas about witchcraft increasingly associated women with the devil. This image from Francesco Maria Guazzo's *Compendium Maleficarum,* an early modern witchcraft manual, vividly portrays contemporary connections between gender, sex, and the devil. *(The Granger Collection, New York.)*

Table 7.1

SEX OF ACCUSED WITCHES

Region	Years	Male	Female	% Female
Southwestern Germany	1562–1684	238	1,050	82
Bishopric of Basel	1571–1670	9	181	95
Franche-Comté	1559–1667	49	153	76
Geneva	1537–1662	74	240	76
Pays de Vaud	1581–1620	325	624	66
County of Namur (Belgium)	1509–1646	29	337	92
Luxembourg	1519–1623	130	417	76
City of Toul	1584–1623	14	53	79
Dept. of the Nord, France	1542–1679	54	232	81
Castile	1540–1685	132	324	71
Aragon	1600–1650	69	90	57
Venice	1550–1650	224	490	69
Finland	1520–1699	316	325	51
Estonia	1520–1729	116	77	40
Russia	1622–1700	93	43	32
Hungary	1520–1777	160	1,482	90
County of Essex, England	1560–1675	23	290	93
New England	1620–1725	75	267	78

Source: Brian P. Levack, *The Witch-Hunt in Early Modern Europe,* 2nd ed. (London: Longman, 1995), 134.

Between roughly 1450 and 1750, approximately one hundred thousand Europeans were tried for witchcraft. The enthusiasm for witch-hunting varied greatly across Europe. About half of the trials took place in the German lands of the Holy Roman Empire, and authorities in the adjacent lands of Poland, Switzerland, and France also conducted large numbers of trials. In contrast, the number of witch trials in Spain and Italy was much lower, probably no more than ten thousand. Across Europe, approximately forty thousand to sixty thousand people were executed as witches, although the rates of execution varied from 90 percent of those tried in the Pays de Vaud (France) to only about 12 percent in Iberia and Italy.[23]

The relationship between witchcraft and women was complex. Scholars consider it a sex-related but not a sex-specific crime, as women were the frequent, but not the only subjects of witchcraft accusations (see Table 7.1). In Denmark, Switzerland, and Hungary, women made up 90 percent or more of those accused. In contrast, in the Baltic nations of Finland, Estonia, and Russia more men were accused than women, and the same was true in the Spanish Kingdom of Aragón and in Iceland. Overall, women were more than 75 percent of those accused of witchcraft. The fact that officials hunted witches in both Catholic and Protestant regions of Europe indicates that adherents of both faiths shared similar ideas about witchcraft and witches and similar fears about women.[24]

It is difficult to create a profile of the typical witch, but certain women were more susceptible to charges of witchcraft than others. Neighbors sometimes denounced women healers and midwives as witches because of their knowledge of women's bodies and their presence at the death of mothers in childbirth and infants. Older women also regularly fell victim to witchcraft charges. Women older than age fifty, although not rare, were less common than they are today. These independent, sexually experienced women could be threatening to other community members. Moreover, women accused of witchcraft may have tended to be older because they had been healers or midwives for many decades, and tensions about their supposed powers had built up over the years.

Finally, the early modern women accused of witchcraft were often poor. Generally, they were not the poorest people in the community, but they lived on the margins of subsistence and had no families to help them. As a result, they often relied on charity for their survival. During economic crises, when these women begged for food from already impoverished neighbors, they provoked guilt and resentment. Women frequently accused other women, reminding us that both men and women believed that women were more likely to engage in witchcraft.

Another component of early modern witch-hunting was the prosecution of cases of demonic possession. Traditionally, people believed that those possessed by the devil could be "cured" by exorcism. In early modern society, women were most often considered possessed, and many believed that women were responsible for causing the devil to enter their bodies and that therefore they had to be punished. Cases of demonic possession often led to multiple accusations of witchcraft. In one of the most famous cases, seventeen Ursuline nuns in a convent at Loudon in southern France allegedly were possessed by demons. The witch trials in Salem, Massachusetts (1692), in which hundreds of people were accused of witchcraft, began with the accusation that two girls were possessed.

The role of sex was clearly evident in trial procedures. Judges frequently searched women's bodies for the devil's mark. Many judges believed that the devil branded his followers with a scar or that witches had an extra nipple. Accused women were stripped and shaved before being thoroughly searched. Although midwives or other women might be trusted to search for the mark, most of the humiliating and erotically charged inspections were done by male judges in front of all-male audiences. Additionally, as mentioned in the previous section, men often watched, touched, or hurt partially naked women during tortures and punishments.

Early modern witch-hunting met a rapid end. By the seventeenth century, as authorities relied more on empirical investigation, the numbers of witchcraft accusations quickly dwindled. As early as 1610–1614, after mass accusations led to a witch panic in Logroño in the Spanish Basque country, Inquisition officials in Madrid put a halt to the trials and investigations. The new Inquisitor used empirical study to prove that the ointments witches allegedly used were harmless and concluded that witchcraft had not taken place. Moreover, some European intellectuals had long expressed skepticism about the existence of witchcraft, asserting that it contradicted the belief in an all-powerful God. By 1700, witchcraft trials had almost entirely disappeared from western Europe, although they continued in Hungary and other parts of eastern Europe for another half century.

Expulsions and New Communities

Early modern Europeans not only feared the existence of witches in their communities, but also the presence of non-Christians. Early modern anti-Semitism was driven by a desire for religious homogeneity that had its roots in the Middle Ages. As a result, by the end of the late Middle Ages, monarchs had expelled Jews from much of northern Europe. Queen Isabel of Castile and her husband, Ferdinand of Aragón, ordered the expulsion of the remaining unconverted Jewish population of the Spanish kingdoms on March 31, 1492. Within six months, Spanish Jews had to accept baptism or leave the country.

Recent scholarship suggests that despite the edict only some of the Spanish kingdoms' eighty thousand Jews left Spain. Approximately ten thousand Jews left the Mediterranean coast in 1492 and 1493, and another thirty-five thousand spent some time in exile in neighboring Portugal and Navarre, where Judaism was still tolerated. To remain in Spain, Jews had to convert to Christianity. Many Jews sincerely converted and quickly assimilated into Christian culture. For those women, this meant altering the family's eating habits (for instance, by including pork), having their children baptized, and attending Mass on a regular basis. However, many women secretly adhered to Jewish tradition and became known as crypto-Jews. These women maintained Jewish culture by continuing to clean meat according to Jewish law. They also followed Sabbath traditions like wearing freshly laundered clothes and avoiding work.

Although the Inquisition had no jurisdiction over Jews who had not yet converted, it took a special interest in crypto-Jews. In fact, during the first fifty years of its existence, the majority of Inquisition cases dealt with recently converted Jews accused of relapsing to their Jewish faith. Female converts from Judaism, *conversas,* were regularly accused of cooking "Jewish" foods, trimming or washing meats according to Jewish law, and/or preparing clean clothing and linens for the Sabbath. Their Christian servants often denounced them. While many conversas confessed to their "crimes" in the hope of avoiding execution, at least one accused Judaizer, María López, argued that she had been falsely accused and that her suspicious laundry and food habits had been those of a conscientious, clean housewife, not those of a clandestine Jew.[25] She was convicted and handed over to the secular authorities for execution. Between 1480 and 1530, thousands of converted Jews were executed as heretics.

After their expulsion from Spain, many Jews fled to Portugal, where they eventually made up nearly a fifth of the Portuguese population. The Portuguese monarchy expected these immigrants to convert, but promised not to introduce the Inquisition for twenty years. When the Portuguese king finally established the Inquisition in 1536, thousands of New Christians fled the country.

As a result of these expulsions, during the sixteenth century the Netherlands became a major center of early modern Sephardic (from the Hebrew word for Spain, *Sepharad*) Jewish culture. Wealthy Sephardic families contributed to its rich, cosmopolitan culture. They built fabulous synagogues that attracted non-Jewish visitors, and patronized artists and musicians. The Duarte family, affluent Antwerp jewelers and diamond merchants, made their home into a center of music and the visual arts. Their daughter, Leonora Duarte (ca. 1610–1678), composed music, and the family was renowned for its musical abilities. Sephardic women benefited from their commu-

nity's economic and social success; they were twice as likely to be literate as their counterparts in the Christian community.[26]

After the expulsions, many Sephardic Jews, like Doña Gracia Mendes Nasi (1510–1569), were caught precariously between Christian and Jewish cultures. Born in Portugal to a recently converted family of Spanish emigrants, she was baptized Beatriz de Luna. She later married the son of a wealthy Spanish Jewish family, Francisco Mendes, who had also recently fled to Portugal. During their short marriage, the crypto-Jewish couple maintained connections with their Jewish heritage and other converso families. When Francisco died, he left Doña Gracia with a daughter and half of his extensive properties. She and her daughter then fled the Portuguese Inquisition for Antwerp, where her husband's family had a successful business in luxury goods. In Antwerp, Doña Gracia grew wealthy through the family business, using her money to aid conversos fleeing the Iberian Peninsula and to support the publication of works by Jewish scholars and rabbis. Her powerful social and business alliances included both Christians and Jews.

Despite her baptism, Doña Gracia continued to practice Judaism and was, therefore, a Christian heretic. To punish her, Holy Roman Emperor Charles V ordered the confiscation of the Mendes family records and assets, but Doña Gracia prevented the destruction of her financial empire by bribing the emperor with a substantial loan. She then dismantled the family business in Antwerp and moved her family and her wealth to the relative safety of Venice. In 1552, she and her daughter moved to Constantinople where they could practice Judaism openly. There, Doña Gracia became a leader in the Jewish community and a great philanthropist and businesswoman who was influential at the sultan's court. She even pressured Jewish shippers and traders to boycott the Italian port of Ancona after the Inquisition burned twenty-six of the city's Jews. Jewish and Ottoman leaders enforced the embargo, which only collapsed after the economic pressure on Ancona's Jewish community became too great. When Doña Gracia died in 1569, twenty thousand people attended her funeral.

While the Netherlands became the center of Sephardic Jewry, large numbers of central European

Jews emigrated to Poland, which became home to the largest Jewish community in the world at the time. The Jewish population grew from approximately one hundred thousand at the end of the sixteenth century to more than five hundred thousand by the middle of the eighteenth century. The Polish monarchy allowed Jews to freely practice their religion and engage in most occupations.

The End of Islam in Western Europe

Unlike the Jewish population, Europe's remaining Muslims were expelled entirely from western Europe. At the end of the fifteenth century, the only significant populations of Muslims lived in the Kingdom of Aragón, where they made up nearly one-third of the population, and in the Kingdom of Granada, the last Muslim stronghold in western Europe. In Aragón, most Muslims worked as farmers or peasants on large estates owned by Christians. When they lived in Christian cities, Muslims were forced to live in ghettos.

With the final destruction of the Muslim kingdom in 1492, Isabel and Ferdinand promised this large minority population a degree of religious toleration. However, under pressure to convert, Muslims in Granada revolted in 1499. After the revolt, the Spanish monarchs declared the treaty null and void, offering Muslims living in the Crown of Castile the choice of conversion or expulsion. Thousands left for North Africa, but many more converted, at least nominally. Many others just kept to themselves, remained loyal to their Islamic faith in private, and hoped to avoid confrontation with Christian officials.

In 1527, in an attempt to end an uprising of Muslim peasants, Charles V reached an agreement with Muslim authorities that the Inquisition would not be too rigorous in seeking out relapsers and that they could retain their own customs for the next forty years. During this transitional period, women were central to the Muslim community's resistance to Christianization. Without mosques, Arabic books, or official religious leaders, the home became the secret center of Islamic life. The fact that Muslims were forced to live in ghettos reinforced the ability of women to maintain Islamic culture in secret. Under the careful supervision of women, families could even continue to celebrate the Muslim holy month of Ramadan in the privacy of their homes, and newborns could be presented in traditional Muslim ceremonies before being taken to the church for baptism. *Moriscas*, Muslim women who had converted to Christianity, hid Arabic books and taught their children Islamic prayers. As a result, Moriscas were frequently denounced to the Inquisition for maintaining Islamic rituals, dietary laws, and fast days, and Christian clerics accused Moriscas of preventing their children from attending compulsory Christian schools.[27]

Not all Morisca resistance took place within the home. When the Morisco population in the mountains outside of Granada revolted in 1568, women armed with stones and roasting spits joined in the rebellion. However, the results were disastrous. Once the revolt was suppressed, the Spanish government dispersed the remaining population across the kingdom. Many were enslaved, and young children were removed from their families to ensure that they were raised as Christians. Finally, in April 1609, King Philip III (r. 1598–1621) decided in favor of the expulsion of the Moriscos. Forced to pay their own passage, authorities herded more than 275,000 Moriscos aboard waiting vessels that left under naval escort for North Africa. Without further research, we can only speculate on the impact of the expulsion on women. Mothers must have suffered as they were forced to leave their young children behind to be converted to Christianity. The expulsion also must have increased their economic stress, as few Moriscos were wealthy and many had to leave most of their belongings behind. Finally, Moriscas were no doubt critical in the establishment of new households in foreign lands.

As both Catholics and Protestants attempted to consolidate authority in their respective territories, they worked to purify their communities of people whom they saw as threatening. Thousands of poor and old women were victims of witch-hunts, and Jews and Muslims faced expulsion in the name of religious homogeneity. Gender played a central role in these events. Regardless of their beliefs or social status, suspicions about women's knowledge and their authority in the home made them particularly vulnerable to marginalization and persecution.

QUEENS, PATRONS, AND PETITIONERS

During the early modern period, many European kingdoms developed into strong, centralized monarchies, a process that has traditionally been viewed as the product of masculine accomplishments on the battlefield and at the negotiating table; however, in their formative periods, powerful female monarchs led many of these nations. Despite obstacles to their rule, these women ruled adeptly, molding gender ideologies to reinforce their authority. Behind the scenes, noblewomen used their resources and influence to support their families and beliefs. By the end of the seventeenth century, even savvy nonaristocratic women dared to enter the political arena and express their political opinions in public.

Unifying Queens

During the late Middle Ages and early modern period, women regularly ruled in Europe, as both queens and regents. They exercised power with authority, never shirking from diplomatic or military confrontation. Indeed, the fifteenth century began and ended with powerful queens successfully unifying large kingdoms and establishing new models for female rule. Margaret of Denmark (1353–1412) rose to power as regent for her son Olaf in 1375. As regent, she consolidated power by forcing the return of royal castles that had been taken by the Hanseatic League, an association of northern German merchants, and laid the groundwork for Olaf's expansion of Danish territory. However, Olaf died suddenly in 1387 and in a curious turn of events, the Danish nobility chose Margaret to succeed her childless son as "guardian" of the kingdom. Quickly, Margaret had the nobility declare her queen of Denmark and the following year she convinced the Norwegian nobles to elect her as their queen following the death of her husband, King Haakon VI (r. 1340–1380). She even won the support of the Swedish nobility who proclaimed her queen of Sweden in 1388. Margaret signed the Union of Kahlmar in 1397, uniting the three kingdoms under one rule. She chose her great-nephew, Erik of Pomerania (1382–1439), as the ruler of the three kingdoms, but she never gave up her guardianship of the thrones. She successfully fought off German incursions until her sudden death in 1412. The Scandinavian union that she created lasted until 1523.

Similarly, Isabel of Castile fought for the consolidation of her kingdom and set the stage for the eventual unification of the Spanish kingdoms under one monarch. Before becoming queen, Isabel and her supporters had to defeat Castile's stubborn nobility, many of whom supported her niece Juana as the legitimate heir to the throne. Isabel secretly arranged to marry Ferdinand, the prince and soon to be king of the neighboring Kingdom of Aragón. While each continued to rule separately in their respective kingdoms, the alliance helped solidify her own succession and Castile's defeat of the Muslim Kingdom of Granada. Isabel further expanded her power when she petitioned for the establishment of a permanent Inquisition. She made certain that it fell under royal, not papal jurisdiction. Isabel brought religious unity to the peninsula by defeating the Kingdom of Granada and expelling the Jewish population. She also strengthened royal authority by placing royal officials in each city and by creating a rural police force.

The Monstrous Regiment of Women

Despite these powerful late medieval precedents, most early modern political thinkers declared that women were unsuited to politics. In one of the most virulent attacks on female rule, in 1558 the Scottish Calvinist John Knox (1505–1572), faced with the rule of Mary Tudor in England, Mary Stuart (1542–1587) in Scotland, and Catherine de Médicis (1519–1589) in France, termed their rule "the monstrous regiment of women." Many thinkers fervently believed that men had to rule over women to maintain the order God created. Clerics, aristocrats, and intellectuals challenged women's right and ability to govern based on their sex. As a result, early modern queens either creatively employed different strategies to overcome opposition to their rule or suffered severe consequences.

Despite the fact that Henry VIII legitimized his daughters' successions in the 1544 Act of Succession, Elizabeth I had to transcend the expectations of her gender and act like a man without appearing manly, and therefore unnatural, in order to govern effectively. Hoping to prevent her enemies from marking her as weak because of her sex, Elizabeth I remained unmarried and childless despite the succession problems that dogged her reign. By remaining the "Virgin Queen," she de-emphasized her sexuality to such a degree that men could respect her as a monarch. Her strategy was largely successful. According to her advisor Robert Cecil, she became "more than a man and in truth somewhat less than a woman."[28]

In contrast, Mary, Queen of Scots fell victim to early modern gender expectations, as her enemies manipulated her through her lovers and husbands. Mary became queen of Scotland before she was a week old, but was reared in France and married the young king Francis II (r. 1559–1560). He died shortly after, but she did not return to Scotland to take the throne until she reached the age of majority in 1561. Although Catholic, she agreed to rule alongside her half brother's Protestant-led government that was in place when she arrived. She faced constant and strong opposition. Her detractors accused her of sexual promiscuity (a typical argument against women's ability to rule), charges that seemed to be confirmed by her many marriages and lovers. Her second husband, Lord Darnley, sided with the nobility against her and had her secretary (and rumored lover) murdered. Accusations of adultery, lust, and "unbridled licentiousness" plagued her. Eventually, Darnley was strangled and blown up in a Protestant plot in which Mary was implicated. She then eloped with the man who had murdered Darnley. Her decision to marry again, this time to a Protestant, caused a revolt by the Catholic nobility. They quickly defeated her armies and forced her to abdicate in favor of her son, who was crowned as James VI (r. 1567–1625) while still an infant. Mary then sought refuge at the court of Elizabeth I. Protestants unfavorably compared the thrice-married Mary to the virginal Elizabeth. When she arrived in England, Elizabeth had her seized and kept under house arrest. The English eventually charged her with conspiracy to assassinate Elizabeth. Elizabeth had Mary tried and executed for treason in 1587. Unlike Elizabeth I, Mary never found a way to move beyond the negative expectations of her sex.

Catherine de Médicis used a different strategy to maintain her authority, basing her rule on traditional expectations of motherhood. In the fourteenth century, the French monarchy invoked medieval Salic laws of inheritance to prevent women from succeeding to the throne; however, women like Catherine regularly ruled as regents for their minor sons. Catherine had little power during the reign of her husband and that of her first son, Francis II, but upon Francis's death in 1560, the government fell entirely into her hands. She ruled as regent for her second son, Charles IX, until he reached the age of majority in 1563, and she dominated him for the duration of his reign. Catherine exerted power in ways that Elizabeth could not. She presented herself as the pious widow, devoted to her late husband and the mother of future kings of France. She put motherhood at the heart of her queenship, making it the source of her power. When she brought peace or formed alliances, it was not as a ruler but as the mother of France. This strategy seems to have worked during her lifetime. In the earliest stages of the Catholic-Protestant conflict, she played the role of the peacemaker, encouraging Huguenot noblewomen to live at court and allowing them to worship as they pleased.[29] She continued to pursue peace, both at home and internationally, but religious partisans on both sides hindered her efforts. Although this emphasis on her femininity brought her power, it also left her vulnerable to attacks. After the plot to assassinate the Protestant leader Gaspar de Coligny (1519–1572) and the deaths of an estimated six thousand other Huguenots in the Saint Bartholomew's Day Massacre, both sides were eager to believe that she condoned if not initiated the violence. Her enemies turned her maternal identity upside down, describing her as a corrupt, unnatural mother who either dominated her children to further her own ambitions or a dangerous mother who put the good of her children over the needs of the state. Catherine's power declined after Charles died and her third son, Henry III (r. 1574–1589), succeeded to the throne.[30]

Other Avenues to Power

Royal women often exercised considerable power even when they did not rule directly. Their ability to affect the course of events through their influence and wealth is most evident as leaders and supporters of both sides in the French Wars of Religion. Well-educated and powerful noblewomen often supported Protestant forces using what historian Sharon Kettering has called "domestic patronage"—their access to economic resources and authority over family members—to support men with certain religious beliefs. Early on, church reformers found support at the French court from Marguerite of Navarre (1492–1549), the influential sister of the French king Francis I (r. 1515–1547). A humanist and author of *The Heptameron* (published in 1559), Marguerite carefully protected religious reformers at court, although she never converted to Protestantism. Madaleine Mailly (d. 1567) was one of the earliest French noblewomen to convert to Calvinism. In an attempt to influence royal policy, she arranged an early meeting between Calvinist pastors and Catherine de Médicis, and although she was imprisoned during the wars, she was influential in arranging the Edict of Amboise (1563) that ended the first of the Wars of Religion. Jeanne d'Albret (1528–1572), the daughter of Marguerite of Navarre, became an enthusiastic supporter of French Calvinism and converted her husband, the king of Navarre, to the faith. She pawned her jewels in 1569 to pay the expenses of a Huguenot army that reconquered the city of Béarn from the Catholics.[31]

Queen regents were frequently able to fulfill their duties without explicitly addressing the issue of gender. Although no Habsburg woman ruled on her own until the eighteenth century, Habsburg women regularly ruled on behalf of their male relatives in the Holy Roman Empire, parts of the Low Countries, and Spain. On four different occasions when the Holy Roman Emperor Charles V left Spain for the wars in Germany, he appointed his wife, Isabel of Portugal (1503–1559), as his regent. Later in his reign, he chose his sister María and his daughter Juana to watch over his Iberian possessions. His aunt, Margaret of Austria (1480–1530), acted as Charles's regent in the Low Countries from 1507 to 1530. At her death, Charles's sister, Mary of Hungary (1505–1558), replaced her and ruled until 1555. As representatives of the most powerful man in Europe, their authority faced few challenges.

Other Habsburg women influenced court politics from behind the scenes. Margaret of Austria (1584–1611) was not only the wife of the Spanish king Philip III and his second cousin, but also the sister of Ferdinand II, the Holy Roman Emperor (r. 1620–1637). She regularly wrote her relatives in central Europe to pressure them with specific demands that were favorable to her husband and to Spain. She also used her influence with Philip to negotiate aid for her brothers, Austrian archdukes who needed funding for their military exploits. Philip's aunt, the Empress María (1528–1603), was a daughter of Charles V and widow of the Holy Roman Emperor Maximilian II. Although she made her home in a Madrid convent, she actively engaged both Philip and his advisors in policy conversations. She acted as a conduit for information between the Spanish and the Austrian courts and promoted the interests of friends and relatives. Philip regularly came to her for political advice. Empress María's voluntary enclosure in the Carmelite convent in Madrid protected her from court gossip and intrigue, and unlike other courtiers, she could regularly speak with the king in complete privacy. Her reputation for piety actually allowed her to undertake political critique that was impossible for other women (and for many other men).[32]

One of the most unconventional examples of female power was Queen Christina of Sweden (1626–1689). Lutheran Sweden, a longtime bystander in Continental politics, came to international prominence during the Thirty Years' War (1618–1648) under the leadership of Christina's father, King Gustav II Adolf (1594–1632). The Thirty Years' War was a complex multinational conflict that highlighted Europe's long-standing political antagonisms and unresolved religious tensions. When Christina came to the throne in 1644 after a twelve-year regency, she was critical in ending the war with the Peace of Westphalia in 1648. However, after the war, she converted to Catholicism. As Swedish law forbade a Catholic from ruling, she abdicated the throne in 1654. Despite her status as a former monarch, Christina refused to submit to traditional gender expectations by either marrying or entering a convent.

Her rejection of the roles of queen, wife, and nun were controversial as was her decision to wear men's clothing while traveling and her well-documented romantic relationship with an Italian cardinal. Instead, Christina went to Rome where she became active in papal and international politics, urging war against the Turks and making unsuccessful attempts to seize the thrones of Naples and Poland. She was also a prominent patron of the arts and sciences. Even without a crown, Christina remained a powerful force in European politics.

Gender, Politics, and the English Civil War

Women also found opportunities for political action when political and religious strife struck England during the last half of the seventeenth century. Unlike other similar bodies in Europe, the English Parliament had acquired significant authority, and its willingness to use that power to limit royal power led to ongoing tensions with King Charles I (r. 1625–1649). Charles further antagonized Parliament with his Catholic sympathies. Despite the fact that he was the head of the Church of England, he married a Catholic and granted Catholics some freedom to practice their religion. Charles also persecuted Puritans, many of whom fled to North America. As the Parliament was overwhelmingly Protestant, these actions eventually provoked the English Civil War (1642– 1649).

Even before the outbreak of war, women attempted to employ the English political system to express their opinions. Although voting had been limited to upper-class men, in the 1640 election to Parliament, some upper-class women attempted to vote for Puritan candidates. Officials rejected their votes, not because it was illegal for them to vote, but they argued that women's support would dishonor the candidates.[33] Nevertheless, Englishwomen believed in their right to take political action, and women boldly asserted their right to petition the government for political change. In 1642, a number of Protestant women led by a brewer's wife named Ann Stagg petitioned Parliament to send troops to put down a Catholic rebellion in Ireland. The petition also called upon the House of Commons to expel the bishops and Catholic nobles from the House of Lords. The next day four hundred more

women and children appeared at the House of Commons demanding a response to the petition. Members of the House of Commons gave it serious consideration.

Once the English Civil War began, women used violence to support their side or to protect their homes and families. In 1643, a mob of women who shouted for peace in the Palace Yard responded to calls to disband by throwing stones.[34] Rumors that women were fighting among the soldiery were pervasive enough that Charles I felt compelled to issue a proclamation intended to prevent women from joining the army by punishing them for wearing men's clothing.[35]

During the Civil War, the majority of English-women remained Anglican or secretly Catholic; however, Protestant radicals split into a number of small sects. Women were particularly attracted to the new congregations. In overall numbers, members of these sects made up less than 5 percent of the population, but women outnumbered men in nearly all of them. These new congregations frequently met in women's homes, and during the early stages, female members frequently preached and prophesied. Mrs. Attaway, a lace maker in London, was a member of a Baptist congregation and held regular religious meetings. By 1645, women preached there regularly on Tuesday afternoons.[36] Many prominent female preachers were members of the Society of Friends, also known as the Quakers. Unlike many sects, Quakers did not preach but spoke when inspired, and they believed that godly inspiration was open to both men and women. Margaret Fell (1614–1702), a Quaker leader, wrote eloquently about women's right to preach. Historian Phyllis Mack has identified more than two hundred female Quaker visionaries, many of whose messages included political as well as religious ideas.[37]

As members of the Levellers, women explicitly connected Christian equality and political equality. The Levellers argued that all men were equal and that the government should be a secular state created by a contract between equal citizens with rights to vote, freedom of speech, and religious toleration. Leveller women took this emphasis on equality even further:

> *That since we are assured of our creation in the image of God, and of an interest in*

Christ, equal unto men, as also of a proportionable share in the Freedoms of this Commonwealth, we cannot but wonder and grieve that we should appear so despicable in your eyes, as to be thought unworthy to petition or represent our grievances to this honorable house. Have we not an equal interest with the men of this Nation in those liberties and securities, contained in the Petition of Right and other good Laws of the Land?

Asserting those rights, in 1649, they petitioned Parliament to release Leveller leaders from prison. However, they were brusquely rebuffed. Parliament refused to accept the petition, telling the women:

That matter you petition about, is of an higher concernment then you understand, that the House gave an answer to your Husbands, and therefore that you are desired to go home, and look after your owne businesse, and meddle with your housewifery.[38]

In the ongoing war between supporters of the king and those of Parliament, Parliamentary forces eventually prevailed. Led by Oliver Cromwell (1599–1658), Parliament tried and executed Charles I in 1649 and a Puritan Commonwealth replaced the monarchy. As head of this Puritan state, Cromwell also faced female critics. Anna Trapnel (fl. 1642–1660), a member of the millenarian Fifth Monarchist sect, was imprisoned for her political prophecies against Cromwell's regime. She was in a trance for ten months from October 1657 to August 1658, during which time she continued to criticize the government.

Cromwell created a state based on Puritan principles that prohibited ostentatious dress and public entertainments. Intolerant of dissent, the government subjected members of other Protestant sects, especially Quaker women, to harassment and imprisonment. Dissatisfaction with Cromwell's regime led to the restoration of the monarchy in 1660. However, religious differences continued to divide the Protestant Parliament from the Catholic kings Charles II (r. 1660–1685) and James II (r. 1685–1688). By

1688, to ensure Protestant rule, Parliament arranged for the succession of James II's eldest daughter, Mary (1662–1694), and her husband, William of Orange (1650–1702). When the couple died without an heir, Parliament chose another woman to rule, Anne, James II's other Protestant daughter (r. 1701–1714). By the end of the seventeenth century, female rule was no longer monstrous, but politically and religiously expedient.

At the end of the Middle Ages, queens were central to the creation of early modern nation states. Although many women came to power during the next two centuries, early modern intellectuals expressed deep suspicions about the abilities of women rulers. Indeed, early modern queens had to develop strategies to negotiate gender expectations. However, queenship was not the only means for women to exercise power. Noblewomen used patronage and familial connections to participate in politics, and by the end of the seventeenth century, Englishwomen asserted their rights through prophecy and petitions.

ART, LITERATURE, AND SCIENCE

Women's increased engagement in public discussions of religion and politics was complemented by their growing visibility in intellectual and scientific debates and the artistic world. A combination of increased literacy and the invention of the movable type printing press significantly increased their participation in discussions about sex and gender. Female artists became famous in their own right and created large bodies of work. However, women continued to be frustrated by their inability to be seen as equals by male writers, artists, and scientists.

Gender Theory and Reality in Early Modern Thought

The debate over the role of women in society, the *querelle des femmes,* that received so much attention from European intellectuals in the late Middle Ages, intensified during the early modern period. Writers from many backgrounds, some known, others anonymous, composed hundreds of texts on the subject of women. Much like their medieval predecessors, most male writers were unquestionably antifeminist, regularly referring to Eve's role in the temptation of Adam and asserting that women were inferior and by nature subordinate to men. Some of the most misogynist, presumably satirical, works questioned whether women were human beings at all.

Whether Catholic or Protestant, most of these male thinkers asserted that women needed to be carefully supervised, and they produced instructional manuals for women that clearly expressed gender expectations and described how women might fulfill those expectations. One such manual, Juan Luis Vives's *The Education of a Christian Woman* (1523), extolled the virtues of chastity, marriage, and subservience to one's husband. According to Vives, "Not only the tradition and institutions of our ancestors but all laws, human and divine, and nature itself, proclaim that a woman must be subject to a man and obey him."[39] Many male writers emphasized the importance of female honor based on virginity or chastity. Male honor was dependent on men's ability to ensure the chastity of their female relatives. Women who were not chaste not only threatened their own reputations but also dishonored their families. Although this emphasis on honor was generally associated with Catholic thinkers, conduct manuals by Protestant authors, such as the Swiss reformer Henry Bullinger (1504–1575), also emphasized the preservation of chastity. In fact, as far away as Russia, men voiced their concerns about female honor. During the sixteenth century, the *Domostroi*, a manual of household management, praised female obedience, submission, and the need to preserve female chastity. Elite Russian women were secluded in the women's quarters, the *terem*, to protect their virginity.[40]

However, even in the societies that produced works advocating the most rigid controls of women, such as Spain and Russia, the emphasis on female honor was not as inflexible as the prescriptive works would have us believe. For instance, in both societies, uxoricide (wife killing) was rare and women of all social classes could use the judicial system to help defend and even restore their honor. Moreover, class played a key role in determining the degree to which a woman was expected to conform to honor codes. Elite women no doubt faced great pressures to be chaste and submit to male control, while nonelite women may have had greater latitude in both their public and private activity.

Women had some male defenders. These intellectuals generally asserted that biological difference did not make women naturally inferior and that only the lack of opportunity (especially in terms of education) kept women from being the equals of men. One of the most important defenses of women was *Of the Nobilitie and excellencye of woman kynde* (1509) by Heinrich Agrippa von Nettesheim (1486–1538), a German humanist. In this work, which was reprinted many times and translated into numerous languages, he argued that Adam was responsible for the Fall, not Eve. According to Agrippa, women were not only equal to men in reason, but superior to men in many ways. He argued that women had the capacity to rule and that society controlled women through marriage laws and convents. Agrippa believed that men should not deny women full economic and political equality.

Women were also active defenders of their sex. Moderata da Fonte's (also known as Modesta dal Pozzo, 1555–1592) *The Worth of Women* (1600) is a conversation among seven women, each of whom proclaim their independence from men. One character, Cornelia, asserts the independence of women, saying, "Wouldn't it be possible for us just to banish these men from our lives, and escape their carping and jeering once and for all? Couldn't we live without them? Couldn't we earn our living and manage our affairs without help from them? Come on, let's wake up and claim back our freedom, and the honor and dignity that they have usurped from us for so long."[41] Fonte contrasts the natural superiority of women with the inferiority of men who are dangerous, unreliable, and liars. She praises singleness and condemns marriage for the way it subordinates women. Ironically, Fonte died giving birth to her fourth child, one day after finishing *The Worth of Women*.

Fonte was far from alone. Among some of the notable treatises in defense of women is that of the young Englishwoman Rachel Speght (1597–ca. 1630). At the age of twenty, she wrote a response to Joseph Swetnam's misogynist tract, *The*

Arraignment of Lewd, Idle, Froward and Unconstant Women (1615). Speght used biblical passages to argue that God had made women and men equal. In fact, in seventeenth-century England, defenses of women outnumbered anti-woman texts three to one.[42] Even fourteen-year-old Sarah Fyge Egerton felt driven to compose a compelling defense of her sex (see **Sources from the Past:** *Female Advocate, A Defense of Women* by Sarah Fyge Egerton).

The *querelle des femmes* intensified during the early modern period, presumably in response to women's increased public activity. Although many writers reaffirmed traditional gender expectations, not all intellectuals readily accepted assertions of female inferiority. Both men and women published passionate responses that promoted the intellectual, moral, and physical equality, and even superiority, of women.

Enlivening the Arts

As intellectuals debated the role of women in society, many successful and innovative female painters thrived. Giorgio Vasari's *Lives of the Painters* (1550) includes a number of women artists whose work was highly regarded. Of those female artists, Sofonisba Anguissola (1532–1625) was the most famous during her lifetime. The eldest of six daughters of an aristocratic family from Cremona, she studied informally with Michelangelo. Anguissola quickly became famous for the naturalness of her portraits and was invited to the court of the Spanish king Philip II to serve as a court painter. Like many female painters who followed in her footsteps, Anguissola excelled at portraying intimate moments. Vasari noted that her paintings were "truly alive and are wanting nothing save speech" (Vasari, *Lives of the Painters*, vol. 3).

While Anguissola worked in Spain, Lavinia Fontana's (1552–1614) artistic talents were being heralded in Bologna. Trained by her father, also a well-known artist and teacher, she supported her family with her paintings. In her father's studio, she met another painter, Gian Paolo Zappi, whom she married in 1577. Zappi appears to have given up his artistic career to assist his wife in her studio, handle the accounts of her numerous commissions, and help care for their eleven children. Fontana is remarkable for the variety of works that she produced. She became famed as a portraitist as well as for her biblical and mythological works. She was also commissioned to paint large public altarpieces, a rare distinction for a woman artist. After moving to Rome around 1603, she created the best known of her public commissions, the altarpiece for the pilgrimage church of San Paolo Fuori le Mura in Rome, *The Stoning of Saint Stephen Martyr*. Although scholars have documented over one hundred works by Fontana, only thirty-two signed and dated or datable works exist, and a smaller number of paintings are attributed to her on stylistic grounds. Nevertheless, hers is the largest surviving body of work by any woman artist active before 1700.

Women's personal experiences often informed their painting. For many scholars, Artemesia Gentileschi (1593–1653) epitomizes the close relationship between art and life. When she was refused admission to art academies because she was a woman, her father, Orazio Gentileschi (1563–1644), a well-known artist, arranged for her to study with a friend, Agostino Tassi (1578–1644). Her early works, like *Susanna and The Elders* (1610), communicate a decidedly feminine point of view. However, Gentileschi is best known for her scenes of graphic violence, especially her *Judith Decapitating Holofernes* (1620). Some feminist art historians assert that this and similar works reflect the violence to which Artemisia had been subjected. At age nineteen, Artemisia was allegedly raped by her instructor, Tassi. The seven-month trial that resulted was quite sensational and did more harm to Artemisia than to her assailant, who served only a brief prison sentence. One month after the trial, Gentileschi married and moved to Florence where she produced some of her finest paintings.

As still lifes and flower paintings grew popular during the seventeenth century, Dutch women like Clara Peeters (1594–ca. 1657), Maria van Oosterwyck (1630–1693), and Rachel Ruysch (1666–1750) found audiences for their talents. Peeters was one of the first painters to work in the genre, and all three women were important innovators in the field.

Despite these successes, female artists faced innumerable obstacles. They had to overcome the traditional male expectation that women could not create art, a perception that made it difficult

Female Advocate, A Defense of Women by Sarah Fyge Egerton

At the age of only fourteen, Sarah Fyge Egerton (1670—1723) wrote this response to the misogynist literature of late-seventeenth-century England. The poem was published without her consent, and her parents banished her to live with relatives in the countryside. She then revised the poem and had it reprinted a year later. Her second volume of poems, Poems on Several Occasions, *was published in 1703.*

Female Advocate or, an Answer to a Late Satyr Against the Pride, Lust and Inconstancy, &c. of Woman. Written by a Lady in Vindication of Her Sex (1686)

Blasphemous Wretch, thou who canst think
    or say
Some Curst or Banisht Fiend usurp't the
    way
When Eve was form'd; for then's deny'd by
    you
Gods Omniscience and Omnipresence too:
Without which Attributes he could not be,
The greatest and supremest Deity:
Nor can Heaven sleep, tho' it may mourn to
    fee
Degenerate Man utter Blasphemy.
When from dark Chaos Heav'n the World
    did make,
Made all things glorious it did undertake;
Then it in Eden's Garden freely plac'd
All things pleasant to the Sight or taste,
Fill'd it with Beasts & Birds, Trees hung
    with Fruit,
That might with man's Celestial Nature suit:
The world being made thus spacious and
    compleat,
Then Man was form'd, who seemed nobly
    great.

When Heaven survey'd the Works that it
    had done,
Saw Male and female, but found Man alone,
A barren Sex and insignificant;
So Heaven made Woman to supply the
    want,
And to make perfect what before was scant:
Then surely she a Noble Creature is,
Whom Heaven thus made to consummate
    all Bliss.
Though Man had been first, yet methinks
    She
In Nature should have the supremacy;
For Man was form'd out of dull senceless
    Earth;
But Woman she had a far nobler Birth:
For when the dust was purify'd by Heaven,
Made into Man, and Life unto it given,
Then the Almighty and All-wise God said,
That Woman of that Species should be
    made:
Which was no sooner said, but it was done,
'Cause 'twas not fit for Man to be alone.
Thus have I prov'd Woman's Creation good,
And not inferior, when right understood:
To that of Man's; for both one Maker had,
Which made all good; then how could Eve
    be bad?
But then you'll say, though she at first was
    pure,
Yet in that State she did not long endure.
'Tis true; but if her Fall's examin'd right,
We find most Men have banish'd Truth for
    spight:
Nor is she quite so guilty as some make;
For Adam did most of the Guilt partake:
For he from God's own Mouth had the
    Command;
But Woman she had it at second hand:
The Devil's Strength weak Women might
    deceive,
But Adam tempted only was by eve.
Eve had the strongest Tempter, and least
    Charge;
Man's knowing most, doth his Sin make
    most large.
But though Woman Man to Sin did lead?

Yet since her Seed hath bruis'd the serpent's
   Head:
Why should she be made a publick scorn,
Of whom the great Almighty God was born?
Surely to speak one slighting Word, must be
A kind of murmuring Impiety:
But still their greatest haters do prove such
Who formerly have loved them too much:
And from the proverb they are not exempt;
Too much Familiarity has bred contempt;
For they associate themselves with none,
But such whose Virtues like their own, are
   gone;
And with all those, and only those who be
Most boldly vers'd in their debauchery:
And as in Adam all Mankind did die,
They make all base for ones Immodesty;
Nay, make the name a kind of Magick Spell,
As if 'twould censure married Men to
   Hell. . . .

But if all Men should of your humor be
And should rob Hymen of his Deity,
They soon would find the Inconveniency.
Then hostile Spirits would be forc'd to
   Peace,
Because the World so slowly would increase.
They would be glad to keep their Men at
   home,
And each want more to attend his Throne;
Nay, should an English Prince resolve that he
would keep the number of of 's Nobility:
And this dull custom some few years
   maintin'd,
There would be none less than a Peer oth'
   land.
And I do fancy 'twould be pretty sport
To see a Kingdom cramb'd into a Court.
Sure a strange world, when one should
   nothing see,
unless a Baudy House or Nunnery.

Or should this Act ere pass, woman would
   fly
With unthought swiftness, to each Monastry
And in dark Caves secure her Chastity.
She only in a Marriage-Bed delights;
The very Name of Whore her Soul affrights.
And when that sacred Ceremony's gone,
Woman I am sure will chuse to live alone.

There's none can number all those vertuous
   Dames
Which chose cold death before their lovers
   flames.
The chast Lucretia whom proud Tarquin
   lov'd,
Her he slew, her chastity she prov'd.
But I've gone further than I need have done,
Since we have got examples nearer home.
Witness those Saxon Ladies who did fear
The loss of Honour when the Danes were
   here:
And cut their Lips and Noses that they
   might
Not pleasing seem, or give the Danes delight.
Thus having done what they could justly
   do,
At last they fell their sacrifices too.
Thus when curst Osbright courted Beon's
   wife,
She him refus'd with hazard of her life.
And some which I do know but will not
   name,
Have thus refus'd and hazarded the same.
I could say more, but History will tell
Many more things that do these excel.

Source: The Emory Women Writers Research Project:
http://chaucer.library.emory.edu/cgi-bin/sgml2html/
wwrp.pl?act=contents&f=%2Fdata%2Fwomen_writers%2F
data%2Fegerton.sgm

for women to find teachers and patrons. They also had to reject cultural norms about female modesty in order to use male models, to paint nudes, and even to paint self-portraits.

Women writers took advantage of increased literacy to express their opinions on particularly female concerns. Veronica Franco (1546–1591) was a Venetian courtesan, a highly paid prostitute, famed for both her beauty and her poetry. As a courtesan, she was free from the social constraints placed on respectable women. Well-educated and cultured, her relationships with powerful men provided her with the influence and finances necessary to edit anthologies and publish her poetry. She deeply believed in women's abilities and recognized their subordination by men. In response to a famous attack by another poet, Franco asserted that women's inequality was not natural but was due to a lack of education. "When we women too, have weapons and training, we will be able to prove to all men that we have hands and feet and hearts like yours." Using the weapons of language and poetry, Franco vowed to show her opponent, "how far the female sex excels your own."[43]

Maria de Zayas y Sotomayor (1590–ca. 1660) used her literary skills to attack the sexual double standard and violence against women in *The Disenchantments of Love* (1647). The disenchantments are ten stories told by guests to entertain a bride-to-be. The tales all include gruesome depictions of women tortured and/or murdered by men whom they loved or trusted. In addition to the violence against women that marks most of the stories, Zayas reveals her disdain for Spanish gender norms when, in the end, all the women who survive in the stories as well as the bride-to-be enter convents where they find safety and comfort away from men.

By the seventeenth century, women began to make their livings from writing. The English author Aphra Behn (ca. 1640–1689) began her career as a successful dramatist. Between 1670 and 1689, Behn had nineteen plays produced on the London stage. However, the use of her talents for profit did not stop her from expressing her views on politics and gender. Her play *The Rover, or the Banished Cavaliers* (1677) voiced her disappointment with the limited options available to women. Her female characters refused to consent to either life in a convent or arranged marriages. These were not merely literary images for Behn; she also served as a spy for the English king.

Women also became more prominent in early modern music as the result of both the Reformation and changes in musical aesthetics. As had been true for centuries, women expressed their religious piety through music. Protestant women including Katherine Zell (1497–1562), a prominent reformer, and the Norwegian noblewoman Inger of Austråt (fl. 1530) composed early Lutheran hymns.

The Catholic Church's desire to control convent life affected the composition and performance of convent music. Some church officials argued that nuns should refrain from polyphonic chant, fearing that such music "distracted [the nuns] from their ceremonial duties and spiritual exercises to which they are dedicated because of the dissolute rhythms they produce in sinuous voices."[44] More broadly, the decree on enclosure hindered nuns' ability to hear new compositions and receive instruction. Nevertheless, Isabella Leonarda (1620–1704), enclosed in an Ursuline convent in Novara, Italy, was amazingly prolific. She composed and published more than two hundred works and was the first woman to publish sonatas.

Dramatic changes also took place in secular music. Prior to the early modern period, vocal performances had been group performances, but during the sixteenth century, composer Giulio Caccini promoted what is often referred to as "the new music," based on solo performances. His daughter, Francesca Caccini (1587–ca. 1645), one of three musical sisters, was not only renowned for her performances of the new music, but she also composed and published dozens of secular and sacred pieces. Her most famous work, *La liberazione di Ruggiero dall'isola d'Alcina* (1625), was the first extant opera by a woman.

Female artists, writers, and musicians flourished during the early modern period. They defied the skeptics who denied their abilities and bravely displayed their passions on canvas, print, and in song. For the first time, people were reading, seeing, hearing, and even purchasing works by women. For a few special artists, it was truly a new age.

Behind Closed Doors: Women in Early Modern Science

During the seventeenth century, European intellectuals increasingly relied on empirical investigation in their attempts to understand the world. This scientific revolution transformed philosophy, biology, physics, and astronomy, yet women remained on the margins of these disciplines. Women were prohibited from earning university degrees or joining the growing number of scientific academies, yet they gained access to scientific study through other avenues. Some women used their noble status to learn from the great thinkers of their time. For example, Princess Elizabeth of Bohemia (1618–1680) corresponded extensively with French philosopher Rene Descartes (1595–1650), and Descartes' work, *The Passion of the Soul* (1649), resulted from her questions about the interactions between the soul and the body. Other women married scientists as a means to pursue scientific study, as did Elizabeth Koopman (1647–1693). Eager for a career in astronomy, she married the prominent German astronomer Johannes Hevelius (1611–1687) and served as his chief assistant.

No matter how they acquired their knowledge or how sophisticated their participation in the sciences, women found little respect among male scientists. When Maria Cunitz (1610–1664), who learned the skills that she used as an astronomer from her father, published her collection of astronomical tables, *Urania propitia*, in 1650, her husband had to deny that the work was actually his in the preface to later editions. Critics also accused her of neglecting her domestic duties by sleeping during the day so she could observe the stars at night.[45]

During the early modern period, the relationship between female and male medical practitioners began to change. Some historians assert that although female healers and midwives had provided most medieval medicine to women, professionally trained physicians gradually removed women from obstetrical care. However, recent scholarship presents a much more complicated picture of early modern medicine. Although male midwives increasingly attended births, especially in emergencies, in most parts of Europe, women continued to prefer female midwives to help during labor. Moreover, professional medical knowl-

Polish Astronomer Johannes Hevelius and Wife Elizabeth Koopman Working Together Using Their Large Brass Sextant (Danzig, 1673). The exclusion of women from university study made it difficult for them to engage in scientific experimentation. However, some women, like Elizabeth Koopman, found scientist husbands whom they worked alongside. *(The Granger Collection, New York.)*

edge and medical theory were not solely available to men, as is evident in the obstetrical treatises written by Louise Bourgeois (1563–1636), midwife to the French queen Marie de Médicis (1573–1642). Midwives' role in childbirth would not be supplanted for another century.[46]

During the early modern period, women vigorously defended their intellectual abilities as a part of the ongoing querelle des femmes. They also found new prominence as artists and writers. However, women continued to be limited in their ability to enter scientific professions. Few in the European intellectual community could comprehend that women might have the rational skills to undertake empirical investigation and analysis.

EUROPEAN EXPANSION

During the religious strife and political consolidation that swept the Continent, early modern Europeans expanded their wealth and power through overseas exploration and conquest. During the fifteenth century, the Portuguese headed east, slowly traversing the coast of Africa in the hope of finding a sea route to the rich kingdoms of the East. They set up colonies in Africa, India, China, and Southeast Asia. By 1492, Christopher Columbus had chosen a westward path to Asia and established permanent contact between Europeans and Native Americans. The consequences of the conquest of the Americas were disastrous. European disease rapidly killed off more than 90 percent of the native population, as Native Americans' immune systems proved unable to resist European diseases such as smallpox and typhus. In the Western Hemisphere, as native peoples from the Mississippi Valley to Peru died, the Spanish, French, Dutch, and Portuguese toppled powerful native empires, converted the survivors, and set up colonies (see Map 7.2). In Africa and Asia, the Portuguese became the great colonial power. Gender roles were critical in the creation of the European empires. From the beginning, European women traveled to these colonial outposts in search of wealth, spiritual fulfillment, or husbands. With them, they brought their religion, their cultures, and their capacity to produce European children. In contrast, native women bore the brunt of the conquest as victims of rape, enslavement, and cultural conquest.

Life on the Periphery: European Women and the Colonization of Asia and the Americas

Although the military conquest was largely a masculine effort, early modern Europeans believed that women were integral to successful colonization. Imperial authorities thought that women would tame the largely unsupervised soldiers and help to establish permanent European settlements. They feared that soldiers and settlers without wives would be unruly and their behavior could compromise the evangelization and "civilizing" processes.

European women arrived in the Americas on Columbus's third voyage to the Caribbean in 1498. Initially, the numbers of female settlers were small, but women traveled to conquer Mexico with Hernán Cortés (1485–1547). Five women were among the founders of the city of Puebla in 1531. Some were single female servants, but many were the wives and daughters of the conquistadores. Between 1598 and 1621, 42 percent of the immigrants to Peru and 32 percent of immigrants to Mexico were female.[47]

Across the Americas and Asia, the scarcity of European women, racial concerns, and individual ambition increased the value of European women in the colonies. They not only produced white children to populate the new colonies, but their dowries were essential to the establishment of colonial businesses. Moreover, the fact that single and widowed Iberian women could inherit, administer, and dispose of property without the intervention of men made the wealthiest women highly sought after. As a result, the colonial powers enacted policies to ensure a regular supply of European women overseas. The Portuguese crown set up a scheme to bring orphan girls and reformed prostitutes to its overseas possessions, and the French undertook a similar project in Quebec. Certain Portuguese orphan girls, living in government-sponsored shelters known as *Recolhimentos*, were chosen to move to the colonies. They had to be between the ages of twelve and thirty, and free of Jewish, Muslim, or African blood. In addition, authorities preferred girls whose fathers had died in service overseas. These "orphans of the king" were sent to both Brazil and to India in small batches and "rewarded" with dowries of minor posts in the imperial bureaucracy. Potential husbands petitioned for the posts and, upon marriage, accepted the jobs as the women's dowries. Once orphanages were set up in Goa (India), local Portuguese orphans were also included in the project. In Portuguese Sri Lanka and a few parts of Portuguese India, some women

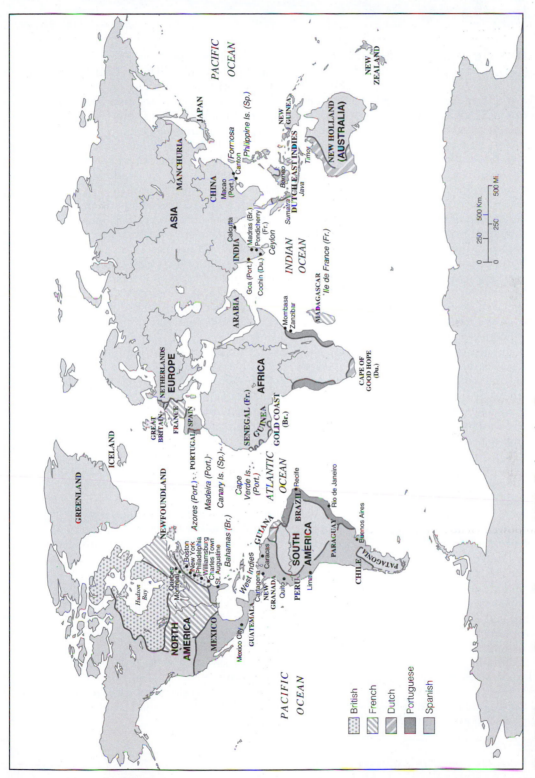

Map 7.2 **European Overseas Expansion, 1715.** Early modern European expansion has often been characterized as a male enterprise, but European women were central to the creation of colonies around the world.

Women's Lives

Catalina de Erauso, Soldier and Adventurer

As early modern explorers and conquerors opened up new continents to European settlement, they also created new possibilities for personal transformations. Catalina de Erauso was born to a well-to-do Basque family in 1592. At the age of four, her parents took her to the Dominican convent to be educated along with her two sisters. However, she hated the religious life, and at the age of fifteen, Catalina escaped from the convent. Erauso made her nun's habit into boy's clothing and cut her hair. She changed her name and began to live as a man.

After working as a boy page in a number of different households, Catalina traveled to the Americas where she could more easily escape detection. After crossing the Atlantic on a Spanish galleon as a cabin boy, she jumped ship at what is now Panama. Passing as a man, she worked for a merchant. Erauso then moved to Peru where she took the name Alfonso Ramírez de Guzmán.

During her stay, she attracted the attention of one of her employer's sisters-in-law. Erauso seems to have reciprocated her affections as, at one point, the two were caught in an intimate moment. However, she never engaged in a long-term relationship with a woman either for fear of being exposed or out of discomfort with her feelings for other women.

After killing a man in a brawl, Erauso joined a group of Spanish soldiers fighting the Araucanian Indians in Chile. Her bravery in battle won her the title of lieutenant. Remarkably, despite living among men in military camps, her secret was never revealed. Supposedly, as a youth, she had used a poultice to dry up her breasts and those who met her rarely noticed that she had no beard. How she dealt with menstruation remains a mystery. She was not discovered until after she killed her brother in a duel and was twice seriously injured in deadly brawls. Fearing death, she confessed her true sex to the bishop and allowed local women to examine her. They confirmed her femininity and her virginity. Upon hearing her story, church officials forced her to live in a convent for two and a half years until word came from Spain that she had not taken vows as a nun and therefore was free to leave.

When Erauso arrived back in Spain, she returned to men's clothing. She was arrested twice more, once in Madrid and again in Piedmont as a Spanish spy. In 1626, she returned to Madrid and requested a pension in reward for her service in the Americas from King Philip IV. In the petition, she explained how she had served as a soldier for his majesty in Peru as a man and her valiant efforts on his behalf. The Council of the Indies approved her request, granting her a pension of eight hundred escudos. Erauso then traveled to Rome, where Pope Urban VIII (r. 1623–1644) granted her a license to continue dressing as a man, despite biblical injunctions against cross-dressing. Sometime between 1626 and 1630, she either wrote or dictated a memoir of her life. She returned to the Americas, where she lived in Mexico as a muleskinner and merchant named Antonio de Erauso. She disappears from the historical record after 1645.

Although born female, Catalina de Erauso found success and independence living as a man. On the one hand, she transgressed gender norms, denying her biological sex for most of her adult life. On the other hand, as a man she accepted masculine notions of violence and power. Known in literature and folklore as the lieutenant nun, Catalina de Erauso was both a product of and a rebel against early modern society.

Sources: Mary Elizabeth Perry, "From Convent to Battlefield: Cross-dressing and Gendering the Self in the New World of Imperial Spain," in *Queer Iberia: Sexualities, Cultures, and Crossings from the Middle Ages to the Renaissance*, ed. Josiah Blackmore and Gregory S. Hutcheson (Durham: Duke University Press, 1999), pp. 394–419; and Catalina de Erauso, *Lieutenant Nun: Memoir of a Basque Transvestite in the New World*, trans. Michele Stepto and Gabriel Stepto (Boston: Beacon Press, 1996).

received their dowries in the form of land or taxes from villages to encourage settlement. In addition, Portuguese officials severely limited the establishment of convents in its Asian possessions. In a setting where white women's reproductive abilities were so valuable, government officials did not want any women taking vows of celibacy. The population of the convent of Santa Clara in Portuguese Macau (now China) was limited to thirty-three nuns, so that few women left the marriage market. Between 1550 and 1755, probably no more than one thousand orphans and reformed prostitutes left Lisbon to colonize the empire; however, the project offers a fascinating look into the use of women to pursue certain racial policies. The goal was always to have more whites in the territories and to perpetuate European culture. However, by the end of the seventeenth century, Portuguese authorities had decided that families were the best means of colonizing its territories. Portuguese women and their husbands traveled to places as diverse as Angola, São Tomé, Mozambique, Monomotapa (modern-day Zimbabwe), and the Maranhão in the interior of Brazil.[48]

The English also wanted more white women in their North American colonies. To make the colony more attractive to women, the first session of the Virginia legislative assembly in July 1619 granted husbands shares of land for their wives so that women could claim land in their own right. They also wrote to England requesting more women. In response, ninety single women arrived later that year. In 1620, authorities requested another hundred women to fill the need for wives among the colonists. Each woman cost 120 pounds of tobacco, six times the cost of a young male servant. Unfortunately, by 1625, three-quarters of these women had died of starvation or disease, and men outnumbered women in Virginia four to one.[49]

Life for white women in colonial possessions must have been difficult. They were far from their families. The customs and gender expectations of their home countries often pressured them to wear heavy clothes that were popular in Europe, but uncomfortable and unhygienic in the tropics. Husbands and fathers often restricted their movements to prevent them from interacting with indigenous men. For all but the most wealthy, the work was hard and the living conditions difficult.

Their husbands and fathers were frequently away on business or defending the settlements, leaving them in charge of large farmsteads and family businesses. In the Catholic colony of Maryland, Margaret Brent (1601–1671) owned thousands of acres of land, which she vigorously protected from mutinous soldiers and government criticism. In peripheral areas like Chile, Angola, and Canada, white women often had few social opportunities. No doubt, their sense of loneliness and isolation was heightened as their husbands entered into sexual relationships with local women and the growing numbers of African slaves in both North and South America.

In the anonymity of Europe's colonies, people could undergo striking transformations. Although thousands of men, women, and children were taken captive by native tribes during the colonial period, most were "redeemed" or, like Hannah Dustin (1657–1737), murdered their abductors and escaped. However, many women who were taken captive in colonial North America chose to remain among their captors. They adopted native dress, bore children to native men, and spoke native languages. They took native names and adopted the religion of the tribe. Their choices shocked their contemporaries, who saw their decisions not only as betrayals of Christian civilization, but also as transgressions of race and gender hierarchies.

A few people took the opportunity to redefine their sexual identities (see **Women's Lives: Catalina de Erauso, Soldier and Adventurer**). Virginia colonist Thomas Hall certainly took advantage of the colonial setting to remake him/herself in ways that confounded colonial officials. In 1629, Hall became the subject of rumors of sexual misconduct that prompted a local investigation. The investigators found that he had been christened Thomasine and raised as a girl, but at the age of twenty-four he had cut his hair, wore men's clothing, and became a soldier. After fighting in France, he resettled in England as a woman. In 1627, Hall returned to life as a man but occasionally wore women's clothing and performed traditional women's work. Hall crossed the Atlantic as a man, but once in Virginia he sometimes wore women's clothing. When asked whether he was a man or a woman, he replied that he was both. A group of women who examined his body concluded that he was a man, but the plantation commander overturned that decision and ordered Hall to wear women's clothing. Authorities never reached a clear conclusion on Hall's gender. The General Court in Virginia eventually sentenced him to wear men's clothing but also to wear an apron to mark him as a woman. In the colonies, gender and even sex could be difficult to unravel.[50]

Women and the Missionary Effort

The European colonies offered new religious opportunities and constraints for women. For example, female monastics in or close to major European settlements were carefully cloistered. Their mission was to pray for the success of the evangelization effort, to provide homes for white women with religious vocations or those who were unmarriageable, and to educate the daughters of colonists. The first convent in New Spain (Mexico) was founded in 1540. Although there were few Spanish women, colonists across the Americas wanted a convent in which to place mestizo (mixed-race) daughters produced by European men's relationships with native women. Nuns taught these girls European ways and protected their virginity until the time came for them to marry. Although in the early years of the conquest, convents eagerly sought out mixed-race students and boarders, as time passed convents often replicated colonial race and class hierarchies. In Spanish America, where women of color were forbidden to take final vows, a two-tiered system developed within many convents. European nuns wore black veils and held monastic offices, while women of color wore the white veil of the novice or lay sister and were not allowed to take final vows or hold offices. In wealthier convents, dozens of black, mixed-race, and native slaves served European white nuns. Many of these slaves were orphaned girls who had been raised in the convent but were not permitted to leave.

In contrast, the first convents were founded in Portuguese Brazil only in the last half of the seventeenth century, nearly two hundred years after the territory's settlement by Europeans. Until that time, European women were in short supply and those few who actively sought the religious life were sent to convents in Portugal. Only when European women were plentiful did the Crown allow for the foundation of the Destêrro Convent in Bahia in 1677. The Destêrro served an elite clientele of Brazil's wealthiest families, protecting and educating their daughters until marriage.

Nuns in peripheral areas brought Christianity and European culture to Native Americans. The French Ursuline convent in Quebec under the supervision of Mother Superior Marie de l'Incarnation (1599–1672) took in Algonquin, Huron, and Iroquois girls. In addition to teaching Christian doctrine and prayer, the sisters dressed their students in French clothing and taught them how to speak French, embroider, and paint. The sisters hoped that the girls would bring Catholicism and French customs to their families when they returned to their villages.[51]

Like Catholic women, the Puritan women who fled persecution in England for the shores of North America could neither evangelize to natives nor engage in any activity that might be construed as preaching to other members of their own communities. Nevertheless, carried away by religious enthusiasm, Anne Hutchinson (1591–1643) began informal prayer groups for Puritan women. When her preaching began to attract large audiences, Boston's clergy and magistrates rebuked her. They eventually excommunicated Hutchinson and banished her from Massachusetts. Quaker women met similar fates. Twenty-six female Quaker preachers journeyed from England between 1656 and 1663, among them Mary Dyer (ca. 1611–1660) who had returned to England and joined the Quakers after hearing Anne Hutchinson preach. In 1657, she returned to New England but was banished from Massachusetts. More than once, she defied the ban and returned to preach. Massachusetts magistrates sentenced her to death for her actions and then commuted her sentence to banishment, but she returned again to Boston. The governor of Massachusetts ordered her to be executed the next day.

Native Women in the Conquest of the Americas

While European women were critical to colonization and settlement, those processes took a heavy toll on native women, especially in the Americas. Thousands of women died, victims of murder and disease. Survivors faced the disruption and destruction of their families, homes, and cultures. Enslavement, rape, and abduction marked native women's experience of conquest.

As slaves or newly conquered peoples, native women frequently served as guides and interpreters for Europeans. Doña Marina (d. ca. 1530) has come to epitomize this interaction between native women and European men. Sold into slavery by her Maya kin, she was either given or sold to the Spanish conqueror Hernán Cortés soon after his arrival on the Mexican mainland in 1519. Upon taking possession of her, Cortés had her baptized and gave her the Christian name Marina. She proved to be a skilled linguist and interpreter whose proficiency included a special form of Nahuatl (the language of the Aztecs) only used in the presence of the emperor. As Cortés's translator during the conquest of the Aztec Empire, she was central to negotiations between Cortés and members of the Aztec Empire and eventually in the meetings between Cortés and the emperor

Doña Marina Translating for Hernan Cortés During His Meeting with the Aztec Ruler Moctezuma (ca. 1560). As Europeans explored and then conquered new lands, Native women often acted as cultural mediators. Whether willingly or by force, they provided European explorers with food, acted as guides, and even translated critical diplomatic moments. *(The Granger Collection, New York.)*

Moctezuma. She later gave birth to Cortes's son, Martín, and many consider her the mother of the mestizo race in Mexico, a title with both positive and negative connotations; she was also called La Malinche, a nativized version of Marina, which has come to mean "traitor."

Abduction was another way that European men controlled native women. Pocahontas (1595–1617), a famous native captive, first entered the historical record in 1607 in Captain John Smith's description of his capture by the Powhatan Indians in Virginia. Although much of Smith's narrative has come under scrutiny (curiously he is rescued on three different occasions by prepubescent native girls), it seems clear that his relationship with Pocahontas began her lifelong contact with the English. Beginning in 1608, Pocahontas (a nickname; her real name was Matoaka) made frequent trips to Jamestown, delivering messages from the Powhatan and arranging for the exchange of food and supplies.

In 1613, English settlers abducted her so that they could exchange her for English prisoners and weapons held by the Powhatan. While in captivity, she converted to Christianity, supposedly becoming the first native in Virginia to do so. In 1614, she married John Rolfe, a prominent settler, changed her name to Rebecca Rolfe, and bore a son. In 1616, Rebecca, her husband, their son, and several other Indian men and women traveled to England. The Indian woman captivated English royalty, and the publicity surrounding her visit sparked interest in the colonies. Sadly, onboard ship, Rebecca Rolfe became gravely ill and died far from her native land. She was buried in England.

Like many native women, Doña Marina and Pocahontas became chattel, taken from their families and exchanged among Europeans, for whom they became critical in the process of cultural exchange. They translated for European men and taught them native languages. They instructed the European men who controlled them about native plants, foods, and customs. Their captors and husbands renamed them, converted them to

Christianity, and introduced them to European ways. In the process, the women often lost much if not all of their cultural identity. In time, they no longer used natives words, ate native foods, wore native clothes, or practiced native religions.

Over the centuries, these women have faced considerable criticism from their own peoples. They have been accused of betraying their race and culture. From the European perspective, they were model women who acted as good Christian women, helping them conquer uncivilized peoples. Whatever the case, they are testaments to survival. They employed their strengths and skills to overcome the traumas of conquest, abduction, slavery, and rape.

Women continued to shape the European colonial experience. In eighteenth-century Latin America, women made up the majority of the population of most colonial Latin American cities. While military might and technological superiority were critical in the early stages of early modern European colonization, the ultimate success of those efforts relied on women's emotional, productive, and reproductive abilities. Through their persistence and determination, European and native women created new colonial cultures.

CONCLUSION

The religious turmoil of the early modern period turned women's lives upside down. Although Protestantism offered women new possibilities for salvation, it often did little to change their place in society. The Catholic Church reacted to the challenge of Protestantism with increased controls on women's sexuality. Across Europe, religious tensions erupted in anti-Semitic violence and witch-hunts. Nevertheless, as women faced increasing criticism for their participation in public life, they found new sources of power, new creative outlets, and new worlds in which they could express their priorities, their personalities, and their promise.

NOTES

1. Merry Wiesner, "Luther and Women: The Death of Two Marys," in *Disciplines of Faith: Religion, Patriarchy, and Politics*, ed. Raphael Samuel, James Obelkevich, and Lyndal Roper (London: Routledge, 1987), 300.

2. Merry Wiesner, "Women and the Reformation," in *The German People and the Reformation*, ed. R. Po-Chia-Hsia (Ithaca: Cornell University Press, 1988), 156.

3. Margaret L. King, *Women of the Renaissance* (Chicago: University of Chicago Press, 1991), 100–101.

4. Amy Leonard, *Nails in the Wall: Catholic Nuns in Reformation Germany* (Chicago: University of Chicago Press, 2005), chapter 4.

5. Cited in Mary Potter, "Gender Equality and Gender Hierarchy in Calvin's Theology," *Signs* 11:4 (Summer 1986): 727.

6. E. William Monter, "Women in Calvinist Geneva," *Signs* 6:2 (1980): 192.

7. Julian Goodare, "Scotland," in *The Reformation in National Context*, ed. Bob Scribner, Roy Porter, and Mikulás Tech (Cambridge: Cambridge University Press, 1994), 102–103.

8. Natalie Zemon Davis, *Society and Culture in Early Modern France* (Stanford: Stanford University Press, 1975), 183.

9. R. Po-Chia Hsia, "Münster and the Anabaptists," in *The German People and the Reformation*, 58.

10. Po-Chia Hsia, "Münster and the Anabaptists," 59.

11. Marybeth Carlson, "Women In and Out of the Public Church in the Dutch Republic," in *Women and Religion in Old and New Worlds*, ed. Susan E. Dinan and Debra Meyers (New York: Routledge, 2001), 118.

12. Diane Willen, "Women and Religion in Early Modern England," in *Women in Reformation and Counter-Reformation Europe: Private and Public Worlds*, ed. Sherrin Marshall (Bloomington: Indiana University Press, 1989), 144.

13. Willen, "Women and Religion in Early Modern England," 146.

14. Diane Willen, "Godly Women in Early Modern England: Puritanism and Gender," *Journal of Ecclesiastical History* 43:4 (1992): 563, 578.

15. Henry Kamen, *The Phoenix and the Flame: Catalonia and the Counter Reformation* (New Haven: Yale University Press, 1993), 326.

16. Marc Forster, *The Counter-Reformation in the Villages: Religion and Reform in the Bishopric of Speyer, 1560–1720* (Ithaca: Cornell University Press, 1992), 237.

17. Mary Elizabeth Perry, *Gender and Disorder in Early Modern Seville* (Princeton: Princeton University Press, 1992), 142.

18. Jaime Contreras and Gustav Henningsen, "Forty-four Thousand Cases of the Spanish Inquisition (1540–1700): Analysis of a Historical Data Bank," in *The Inquisition in Early Modern Europe*, ed. Gustav Henningsen and John Tedeschi (Dekalb, IL: Northern Illinois University Press, 1986), 114.

19. María Helena Sánchez Ortega, "Sorcery and Eroticism in Love Magic," in *Cultural Encounters: The Impact of the Inquisition in Spain and the New World*, ed. Mary Elizabeth Perry and Anne J. Cruz (Berkeley: University of California Press, 1991), 82.

20. William E. Monter, *Frontiers of Heresy: The Spanish Inquisition from the Basque Lands to Sicily* (Cambridge: Cambridge University Press, 1990), 281–282, 316–317.

21. P. Renée Baernstein, *A Convent Tale: A Century of Sisterhood in Milan* (New York: Routledge, 2002), 88.

22. Ulrike Strasser, "Cloistering Women's Past: Conflicting Accounts of Enclosure in a Seventeenth-Century Munich Nunnery," in *Gender in Early Modern German History*, ed. Ulinka Rublack (Cambridge: Cambridge University Press, 2002), 225.

23. Brian P. Levack, *The Witch-hunt in Early Modern Europe* (New York: Longman, 1995), 23.

24. Levack, 133.

25. Reneé Levine Melammed, "María López. A Convicted Judaizer from Castile," in *Women in the Inquisition: Spain and the New World*, ed. Mary E. Giles (Baltimore: The Johns Hopkins University Press, 1999), 58–59.

26. Daniel Swetschinski, *Reluctant Cosmopolitans: The Portuguese Jews of Seventeenth-Century Amsterdam* (London: The Littman Library of Jewish Civilization, 2000), 88.

27. Mary Elizabeth Perry, "Patience and Pluck: Job's Wife, Conflict and Resistance in Morsico Manuscripts Hidden in the Sixteenth Century," in *Women, Texts, and Authority in the Early Modern Spanish World*, ed. Marta V. Vicente and Luis R. Corteguera (Burlington, VT: Ashgate Press, 2003), 94.

28. Anne MacLaren, "Gender, Religion, and Early Modern Nationalism: Elizabeth I, Mary Queen of Scots, and the Genesis of English Anti-Catholicism," *American Historical Review* 107:3 (June 2002): 759.

29. Nancy Roelker, "The Appeal of Calvinism to French Noblewomen in the Sixteenth Century," *Journal of Interdisciplinary History* 2 (1972): 400.

30. Elaine Kruse, "The Blood-Stained Hands of Catherine de Médicis," in *Political Rhetoric, Power, and Renaissance Women*, ed. Carole Levin and Patricia A. Sullivan (Albany: SUNY Press, 1995), 146.

31. Sharon Kettering, "The Patronage Power of Early Modern French Noblewomen," *Historical Journal* 32:4 (December 1989): 825.

32. Magdalena S. Sánchez, *The Empress, The Queen, and the Nun: Women and Power at the Court of Philip III of Spain* (Baltimore: The Johns Hopkins University Press, 1998).

33. Sara Mendelson and Patricia Crawford, *Women in Early Modern England, 1550–1720* (Oxford: Clarendon Press, 1998), 396–397.

34. Alison Plowden, *Women All on Fire: The Women of the English Civil War* (Phoenix Mill, England: Sutton Publishing, 1998), 62.

35. Plowden, 67.

36. Patricia Crawford, *Women and Religion in England, 1500–1720* (London: Routledge, 1993), 135.

37. Phyllis Mack, "Women as Prophets During the English Civil War," *Feminist Studies* 8 (1982): 24.

38. Ann Hughes, "Gender and Politics in Leveller Literature," in *Political Culture and Cultural Politics in Early Modern England*, ed. Susan D. Amussen and Mark A Kishlansky (Manchester: Manchester University Press, 1995), 163.

39. Juan Luis Vives, *The Education of a Christian Woman: A Sixteenth-Century Manual*, ed. and trans. Charles Fantazzi (Chicago: University of Chicago Press, 2000), 193.

40. Natalia Pushkareva, *Women in Russian History: From the Twelfth to the Twentieth Century*, trans. Eve Levin. (Armonk, NY: M. E. Sharpe, 1997), 88–93.

41. Moderata da Fonte, *The Worth of Women: Wherein Is Clearly Revealed Their Nobility and Their Superiority to Men*, trans. Virginia Cox (Chicago: University of Chicago Press, 1997), 237.

42. Frances Teague and Rebecca De Haas, "Defenses of Women," in *A Companion to Early Modern Women's Writing*, ed. Anita Pacheco (London: Blackwell, 2002), 250.

43. Veronica Franco, "A Challenge to a Poet Who Has Defamed Her," *Poems and Selected Letters* ed. and trans. Ann Rosalind Jones and Margaret R. Rosenthal (Chicago: University of Chicago Press, 1998), 163,165.

44. Kimberlyn Montford, "L'Anno Santo and Female Monastic Churches: The Politics, Business and Music of the Holy Year in Rome (1675)," *Journal of Seventeenth-Century Music* 6:1 (2000): par. 3.3 http://www.sscm-jscm.org/jscm/v6/no1/Montford.html

45. Londa Schiebinger, *The Mind Has No Sex: Women in the Origins of Modern Science* (Cambridge, MA: Harvard University Press, 1989), 80–81.

46. Lianne McTavish, *Childbirth and the Display of Authority in Early Modern France* (Aldershot, England: Ashgate Press, 2005), esp. 2, 43, 103.

47. Auke P. Jacobs, *Los movimientos migratorios entre Castilla e HispanoAmerica durante el reinado de Felipe II, 1598–1621* (Amsterdam: Editions Rodopi, 1995), 281.

48. Timothy J. Coates, *Convicts and Orphans: Forced and State-Sponsored Colonizers in the Portuguese Empire, 1550–1755* (Stanford: Stanford University Press, 2001), esp. 143, 155, 173.

49. Kathleen Brown, *Good Wives, Nasty Wenches, and Anxious Patriarchs: Gender, Race, and Power in Colonial Virginia* (Chapel Hill: University of North Carolina Press for the Institute of Early American History and Culture, 1996), 80–83.

50. Brown, 75–80.

51. Natalie Zemon Davis, *Women on the Margins: Three Seventeenth-Century Lives* (Cambridge: Harvard University Press, 1995), 96–97.

SUGGESTED READINGS

Brown, Kathleen. *Good Wives, Nasty Wenches, and Anxious Patriarchs: Gender, Race, and Power in Colonial Virginia*. Chapel Hill: University of North Carolina Press for the Institute of Early American History and Culture, 1996. Brown examines not only the role of women in Colonial British America, but also the interactions between white settlers and native and African Americans.

Davis, Natalie Zemon. *Women on the Margins: Three Seventeenth-Century Lives*. Cambridge, MA: Harvard University Press, 1995. These portraits of a Catholic nun, a Jewish woman, and a Dutch artist bring the complex world of early modern women to life.

Giles, Mary E. *Women in the Inquisition. Spain and the New World*. Baltimore: The Johns Hopkins University Press, 1999.

Levack, Brian P. *The Witch-hunt in Early Modern Europe*. 2nd ed. London: Longman, 1995. This works provides the most detailed and the broadest examination of the phenomenon of witch-hunting.

Schiebinger, Londa. *The Mind Has No Sex: Women in the Origins of Modern Science*. Cambridge, MA: Harvard University Press, 1989. This pioneering study looks at the changing roles of women during the scientific revolution.

Chapter 8

Whose Enlightenment, Whose Revolution? 1700–1815

Women's March on Versailles, (October 1789). In the French Revolution, women's public protests and violence changed from demands for food for their families to demands for equality and citizenship. (Musée Carnavalet, Paris, France/ RMN/Art Resource, NY.)

The eighteenth century was a period of intense social, political, and intellectual change. Class differences increased as the nobility lived in luxury while peasants continued to starve. Inspired by the scientific revolution, Enlightenment intellectuals debated the inevitability of social and gender inequality and laid the groundwork for the revolutions in the Americas and France. They also struggled with the question of whether women could be citizens or whether motherhood demanded their confinement to home and domesticity. Women were both patrons of and participants in these debates. The impact of the Enlightenment was not the same everywhere. In Austria, Prussia, and Russia, Enlightened rulers manipulated gender expectations in different ways to maintain their authority. The Enlightenment also inspired new artistic forms, and women critiqued their experiences through their artistic participation. Ultimately, the revolutions in North America and France brought short-term gains to women and raised new issues about the nature of political participation.

SOCIETY AT THE END OF THE OLD REGIME

Increasing class tensions marked the end of the Old Regime. The aristocracy lived in luxury and had almost exclusive access to political power. Although the wealthiest members of the middle class could live like the aristocracy, they lacked the status and privileges that came with nobility. At the bottom of the social hierarchy, poor women struggled to make ends meet, resenting the ostentatious luxury and leisure of the upper classes. Although these tensions were nothing new, changing economies accentuated class divisions.

Royal and Aristocratic Women

Wealth and leisure defined the lives of aristocratic women. Their families' personal holdings were often enormous. In Hungary, 40 percent of the land belonged to 150 or so families.[1] In Naples, eighty-four noble families controlled at least ten thousand peasants each, over two million people

Chapter 8 ❖ Chronology

1720	Rosalba Carrira paints in Paris
1740	Emilie du Châtelet published translation and commentary on Newton's *Principia mathematica*
	Maria Theresa first woman ruler of the Habsburg monarchy
	Prussia invades Silesia, initiating the War of Austrian Succession
1757	Louis XVI bans the *Encyclopédie*
1758	Jean-Jacques Rousseau writes *Emile*
1759	Marie Thiroux d'Arconville publishes *Ostéologie*
1764	Catherine the Great founds first secular school for girls in Russia
1776	Declaration of Independence, start of American Revolution
1786	Carona Schröter publishes first of two collections of songs
1789	Start of French Revolution
1791	Olympe de Gouge writes *Declaration of the Rights of Women and Female Citizen*
1792	Mary Wollstonecraft publishes *Vindication of the Rights of Woman*
1793	Executions of Marie Antoinette and Louis XVI
1804	Napoleonic Code
1807	New Jersey terminates women's right to vote
1815	Napoleon defeated at Waterloo

total.[2] This wealth allowed aristocratic women to live in remarkable opulence. Palaces, like that of Queluz built by the Portuguese king consort Dom Pedro III (1717–1786) between 1747 and 1780, held splendid furnishings imported from around the world. A lavish life required an elaborate wardrobe. When Empress Elizabeth of Russia (1709–1762) died, she left fifteen thousand dresses in her wardrobe, and the trousseau of Archduchess Maria Josepha of Austria (1699–1757) included ninety-nine dresses made of rich silks decorated with gold and silver lace.[3] The aristocracy filled their considerable leisure time with racing, card playing, balls, and other social events.

Aristocratic women's sole duty was to produce male heirs who would perpetuate the lineage and increase the family's political and economic power. Families looked for suitable matches based on political connections and family wealth. Elite women married around age sixteen, nearly a decade younger than most peasant women, and their husbands were often considerably older. By marrying young and sending their children out to wet nurses, noblewomen tended to have large families. In France at the beginning of the century, noble families had an average of 6.5 children.[4] Considering that nearly half of all children did not live to adulthood, noblewomen often had more than ten pregnancies in a lifetime.

Some historians argue that aristocratic attitudes toward motherhood changed considerably over the eighteenth century. At the beginning of the century, elite mothers often took little interest in their children. Their wealth allowed them to employ large numbers of servants to cook, clean, sew, attend to the needs and wants of their masters and mistresses, and take care of the children. One French noblewoman remembered her childhood as a time of neglect and frequent accidents. "My mother . . . neglected me a little, and left me too much in the care of the women [servants], who neglected me also."[5] However, as the century progressed, elite society began to emphasize the importance of maternal love. In his 1758 novel *Emile,* the Swiss social theorist Jean-Jacques Rousseau (1712–1778) encouraged mothers to breastfeed to strengthen the maternal bond. Letters between husbands and wives and between female friends indicate a greater interest in child-rearing. Even the French queen, Marie Antoinette (1755–1793), had a model dairy farm built for her and her ladies in waiting so that they could "return to nature" and practice nurturing. Increasingly, mothers looked after their children's education and supervised nannies, governesses, and tutors. Both breastfeeding, which suppressed fertility, and an increased use of birth control led to a decline in the number of children born to noblewomen.

Despite the importance of marriage, family strategies prevented many noblewomen from marrying. Nearly one-third of elite Englishwomen never married because their families could not afford dowries or find appropriate spouses.[6] Because women assumed the status of their husbands, noblemen could find spouses among the daughters of the urban elite, but sisters who married down in the social hierarchy brought shame to their families. As a result, many women remained single, living at home and receiving only modest inheritances. These women were doubly disappointed; they were unable to fulfill the goals of marriage and motherhood for which they were raised and unable to afford the lifestyle of their class.

Aristocratic women's wealth gave them access to court life and royal politics. Indeed, many contemporaries complained that women had taken over politics. Some women used their sexuality to achieve their personal and political goals. Claudine-Alexandrine Guérin de Tencin (1681–1749) first seduced the French regent Philippe Duc d'Orléans (1674–1723) and then became the mistress of the abbé Dubois (1656–1723), who went on to become an archbishop and cardinal. Through her liaisons, she hoped to promote the career of her less ambitious brother, Cardinal Pierre Guérin de Tencin. Even more influential was Jeanne Poisson, mistress to the French king, Louis XV (r. 1715–1774), and better known as the Marquise de Pompadour (1721–1764). Her affair with the king brought her more than riches; she controlled all access to the king and placed her allies in important political positions.

Increasingly, the new elites who had earned great fortunes from business rather than family wealth clamored to become members of the aristocracy. They wanted access to the power and privileges that came with hereditary titles. Eager for alliances and money for the treasury, the French monarchy sold noble titles to those ambitious families. As a result, over the course of the century, the French aristocracy nearly doubled in size.

Women and Rural Life

As had always been true, peasant women produced much of the wealth enjoyed by elite women. Although rural women's work remained much as it had for centuries, overseas trade, increased consumption and manufacturing, and new farming techniques changed the organization of peasant women's work. Across Europe, peasant households were less often self-supporting. Women now produced goods and food for markets in a process known as *protoindustrialization.*

Landowners drove much of the change in rural life. They introduced a variety of new farming techniques and new crops like the potato and the turnip, which allowed for more efficient use of land and healthier, more productive livestock. Just as important, landowners enclosed fields, forcing thousands of peasant families off lands that they had worked for generations. After enclosure, peasants no longer farmed primarily for themselves, but to harvest crops that would be sold in the marketplace and whose profits went to the landowner.

While peasant men continued to work in the fields, businessmen purchased raw materials such as linen, cotton, or wool and employed peasant women to turn it into cloth. Some women produced the entire product from thread to finished cloth, while others completed only one part of the production process, such as spinning or weaving. The businessman returned to collect the finished product, paying the women by the piece. He then sold the cloth at regional, national, and international markets. This process is known as "cottage industry," since it took place in peasant cottages, or as the "putting-out system." Although this system of production was not new, it became much more common in the eighteenth century. Women's paid labor integrated easily into their traditional household duties. The cash they earned paid for the goods that their families no longer produced. Often, women earned the only cash families ever saw.

Their ties to national and international economies left women and their families increasingly vulnerable to economic crises. The changing price of manufactured goods affected families' survival, and crop failures in France in 1725, 1739–40, 1752, and 1768, caused an increase in bread prices and hunger. One French police officer testified that a pregnant woman, desperate to feed her children, had come up to him before a riot crying, "Help me, help me. My husband and me and my three children will starve to death if you don't get us corn [grain]. I'll stab myself before your very eyes."[7] A group of women then attacked the local grain store. Unable to grow their own food and without the cash to buy basic foodstuffs, women resorted to violence to feed their families.

In eastern Europe, the living and working conditions of peasants declined as most were forced into serfdom. Faced with lower profits and higher labor costs, aristocratic Austro-Hungarian, Polish, Prussian, and Russian landowners held on to their shrinking rural workforce by tying them to the land. Peasants owed their lords as many as three hundred days of labor a year in exchange for a plot of land and a house. Typically, they supplied their own tools and draft animals, which added to their burden. Life was hard and living conditions squalid. Attempts to flee brought severe penalties. In many areas, serfs were no better off than slaves. In Poland, landlords had the power of life and death over their serfs until 1768. The impact on women was especially severe. To alleviate their labor shortage, eastern European lords encouraged or coerced their serfs into marrying early and raising more children. Russian peasant women could expect to marry in their early teens and bear numerous children. Widows made up the poorest segment of the serf population; often lacking male help to perform the onerous labor services, they had to sell off livestock and household goods to feed and support themselves.

These harsh conditions did not prevent thousands of serf families from either fleeing to cities or revolting against their lords. In Russia, seventy-three peasant uprisings took place between 1762 and 1769. After nearly one-quarter million Bohemian peasants died between 1770 and 1772 from famine, the survivors launched a massive revolt in 1774.

Although life expectancy increased during the eighteenth century, rural life was still very difficult, especially for those trapped in serfdom. With poor medical care and long workdays, malnutrition and poor hygiene remained constant threats. For women, this meant continued high rates of death from childbirth and high infant mortality rates.

Urban Women

While peasant women toiled in their homes and fields, cities became the centers of a new consumer-oriented society that fostered new values and behavior. New manufacturing techniques and cheaper raw materials now made it possible for nonelite women to afford items that had been previously beyond their reach. Many of those goods imitated the styles of the wealthy. They bought fashionable clothing and home furnishings rather than utilitarian goods. At all levels of urban society, women's wardrobes became larger and more expensive. Manufacturers and shopkeepers encouraged this consumption by advertising the latest fashions from Italy and France in newspapers. The first color fashion advertisements appeared in the British publication *The Lady's Magazine* in 1771. Ads targeted women, as they made most of the basic household expenditures, and manufacturers eagerly accommodated women's changing tastes. When British women sought to make their skin pale by washing in arsenic, they then wanted black tea sets to set off their skin. Josiah Wedgwood (1730–1795), who had pioneered the mass production of fine china, quickly capitalized on this trend by producing an inexpensive set of black china.[8]

Formerly exotic goods like coffee and tea became commonplace and changed urban society. Coffeehouses replaced taverns as public gathering spots where men met to discuss business and politics. To distinguish themselves from lower-class taverns, coffeehouses prohibited swearing, gambling, and fighting on their premises. Teahouses and tea drinking became associated with women and feminine behavior. Some moralists even worried that women's control of tea serving would lead to a rise in effeminate men and a weakened military.[9]

Nevertheless, tea imports increased steadily throughout the eighteenth century, especially in England. Tea gardens and teahouses such as the Golden Lion, opened by the Twinings Company in 1706, catered to women. Men and women also drank tea at home, and by the 1740s, English women routinely presided over afternoon tea. At tea, parents taught their children upper-class manners, emphasizing that moderation, self-control, and domestic order conferred respectability rather than birth and wealth.

The city offered women a wider array of life choices than the countryside. Although most women married, between 15 and 25 percent of urban middle-class women remained single.[10] As sons and daughters inherited equally, middle-class single women often used their inheritances to set up their own households in the city. Others shared lodgings with another woman or a relative. Over the course of the eighteenth century, illegitimate births in much of the rest of Europe more than doubled, evidence that many of these single women did not wait for marriage to engage in sexual relationships. Other women chose to spend their time with women, both as friends and as lovers. To support themselves, single women worked in occupations that their socially mobile families found acceptable, such as milliners, shopkeepers, and glovers. Single women with some education became governesses and boarding school teachers.

European cities were also home to a range of working-class women whose work options reflected the growing urban economy. Although some were born in the city, most had moved from the countryside seeking a better life. Domestic service drew the largest numbers of young women to urban areas. During the eighteenth century, one-quarter of London's women worked in domestic service. Changes in the cloth industry also offered women new work opportunities, as the growth of overseas trade brought in more raw materials and new manufacturing techniques weakened the guild system. In Florence, thousands of women wove silk cloth for a living; in German cities, they dominated the spinning industry; and in France they made lace. With such a variety of occupations available, many women found they did not have to marry to support themselves. In London between 1695 and 1725, 78 percent of single women and 71 percent of widows claimed that they were wholly self-supporting.[11]

However, the changing economy endangered widows' abilities to earn livings. As guild masters saw their livelihoods threatened, they tried to protect themselves by excluding women from the few remaining guilds. Legislation prevented widows from taking over their deceased husbands' trades and, as a result, widowhood in urban areas became increasingly associated with poverty. Across Europe, urban widows tended to be poorer than women living in households headed by men. Many rented dank and cramped rooms and had little opportunity to enjoy urban life.

Most urban married women also worked. One historian found that between 1695 and 1725, 60 percent of London wives who testified in court claimed that they were at least partially employed. No doubt, many more women worked informally for or with their husbands.[12] The wealthier a woman was, the less likely she was to work outside the home for pay. However, her domestic work, including the supervision of servants, left her with little leisure time.

Differences between social classes intensified during the eighteenth century. Elite women lived in magnificent palaces, surrounded by the finest clothing and furnishings that money could buy. They built their success on the labor of peasant women, whose livelihoods became increasingly fragile as family economies became integrated into regional and national markets. At the same time, successful middle-class women enjoyed the benefits of an ever more consumer-oriented society.

The differences among women reflected broader social divisions that would erupt in violence in many parts of Europe by the end of the century.

ENLIGHTENMENT IDEAS

Conscious of the increasing disparities in wealth and driven by the intellectual achievements of the scientific revolution, intellectuals began to explore the possibilities for changing society. In this intellectual revolution, known as the Enlightenment, thinkers used rational observation to understand the laws that governed the universe, nature, and social and political organization. They questioned the legitimacy of monarchies and the social order, as well as the role of women in politics and society. Although male intellectuals used a wide array of scientific and philosophical arguments to marginalize women from scholarly and political pursuits, across Europe, women found innovative ways to participate in intellectual debate and artistic achievement.

Women and the Birth of Modern Science

At the end of the seventeenth century, scientific inquiry captured the imagination of many. Interested men and women observed and experimented in an effort to explain the natural world. Mathematics became particularly popular, and women of all classes attended public lectures on mathematics and astronomy. Several popular publications, such as the *Ladies' Diary* published in England from 1704 to 1841, promoted women's education in the "mathematical sciences."[13] Many aristocratic women used their connections to explore the world of science. Emilie du Châtelet (1706–1749) took advantage of this new enthusiasm. Emilie married the Marquis du Châtelet when she was nineteen years old. While raising three children, she surrounded herself with mentors who instructed her in science and mathematics. Her most famous association was with Voltaire (1694–1778), the French writer and satirist with whom she formed a close physical and intellectual relationship. He introduced her to Newtonian physics, and she actively participated in the debates about the role of metaphysics in natural science that raged between the Newtonian and Cartesian (followers of Descartes) thinkers in France. In 1740, she published her French translation and commentary on Newton's *Principia mathematica*.

Female artisans also became interested in scientific inquiry. Maria Sibylla Merian (1647–1717) learned illustration, engraving, and painting from her father. After successfully printing textiles for many years, she began to study nature in search of better colors and new images for her textiles. Merian illustrated the works of other naturalists, and then in 1699, she set sail for the Dutch colony of Surinam to continue her research into plants and insects. She returned to Amsterdam in 1701 to begin her major scientific work the *Metamorphosis Insectorum Surinamensium,* an illustrated study of New World insects.

However, men continued to limit women's access to higher education and the most elite intellectual circles. Officially unable to attend universities, few women could obtain the university degree required to do scientific research in academies or universities. Laura Bassi (1711–1778) held a chair in physics, and Maria Gaetana Agnesi (1718–1799) succeeded her father as professor of mathematics at the University of Bologna. Agnesi felt closely connected to other ambitious women. She dedicated her most famous mathematical treatise to Maria Theresa of Austria (see below). In the dedication she noted, "Nothing has encouraged me as much as your madam being a woman, which luckily applies to me."[14] Maria Theresa sent Agnesi a basket of jewels in appreciation. However, these women were exceptional. Most of the newly formed scientific societies, such as the Royal Society of London (1662), the Parisian Royal Academy of Science (1666), or the Royal Society of Sciences in Berlin (1700) also excluded women from membership, thus denying women the economic and intellectual networks that Europe's male intelligentsia gained from their membership.

Science was men's work, and most women who wanted to pursue scientific investigation could only do so as assistants to their fathers, husbands, and brothers. Caroline Herschel (1750–1848), born in Hanover, Germany, served as her brother's assistant while he was astronomer to King George

MARIA SIBILLA MERIAN
Nat. XII. Apr: M.D.C.XLVII. Obiit XIII. Jan: M.D.C.CXVII.

MARIA SIBYLLA MERIAN (1647–1717). Merian's work as an artist for silk cloth led to her interest in the natural world. She traveled to Surinam to catalogue, collect, and illustrate the insects' life there. *(Offentliche Kunstsammlung Kunstmuseum, Basel.)*

III of England (r. 1760–1820). She could only have access to his high-quality telescopes when her brother traveled, yet between 1789 and 1797, she discovered eight comets and three nebulae and published her *Catalogue of Stars* with the Royal Society. Nonetheless, she described herself as "a well-trained puppy-dog," not an independent thinker.[15]

Enlightenment Ideas About Women

As Enlightenment thinkers explored the basic structures of nature and society, debates about gender revolved around the nature of sex differences and their role in social organization. Although French philosopher René Descartes

(1596–1650) did not directly address the issue of gender, his ideas became central to Enlightenment defenses of women's intellectual abilities. According to Descartes, the mind functioned independently of the body. Men's bodies differed from women's bodies only in the sex organs; therefore, all minds were potentially equal. This idea led many followers of Descartes to reconsider their views on women. Philosopher and former Jesuit Francois Poullain de la Barre (1647–1725) said, "When I was a scholastic, I considered [women] scholastically, that is to say, as monsters, as beings inferior to men, because Aristotle and some theologians whom I had read, considered them so." Changed by his encounter with Cartesian ideas, Poullain de la Barre later enthusiastically proclaimed, "The mind has no sex."[16]

Similarly, political theorist John Locke (1632–1704) almost unintentionally provided a philosophical foundation for women's political roles. In his *Two Treatises on Government* (1680–1690), he refuted traditional justifications for absolutism and in doing so, he provided a critique of patriarchy. Supporters of absolutist monarchies argued that the king was analogous to a father and children were to honor their father. However, Locke pointed out that the biblical commandment was to honor fathers *and mothers*. Moreover, Locke asserted that marriage was a voluntary relationship, and while husbands might rule their wives, that hierarchy was not inevitable.[17]

However, not everyone agreed with these radical views of human equality. Eighteenth-century anatomists began to reconsider the theories of bodily humors that had dominated classical and medieval understandings of the body and sex differences. In the process, they formulated views of male and female bodies that emphasized sex differences beyond those found in the reproductive organs. Marie Thiroux d'Arconville (1720–1805) played a critical role in both defining and illustrating these differences. Although she argued that women should not get involved in medicine, in 1759, she produced the most important illustrations of the female skeleton of her time. Published under a male pseudonym, her *Ostéologie* became the standard view of female skeletons, with a small head, enlarged pelvis, and narrow ribs.[18] Such a body was perfect for childbearing, but

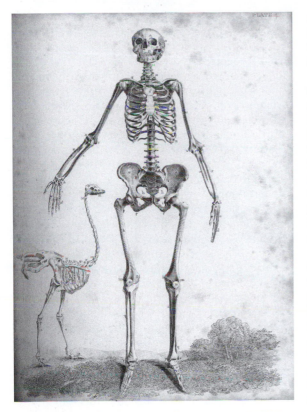

D'ARCONVILLE'S FEMALE SKELETON (1759). Marie Thiroux d'Arconville produced the standard view of female skeletons, with a small head, enlarged pelvis, and narrow ribs. *(Courtesy Special Collections, Dalhousie University Archives and Special Collections.)*

woefully inadequate for intellectual or physical exertion.

The new belief that women's bodies differed fundamentally from men's and were not just inferior versions of them was known as *complementarity*; men's and women's bodies had differing but complementary roles in society and biology. Complementarity had profound social implications. On the one hand, because anatomists believed that women's bodies were designed only for motherhood, they came to view the womb as an amazing organ, instead of the source of hysteria and confusion advanced by Aristotle. On the other hand, complementarity provided the basis for the idea that women were built for domesticity

and child-rearing, and men were built for rule, rationality, and public duties. This understanding of sex differences justified the different educations and political rights that men and women received.

Rousseau was a vocal advocate of complementarity. Men and women were physically, intellectually, and morally different and those innate and unalterable differences determined women's inferior place in society.[19] Tapping into the new emphasis on domesticity that was sweeping Europe, Rousseau believed that women had the capacity to develop, learn, and grow, but that their talents lay only in the domestic realm. Thus, women's education must be different from men's in order for them to reach their full potential as mothers and helpers to their husbands.

Although popular, Rousseau's ideas faced criticism. The Marquis of Condorcet (1745–1793) argued that granting women rights did not imply a social revolution, only that it would give them basic rights due to all humans. Because society had advanced to a peaceful, sedentary, and civilized level, it should foster greater equality between men and women. Condorcet also believed that the physical differences between men and women should not stand in the way of social equality and citizenship. There were many physical differences between people, not the least of which were differences between men and women. To those who believed that pregnancy made women incapable, Condorcet responded that other people became incapacitated by rheumatism or ill with gout. To those who argued that women had not made important scientific discoveries or written literary masterpieces, he replied that was also true of most men.[20] At the heart of Condorcet's disagreement with Rousseau and other proponents of complementarity was whether the social differences between men and women were natural or, to use a modern phrase, "socially constructed."

The *Salonières* and the Philosophes

Enlightenment thinkers debated these and other issues in intellectual gatherings known as *salons*, most of which were organized and supported by noble and bourgeoisie women. Salons took place in private homes and women, the *salonières*, presided over them. At a salon, intellectuals, usually men, debated ideas, read new literature, and performed music. The men who embraced this new emphasis on intellectual inquiry, particularly in order to critique religion and politics, called themselves *philosophes*.

Although many salon participants were connected to the king, the salon as an institution was the antithesis of the monarchy in its appreciation of criticism, debate, and republican sentiments. In fact, the salon had much in common with the workshop, because members saw it as a place of work, not play, and like a workshop, it depended on the labor of both men and women. Although members valued wit, good manners, and a pleasant personality, in a salon one also had to produce, debate, and defend ideas; frivolous activities such as gambling and parlor games were largely absent. One of the leading salonières, Marie-Thérèse Rodet Geoffrin (1699–1777), specifically rearranged the schedule of her salon to encourage its work. Instead of hosting the traditionally sociable late-night supper, she moved her salon to one o'clock in the afternoon so as to leave the afternoon free for conversation. To focus discussions, she held her Monday salon for artists and her Wednesday salon for writers. This regular schedule made the salon a social center for those who saw themselves as public intellectuals or as they referred to themselves, "citizens in the Republic of Letters."[21]

Mentoring between women also made the salon much like an artisan's workshop. For instance, salonières served informal apprenticeships before opening their own salons. Geoffrin began her salon career as a very young, devout wife of a man five times her age. To educate herself, she attended the salon of her neighbor, Claudine-Alexandrine Guérin de Tencin. When Tencin died in 1749, Geoffrin formalized her own salon. In turn, Geoffrin "trained" Suzanne Necker (1739–1794) and Julie de Lespinasse (1732–1776) who eventually ran their own salons in concert with Geoffrin. Julie de Lespinasse, the illegitimate daughter of a countess, had no dowry and few prospects in eighteenth-century society. Her letters acknowledge the value of the friendships that she had formed in salons. For the salonières, salons offered ideas, friendship, leadership, and work in contrast to the rest of elite society where women were only expected to be beautiful when they were not producing heirs. In fact, historian Dena

Goodman has argued that the salon's primary relationship was not between a woman and a group of men, but between female mentors and their students.[22]

Women set the agenda for much of the debate and scholarship that emerged from the salons. Members of Julie de Lespinasse's salon planned the *Encyclopédie,* the most ambitious Enlightenment project; indeed her salon came to be known as the "laboratory of the *Encyclopédie.*"[23] Initially intended to be a translation and expansion of a popular English encyclopedia, it soon became an undertaking in its own right, embodying, so its editors believed, the spirit and goals of the Enlightenment. Two Frenchmen, Denis Diderot (1713–1784) and Jean Le Rond d'Alembert (1717–1783), the illegitimate son of the salonière Tencin, directed this work. They attempted to use the expertise of a variety of thinkers to catalogue and explain all human knowledge.

The editors funded production of the *Encyclopédie* through subscriptions, a new system recently imported from England. They increased circulations by bringing out cheap editions and abridged versions, and with the appearance of pirated copies, the *Encyclopédie* enjoyed a wide audience. Because of its broad readership and its open examination and criticism of many aspects of society, such as organized religion and monarchies, the king of France banned the *Encyclopédie* in 1757, forcing it underground after only seven volumes had been published. Soon thereafter, Madame de Pompadour came to the project's defense at a dinner party attended by the king. The host raised the question of how gunpowder was made and Madame de Pompadour countered by wondering about the ingredients of face powder. She then added that had the king not banned the *Encyclopédie,* they might know the answers to these and other interesting questions. The king then sent for his own copies, which had not been confiscated, and soon thereafter allowed Diderot and d'Alembert to continue their work.[24] When completed in 1766, the project consisted of seventeen volumes of articles and eleven volumes of illustrations. Despite the important role that Lespinasse played in fostering this project, only two women actually contributed to it. Both articles were on garments or fashion, and one of these women remains anonymous.[25]

The most famous salons were in France, but the idea spread to other parts of Europe, where salons often took on other agendas. In Prussia, Berlin's salons attracted Jews and Christians from all walks of life, and Jewish women ran some of the most influential gatherings. They introduced French style and culture to attendees and emphasized common interests over their cultural differences. One of the products of the Prussian salons was Moses Mendelssohn (1729–1786), the father of the Jewish Enlightenment known as the *Haskalah*, which encouraged Jews to study secular subjects and to assimilate into European society. Mendelssohn attempted to integrate reason into Jewish understandings of God, and his daughter, Dorothea von Schlegel (1763–1839), carried on this intellectual inquiry with her own popular salon. Although the salons offered Jewish women new educational opportunities, they also attracted them away from their traditional culture. Many Jewish salon women took Christian names, divorced their Jewish husbands, converted, and married Christian men.[26]

In Spain, female participants in the Enlightenment did not criticize Catholicism or the monarchy as they did in France, but directed their attention to social reforms. In Madrid, a group of about thirty women formed a women's council attached to the Economic Society of Madrid, whose work focused on women's education and the reform of foundling hospitals. As the first female member of a Spanish Economic Society, Josefa Amar y Borbón (1749–1833) turned her considerable intellectual powers to translating and composing treatises on new agricultural techniques for the Royal Aragonese Economic Society. She argued passionately for female membership in the Economic Society. She also created her own catalogue of worthy women for other women to emulate and produced an important work on women's education.[27]

In England, women gathered in reading groups to discuss ideas and promote social change (see **Women's Lives**: Lady Mary Wortley Montagu). These reading societies drew some of their inspirations from the writings of David Hume (1711–1776) and other Scottish Enlightenment thinkers. He argued for women's education and their important role in civilizing society. Members of these reading groups often pooled their resources to open their own libraries or publish their own books and pamphlets. One of the most famous of these groups was the *bluestockings*, who focused on women and women's social concerns. Led by Elizabeth Montague (1720–1800), they challenged the limitations placed on women, in particular the frequency with which women had to marry for money or social standing and the vapid pleasure-seeking lives that often followed such marriages. Among the most active English bluestockings, Hannah More (1745–1833) wrote and spoke publicly on behalf of women's education, and Elizabeth Carter (1717–1806) translated Greek classics and was fluent in many other languages. Samuel Johnson (1696–1772), the great lexicographer, declared of Carter that she "could make a pudding as well as translate Epictetus [first century C.E.] and work a handkerchief as well as compose a poem."[28]

Run by women and organized around the principles of mutuality and friendship, the salon was the opposite of the academy, which excluded women and likened academic debate to combat. However, in the end, the association of the salon with femininity was the salon's undoing. The most pointed attack came from Rousseau. He argued that society grew out of man's need to be judged by others and that putting the role of judge in the hands of women, as was done in the salons, was corrupt. Salons feminized knowledge and made thinkers effeminate or womanish. These and other criticisms had their effect. By the end of the century, the new professional and scientific academies and the resurgence of universities had eclipsed the great influence of the salons. Yet the role of women in salons meant that for most of the century, gender, either implicitly or explicitly, was a regular topic of conversation.

The Enlightenment arose out of the passion for intellectual inquiry brought about by the scientific revolution. Although male scientists often excluded women from traditional but important educational and research institutions, many women found alternative avenues to scientific exploration. The desire for a greater understanding of the world around them led to passionate debates over sex differences, the nature of government, and social hierarchies. If men's and women's minds were equal, then society needed to be reformed to reflect that

Women's Lives

Lady Mary Wortley Montague

Lady Montague's life exemplifies the opportunities and limitations of the Enlightenment. She traveled extensively, engaged in literary debates about the rights and privileges of women, and applied her observations to improving society. Resistance to her and her ideas reveals the limits of the Enlightenment when it came to gender.

Born Mary Pierrepont, the eldest daughter of a Yorkshire gentry family, Lady Montague received a limited education but taught herself Latin in order to read Ovid. Her father then arranged to have her taught Italian and French. Instead of marrying a suitably rich aristocrat, Mary eloped with Edward Wortley Montague, the brother of a girlhood friend. Edward believed that women should be educated and was impressed with his wife's erudition.

In 1714, Edward became Lord of the Treasury and moved his family to London where Lady Montague joined London's literary scene. She became a close friend of poet and social critic Alexander Pope (1688–1744) and began writing. Although relatively few works appeared in her name, she was instrumental in developing a genre of writing, town eclogues, which celebrated urban life, particularly London, in the way that pastoral literature idealized the countryside.

In 1716, the couple traveled to Istanbul where her husband had been appointed ambassador. Lady Montague toured the country, learned Turkish, visited with harem women, and often dressed in local clothing. She kept a journal of her observations, which served as a source for her letters back home and her famous *Embassy Letters,* fifty-two letters written or assembled shortly after she returned to London in 1718 and published after her death.

In Turkey, she observed inoculations for smallpox, a practice unknown in Europe. Lady Montague had been scarred by the disease before leaving for Turkey and when an epidemic threatened London in 1721, she had her children inoculated. However, when some patients died after being inoculated, doctors and scientists condemned her and the practice of inoculation, accusing her of feminine gullibility.

Lady Montague's notoriety reached into the literary and political world. In 1722, when she rejected Pope's declaration of love, he began a sustained and public attack on her. He accused her of infidelity, manliness, and lesbianism. Lady Montague composed public replies published under a pseudonym. Her replies only made Pope angrier and his attacks threatened her husband's political career. In response, Lady Montague turned to writing political commentary in defense of her husband's political party. These tracts were also published anonymously. They were a huge success, but did not restore her reputation and that of her husband.

In 1734, Lady Montague left England for a self-imposed exile in France and Italy. Some claimed that she was following a lover, but she never lived with one. She traveled extensively and even managed a farm in Italy. She lived on the Continent for twenty-seven years, corresponding with her husband and daughter regularly. Her husband gave her a generous allowance, but they never met again.

Meanwhile, her daughter, also Mary, had married one of King George III's (r. 1760–1820) most trusted advisors. The younger Mary, fearing the impact of her mother's unorthodox ways on her own husband's reputation, destroyed her mother's journals after she died and tried unsuccessfully to prevent the publication of *The Embassy Letters.*

Lady Mary Wortley Montague was an adventurer, deeply influenced by the scientific and romantic ethos of the period. She immersed herself in Turkish culture and society and tried to pursue the new ideas current in intellectual circles. Her success threatened many. In her confrontations with Pope and British physicians, she faced the limitations of her society and her sex, even as she broadened their horizons with her writings.

Sources: Robert Halsband, ed., *The Complete Letters of Lady Mary Wortley Montague,* 3 vols. (Oxford: Oxford University Press, 1965–67); and Isobel Grundy, *Lady Mary Wortley Montague* (Oxford: Oxford University Press, 2001).

equality. The emphasis on intellectual equality was most evident in the salons that appeared across Europe. Organized and supported by women, these intellectual gatherings produced some of the great achievements of the Enlightenment.

THE ENLIGHTENMENT IN EASTERN EUROPE AND RUSSIA

Many Europeans reacted to the Enlightenment with horror, afraid of its potential to disrupt the social hierarchy and monarchical authority. However, even the most absolute monarchs of the period expressed some interest in pursing limited reforms based on Enlightenment ideas. As *enlightened despots*, they implemented changes that benefited their kingdoms and increased monarchical power. Enlightened monarchs in Austria and Prussia used gender in very traditional ways to both maintain power and impose reform, while in Russia, absolutist pressures tempered enthusiasm for Western ideas.

Gendering Enlightened Absolutism in Austria and Prussia

The Habsburg monarchy ruled over Austria, Hungary, and Bohemia, the southern Netherlands, and parts of Italy and the Balkans, was one of the most powerful absolute monarchies in the West. However, the Habsburg rulers constantly struggled to maintain control over this multicultural, multilingual, and multireligious empire. By the eighteenth century, a succession crisis threatened to end centuries of Habsburg rule. Historically, the Habsburg monarchy had excluded women from the throne based on medieval Salic law that had prohibited women from inheriting property. In an effort to keep Habsburg possessions intact, Emperor Charles VI (r. 1711–1740) spent much of his reign persuading the many territories under Habsburg rule and the rest of Europe to accept the Pragmatic Sanction, a decree that provided for his daughter's succession and the indivisibility of Habsburg lands. When Maria Theresa (r. 1740–1780) succeeded him, she became the first female ruler in the dynasty's 650–year history.

When Maria Theresa became empress at the age of twenty-three, she was four months pregnant and woefully unprepared to govern. Despite her father's work on behalf of the Pragmatic Sanction, he had done little to educate her to rule and had even excluded her from official meetings. Charles just assumed that Maria Theresa's husband would be the true power behind the throne.[29]

From the outset, she faced regular challenges to her authority. Almost immediately Bavaria, France, Prussia, and Saxony reneged on their support of the Pragmatic Sanction. Prussia invaded Silesia, initiating the War of the Austrian Succession. Soon, France, Spain, and Prussia formed a coalition against her. Things at home were no better. Her own subjects knew little about her and hated her French-speaking husband.

However, Maria Theresa proved to be an adept ruler, who was always willing to use her femininity to her advantage. In 1741, she went to the Hungarian diet to request military support. She stood before the Hungarian nobles with her four-month-old son in her arms and tears in her eyes. Her feminine wiles and some skillful negotiation persuaded the Hungarians to raise an army of fifty-five thousand men on her behalf.[30] With their aid, Maria Theresa quickly recovered her occupied lands. In 1742, she sent a letter and picture of herself and her infant son to the commander of her army hoping to rally him and his troops with a rousing reference to her femininity:

> *Here you see before you a queen and her masculine inheritance who have been abandoned by the whole world. What do you think will become of this child? Look at this poor woman who must place in your loyal hands, herself, her whole power, her authority, and everything that our empire stands for and is capable of achieving. Act, O hero and true vassal, as if you will have to justify yourself before God and the world.[31]*

Her military successes attracted Austria's traditional allies especially England. The war dragged on, but when peace was negotiated in 1748, Maria Theresa emerged with her claim to the monarchy secure (see Map 8.1).

Domestically, Maria Theresa liked to be called "Mother of the Country," *Landesmutter*, and she skillfully introduced a wide array of reforms that affected nearly all aspects of life in her domains. She revised the Austrian law code and abolished judicial torture. Within a decade, her administrative reforms had doubled state revenue and professionalized the civil and military bureaucracies. Despite her personal piety, she decreased the power of the church, particularly the Jesuit Order that controlled most educational institutions. When the pope suppressed the order in 1771, Maria Theresa appropriated its holdings to help finance expansion of the public school system. She believed that her subjects should be educated, as education was an avenue to greater productivity, better armies, stronger morality, and orthodox Catholicism. She also decreased the work required of serfs and abolished some feudal dues. However, her commitment to her people came from her personal piety and humanitarian concerns rather than an Enlightenment sense of social justice. She supported the social hierarchy that allowed her and her nobles to control most of the population and believed that calls for liberty and freedom would lead to chaos and disorder.

When not actively engaged in governing her empire, Maria Theresa was dedicated to her family. She was remarkably fertile. She gave birth to sixteen children, five sons and eleven daughters, and used their marriages in to the ruling houses across Europe to secure important alliances. Her most famous match was the marriage of her youngest daughter, Marie Antoinette, to the future French king, Louis XVI (r. 1774–1793). After her husband's death in 1765, Maria Theresa assumed the title *kaiserinwitwe*, empress-widow, cultivating the image of the sad widow and dressing in mourning for the rest of her life.[32]

From 1765, Maria Theresa ruled the hereditary Habsburg lands jointly with her son Joseph II (r. 1765–1790) until her death in 1780. More influenced by Enlightenment thought than his mother, Joseph II abolished serfdom in 1781 and reversed many of Maria Theresa's policies that had been motivated by religious intolerance. In 1745, she had expelled the Jews from Prague, accusing them of siding with Prussia against her. Joseph II condemned this decision and lifted the prohibition. He allowed Protestant clergy to proselytize, as long as they did not insult Catholicism. He continued his mother's policy of closing contemplative monasteries and limiting new monastic vocations, a process that constrained the opportunities for many aristocratic women He also ended censorship of the press and curtailed the activities of the secret police. Unfortunately, his progressive ideas met with considerable criticism, and the nobility and the clergy compelled him to rescind many of his reforms on his deathbed.

While Maria Theresa promoted an image of a powerful mother in Austria, her greatest rival, Frederick II (r. 1740–1786), fashioned a masculine, military society in neighboring Prussia. Frederick, who came to the throne only five months before Maria Theresa, viewed himself as the consummate enlightened monarch. He was an intellectual, a poet, a musician, and a lover of French culture. However, in reality, he was one of the most conservative monarchs in Europe.

By the end of the eighteenth century, Prussia had become the dominant military power on the European continent. Frederick's father, Frederick William I (r. 1713–1740), had created this powerful military by raising taxes, re-enserfing the peasantry, employing new technologies and strategies to modernize the troops, and setting up military academies. By 1740, the army had become the preeminent institution in the country, and Frederick was eager to use it to expand his territories. Upon coming to power, he rejected the Pragmatic Sanction and invaded Silesia in 1740, challenging Maria Theresa's succession to the throne.

To sustain his aggressive foreign policy, Frederick created a masculine culture focused on the military. The officers all came from the nobility, and the troops were conscripted peasants. His taxation system and bureaucracy were designed to support the army and he maintained a close alliance with the *Junkers*, the landed aristocracy who served as the officers in his army. To improve the health of the soldiers and the women who bore them, Frederick moved villages to more fertile lands and introduced potato cultivation. Frederick believed that social segregation ensured strict military discipline, and he used legislation to enforce class distinctions. Noble officers could not socialize with commoners, and he prohibited marriages between people of different social standings. Each social group paid different taxes and a noble could

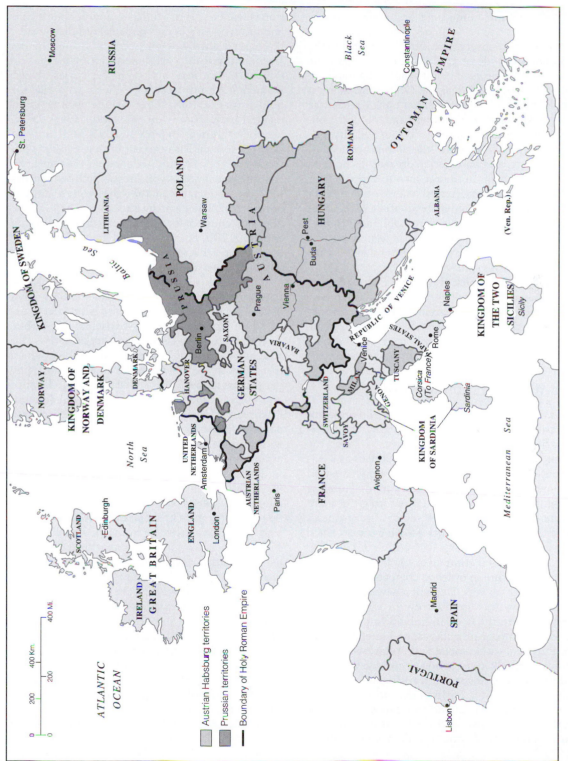

Map 8.1 EUROPE IN 1789. When Maria Theresa became the first woman to rule Habsburg lands, she adopted a policy of "enlightened despotism," tempering centralized rule with Christian charity.

not sell land to a commoner or a member of the middle class.

Frederick's conservative ideas are evident in the Prussian law code of 1747. The code reveals the contradictory views of gender that Enlightenment thought provoked in Prussia. On the one hand, it proclaimed both sexes as equal unless otherwise indicated by law. On the other hand, the code contained numerous exceptions to that equality. For instance, it declared that "the man is the head of the marriage, and his decision prevails in common affairs" and went on to urge men to support their wives appropriately, unless they could not, at which point wives had to be content with lower social standing. Women were "obligated to preside over the household." Thus, in legal terms, the code designated public life as men's sphere and the home as women's sphere.[33]

Although Frederick II may have wanted to be remembered for his enlightened ideas, his conservative reforms and laws reinforced class distinctions and traditional gender norms. Moreover, the centrality of the Prussian military created a masculine culture based on hierarchy and obedience.

The Westernization of Russia

Until the eighteenth century, Russia had only limited contact with western Europe. Only the determination of Peter I, also known as Peter the Great (r. 1682–1725), finally ended Russia's isolation. During his reign, he brought western European culture to Russia and made Russia a recognized European power. Although peasant women lives remained the same, elite women's lives changed dramatically as Peter transformed Russian society.

Peter believed that Russia had to adopt European culture in order to compete successfully with Western powers. He built a new capital in St. Petersburg with western European–style architecture. At court, the Russian nobility spoke French, dressed in European fashions, and attended western European–style social gatherings, where men and women talked, ate, and danced together. Peter did not achieve this social transformation easily. Most memorably, he insisted that nobles cut their beards. Noble women had to wear Western-style clothing that showed off the waist and the bust and left their heads uncovered, instead of tradi-

tional Russian tunics, cloaks, and kerchiefs that had hid women's bodies and covered their heads. He moved elite women out of seclusion in the *terem* and encouraged them to mix with men in public celebrations and court festivities. These women were not necessarily well prepared for public interactions. One British visitor commented on Russian women's awkwardness, stating they "appear indeed perfectly well dressed after the foreign Fashion; but in conversation with strangers, they cannot yet conquer their in-born bashfulness and awkwardness."[34] Other visitors to Peter's court noted that the women danced poorly and that Peter had to post guards at the doors of court balls to stop guests from leaving early. In 1700, Peter expanded his reforms to the lower classes, decreeing that women in towns also adopt Western dress.[35]

Peter used his family to model behavior and appearance. His half sister Praskovia Saltykova (1664–1723) was one of the first women at court to adopt European dress, participate in public assemblies, and host European-style parties. Her daughters received European educations, which focused more on language and natural philosophy than the traditional terem education of needlework and religious piety. When they were old enough, Peter married his nieces to European, not Russian, nobles in order to expand his political connections with western Europe. When Praskovia died, Peter arranged a grand European-style funeral.

Peter's second wife, Catherine I (1684–1727), was a Lithuanian peasant whose intelligence and interests matched Peter's. She came to Peter's attention after one of his field marshals captured her and made her his mistress. Peter married Catherine in 1712 and crowned her his consort in 1724. Peter included Catherine in his government, and when he died in 1725, she ruled successfully for two years, continuing Peter's pro-Western policies. For example, she sponsored expeditions to Siberia in search of furs for export; one expedition discovered the Bering Strait between Russia and Alaska. She also founded the Russian Academy of Sciences.

Catherine came to power because Peter declared his right to designate his successor. In fact, for much of the eighteenth century, women ruled Russia. After Catherine's death, Peter's great-niece Anna (r. 1730–1740) ruled, followed by his daughter Elizabeth (r. 1741–1760), and finally Catherine II (r. 1762–1796). Her son, Paul I (r. 1796–1801), then established hereditary rule, excluding women from the throne.

Russia's enthusiasm for Western ideas and practices continued but without much direction or commitment until the reign of Catherine II "the Great." Born Sophia Frederika Augusta, the daughter of a minor German prince, she married Tsar Peter III in 1733 at the age of fourteen. She took the name Catherine when she converted to Russian Orthodoxy. Unlike her husband whose only interest was drilling his troops, Catherine enthusiastically read Enlightenment writers. When she discovered that her husband wished to concede vast tracks of land won by Russians in hard-fought battles to Prussia, she led a coup and had Peter killed. She then ruled on her own, styling herself as an Enlightened ruler, but actually ruling as an absolute monarch.

Catherine's rule was filled with contradictions. On the one hand, she was a great supporter of education and the arts. She opened the first secular school for elite girls in 1764 and followed with plans for public schools in 1786. She also founded the Free Economic Society that produced up-to-date information on agriculture and industry. She corresponded with Voltaire and promoted many noble women to positions of public responsibility. Among them, Princess Ekaterina Vorontsova-Dashkova (1743–1810) became one of the great intellectuals of the Russian Enlightenment. She was the first women president of the Academy of Sciences and the Academy of the Study of the Russian Language. Vorontsova-Dashkova traveled around Europe, met Diderot and Voltaire among others, and oversaw the publication of the first Russian dictionary. She was also a naturalist, particularly interested in mineralogy.[36]

On the other hand, the condition of most of Russia's population worsened during Catherine's reign. Continual warfare and an ostentatious nobility cost the Russian peasantry dearly. Although initially Catherine expressed some interest in reforming serfdom, a series of rebellions prompted a change in her attitude. She issued decrees in 1765 and 1767 that reduced the serfs nearly to slave status. It became illegal for a serf to file a complaint against his or her master. Lords could sell serfs away from their families or exile them to Siberia for minor infractions. Class tensions came to a head in 1773 when a local uprising led by Emilian Pugachev (ca. 1740–1775), an illiterate Cossack (an ethnic group known for their military prowess) who claimed to be Catherine's murdered husband, erupted into an enormous peasant rebellion. It took two years and extreme measures to put it down. After the rebellion, Catherine dropped all pretense of enlightenment or liberalism, ruling harshly for the rest of her life.

The spread of Enlightenment ideas across Europe prompted some absolutist monarchs to pursue limited reforms. The absolutist rulers of the Habsburg monarchy and Prussia were both heavily influenced by gender expectations in their paths to reform. Maria Theresa of Austria relied on traditional representations of femininity to maintain power during her reign, and Frederick II of Prussia consciously created a very masculine, military culture during his. In Russia, although elite women benefited from the monarchy's Westernization policies, most Russian women experienced no improvement in their lives. For many, Enlightenment ideas about social reform and reconsiderations of gender expectations were too dangerous to even consider.

WOMEN, ART, AND CULTURE IN THE EIGHTEENTH CENTURY

During the late seventeenth and eighteenth centuries, changes in the art world transformed artisans into artists and provided women with a wide array of new opportunities. However, much like scientific inquiry, men worked to exclude women from the highest levels of artistic recognition. They attacked not only women's talents, but also the genres of painting, music, and literature typically associated with women. Nevertheless, women not only excelled at art, but created new forms of expression in painting, music, and literature that addressed the limitations of their gender.

Women as Professional Artists

The creation of artistic academies, such as the French Royal Academy of Painting and Sculpture founded in 1648, clearly established the position of the artist as a trained theoretician, not a tradesman or an amateur; however, painting's transition from a guild-controlled occupation to a profession did nothing to aid the artistic careers of women. The Royal Academy offered a rigorous course of instruction and hosted juried art shows that attracted thousands of visitors. It also established a hierarchy of painting genres. History paintings with their representations of Enlightenment themes of advancing civilization and republican sentiments were the most prestigious form, followed by portraiture, still life, and landscape. However, the Academy prevented women from obtaining the skills necessary to participate in the most prestigious genres. Women could not attend human drawing classes because it would expose them to naked bodies. This restriction made it difficult for women to get the training necessary to execute history scenes. Instead, women were relegated to portraiture, still lifes, and landscapes, the lesser forms of painting.

Fortunately, urban middle-class tastes helped to cultivate women's talents. They often hired women to immortalize their social and economic success in portraits and encouraged their daughters to learn painting and drawing because of the new availability of prepared colors, colored chalk, and inexpensive paper.

Indeed, paintings were often important illustrations of the emphasis on family and domesticity that men like Rousseau promoted. Images of mothers and women performing women's traditional "minor arts" of embroidery or sewing became particularly popular, such as depicted by Catherine Read's (1723–1778) *Lady Anne Lee Embroidering* (1764).

Despite these attempts to feminize certain artistic media and subjects, women transformed even popular genres. The Venetian painter Rosalba Carriera (1675–1757) revolutionized the use of pastels. By employing white chalk over a darker under drawing, she was able to create luminescent highlights. In 1720, she joined a group of artists in Paris working in the sensuous rococo style, popular among the wealthy urban elite. Carriera was so influential that the royal family commissioned her to paint the ten-year-old monarch, Louis XV. She was accepted as a member of the Roman Academy in 1705, and in 1720, she was elected to the Royal Academy in France, which had not admitted a woman in thirty-eight years. After Carriera, the Academy returned to its original policy of excluding women.[37]

In contrast to the restrictive policies of the Royal Academy, the *Académie de Saint-Luc*, founded in 1751, not only allowed women artists to exhibit, but its membership included a wide array of women artists and artisans. The two most famous French female painters, Adélaïde Labille-Guiard (1749–1803) and Elisabeth-Louise Vigée-Lebrun (1755–1842), began their careers there. The popular press created a rivalry between them, encouraging critics to compare the women to each other, rather than to their male contemporaries. However, this supposed rivalry generated accusations of sexual immorality and obscured both the quality of these women's works and the similarities in their styles. Labille-Guiard and Vigée-Lebrun were famed for introducing a "natural" and unencumbered image of women and motherhood into aristocratic portraiture, and their works reflect elite women's increasing emphasis on maternity and domesticity.[38] In particular, Vigée-Lebrun's famous painting of Marie Antoinette tried to redefine the foreign-born queen as a tender mother and domesticated queen.[39]

Breaking the boundaries of genre, Angelica Kauffmann (1741–1807) became renowned as one of the great history painters of her day. Having studied in Italy, she returned to her native England in 1766 and two years later was one of the founding members of the Royal Academy of Arts in London. She clearly fostered her unique position as a female history painter by consciously choosing subjects that had not been portrayed before and giving them innovative interpretations. Her royal patrons included Emperor Joseph II of Austria, Catherine II of Russia, and Queen Carolina of Naples (1752–1814). Engravers often copied her paintings and used them as china patterns and other decorative pieces, allowing her ideas to reach beyond those who could attend urban art exhibitions.[40]

Music

During the eighteenth century, although religious music was still popular, public secular music began to draw large audiences and created new opportunities for talented women. In fact, the most eminent names in eighteenth-century music, Antonio Vivaldi (ca. 1680–1743), Franz Josef Haydn (1732–1809), and Wolfgang Amadeus Mozart (1756–1791), employed female musicians, taught female students, and competed with female composers. Among the most celebrated female composers was Maria Theresia von Paradis (1759–1824). She studied with Mozart's rivals Leopold Kozeluch (1747–1818) and Antonio Salieri (1750–1825), and both Mozart and Haydn composed pieces for her. Mostly blind, she wrote more than thirty works, including at least five operas, as well as cantatas and numerous piano pieces.

In Venice, four *Ospedali*, or conservatories, trained talented orphan boys and girls. Donations and noble patronage provided the children with quality educations and dowries for the girls. The girls received ten years of rigorous training and those who completed the course could stay on at the conservatory as *maestrae*. Their concerts drew audiences from all over Europe. Antonio Vivaldi composed many of his celebrated works for the choirs and orchestras of girls in the *Ospedale della Pietà*. At least twenty-eight concertos were for violinist Anna Maria della Pietà (ca. 1689– after 1750). Although she never performed outside the conservatory, she was hailed as the greatest violinist in Europe. For other students of the Ospedale, a career in performance and teaching provided an alternative to marriage. Although generally women could not marry and maintain the status of maestrae, Maddalena Lombardini (later Sirmen) (1745–1785) was the exception. The daughter of poor aristocrats, she was raised in an ospedale and became both a virtuoso violinist and composer. Her talent was so great that she received permission to train with notable musicians outside of the conservatory and to occasionally tour with them as a singer, solo violinist, and a member of an opera orchestra. Sixty years after her death, her music was still in print and regularly performed.

Female opera singers gained increasing renown during this period, although they often had to compete with *castrati*, castrated men whose voices remained high, for roles. However, private training with male teachers, the gender-bending of operatic roles, and the androgynous or effeminate

castrati left women vulnerable to questions about their morality and sexuality. One exception was Faustina Bordoni (later Hasse) (1700–1781), whose noble background afforded her the best private teachers and lifted her above the suspicions associated with opera. She made her debut at age sixteen and became a star on the great stages of Europe. In the 1720s, she sang with Frederic Handel (1685–1759) in London. She then married operatic composer Johan Adolph Hasse (1699–1783), and both went to work at the court of Dresden, where she earned twice his salary.[41]

Choral music, which blended Protestant musical styles of Germany and the operatic traditions of Italy and France, also enjoyed great popularity. German concertmaster Johann Adam Hiller (1728–1804) of Leipzig argued for the inclusion of women's voices in choral music, and in 1771, he opened a school for male and female singers. He taught Corona Schröter (1751–1802), who went on to perform in royal German courts as a singer and actress and moved in the highest intellectual circles. In 1786 and 1794, she published two collections of her own songs, called *lieder,* experimenting with a range of styles, some drawn from the folk tradition.

Literature by and for Women

With the expansion of literacy, women produced and purchased books, pamphlets, and newspapers as never before, and the formation of lending libraries gave a broad segment of society access to the world of literature. One enthusiastic Spanish intellectual declared that the *Biblioteca Real,* which opened in Madrid in 1722, was "full of the best Spanish books which anyone is allowed to read."[42] As more people demanded printed material, literary styles multiplied and the printing industry expanded to accommodate the tastes of the reading public.

To meet the demands of this reading-hungry public, women founded popular magazines directed at female audiences. In England, Sarah Trimmer (1741–1810), who along with Hannah More had instigated the Sunday school movement, founded *The Family Magazine* in 1788. Their goal was to introduce middle-class manners, morals, and interests to the lower classes. To this end, Trimmer also wrote a religious history for young people in 1805. Women often risked their lives by expressing radical political opinions in the press. In Naples, Italy, Eleanor Pimentel (1752–1799) founded the republican newspaper the *Il Monitore*. She supported education for the lower classes, arguing that illiteracy hindered true political reform. When the monarchy cracked down on its opponents in 1799, she was arrested and executed.[43]

The eighteenth century saw the rise of the female novelist. Extremely popular among European women, the novel was a flexible form that allowed the author to include social commentary and explore personal development while entertaining the public. By the end of the century, female novelists nearly outnumbered male ones. As a popular genre, female authors had to find ways to express themselves while meeting the demands of critics and the reading public. Critics urged female novelists to avoid bawdy, sexually explicit prose in favor of sentimental tales of virtuous heroines, while the middle class, who purchased most novels and had the time to read them, wanted authors to write about family issues, interpersonal relationships, and feelings.

Novels in the form of letters became very popular. One of the first of these epistolary novels was *The Persian Letters* (1721), by Charles-Louis de Secondat, Baron de Montesquieu (1689–1755). Through the fictional letters of two Persians, Rica and Usbek, who are visiting Paris at the end of Louis XIV's reign, Montesquieu mocked French society and questioned its restrictions on women. Montesquieu likened Usbek's dominance of the wives in his harem to that of a despotic monarch who deprived his subjects of their happiness. After the success of *The Persian Letters*, Françoise de Graffigny (1695–1758) used the same medium of fictional letters to discuss women's roles in society. Whereas Montesquieu presented a male-voiced debate over the relative merit of a wife's fidelity or freedom, in *Letters from a Peruvian Woman* (1747), Graffigny chronicled the travels of Zilia, an Incan princess. Captured and sent to France, most of the letters are to her Peruvian lover, who in the end, betrayed her. Zilia admires French culture, even as it treats her with disdain. In her Spanish translation of *Letters from a Peruvian Woman,* María Romero Masegosa y Cancelada manipulated Graffigny's social commentary to suit Spanish concerns. She refashioned Graffigny's

negative portrayal of Spanish conquest into something more positive. Rather than maintain the common Enlightenment stance that Catholicism was a source of ignorance and superstition, Romero argued in her translation that hypocrisy and ignorance were far more dangerous.[44]

Gothic novels also became popular among women writers. Ann Radcliffe (1764–1823) wrote five such novels between 1789 and 1797. This style owed much to both the Enlightenment and colonial expansion. Gothic novels favored exotic locations, heavy atmospheres, and a standard plot of danger, lost inheritances, hidden crimes, and interactions with the supernatural. Authors contrasted scientific discoveries, travel, and empirical observation by the hero and heroine with the villain's superstitious behavior. Characters traveled to Catholic countries, where such "enlightened inquiry" was forbidden and whose "backward" customs set up obstacles for the hero to overcome. This genre became even more popular as industrialization and colonization expanded during the next century.

Readers' changing tastes did not prevent women writers from criticizing society. German author Sophie von La Roche (1731–1807), author of *The Story of Miss Von Sternheim* (1771), created a heroine, Sophie, who grew in wisdom and accomplishments as she fled a bad marriage and a seductive prince. While focusing on Sophie's personal moral development, von La Roche used her as a medium to express concerns about women's role in society at large. Similarly, Jane Austen (1775–1817) wrote with great irony and wit about women's lack of money, their need to make a good marriage, and the shallowness and greed of English society. Through observations of her characters, such as Elizabeth Barrett in *Pride and Prejudice* (1813), Jane Austen criticized society's constraints on women.

Until recently, women's artistic endeavors from the eighteenth century have been largely ignored. Their paintings fell into obscurity, their musical compositions were lost, and many of their novels only had one printing. Yet contemporaries noted the growth in women's artistic production, and the enthusiasm with which women engaged in artistic pursuits brought their ideas to larger audiences than ever before. Even as men sought to limit women's artistic activity, female artists persistently challenged those constraints.

GENDER IN THE COLONIES

During the eighteenth century, Europe's changing relationship with its colonial possessions altered the lives of women of all races and classes. European nations' increasing dependence on their colonies to supply the raw materials for the early stages of their industrial development came at the expense of women from Mexico to Calcutta and the expansion of the slave trade. At the same time, Enlightenment critiques of tyranny and debates about individual rights laid the foundation for the American Revolution. On both sides of the Atlantic, women fought for republican liberty and struggled with the social and moral implications of slavery.

Colonial Economies

During the seventeenth century, to ensure control over their expanding colonial possessions, many European nations adopted French minister of finance Jean-Baptiste Colbert's (1619–1683) economic policies aimed at increasing the power of the state. In terms of colonial economics, these *mercantilist* policies tightly regulated trade between the mother country and the colony. The colony extracted raw materials, which were then shipped to the mother country to be manufactured into finished goods. Laws required that colonists then buy the finished goods only from the mother country. They could not buy cheaper goods elsewhere, nor were they encouraged to manufacture their own finished products.

Mercantilism led to the expansion of enormous plantations across the Americas, most of which relied on slave labor. Because of the transient nature of colonial life, women often managed these large estates. For example, when Eliza Lucas Pinckney (1722–1793) was sixteen, her father left her in charge of the family plantation on the island of Antigua. After the family moved to South Carolina, he became lieutenant governor and again left his family and estate in her hands. An able and innovative manager, Eliza introduced indigo (a plant that produces a bright blue dye) on her plantation worked by hundreds of slaves. This crop quickly became the foundation of South Carolina's agricultural economy. Eliza married and bore four children, but she continued her pur-

suit of agricultural innovations, experimenting with hemp and flax, and revived the silk industry in the region. After her husband's death, she managed many of his properties.

With its victory over France in the Seven Years War (1756–1763), England added Canada, all of France's North American territories east of the Mississippi River, and most of France's possessions in India to its already extensive empire. In India, rather than directly administer its Indian possessions, the British government relied on the British East India Company to represent it and facilitate trade. These kinds of state-sponsored trading companies were very popular across Europe. Individuals invested in the companies, receiving a portion of the profits in return. Women eagerly participated in these financial opportunities. Women made up more than one-third of the investors in the East India Company in 1756. Interestingly enough, the majority of these female investors were not Englishwomen, but Dutch widows and single women attracted by the stability of the British company.[45]

The English government gave the East India Company extensive control over its dominions. Between 1763 and 1857, the East India Company directly managed many formerly independent Indian states and reduced others to vassal or dependent status with a native army led by a few European officers. It established major settlements in Bombay, Madras, and Calcutta, where white merchants and soldiers lived separate from the Indian population. At least during the eighteenth century, few English women traveled to India. Some wives of company employees settled with their husbands, but soldiers were prohibited from taking their wives. English society, both at home and in India, assumed that single women who emigrated to India were only seeking rich husbands. A ceremony called "sitting up" displayed newly arrived single women to marriageable men, and the women were referred to as "the fishing fleet."[46]

The Company ruled harshly and without regard for local custom, while making huge profits by exporting spices, cotton cloth, and tea to Europe. Indian women worked in the tea fields, harvested cotton and spices, and spun, wove, and dyed cotton into colorful cloth. Because female labor was cheap, the East India Company was able to export these goods inexpensively to England.

European demand for cotton and the British East India Company's successes led to important technological innovations. Manufacturers developed a series of new technologies to speed spinning and weaving, including the flying shuttle and the spinning jenny. In terms of colonial trade, these inventions had a powerful impact. With the ability to easily harvest and finish cotton at home, English merchants no longer needed to buy finished cloth from India, and by 1830, India's cotton trade was dead, putting thousands of women out of work.

Slavery and the Abolitionist Movement

Enlightenment ideas clashed with European economic growth over the issue of slavery. As economies boomed, the production of raw materials for use in Europe and the United States soared, and the United States increasingly relied on slave labor to keep up with demand. Over the course of the century, the British exported more than three million slaves from West Africa to its colonies and former colonies in North America and the Caribbean.

Male slaves outnumbered women by about two to one. Although some slave women worked in plantation houses caring for children, cooking, and cleaning, most worked in the fields planting and harvesting cotton. Slave owners routinely separated mothers and children and had little respect for the emotional ties between men and women. Women were brutalized and raped by slave traders and masters, and while infant mortality was much higher among slave than free women, those infants who survived assumed their mother's slave status.

Europe also had a small population of slaves. European elites prized African children as house slaves, where they served as accessories to the elite's lavish lifestyles. In addition, runaway and freed slaves established communities in places like London and Bristol. One scholar has estimated that there were as many as fourteen thousand blacks in eighteenth-century England.[47] These communities cultivated some of the earliest resistance to slavery, sheltering runaways and writing accounts of the slave trade.

Some of the most radical Enlightenment thinkers opposed slavery and were horrified to realize that their refined lifestyles and creature comforts depended on the wealth produced by slaves. The philosophe abbé Guillaume Thomas François Raynal (1713–1796) pointedly reminded his readers, "They [African slaves] are tyrannized, mutilated, burnt, and put to death, and yet we listen to these accounts coolly and without emotion. The torments of a people to whom we owe our luxuries, can never reach our hearts."[48] To address the issue, in 1788, Jacques-Pierre Brissot de Warville founded the Society of the Friends of Blacks, a French antislavery group. Unfortunately, both the ideals and most members of the Society would fall victim to the violence of the French Revolution.

England had a much larger and longer-lived abolition movement. Led by Hannah More, a bluestocking who grew up in the slave-trading town of Bristol, England, and Anna Laetitia Barbauld (1743–1825), Englishwomen pressed for abolition on both sides of the Atlantic. Quaker women, who were allowed to travel and preach, became important in these transatlantic discussions. For example, Mary Peisley (1717–1757) of County Kildare in Ireland and Catherine Phillips (1727–1794) of Worcestershire, England, traveled extensively in the United States organizing and speaking to groups of Quakers about abolition. Women also collected money for antislavery groups and gathered signatures for antislavery petitions that they submitted to Parliament. Many women boycotted sugar grown with slave labor. Antislavery literature enjoyed great popularity in England. One of the most famous antislavery pieces, *A Poem on the Inhumanity of the Slave-Trade* (1788), was written by Ann Yearsley, a working-class woman who sold milk for a living. Irish abolitionist poet Mary Birkett (1774–1817) admonished women to consider the role of slaves when buying goods: "yes, sisters, to us the task belongs / 'Tis we increase or mitigate their wrongs. / If we the produce of their toils refuse, / If we no more the blood-stain'd lux'ry choose."[49] England and the United States criminalized the slave trade in 1806. However, the impact of those decisions was limited as slavery remained legal in the Americas.

The American Revolution

Inspired by Enlightenment criticisms of absolutism and debates over individual rights and social equality, colonists in British America began to agitate for representation in the English Parliament. Much of this rhetoric was highly gendered, likening England to a corrupt and evil mother and the colonies as strongholds of manly virtue. Politician John Adams (1735–1826) worried about the threat of European "elegance, luxury, and effeminacy" on "colonial vigor, industry, and frugality."[50] Female writer Mercy Otis Warren (1728–1814) of Massachusetts understood the gendering of the colonial relationship quite differently. In her anonymously published

EUROPE SUPPORTED BY AFRICA AND AMERICA, WILLIAM BLAKE (1796). Beliefs in women's need for domination and support were employed by intellectuals to conceptualize the relationship between Europe and the colonies. *(The Bridgeman Art Library.)*

satire, *The Adulateur* (1772), villainous governor Rapatio figuratively set out to rape the colony.

Colonists were particularly outraged at progressive increases in their taxes, much of which was used to pay for England's wars. The Stamp Act of 1765 taxed all paper, including newspapers, legal documents, and stationery. Angry mobs of men and women rioted and Parliament withdrew the tax the next year. However, Parliament also reaffirmed its right to tax the colonies in the Declaratory Act, and in 1767, the Townsend Act imposed new duties on all imports into the thirteen colonies, prompting colonists to boycott British products.

The boycotts that arose in response to the Townsend Act drew women into politics in unprecedented ways. The most famous of these political acts was the tea boycott, which followed the Tea Act of 1773. In 1773, Parliament withdrew the Townsend Act but replaced it with a tax on tea. Colonists retaliated by boycotting tea. The success of the boycott required male organizers winning over women to the cause, because purchasing tea, like all foodstuffs, was a part of women's domestic work. Newspaper editorials called upon women to participate in the boycott, and, in response, both individuals and groups of women publicly asserted their opposition to British taxes. In 1774, one landlady refused to serve tea to John Adams, even though he specifically requested smuggled, untaxed tea. In Boston in 1773, three hundred women publicly agreed to refrain from serving any tea, and in October 1775, fifty-one women from North Carolina publicly declared their support of the tea boycott. Conversely, prominent Loyalist women drank tea in public as an assertion of their political stance.[51] Other boycotts included women organizing or hosting spinning bees to make their own cloth, in order not to buy cloth manufactured in England. Such political behavior on the part of women shocked many, and British newspapers lampooned colonial women's efforts.

Women's efforts did not end with the outbreak of war in 1776. Although General George Washington (1732–1799) did not like the large numbers of women in his camps, his continually undersupplied army needed women to make uniforms, cook food, tend the sick and wounded, and do anything necessary to keep the colonial army fighting. Women even raised money to help the revolutionary forces. In Philadelphia, New Jersey, and Maryland, women went door-to-door soliciting money to help the troops, an act which would have been shocking in other circumstances.[52]

Many women took up arms to defend their houses and farms. After Margaret Corbin's (1751–ca.1800) husband died during an assault on Fort Washington, she loaded his cannon and fired until she was wounded by enemy fire. The Continental Congress granted her a pension as a disabled soldier. However, a few women fought in the army disguised as men. Perhaps the most famous is Deborah Samson (1760–1827), who was only discovered when she fell sick with a fever, after fighting for two years. When she died, her husband received a pension as a widower of a revolutionary soldier.

The American Revolution, like all wars, was dangerous for noncombatants. Both British and American troops plundered towns and farms and killed civilians. The British practice of billeting troops in civilian homes left women particularly vulnerable to sexual assault. Hunger, disease, and economic devastation left many families ruined, not to mention the many women widowed by the rebellion.

With the defeat of the British in 1781, the elite men who had led the Revolution debated the qualifications for citizenship in the new nation. From the outset, some had argued that women who met property requirements should be granted certain rights as citizens. Indeed, Abigail Adams (1744–1818) admonished her husband, John, to grant women rights, noting that, "all men would be tyrants if they could. If particular care and attention is not paid to the ladies, we are determined to foment a rebellion, and will not hold ourselves bound by any laws in which we have no voice or representation" (*Letter from Abigail Adams to John Adams, March 31, 1776*). However, the Declaration of Independence, issued only three months later, stated only that "all men are created equal." The presumption of women's inequality persisted throughout the creation of the legislative and judicial institutions of the new nation. Women were neither involved in their formation nor allowed to serve in their halls.

However, at least at first, individual states had considerable freedom in defining citizenship within their borders, and some propertied women had limited voting rights in New York, New Hampshire, New Jersey, and Massachusetts. Moreover, New Jersey's Constitution of 1776 gave all inhabitants worth fifty pounds and over the age of twenty-one the right to vote regardless of race or gender, and its election law of 1790 refers to voters as both "he" and "she." As married women had few independent legal rights, only single and widowed adult, property-owning women met New Jersey's criteria as voters. Yet, by 1784, the tide had turned and all states except New Jersey had rescinded women's voting rights. Following their lead and encouraged by charges of voter fraud, New Jersey legislators terminated women's right to vote in 1807.

Instead of supporting women as active voting citizens, American leaders created a new political role for women that historian Linda Kerber has called *Republican motherhood*. That is, rather than direct engagement in politics as a citizen, a woman's role as mother determined her participation in politics. She was to train her children in civic virtue, educate her sons for civic participation, and correct her husband when he failed to uphold civic values.[53] Women could not be citizens in the United States; they could only contribute to the political culture of the new nation through their influence over men.

Women in Spanish America

In Spanish America, Enlightenment intellectuals had to negotiate the strong presence of the Catholic Church and a strong monarchy back in Spain. There were few calls for republican government and almost none for social equality, yet eighteenth-century intellectual and economic trends still shaped Spanish colonial life. In particular, the Spanish monarchy attempted to reformulate the mother country's relationship with its colonies to increase its colonial income to pay for its Continental wars and the defense of its extensive colonial borders.

Women in Spanish America played an ever-larger role in the changing economy. In addition to administering large estates, wealthy white women often invested in companies that manufactured or sold goods. Doña María Paulía y Aguirre (d. 1789), the daughter of one of Mexico City's most important textile factory owners and widow of a

wealthy merchant, owned a store and two factories. Some women, like María Magdalena de
Mérida of Caracas, could be quite successful. The
widow of a military man, she increased her husband's estate by two thousand silver pesos in the
first five years after his death.[54]

Farther down the social scale, women owned
shops or worked in factories. According to a 1795
survey of Mexico City, 7 percent of the shop owners were women.[55] In cloth production and some
areas of food preparation, women were so numerous that by the end of the eighteenth century,
guilds began to admit them. Women also worked
in cigarette factories. Indian and mestiza women
(part Indian and part European) dominated the
manufacturing and retail of some alcoholic bever-
ages, and women of all races worked in domestic
service, although white women generally did not
do the most menial jobs, leaving those tasks to
women of color—Indians, black women (both
free and enslaved), and mestizas and mulattas
(part black and part European). In the countryside, poor free and slave women worked in the
fields and the mines.

White women in Spanish American cities tried
to emulate the lavish lifestyles of their European
relations. They imported expensive clothes and
jewelry and were attended by entourages of black
or mixed-race servants. Since wealthy European
women were in short supply, they often married
young and had many children. Francisca Moreno
de Mendoza, the wife and daughter of military
men, married at fifteen and had sixteen children,
one child every thirteen months for the next
twenty-one years.[56]

As far away as Bógota, elite Spanish women
tried to form their own versions of European
salons. Doña Manuela Sanz de Santamaría held a
weekly salon called *El Buen Gusto*, where attendees discussed science, literature, and radical politics. However, unlike Spain or France, we have no
female writers commenting on women's status in
the colonies. Woman may not have participated in
these debates due to the conservative nature of the
Enlightenment in Spanish America and the rarity
of advanced female education.

The most dramatic change in the lives of Spanish
American women came with the Spanish monarchy's regulation of marriage. In Catholic countries,
the church had sole authority over marriage,
emphasizing an individual's free will and the right to
marry even without parental consent. However,
many Spanish thinkers believed that the growth of
the nonwhite population in Spanish America threatened the social and racial hierarchy because women
married men who were not their social, economic,
or racial equals. As a part of its program to remove
authority from the church, the Spanish monarchy
issued the Royal Pragmatic in Spain in 1776 and in
Spanish America in 1778. The Pragmatic protected
families from "unequal" marriages and preserved
the social and economic hierarchy by requiring a
parent's or guardian's consent to all marriages under
threat of disinheritance. Although the crown
intended to prevent interracial marriage, parents
used it to stop marriages of unequal status or
wealth. The Pragmatic resulted in a flood of lawsuits, like that of Don Manuel Valdivieso y Carrión
from Quito Ecuador, who sued Juan Teodoro
Jaramillo, his daughter's fiancé. Don Manuel argued
that Jaramillo was of too low a social standing for
his daughter and he wanted the royal authorities to
intervene and prevent the marriage.[57] For women in
Spanish America, the Enlightenment was less about
freedom and more about increased government regulation and control.

Women did not always benefit as colonial society
became a testing ground for Enlightenment ideas.
Although North American women challenged
British rule, their participation went unrewarded
as men relegated them to the margins of American
politics. In Spanish America, many European
women lost the critical right to choose their own
marriage partners as the monarchy used marriage
laws to reinforce social, economic, and racial hierarchies. Nevertheless, many women adopted
Enlightenment ideas of social equality, working
tirelessly to end the injustice of slavery.

WOMEN AND THE FRENCH REVOLUTION

The most radical manifestation of the Enlightenment was the French Revolution (1789–1798).
Revolutionaries developed doctrines of human
rights and citizenship and fostered institutions
that opened politics to all levels of society. Unlike

the American Revolution, where women's involvement drew largely on their domestic experiences, French women's participation in the Revolution was much more extensive, as they questioned the quality of their citizenship and their place in the new revolutionary society.

Women and the Start of the Revolution

One of the major issues that led to the French Revolution was the absolutism of King Louis XVI. Known for his harsh and inconsistent laws and his wild spending habits, he exacerbated an ongoing fiscal crisis, which he and his ministers tried to resolve by raising the already high taxes. Peasants and urban laborers bore the brunt of these taxes, from which the nobility and rich middle classes were exempt. Much of the population also resented the church, which they saw filled with unproductive, frivolous, and immoral aristocrats whose prying eyes and greed further burdened the population. Food shortages in the late 1780s brought these tensions to a head.

In 1788, the king again raised taxes, but the nobility resisted, and in desperation, the king and his ministers summoned the Estates General, an assembly representing the three estates of society (the clergy, the nobility, and the common people) to approve new taxes. The Estates General had not met since 1614, as French monarchs had ruled with limited input from their subjects. Much had changed in the intervening century and a half. By 1788, the Third Estate included not only the peasantry, but also the urban middle classes, some of whom were richer than the nobility. Calling the Estates General necessitated elections for deputies to represent the three estates. Traditionally, few people had participated in this process, but in the Enlightenment spirit of public debate, intellectuals and officials widely publicized the election and men and women of all classes enthusiastically debated political issues. Local deputies assembled lists of people's concerns. Assembling the lists of grievances involved both men and women of all classes in the political process. Female artisans wanted protection for their crafts and rural women wanted better prices for their grain, and women across France complained about unhappy marriages.[58] These complaint books demonstrate

French women's determination to be a part of political reform.

Once the Estates General assembled in Paris in the late spring of 1789, the members quickly realized that the king had no interest in their reform agenda. In anger, the Third Estate split off and formed a new body called the National Assembly. Members of the National Assembly drew on Enlightenment ideas that state power resided with the people, not an absolutist monarch. They argued that they had a mandate to govern from the people and vowed not to disband until they created a new constitution for France.

The National Assembly worked throughout 1789. They kept the people apprised of their efforts despite resistance from the king, who refused to acknowledge the Assembly's legitimacy. On July 14, an angry mob of men and women stormed the Bastille prison. Although largely a symbolic act, it demonstrated the people's strong opposition to royal power. In August, the National Assembly abolished all feudal privileges and sent to the king a *Declaration of the Rights of Man and Citizen*, which stated that based on natural law, the people were the source of his sovereignty, and that he could not rule without their consent. Throughout the summer, people demonstrated in Paris and other cities almost daily. Women played a key role in these disturbances. Police reports even include accounts by women who felt coerced into joining for fear of reprisals by other women. Although women had long been part of mob violence and demonstrations, the events of the summer of 1789 gave new meaning to their actions and drew a larger cross section of women.

When the king refused to ratify the *Declaration of the Rights of Man and Citizen*, a mob of women, angered by high bread prices and food shortages, marched on the king's palace of Versailles, outside of Paris. Demanding that the king and his family move back to Paris, they broke into the palace and killed two bodyguards. A small delegation met with the king and his queen, Marie Antoinette, and fearing more violence, the king and queen returned with the women to Paris where they were kept under guard.

With the royal family under lock and key, the National Assembly began a radical restructuring of French government and society (see **Sources from the Past:** Marie-Madeleine Jodin on Women's Rights). They created a new national administration, eliminated church power, and ended privileges based on birth. They instituted new holidays, such as Bastille Day, adopted the Tricolor flag, and tried to impose a new state religion dedicated to the Supreme Being. The Assembly also abolished slavery in the colonies. In 1792, the National Assembly adopted a new set of laws designed to end the patriarchal family, which reformers argued replicated the relationship between the king and his subjects. The laws ended distinctions between legitimate and illegitimate children and primogeniture, allowing younger sons and daughters to inherit. New laws made it easier for women to file for divorce. However, women did not gain full equality. Basing citizenship on the concept of "public utility," the constitution classified women with foreigners, domestic servants, and men who could not pay the value of three days of labor as passive citizens, unable to vote. Men who paid this rate were active citizens and could vote. Although radical for the time, the National Assembly could not disassociate women from the domestic realm.

By 1791, the church and the nobility who had fled into exile began financing a counterrevolutionary movement. The king and his family escaped Paris with the intent of joining supporters at the Belgian border. On the way, revolutionaries recognized, captured, and brought them back to Paris where they faced a hostile crowd. The royal family's arrest ushered in a new phase of the Revolution. Whereas the revolutionaries had been fighting for liberty and an end to what they saw as feudal traditions that privileged the aristocracy, the next phase focused on citizenship and equality and brought increased revolutionary activity by urban women.

Women and the Radical Phase of the French Revolution

The new government faced many problems. When Louis fled, the National Assembly suspended his executive powers. To prove its legitimacy, the Assembly assumed France's massive debts and suffered a devastating combination of rising prices and no new sources of revenue. Tensions developed between urban radical revolutionaries and the National Assembly, and Austria amassed armies along France's borders.

A variety of political clubs, such as the radical *Cercle Social* and the Cordeliers Club, contributed to Parisians' radicalism. The Cercle Social was the first club to admit women. Members challenged the legitimacy of both the king and the National Assembly. The Cercle Social argued that women should be granted citizenship and without that provision, France's democracy was incomplete. One male member declared: "Women be a citizen! Until now you have only been a mother."[59] Members of the club did not accept the idea that motherhood disqualified women from equal rights.

On July 17, antagonisms between the people of Paris and the National Assembly came to a head. The National Assembly's troops fired on a peaceful demonstration at the Champ de Mars, killing dozens of people. The massacre outraged the citizens of Paris, who believed that the National Assembly had betrayed them and that their constitution of 1791 was invalid.

The next year, revolutionary leaders encouraged women to challenge the constitutional monarchy by demanding the right to carry a pike: an affordable and easy-to-use weapon of self-defense. It became a symbol of equality, independence, and the recovery of liberty. In newspapers, at clubs, and on broadsheets, men and women debated women's ability to carry pikes. Pauline Léon (1768–after 1793), who had been at the massacre at Champ de Mars, presented a petition of more than three hundred signatures to officials and declared, "You cannot refuse us and society cannot remove from us this right which nature gives us, unless it is alleged that the Declaration of Rights is not applicable to women and that they must allow their throats to be slit, like sheep, without having the right to defend themselves."[60] While the National Assembly debated, the mayor of Paris granted them this right, thus creating a model of women's citizenship that combined their right to defend themselves with their civic obligation to defend the nation. By the spring of 1793, Léon and other women used this new authority to form an all-women's political group, the Society of Revolutionary Republican Women, which

Marie-Madeleine Jodin on Women's Rights

Marie-Madeleine Jodin (1741–1790) was an actress, a protegée of the great philosophe Diderot, and a strong advocate for women's rights. Published at the height of the French Revolution, her argument that women should be granted full citizenship based on their moral perfectibility is a sharp critique of Rousseau's ideas about women. Jodin's treatise may be the first signed, female-authored, feminist work of the Revolution.

LEGISLATIVE VIEWS FOR WOMEN ADDRESSED TO THE NATIONAL ASSEMBLY BY MADEMOISELLE JODIN

Now that the French have declared their zeal for the regeneration of the State and for basing its happiness and glory on the eternal foundations of Virtue and Law, the thought has struck me that my sex, which constitutes an attractive half of that fair Empire, could also claim the honour, and even the right, of contributing to the public welfare; and that in breaking the silence to which politics seems to have condemned us, we could usefully say: 'And we too are Citizens.'

As such, have we not our rights as well as our duties, and must we remain purely passive at a moment when all fruitful thinking about the public good must also touch on this delicate point, the happy bond which attaches us to good? No, there is a plan necessary to the health of our Legislation; and this plan, founded upon ancient and pure foundations, shaken by the vicissitudes of time and the alteration of manners, can only, it seems to me, be revived by ourselves.

I mean to do no more than announce this plan. The programme is a simple one; it invites my fellow Citizenesses to take part in an undertaking altogether worthy of them and of the motives which led me to conceive it. Happy woman that I am! Able to pay to my country the debt, not of talents, but of the heart; and to my sex, that of my esteem.

LEGISLATIVE VIEWS FOR WOMEN

At a time when true Philosophy is beginning to enlighten all minds, when the defeat of Despotism leaves the prejudices which owed their existence to it helpless and without defence, shall the weaker sex, excluded by force from public deliberations, demand its inalienable rights in vain? Shall that essential half of Society not have any share in the legislative Code proclaimed in the name of Society as a whole? I can picture the reason and equity which animate the august Assembly of Representatives of the Nation, amazed that these questions have not been raised before, hastening to welcome them. So let us obey the general impulse which directs all ideas towards the goal of liberty regained, a liberty usurped by oppression from all of us equally. . . .

Do you wish to raise us to great things? All that is necessary is to excite our emulation. Now, this can only be brought about by a new mode of political organization—one which grants full rights to opinion and frees us from the species of tutelage which, in a sense, separates us from public concerns, leaving us linked with them only by our heart's vows and irresistible attraction to that imperious sex which enslaves our wills as it does our affections. But whilst the subordination thus inseparable from our condition bends us under its Laws, it has not succeeded in stifling our sense of our rights. We claim them today, Sirs, when a new scheme of Legislation is to consider the bonds connecting us with civic harmony. If our private advice has benefited you, when esteem and love have admitted us into your confidence, what even greater advantages will you not derive from our gratitude (for we shall have to owe it to your goodwill) when you restore to us the rights which are ours by Nature and by the social compact. . . .

Love of country, of liberty and of glory animate our sex as much as they do yours, Sirs; we are not, on this earth, a different species from yours. The mind has no sex, any more than does Virtue; but the vices of intelligence and the heart belong almost exclusively to your sex. It is painful for me to declare this harsh truth, but one is sometimes allowed to take one's revenge. . . .

We deserve no fewer eulogies, and no less censure, than yourselves, Sirs. Some women are the shame of their sex, some are its glory; nothing will curb the former in vice, nothing will arrest the latter in the painful path of Virtue. Your sex is not more free than ours from this contrast; for what motives, then, could you pronounce a *nolle prosequi* on this demand of ours to the right to contribute with you to the public welfare, in the legal sphere which concerns us alone? One sex has not been appointed the oppressor of the other, and these ridiculous debates about superiority offend against Nature. You are born our friends, not our rivals, and we emulate you. To reduce us to slavery is to abuse a force which was given you to defend us; it is to deprive Society of what gives it charm and life. . . .

The empire which we wield through beauty is only given us for the good of the human species. The character of the male, destined to strong actions, has a roughness which it is our task to correct; a gentleness in our manners, even more than in our features, is designed to soften that natural pride of yours which otherwise degenerates into ferocity. From every point of view, man would be less perfect, less happy, if he did not converse with women. He who is insensible to commerce with women, who refuses it, has an inflexibility that renders his very Virtues dangerous. . . . In our absence, Sirs, your imagination is inactive, your productions are without grace, your philosophy is sombre and harsh; in your absence, ours become too frivolous. It is by commerce with you that our talents and qualities develop and acquire solid-ity. From this exchange of mutual aid there flows a happy concord which brings both of us nearer to perfection, the faults of one sex correcting those of the other, and in this way women, whatever you do, will always be central to life in Society. Your having charge of public affairs only reinforces our value. The human species conducting itself more by the heart than by the mind, the direction of public affairs, whoever is responsible for it, is always influenced by what is loved. Accordingly, Sirs, you will always do what we want. Where women command, men reign, and when women reign, they prove that they possess the science of government in the highest degree.

The English were never so powerful as under the reign of Elizabeth. Women in France, though excluded from the throne, have none the less played their part in government during various royal minorities. Queen Blanche proved that she deserved more than a mere regency; her maxims are the Code of good kings. Catherine II, reigning in the north at this moment, will be the model for conquerors. Though the snarls of jealous pride endeavour to tarnish the splendour of her great qualities, she will none the less occupy an honourable place in history! The men of Rome, too jealous of their own authority, allowed women no part in government; but in France, where custom and Nature grant them an influence, one could not fail to benefit by entrusting to them Legislation on manners and morals, . . .

If order, the foundation of Society, depends especially on the Virtue and decency of women, if regard for this constitutes their honour, as your 'point of honour' is courage, and if your Laws—refer matters of masculine honour to a unique and supreme tribunal, why should we not have ours too? . . .

Source: Felicia Gordon and P. N. Furbank, *Marie Madeleine Jodin, 1741–1790: Actress, Philosophe and Feminist* (Burlington, VT: Ashgate Press, 2001), 176–191.

worked to curb prices on food and limit the influence and power of the aristocracy.

Gender did more than inform the debates over citizenship. Revolutionaries also used sexually charged rhetoric to press their claims and humiliate the royal family. Some pamphlets even argued that the right to sex with anyone, in any position, was a natural and inalienable right. The queen, Marie Antoinette, was a particularly popular subject. Her foreign origins, frivolous nature, and her difficult relationship with the king, who was impotent for the first seven years of their marriage, inspired anonymous attacks, satires, and criticisms in both newspapers and broadsides. One frequent accusation, featured in such pamphlets as *The Royal Dildo* or *The National Bordello Under the Auspices of the Queen*, was that she was a lesbian. Anonymous writers asserted that because the king could not satisfy her, she found comfort in the arms of other women and in the bed of her brother-in-law. By questioning the queen's sexuality, pamphleteers criticized the royal family and the aristocracy for adhering to a different moral code than the rest of the nation, further undermining the legitimacy of the monarchy.[61]

As the violence escalated, it became clear that the Parisian revolutionaries were far more radical than their rural counterparts. Most peasants had fairly conservative political ideas. They were happy to have their taxes lowered and were not opposed to the republic, but they disagreed with the extreme goals of the Revolution. Rural women particularly resisted the campaign to de-Christianize the nation, which they saw as an attack on their families and traditions. They believed the abolition of church bells, which regulated the day, and the ecclesiastical calendar, which ordered the year, as too radical. Instead of the Trinity and the Virgin Mary, the Revolution promoted alternative deities such as the Supreme Being, Reason, and Liberty. This part of the revolutionary program failed dramatically and villagers engaged in both active and passive resistance to it. For example, in 1794, a governmental official arrived in a Loire village to preach on the Supreme Being at the local Temple of Reason. When he began, the women stood up, turned around, and lifted their skirts revealing naked backsides.[62] Women could also secretly

MARIE ANTOINETTE AND HER CHILDREN (1788). Elisabeth-Louise Vigée-Lebrun's (1755–1842) picture of the unpopular queen in a domestic setting did not change her image with the public. They were unable to see her as maternal, but only as frivolous and decadent. *(Art Resource, NY.)*

baptize an infant, pray over a dying person, or provide a Christian burial service at night—all in opposition to revolutionary dictates.

Women who supported the Revolution became more radical and more vocal, articulating distinct political programs from men. Two pieces of writing stand out as statements on women's rights in the new nation: Olympe de Gouge's *Declaration of the Rights of Woman and Female Citizen* (1791) and Mary Wollstonecraft's *Vindication of the Rights of Woman* (1792). Both women had been on the fringes of the salons, and Enlightenment thinking influenced their ideas. Olympe de Gouge (ca. 1748–1793) came from an uneducated, provincial family, but she later claimed to be the illegitimate child of a nobleman. At sixteen, she married a man she did not love and had at least one son.

She left her husband for Paris in 1770, where she developed her political ideas living on the fringes of the salons, supported by a male companion. During the Revolution, she frequented many of the radical political clubs and wrote political pamphlets and political dramas. Her most famous work, her *Declaration,* was largely unknown during her lifetime. Modeled on the *Declaration of the Rights of Man and Citizen*, published by the National Assembly, it was a call for action by women. She based women's right to citizenship on the fact that women gave birth to citizens, an act that contributed to the state. Therefore, women should be granted equal citizenship with men. For de Gouge, gender and sex differences were important, but they did not justify political exclusion. She also demanded equal opportunities in employment and women's right to economic support by the fathers of their children.[63]

Mary Wollstonecraft (1758–1797), an English journalist and teacher, became involved in the French Revolution when she moved to France. Her *Vindication of the Rights of Woman* celebrated women's involvement in the Revolution and challenged Rousseau's belief that women should have only limited education. According to Wollstonecraft, because women were rational creatures, they had a right to the same education as men in order to develop the dignity of their work as partners to their husbands in the household. Without such education, women could not adequately perform the natural duties of motherhood. She also decried conceptions of women's femininity, believing that they developed out of women's dependence on men and kept them in an inferior position. The equal treatment of the sexes should result from their separate but equal human duties to community and nation.

Increased radicalism led to more violence. In August of 1792, the constitutional monarchy collapsed. In January of 1793, after a brief trial, the king was executed for treason and a new legislative body, the National Convention, took over the government. The National Convention tried the queen separately on charges that included incest and executed her as well.

With the ongoing war with Austria needing urgent attention, the National Convention turned over concern for counterrevolutionaries to the Committee of Public Safety, a group of twelve men lead by Maximilien Robespierre (1758–1794). Relying on Rousseau's rhetoric, Robespierre argued that sovereignty resided with the people and that he would root out all opposition to their will. However, he ruled as a virtual dictator and executed twenty-five thousand people for their real and imagined counterrevolutionary beliefs or activities. In July of 1793, Charlotte Corday (1768–1793) assassinated Jean-Paul Marat (1743–1793), the radical pamphleteer, while he bathed. Corday, outraged that Marat had supported Robespierre and what became known as the Reign of Terror, wanted to avenge his betrayal of the Revolution. For this act, she was guillotined in 1793. Ironically, because Olympe de Gouge had dedicated her *Declaration of the Rights of Women* to the queen, she was executed as a royalist in 1793.

The Committee of Public Safety found women's agitation so threatening that they outlawed women's political groups such as the Society of Revolutionary Republican Women. Later the Committee banned women from attending public meetings or assembling in groups. At the same time, the government also imposed price controls on foodstuffs, which won the support of many women. A combination of the Terror's violence and legislation that prevented women's participation as citizens pushed women back into their homes.

Robespierre's popularity declined as his fanaticism grew. The National Convention began refusing to pass his decrees, and in September 1794, the Committee of Public Safety executed Robespierre as an enemy of the state, ending the Terror. A new, governing body, called the Directory, was elected and took over the government. Made up of many members of the previous National Convention, the Directory withdrew from the radical ideas of the Revolution and tried to negotiate between royalists and radical republicans. Because of its general Napoleon Bonaparte (1769–1821), the Directory achieved considerable military success, expanding France's territory to include Belgium, the Netherlands, Switzerland, and much of Italy. However, it was unable to reconcile opposing political factions. In 1798, Napoleon overthrew the Directory and declared himself the leader of the new French government. In 1802, the French people gave him the title "consul for life."

Women and the Napoleonic Era

Following his conquest of France, Napoleon turned his attention to the rest of Europe. In 1801, Napoleon defeated Austria. In 1802, he signed a treaty with Great Britain that assured his continued rule of the Low Countries and the rest of Italy. In 1804, Napoleon crowned himself emperor. By 1806, the Holy Roman Empire had collapsed and Napoleon controlled its territories. He conquered Spain and Portugal and had weakened Russia, Austria, and Prussia through diplomatic maneuvers and outright military defeat. By the 1807 Treaty of Tilsit, he dominated Europe (see Map 8.2). His conquests made him adored in France and reviled throughout the rest of Europe.

Napoleon created a highly efficient and centralized government to regulate the lives of his subjects. At the heart of his government was the 1804 legal reform called the Napoleonic Code, which he imposed on all social classes and all conquered territories. The Code was a radical departure from traditional ideas of law and privilege. There were no exceptions for the rich and aristocratic and no feudal privileges. At the same time, it was very conservative, enshrining Napoleon's belief in separate spheres for men and women. Napoleon believed that women needed protection, not liberty. He did not believe that they could be citizens, or that they should have public legal rights. He had vivid memories of women marching with weapons in the French Revolution and wanted to ensure that women never took up arms against him. By reestablishing the patriarchal family and subordinating women to male authority, the Napoleonic Code undid most of the social and legal gains French women made in the Revolution.

Central to redefining women's status were changes to the laws surrounding married women and marriage. The Code also made it difficult for married women to inherit property. While married a woman could not undertake legal transactions without her husband's permission and she could not appear in court. Her husband controlled any property she brought to the marriage, and it became difficult for women to inherit property. The Code made it harder for a wife to initiate divorce than a husband. A wife's adultery was grounds for divorce without her consent, but a woman could only sue for divorce without her

husband's permission if he kept his mistress in the same house with his wife. In keeping with the idea that women needed protection, these divorce laws tried to protect middle-aged women from abandonment. Even if both parties agreed to the divorce, the Code forbade it if it was within the first two years of marriage, if the wife was over forty-five years old, or if the couple had been married for more than twenty years.[64] The Code served as a model for the legal codes of Italy, Portugal, Spain, and parts of Switzerland.

To enforce his Code, Napoleon created an extensive bureaucracy that kept track of population size, how many children women had, how much land families owned, how much money they earned, and what they thought about him and his government. With this information, he created a taxation and military system that helped further his conquests and silenced political opposition. His bureaucracy changed the relationship between women, families, and the state.

Napoleon's imperial ambitions required an immense army. Napoleon argued that families should willingly work and fight for his empire, and that women should bear and raise the sons who would sacrifice themselves for him and the greater glory of France. Motherhood was not just a biological function, it was also a patriotic duty. His bureaucracy identified male babies and kept track of them as they grew to military age. Since not enough men would volunteer, Napoleon conscripted most of his army. Scholars estimate that between 1799 and 1812, Napoleon had 1.3 million men in arms.[65] An army of six hundred thousand, over half of whom came from outside of France, invaded Russia.

Conscription created hardship and disrupted families. Although the rich could pay someone to serve in the military for them or pay the fines imposed for resisting the draft, the working and peasant classes could not. Familiar with the soldiers' stories of poor treatment, loneliness, and homesickness, large numbers of men resisted conscription. Throughout 1802 and 1803, entire villages in Italy violently resisted conscription by burning birth registers, draft notices, and other evidence of military eligibility. Government officials responded by imposing travel restrictions, which hindered peasants' ability to flee. These regulations also limited women's ability to go to mar-

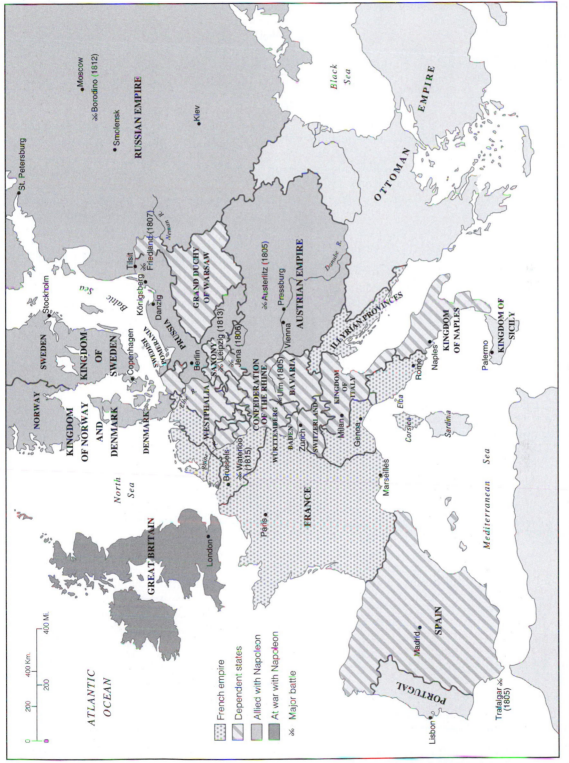

Map 8.2 Napoleonic Europe in 1810. Napoleon's conquest put most European women under his restrictive legal code.

ket and men's ability to search for work or follow their herds to better grazing. Women frequently helped individual men resist the draft by hiding them in barns, cellars, or in nearby woods, and by supplying them with food and clothing until the recruiters left. In 1805, police in the department of Seine-et-Oise arrested and punished a woman for providing shelter for numerous deserters.[66] Widows, even elderly widows, offered themselves as brides to young men to make them ineligible for the draft. In 1809, Gerolamo Uglio of Breme (Italy) married a seventy-two-year-old widow in an effort to avoid the draft.[67] Napoleon's desire for a glorious empire imposed great hardship on the European peasantry.

Women and Resistance to Napoleon

Napoleon's charismatic personality and military success made him immensely popular in France. However, he did not rule unopposed. Liberals were unhappy with military rule and limitations on their ability to participate in government. Monarchists wanted a strong king and a restoration of aristocratic privilege. The working classes resented the imposition of harsh rules, conscription, taxes, and limited suffrage. Outside of France, his conquered subjects hated him.

One of Napoleon's most celebrated opponents was the novelist and essayist Germaine de Staël (1766–1817). De Staël was born to a wealthy Swiss family but lived nearly all of her life in France, where she received an excellent education and traveled in the best social circles. The heroines of her romantic novels lived in worlds quite different from the society that Napoleon envisioned. In *Delphine* (1802), the story of an impetuous but generous heroine, her characters argued for the need for divorce, criticized stifling social conventions, and discussed the benefits and problems of the Revolution. In *Corinne* (1807), de Staël's descriptions of Italy drove home the point that great civilizations had existed before Napoleon and that their citizens had enjoyed greater freedoms than they did under the emperor. De Staël's work *On Germany* celebrated German culture and ideas as the antithesis of Napoleonic France. Although Napoleon originally permitted its publication, upon learning of its contents, he changed his

mind. De Staël escaped France just ahead of the police with a copy of the manuscript and published it in Britain in 1813. De Staël's opposition to Napoleon cost her dearly. Not only was she was forced into exile several times, but she saw many of her friends and lovers persecuted, and Napoleon's secret police and spies continually followed and harassed her.

Outside of France, Napoleon and his troops faced strong opposition. The most serious revolt erupted in Spain in 1808. Monarchists, Catholics, and Spanish patriots rebelled when Napoleon replaced the Spanish king with his brother Joseph Bonaparte (r. 1808–1813). Spanish women risked their lives for their country's independence and Spanish accounts hailed their valor. Agustina of Aragon took over the firing of cannons in defense of the city of Zaragoza after the men had been killed. Her quick actions reportedly saved the city and later she received a medal, an officer's commission, and a military pension for her bravery.[68] Spanish women taunted also French soldiers and impugned their masculinity. When the French soldiers went on parade in Madrid in May of 1808, a group of "beautiful young women" straddled the French cannons and yelled at the French soldiers, "Your dinky pistols do not frighten those of our regiment."[69]

Napoleon's conquests brought war to much of Europe. As in every other era, women accompanied men into battle. Although "camp followers" had unsavory reputations, most were not prostitutes but soldiers' wives with nowhere else to go. By holding lotteries, the British military maintained strict quotas on the number of women allowed to follow regiments. Women who won their lottery received official rations, although less than their husbands. To augment their meager rations, women bartered, took in mending, or simply stole. The British general leading the army in Spain repeatedly issued orders prohibiting women from pillaging local gardens. Following the army meant marching with them, sleeping outside in tents or huts (often close to battle), and facing the danger of snipers and attack. When James Anton of the Forty-Second Highlanders sailed to Spain to fight Napoleon, his wife, Mary, accompanied him. He turned his daily rum ration over to the ship's cook so that he and Mary could sleep undisturbed in one of the lifeboats. Mary commented that they were the "most comfortable of the uncomfortable."[70]

The scarcity of women turned them into a commodity. When camp life or marital life became too difficult, soldiers made a practice of "selling their wives" to other men. A German soldier serving in Spain wrote, "In Palermo I had also the opportunity of witnessing the singular English custom of the sale of wives. A soldier of the 10th regiment of infantry sold his wife to a drummer for two pounds sterling; he, however, did not keep her long, but parted with her to the armourer of the regiment for two Spanish dollars."[71] Women were not always the innocent victims. One Anne Duke, tired of her husband, took up with the higher-ranked soldier who "purchased" her from her husband. Her new "husband" left her behind when he was transferred to another post and Anne found another "husband' of even higher rank.[72]

In 1812, Napoleon turned on his former ally, Russia, but the harsh combination of winter weather, lack of food, and the Russian army handed Napoleon a major defeat. Most of his army never returned. He then attacked Prussia and Austria, who quickly formed a coalition with Great Britain to defeat him in 1814. The coalition exiled Napoleon to the island of Elba off the coast of Italy. They then installed a Bourbon king, Louis XVIII (r. 1814–1824), the brother of the executed Louis the XVI, as France's ruler. (Louis XVI and Marie Antoinette had a son who died in prison. He never ruled but is considered Louis XVII.) In February 1815, Napoleon escaped from Elba to reclaim his empire; however, within months, the British, led by the Duke of Wellington (1769–1852), defeated Napoleon at the Battle of Waterloo. The coalition exiled Napoleon again, this time to the rocky and desolate island of Saint Helena off the coast of Africa, where he died in 1821.

After Napoleon's defeat, the victors, Britain, Prussia, Russia, and Austria, gathered at the Congress of Vienna to divide Napoleon's conquests and redraw the map of Europe. The settlement was very harsh, pushing the borders of France back to its 1792 territory and imposing reparations. The Congress compensated the victors for their participation in the wars and balanced Europe's military power in the hope of preventing further conflict.

CONCLUSION

In the eighteenth century, debates about women's political participation reached new heights. Encouraged by Enlightenment ideas and pushed by economic change, women marched in the streets, debated in salons, and fought on the battlefield. However, many continued to believe that women were only fit for motherhood, did not need citizenship, and did not belong in politics. In the end, the few citizen rights that women won in the American and French Revolutions would be short-lived. Conservative thinkers and monarchs pushed women to embrace motherhood and domesticity over voting and economic independence. Nevertheless, women found outlets for their ideas and emotions in art, and debate about women's proper roles would provide the basis for political and social action in the nineteenth century.

NOTES

1. Jerome Blum, *The End of the Old Order in Europe* (Princeton: Princeton University Press, 1978), 25

2. Isser Woloch, *Eighteenth-Century Europe: Tradition and Progress, 1715–1789* (New York: Norton, 1982), 80–81.

3. Aileen Ribeiro, *Dress in Eighteenth-Century Europe*, 2nd ed. (New Haven, CT: Yale University Press, 2002), 77.

4. Cissie Fairchilds, "Women and Family," in *French Women in the Age of Enlightenment*, ed. Samia I. Spencer (Bloomington: Indiana University Press, 1984), 101.

5. Quoted in Fairchilds, 100.

6. Lawrence Stone, *The Family, Sex and Marriage in England, 1500–1800* (New York: Harper and Row, 1977), 44, 47.

7. Quoted in Olwen Hufton, *The Prospect Before Her: a History of Women in Western Europe* (New York: Alfred Knopf, 1996), 473.

8. Neil McKendrick, Colin Brewer, and J. A. Plumb, *The Commercialization of Eighteenth-Century England* (Bloomington: Indiana University Press, 1982), 76.

9. Ross W. Jamieson, "The Essence of Commodifications: Caffeine Dependencies in the Early Modern World," *Journal of Social History* 35:2 (Winter 2001): 284.

10. E. A. Wrigley and R. S. Schofield, *The Population History of England, 1541–1871* (Cambridge: Cambridge University Press, 1989), 262–265.

11. Margaret R. Hunt, "The Sapphic Strain: English Lesbians in the Long Eighteenth Century," in *Singlewomen in the European Past, 1250–1800*, ed. Judith M. Bennett and Amy M. Froide (Philadelphia: University of Pennsylvania Press, 1999), 280.

12. Margaret R. Hunt, *The Middling Sort: Commerce, Gender, and the Family in England, 1680–1780* (Berkeley: University of California Press, 1996), 128.

13. Londa Schiebinger, *The Mind Has No Sex? Women in the Origins of Modern Science* (Cambridge, MA: Harvard University Press, 1989), 41.

14. Quoted in Maria Cieslak-Golonka and Bruno Morten "Two Women Scientists of Bologna," *American Scientist* 88 (January 2000): 68.

15. Schiebinger, 262.

16. Quoted in Schiebinger, 174, 176.

17. Linda K. Kerber, "The Republican Mother: Women and the Enlightenment—An American Perspective," in *Toward an Intellectual History of Women*, ed. Linda Kerber (Chapel Hill: University of North Carolina Press, 1997), 43–44.

18. Schiebinger, 197.

19. Schiebinger, 221–222.

20. Schiebinger, 232.

21. Dena Goodman, *The Republic of Letters: A Cultural History of the French Enlightenment* (Ithaca, NY: Cornell University Press, 1994), esp. 74, 90–91.

22. Goodman, *The Republic of Letters*, 76.

23. Sara Ellen Procious Malueg, "Woman and the *Encyclopédie*," in *French Women in the Age of Enlightenment*, 260.

24. Malueg, 259.

25. Mme Delusse wrote the commentary for two plates in volume 22, and an anonymous woman wrote the entries for "Falbala," and "Fontange," both decorative elements in women's clothing. Malueg, "Woman and the *Encyclopédie*," 260–261.

26. Deborah Hertz, "Emancipation Through Inter-marriage? Wealthy Jewish Salon Women in Old Berlin," in *Jewish Women in Historical Perspective*, 2nd ed., ed. Judith Baskin (Detroit, MI: Wayne State University Press, 1998), 193–204.

27. Constance A. Sullivan, "Constructing Her Own Tradition: Ideological Selectivity in Josefa Amar y Borbón's Representation of Female Models," in *Recovering Spain's Feminist Tradition*, ed. Lisa Vollendorf (New York: Modern Language Association of America, 2001), 142.

28. *Johnsonian Miscellanies*, vol. 2, ed. George Birkbeck Hill (London: Constable and Co., 1966), 11.

29. Charles Ingrao, *The Habsburg Monarchy, 1618–1815* (Cambridge: Cambridge University Press, 1994), 150.

30. Ingrao, 155.

31. Quoted in Karl A. Roider Jr., *Maria Theresa* (Englewood Cliffs, NJ: Prentice Hall, 1973), 23.

32. Michael E. Yonan, "Conceptualizing the *Kaiserinwitwe*: Empress Maria Theresa and Her Portraits," in *Widowhood and Visual Culture in Early Modern Europe*, ed. Allison Levy (Burlington, VT: Ashgate Press, 2003), 113.

33. Marion W. Gray, *Productive Men, Reproductive Women: The Agrarian Household and the Emergence of Separate Spheres During the German Enlightenment* (New York: Berghahn Books, 2000), 162.

34. Quoted in M.S. Anderson, *Peter the Great* (London: Thames and Hudson, 1978), 123.

35. Lindsey Hughes, *Russia in the Age of Peter the Great* (New Haven, CT: Yale University Press, 1998), 187–188.

36. Natalia Pushkareva, *Women in Russian History from the Tenth to the Twentieth Century*, trans. Eve Levin (New York: M. E. Sharpe, 1997), 149–150.

37. Whitney Chadwick, *Women, Art, and Society* (London: Thames and Hudson, 1990), 143.

38. Chadwick, 161, 166, 168.

39. Melissa Hyde, "Under the Sign of Minerva: Adélaïde Labille-Guiard's *Portrait of Madame Adélaïde*," in *Women, Art, and the Politics of Identity in Eighteenth Century Europe*, ed. Melissa Hyde and Jennifer Milam (Burlington, VT: Ashgate Press, 2003), 144.

40. Wendy Wassyng Roworth, "Ancient Matrons and Modern Patrons: Angelica Kauffman as a Classical History Painter," in *Women, Art, and the Politics of Identity in Eighteenth Century Europe*, esp. 197.

41. Barbara Garvey Jackson, "Musical Women of the Seventeenth and Eighteenth Centuries," in *Women and Music*, ed. Karin Pendle (Bloomington: Indiana University Press, 1991), 116.

42. Quoted in Nigel Glendinning, *A Literary History of Spain: the Eighteenth Century* (London: Ernest Benn Limited, 1972), 18.

43. Bonnie Smith, *Changing Lives: Women in European History Since 1700* (New York: D. C. Heath, 1988), 112.

44. Theresa Ann Smith, "Writing Out of the Margins: Women, Translation, and the Spanish Enlightenment," *Journal of Women's History* 15:1 (Spring 2003): esp. 116.

45. H. V. Bowen, "Investment and Empire in the Later Eighteenth Century: East India Stockholding,

1756–1791," *Economic History Review* 42:2 (1989): 202.

46. P. J. Marshall, "The White Town of Calcutta Under the Rule of the East India Company," *Modern Asian Studies* 34:2 (2000): 312.

47. Gretchen Holbrook Gerzina, *Black London: Life Before Emancipation* (New Brunswick: Rutgers University Press, 1995), 5.

48. Quoted in Dena Goodman, "Women and the Enlightenment," in *Becoming Visible: Women in European History*, 3rd ed., ed. Renate Bridenthal, Susan Mosher Stuard, and Merry E. Wiesner (Boston: Houghton Mifflin, 1998), 241.

49. Clare Midgley, *Women Against Slavery: The British Campaigns, 1780–1870* (London: Routledge, 1992), 15, 36.

50. Quoted in Sara Evans, *Born for Liberty* (New York: Free Press, 1989), 47.

51. Evans, 49–50.

52. Evans, 50.

53. Kerber, 58.

54. Susan Migden Socolow, *The Women of Colonial Latin America* (Cambridge: Cambridge University Press, 2000), 113.

55. Socolow, 113.

56. Socolow, 86.

57. Christian Büschges trans. "Don Manuel Valdivieso y Carrión Protests the Marriage of his Daughter to Don Teodoro Jaramillo, a Person of Lower Social Standing, Quito, 1784–85," in *Colonial Lives: Documents on Latin American History, 1550–1850*, ed. Richard Boyer and Geoffrey Spurling (Oxford: Oxford University Press, 2000), 224–235.

58. Darline Gay Levy and Harriet B. Applewhite, "A Political Revolution for Women? The Case of Paris," in *Becoming Visible*, 270.

59. Quoted in Gary Gates, "The Powers of Husband and Wife Must Be Equal and Separate: The *Cercle Social* and the Rights of Women, 1790–91," in *Women and Politics in the Age of Democratic Revolution*, ed. Harriet B. Applewhite and Darline G. Levy (Ann Arbor: University of Michigan Press, 1990), 172.

60. Quoted in Levy and Applewhite, "A Political Revolution for Women?" 280.

61. Elizabeth Colwill, "Pass as a Woman, Act Like a Man: Marie-Antoinette as Tribade in the Pornography of the French Revolution," in *Marie-Antoinette: Writings on the Body of a Queen*, ed. Dena Goodman (London: Routledge, 2003), 139–169.

62. Olwen Hufton, "Counter-Revolutionary Women," in *The French Revolution in Social and Political Perspective*, ed. Peter Jones (London: Arnold, 1996), 299.

63. Joan W. Scott, *Only Paradoxes to Offer: French Feminists and the Rights of Man* (Cambridge: Harvard University Press, 1996), 33ff.

64. Theresa McBride, "Public Authority and Private Lives: Divorce after the French Revolution," *French Historical Studies* 17:3 (Spring 1992): 750.

65. Alexander Grab, "Army, State, and Society: Conscription and Desertion in Napoleonic Italy (1802–1814)," *The Journal of Modern History* 67:1 (March 1995): 26; Eric A. Arnold Jr., "Some Observations on the French Opposition to Napoleonic Conscription," *French Historical Studies* 4:4 (Autumn 1966): 453.

66. Arnold, 455.

67. Grab, 41.

68. John Lawrence Tone, "Spanish Women in the Resistance to Napoleon, 1808–1814," in *Constructions of Spanish Womanhood: Female Identity in Modern Spain*, ed. Victoria Lorée Enders and Pamela Beth Radcliff (Albany, NY: SUNY Press, 1999), 263.

69. Quoted in Tone, 259.

70. Quoted in F. C. G. Page, *Following the Drum: Women in Wellington's War* (London: Andre Deutsch, 1986), 39.

71. Quoted in Page, 50.

72. Page, 51–54.

SUGGESTED READINGS

Brophy, Elizabeth Bergen. *Women's Lives and the Eighteenth-Century English Novel*. Tampa: University of South Florida Press, 1991. A study of the relationship between the presentation of everyday life in eighteenth-century novels and the social history of ordinary women.

Goodman, Dena. *The Republic of Letters: A Cultural History of the French Enlightenment*. Ithaca, NY: Cornell University Press, 1994. Feminist history of the salons that argues for the centrality of women's roles in the Enlightenment debates that preceded the Revolution.

Kerber, Linda. *Towards an Intellectual History of Women*. Chapel Hill: University of North Carolina Press, 1997. Collection of essays that looks at the issues of women's political identity and involvement in the American Revolution and early republic.

Schiebinger, Londa. *The Mind Has No Sex? Women in the Origins of Modern Science*. Cambridge, MA: Harvard University Press, 1989. Looks at how the changing understanding of sex differences gave rise to the idea that science was a masculine enterprise.

Scott, Joan Wallach. *Only Paradoxes to Offer: French Feminists and the Rights of Man*. Cambridge, MA: Harvard University, 1996. An analysis of the paradox of French feminists' demands that both accept and reject the significance of differences between men and women with respect to citizenship.

Valenze, Deborah. *The First Industrial Woman*. Oxford: Oxford University Press, 1995. A study of the underlying gender assumptions behind women's work at the beginning of the Industrial Revolution.

Index

women of, 88, 89, 90; political violence in the, 86; population of late,
85; senatorial class of the, 98; service
occupations in, 96, 97; urban life in
the, 96–97, 98; witch-hunting in,
231; women and religion in, 84, 85
Roman Republic: economy of, 78;
Etruscans and the, 70–71, 72; expectations of women, 73; family and
the, 79–80, 81; founding of, 69; gender roles of, 80; Greek influence on,
77, 78; Iberian conquest and, 77;
imports and, 78; legends of women
and the, 74; lifestyle, 78; marriage
and divorce in, 81–83, 84; patricians
and plebians, 73, 74; priorities of
the, 73; professional class of the, 80,
81; slavery and the, 78, 79; structure
of government for, 73, 74; Struggle
of the Orders, 74; themes of history,
72; Twelve Tables and, 79; warfare
and the, 75–76, 77; women and the,
72, 74, 77, 79; women and warfare
of, 75, 77
Rome, Imperial: colonial lifestyle of,
91, 92–93; marriage and, 91; women
in, 91–102
Romero Masegosa y Cancelada, María,
274
Rousseau, Jean-Jacques, 258, 263, 265
The Rover, or the Banished Cavaliers
(Behn), 244
Rowley, Alice, 204
Royal Academy of Arts, 272
Royal Aragonese Economic Society,
265
Royal Society of London, 261
Royal Society of Sciences, 261
Rufus, Musonious, 99
Russia: Academy of Sciences, 271;
Academy of the Study of the
Russian: Language, 271; Bering
Strait, 270; class tensions in, 271;
divorce customs and, 158; Enlight-
enment, 271; European culture and,
270; expeditions and, 270; female
honor and, 240; mixing of sexes in
public, 270; Napoleon and, 286,
289; peasant rebellion in, 259, 271;
Saint Olga and, 157; slave trade and,
188; uxoricide and, 240; Vikings
and, 157; witchcraft in, 231; women
rulers of, 270, 271
Russian Academy of Science, 270
Ruysch, Rachel, 241

Sabitu, 13
Sagas, 154
Saint Bartholomew's Day Massacre,
222, 236
Saints: Christian monastic, 125; ideals
for, 151; intercession and, 219;
Middle Ages and women, 196, 197;
mystical experiences of, 197; women
and devotion to, 201, 202. *See also*
Individual saints
Salic Code, 145
Salieri, Antonio, 273
Salonières, 263
Salons, 263, 264–266, 267, 279, 284
Saltykova, Praskovia, 270
Samson, Deborah, 278
Sanhedrin, 110
Sanz de Santamaría, Manuela, 279
Sappho, 44, 45
Sargon the Akkadian, 8, 11, 14
Saxony, 267
Schlegel, Dorothea von, 265
Schröter, Corona, 273
Scientific revolution, 245, 246, 261.
See also Enlightenment
Scotland: John Knox and, 222, 235;
Mary, Queen of Scots and, 236; Mary
Stuart of, 235; Scottish Enlighten-
ment, 265; Vikings and, 154
Scriptoria, 153
Secondat, Charles-Louis de, 274
The Secret Histories (Prokopios), 133
Seleucus I (Seleucid king), 61
Senworsret I (king of Egypt), 20
Sephardim, 233
Septimus Severus (Roman emperor), 91
Serfs: Joseph II and, 268; legal rights
of, 168; reduced to slave status, 271;
urban population and, 170
Sergius III, Pope, 174
Seven Years' War, 275
Severa, Claudia, 92
Sex and sexuality: of Ancient
Egyptians, 21; Ancient Greece and
homosexuality, 44, 45; Ancient
Greeks view of, 42, 43; of Ancient
Israelites, 29, 30; artistic rivalry and,
272; Black Death and, 192, 193;
Caligula's court and, 92; Catholic
Church and, 226; chivalric culture
and, 164; city-states and homosexu-
als, 206; in Classical Greece, 53–58,
59; clerical celibacy and, 175; the
Genevan Consistory and, 222;
Council decrees on, 226, 227; differ-

ences of men and women, 262; exile
and promiscuity of, 91; French revolutionaries use of, 284; "fruitful
intercourse" and, 100–101; gender
debate and, 249, 250; gender expectations of queens and, 236; gender
versus, 1; Inquisition and, 227, 228;
interfaith relationships and, 189;
Jean de Meun and, 209; Jesus' view
on, 115; Marie Antoinette and, 284;
medieval laws and, 186; medieval
society and, 170; of Mesopotamians,
11, 12; Mishnaic system and, 110;
Montanists and, 117; Muslim
women and, 190; Paul's view of,
112; penitentials and, 171; personal
and political goals with, 258; priests
and concubinage, 226; in the
Roman Empire, 97, 98; Roman's
view of, 77, 78; Roman women and
freedom of, 88; single women and,
260; slaves and, 249; Spartan homosexuality and, 52; of Spartan
women, 52; value of reproductive
abilities, 249; Vestal virgins of Rome
and, 84, 85; Virgin Mary and, 122;
women and witchcraft with, 230;
women musicians and, 273; women
servants and, 187
Seymour, Jane, 224
Shenoute, 125
Shîmatum, 8
Shiptu, 8
Shulgi, 12
Shulgisimti, 12
Shu-Sîn, King, 9
Siberia, 270
Sigibert (Frankish king), 146
Silesia, 268
Singers: Faustina Bordoni, 273; school
for male and female, 273. *See also*
Musicians and music
Sirmen, Maddalena (Lombardini), 273
Slaves and slavery: abolitionist move-
ments and, 276, 277; Ancient Greek
and, 48; antislavery groups and, 276;
Christian deacons and, 121, 122;
Christianity and, 113; diversity of,
187, 188; French National Assembly
and, 281; impact of mercantilism on,
275; Inquisition and, 228; intermar-
riages of, 188; Islamic Spain and,
161; of Jews, 108; marriage and, 21;
Morisca resistance and, 234; Muslim
adulterous women and, 190; native